NAVIGATION
ADVANCED
MATES/MASTERS

SECOND EDITION

Captain Nadeem Anwar

Witherby Seamanship International
A Division of Witherby Publishing Group Ltd

4 Dunlop Square, Livingston, Edinburgh, EH54 8SB, Scotland, UK
Tel No: +44(0)1506 463 227 - Fax No: +44(0)1506 468 999
Email: info@emailws.com - Web: www.witherbyseamanship.com

First edition published 2006
Second edition published 2015

ISBN: 978-1-85609-627-0

British Library Cataloguing in Publication Data
A catalogue record for this book is available from the British Library.

Cover image: BA Chart 105: 'Cromer Knoll and the Outer Banks' - NOT TO BE USED FOR NAVIGATION

This book has been partly derived from material obtained from the UK Hydrographic Office, Her Majesty's Stationery Office.

THIS PRODUCT IS NOT TO BE USED FOR NAVIGATION.

The UK Hydrographic Office (UKHO) and its licensors make no warranties or representations, express or implied, with respect to this product. The UKHO and its licensors have not verified the information within this product or quality assured it.

Printed by The Print Network, Penrith, UK

Published by

Witherby Publishing Group Ltd
4 Dunlop Square, Livingston,
Edinburgh, EH54 8SB,
Scotland, UK

Tel No: +44(0)1506 463 227
Fax No: +44(0)1506 468 999

Email: info@emailws.com
Web: www.witherbys.com

NAVIGATION
ADVANCED
MATES/MASTERS

SECOND EDITION

Captain Nadeem Anwar

Captain Nadeem Anwar

Captain Nadeem Anwar, FNI, MSc, BSc, ACII, CertEd, PGCEL, Master Mariner, is a Curriculum Manager at Fleetwood Nautical Campus, UK.

Captain Anwar has written several other books including *'Ballast Water Management'* and *'Passage Planning'*. He has also contributed to various other titles, developed training courses and written a range of training materials. He also provides consultancy services to marine-training providers and shipping companies.

Captain Anwar has 14 years experience of being at sea on a variety of ships, including multipurpose vessels, car carriers, VLCC, OBO, O/O, Gas and Chemical Tankers. He has substantial experience of being at a senior level on board ships, including being in command. He has navigated worldwide and gained substantial experience of different extreme environmental conditions and sea areas, gaining a wealth of navigational experience.

He has had a successful career as an academic and a professional. In 2005, he achieved an MSc in Maritime Operations with a Distinction (Liverpool John Moores University) as well as an Advanced Diploma in Insurance (through the Chartered Insurance Institute, London).

Captain Anwar was recently in the Arabian Gulf, where he was exposed to modern developments and current industrial practices. His consultancy base expanded significantly while working in the Gulf as the Managing Director of leading international companies.

Author's Preface

Navigational inaccuracies have mainly been the source of most of the catastrophic maritime disasters. The industry is heavily legislated and more regulations are likely to be developed in the near future. It is important to understand that it is the basic skills of the seafarers, especially the navigators who are the main stay of maritime safety.

There are increasing concerns about the competence and skills of seafarers, in particular the navigation watchkeepers. The training and development of seafarers is time consuming, costly and demanding. There is also the need to keep the knowledge current by staying abreast of the new developments and practices.

This book is aimed at the navigator of today and of the future. The increasing workload on the watchkeeper demands simple methods of working and, clear and concise instructions, so that the navigator can spend more time concentrating on watchkeeping. The methods of working used in the book are not just easy to follow for learning, but are also for on board applications. It contains a number of worked examples, plots, templates for working and exercises to allow the navigator to gain basic and advanced navigation skills. The book not only mentions the methods, it explains the methods.

The future of maritime safety, to a large extent, relies on advanced navigational skills. The book is aimed at Masters and senior navigation officers and would also be beneficial for the junior navigation officers as it would help them to gain knowledge and develop skills for shipboard applications, and also for future career progression.

Contents

Regulatory Requirements

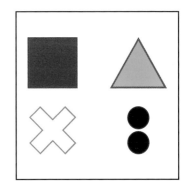

Shipping is a globalised industry and, as it must work to common international standards, legislation is very important. This legislation affects all aspects of shipping, from construction to safe operations, with navigation being no exception.

In consultation with its Member States and using expert help from relevant sub-committees, the International Maritime Organization (IMO) produces draft proposals. Once a pre-determined number of the Member States, who between them have a certain percentage of world tonnage, agree to a proposal, the Convention is enforced.

While the actual regulations a ship should follow will be the national law of the country (flag State) where it is registered, the Conventions provide the minimum standards for international trading. The ship must also meet any port and coastal state standards, these may be different to, but often of a higher standard than, the IMO Conventions.

Navigation and the issues relating to it are covered under international instruments such as SOLAS, STCW and Collision Regulations. The flag States will also advise their own ships through regulations, codes and notices. The main areas covered include:

- Training and certification (covered under STCW'78/95 as amended 2010)
- safety of navigation (covered under SOLAS Chapter V, National Laws and the Bridge Procedures Guide by ICS)
- carriage of navigational equipment and publications (covered under SOLAS and National Laws)
- management (covered under ISM Code in SOLAS'74)
- collision regulations (COLREGS'72)

The significance of some of these codes and regulations are discussed briefly in this chapter. Some non-statutory requirements are also covered for completeness.

1.1 STCW

The International Convention on Standards of Training, Certification and Watchkeeping for Seafarers (STCW) was adopted by the International Conference on Training and Certification of Seafarers on July 7th, 1978. The 1978 STCW Convention (known as STCW'78) came into force on April 28th, 1984. Various amendments have subsequently been adopted. The 1991 amendments relate to the Global Maritime Distress and Safety System (GMDSS) and were adopted on December 1st, 1992. The 1994 amendments relate to special training requirements for tanker personnel and were adopted on January 1st, 1996. In the 1995 amendments, there was a complete revision of the annex of the 1978 STCW Convention. Including the following:

- Clarification of the standards of competence required
- qualification requirements for trainers and assessors
- provision of effective mechanisms for enforcement
- provision of mechanisms for greater flexibility in the assignment of functions on board ship, broadening seafarers career opportunities.

The Convention set out the minimum global standards of knowledge, understanding, experience and professional competence required by the Member States. The STCW 1995 came fully into force on 1 February 2002 and is generally referred to as STCW'95.

The 2010 amendments, known as the Manila amendments, to the Convention and Code were adopted by resolutions 1 and 2. The amendments updated the standards of competence required, particularly in light of emerging technologies, to introduce new training and certification requirements and methodologies, improve mechanisms for enforcement of its provisions, and detailed requirements on hours of work and rest, prevention of drug and alcohol abuse and also medical fitness standards for seafarers.

Function: Navigation at the Management level

The following are the required Competencies:

- Plan a voyage and conduct navigation
- determine position and the accuracy of resultant position fix by any means
- determine and allow for compass errors
- coordinate search and rescue operations
- establish watchkeeping arrangements and procedures
- maintain safe navigation through the use of information from navigation equipment and systems to assist command making decisions
- maintain safety of navigation through the use of ECDIS and associated navigation systems to assist command decision making
- forecast weather and oceanographic conditions
- respond to navigational emergencies
- manoeuvre and handle a ship in all conditions
- operate remote controls of propulsion plant and engineering systems and services.

Table 1.1   STCW navigation function

The STCW Code stipulates the minimum training and certification requirements for Masters, Chief Mates, OOWs and ratings. They are governed by the STCW Regulations and take the ship's gross tonnage and near/non-near coastal voyages as criteria. It will always be a factor in deciding the safe manning levels of ships.

1.2 Safe Manning

IMO and Flag States establish the guidelines for the safe manning of ships. A ship's minimum safe manning level should be established taking into account all the relevant factors. When calculating the safe manning level, the following factors should be considered:

- Frequency of port calls, the duration and nature of the voyage
- the trading area(s), waters and type of operations the ship is involved in as well as any special requirements that the trade or operation specify
- the number, size in kW and the type of main propulsion units and auxiliary machinery
- the type of ship, its size and layout, type of ship and layout
- ship's construction and the equipment that is on board
- the type of cargo being carried or the operational requirements
- maintenance methods
- extent of training that is carried out on board
- how crew will deal with emergency situations that may arise
- the navigational duties and responsibilities as set out in STCW, including:
  - plan and carry out safe navigation
  - safe navigational watch must be maintained
  - manoeuvre and handle the ship in all conditions and during all operations

- moor and unmoor the ship safely
- maintain safety while in port.

Cargo handling and stowage:

- Plan and monitor that the cargo is safely loaded, stowed, secured, carried and unloaded.

Ship specific operations:

- The type and duration of operation(s) that a ship undertakes as well as the environmental conditions.

Ship operations and looking after personnel on board:

- The safety and security of all personnel on board must be maintained and lifesaving, fire fighting and other safety systems must be kept in operational condition. Including being able to muster and disembark passengers and other nonessential personnel
- watertight closing arrangements must be operational and maintained
- perform necessary operations to protect the marine environment
- provide medical care on board
- administrative tasks that are required for the ship's safe operation should be carried out
- participate in safety drills and exercises that are mandatory.

Marine engineering tasks and duties:

- Operate and monitor the ship's main propulsion and auxiliary machinery
- a safe engineering watch should be maintained
- manage and carry out fuel and ballast operations
- the ship's engine equipment, system and services must be maintained.

Electrical, electronic and control engineering duties:

- Able to operate the ship's electrical and electronic equipment
- keep the ship's electric and electronic systems maintained.

Radio communications:

- Information should be transmitted and received by using the communication equipment on board
- maintain a safe radio watch
- able to maintain communication if there is an emergency.

Maintenance and repair:

- Maintenance and repair work should be carried out to the ship, its machinery, equipment and systems, as appropriate to the maintenance and the repair systems used.

Safe manning level's should also take account of:

- Management of a ship's safety functions when it is underway, not underway or operating in an almost stationary mode
- qualified deck officers should be available to ensure that the Master does not have to keep regular watches, by doing this a three watch system can be adopted. This may not apply to smaller vessels
- qualified engineering officers should be available to ensure that the Chief Engineer is not required to keep regular watches, by doing this a three watch system can be adopted, apart from on vessels that have limited propulsion power or where unattended machinery spaces are provided
- maintaining the appropriate occupational health and hygiene standards on board
- proper food and drinking water for all persons on board.

1.3 SOLAS Chapter V

Chapter V identifies certain navigation safety services that contracting Governments should provide. It outlines the operational provisions that apply to all ships on all voyages. The subjects covered include:

- A general obligation for Masters to assist those in distress
- maintaining meteorological services for ships
- ice patrol service
- routeing of ships
- maintenance of search and rescue services.

Chapter V requires Contracting Governments to ensure that all ships are manned sufficiently and efficiently from a safety point of view. The chapter makes it mandatory for Voyage Data Recorders (VDR) and automatic ship identification systems (AIS) to be carried for certain classes of ship.

1.3.1 Reports by the Master

SOLAS V Regulation 31 states that a ship's Master who meets with any of the following conditions' must make a report (preferably in English), by all available means, to all other ships in the vicinity as well as the relevant authorities. These messages should be sent on DSC, R/T and INMARSAT.

- Tropical storms
- winds of force 10 and above, when there was no warning
- air temperatures below freezing, associated with gale force winds that have caused severe icing
- dangerous ice
- a dangerous derelict.

Each message should be preceded with SECURITE or PAN PAN as appropriate. Table 1.2 shows the Chapters of SOLAS V Regulations.

SOLAS V – List of Regulations	
Regulation	**Title**
1	Application
2	Definitions
3	Exemptions and equivalents
4	Navigational warnings
5	Meteorological services and warnings
6	Ice patrol service
7	Search and rescue services
8	Life-saving signals
9	Hydrographic services
10	Ship's routeing
11	Ship reporting services
12	Vessel traffic services
13	Establishment and operation of aids to navigation
14	Ship's manning
15	Principles relating to bridge design, design and arrangement of navigational systems and equipment and bridge procedures
16	Maintenance of equipment
17	Electromagnetic compatibility
18	Approval, surveys and performance standards of navigational systems and equipment and voyage data recorder
19	Carriage requirements for shipborne navigational systems and equipment
19-1	Long-range identification and tracking of ships
20	Voyage data recorders
21	International Code of Signals and IAMSAR Manual
22	Navigation bridge visibility
23	Pilot transfer arrangements
24	Use of heading and/or track control systems
25	Operations of steering gear
26	Steering gear: testing and drills
27	Nautical charts and nautical publications
28	Records of navigational activities and daily reporting
29	Life-saving signals to be used by ships, aircraft or persons in distress
30	Operational limitations
31	Danger messages
32	Information required in danger messages
33	Distress situations: obligations and procedures
34	Safe navigation and avoidance of dangerous situations
34-1	Master's discretion
35	Misuse of distress signals

Table 1.2   SOLAS V Regulations

SOLAS V – Regulation 19 (Summary)
All Ships, regardless of size, shall be provided with:
<ul><li>A properly adjusted standard magnetic compass independent of power supply, to determine the ship's heading and display the reading at the main steering position</li><li>A pelorus or compass bearing device, or other means, independent of any power supply, to take bearings over an arc of the horizon of 360°</li><li>Means of correcting heading and bearings to true at all times</li><li>Nautical charts and nautical publications; ECDIS</li><li>Back-up arrangements; complied with by a second stand-alone ECDIS</li><li>Global Navigation Satellite System receiver or a terrestrial radio navigation system</li><li>On vessels of less than 150 GT; Radar reflector, or similar arrangement to enable detection by ships navigating by 9 and 3 GHz Radar</li><li>Sound reception system on ships with totally enclosed bridge</li><li>Telephone or other means to communicate heading information to emergency steering position</li></ul>
All Ships of 150 GT and upwards and passenger ships, regardless of size, shall be provided with:
<ul><li>A spare magnetic compass, or other means to determine the ship's heading and display the reading at the main steering position</li><li>A daylight signalling lamp with independent power supply as well</li></ul>
All Ships 300 GT and upwards and passenger ships regardless of size, shall be provided with:
<ul><li>Echo sounder</li><li>9 GHz Radar</li><li>Electronic plotting aid, or other means, to plot electronically the range and bearing of targets to determine collision risk</li><li>Speed and distance measuring device, or other means to indicate speed and distance through the water</li><li>Properly adjusted transmitting heading device, or other means, to transmit heading information for input to radar and plotting aid</li></ul>
<ul><li>AIS (specific rules regarding size of vessels apply)</li></ul>
On vessels of 500 GT and over
<ul><li>Gyro Compass</li><li>Gyro heading and bearing repeater</li><li>Rudder, Propeller, Pitch, RPM indicators</li><li>An automatic tracking aid</li></ul>
All ships of 3,000 GT and over:
<ul><li>A 3 GHz Radar, or another 9 GHz Radar</li><li>A second automatic tracking aid</li></ul>
All ships of 10,000 GT and over:
<ul><li>ARPA</li><li>Auto Pilot</li></ul>
All ships of 50,000 GT and over:
<ul><li>Rate of Turn Indicator</li><li>Speed and distance measuring device, or other means to indicate speed and distance over the ground</li></ul>

Table 1.3   SOLAS V - Regulation 19 – Summary of requirements

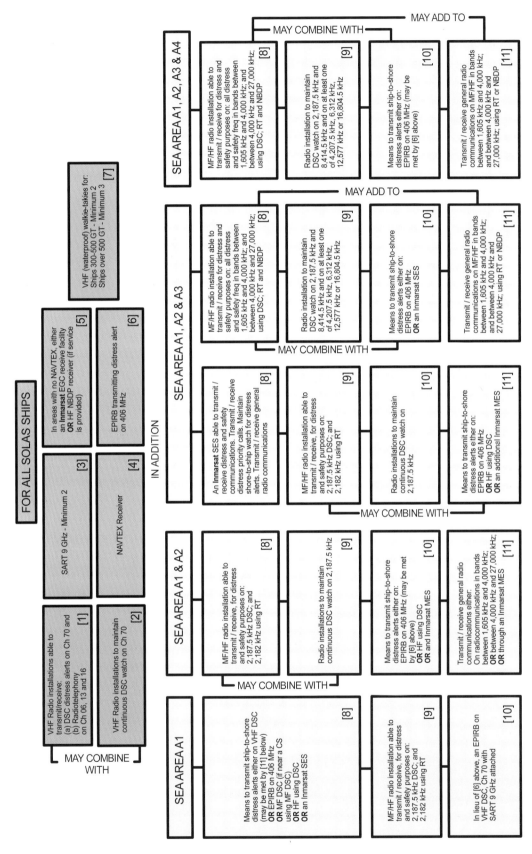

Figure 1.1 GMDSS carriage requirements

1.4 ISM Code

Analysing any accident or incident generally shows that there has been an element of human error or management failure, as do so-called 'equipment failure' or 'Act of God' incidents. Equipment or machinery may not have been maintained adequately, too much reliance may have been placed on a single system or decisions may not have been made in time. Management can be an issue where an error of judgment or an individual's mistake should have been spotted and corrective action taken. To overcome these human error and management issues, general principles and objectives to promote good management and operating practices within the industry as a whole were introduced into shipping through the ISM Code under SOLAS.

The full title of the ISM Code is: '*The International Management Code for the Safe Operation of Ships and for Pollution Prevention*'. Its objective is to ensure safety, prevent human injury or loss of life and to prevent property and the environment from being damaged. Navigation safety is a significant achievement of these objectives.

Most recent amendments have come into force on 1/1/2015.

1.4.1 SMS

This Code reinforces the owner or company's responsibility to ensure the proper management and operation of the ship. The owner or company is required to develop, implement and maintain a Safety Management System (SMS) for the company and ship to use in order to meet the objective. An SMS must have the following relevant functional requirements.

With particular reference to the safety and environment protection policy, the SMS should include a clear statement on the navigation policy of the company. This can be brief, highlighting the company's general aims that should be achieved through safe navigation.

This is a full set of instructions and procedures for carrying out safe ship operations and environmental protection, while satisfying the applicable international and flag state requirements. Generally, this is a large part of SMS. The Code requires procedures to be available for all aspects of operations, implying that all known aspects of navigation are covered. The procedures provide clear instructions that are in line with company policy, to prepare for navigation, execution and monitoring, including how relevant

records should be kept and the performance review. The procedures will define the safety limits to be applied and maintained in particular circumstances. It also covers the maintenance and upkeep of equipment and associated materials.

An organisational structure defining the levels of authority and lines of communication amongst and between the company and shipboard personnel. In addition to general watchkeeping duties, the Master may delegate responsibility for certain aspects of navigation to the officer(s).

The procedures for reporting non-conformities within the provisions of the ISM Code, as well as accident reporting, are fully covered in the operation procedures.

Procedures for readiness and response to emergency situations. The company will supply the ship with standard contingency plans, its procedures for response and communication to the Master are also established in this section.

Procedures for detailing internal audits and reviews. This sets out how performance can be measured, how deficiencies in procedures should be determined, what resources are required and how to use an audit to improve performance.

1.4.2 The Master's Responsibility

The Master must ensure that all officers and crew with navigational duties are fully aware of the company's policy on navigation and understand the established procedures. The Master should also determine the competence of individuals before allocating responsibilities. Finally, the Master must ensure that all individuals are fit for duties and are adequately rested.

Training is considered as the best motivator. Personnel with navigation duties should be trained fully on the equipment that they will use for navigation.

The Master should write a full set of standing orders (see 1.12.1) for the watch officers, supplemented by night orders (see 1.12.2) and also bridge orders where required. Standard marine vocabulary should be adopted for all bridge communications.

All international and flag state requirements must be followed to the Master's satisfaction. The operational status of mandatory equipment including Automatic Identification Systems (AIS), VDR, relevant records (Radio), regular reporting (danger messages and reporting systems) and receipt of information (MSI) must meet the necessary standards.

The Master should review the ship's navigation before the voyage begins, when it is in progress and once it is complete. The process starts with ensuring that the appropriate resources are available and that all personnel are competent and properly trained. Passage plans must be completed in a timely manner and contain enough detail to ensure the ship's safe navigation on its current passage, taking account of the environment. During the performance stages of the voyage, the stipulated watchkeeping resource (in the passage plan) should be maintained and the ship's safe and efficient progress checked regularly. On completion, or if there were any problems, review all the information and records to determine any possible improvements that could be made on future voyages. Where necessary, these include:

- Additional resources required
- additional training
- proposed amendments of procedures required
- lessons to be learnt and communicating them to others.

The Master has overriding authority in cases involving safety and pollution prevention. While the Master can override procedures to complete operations safely, they cannot be amended permanently. Amendments can only be made by the owner, ie the company. The Master may follow advice from external authorities such as routeing instructions but can choose to override these to ensure the safety of the ship and to prevent the environment from being damaged.

1.4.3 Simplified Compliance

Knowledge of the current international and flag state requirements and ways to comply with them are important for complying with the ISM Code. Whether it is navigation, collision avoidance, navigation equipment or radio and communications, a few basics apply in all cases. These can be summarised as follows:

- Equipment must be approved in line with the requirements
- there must be sufficient equipment as stated by the requirements
- personnel must be familiar with and trained on using all equipment
- personnel must have full knowledge of the procedures that are to be followed
- proper records, whether they are automatic or human interface, must be maintained
- records must be maintained for the specified periods
- checklists must be reviewed regularly
- valid documents must be available at all times
- crews must be able to communicate clearly

- risk assessment principles and techniques should be completed for all identified risks
- regular assessments and monitoring should be carried out
- the SMS should not be different to the law, although the company may choose to make their own requirements more stringent for added safety.

Author's Note:

Critics of the Code will argue that "If all procedures are in place, what is the need for training"? But procedures are for guidance only and are generic. Not all situations are the same. Those responsible for navigation must have detailed knowledge and understanding of the tasks and their duties in order to deal with all types of circumstances and scenarios. This also applies to instructions from external bodies. A Master, fully competent on navigational issues, can make a sound judgement on whether or not to follow the given advice or guidance or to prepare his own plans to meet the requirements ensuring the safety of the ship, crew and environment.

Another debate is the perceived conflict between the requirements under the ISM Code to produce a wide range of documents and reports as part of its SMS and the consequential production of potentially self incriminating evidence that could be used against those who produce that evidence. This text is not where the right or wrong answers to the conflicting position should be stated. The only comment by the author is that compliance with the Code – and the SMS – is a legal requirement and where it demands records to be maintained, these records cannot be avoided. In addition, the Code is designed to ensure safety and prevent accidents or incidents. Where these are still happening, something is going wrong and the authorities should use some tools to teach appropriate lessons. The issue of using records for commercial cases is beyond the scope of this text.

1.5 Bridge Procedures Guide

Produced by the ICS this publication is designed to make mariners aware of good operating practices and efficient bridge organisation. It ensures that similar actions are taken on the bridges of all ships.

1.5.1 Contents

1.5.1.1 Part A

Covers guidance to Masters and navigating officers on the following topics:

- Bridge resource and bridge team management

- passage planning in ocean waters and also in restricted waters, pilotage, ship's routeing, ship reporting systems and vessel traffic services
- duties of the OOW with regard to watch-keeping, navigation, communication, pollution prevention and in emergency situations the operation and maintenance of bridge equipment.

There are also Annexes containing the formats used for pilotage, lists of distress frequencies and guidance on steering-gear test routines.

1.5.1.2 Part B

Provides bridge checklists for routine bridge procedures including:

- Familiarisation with bridge equipment
- preparation for sea
- preparation for arrival in port
- pilotage
- passage plan appraisal
- navigation in coastal waters
- navigation in ocean waters
- anchoring and anchor watch
- navigation in restricted visibility
- navigation in heavy weather or tropical storm areas
- navigation in ice
- changing over watch
- calling the Master.

1.5.1.3 Part C

Provides checklists that can be used during emergencies, including:

- Main engine or steering failure
- collision
- stranding or grounding
- man overboard
- fire
- flooding
- search and rescue
- abandonment of the ship.

A revised edition of 'Bridge Procedures Guide' will be available shortly.

1.6 BNWAS

The requirements making it mandatory to have a bridge navigational watch alarm system (BNWAS) fitted to all passenger and cargo ships are stated in the amendments made to SOLAS Chapter V Regulation 19 that were adopted by the IMO on 5th June 2009 in Resolution MSC.282(86).

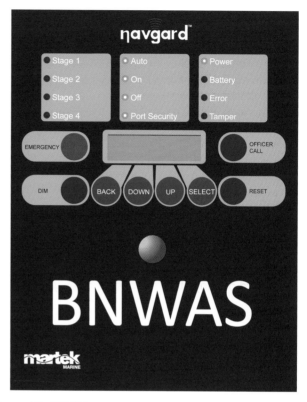

Figure 1.2 BNWAS

The following subparagraph is added to paragraph 2.2 of the regulations:

.3 a bridge navigational watch alarm system (BNWAS), as follows:
.1 cargo ships of 150 gross tonnage and upwards and passenger ships irrespective of size constructed on or after 1 July 2011;
.2 passenger ships irrespective of size constructed before 1 July 2011, not later than the first survey* after 1 July 2012;
.3 cargo ships of 3,000 gross tonnage and upwards constructed before 1 July 2011, not later than the first survey* after 1 July 2012;
.4 cargo ships of 500 gross tonnage and upwards but less than 3,000 gross tonnage constructed before 1 July 2011, not later than the first survey* after 1 July 2013; and
.5 cargo ships of 150 gross tonnage and upwards but less than 500 gross tonnage constructed before 1 July 2011, not later than the first survey* after 1 July 2014. The bridge navigational watch alarm system shall be in operation whenever the ship is underway at sea;
.4 a bridge navigational watch alarm system (BNWAS) installed prior to 1 July 2011 may subsequently be exempted from full compliance with the standards adopted by the Organization, at the discretion of the Administration."

The purpose of BNWAS is to monitor the watchkeeper for any sign of disability that may lead to marine accidents. A watch officer is required to press the button on a Timer Reset Panel or to operate the navigation equipment, eg ECDIS, Radar etc, at certain intervals. When the officer does not press the button within pre-set intervals, visual and audible alarms will be generated in the wheelhouse. If the officer doesn't respond to the alarm, the system transfers the alarm to the Cabin Panels installed in other sections of the ship, in order to inform the Master/backup officers of the watch officer's incapacity.

1.7 Buoyage

IALA (The International Association of Marine Aids to Navigation Lighthouse Authorities) has set the design and standard of buoys that are used for navigational purposes.

It divides the world into two regions, A and B, for the purpose of Lateral Marks. B includes all of the Americas, Japan, Philippines and South Korea. The cardinal marks are uniform throughout the world.

1.7.1 Direction of Buoyage and Distance

Direction of buoyage can be found either from navigational charts or sailing directions. Locally, it is the direction taken by the mariner from seaward when approaching a harbour, river, estuary or other waterway. It is usually determined by the buoyage authorities and tends to be clockwise around continental landmasses.

There is no specified minimum distance that a buoy should be passed. Looking at the chart, the proximity to hazards, ship's draught and the amount of sea room can assist in deciding the safe distance that should be maintained. In congested waters the distance is not expected to be large. When following the lateral marks, the ship should remain as close to the mark on the starboard hand side of the ship as appropriate.

- When proceeding with the direction of buoyage, use the starboard hand marks
- when going against the direction of buoyage, use the port hand marks.

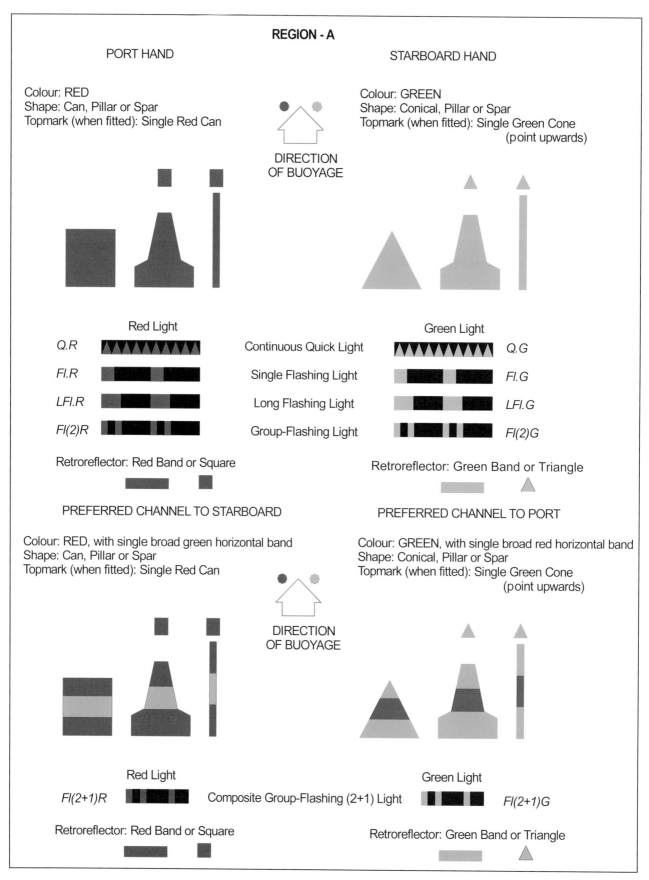

Figure 1.3 IALA lateral marks "Region A"

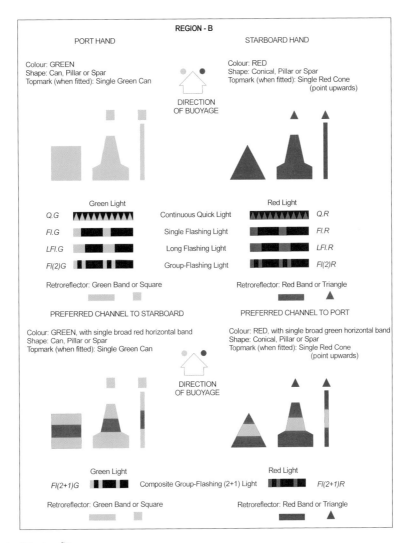

Figure 1.4 IALA lateral marks "Region B"

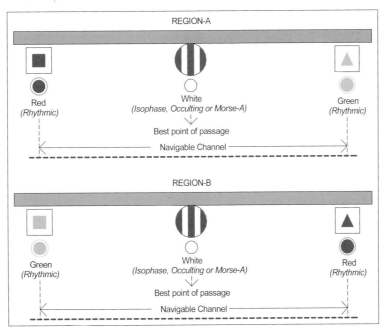

Figure 1.5 IALA lateral marking under bridges

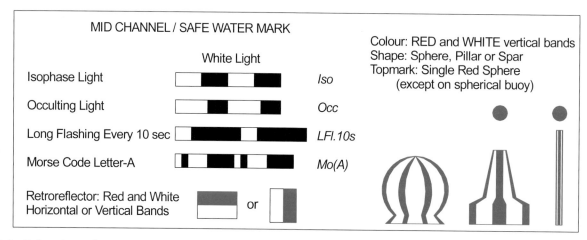

Figure 1.6 Safe water mark

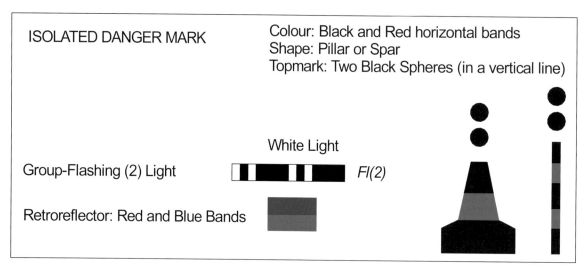

Figure 1.7 Isolated danger mark

1.7.2 Special Marks

Special marks are used to indicate:

- Cables or pipelines
- recreational areas
- ocean data acquisition systems
- firing or military exercise zones
- termination points of Traffic Separation Scheme, where required
- spoil ground
- channel within a channel.

Author's Note:
To remember this, take the first letter of each to spell CROFTS Ch.

SPECIAL MARKS

Colour: YELLOW
Shape: Conical, Can, Sphere, Pillar, Spar or Cylinder
Topmark: Optional - Single Yellow St Andrew's Cross
     (except on spherical, conical or can buoy)

Yellow Light, any rhythm except that used for white lights

Retroreflector: Yellow Band

Figure 1.8   Special marks

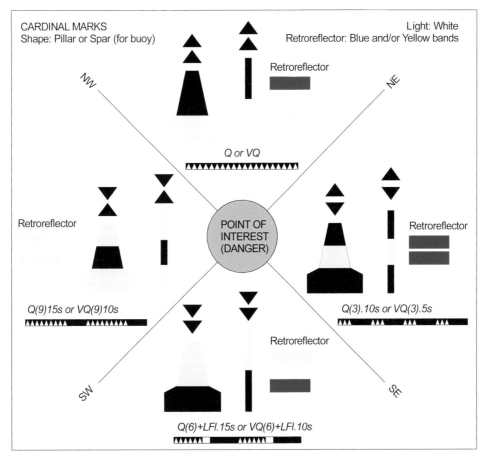

Figure 1.9   Cardinal marks

1.7.3 New Dangers

New dangers are marked by one or more cardinal or lateral marks as required by the IALA system. If lights are fitted, they will be quick or very quick.

Where it is particularly dangerous, at least one of the marks will be repeated at close intervals, by an identical mark as soon as practical.

A RACON using morse code D, with a signal length of one nautical mile on a radar display, can be used on the repeated mark.

IALA has developed an emergency 'wreck marking buoy'. It is in the form of a pillar or spar buoy, with yellow and blue vertical stripes, and has a yellow and blue alternating flashing light that has a nominal range of 4 nm.

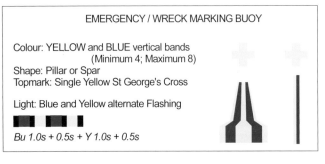

EMERGENCY / WRECK MARKING BUOY

Colour: YELLOW and BLUE vertical bands
(Minimum 4; Maximum 8)
Shape: Pillar or Spar
Topmark: Single Yellow St George's Cross

Light: Blue and Yellow alternate Flashing

Bu 1.0s + 0.5s + Y 1.0s + 0.5s

Figure 1.10 Wreck marking buoy

1.8 ISPS

The provisions of the International Ship and Port Facility Security Code (ISPS) may have a bearing on navigation. Areas with heightened security threats should be avoided at the planning stage or passed at an increased distance, and transits should be completed allowing for these additional precautions.

The ship's officers should be aware of any potential evasive manoeuvres, as indicated in the ship's security plan. Similarly, depending on the port's security level, the ship should either be able to stay clear of port or be ready to leave port at very short notice if the conditions dictate. There should be contingency plans available for all eventualities in a tabular format that can be transferred to the navigational charts as and when required.

1.9 Pollution

The navigator is responsible for advising the relevant departments about the distances from the nearest land, ie the base line, depth of water (for chemical tankers and ballast water exchange) and the presence of the ship in special areas. He should also obtain specific authority from the bridge before allowing any MARPOL-controlled discharges from the ship.

1.10 Guidance from a Flag State

IMO Conventions can either be adopted by a flag State to form its own law or, the flag State may produce legislation fulfilling the requirements of the relevant IMO Convention also enhancing them. In addition, the flag State may also provide guidance in the form of codes of practice or guidance notices related to specific areas. This occurs when:

- New legislation is introduced
- an enquiry into an accident has identified poor practice
- there are issues involving safety and pollution prevention
- the industry has to be notified of a change.

The flag State administration may also issue notices. The UK's MCA issues notices in three series:

1.10.1 Merchant Shipping Notices (MSN)

These are related to UK legislation and contain information to comply with it. They contain technical details relating to statutory instruments and regulations and are also numbered in sequence with the prefix MSN. They are related to publications including COSWP, LSA regulations, SOLAS.

1.10.2 Marine Guidance Notes (MGN)

Providing guidance and advice to improve the safety of shipping. They are concerned with issues that relate to the safety of life at sea and pollution prevention. They are sequentially numbered with the prefix MGN. Examples are Navigation in Dover Strait, Navigation in fog, STCW and MARPOL.

1.10.3 Marine Information Notices (MIN)

Intended for a limited readership and are valid for a limited period of time only. They provide information regarding training establishments, equipment manufacturers and research results.

1.10.4 Carriage Requirements for Publications

Flag States also require certain bridge publications to be carried. For example, the following are required under UK law:

- A full set of navigational charts, fully corrected and the latest edition, including the chart catalogue. These can be approved electronic charts
- notices to mariners

- annual summary of notices to mariners
- International Code of Signals
- mariners handbook
- sailing directions
- list of radio signals
- list of lights
- tide tables
- tidal stream atlases
- MSN (Merchant Shipping Notices), MIN (Marine Information Notices), MGN (Marine Guidance Notices)
- Nautical Almanac
- operating and maintenance instructions for the ship's navigational equipment.

1.11 Voyage Data Recorder

For operational and legal reasons, ships are required to maintain extensive records. These records allow performance to be analysed and proof that legislation has been complied with.

There are two main problems with traditional methods of record keeping:

- Manipulation and falsification of records by unscrupulous individuals
- loss of all evidence and records if the ship is lost or there is a major fire.

Considering the aviation industry's experiences with the Black-Box, the IMO has made it mandatory for ships to be fitted with a 'Voyage Data Recorder' (VDR). The main purpose of the VDR is to make data available after an incident so investigators can gain a better understanding of the events that led up to it, particularly where the ship is lost without trace, records have been lost or the crew have perished due to the accident. The requirement is part of SOLAS Chapter V. The following ships must be fitted with a VDR:

- Passenger ships built on or after 1st July, 2002
- Ro-Ro passenger ships built before 1st July, 2002, but no later than the first survey on or after 1st July, 2002
- passenger ships (not Ro-Ro passenger ships) built before 1st July 2002, but no later than 1st January, 2004
- ships (not passenger ships) of 3,000 GT and upwards, built on or after 1st July, 2002
- VDRs must meet the minimum performance standards specified by the IMO. A VDR consists of:

  - a main unit that can be connected to a download device
  - a protective capsule housing the device
  - records of the previous twelve hours of data
  - external cables
  - a reserve power source
  - an acoustic beacon.

The VDR automatically maintains records of a number of parameters on a ship for the last twelve hours.

Data	Source
Date and Time	Using a source external to the ship (GPS)
Ship's Position	Electronic positioning system
Speed (water or ground)	Ship's speed log or designated equipment
Heading	Ship's compass (Gyro)
Bridge Audio	8 microphones
Communications audio	VHF and other R/T units
Radar (post display)	Screen dump every 12 seconds
Water depth	Echo sounder
Main alarms	All mandatory alarms on the bridge
Rudder order and response	Steering gear and autopilot
Engine order and response	Telegraphs, controls, thrusters
Hull opening status	All mandatory status information displayed on the bridge
Watertight and fire door status	All mandatory status information displayed on the bridge
Acceleration and hull stresses	Hull stress and response monitoring equipment where fitted
Wind speed and direction	Anemometer where fitted
Last 12 hour data	*Analysis report of data*

Table 1.4 VDR recorded data

The equipment should be approved before installation. Throughout the ship's life, the VDR system and all its sensors must be tested annually. The test should be conducted in conjunction with the relevant statutory survey, ie, for Passenger Ship Safety Certificate (PC), Cargo Ship Safety Certificate (CSC) or Cargo Ship Safety Equipment Certificate (SEC). The survey must be within the period permitted by the Harmonised System of Survey and Certification, three months before the due date for PC, and +/- three months of the due date for CSC and SEC surveys. Once the tests have been completed successfully and there is satisfactory performance, the administration will issue a performance test certificate to the ship, which must be kept on board. The tests include verification of the accuracy, duration and recoverability of the recorded data. Tests and inspections must also be conducted to determine the serviceability of all protective enclosures and devices fitted. To prevent any over-writing of data, it is important to turn the VDR off shortly after arriving in the port where the test is to be performed.

During an emergency, it is important that the Master downloads the data early to prevent it from being any over-written. This is important for investigation and evidence purposes. If the emergency situation continues for a significant period of time subsequent downloads, at less than twelve hours intervals, should be carried out. Some companies have procedures for VDR data to be downloaded at less than twelve hour intervals so access to the entire voyage data is available for analysis and investigation, when required.

1.12 Standing and Night Orders

Shipping is governed by various conventions, codes and guidelines at national and international levels. These provide the framework where the officers' duties are performed routinely and at times in extra-ordinary circumstances. The owner's SMS provides operational procedures that are based on the owner's navigation policy. These should work without any conflict within the SMS and applies to every ship.

1.12.1 Standing Orders

1.12.1.1 Criteria for Standing Orders

The Company may have standing instructions for navigation, however the Master should also provide standing orders to explain the requirements to the officers. These might relate to the Master's own experiences, points that have caused concern in the past or lessons that have been learned. The standing orders will reflect the type of ship, trading pattern, personnel forming the bridge team and their experience, these are all specific to the ship and

her crew. The Master must ensure that the officers understand the content of the orders.

1.12.1.2 Purpose of Standing Orders

The Master should provide standing orders that clearly set out his requirements to the officers. The standing orders will be supplemented daily by night orders. These orders set the general standards required of the watchkeepers. The standing orders should be used to supplement other available publications, eg Bridge Procedures Guide, SMS, etc. A copy should be available on the bridge and all the officers should sign it. The purpose is:

- To lay down the ground rules of the Master's expectations of his officers in various circumstances
- to reinforce practices that the Master expects to be followed
- to create a relationship where mutual confidence is established
- to increase the responsibility of the officers without imposing limitations
- to ensure that one person's mistake does not put the ship in danger
- for officers to check their own and verify others work when handing or taking over the watch. This should also apply to times under pilot
- officers will know when the Master expects to be called and the Master knows that the OOWs will follow his instructions.

Consideration should be given to the special circumstances that exist every time the Master takes over command. These will relate to the particular ship and also to the officers and crew serving on her. The temptation is to use one set of tried and tested Master's standing orders without any adjustments being made for each ship. As well as being a mistake it is also a lost opportunity to address the special needs and circumstances of each different command.

SO should start with a general section covering factors that are common to all watchkeeping situations. Some examples that should be covered are:

- Manning levels on the bridge
- keeping a lookout
- protection of the marine environment
- distress situations
- use of navigational equipment
- testing of navigational equipment
- safe passing distances
- calling the Master
- special circumstances, that exist every time the Master takes over command.

This section should be followed by more detailed advice covering the following watchkeeping situations:

- Preparation for arrival/departure
- ocean passages
- coastal passages
- TSS and confined waters
- navigating with a Pilot on board
- heavy weather
- ice
- TRS
- at anchor
- in port
- ship operations.

The Master should sign and date all standing orders, all watchkeepers should then read and also sign the standing orders indicating that they understand and will comply with them.

1.12.2 Night Orders

- These are specific instructions given to watchkeeping officers in a given situation and are supplementary to the standing orders
- they cover periods when the Master is absent from the bridge at night
- these instructions allow the OOW to take action to ensure the ship's safety and also allows sufficient time for the Master to take command of the ship
- it must be understood that these instructions are intended to increase the responsibility of the OOW and are not meant to impose limitations
- the information contained in the night order should not be a repetition of the aspects of the passage plan that the OOW already knows. They should be instructions based on the Master's knowledge and experience that would allow the passage plan and general navigational duties to be performed better
- details of when to serve various notices, call crew, call the Master, send or receive messages and the changes required in the status of machinery are common examples

- operational circumstances during the night are also covered under these orders, eg any ongoing operations. Night orders would give courses, RPM, manned/UMS, clock changes and anything that was occurring, such as a fire pump under repair, cargo ventilation, gasfreeing, hatch lids or doors that are deliberately left open. It may also include handling the ship during heavy weather or other hazardous situations
- navigational aspects are detailed including position/ area, course and speed. The night orders should provide instructions on the security level and readiness to combat security related threats
- advice on using specific navigational equipment and the special set up for the navigational needs, including radar set up, the radar range scales to use, radar performance checks to perform, ranges where coast or features are likely to be detected on radar considering the environmental conditions, using an echo sounder and its set up, the necessity to cross check a position using different methods, etc
- details of weather and changes that are likely to be encountered and their effect on course keeping, unusual currents and/or tidal streams
- manning levels to be maintained at different stages, including the need for additional personnel
- specific actions to be taken regarding navigation, eg when making landfall, and specific guidance on what to do if detections are not made at the expected times
- radio channels/frequencies to guard and any reports to be made
- each OOW should sign the night order book
- it should be maintained as an important record of on board events.

The aim of providing standing orders and night orders is to make the framework clear that the OOW or duty officer is expected to work in. It avoids any question of 'but I wasn't told to do so' by the officers.

2 Passage Planning

Safety at sea is the primary concern of any mariner, but it must be achieved alongside the commercial requirements of a voyage. It is critical that a ship completes its operations safely and efficiently. The majority of studies into maritime casualties have highlighted human error as one of the most significant contributory factors in an incident. Careful planning plays a significant part in reducing these errors, creating an environment for safety and commercial success. Passage Planning is a recommendation for ensuring safety at sea.

There are international, national and company specific recommendations for passage planning. These may be in the form of IMO guidelines, ICS – Bridge Procedures Guide, MCA – A Guide to the Planning and Conduct of Sea Passages, MCA – MGNs and MSNs and part of Company Safety Management System. In particular, SMS provides detailed instructions for it.

A bridge team consists of several individuals who may have different levels of knowledge, skills and experience. As well as being a requirement, passage planning serves a useful purpose in ensuring that the bridge team follows agreed consistent procedures and standards. In looking at the technical skills, consideration must be given to the techniques involved in preparing for and conducting the proposed passage.

The passage plan should make it easier for the bridge team to navigate the ship safely. It should be comprehensive, detailed and easy to interpret. The full procedure has four stages:

- Appraisal
- planning
- execution
- monitoring.

The first two stages are the preparatory ones. Stages three and four are the essential elements of voyage execution and confirm that the voyage is being conducted according to the plan. The procedure must be supported by good information and data.

2.1 Appraisal

Before embarking on any venture, the personnel controlling or playing a part in it, must understand the risks that are likely to be involved. The purpose of appraisal is to provide a clear indication of all the danger areas, areas where it will be possible to navigate safely, including any existing routeing or reporting systems and vessel traffic services, as well as areas where marine environmental protection considerations apply.

During appraisal, all relevant information to the passage is gathered and the risks are examined. The following items should be taken into account when voyage and passage planning:

- The condition and state of the ship, its stability and its equipment, any operational limitations, its permissible draught at sea in fairways and ports, its manoeuvring data, including any restrictions
- any special characteristics of the cargo, particularly if hazardous, its distribution, stowage and securing on board the ship
- the provision of a competent and adequately rested crew who are able to undertake the voyage or passage
- requirements for up-to-date certificates and documents concerning the ship, its equipment, crew, passengers or cargo
- appropriate scale, accurate and up-to-date charts should be used for the intended voyage or passage, as well as any relevant permanent or temporary notices to mariners and existing radio navigational warnings
- accurate and up-to-date sailing directions, lists of lights and radio aids to navigation
- any relevant up-to-date additional information, including:
  - mariners' routeing guides and passage planning charts, published by competent authorities
  - current and tidal atlases and tide tables
  - climatological, hydrographical and oceanographic data, including other appropriate meteorological information

- availability of services for weather routeing, eg information contained in Volume D of the World Meteorological Organization's Publication No. 9
- existing ships' routeing and reporting systems, ship traffic services and marine environmental protection measures
- volume of traffic likely to be encountered throughout the voyage or passage
- if a pilot is being used, information relating to pilotage, embarkation and disembarkation including the exchange of information between the Master and pilot
- available port information, including information that relates to the availability of shore-based emergency response arrangements and equipment
- any additional items pertinent to the type of ship or its cargo, the particular areas where the ship will traverse and the type of voyage or passage being undertaken.

2.1.1 Use of Publications

Detailed information is required so that decisions regarding the overall conduct of the passage can be made. This information is taken from several sources, such as regular publications or notices provided in response to events. Instructions from parties influencing the venture, eg owners and charterers, will also be part of the appraisal.

Choosing which authority's publication to use will depend on the Chart Outfit carried on board, the availability of local publications and legal requirements for carriage, for example charts for coastal or inland waters.

2.1.1.1 Chart Catalogue

The United Kingdom Hydrographic Office (UKHO) publishes The Catalogue of Admiralty Charts and Other Hydrographic Publications (NP131) annually. It shows the area that BA charts and other BA publications cover. The Defence Mapping Agency (DMA) of the USA produces a similar document, the CATP2V01U. The US version shows the areas the US charts and other publications cover.

2.1.1.2 Navigational Charts

These are a very significant source of information. Most merchant vessels carry UKHO or US charts. Some areas of the world are covered in greater detail by charts that are published by local hydrographic authorities. In some parts of the world it may be a requirement to use local charts. UKHO charts are published on a large scale allowing safe navigation in the coastal waters of the UK, the Commonwealth and some Middle Eastern countries. For other areas the policy is to publish enough charts to allow the mariner

to cross the oceans and proceed along the coasts to reach the port approaches safely.

2.1.1.3 Sailing Directions and Pilot Books

'Admiralty Sailing Directions', or 'Pilot Books' as they are commonly known, are published by the UKHO in volumes. These provide worldwide coverage and are intended to complement the Admiralty charts. They contain descriptions of:

- The coast
- off-lying features
- tidal streams and currents
- directions for navigation in complicated waters
- information about channels and harbours
- navigational hazards
- buoyage systems
- pilotage
- regulations
- general notes on countries covered by the volume
- port facilities
- seasonal currents
- ice
- climatic conditions with direct access to the sea.

Sailing directions are published by the DMA in the series SDPUB 121-200. Some provide information similar to Ocean Passages for the World and are referred to as Planning Guides. Other publications contain information similar to Pilot Books and can be referred to en-route.

2.1.1.4 Ocean Passages for the World (NP136)

Published by the UKHO, it contains information on planning ocean passages, oceanography and currents. It also provides recommended routes and the distances between the world's principal ports as well as details about winds, weather, currents and ice hazards that may be encountered. Ocean Passages also contains diagrams and chartlets for the main ocean routes for power vessels and sailing ships.

2.1.1.5 Routeing Charts and Pilot Charts

These contain basic routeing instructions, together with meteorological details, they are published for the main oceans for a twelve-month period. The information includes limits of load line zones, routes and distances between principal ports and focal points, ocean currents, wind roses and ice limits. Inset chartlets and texts include air, dew point and sea temperatures, barometric pressure, diurnal variation and the incidence of fog, gales and storms.

Routeing charts are published by the UKHO as Chart numbers 5124-8. Similar meteorological charts are published by the DMA and are known as Pilot Charts.

2.1.1.6 Admiralty List of Radio Signals (ALRS)

The UKHO publishes this list in 6 volumes:

- Volume 1 - Maritime Radio Stations NP281, 2 Parts
  Global marine communications service, ship reporting systems, medical advice by radio, quarantine reports, locust reports, CRSs, coastguard stations, piracy and armed robbery reports, alien smuggling reporting, radio regulations in territorial waters
- Volume 2 - Radio Aids to Navigation, D/F, Radar beacons, Satellite
  Navigation systems, legal time, radio time signals and electronic position fixing system
- Volume 3 - Maritime Safety Information Services, 2 Parts
  Radio facsimile broadcasts and weather services, navigational warnings (WWNWS and NAVTEX), weather routeing services, global marine meteorological services, meteorological codes for shipping use. (See Chapter 11 for more on this)
- Volume 4 - Meteorological Observation Stations
- Volume 5 - Global Maritime Distress and Safety System (GMDSS) (See Chapter 11 for more on this)
- Volume 6 - Pilot Services, Vessel Traffic Services and Port Operations, 5 Parts.

Similar information is available in the DMA publications of the USA.

2.1.1.7 List of Lights and Fog Signals

These are published by the UKHO in eleven volumes and provide worldwide coverage. A UKHO digital version of the List of Lights and Fog Signals is also available, covering the world in ten areas. The digital version is corrected using diskettes, that are issued weekly. The US Coast Guard (USCG) publishes seven volumes of Light Lists and Fog Signals, covering the US coast and Great Lakes. Light Lists published by the DMA cover the rest of the world.

2.1.1.8 Notices to Mariners

The UKHO and DMA publish notices to mariners in weekly editions. The contents include:

- Index
- admiralty notices to mariners
- navigational warnings
- corrections to the Admiralty sailing directions
- corrections to the Admiralty list of lights and fog signals
- corrections to the Admiralty list of radio signals (ALRS).

Digital versions of Notices to Mariners are also available. They are used to correct digital charts (ECDIS, ENC, and ARCS) and digital lists of lights.

2.1.1.9 Ship's Routeing

Published by the IMO. This book contains information on all routeing, traffic separation schemes (TSS), deepwater routes and areas to be avoided. Similar information can be found on charts and is also contained in the sailing directions.

2.1.1.10 Tide Tables

The UKHO annually publishes four volumes of the Admiralty Tide Tables (ATT) that cover the world. 'TOTAL TIDE', a digital CD version of UKHO Tide Tables, uses computers to provide tidal information and covers the world in ten areas. Paper and digital versions also provide tidal stream data. The US National Ocean Service also publishes worldwide tables.

2.1.1.11 Tidal Stream Atlases

Published by the UKHO and cover the waters of North West Europe and Hong Kong. Total Tide provides worldwide tidal stream information. Some port authorities publish their own tidal stream atlases. The US National Ocean Service publishes tidal current tables that cover the Atlantic Coast of North America and the Pacific Coast of North America and Asia.

2.1.1.12 Co-Tidal and Co-Range Charts

These are published for waters where tidal conditions are particularly significant to safety and critical for navigation.

2.1.1.13 Load Line Chart

Load line zones are shown in Ocean Passages for the World and in BA Chart D6083. The chart shows the boundaries of the zones and the applicable dates for seasonal zones.

2.1.1.14 Nautical Almanac and Tables

These provide essential navigational information of certain events, eg sunrise and sunset.

2.1.1.15 Distance Tables

The UKHO and DMA produce tables giving coastal and ocean distances. Some independent companies, such as Reed's or BP, also produce distance tables.

2.1.1.16 The Mariner's Handbook

This book is published by the UKHO. It contains advice and recommendations on navigation and general information that is of interest to the mariner.

2.1.1.17 Passage Planning Charts – 5500 Series

These are available for certain parts of the world, eg the Dover Straits, Malacca Straits and the Red Sea.

They contain useful information in the form of text and diagrams.

2.1.1.18 Annual Summary of Admiralty Notices to Mariners

Published by the UKHO, it contains information and UK legislation that is relevant to British shipping.

2.1.1.19 Merchant Shipping Notices

This series of notices is published by the MCA and MAIB.

MSNs contain statutory information that must be complied with.
MGNs contain advice and recommendations on matters concerning safety of life at sea and pollution prevention.
MINs contain information that is for limited readership and is intended to support information about the services available to the industry. These have an expiry date.

2.1.2 Other Sources of Information

2.1.2.1 Climatic Information

Climatic information can be obtained from:

- Pilot books
- pilot charts
- The Mariner's Handbook
- Ocean Passages for the World
- Meteorology for Mariners.

2.1.2.2 Weather Reports

These are significant just before the voyage starts and during it. They are used for reviewing the passage plan once the ship has embarked on the voyage. Sources of weather information include:

- Radio weather reports
- NAVTEX (See Chapter 11)
- port authorities
- other shipping.

2.1.2.3 Navigational Warnings

These contain the most recent changes to navigational aids and hazards. They are obtained from:

- Radio
- INMARSAT/SafetyNET (See Chapter 11)
- NAVTEX
- Vessel Traffic Services (VTS)
- harbour authorities.

Navigational warnings are also published in the Annual Summary of Admiralty Notices to Mariners and the weekly editions of Notices to Mariners.

2.1.2.4 Onboard Navigation Systems Technical and User Manuals

These are supplied with the navigational equipment when it is installed on board. All officers using the equipment should read and understand the user manuals.

2.1.2.5 Manoeuvring Data and Draught Information

Full manoeuvring characteristics information in various conditions throughout the voyage are required to determine the wheel-over positions and the ship's ability to follow the track in safety, while taking into account the width of channels and planned speeds. These characteristics will determine the amount of sea room that the ship requires and the clearances over and under obstructions.

2.1.2.6 Owner's and Charterer's Instructions

Instructions relating to bunkering, storing and routeing from the C/P may leave the Master with a limited choice. In complying with these instructions, it must be remembered that the ultimate responsibility for the safety of the ship rests with the Master, who has overriding authority in all cases concerning safety and pollution.

2.1.2.7 Routeing Advice

Some routeing agencies may provide advice on the route to be followed, based on the ship and weather that is likely to be experienced.

2.1.2.8 Passage Records and Personal Experience

Records of the ship's past performance under similar conditions are valuable when deciding on a route. The Master, officers and crew members personal experiences of the intended ports and areas may also be a useful source of information.

2.1.2.9 Other Publications and Authorities - Information from other Ships

Consult the Guide to Port Entry, any Port handbooks, information from Agents and P&I correspondents regarding local regulations, facilities, approaches, mooring and watchmen requirements. Observations made by other ships regarding weather encountered and the conditions experienced in the areas and ports to be visited may be considered up-to-date, but should always be used with caution.

Use an appropriate checklist to ensure that nothing is left to chance and that all aspects have been covered. Table 2.1 is a combined checklist for appraisal, planning and other aspects of passage planning.

Checklist Questions		References/Remarks
a) General Information 1. Are there any Port/Pilot/Agent/Charter's instructions for the intended passage?	☑	→ ....
2. Does the Company have any special instructions pertaining to the route?	☐	→ ....
3. Has the Master given any particular instructions?	☐	→ ....
4. Has the ship been to the present destination port(s) in the past? (If so, the record of previous passage can help identify the route and the navigation officer can construct a new with amendments)?	☐	→ Date of Voyage/Copy of previous Passage Plan → ....
5. Is there any watchkeeping officer on board who has already been to that area/port?	☐	→ Name/Record of Information obtained → ....
b) Publications 1. Is there any requirement for the use of local publications/navigational charts?	☐	Yes/No (If YES, Sheet No.) ....
2. Are there any local publications required and available for departure and destination port?	☐	→ Yes/No (If YES, Sheet No.) ....
3. Are the following publications present on board and corrected up to date?		
a. Chart Catalogue (NP 131)	☐	→ Edn. ... ...
b. Navigational Charts - the largest scale available	☐	→ Corrected to ANM ... ...
c. Routeing Charts	☐	→ Edn. ... ...
d. Admiralty Notices to Mariners/Annual Summary	☐	→ Latest ANM on board ... ...
e. Sailing Directions	☐	→ Edn. ... ... Corrected to ANM ....
f. Tide Tables	☐	→ Edn. ... ...
g. Tidal Stream Atlas		→ Edn. ... ...
h. List of Lights	☐	→ Edn. ... ... Corrected to ANM ....
i. List of Radio Signals	☐	→ Edn. ... ... Corrected to ANM ....
j. Guide to Port Entry	☐	→ Edn. ... ...
k. Mariner's handbook	☐	→ Edn. ... ... Corrected to ANM ....
l. Ocean Passages for the World	☐	→ Edn. ... ... Corrected to ANM ....
m. Ships Routeing (IMO)	☐	→ Edn. ... ...
n. Load line chart	☐	→ Edn. ... ...
o. Other	☐	→ Edn. ... ...
4. Additional Publications		
a. MSNs, MGNs, MINs		→ Location on bridge ....
b. Manual for all the navigational equipment on bridge		→ Location on bridge ....

c. International Code of Signals		→ Edn. … … … …………
d. Admiralty/other Distance Tables		→ Edn. … … … …………
e. Chart Correction Log (NP133A)		→ Edn. … … … …………
f. IALA Buoyage System (NP735)		→ Edn. … … … …………
g. Symbols & Abbreviations (BA Chart 5011)		→ Edn. … … … …………
c) Vessel & Cargo 1. Is there any bunker port diversion to consider bunkering?	☐	→ Yes/No (If YES, Sheet No.) ……………………
2. Is the ship loaded or in ballast? (For ships manoeuvring data)	☐	→ Loaded/In Ballast
3. Has the pilot card been updated? (If possible, obtain a copy and attach with passage plan)		→ Yes/No (If YES, Sheet No.) ……………………
4. Does the ship have sufficient UKC?	☐	→ UKC ……………… m/ft
5. Has the pilot boarding area been considered for manoeuvring to provide lee for the pilot boat?	☐	→ Yes/No (If YES, Sheet No.) ……………………
6. Are there any overhead cables/bridges in the passage for consideration of air-draft?	☐	→ Yes/No (If YES, Sheet No.) ……………………
7. Are there any special Cargo Condition/ Requirements that may affect the passage plan?	☐	→ Yes/No (If YES, Sheet No.) ……………………
d) Weather 1. Does the plan take Meteorological conditions into account?	☐	→ ………………………
2. Have the latest weather forecasts/warnings been obtained and checked?	☐	→ …………… **Sheet No.** …………………………
3. Does the ship follow advice from any weather routeing service?	☐	→ …………… **Sheet No.** …………………………
4. Have the latest Navigational Warnings been taken into account?	☐	→ ………………………
e) Watch keeping Personnel 1. Has the requirement for OOW/Lookout doubling up watches been considered with respect to adverse weather/restricted visibility?	☐	→ …………… **Sheet No.** …………………………
2. Has the crew calling points for anchor/ berthing stations, piracy watches been established and noted on the chart/passage plan?	☐	→ …………… **Sheet No.** …………………………
3. Have the rest hours for watchkeepers been considered?	☐	→ …………… **Sheet No.** …………………………
f) Passage 1. Are there any mandatory ship reporting schemes?	☐	→ ………………………
2. Has the position of pilot boarding/ disembarkation been established?	☐	→ ………………………
3. Has clock adjustment with respect to local times been considered and times/positions noted on the chart to advance/retard clocks?	☐	→

4.	Has the condition & availability of anchorage berths been considered?	☐	→	....
5.	Is risk assessment carried out for predicted areas of danger?	☐	→	....
g)	**Plan**			
1.	Have the following been marked/drawn on the chart?			
	a) Courses as recommended by local/ international regulations, company & Master's instructions	☐	→	References....................................
	b) Margins of safety as required by the Master/company	☐	→	References....................................
	c) Wheel over points	☐	→	....
	d) VTS or other reporting points marked on the chart and noted in the Passage Plan sheet	☐	→	.... **Sheet No.** ....
	e) Pilot boarding position and alternative pilot boarding position in case of adverse weather	☐	→	References....................................
	f) Speed reduction points	☐	→	.... **Sheet No.** ....
	g) Notices to engine room	☐	→	.... **Sheet No.** ....
	h) Abort points	☐	→	.... **Sheet No.** ....
	i) Point where call is given to ship's Crew for anchor/berthing stations		→	.... **Sheet No.** ....
	j) Sequence of charts for the passage	☐	→	marked on charts
	k) Cross Index Range (CIR) for Parallel Indexing	☐	→	.... **Sheet No.** ....
	l) Tides and currents	☐	→	.... **Sheet No.** ....
	m) Predicated areas of danger and no-go areas	☐	→	marked on charts
	n) Radar Conspicuous objects eg hills, RACONS etc	☐	→	marked on charts
	o) Transit & clearing bearings	☐	→	marked on charts
	p) Position indicating when to move onto the next chart along with Chart Number	☐	→	marked on charts
	q) Waypoint number on each waypoint	☐	→	marked on charts
	r) Position on chart where additional navigation aids are required to be switched on	☐	→	marked on charts
	s) Specific meteorological information relating to any area, eg haze, dust storms, areas of restricted visibility	☐	→ →	marked on charts References...............
	t) Navigational warnings, preliminary and temporary chart corrections from notices to mariners	☐	→ →	marked on charts References...............
	u) Areas of special marine environmental protection consideration	☐	→ →	marked on charts References...............

v) Minimum under keel clearance required particularly in shallow waters	☐	→ →	marked on charts References................
2. Have the primary & secondary means of position fixing been agreed on?	☐	→	Recorded in passage plan sheet
3. Have the position plotting intervals been agreed on for each leg?	☐	→	Recorded in passage plan sheet
4. Has a way been identified to verify the datum on a navigational chart with the Datum in the GPS	☐	→	Recorded in passage plan sheet
5. Are there any contingency plans available for the following?			
• Failure of electronic navigational aids		→	.... **Sheet No.** ....
• Man overboard	☐	→	.... **Sheet No.** ....
• Fire	☐	→	.... **Sheet No.** ....
• Steering gear failure	☐	→	.... **Sheet No.** ....
• Main engine failure	☐	→	.... **Sheet No.** ....
• Helicopter operations	☐	→	.... **Sheet No.** ....
• Radar failures	☐	→	.... **Sheet No.** ....
• Piracy/armed robbery/terrorist activity	☐	→	.... **Sheet No.** ....
• Distress	☐	→	.... **Sheet No.** ....
• Unavailability of Pilot/ OOW/lookouts/ helmsman	☐	→	.... **Sheet No.** ....
• Adverse weather/visibility	☐	→	.... **Sheet No.** ....
6. Are all officers and crew fully familiar with relevant bridge equipment and procedures?	☐	→ →	Yes/NO, If not reference to company procedure ....
7. Have OOWs and crew been briefed about the passage plan?	☐	→	Signature on passage plan sheet
8. Have all OOWs seen, understood and signed the passage plan?	☐	→	Signature on passage plan sheet
9. Has the Master checked & approved the plan?	☐	→	Signature on passage plan sheet

Table 2.1 Checklist

Through appraisal, the Master should be satisfied that the charts are the largest scale for the passage, are on board and that all charts and publications are corrected up to date, having taken navigational warnings into account. Apply all T & P corrections that are in force.

The appraisal process should result in the navigation officer and Master gaining knowledge of the following (but not limited to):

- The general choice of routes that can be followed
- the availability of the largest scale charts and the relevant publications being on board, along with any corrections
- the distances between the departure and destination positions on various route options

- the draught at departure and various stages of the passage, taking into account the passage consumption, bunkering options and any transfers of fuel and cargo on passage
- minimum depths on the various route options
- the tidal conditions at critical stages of the route options
- proximity to hazards on the different route options
- reliability of the ship's machinery and equipment
- the load line zones that will be passed on the various route options
- recommendations in Ocean Passages and Sailing Directions
- advice from shore routeing services
- the climatic conditions on various route options
- past, present and forecast weather

- the routeing schemes expected to be used on the various route options
- direction of flow, type and volume of traffic that is likely to be encountered
- times of sunrise, sunset and duration of daylight and darkness
- navigational aids, radio and terrestrial, that will be available for position monitoring
- the ship's manoeuvring characteristics and how the ship would manoeuvre or handle in different areas
- search and rescue arrangements along the route
- likely ports of refuge, shelter locations or anchorages
- considerations for a suitable landfall for the various route options
- restrictions created by the nature of the cargo or type of operations
- security threats or guidance from flag or coastal states.

Once the relevant sections of the appropriate publications have been studied as well as all the associated material, reports, requirements and warnings, the navigation officer will provide outline route options to the Master. Based on the available information, while keeping the safety of the ship, crew, passengers and cargo as a priority, the Master will select the most appropriate option.

2.1.3 Chart 5500

The 5500 series of charts is the British Admiralty (BA) Series of World Passage Planning Charts. Chart 5500:

- Is very important for all vessels transiting the English Channel and using ports of NW Europe
- contains details to assist with passage planning and to ensure a safe passage through the Channel
- includes advice on appraisal, planning, execution and monitoring
- has pilot boarding areas specially marked for deep draught vessels, where the pilot comes aboard by helicopter.

2.1.3.1 Passage planning for special classes of vessels

- Deep draught vessels and vessels bound for Europort are given specific instructions regarding the routes they are to follow, reporting points, pilot boarding points and alteration points for joining and leaving the TSS
- for ships that are constrained by their draught, information is provided regarding the need for adequate UKC.

2.1.3.2 Routeing

- Routes used by ferries and passenger ships are marked.

General recommendations

- The Dover straits is an area of high traffic congestion, the details of the TSS being used and the Master's legal obligations under COLREGS are discussed in detail.

Specific regulations

- The special regulations that apply to the TSS are summarised within the passage plan chart
- with regard to the electronic position fixing equipment to be fitted on board to improve navigation, recommendations for ships of over 300GT are included
- the limits of the chart and the numbers used for the passage are printed on the chart.

2.1.3.3 Radio Reporting System

- All ships using the English Channel are required to report at various points to the UK and French maritime authorities while using the TSS off Ouessant, Cape Gris Nez and the Dover coast guard
- guidance regarding special reporting arrangements and reporting points for ships carrying oil or a dangerous cargo are given in detail
- radio reporting procedures to the port of destination, along with complete details of cargo and ship's navigation capabilities, are mentioned
- tanker checklists and documents to be produced to authorities are given.

2.1.3.4 Maritime Radio Service

- Details of stations operating in the area, along with their times of transmission, types of messages, eg navigational warnings, weather messages, storm warnings, are given. Details of NAVTEX service.

2.1.3.5 Radio Beacon Service, Tidal Information and Services

- Offshore tidal data with an illustration/examples of using co-tidal, co-range lines are explained
- maximum tidal stream rates in relation to HW Dover are included.

2.1.3.6 Pilotage Services

- Details of requests for deep sea pilots for respective ports, and the relevant communications required, are available
- rendezvous points for helicopter/pilot transfer and procedural action are provided.

2.1.4 Charts and Associated Publications – Reliance

The Admiralty along with other establishments that publish charts and associated publications, try to ensure that their published information is accurate. However, it is possible that the information may not always be complete, so the Master must decide on how much reliance should be placed on a chart or publication.

2.1.4.1 Factors Affecting Chart Reliability

To establish reliability, examine the chart. The mariner checks:

Source Data:
A chart uses information from many sources, the most important being the survey. Recent charts will either have source data information printed on them or will include a source data diagram.

Careful examination will show:

- When the survey was done
- the method of the survey, eg by echo sounder, hand lead, side sonar
- the authority conducting the survey, eg Royal Navy, port authorities, foreign governments or oil companies
- the method of determining positions, eg DGPS or other, close to/away from land, how accurate a survey of positions on land is
- the scale of the survey.

A major factor that contributes to a chart's accuracy is the ability of the hydrographer to collate all the information. In this respect, Information Technology has added to the reliability of a published chart. However, the mariner should note that certain areas of a chart may not have been covered by a survey.

Scale:
The scale of the chart is very important. The largest scale charts should be used as they contain the most detailed information and are generally corrected first. On smaller scale charts, particularly ocean areas, the information is sparse and charted dangers may be incorrect regarding position, least-depth and extent.

The scale of a chart is normally the same as the scale of the survey, especially with modern larger-scale charts. Small-scale charts may be published from a larger scale survey, but it is unlikely that an older small-scale chart will have been published from a larger scale survey.

Area of Usage:
If a particular area of a sea or ocean is not frequently used for navigation, it is unlikely that there will be any detailed information available.

Positioning:
The datum relates to a particular positioning system, eg WGS 84 or PZ 90. Position-fixing devices are able to relate WGS 84 to another datum, but the positions may not always agree with the charted positions used by the Hydrographic Office, even if the stated horizontal datum was the same.

Graduation on Plans:
Some older charts did not have graduations on plans of ports and harbours. On un-graduated plans, it will be difficult to determine a position accurately. However, newer charts are published with graduations on the plans and the older charts are being revised.

Distortion of Paper:
The paper that a chart is printed on can become distorted, although the resulting errors are unlikely to be significant.

Depth Criteria:
Many hydrographic offices use different depth criteria for dangerous and non-dangerous wrecks.

Soundings:
The normal way to obtain soundings of the seabed uses a surveying vessel to produce a systematic series of profiles covering the entire area. The scale of the survey should allow sufficient plot lines to indicate the seabed's configuration.

- A line, that may be many miles wide on a chart, only represents a narrow width of the echo sounder's beam. Soundings by lead line only represent an area of a few centimetres
- older exploratory surveys indicate random soundings where checks were carried out.

Changes in Depths:
An unstable seabed may cause a change of soundings.

Quality of Bottom:
On a chart, the nature of the bottom shown only represents the upper layer.

Magnetic Variation:
Charts indicate the magnetic variation and yearly change. The actual change can be very different to the charted change.

Corrections:

Some charted areas generate many corrections. The following questions should always be asked:

- Is the chart corrected up-to-date
- have all the corrections been made?

2.2 Planning

A plan cannot be made without the necessary information being available. The planning stage must follow the appraisal. This involves laying out tracks, calculations, instructions, setup of equipment and programmes, as well as the relevant references. A plan can be prepared in several formats. Almost all companies under the ISM Code have laid down detailed procedures in the SMS about passage planning. It is likely to be a combination of tabular, narrative, plotting and digital file format.

2.2.1 Berth-to-Berth Planning

At all times, the responsibility for safe navigation of the ship rests with the Master and OOW. During the planning stages, attention should be given to all the possible dangers of navigation. The passage plan acts as a benchmark for the bridge team, the Master must ensure that all relevant information was considered when the plan is prepared. The bridge team can then execute the passage plan and monitor the ship's progress effectively. If there is no plan, execution and monitoring have no comparison points.

The passage between the pilot ground and berth is critical. It may be through congested waters, in close proximity to hazards and with a reduced UKC. The passage may also take the ship close to expensive property, port facilities and other vessels. Pilots are employed for their extensive local knowledge and expertise. The pilot arrives on board with a plan to guide the ship and outlines the planned passage to the berth (or pilot station) to the Master. The pilot also advises the Master of the passage that the vessel will follow. A berth-to-berth plan provides:

- Knowledge of all hazards and actions to be taken during voyage
- agreement on a common plan to be used in pilotage waters
- allows the ship's position to be monitored at all times
- an awareness of the pilot 's intention at all times
- the pilot's advice, it can be cross-checked and clarified by the pilot if there is any doubt.

If the pilot, for whatever reason, cannot perform his duties, the plan helps the bridge team to maintain the ship's safety until a replacement pilot arrives.

2.2.2 Passage Plan Format

The end product should follow the preferred format of the company SMS. The best approach is to:

- Complete the plan on the largest-scale navigational charts
- document the plan in a tabular format (Table 2.3 is a suggested format)
- provide instructions to the bridge team in a passage plan note book (Table 2.2). Computer-based files are also useful.

Waypoint or Leg No	References	Notes/ Instructions
Names/ numbers and positions of waypoints Leg/Track references	• Coastal Features for position fixing • navigational aids • directions • hazards • weather • currents/tides/tidal streams • security threats • routing schemes • regulations	Specific instructions to the bridge team about conduct of passage

Table 2.2   Recommended format for passage plan notebook

There have been debates about too much information being included on the chart. A navigator usually relies on three basics:

- Sight and hearing
- instruments
- navigational charts/plans.

It may be prudent to have the maximum amount of detail on the chart, but leaving sufficient room for plotting fixes. Details can be left in the documents or booklets backing up the chart, references to them should be marked on the charts. In congested waters, where the navigator does not have the time to read a file of papers, more information can be added to the chart. To avoid overcrowding, information should be written on land or away from the intended course line, with arrows pointing to the track.

PASSAGE PLAN

Vessel: ....

Voyage No: ....

From: ....

To: ....

Berth: ....
(Name of Berth/Wharf/Anchorage)

Prepared by: ....
(Navigation Officer)

Date: ....

Approved by: ....
(Master)

Date: ....

OOW2: ....

OOW1: ....

References: (Write Vol No and Page Nos for quick reference)

Publication Correction: Date .... ANM No ....

Sailing Directions: ....

ALRS: ....

ATT: ....

ALLFS: ....

Ocean Passages: ....

NAVTEX Stations: ....

VHF Channels: ....

PAGE

.... of ....

Drafts

F: .....m

A: .....m

Chart(s)		Waypoints				Course° T				
Number	Datum	Name	Lat	Long		Speed	Eng Order			
	No									

Distance and Time to go					Min.Depth/UKC m				
Next Waypoint		Total							
Distance	Time	Distance	Time						

Parallel Index		WO		Position Fixing		Current Tidal Stream	Master's instructions
Reference Mark	CIR	Reference Mark	Bearing x Range	Frequency (min)			Hazards
				Primary		Set	Weather
				Secondary		Rate	Contingency
							Remarks

Position Fixing — Primary: Vis/Radar/GPS .... Vis/Radar/GPS .... Vis/Radar/GPS ....

Position Fixing — Secondary: Vis/Radar/GPS .... Vis/Radar/GPS .... Vis/Radar/GPS ....

Table 2.3 Passage planning table

2.3 Summary of General Principles

The navigation officer must adopt:

- A consistent pattern for work and adhere to it throughout the passage plan. Frequent changes in the symbols/legends or abbreviations used on charts or passage plan lead to confusion
- an advance warning system on charts and in passage plan sheets, eg Next chart No. Similarly, other hazards, including high traffic density, fishing grounds, crossing traffic, shallow waters, etc can also be indicated before they are expected.

All charts should be studied carefully in conjunction with the sailing directions, navigational warnings and weather reports, areas of danger should be identified. These predicted areas of danger should be marked as no-go areas. Courses should be plotted on the largest scale charts and be clear of predicted danger areas, allowing for a margin of safety as determined by local and company regulations as well as the Master's instructions. When establishing margins of safety, the navigation officer must keep contingencies in mind, eg if the ship's steering gear fails or an engine breaks down.

When course alterations are shown on the charts, the WO (wheel over) positions should be identified and the range(s)/bearing(s) from clearly identifiable, conspicuous shore objects/radar targets be given. Where there are visual means of position fixing available, using the GPS should be secondary. Remember, the visual or even radar position fixing is from objects that can be physically seen. Where possible, beam bearings should be used for alterations.

When transferring positions or courses between charts, ranges and bearings from fixed objects must be used. Establish 'Points of no return', particularly in approaches to narrow passages, night passage or when passing over river bars with a critical height of tide. These must be finalised by the Masters' specific instructions and preferences with respect to their own vessel handling characteristics. In any circumstances, these points are the areas where the ship cannot return to sea and must continue to the next available exit where she can safely berth, anchor or return to sea.

Use this guideline to place marks on charts that will not cause clutter or confusion:

- Courses, always TRUE, in three digit notation and distance of each leg, DTG to destination, eg pilot boarding ground
- margins of safety as required by the Master/company
- position fixing frequency for each leg of the passage
- wheel-over (WO) points

- reporting points. If there are any stations to be called, their IDs, VHF channel and position where it is to be called
- pilot boarding/disembarkation position(s)
- speed reduction points
- position where notice is given to the engine room
- abort points/points of no return
- indication on the course line where notices are to be given to additional watchkeepers, helmsmen and lookouts
- sequence of charts for the passage
- parallel Index Lines along with PI distances
- set and rate of current, height of tide, tidal window for critical areas
- areas of danger and no-go areas
- radar/visually conspicuous objects, eg mountains peaks, RACONs, lighthouses
- next Chart, along with its number and an indication of when to move to the next chart
- transit bearings for a quick check of compass error and clearing bearings, to clear a specific hazard, particularly when making approaches in narrow channels
- waypoint number on each waypoint, so that it refers to the passage plan sheet, GPS and ECDIS (if used)
- position on the chart where it is required to switch on certain navigation aids, eg the echo sounder
- navigation warnings, preliminary and temporary chart corrections from notices to mariners
- specific meteorological information that is available, eg dust storms, restricted visibility, sea, swell and wind conditions
- radio frequencies/channels, station identifiers and message types
- areas requiring specific marine environmental protection considerations
- minimum UKC, particularly in shallow water areas
- chart datum is usually given on the chart. Highlight any chart that has different datum to notify the OOWs
- references to contingency plans for alternative actions to maintain safety of life, environment, ship and the cargo.

Where an approved ECDIS (Electronic Chart Display Information System) is used for passage planning, routes and hazards can be marked on the display itself.

2.3.1 Explanation of Planning Methods

2.3.1.1 Wheel-Over (WO)

At the planning stage, the wheel-over point calculations require the following:

- Loaded condition of the ship-loaded, ballast or Intermediate condition. This is used to select the turning circle diagram/appropriate table

- change of course in degrees, between one track and the next
- helm angle to be used. This may vary with the proximity of hazards. The nearer the hazard, the larger the angle, to keep the ship as close as possible to the planned track or to make a tight turn
- speed of the ship while making the turn
- depth of water, effect of shallow water on the turning circle and the increase in draught while turning.

Obtain the advance and transfer from the appropriate turning circle diagram or tabulated information. For example, a ship on a course of 270°T has to alter course to 310°T. Assuming the advance is 4.7 cables and the transfer is 0.9 cables for a 40° alteration based upon 20° helm:

- At way point 'B', extend the present course line 270° T
- at any point 'X' on this line, draw a perpendicular line 'XY' towards the alteration, so that 'XY' = Transfer

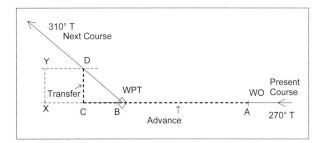

Figure 2.1   Wheelover point determination

- at 'Y', draw a line parallel to 'BX', so that it cuts the next course line 310°T. The point where the parallel line cuts the next course line is 'D'. If a line was drawn at 'D' that was parallel to 'XY', point 'C' would be obtained on the extension of the present course line
- from 'C', measure the Advance backwards, ie in direction 090° T (reciprocal of 270° T) to obtain point 'A'. 'A' is the wheel-over point, where 'CA' equals Advance
- a setsquare marked with the required transfer can be used to obtain point 'C' and 'D' by simply sliding it across the original course line until the transfer mark coincides with the new course line.

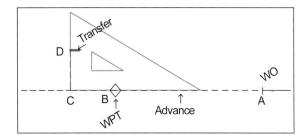

Figure 2.2   Marking wheelover with a set square

A formula can be used to determine the wheel over distance from the waypoint:

Distance backwards from WPT (AB) = Advance - (transfer ÷ tan of course alteration°)

Please note: This method is based on the advance and transfer for the helm angle used and does not allow for any steadying helm to counteract the swing of the ship. Also, during the execution and monitoring, the sea state, current or tidal stream and wind effect on the ship may cause errors. Cross track error would require an adjustment of wheel-over point.

Another method that can be used for planning wheel-over is the constant radius turn. The distance travelled by the ship or the time taken before she begins to turn is the inertia distance (AC). This will vary depending on the speed and helm angle used. During the turn as the speed reduces, the helm angle should be adjusted (reduced) to maintain radius.

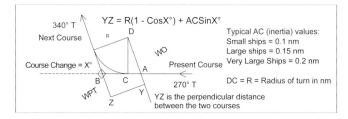

Figure 2.3   Wheelover - constant radius turn

Parallel indexing can be used to monitor the ship during the turn (see 6.5.1). Alternately, VRM set at the required range from a fixed object (clearing range) can also be used to monitor the turn, especially if it is a constant radius turn. The object selected in this case should be at the centre of curvature of the turn.

2.3.1.2 Position Fixing Frequency

Decide this frequency for every leg of the passage. These are the main factors affecting the frequency of the fix:

- Proximity to hazards
  If hazards are close to the intended passage, plot positions more frequently so that corrective action can be taken before the ship gets too close.

- Speed
  A faster ship will cover more distance in a given time than a slower one, as a result it will get close to dangers more rapidly.

- Draught
  Ships with a deeper draught have limited sea-room to manoeuvre. Positions should be plotted more

frequently to ensure that the ship remains within the intended channel.

- Displacement
  Larger displacement means more momentum, these ships take time to turn or manoeuvre.

- Environmental factors
  In areas where extraordinary set, drift or leeway is being experienced, especially towards a hazard, the fixing frequency should be increased.

- Traffic Density
  A ship must take avoiding action for traffic. The bridge team must be aware of the available sea room to execute such actions. Positions should be plotted more frequently to keep the OOW informed of the searoom.

- Manoeuvring characteristics
  Vessels with larger turning circles or stopping distances must be aware of searoom for basic manoeuvres including course alterations and corrective actions.

The fix frequency should be set so that the ship is not in danger between fixes and to ensure that avoiding action can be taken to maintain the ship's safety in case of a deviation. There should be sufficient time and sea-room from a worst case position to still take avoiding action. Generally, use continuous-monitoring techniques in hazardous areas where fixing is time consuming, but it should not be used as an alternative to position fixing.

Author's Note:
There are two rules of thumb on coastal passages for position fixing frequency:
1. The interval between fixes should be half the time it takes to run out of the margin of safety
2. The interval between markings should be approximately 5 cm apart on the largest scale chart.

2.3.1.3 Abort and Point of No Return

An abort is the position that a ship can abandon her passage and maintain safety or return. This may be used for the following reasons:

- Change or deviation from the approach line
- machinery, equipment or instrument malfunction or failure
- instructions from the harbour authority, eg pilot, tug or berth availability
- change in the elements of nature, eg wind, poor visibility, etc
- blockage of the approach, channel or berth, eg navigational hazard, other ship or for security reasons.

The marking of an abort requires careful consideration, there should be sufficient sea room for the ship to undertake any of these manoeuvres in safety:

- Turn around
- stop in safe waters
- anchor.

A passage plan should incorporate a return or manoeuvre plan for execution at this position.

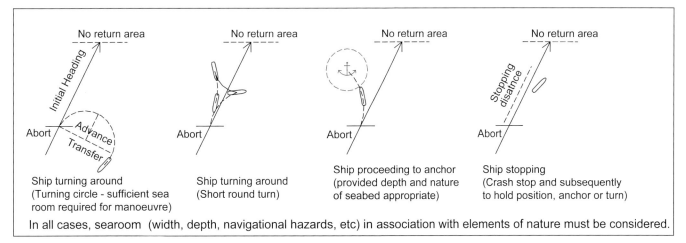

Ship turning around
(Turning circle - sufficient sea room required for manoeuvre)

Ship turning around
(Short round turn)

Ship proceeding to anchor
(provided depth and nature of seabed appropriate)

Ship stopping
(Crash stop and subsequently to hold position, anchor or turn)

In all cases, searoom (width, depth, navigational hazards, etc) in association with elements of nature must be considered.

Figure 2.4 Abort manoeuvres

Once the abort has been passed, the ship enters the no return part of the passage and remains fully committed. Any problems or changes in circumstances would now have to be dealt with through the initiation of contingency plans for the passage.

2.3.1.4 Under Keel Clearance (UKC)

This formula should be used to calculate the 'least-charted depth' that a ship is able to safely navigate in:

> UKC + Draught = Least-charted depth + predicted height of tide

When determining UKC, consider:

- Weather conditions and state of sea, on all legs of the passage
- the ship's rolling and pitching movement
- uncertainties in charted depth
- uncertainties in the ship's draught, accuracy of draught measurement, variation in consumption and resulting errors in draught or change of trim
- tidal levels below expected (negative tidal surges)
- squat of the ship at a given speed (maximum speed should be stated)
- possible alterations in depth since the last survey
- areas of mobile bottom
- offshore areas with developments that result in reduced depths (sometimes up to 2 m) over pipelines and similar underwater objects
- OREI areas where due to development work, flow of current or tidal stream, can effect depths, as well as a possible reduction in depth due to submarine power cables
- recommended routes for deep draught vessels
- inaccuracies in tidal predictions and offshore depths
- possibility of determining tidal height in all areas (including offshore)
- the fact that high pressure is known to reduce the water level by several centimetres
- skills of the navigator to determine the tidal height and refer it correctly to the chart datum.

2.3.1.5 Squat

A ship will experience different effects in shallow water, and is often known as the shallow water effect. The speed in shallow water leads to the water level being lower around the hull and may cause a change of trim. This is called squat and is difficult to quantify. It is expected to occur when depth is less than 1.5 the draught.

A ship's manoeuvring data provides information on squat values. During passage planning, the UKC should take squat into account. The allowance for squat should be the greater of these values:

- Value of squat from the ship's manoeuvring data
- speed^2 (in knots) ÷ 100 in metres
- 10% of the draught
- 0.3 metres for every 5 knots of the ship's forward speed

2.3.1.6 Landfall

Consider these factors when planning for landfall:

- Use the largest-scale charts
- at landfall points, there should be clear water all round and in the vicinity of the line of approach
- avoid areas of poor visibility if landfall is to be made on a lighthouse
- when making landfall on a light, raising distances should be determined for the different visibility conditions that may be encountered
- where ground is open to weather, low clouds can form. Avoid approaching land or islands from a windward direction
- use caution in areas that are subject to strong tidal streams
- points of landfall and approaches should provide more than one method of monitoring your position, visual, radar and electronic aids to navigation, including the echo sounder
- avoid low-lying islands as they may not be visible at a reasonable distance, even during clear daylight
- avoid straight coastlines. Instead, go for areas with prominent headlands or coastal features
- avoid lee shores with strong onshore winds
- avoid (or consider carefully) areas of high traffic density
- avoid using floating aids (even LANBY's with RACON), unless absolutely necessary. If you have to use them, confirm their position by other means
- celestial observation can be used for checking landfall approaches
- determine conditions, contingency plans and abort positions
- when a landfall position has been chosen, assess its adequacy for daylight, darkness and reduced visibility.

The navigator must appreciate that there is a difference between planning and execution, once the landfall is planned, specific bridge procedures must be followed to ensure that the landfall is made successfully. The procedures that follow should be used when **Making Landfall**:

- Use and complete the checklist from SMS for making landfall
- carry out a navigational risk assessment
- test all bridge equipment, steering controls and gear, main engine controls, etc

- check with the department heads that the ship's stability is adequate, that ballast has been added or adjusted as required and that the correct draught is reported to the bridge
- determine the gyro error and deviation for the magnetic compass and also all other bridge equipment for errors
- ensure that the largest scale corrected charts are in use
- obtain latest navigational warnings/MSI using NAVTEX and all available methods, navigational charts should be updated with the navigational warnings and all T&P corrections
- obtain the latest weather reports and forecasts
- work out the tidal stream/current information and height of the tide
- notify the engine room of landfall, advise them of when the engine must be put on stand-by, and of any other requirements, eg power for deck equipment
- ensure that bridge manning is as specified in the SMS, Standing Orders and Passage Plan requirements. This may include, but is not limited to, an additional watchkeeping officer, additional lookout and helmsman
- inform the Master as per point marked on the chart
- inform crew and ensure that anchors are cleared in time
- make reports to the relevant authorities and parties
- keep watch on Ch 16 and other channels as required
- inform all departments of the distances from the nearest land, entry to a special area, in order to comply with MARPOL requirements
- obtain position using Celestial Observations to verify the position by the GPS or another position fixing system being used in the open sea

- verify the course made good and compare it with DR and EP based on the course, speed and elements of nature that are being experienced
- work out the maximum distances that the radar can detect the coast, geographical and luminous ranges of lights, times when passing depth contours
- the echo sounder should be kept on at the appropriate depth scale
- ensure that both radars are functional, one on ground stabilised mode for navigational purposes and the other on water track. Use long range scanning to detect the coast in time. One radar should be on long pulse
- plot the position using different methods, including radar, visual, DGPS, GPS and verify against each other and DR/EP
- if using ECDIS, ensure that it is correct
- set up PI on radar and plot positions as set out in the passage plan intervals.

2.3.1.7 Changing Charts

Use the range and bearing from a common fixed point to transfer a position from one chart to the next. Alternatively, use the latitude on a common meridian to transfer the course from one chart to the next. Use meridional parts (MP) of the latitude at the common meridian. For a rhumb line, the tangent value is always the same: d.long is obtained between the initial longitude 'A' and the common meridian between two charts 'C'.

DMP2 = d.long/tan course
MP2 = MP1 +/– DMP2

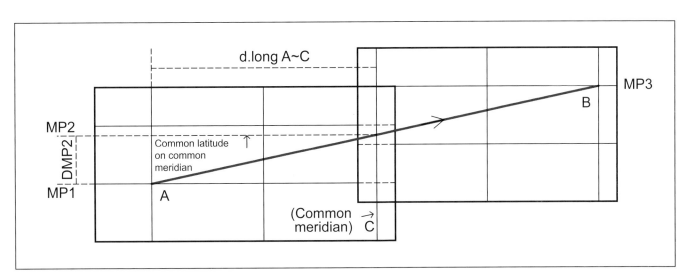

Figure 2.5 Plotting a course using DMP

This method can be used for laying courses on charts in general. Between two waypoints, the course may not be an exact degree of the true direction from 000° to 360°. If any fraction is involved, using the above method simplifies plotting.

2.3.1.8 Traffic Separation and Routeing Schemes

This is an extract from the IMO Routeing Guide for Ships.

"The purpose of ships' routeing is to improve the safety of navigation in converging areas and in areas where the density of traffic is great or where freedom of movement of shipping is inhibited by restricted sea room, the existence of obstructions to navigation, limited depths or unfavourable meteorological conditions."

The precise objectives of any routeing scheme will depend upon the particular hazardous circumstances that it is intended to alleviate, but may include some or all of the following:

1. The separation of **opposing streams of traffic** so as to reduce the incidence of head-on encounters
2. The reduction of dangers of collision between **crossing traffic** and shipping in established traffic lanes
3. The **simplification of the patterns** of traffic flow in converging areas

4. The organisation of safe traffic flow in areas of **concentrated offshore exploration** or exploitation
5. The organisation of traffic flows in or around areas where navigation by **all ships or by certain classes of ship is dangerous or undesirable**
6. Organisation of safe traffic flow in or around or at a safe distance from **environmentally sensitive area**(s)
7. The reduction of risk of grounding to providing special guidance to vessels in areas where **water depths are uncertain or critical**
8. To route traffic **clear of fishing grounds** or the organisation of traffic through fishing grounds.

2.3.1.9 Traffic Separation Scheme (TSS)

The provisions of Rule 10 should be applied when navigating in or in the vicinity of a TSS. Figure 2.6 illustrates the preferred tracks that ships should follow for their intended passages. Where navigational hazards do not allow full compliance, the preferred tracks may be adjusted. When navigating within the TSS, particular attention should be paid to collision avoidance manoeuvres. A vessel must comply with Rule 10 and all other collision avoidance rules simultaneously. Care should be exercised in precautionary areas and at roundabouts, where traffic might be converging and exiting in different directions.

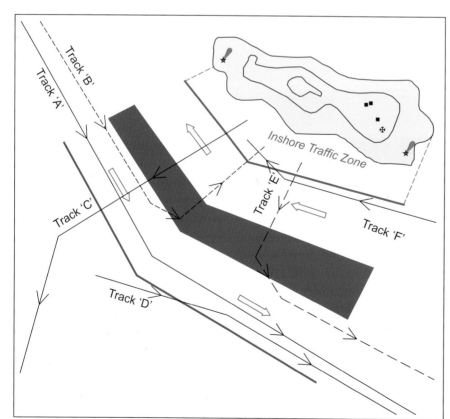

Track 'A' - Through traffic

Track 'B' - Traffic using a lane and crossing other lane to reach inshore zone. Notice the small angle at which it leaves the lane to reach separation zone and altering course within the separation zone

Track 'C' - Traffic crossing TSS at right angles

Track 'D' - Traffic joining lane from the side

Track 'E' - Traffic leaving the inshore zone, crossing one lane and joining the other lane at a small angle

Track 'F' - Traffic leaving the lane at a small angle

Figure 2.6   Tracks for navigation through a TSS

The following rules should be complied with:

- A ship should avoid a TSS by a wide margin if it is not using it
- ships that are using a TSS lane should proceed in the appropriate traffic lane and travel in the direction of traffic flow for that lane. The ship's track should be parallel or as close to parallel as possible to the sides of the lane
- ships should attempt to join or leave a TSS at a termination point. When a ship joins or leaves a TSS it must do so at as small an angle as possible to the general direction of the traffic flow
- when a ship has to cross a TSS, it should do so at right angles to the general direction of the traffic flow for the lane. Where possible the lane should be crossed in one go. If one lane has to be crossed to get to the next, then the course must be altered in the separation zone. When a ship is proceeding in a lane, it is not acceptable to make a 90° turn in the lane to either cross, partly cross or to join another lane
- in UK waters the penalty for a ship not complying with a TSS is £50,000 ($90,000 US approximately)
- ships should keep clear of separation lines or zones. Unless it is joining or leaving from the side, the rule suggests that the course should be plotted clear of the sides. During the passage planning stage, navigators should pay attention to the position of the ship's track on the correct side of the TSS to avoid other traffic from being disrupted
- ships should navigate with caution at the lanes termination points
- the stress of traffic should not be used as a reason to enter the inshore zone
- ships should avoid anchoring in a separation scheme or in other areas that are near to the TSS termination
- additional routeing measures are in the form of deepwater routes. Vessels that meet the criteria for their use should follow the deep water route. Other vessels should avoid the deep water channel by a reasonable distance.

2.3.1.10 Adopted and Non-Adopted Routeing Schemes

Some schemes are not adopted by the IMO and only the local regulations apply. In these cases it is essential that there is a clear understanding of the local regulations.

Adopted Schemes:
- Routeing schemes adopted by IMO
- provisions of Rule 10 of COLREGS apply fully
- these schemes are in international waters, although exceptions apply

- the sponsoring government should make arrangements for monitoring and policing of the scheme
- they are intended for use by all vessels, during the day and night, in all weathers, in ice-free waters or under light ice conditions where no extraordinary manoeuvres or assistance from ice-breakers is required.

Non-adopted Schemes:
- These routeing schemes are established by national governments or local authorities and have not been adopted by the IMO, although the scheme may be approved by IMO
- the rules and regulations are laid out by these authorities and may not conform to Rule 10. Modifications of Rule 10, as well as other COLREGS rules, may be applied by the local administration. It is important that they are fully understood.

2.3.1.11 Anchor Plan

Various factors influence the choice of an area for anchorage. For routine anchoring, when the ship is required to wait outside or inside the harbour area, the port authority will usually define the anchorage area. Port, pilotage or VTS authorities may advise the ship to proceed to a particular anchorage or position for anchoring. Some ports have clearly charted anchorages for ships to use. For commercial reasons, a ship may be required to anchor within the commercial limits of the port.

There may be circumstances when a ship has to anchor either without appropriate instructions or due to an emergency. Careful appraisal of the navigational chart, Pilot Books and the current and forecasted weather conditions will allow the Master to choose a safe area for anchoring. The choice of anchoring position depends on the following factors:

- Size of the ship, including windage area of the ship's hull, superstructure and cargo
- depth of water for maximum anchoring depth as well as for draught and UKC
- holding ground, depending on the type of seabed
- type of anchor and its holding power
- strength of wind, current or tidal stream
- length of time the ship intends to stay at anchor
- sea room available for swinging and manoeuvring
- draught and windage area
- proximity to dangers, submerged or on the surface
- underwater obstructions
- proximity to routes taken by passing or harbour traffic
- forecast and actual weather conditions
- availability of shelter

- commercial limits of the port
- availability of position monitoring landmarks (transit/ anchor bearings)
- instructions from the port authority, agent or owners/ charterers
- security, as piracy is common in some areas
- health, ships should stand off ports where malaria is prevalent
- on arrival at the anchorage area:
  - distance from other ships already at anchor
  - distance from the line astern of ships already at anchor.

The plan should include a marking of the anchoring position, any wheel-over bearings, steering bearing, let-go bearing and distances to go. Details can also be added of engine manoeuvres to reduce speed during approach. Use current/tidal stream or wind to decide the final approach. When this is known in advance, it should be incorporated in the plan.

- Scope of cable: depth m × 3 = X m ÷ 27.5 m = Y Shackles, minimum of three shackles in any case (add distance from deck to water level)
- in depths of 30 m or over, lower one shackle into the water and then let go

- in depths of 60 m or over, walk back anchor all the way and do not let go
- at the time of letting go, take a range and bearing from the beacon and note the ship's heading. Also, note the GPS position
- to mark the anchor position on the chart, apply the ship's length forward of the wheel house, in the direction of the ship's heading at the time of 'let go'
- draw the anchor circle with a radius = ship's length + forecastle to anchor position
- (Forecastle to anchor position)^2 = (Scope of Cable)^2 − (Depth)^2.

2.3.1.12 Risk Assessment (also see 5.7)

The plan should take into account all the risks that are likely to occur on the passage. The navigational risk assessments for these types of hazard should be completed and recorded. These should be available for the execution and monitoring stages.

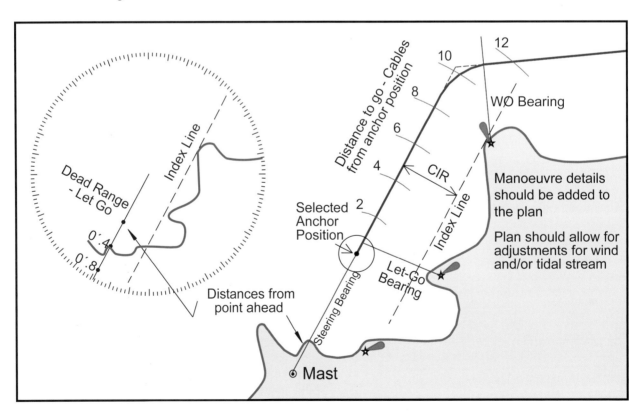

Figure 2.7 Anchor plan and radar set –up

2.4 Execution

Once the plan is prepared, discussed among the bridge team and approved by the Master, the plan can be executed when the ship departs. Execution is based on the methods and resources determined in the planning stage. When the voyage starts, arriving at various critical stages is important, as some of the initial and subsequent details depend on this time. The ETD and ETAs are calculated accurately and passed on to the relevant parties. The strategy to execute the passage plan depends on:

- Availability, reliability and status of the navigational equipment on board
- ETAs at focal points, consideration of the tides and traffic congestion. Other ships in the same area may be planning to catch the same tide
- use of ship's personnel at various stages of the passage
- possibility of reduced visibility and a change in meteorological conditions
- reliance of navigational marks with reference to day versus night approach, particularly around predicted areas of danger
- meteorological conditions, particularly in areas that are known to be affected by frequent periods of low visibility, as well as weather routeing information
- daytime versus night time passing of danger points, and any effect that this may have on position fixing accuracy
- traffic conditions, especially at navigational focal points.

Execution includes these tasks:

- Operation of the ship's navigational aids and communication equipment
- ship's propulsion, manoeuvring and handling
- maintenance of navigational and other charts, publications and their status regarding the dates of publication
- navigational observations and calculations
- maintenance records
- amendment of passage plans as required and making note of any deviations
- obtaining meteorological/navigational warnings and/or forecasts
- participation in local and/or international Ship Reporting Schemes, eg local VTIS, AMVER, AUSREP and JASREP.

It is important that the Master considers whether any particular circumstance, eg a forecast of restricted visibility in an area where position fixing using a visual means at a critical point is an essential feature of the voyage or passage plan, introduces an unacceptable hazard to the safe conduct of the passage. And whether that section of the passage in the current or anticipated conditions should be attempted. The Master should also consider the specific points of the voyage or passage where additional deck or engine room personnel may be required.

2.4.1 Bridge Resource Management

Many accidents have been due to organisational errors. These include insufficient information at the planning stage and/or a lack of communication between the bridge team members.

The following are examples:

- Failure to identify hazards
- failure to allocate responsibilities
- failure to prioritise tasks
- inadequate assistance to the OOW, Master and/or pilot
- insufficient monitoring
- reliance on unsupported information
- over-reliance on electronic navigational aids
- hesitation in reporting a deviation from the passage plan and a failure to seek assistance.

Bridge Resource Management or Bridge Team Management is the skill that balances efficient and successful administration with the organisation of all available resources so voyages are conducted safely. Available resources vary from ship to ship, just as individual capabilities vary from person to person. First, establish the available resources, then balance the abilities and limitations of the ship's personnel to achieve a safe passage. These are the key areas that require the available resources to be allocated:

- The Ship's Navigational Aids and electronic equipment (GPS, Radar(s), ARPA, ECDIS, Echo Sounder, NAVTEX, Compass (gyro, magnetic or satellite compass), communication equipment (GMDSS), sextant, AIS
- characteristics of the ship, eg propulsion, manoeuvrability, bow/stern thrusters
- navigational, also other charts and publications and their validity
- meteorological conditions (visibility, wind, tide and currents)
- local and/or international Ship Reporting Schemes (local VTIS, AMVER, AUSREP, JASREP)
- experience and availability of the officers and ratings, particularly those involved in watchkeeping, with attention to fatigue and rest hours for each person involved

- availability or non-availability of pilot(s) in certain areas
- a comprehensive passage plan where all the resources are identified and used.

Bridge resource management highlights internal dangers (machinery, equipment and personnel) and external dangers (weather, UKC and navigational hazards) to the ship. To maximise the available resources, the bridge team must be aware of their responsibilities. They must know the agreed procedures for the intended passage and, to avoid confusion at a later stage, any concerns must be raised immediately.

Decisions may be questioned in order to clarify a situation, but not to challenge the authority of the Master or to disregard the on board chain of command. All team members must know their roles and responsibilities before the voyage begins. Members of the bridge team should know their individual tasks and schedule the time required to complete them, such as the position-fixing intervals defined in the passage plan. During execution and monitoring, any variations and deviations to the plan should be recorded in the appropriate logs and the remarks column of the checklists.

2.5 Monitoring

The passage plan should be available at all times on the bridge, so that bridge officers have immediate access and reference to the details of the plan.

The ship's progress in accordance with the voyage and passage plan should be closely and continuously monitored. Any changes that are made to the plan should be consistent with these guidelines and clearly marked and recorded.

It is essential to ensure that the ship proceeds safely and efficiently on its intended passage. The final stage is to monitor the ship's progress along the planned route, closely and continuously. Monitoring begins immediately when the passage starts and runs alongside execution. There are times when an early warning from monitoring may cause a change in execution.

It is the Master's duty to ensure that the watchkeeping officers are comfortable in calling whenever they are in any doubt (or have problems) in following the planned route. Generally, watchkeeping officers are not authorised to amend the passage plan without the Master's specific instructions. But if immediate action is required and the Master is absent, the watchkeeping officers can take action to maintain the safety of navigation. This is only possible if efficient monitoring

makes them fully aware of the ship's position and movement. The navigator is also required to keep a check on all aspects of the passage plan, including heavy weather or navigational warnings, that may force the bridge team to deviate from the existing plan. Contingency planning should be part of the overall passage plan.

2.5.1 Position Fixing

Use these methods to obtain the position of a ship:

- Visual bearings and observations of terrestrial objects
- ranges by visual observations
- radar ranges and bearings
- use of soundings
- terrestrial radio aids to navigation
- satellite systems
- celestial observations.

In addition, other methods can be used to monitor the progress of the ship continuously. These may be based on visual techniques, parallel indexing using radar and satellite systems with or without using an ECDIS system.

2.5.1.1 Choice of Objects

- Objects that are to be used for visual and radar position fixing should be charted, as the bearings or ranges will have to be plotted on the chart from their symbols. Objects should be easily identifiable
- objects should be spread well apart to provide a good angle of cut between the position lines or ranges. The preferred angle is 90° between two objects and three marks at 60°. The angle should not be less than 30°
- objects should be selected so that the objects and ship do not end up on the perimeter of a circle, as the position can be plotted anywhere on the circle and errors in the compass may not be evident from the fix. If the objects are on a straight line the problem can be avoided
- objects should be observable from the same compass repeater to save time between observations
- it is preferable to select objects that are closer to the ship, as any error in the fix due to errors in position lines will be less significant over shorter distances
- when the ship is in a channel, the objects should be on the same side of the channel to avoid any errors caused by datum inaccuracies
- objects in transit are a good option as the bearing is not subject to compass error. In fact, the compass error can be determined from a single observation
- objects should be ahead of the ship rather than astern.

2.5.1.2 Procedure for Fixing

- The navigator should check the chart to identify the best objects to use for fixing the position. Note the names of these objects and the expected bearing or range based on the projected EP or DR. Select at least three objects
- locate the objects visually, or on radar, and identify them correctly
- at the required time, take bearings, or ranges on radar, and note them along with the exact time
- bearings of objects forward and aft of the beam should be observed first. Bearings of objects near the beam should be observed last at the required time of position. This is because bearings abeam are likely to change more rapidly
- the ranges of points abeam should be taken first as these change the least. Then those ahead and aft should be taken
- plot bearings and ranges on the chart. Use the correct symbols to mark the point of intersection. Write the time to the fix symbol
- any cross-track tendency and speed/course made good should be checked. Any required course correction should be allowed
- the EP/DR should be run-up for the next time of observation as set by the planned fix frequency. Recheck the chart for any hazards that the ship may pass before the next fix. From the run-up EP/DR, note the bearings and ranges for the next fix
- give the highest priority to position fixing by visual bearings
- floating objects, eg buoys or beacons, should not be used for position fixing unless the accuracy of their position has been established
- allow for errors of compass, sextant and other navigational aids/equipment
- the interval between fixes should be pre-agreed and consistent. This helps to make a judgment on the estimated position of the ship in future.

2.5.2 Visual Monitoring Techniques

Visual monitoring techniques should be employed where they are available. After correct identification, visual observations of fixed objects are the most reliable. Some of the significant methods are explained below.

2.5.2.1 Vertical Danger Angle

If the ship is to pass a total distance of 13.5 cables (7 + 6.5) [13.5 × 185.2 m = 2,500.2 m] from the lighthouse, an arc should be drawn with a radius of 13.5 cables with the lighthouse at the centre on the chart. At any point on this arc, the angle of the ship between the sea level and lantern should be the same.

If the light is 36 m above MHWS, which is 5 m above chart datum and the height of tide is 3 m, the effective height of light above sea level is 36 + 5 – 3 = 38 m.

$$\text{Tan } \theta = \text{Height/Distance}$$
$$\theta = 0° \, 52'.2$$

Using a sextant, if the reflected image of the lantern appears below sea level, the ship is in safety and outside the arc. If the charted height is used, instead of allowing for the height of the tide, the ship will be further away from danger at the calculated angle.

If no allowance is made for the height of tide and the same angle is used with charted height (HAT, MHWS or MHHW) of the light (36 + 5 = 41 m), the calculated distance is less than the actual distance:

Distance = 41/tan 0° 52'.2 = 2,700 m = 14.6 cables

This adds to the safety margin, unless there was also a danger on the other side of the ship. Note that the observer's height on the ship makes very little difference and is not used in this calculation. As the angle is so small, the angle (angle of elevation) at the foot of the lighthouse (waterline) is treated as 90°, or top of the lighthouse (lantern) is treated as 90° (angle of depression).

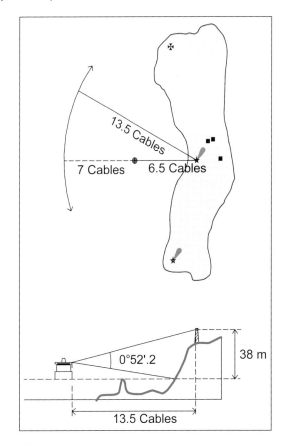

Figure 2.8 Vertical danger angle

2.5.2.2 Clearing Marks

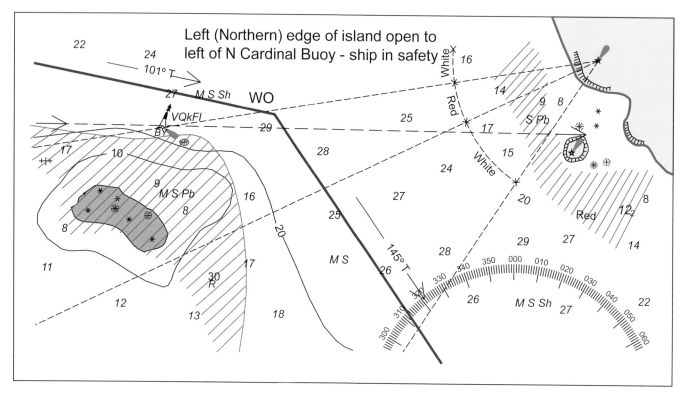

Figure 2.9   Use of clearing mark

The ship's safe approach can be monitored where two marks are used in conjunction. Once a safe bearing has been determined, the furthest of the selected marks should remain open to the side that the ship lies. In Figure 2.9, the ship will be safe if the island remains open to left of the North Cardinal buoy.

2.5.2.3 Horizontal Danger Angle

Once the safe distance from a hazard has been determined, ie 7 cables, mark the chart with the safe distance to pass. Then determine the horizontal angle between two fixed objects that, by preference, should be the same distance either side of the hazard.

In Figure 2.10, the safe distance is 81°. If the angle measured at the ship is equal to or less than the danger angle, the vessel will remain in safety. Where there are hazards either side of the track, repeat the same procedure for a point the same distance inside of the other hazard. In Figure 2.10 this is 50°. In this case, if the angle is more than 50°, the ship will remain in safety.

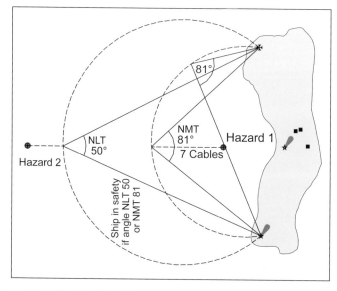

Figure 2.10   Horizontal danger angle

If the angle at the ship is no less than (NLT) 50° or no more than (NMT) 81°, the ship will remain in safety.

2.5.2.4 Horizontal Angle Fix

In Figure 2.11:

C Brg 1 = 048° C Difference between 1 and 2 = 47°
C Brg 2 = 095° C Difference between 2 and 3 = 39°
C Brg 3 = 134° C Complement 1-2 = 90° - 47° = 43°
Complement 2-3 = 90° - 39° = 51°

The Horizontal Angle can be used for fixing. In this case, objects should be selected so that they and the ship do not end up on the perimeter of a circle. This is because the position can be plotted anywhere on the circle. To avoid this problem, objects should be on a straight line. Using the complements, two position circles are plotted. The fix can be used to determine the error in compass, as the fix is not based on the bearings themselves but on the difference of angle between the pairs.

Compass error 1 = 048° C ~ 050° T = 2° E
Compass error 2 = 095° C ~ 097° T = 2° E
Compass error 3 = 134° C ~ 136° T = 2° E

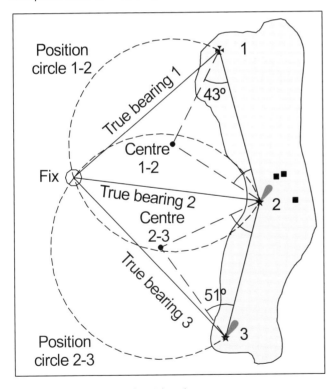

Figure 2.11   Fix using horizontal angle

If the incorrect bearings have been plotted directly, use the format station pointer to obtain the correct fix. The true bearings can then be read from the chart. In both the cases, the cocked hat in terrestrial fixes can be resolved.

2.5.2.5 Sector Lights

Sectors of coloured lights can be used to indicate the presence of navigational hazards and the safe water around them. These lights show different colours when viewed from different bearings.

The limits of the sectors are marked on navigational charts. This method of monitoring can only be used in good visibility.

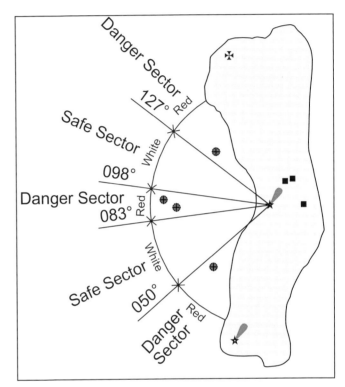

Figure 2.12   Use of coloured sectors

2.5.2.6 Clearing Bearings

In the vicinity of hazards, the clearing bearings of selected objects should be determined and marked on the chart during planning to set the safety margins and for monitoring. These bearings should be determined as Not More Than (NMT) or Not Less Than (NLT).

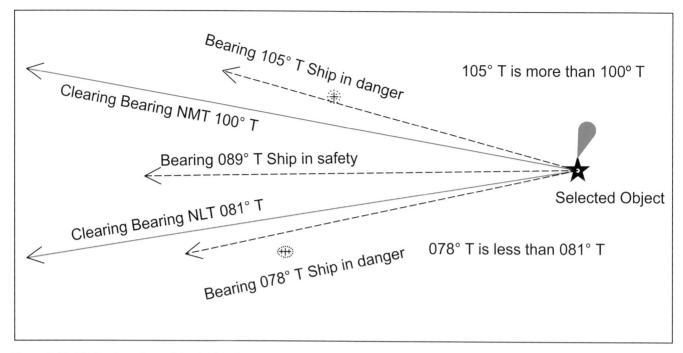

Figure 2.13 Explanation of use of clearing bearings

2.5.2.7 Leading Lights/Marks

The principle is to keep the marks or lights in transit.

- If the nearer mark is opening to starboard, the ship is to the left of the intended track
- if the nearer mark is opening to port, the ship is to the right of the intended track.

This method of monitoring can only be used in good visibility.

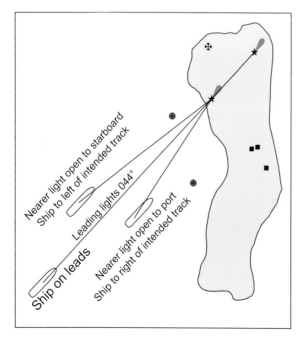

Figure 2.14 Use of leading lights

2.5.3 Ship's Profile and Datum Shift

The position plotted on the chart represents a part of the bridge or the scanner's position. Some parts of the ship are away from this point. Depending on the scale of the chart being used and the size of ship, these points may be in or approaching danger. It is important to know the corresponding size of the ship for the respective chart so the navigator is never in doubt about a hazard's proximity and the time or distance to it.

Simple cardboard models of the profile and shift for the different charts to be used during the passage can be a valuable addition to the chart table.

Natural scale, dimensions of the chart and correction for datum should be used to calculate this. The models cannot be used on a smaller-scale chart as the vessel's profile would be too small.

Natural scale 1:12,500 at latitude 21° 30′ N
Dimensions 965 mm × 635 mm (d.lat = 0° 5′.21)
[ie 1 nm = 185.2 mm]
Corrections for datum 0′.17 N, 0′.06 E
Ship's profile (for L = 300 m × B = 50 m) is 30 mm × 5 mm
Datum shift is 019°T × 33.4 mm (0′.18)

In electronic charts, the ship's profile can be automatically generated for the scale in use.

Depending on the navigation system being used and the datum of the chart, there may be a discrepancy

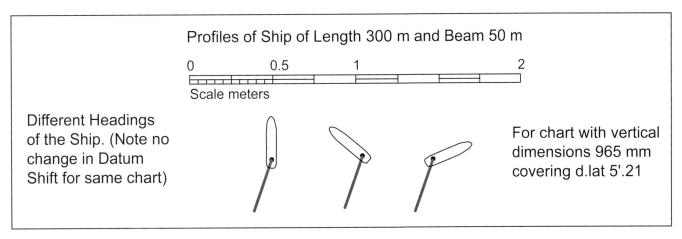

Figure 2.15 Profile and datum shift

between the plotted position and the actual position, ie if it is not corrected before plotting.

It is better to apply datum shift separately as the ship may not always be on the same heading as when the profile and shift model was prepared.

2.5.4 Non-Visual Monitoring Techniques

Using continuous monitoring techniques does not relieve the OOW from plotting the ship's positions at the planned fix frequency. Parallel indexing, maps and navigation lines are used on radar for continuous monitoring. This is explained in detail in sections 6.5.1, 6.5.2 and 6.5.3.

Terrestrial radio and satellite navigation systems can be used for continuous monitoring through use of cross track error and alarm, arrival alarm and course to steer alarm. Reliance on continuous monitoring systems must remain within the limitations of the base system in use. If the positioning system has an error of $0'.5$, the monitoring may be constantly in error.

Use of XTE on GPS etc, allows monitoring of ground track and speed made good against ship's course and speed. It is also useful to monitor DR and EP.

2.5.4.1 Discrepancy in Positions

If there are random errors, generally the position plotted from terrestrial observations will result in a cocked-hat, the intersection of the position lines closest to the hazard should be selected as the ship's position.

If there is a discrepancy in positions that have been plotted based on different systems, the above principle should still be put to practice. However, the mariner

must carefully analyse the situation and should take into account the circumstances and reasons for the possible discrepancy before accepting a position.

The situation could be of particular concern when hazards are approached in the open sea/ocean. For example, if a ship is to pass an isolated set of rocks, small island or shoal in open sea but positions have been obtained that place her in different locations. Generally, the position that is nearest to the hazard should be assumed and avoiding action should be taken.

In Figure 2.16, the ship is required to pass the isolated rock with the lighthouse at 12 nm. It is assumed that the three positions have been plotted using Radar, GPS and Stellar Observations at twilight. Full analysis should be completed:

- If star sight is correct, the ship is approximately 10 nm South of the intended track. If stars are selected carefully and sight is taken correctly, then the position error should not be more than 1 to 2 nm
- the GPS position puts the ship on track, although there should be no selective availability, there is no assurance that the system is functioning correctly
- the Radar generated position is a single range and bearing. This puts the ship about 4 nm South of the intended track. In addition, the radar range may be accurate but bearing may not be. Also the radar range of light is 23 nm. This may cause doubt as the range and bearing could have been from another passing ship. As the bearing is not a visual bearing doubt exists
- the only position described above that is based on visual identification is Star Sight.

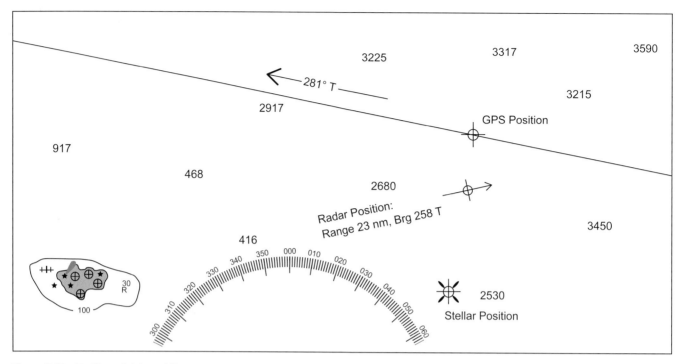

Figure 2.16 Profile and datum shift

In this situation, the ship should immediately alter course to NW or NNW. While the ship cannot obtain soundings at its current position, the echo sounder should be switched on to obtain a warning when the depth is less than 500m. On the radar the parallel indexing should be set up on the lighthouse. GPS positions should also be plotted regularly to identify the trend in the track being made and the set being experienced. If night is approaching, lookouts should focus on detecting lights, in daylight they should be attempting to visually detect the lighthouse.

Author's Note:
The operation of a ship is a complex task. The navigation officers and Master are required to perform a number of tasks simultaneously. The environment can be hostile. The legal requirements surrounding shipping are very stringent. Any error or omission can result in a disaster. With high costs, public and environment damage liability bills increasing all the time, the mariner and the ship operators must ensure that ships are operated as safely as possible. Effective voyage planning is only one of the steps towards ensuring the safety of operations.

2.6 Summary

Waters	Congested		Coastal		Open	
Visibility	Good	Poor	Good	Poor	Good	Poor
Visual	P		P			
Continuous visual monitoring techniques	P		P			
Parallel Indexing/ Electronic monitoring	S	P	S	P		
Radar	S	P	S	P		
LORAN C			S	S	S	S
DGPS		S		P/S		
GPS				S	P	P
Celestial				S		

Table 2.4 Primary and secondary position fixing/monitoring methods

3 Sailings

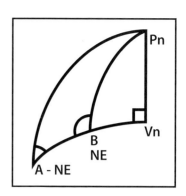

Basic mathematics is used to determine the course, distance and other relevant details of the passage between two points on the surface of the earth. Some methods use plane trigonometry, while others use spherical trigonometry. Before moving on to actual principles and calculations involving sailings, it is useful to identify and explain some of the relevant terms.

3.1 The Terrestrial Sphere

Spherical trigonometry is based on a perfect sphere. For relational purposes, the Earth is assigned a grid system and reference identifiers. The reference system is based on arithmetic, geometric and trigonometric terminology. The Earth is not a perfect sphere, it is an oblate spheroid. It spins on an axis, its extremities are identified as Poles, that are designated North and South providing the basic direction reference on the earth's surface. The true directions are measured as angles from the line(s) joining the North and South Poles. The imaginary lines running from the North

to South Poles are called meridians. The meridian passing through Greenwich, London is called the Prime Meridian or Greenwich Meridian and is assigned 0°. An imaginary line divides the Earth into two halves and is called the Equator. Meridians are perpendicular to the equator. The equator is a Great Circle. Meridians are semi-Great Circles. A meridian where an observer is located is called the Upper Meridian. A meridian on the other side of the Earth, ie 180° away from the observer, is called the Lower Meridian.

A circle on the surface of a sphere, that has a plane passing through the centre of the sphere, is called a Great Circle. There is only one Great Circle possible through two points on the surface of a sphere, unless the points are 180° apart, ie the points are at two ends of a diameter, allowing infinite Great Circles through the two points, eg meridians as Great Circles through the poles. A circle on the surface of a sphere, that does not have a plane passing through the centre of the sphere, is called a Small Circle. Lines running East-West on the

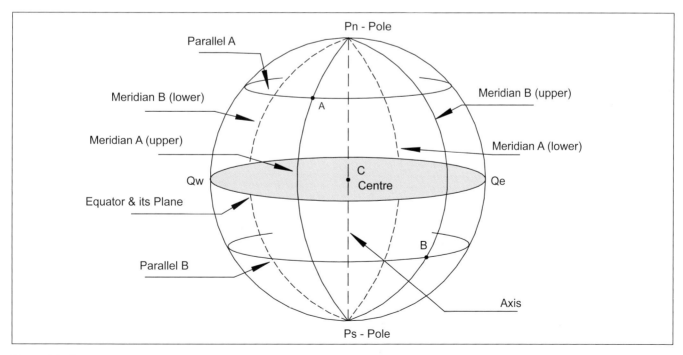

Figure 3.1 Terrestrial references

earth's surface, where the plane is parallel to the plane of the equator, form small circles known as Parallels of Latitude.

3.1.1 Position Reference

On the Earth's surface, positions are referred to using the plane of the equator and the plane of the prime meridian. The latitude of a location is the angle between the plane of the equator and the line perpendicular to the surface of the earth at that place. It is measured north or south of the equator from 0° to 90°. Where 0° is the equator and the 90° points are the poles. This is the Geographic Latitude of a Place and is indicated as xx° yy´.y.

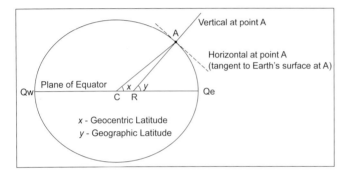

Figure 3.2 Latitudes

Geocentric latitude is either the arc of a meridian or the angle at the centre of the Earth between the plane of the equator and a line from the centre of the Earth through a parallel passing through the point.

Longitude is either the arc of the equator or the angle at the poles contained between the Prime meridian and the meridian through that point. Longitude is measured between 0° and 180° and is named East or West

depending on the relative location East or West of the Prime meridian and is indicated xxx° yy´.y.

The difference in latitude (d.lat) is the arc of the meridian or the angle at the centre of the Earth, between the two parallels of latitude, through the two places. It is named North or South depending on the direction of the second place from the first.

The difference in longitude (d.long) is the shorter arc of the equator or the smaller angle at the pole between the meridians passing through the two places. It is named East or West depending on the direction of the second place from the first.

Example 3.1
Find the d.lat and d.long between the following pairs of positions:

A:	50° 35´ N		000° 00´	
B:	61° 28´ N		013° 35´ W	
d.lat	**10° 53´ N**	**d.long**	**13° 35´ W**	
B:	61° 28´ N		013° 35´ W	
D:	36° 42´ S		093° 45´ E	
d.lat	**98° 10´ S**	**d.long**	**107° 20´ E**	
D:	36° 42´ S		093° 45´ E	
B:	61° 28´ N		013° 35´ W	
d.lat	**98° 10´ N**	**d.long**	**107° 20´ W**	
B:	61° 28´ N		013° 35´ W	
E:	61° 28´ N		175° 28´ E	
d.lat	**00° 00´**	**d.long**	**189° 03´ E**	
			- 360°	
			170° 57´ W (-170° 57´)	

Remember:
d.lat

SAME NAMES	–	SUBTRACT
DIFFERENT NAMES	–	ADD

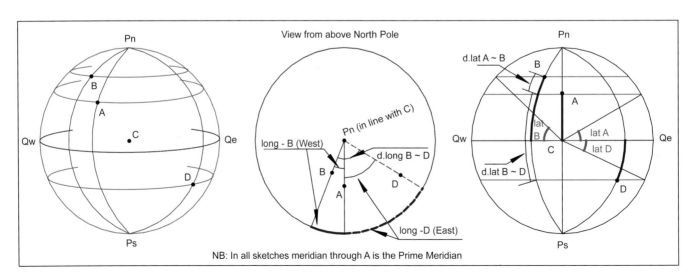

Figure 3.3 Latitude, longitude, d.lat and d.long

Always name it towards the direction of movement N or S.

d.long

SAME NAMES	–	SUBTRACT
DIFFERENT NAMES	–	ADD

always name it towards the direction of movement E or W. If the result is over 180°, subtract from 360° and reverse the sign, as d.long is the shorter arc or smaller angle.

The Earth's maximum diameter is across the equator and its minimum is across the poles. The difference between these two diameters is approximately 24 miles, compared to the average diameter of 6876 international nautical miles it is very small, for most practical purposes the Earth is considered to be a perfect sphere.

3.1.2 Direction Reference

For navigation purposes, the direction on the Earth's surface is measured as an angle from the meridian where the observer is located. There are two commonly used systems for indicating direction:

Quadrantal notation
The angles are measured from North to East or West, and South to East or West, 0° to 90°.

Three figure notation
The angles are measured clockwise from the North 000° to 360° (000° and 360° are the same and indicate the direction of true North).

000° is North
045° is N 45° E (000° + the angle 45°) (First Quadrant)
090° is East
162° is S 18° S (180° - the angle 18°) (Second Quadrant)
259° is S 79° W (180° + the angle 79°) (Third Quadrant)
312° is N 48° W (360° - the angle 48°) (Fourth Quadrant)

Angles are measured in degrees and minutes. For practical purposes, and examinations, courses should be reported to the nearest half degree.

Angle of 45° 12´ north of east is reported as 045°
Angle of 45° 35´ north of east is reported as 045°.5
Angle of 45° 48´ north of east is reported as 046°

True Course is the angle between True Meridian and the ship's head, it is measured between the meridian and ship's fore and aft line. The ship's heading should not be confused with the true charted tracks, as a correction may have been applied.

True Bearing of an object is the angle at the observation point between True Meridian and the line joining the observation point and object. Ships obtain bearings of fixed objects for plotting position, but state their bearing from fixed objects when reporting their own or other positions.

A Gyro compass points along the meridian to the True North, but it may develop errors. If there are no errors, the courses measured are true. The error needs to be known and applied. As a rule:

Gyro High   Steer High
Gyro Low   Steer Low

If the gyro error is 2° High and the course to steer is 315° T, the gyro course would be 317° G. Any observed bearings would have the same error. For the same error, if a gyro bearing is 124° G, the true bearing is 122° T.

Similarly, if the gyro is 2° Low and the course to steer is 315° T, the gyro course would be 313° T and for a gyro bearing of 124° G, the true bearing would be 126° T.

Relative Bearing is the angle between the ships fore and aft line and the line that joins the observation point and the object. The main purpose of relative bearings is to know where objects of interest are in relation to own ship. To convert these bearings into true bearings, the ship's true heading should be applied.

Relative Bearing 135° R (R is always after the degrees)
True Heading   210° T
True Bearing   345° T (if over 360°, subtract 360°)

Relative bearings can be stated from 000° to 360° relative, or 0° to 180° Red or Green, it depends whether the object is on the port or starboard side. G for green and R for red is always used as a prefix, eg R 45° is 315° R.

Magnetic meridians are lines that join the Earth's magnetic poles. As the magnetic poles are not at the same place as the Earth's geographic poles, there is a difference between the magnetic and geographic meridians. The difference is measured as an angle and is known as Variation. As the Earth's magnetic field is not uniform, variation will be different in different places. Due to the Earth's magnetic poles changing constantly, the value of variation at a place is not the same at all times. On navigational charts, the value and annual change are stated either on the compass roses or lines of equal magnetic variation, the isogonic lines.

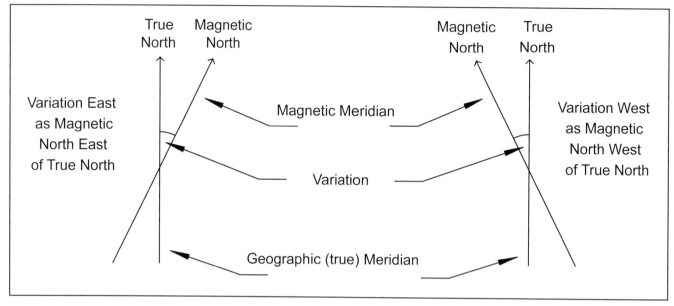

Figure 3.4 Variation

As the ship is made of mild steel, the ship's structure acquires a magnetic field of its own, having an effect at the compass position. This magnetism causes deviation of the magnetic compass needles. Deviation is the angle between the magnetic meridian and the line joining the North and South marks on the compass card (pointing to the Compass North). Deviation is measured East or West from magnetic north. Deviation changes with the ship's heading but remains constant for that same heading. Compass Error is the combined effect, ie the arithmetic sum of variation and deviation. As a rule:

Error E**ast**   Compass L**east**
Error W**est**   Compass B**est**

Table 3.1 and Figure 3.5 demonstrates this relationship.

True Co	Variation	Magnetic Co	Deviation	Compass Co	Compass Err
315° T	14° W	329° M	12° W	341° C	26° W
034° T	10° W	044° M	5° E	039° C	5° W

Table 3.1   Magnetic variation

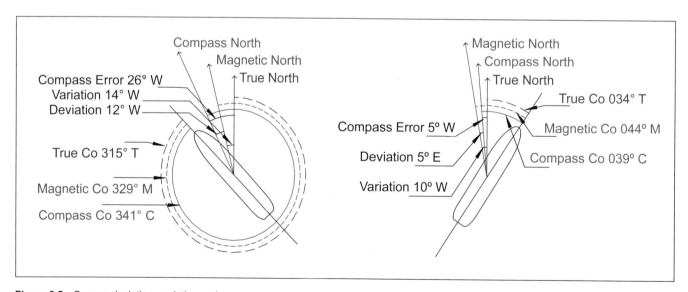

Figure 3.5   Course, deviation, variation and compass error

3.1.3 Distances

For general navigational purposes' distances are measured in Nautical Miles. However, there are several different units used for distance measurement.

A Sea Mile is the length of one minute of arc measured along the meridian in the latitude of a given position. The one minute of arc (1′) subtends an angle of 1′ at the centre of curvature of that place.

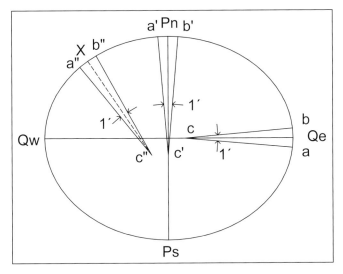

Figure 3.6 The sea mile measurement

At a given place X, the centre of curvature of the Earth is c", with the radius of curvature as c"X. At c" an angle of 1′ subtends an arc a"-b", with X at its middle. The arc (a"-b") is the sea mile in that latitude X. In Figure 3.6, the sea mile, a-b, is shortest at the equator and is 1,842.9 m. At the pole, a'-b' is the longest and is 1,861.7 m. It has a mean value of 1,852.3 m at 45° latitude.

A standard fixed length of 1,852 m is known as the International Nautical Mile.

The distance is stated in minutes of arc and the minute symbol is (′). When a fraction is involved, the minute symbol should be placed before the decimal place, eg 25.3 nautical miles is written as 25′.3.

Geographical Mile is the length of 1′ of arc measured along the equator. As the equator is a circle, the length of a geographical mile is the same, 1,855.4 m. With WGS 84, the geographical mile is 1,855.32 m.

The Statute Mile is a length of 1,760 yards (1,609.3 m) and is also termed Land Mile.

A Kilometre equals 1,000 m. (In all above cases, m stands for metres)

3.2 Parallel Sailing

A ship that steers at 090°T or 270°T would not change its latitude, provided no external forces are acting on the ship. This means that the departure and arrival positions are on the same latitude. This type of sailing is called Parallel Sailing. The distance covered by the ship can be related to a change of longitude (or vice versa) and is equal to a departure between the two positions along the given parallel of latitude.

This is type of sailing was commonly used by Sailing Ships before and during the 19th Century.

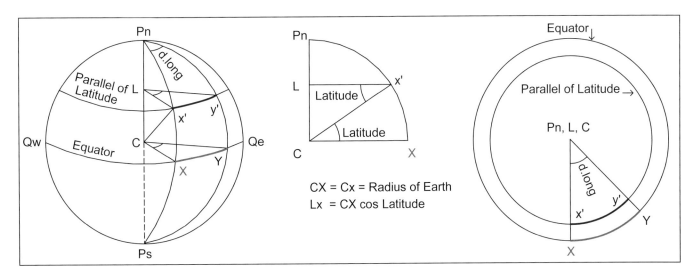

CX = Cx = Radius of Earth
Lx = CX cos Latitude

Figure 3.7 Parallel sailing

When a ship is travelling along any parallel of latitude, x´y´, the d.long is XY. Numerically the distance x´y´ is less than XY. As an angle, x´y´ and XY are the same, ie, d.long is the same. CX is the radius of the earth and Lx´ is the radius of the parallel and is equal to CX cos Latitude. The nearer the parallel of latitude is to the pole, the shorter x´y´ becomes, ie at higher latitudes. It becomes zero at the pole (90° latitude).

When viewed from the pole, the equator and the parallel of latitude are concentric circles.

Arc x´y´/Arc XY   = dep/d.long   = radius Lx´/radius CX

or,

    dep/d.long   = radius Lx´/radius Cx´ (as CX = Cx´
                                 = Radius)

Since triangle CLx´ is right angled:

    Lx´/Cx´   = cos Latitude

That is:

    dep/d.long   = cos Latitude

or,

    departure   = d.long × cos Latitude

Parallel sailing uses the conversion of departure along the parallel of latitude into difference of longitude, assuming the earth is a perfect sphere.

Example 3.2

Find the distance travelled by a ship on a course of 090° T at latitude 45° N, if its longitude changed by 20°. If latitude was 60° N, find the distance

    20°   = 20 × 60   = 1,200´ of arc

For 45° N:
    Dep   = d.long cos Latitude
    x´y´   = XY cos Latitude
    dep   = d.long × cos Latitude   = 1,200 × cos 45°
               = **848´.5**

For 60° N:
    Dep   = 1,200 × cos 60°
           = **600´**

Example 3.3

A ship in position 41° 10´ S 032° 45´ W is steering a course of 090° T at a speed of 16 knots. Find the longitude reached after 22 hours of steaming.

Distance covered in 22 hours = 22 × 16 = 352´ = dep
    d.long   = dep/cos Latitude

           = 352/cos 41° 10´ = 352/0.752798
           = 467´.6 ÷ 60   = 7° 47´.6 E (E as
                                course is 090° T)

Longitude reached
        = 032° 45´ W ~ 7° 47´.6 E = **024° 57´.4 W**

3.3 Plane Sailing

Plane sailing is when a ship sails along any rhumb line between positions that are not situated on the same parallel of latitude or meridian of longitude. In plane sailing, the d.lat, departure, distance and course may be considered as forming the plane of a right-angled triangle. Various trigonometric functions can be applied to obtain a few navigational formulae.

    Departure   = distance × sin course

    d.lat   = distance × cos course

    tan course   = departure ÷ d.lat

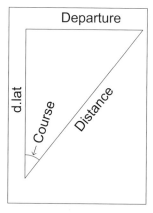

Figure 3.8   Plane triangle

Plane sailing is a method of solving d.lat, departure, distance and course related problems. As the earth is not flat, plane sailing only provides reasonably accurate results up to a distance of 600´.

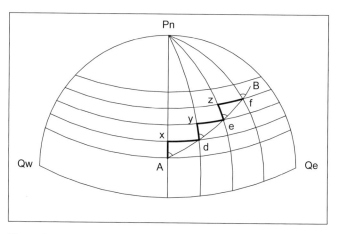

Figure 3.9   Plane sailing

In Figure 3.9 assume that rhumb line AB is cutting a number of parallels and meridians, so that the parallels are an equal d.lat apart. The rhumb line cuts the parallels at A, d, e, f and B. Through these points, the meridians cut the parallels at x, y and z forming right-angled triangles Axd, dye and ezf.

In these triangles, the angles at points x, y and z are right angles. Angles xAd, yde and zef are equal and are the course angles from Pn, ie North Pole. As the parallels are an equal distance apart, lines Ax, dy and ez are also equal in length.

The small triangles are equal in all respects. As the triangles are very small, they are considered as plane right-angled triangles. In triangle Axd:

For d.lat
Ax	=	Ad × cos course
multiples of Ax	=	multiples of Ad × cos course
d.lat	=	distance × cos course

For departure
Xd	=	Ad × sin course
multiples of xd	=	multiples of Ad × sin course
dep	=	distance × sin course

For course
tan course	=	xd/Ax (or multiples of xd, Ax)
tan course	=	departure/d.lat

Example 3.4
Find the distance travelled and course steered by a ship that has moved 45′ to the south and 30′ to the west of its initial position.

Here d.lat = 45′ and dep = 30′
tan course	= dep/d.lat	= 30/45	= 0.66667
course	= 33°.7 or	= S 33°.5 W	**= 213°.5 T**
distance	= d.lat ÷ cos course	= 45 ÷ cos 33.7	**= 54′.1**

Example 3.5
If a ship covers a distance of 35′ in a general north easterly direction and changes its latitude by 20′, find the course it has steered.

d.lat	= distance × cos course		
20	= 35 × cos course		
cos course	= 20/35	= 0.57143	
course	= 55°.1	**= N 55°E or 055°T**	

3.3.1 Use of Mean Latitude

The Earth's surface is not flat. When a ship is on a rhumb line 'not sailing either north-south or east-west', the Earth's curvature must be taken into account when calculating a position.

In Figure 3.10, for a rhumb line between positions A and B, the d.long is a"b". The departure along the parallel through A is Ab' and departure through the parallel of B is a'B. The diagram shows that Ab' is larger than a'B.

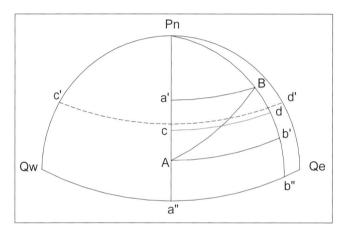

Figure 3.10   Mean latitude

To calculate the correct position of B, the departure from A to B should be along a parallel between A and B, shown here as c'd'. When latitudes of A and B are not too high and the d.lat between A and B is fairly small, the departure can be taken as the latitude at the mathematical mean between latitudes of A and B, ie, cd. This is called the Mean Latitude.

Using:
Cd	=	a"b" × cos a"c	(a"c = b"d)
Departure	=	d.long × cos mean latitude	

Plane sailing should not be applied for distances that exceed 600′. The formula above lacks mathematical accuracy, except where A and B are on the same parallel of latitude. In low latitudes, the discrepancy caused by the Earth's curvature is less. Nautical tables make reference to Middle Latitude, which is the Corrected Mean Latitude between two parallels, say c'd'. It is particularly useful in high latitudes as using Mean Latitude alone in these conditions can result in a larger discrepancy in your position.

For corrected mean lat:
    sec Lat   =   DMP/d.lat (minutes of arc)

Example 3.6

If a ship departs from position 24° 30′ N 038° 20′ W for 22° 45′ N 039° 35′ W, Calculate the course and distance travelled by the ship.

	24° 30′ N		038° 20′ W
	22° 45′ N		039° 35′ W
d.lat =	01° 50′	S dep =	001° 15′ W
	(110′)		(75′)
mean lat	=		½ (24° 30′ + 22° 40′) N
	=		23° 35′ N

dep	=	d.long × cos mean lat
	=	75 × cos 23° 35′
Dep	=	68′.74 W
tan course	=	dep/d.lat
	=	68.74/110 = 0.62487
course	=	S 32° W = 212° T
distance	=	d.lat/cos course
	=	110/cos 32° = **129′.7**

Example 3.7

If a ship departs from position 34° 20′ S 040° 30′ W on a course of 033°T for 350′, determine the position reached.

d.lat	=	distance × cos course
	=	350 × cos 33 = 293′.5
	=	04° 53′.5 N
arrived lat	=	34° 20′ S ~ 04° 53′.5 N
	=	**29°26′.5 S**
mean lat	=	½ (34° 20′ + 29° 26′.5) S
	=	31° 53′.25 S
dep	=	distance × sin course
	=	350 × sin 33
	=	190′.6236623
d.long	=	dep/cos mean lat
	=	190′.6236623 ÷ cos 31° 53′.25
	=	224′.5 ÷ 60 = 3° 44′.5 E
arrived long	=	040° 30′ W ~ 3° 44′.5 E
	=	**036°45′.5 W**

3.3.2 Application of Traverse Sailing

When a ship sails on a number of consecutive legs, the combination is known as traverse sailing. The individual legs of the ship's track form part (hypotenuse) of the plane of the right-angled triangles. A traverse table can be used to obtain d.lat and departure for any course and distance up to 600′. It can also be used to convert departure to d.long or vice versa. The plane sailing

formulae should be used to calculate more accurate results.

Using a calculator with the formulae will avoid the need for interpolation between sets of figures. Traverse sailing can be very useful when the ship has steered various legs during the day.

To determine the final position, calculate the net d.lat and departure from the start position. This can be done by using a tabular presentation as shown in Example 3.8.

Example 3.8

A ship in position 22° 30′ N 061° 40′ E at 1230, is engaged in an exercise and steers the following courses and speeds for the stated time intervals.

Time Interval	Course	Speed
1230 – 1300	155° T	14 kts
1300 – 1315	030° T	10 kts
1315 – 1345	340° T	16 kts
1345 – 1430	270° T	10 kts

Determine the ship's position at 1430, if a current of 040°T at 3 knots is known to be setting throughout.

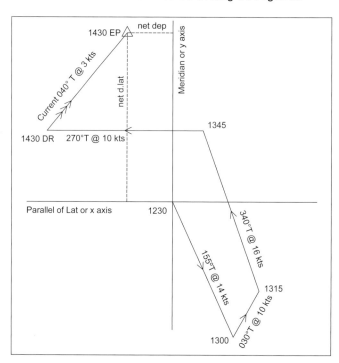

Figure 3.11   Days work (for use with example 3.8)

Time	Course	Speed	Dist	d.lat		dep	
				N	S	E	W
1230 – 1300	155° T	14 kts	7´		6´.3	3´.0	
1300 – 1315	030° T	10 Kts	2´.5	2´.2		1´.3	
1315 – 1345	340° T	16 kts	8´	7´.5			2´.7
1345 – 1430	270° T	10 kts	7´.5	0	0		7´.5
Current – 2 hrs	040° T	3 kts	6´	4´.6		3´.9	
			Total	14´.3	6´.3	8´.2	10´.2
				Net d.lat = 8´.0 N		Net dep = 2´.0 W	

arrived lat	= 22° 30´ N ~ 00° 8´.0 N	= 22° 38´ N
mean lat	= ½ (22° 30´ + 22° 38´)	= 22° 34´ N
d.long	= 0° 2´.2 W	
arrived long	= 061° 40´ E ~ 0° 2´.2 W	= 061° 37´.8 E
Position at 1430 = **22° 38´N**		**061° 37´.8 E**

A traverse table was used to solve this particular example, but using a calculator would improve accuracy. If required, extra columns can be added, eg for leeway.

3.4 Mercator Sailing

Determining a position that is reached after sailing along a rhumb line over a long distance that changes the latitude and longitude simultaneously, ie in directions other than north-south or east-west, must allow for curvature of the earth.

A method known as Mercator Sailing uses the difference of meridional parts (DMP), instead of d.lat/d. long, and departure provides greater accuracy.

Meridional parts can be found in nautical tables. The following formula should be used for the calculation of the sphere:

Meridional parts = 7915.7045 $\log_{10}$
(tan (45° + Latitude°/2))

The formulae for calculating Mercator course and distance are:

tan course	= d.long/DMP
distance	= d.lat × sec course
	(use a calculator, that can register the course to at least six decimal places)

distance	= d.lat/cos course
distance	= dep × cosec course
	(use tables, especially when the course is 60° to 90°, dep should be from corrected mean latitude)

The distance is given in geographical miles.

Example 3.9
Determine the Mercator course and distance between 20° 24´ S 057° 26´ E and 34° 10´ S 112° 28´ E.

	Lat	MP	Long
Departure position:	20° 24´ S	1242.56	057° 26´ E
Arrived position:	34° 10´ S	2170.41	112° 28´ E
d.lat	13° 46´ S (826´)	DMP 927.85	d.long 055° 02´ E (3302´)

tan course	= d.long/DMP	= 3302/927.85
		= 3.558765
course angle	= 74°.30482997	
course (to 0°.5)	= S 74°.5 E	= 105°.5 T
distance	= d.lat/cos course	
	= 826/cos 74°.30482997	
	= 3053´.4 or 3053´ (to the nearest mile)	

Example 3.10
If a ship departs from position 46° 14´ N 125° 36´ W on a course of 237° T and covers 7076´, find the position reached.

Course	= 237° T	= S 57° W
d.lat	= distance × cos course	= 7076 × cos 57°
	= 3853´.9	= 64° 13´.9 S
arrived lat	= 46° 14´ N ~ 64° 13´.9 S	= 17° 59´.9 S

departure lat	46° 14´.0 N	MP	3118.83
arrived lat	17° 59´.9 S	MP	1090.885
		DMP	4209.715

d.long	= tan course × DMP	= tan 57° × 4209.715
	= 6482´.4	= 108° 02´.4 W
departure long	= 125° 36´.0 W	
d.long	= 108° 02´.4 W	
	= 233° 38´.4 W	
	−360°	
arrived long	**= 126° 21´.6 E**	

(Subtraction of 360° has only been carried out as the result was above 180°)

3.5 Great Circle Sailing

A Great Circle is a circle on the surface of a sphere, its plane passes through the centre of the sphere. The Great Circle divides the sphere into two.

A Great Circle is the most direct route between two places on the Earth's surface. The shorter arc of the Great Circle between the two places is the shortest distance between these places. In Figure 3.12 it is identified as arc AB. On the surface of the sphere this arc/circle through A and B has the greatest radius and the least curvature.

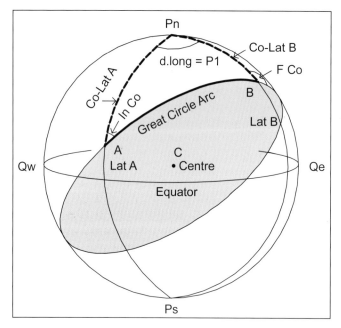

Figure 3.12   Great circle

Great Circles are most useful when latitudes are high and the d.long is significant. The saving in distance may not be significant in low latitudes, with a smaller d.long or when crossing the equator. But there are other reasons for using a Great Circle when routeing ships. These include avoiding adverse currents or winds or for taking advantage of favourable winds or currents.

Calculations involving Great Circles are solutions of a spherical triangle with Pole, A and B as the three corners. Spherical triangles have several properties, including:

- All sides are less than 180°
- all angles are less than 180°
- the sum of the three angles is more than 180°, but less than 540°
- the largest angle is opposite to the longest side
- the smallest angle is opposite the shortest side
- the sum of any two sides is always greater than the length of the third side.

In all Great Circle calculations, the Earth is assumed to be a perfect sphere. In the formulae used in this section:

- Where two letters are used a side is indicated
- where a single letter is used, it indicates an angle.

The three angles and sides of the spherical triangle are:

- P_1 d.long.
- A Initial Course angle.
- B Final Course angle.
- PA Co-lat A (It is an arc of meridian through point A).
- PB Co-lat B (It is an arc of meridian through point B).
- AB Distance (It is an arc of a Great Circle through points A and B).

The direction of d.long, East or West, should be determined carefully as it is a component of the course. Calculations are performed relative to one of the poles, North or South. This pole is referred to as the elevated pole. If both latitudes are in the same hemisphere, the pole of that hemisphere is selected as the elevated pole.

If the latitudes are in different hemispheres, calculations can be performed from any pole. But it is better to work from the pole of the hemisphere that has the starting position in it, as naming the initial course would be convenient.

Figure 3.13 illustrates the elevated poles and working of Co-latitudes, PA and PB.

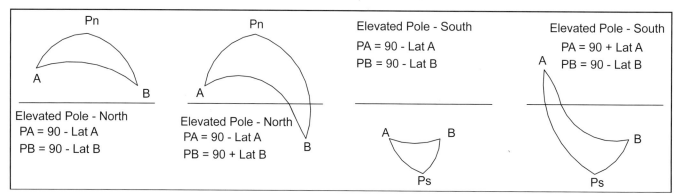

Figure 3.13   Elevated poles

3.5.1 Distance

The cosine method can be used for distance calculation when a scientific calculator is being used.

$$\cos AB = \sin PA \sin PB \cos P1 + \cos PA \cos PB$$

The above formula can be adapted using latitudes directly, avoiding the need for applying co-latitudes, as follows:

$$\cos AB = \cos \text{lat } A \cos \text{lat } B \cos P1 \pm \sin \text{lat } A \sin \text{lat } B$$

If latitudes are in the same hemisphere, ADD (use +), if the latitudes are in different hemispheres, SUBTRACT (use -).

While working with a calculator, it is recommended that all the decimal places are used in calculations and the final result either saved in memory or recorded accurately as it may be required for later calculations.

Generally, five decimal places gives an accurate answer, a problem may arise when shifting the figures from the calculator to the paper and vice versa. If the calculator comes up with a minus sign (-) during the calculations, disregard the minus sign.

Using the Haversine formula:

$$\text{hav } AB = \text{hav } P1 \sin PA \sin PB + \text{hav } (PA \sim PB)$$

In all cases, the arc AB is calculated in degrees and minutes. Multiply the result by 60 to obtain the distance in nautical miles. The distance as an answer should be reported to the nearest mile, but the full value of AB should be used for subsequent calculations, in the same way as for the course calculations.

3.5.2 Courses

Course – Initial:

$$\cos A = \frac{\cos PB - \cos PA \cos AB}{\sin PA \sin AB}$$

Course – Final:

$$\cos B = \frac{\cos PA - \cos PB \cos AB}{\sin PB \sin AB}$$

The course angle in a spherical triangle is an interior angle between the meridian and the Great Circle track. Depending on the method of working, it is related to the pole where the co-lat is applied in a cosine formula.

The navigator needs the knowledge and skills to convert the interior angles to Initial and Final Courses. Basic geometry can be useful:

Where two straight lines intersect, opposite angles are equal, in Figure 3.14 x = y, and the sum of adjacent angles is 180° (x + z = 180°, or z = 180° - x).

If position A is in the Northern hemisphere, with the North pole as the elevated pole and an initial course angle is 45°, the courses would be 045°T (N45°E) for an East d.long or 315°T (N45°W) for a West d.long. If the same angle is 120°T, the courses would be 120°T (S60°E) for an East d.long or 240°T (S60°W) for a West d.long.

If the final course angle is 45° with a North elevated pole, the final course would be 135°T (S45°E) for an East d.long or 225°T (S45°W) for a West d.long. Figure 3.15 illustrates different scenarios as sketches. When drawing sketches, the meridian of vertex should be drawn as a perpendicular, with other positions relative to it.

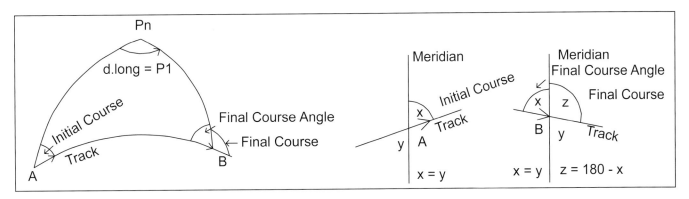

Figure 3.14 Courses and angles

Use the ABC method to determine Courses:

Initial Course:
A = tan lat A ÷ tan P1
B = tan lat B ÷ sin P1
C = A ± B
Tan Course = 1 ÷ (C × cos lat A)

Final Course:
A = tan lat B ÷ tan P1
B = tan lat A ÷ sin P1
C = A ± B
Tan Course = 1 ÷ (C × cos lat B)

(Lat A and B, Same Names Sum, Different Names Difference)

With this method, the course names can be based on the signs of C and d.long.

In all cases, courses should be reported to the nearest half degree. For subsequent calculations, for example the vertex calculation, use the full value.

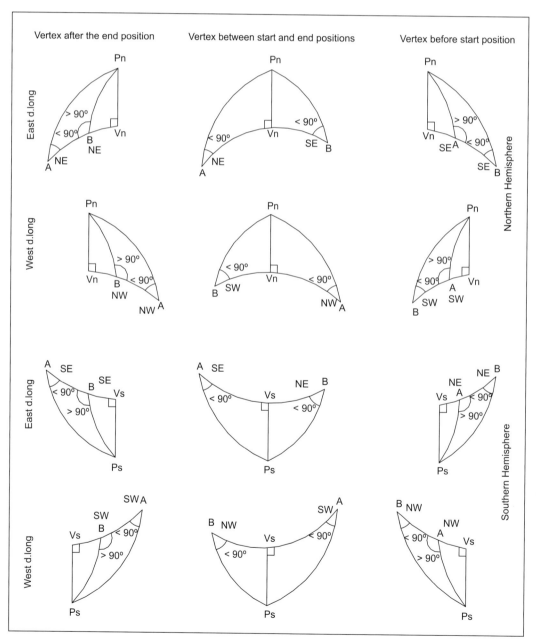

Figure 3.15 Naming of great circle courses

3.5.3 Napier's Rules and Trigonometric Identities

sin of Middle Parts = Product of tan of Adjacent Parts
sin of Middle Parts = Product of cos of Opposite Parts

$\sin \theta$ = $\cos (90° - \theta)$ [sin = sine]
$\cos \theta$ = $\sin (90° - \theta)$ [cos = cosine]
$\tan \theta$ = $\cot (90° - \theta)$ [tan = tangent]
$\cot \theta$ = $\tan (90° - \theta)$ [cot = cotangent]
$\tan \theta$ = $1 \div \cot \theta$
$\tan \theta$ = $1 \div \tan (90° - \theta)$

Effort has been made to work all examples with sin, cosine and tangent only.

3.5.4 Vertex

Vertex is the point along the Great Circle that is nearest to the pole in the hemisphere, ie the point where the Great Circle reaches the maximum latitude. Each Great Circle, other than the equator, has two vertices:

- V_N in the northern hemisphere
- V_S in the southern hemisphere.

At the vertex, the course angle is 90°, ie 090°T or 270°T, depending on the direction of d.long. Vertex is noted as latitude and longitude. Both vertices are 180° apart in longitude.

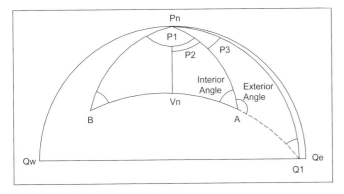

Figure 3.16   Vertex and equator crossing

In triangle PAV, PA and initial course A are known.

- d.long APV = P2 needs to be determined to find the longitude
- PV needs to be determined to find the latitude.

In the cartwheel sketch below, values have been entered clockwise from V. Co – stands for complement (90° - angle).

It is important to use PA and A for both calculations, d.long and latitude of vertex, and not any other quantity that has been determined during the vertex calculation. Any error in the working would be carried into the result.

Using Napier's Rule: sin mid part = product of cos of opposite parts

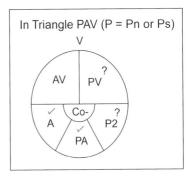

In Triangle PAV (P = Pn or Ps)

$\sin PV = \cos (co - PA) \times \cos (co - A)$
$\sin PV = \cos lat A \times \sin A$
$\cos lat V = \cos lat A \times \sin A$

$$\boxed{\cos lat V = \cos lat A \times \sin A}$$

Using Napier's Rule: sin mid part = product of tan of adjacent parts

$\sin (co – PA)$ = $\tan (co – P2) \times \tan (co - A)$
$\cos PA$ = $\cot P2 \times \cot A$
$\tan P2$ = $\dfrac{1}{\sin lat A \times \tan A}$

$$\boxed{\tan P2 \quad = \quad \dfrac{1}{\sin lat A \times \tan A}}$$

If a vertex is to be worked relative to position B, the latitude B and final course should be used in the above formulae.

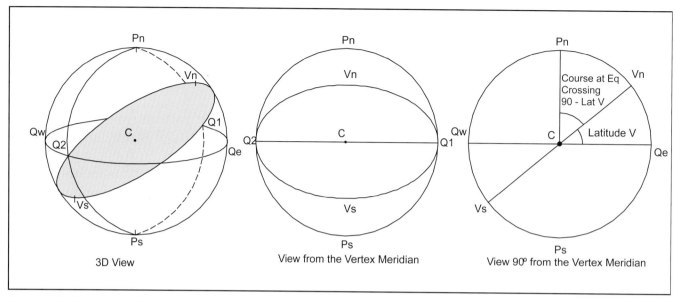

Figure 3.17   Relationship of great circle vertices and equator crossing

Having calculated one vertex, the other can be determined by reversing the sign of latitude and applying a d.long of 180° to the meridian of the first vertex (and not changing sign of longitude, unless one longitude is 090°).

3.5.5 Crossing the Equator

Each Great Circle, other than the equator, crosses the equator at two points. These points are 180° apart in longitude and are at 90° in longitude from either vertex. If the vertex is known, the point is at a d.long of 90° from the vertex longitude. Care should be taken to apply the d.long in the correct direction east or west of the vertex meridian.

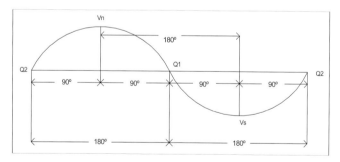

Figure 3.18   Great circle vertices and equator crossing

3.5.5.1 Longitude of Equator Crossing

If the vertex is not required, the longitude can be determined directly. In Figure 3.16 in triangle PAQ1, PA and the initial course angle A are known. In this case a side of 90° is being used with Napier's Rules. The result may have to be taken off from 180° to obtain the correct meridian East or West of position A (see Example 3.12).

It should be noted that course A is an exterior angle. If course A is the interior angle of the triangle, where the crossing point lays on the track between A and B, see Example 3.11, a minus (-) should be applied to the right hand side of the equation. The angle (P3) is the d.long between A and Q1 and the direction is always from A to Q1.

Using Napier's Rule: sin mid part = product of tan of adjacent parts

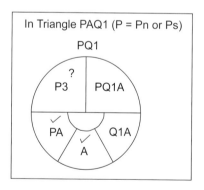

$\sin (co - PA) = (-) \tan P3 \times \tan (Co - A)$
$\cos PA = (-) \tan P3 \times \cot A$
$\tan P3 = (-) \cos PA \div \cot A$
$\tan P3 = (-) \sin lat A \times \tan A$

$\boxed{\tan \text{d.long } P3 = (-) \sin lat A \times \tan A}$

d.long APQ1 = P3 should be applied to the longitude of A to obtain longitude where the Great Circle track crosses the equator.

3.5.5.2 Course at Equator Crossing

If the vertex is known, the course is 90° minus the latitude of vertex. Care should be taken when naming the course so that it is in the correct direction of progress of track. For example, when crossing from N to S with E d.long, course = S xx° E.

However, if the vertex is not required, the course can be determined directly. In triangle PAQ1, PA is known, as is the initial course angle A.

Using Napier's Rule: sin mid part = product of cos of opposite parts

sin PQ1A = cos (co - PA) × cos (co - A)
sin PQ1A = cos lat A × sin A

> sin PQ1A = cos lat A × sin A

3.5.6 Latitude at a Meridian

The Great Circle track is transferred to a Mercator chart as a series of short rhumb lines. For this reason, meridians are selected with a d.long of 5° to 10°, depending on the speed of the ship and the latitude. Latitudes are determined for these meridians using Napier's Rules.

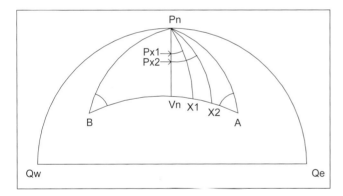

Figure 3.19 Great circle waypoints

In triangle PVX, PV is known (co-lat of Vertex). The second known value is d.long between longitude of the vertex and the longitude of the meridian in question, ie the angle VPX = Px. The side PX must be determined, which is the co-lat of the parallel at X.

Using Napier's Rule: sin mid part = product of tan of adjacent parts

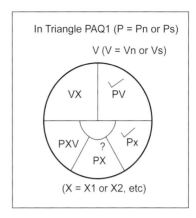

sin (co - PX) = tan PV × tan (co - PX)
cos PX = tan PV × tan lat X
tan lat X = cos PX × tan lat V

> tan lat X = cos d.long PX × tan lat V

This method makes use of the vertex position.

In a particular question: if the vertex is not required to be worked out, a direct formula can be used to obtain this latitude.

$$\tan \text{lat } X = \frac{(\tan \text{lat } A \times \sin \text{d'long } BX) + / - (\tan \text{lat } B \times \sin \text{d'long } AX)}{\sin \text{d'long } AB}$$

For Latitudes with the same names, use plus. For Latitudes with different names, use minus.

Further equations and calculations of distances off a point or hazard are shown in Example 3.11.

Example 3.11
A ship in position 04° 45′ N, 081° 13′ W, is to follow a Great Circle track to 41° 48′ S, 176° 35′ E. Find:

- *Distance*
- *initial and final courses*
- *position of vertex in the southern hemisphere*
- *longitude where GC crosses the equator*
- *course when GC crosses the equator*
- *it is reported that a navigational hazard existed at 26° 20′ S, 120° W. Calculate the distance off:*
  - *on the meridian of 120° W from the hazard at 26° 20′ S*
  - *along the parallel of 26° 20′ S from the hazard at 120° 00′ W*
  - *CPA off the hazard*

A	Lat 04° 45′ N	PA 85° 15′	Long	081° 13′ W
B	Lat 41° 48′ S	PB 131° 48′	Long	176° 35′ E
			d.long (P1)	102° 12′ W

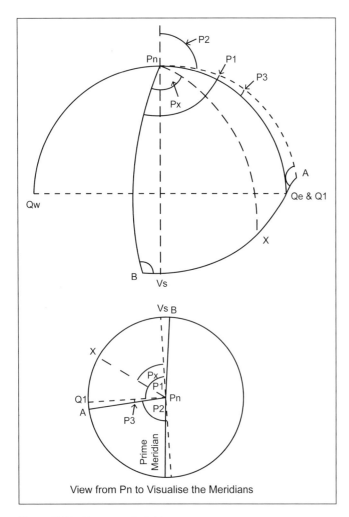

Figure 3.20 For example 3.11

Distance

cos AB = (sin PA sin PB cos P1) + (cos PA cos PB)
= (sin 85° 15′ sin 131° 48′ cos 102° 12′) +
(cos 85° 15′ cos 138° 48′)

= − 0.21219086

AB = 102.2507733 = 102 15.05 × 60 = 6135′.1

Dist = **6135′**

Initial Course

$$\cos A = \frac{\cos PB - \cos PA \cos AB}{\sin PA \sin AB}$$

= [cos 131° 48′ − (cos 85° 15′ cos 102° 15′.05)]
÷ (sin 85° 15′ sin 102° 15′.05)

= −0.666372396

Course = 131°.7876982 = 131° 47′.3 = S 48° W
= 132° T or

Using A B C:

$$A = \frac{\tan \text{lat A}}{\tan \text{d.long P1}} = \frac{\tan 04° 45′}{\tan 102° 12′} = 0.01796547 \text{ N}$$

$$B = \frac{\tan \text{lat B}}{\sin \text{d.long P1}} = \frac{\tan 41° 48′}{\sin 102° 12′} = 0.914762279 \text{ S}$$

C = A ~ B = 0.896796808 S

$$\tan \text{Co A} = \frac{1}{C × \cos \text{lat A}} = \frac{1}{0.932727749 × \cos 4° 45′}$$

= 1.118922731

Course = 48° 12′.7 = **S 48°W**

Final Course

$$\cos B = \frac{\cos PA - \cos PB \cos AB}{\sin PB \sin AB}$$

= [cos 85° 15′ − (cos 131° 48′ cos 102°
15′.05)] ÷ (sin 131° 48′ sin 102° 15′.05)

= − 0.080471926

B = 94° 36′.9 (this is the interior angle. Exterior
angle = 180° - 94° 36.9)

Course = 85° 23′.1 = N 85°.5 W or 274°.5 T

Using A B C:

$$A = \frac{\tan \text{lat B}}{\tan \text{d.long P1}} = \frac{\tan 41° 48′}{\tan 102° 12′} = 0.193311952 \text{ N}$$

$$B = \frac{\tan \text{lat A}}{\sin \text{d.long P1}} = \frac{\tan 04° 45′}{\sin 102° 12′} = 0.085013547 \text{ N}$$

C = A ~ B = 0.108298405 N

$$\tan \text{Co B} = \frac{1}{C × \cos \text{lat B}} = \frac{1}{0.108298404 × \cos 41° 48′}$$

= 12.38637637

Course = 85° 23′.1 = **N 85°5 W**

Vertex

cos lat V = cos lat A × sin A
= cos 04° 45′ × sin 131°.7876982
= 0.74305834

lat V_s = 42° 00′.4 S

$$\tan P2 = \frac{1}{\sin \text{lat A} × \tan A}$$

$$= \frac{1}{\sin 4° 45′ × \tan 131°.7876982}$$

= − 10.79261029

= − 84° 42′.4 (− sign indicates it is an
exterior angle)

= 84° 42′.4 E

long V_s = 081′ 13′ W ~ (180° − 84° 42′.4)
(to apply westerly)

= **176° 30′.6 W**

Longitude at Equator crossing

tan d.long P3 $= - \sin \text{lat A} \times \tan A$

$= - \sin 4° 45' \times \tan 131°.7876982$

$= 0.09265599$

$= 5° 17'.6$ W (see 3.5.5.1)

long Q1 $= 081' 13'$ W ~ $5° 17'.6$ W $= 086° 30'.6$ W

Check from Vertex Meridian:

$= 176° 30'.6$ W ~ $90°$ **$= 086° 30'.6$ W**

Course at Equator crossing

sin PQA $= \cos \text{lat A} \times \sin A$

$= \cos 4° 45' \times \sin 131°.7876982$

$= 0.743058264$

Course $= 47° 59'.6$ $=$ S 48° W

Check from Vertex Latitude:

$= 90°$ ~ $42° 00'.4$ S $=$ S 47° 59'.6 W

$=$ S 48°W

Distance off from 26° 20' S along meridian of 120° W

d.long PX $=$ Vertex meridian ~ 120° W

$= 176° 30'.6$ W ~ $120°$ W $= 56° 30'.6$

tan lat X $= \cos \text{d.long PX} \times \tan \text{lat V}$

$= \cos 56° 30'.6 \times \tan 42° 00'.4$

$= 0.496951508$

lat X $= 26° 25'.5$ S

lat of hazard $= \underline{26° 20'.0 \text{ S}}$

Distance off $= 5'.5$ South of Hazard

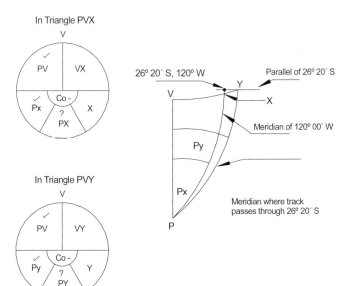

Figure 3.21 For example 3.11

Distance off from 120° 00' W along parallel of 26° 20' S

Sin of middle part $=$ Product of Tan of Adjacent Parts

sin (co – Py) $= \tan PV$ $\times$ $\tan (\text{co - PY})$

cos Py $= \tan PV$ $\times$ $\tan \text{lat Y}$

cos Py $= \tan \text{lat Y}$ $\div$ $\tan \text{lat V}$

cos Py $= \tan 26° 20'$ $\div$ $\tan 42° 00'.4$ S

$= 0.549574469$

Py $= 56° 39'.7$ W

Long Y $= 176° 30'.6$ W ~ $56° 39'.7$ W

$= 119° 50'.9$ W

d.long $= 120° 00'$ W ~ $119° 50'.9$ W

$= 0° 09'.1$ $= 9'.1$

Dep $=$ d.long $\times \cos$ lat

$= 9'.1 \times \cos 26° 20'$

$= 8'.2$ (E of stated position)

CPA Distance

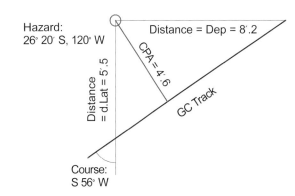

Figure 3.22 For example 3.11

Tan Course $=$ Dep/D.lat $= 8.2/5.5$ $= 1.490909091$

Course $=$ S 56° 08'.9 W

CPA Distance $= \sin$ Co $\times 5.5$ $= 4'.6$

These problems can be worked out using templates that only require figures to be entered into cells. These templates can also be created as computer spreadsheets.

Example 3.12

A ship has to follow a Great Circle track from 32° 54' N, 141° 48' E to 36° 42' N, 120° 37' W. Calculate the distance, initial and final courses, position of vertex and the latitude where the track crosses the 180° meridian.

Template for Great Circle Calculations

lat A	32 54 N	PA	57 06	long A	141 48 E
lat B	36 42 N	PB	53 18	long B	120 37 W
				d.long ^	097 35 E

Mark A and B correctly considering the d.long and respective latitudes

Distance

Distance			
sin PA	sin	57 06	1
sin PB	sin	53 18	2
cos ^P1	cos	097 35	3
1 x 2 x 3 = 4		-0.08883914	5
cos PA	cos	57 06	5
cos PB	cos	53 18	6
5 x 6 = 7		0.32461471	
4 + 7		0.23577557	
cos AB	cos^{-1}	76 21.8	
AB		4581.8 =	4582
Distance	AB x 60		

Initial Course - Using A B C method

tan lat A	tan	32 54 N		9
tan^P1	tan	097 35		10
A	9 ÷ 10 = 11	N	-0.08613	12
tan lat B	tan	36 42 N		12
sin ^P1	sin	097 35		13
B	12 ÷ 13 = 14	N	0.751954	
C	11 ~ 14 = 15	N	0.838081	
cos lat A	cos	32 54 N		16
tan I Co	1 ÷ (15 x 16)		-1.42112	
I Course =	tan^{-1}	54 52	N 55E	

Final Course - Using A B C method

tan lat B	tan	36 42 N		17
tan ^P1	tan	097 35		18
A	17 ÷ 18 = 19	N	-0.09923	20
tan lat A	tan	32 54 N		20
sin ^P1	sin	097 35		21
B	20 ~ 21 = 22	N	0.652637	
C	19 ~ 22 = 23	N	0.751871	
cos lat B		36 42 N		24
tan F Co	1 ÷ (23 x 24)		1.658838	
F Course =	tan^{-1}	58 55	S 59 E	

Vertex

Latitude			
cos lat A	cos	32 54 N	25
sin A	sin	54 52	26
cos lat V	25 x 26	0.68665377	
Lat V =	cos^{-1}	46 38 N	

Longitude			
sin lat A	sin	32 54 N	27
tan A	tan	54 52	28
tan ^P2	1 ÷ (27 x 28)	1.29549773	
d.long^P2	tan^{-1}	52 20.1 E	
long A		141 48 E	
Long V		165 51.9 w	

Equator Crossing

Longitude			
sin lat A	sin	32 54 N	29
tan^A	tan	54 52	30
tan d.long ^P3	29 x 30	0.771904	
d.long ^P3		37 39.9	31
	180 - 31	142 20.1	32
long Q	long A~32	075 51.9 w	

Course			
cos lat A	cos	32 54 N	33
sin ^A	sin	54 52	34
sin ^PQA	33 x 34	0.686654	
PQA	sin^{-1}	43 21.9	S 43 E

Waypoint Latitudes

long V		165 51.9 W	
long of X		180	
d.long^Px		14 08.1	
cos d.long^Px	cos	14 08.1	35
tan lat V	tan	46 38	36
	35 x 36	1.026649	
lat X	tan^{-1}	45 45.2	

d.long of all the required points can be obtained by taking the difference from vertex longitude.

Rest of the calculation is as above for all meridians

3.6 Composite Great Circle

There are occasions when a limit is imposed on a ship, or the Master may not want to proceed to a higher latitude. In order to obtain the shortest possible distance, a composite route is followed, ie a combination of one or two Great Circle legs and a parallel leg. Limits may be imposed on the maximum latitude a ship can sail due to:

- Load lines
- C/P clauses
- insurance – trading warranties
- crew agreement clauses
- routeing advice
- recommended route
- the need to avoid dangers
- the need to avoid unfavourable weather.

The limiting latitude is the vertex of the Great Circles. As the course at the vertex is 90°, Napier's Rules can be used to perform calculations.

In triangle PAV1, sides PA and PV1 are known. Side AV1 gives the first distance, angle A the initial course and angle P1 the d.long. Remember to only work with PV1 and PA.

For distance:

Using Napier's Rule: sin mid part = product of cos of opposite parts

sin (co - PA)	=	cos PV1	×	cos AV1
cos AV1	=	cos P	÷	cos PV1
cos AV1	=	sin lat A	÷	sin lat V1

$$\cos AV1 \;=\; \frac{\sin lat A}{\sin lat V1}$$

For course:

Using Napier's Rule: sin mid part = product of cos of opposite parts

sin PV1	=	cos (co - PA)	×	cos (co - A)
cos lat V1	=	sin PA	×	sin A
sin A	=	cos lat V1	÷	cos lat A

$$\sin A \;=\; \frac{\cos lat V1}{\cos lat A}$$

For d.long:

Using Napier's Rule: sin mid part = product of tan of adjacent parts

sin (co – P1)	=	tan PV1	×	tan (co - PA)
cos P1	=	cotan lat V1	×	cotan PA
cos P1	=	tan lat A	÷	tan lat V1

$$\cos P1 \;=\; \frac{\tan lat A}{\tan lat V1}$$

Readers should try to derive equations for triangle PBV2. In this case, the d.long would be the angle P3.

The third leg, V1V2, can be calculated using the parallel sailing formula.

d.long P2	=	d.long P – (P1 + P3)
distance V1V2 (dep)	=	d.long P2 × cos limiting lat

Total distance AB	=	AV1 + V1V2 + V2B

Example 3.13

Find the distance, initial course and final course along the composite Great Circle track between Cape Agulhas (34° 54′ S, 020° 01′ E), and Cape Leewin (34° 26′ S, 115° 04′ E) applying 40° S as the limiting latitude.

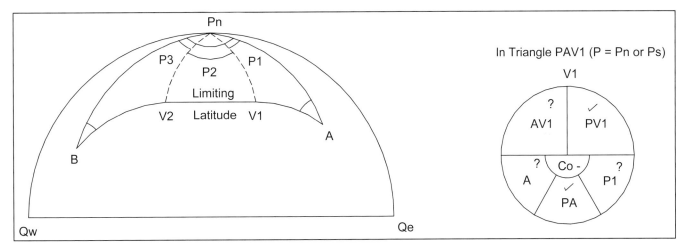

Figure 3.23 Composite great circle

cos AV1	= sin lat A ÷ sin lat V1
	= sin 34° 54′ ÷ sin 40°
	= 0.890100967
	= 27° 06′.8
Distance	= 1626′.8
cos BV2	= sin lat B ÷ sin lat V2
	= sin 34° 26′ ÷ sin 40°
	= 0.879679276
	= 28° 23′.8
Distance	= 1703′.8
sin A	= cos lat V1 ÷ cos lat A
	= cos 40° ÷ cos 34° 54′
	= 0.934027545
	= 69° 04′.3
Course	= S 69° E
sin B	= cos lat V2 ÷ cos lat B
	= cos 40° ÷ cos 34° 26′
	= 0.928781131
	= 68° 14′.7
Course	= N 68° E
cos P1	= tan lat A ÷ tan lat V1
	= tan 34° 54′ ÷ tan 40°
	= 0.831378821
	= 33° 45′.5 E
cos P3	= tan lat B ÷ tan lat V2
	= tan 34° 26′ ÷ tan 40°
	= 0.817029513
	= 35° 12′.7 W
d.long P2	= d.long P − (P1 + P3)
	= 95° 03′ − (33° 45′.5 + 35° 12′.7)
	= 26° 04′.8
distance V1V2 (dep)	= d.long P2 × cos limiting lat
	= (26° 04′.8 × 60) × cos 40°
	= 1198′.7

Total distance AB	= AV1 + V1V2 + V2B
	= 1626′.8 + 1198′.7 + 1703′.8
	= 4529′.3
	= 4529′

3.7 Practical Applications

3.7.1 Use of Gnomonic Chart

Gnomonic charts are based on the perspective projection of the surface on to the tangent plane of a sphere. These charts are for polar-regions, high latitudes covering ocean areas and port plans.

A straight line drawn on a gnomonic chart represents a Great Circle. The meridians will not be parallel unless the tangent point of projection is on the equator. As the meridians are at an angle, rhumb lines will not appear as straight lines. Similarly, angles are also distorted, except for the tangent point of the projection. The ocean charts cover a large area and are of a small scale. The graduations are different and care must be taken when plotting or reading off the position. Meridians and parallels are drawn as solid lines at five degree intervals. Intersections of intermediate meridians or parallels are indicated by crosses at their junction points. Some charts have 30′ marked as dots. In Figure 3.24, the position 36° 30′ S, 020° 15′ E has been plotted.

A gnomonic chart is a valuable tool for deciding on the route that is to be taken without performing calculations. Once the track is plotted on a gnomonic chart, the Master and navigators can see at a glance the maximum latitude to be reached and whether the track would take the ship close to any known hazards. It can also be seen whether the limiting latitude is being crossed or not.

A great circle track from Position A: 36° 30′ S, 020° 15′ E to Position B: 35° 30′ S, 136° 30′ E is created by joining A to B with a straight line. The maximum latitude reached is 54° 10′ S. A composite great circle track between the same positions with a limiting latitude of 40º S, reaches this parallel at 052° 30′ E and leaves it at 105° 30′ E. These points should only be used to make routing decisions.

For composite tracks, the points where the limiting latitude will be joined and left on a composite Great Circle track can be identified. As the scale of the chart is very small, the tangents to the limiting latitude parallel should be drawn with care. When reading the

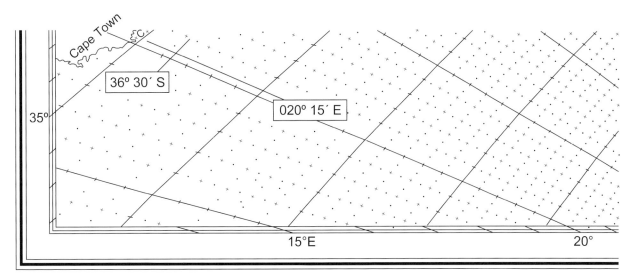

Figure 3.24 Position on gnomic chart

longitude in case of vertex, if it is not possible to make out the meridian, then two points where the track cuts a common parallel should be marked carefully. The longitude of these marks should be determined. The required meridian is half the d.long between these two meridians. In no case should a linear measurement be used to determine the longitude.

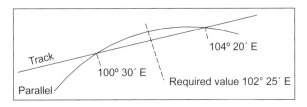

Figure 3.25 Selecting the required meridian of vertex

Once the route has been decided, the gnomonic chart can assist with plotting the selected Great Circle, or composite route, to a Mercator chart. After deciding on the d.long interval, the latitudes can be read off from the gnomonic chart. It is good practice to select the whole longitude degrees at 5° or 10° intervals and not a d.long from the start position. These waypoints can then be transferred to a Mercator chart for plotting a succession of small rhumb lines. It is important to know the route the ship is following, even on small scale ocean charts. It is poor practice to follow the GPS bearing to the next waypoint without having any route plotted on an ocean chart. Plotting tracks on the charts is always done after a careful scan of the charts for hazards. Similarly, the practice of using Mercator plotting sheets for position fixing on ocean passages, instead of the navigational chart, should never be allowed.

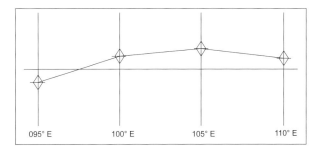

Figure 3.26 Waypoints on mercator chart for plotting rhumb lines

- For GC route the initial and final positions should be plotted on the gnomonic chart and should be joined by a straight line
- it should be checked that the proposed track does not pass over any land or islands, limiting latitude etc and will provide the maximum latitude reached
- as the track crosses meridians at selected and appropriate intervals, latitude should be read from the gnomonic chart. This provides the waypoints to be transferred to the Mercator chart
- these waypoints on navigational charts are joined by a series of small rhumb lines
- this charted track should be checked to pass clear of navigational hazards
- the process should be repeated to plot the track on the routeing chart and checked for the following:
  - ocean currents
  - prevailing winds
  - gale force winds
  - load line requirements
  - ice limits
  - visibility
- an appraisal of the route can then be made.

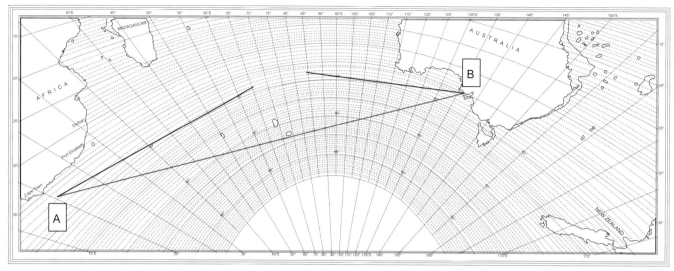

A great circle track from Position A: 36° 30′ S, 020° 15′ E to Position B: 35° 30′ S, 136° 30′ E is created by joining A to B with a straight line. It would be noticed that the maximum latitude reached is 54° 10′ S.

A composite great circle track between the same positions with limiting latitude of 40° S, reaches the parallel at 052° 30′ E and leaves it at 105° 30′ E. **These points should only be used to make routing decisions. When calculating distances on these routes, the calculations should be performed using the appropriate formulae.**

Figure 3.27   Plotting of Great Circle and Composite Tracks

3.7.2 Modifying the Routes

It may be necessary to modify the recommended route in order to comply with the overriding operational conditions.

Example 3.14

A ship is on a voyage from Brisbane (Australia) to Valparaiso (Chile). The Master wishes to take advantage of the shortest possible route without contravening Load Line Rules. The ship is loaded to the Summer marks. 245 tonnes of fuel and water must be consumed, before the ship can enter the Winter zone at 33°S. The ship has a service speed of 16 knots and consumes 25 tonnes of fuel and water per day.

Departure position 26° 49′ S 153° 10′ E Landfall position 33° 00′ S 071° 37′ W. Calculate the shortest legal distance for the voyage.

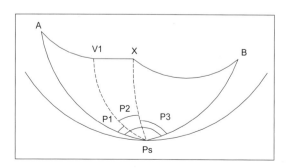

Figure 3.28   Sketch for use with example 3.14

Time required to consume 245 tonnes = 245/25

$$= 9.8 \text{ days}$$

Distance to be travelled in this time $= 9.8 \times 24 \times 16$

$$= 3763'.2$$

For distance:

cos AV1	= sin lat A ÷ sin lat V1	
cos AV1	= sin 26° 49′/sin 33°	= 0.828323229
AV1	= 34° 04′.4 × 60	= 2044′.4

For d.long:

cos P1	= tan lat A ÷ tan lat V1	
cos P1	= tan 26° 49′/tan 33°	= 0.77840407
P1	= 38° 53′.1 E	

Remaining distance to sail along parallel of 33° S   = 3763′.2 − 2044′.4

$$= 1718'.8$$

d.long (P2)   = dep/cos lat = 1718′.8/cos 33°

$$= 2049'.4 = 34° 09'.4 E$$

long X   = long A ~ (P1 + P2) = 153° 10′ E ~ (38° 53′.1 + 34° 09′.4)

= 226° 12′.5 − 360° =133° 47′.5 W

PX	= 90° − 33° 00′	= 57°
PB	= 90° − 33° 00′	= 57°
P3	= 133° 47′.5 W ~ 71° 37′ W	= 62° 10′.5

$\cos XB$ = $(\cos P3 \times \sin PX \times \sin PB) + (\cos PX \times \cos PB)$

= 0.624944715

XB = $51° 19'.3 \times 60 = 3079'.3$

Distance = $3763'.2 + 3079'.3 = 6842'.5$

Answer = **6843'**

Note: The landfall position latitude and the limiting latitude are the same. Some make the mistake of continuing to proceed along the parallel of latitude. Remember that parallel is not a Great Circle, therefore it is not short. However, if this question involved a limiting latitude other than for load line reasons, the only choice would be to proceed along the parallel after the first composite Great Circle leg. Refer to Figure 3.30 for presentation of the route on a Gnomonic Chart.

Example 3.15

A ship is on a voyage from New Caledonia (SW Pacific) to Iquique (Chile). The Master wishes to take advantage of the shortest possible route without contravening Load Line Rules. The ship is loaded to the Summer marks. 135 tonnes of fuel and water must be consumed, before the ship can enter the Winter zone at 33°S. The ship has a service speed of 12.5 knots and consumes 25 tonnes of fuel and water per day. The departure position of New Caledonia is 23° 00' S 166° 00' E Landfall position off Iquique is 20° 12' S 070° 10' W. Calculate the shortest legal distance for the voyage.

Time required to consume 135 tonnes = 135/25
= 5.4 days

Distance to be travelled in this time = $5.4 \times 24 \times 12.5$
= 1620'.0

To calculate the initial distance to reach the limiting latitude on a composite route:

$$\cos AV_1 = \frac{\sin \text{lat } A}{\sin \text{lat } V_1}$$

$\cos AV_1$ = $\sin 23° 00'/\sin 33°$ = 0.717413008

AV_1 = $44° 09'.5 \times 60$ = 2649'.5

This distance is more than the distance required to consume the excess load, the vessel cannot embark on a GC as a tangent to the limiting latitude of 33° S.

The ship can now plan and choose from the direct GC or a combination of two GC's.

If the ship embarks on a direct GC, checks must be carried out to confirm if the excess load has been consumed before to crossing the limiting latitude.

For this purpose the initial course of direct GC must be calculated first.

Long A 166° 00' E
Long B 070° 10' W
d.long (P_1) 123° 50' E

Using ABC:

$A = \dfrac{\tan \text{lat } A}{\tan \text{d.long } P_1} = \dfrac{\tan 23° 00'}{\tan 123° 50'} = 0.284518881\text{S}$

$B = \dfrac{\tan \text{lat } B}{\sin \text{d.long } P_1} = \dfrac{\tan 20° 12'}{\sin 123° 50'} = 0.4429346 \text{ S}$

$C = A \sim B = 0.727453481 \text{ S}$

$\tan \text{Co A} = \dfrac{1}{C \times \cos \text{lat } A} = \dfrac{1}{0.727453481 \times \cos 23°}$

= 1.49337436

= 56° 11'.6 (56.19276783)

Course = S 56° E

Assume the distance to steam to consume the excess load is AC/AD. AC and AD = 1620' = 27°

If the ship embarks on a direct GC, will the excess load be consumed before crossing the limiting latitude of 33° S, assume this happens at point D on the direct GC. AD & AC = 1620/60 = 27°

Re-write the GC equation to determine the polar distance PD when the excess load is consumed.

Cos PD = $(\text{Cos } A \times \text{Sin } PA \times \text{Sin } AD) + (\text{Cos } PA \times \text{Cos } AD)$

Cos PD = $(\text{Cos } 56.19276783° \times \text{Sin } 67° \times \text{Sin } 27°) + (\text{Cos } 67° \times \text{Cos } 27°)$

Cos PD = 0.580664009

PD = 54° 30'.2

Latitude of D = 35° 29'.8 S

The same colour scheme has been used on the Gnomonic Chart to show the routes. This latitude is more than the limiting latitude of 33° this is why the ship must embark on the route A to C, then C to B on two separate GC's. Refer to Figure 3.30 for presentation of a route on a Gnomonic Chart.

Re-write the GC equation to determine the d.Long for this distance AC, if this GC terminates at the limiting latitude of 33° S.

$\text{Cos } P1 = \dfrac{\text{Cos } AC - (\text{Cos } PC \times \text{Cos } PA)}{(\text{Sin } PC \times \text{Sin } PA)}$

$\text{Cos } P1 = \dfrac{\text{Cos } 27° - (\text{Cos } 57° \times \text{Cos } 67°)}{(\text{Sin } 57° \times \text{Sin } 67°)}$

Cos P1 = 0.878495869

P1   = 28° 32´.3 E
Longitude of C = 166° E ~ 28° 32´.3 E = 165° 27´.7 W
Long B   070° 10´.0 W
D Long P2 =   095° 17´.7 E
cos CB = (sin PC sin PB cos P_2) + (cos PC cos PB)

= (sin 57° sin 69° 48´ cos 095° 17´.7) + (cos 57° cos 69° 48´)
= 0.11542763
CB   = 83.37170927   = 83.37170927 x 60   = 5,002´.3
Total Legal Dist = 5,002´.3 + 1,620 = 6,622´.3 = 6,622´

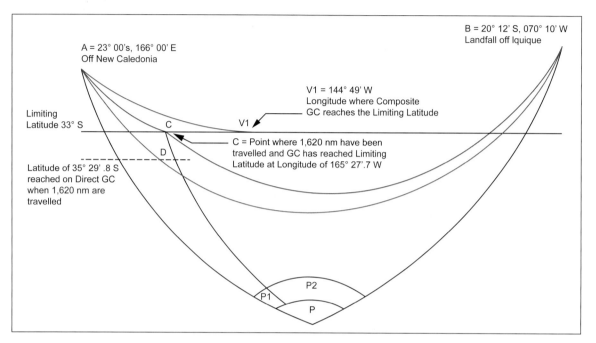

Figure 3.29   Sketch for use with example 3.15

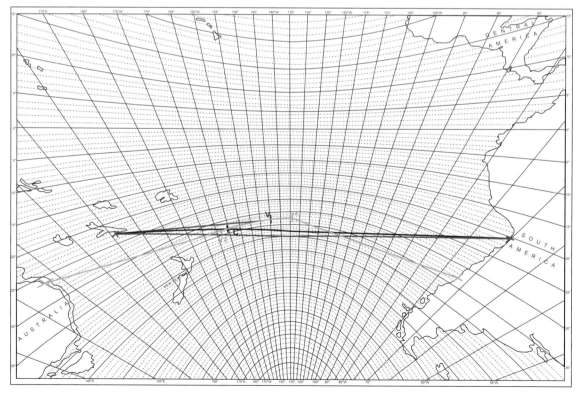

Figure 3.30   Sketch for use with examples 3.14 and 3.15

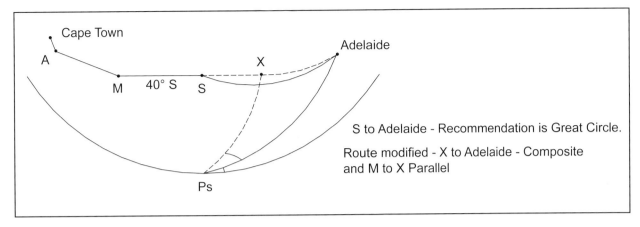

Figure 3.31   Sketch for use with example 3.15

Example 3.16

A ship undertakes a passage from Cape Town (33° 53′ S, 018° 26′ E) to Adelaide, South Australia (34° 38′ S, 138° 23′ E), through the South Indian Ocean during January. The C/P limits the ship from crossing the parallel of 40° S. Identify the route to be followed from the extract of Ocean Passages and calculate the distance on the route, complying with CP instructions.

The ship proceeds to WPT A (36° 45′ S, 019° 00′ E) and then to WPT M (40° 00′ S, 055° 00′ E) following rhumb lines. From waypoint M, the ship proceeds along the parallel of 40° S up to the point where it can follow the last leg as a composite Great Circle.

Note: As the ship cannot cross 40° S parallel, WPT S is not really material. It would be advisable to determine a new point from where to start the final composite Great Circle leg. Once this new point is known, the d.long between WPT M and this new point can be used to determine the parallel distance. A sketch of the potential problem would avoid unnecessary steps.

Leg 1

Cape Town	33° 53′ S	018° 26′ E
WPT A	36° 45′ S	019° 00′ E
d.lat	02° 52′ S d.long	000° 34′ E
	(172′)	(34′)

Mean lat $= 33° 53′ S + ½ (02° 52′) = 35° 19′ S$

Dep $= d.long × cos$ Mean lat $= 34 × cos 35° 19′ = 27′.74$

tan co $= dep/d.lat = 27′.74/172′ = 0.161296289$

Co $= S 9°.162680246 E$

Distance $= d.lat/cos co = 172′/cos 9°.162680246 = $ **174′.2**

Leg 2

WPT A	36° 45′ S	MP	2359.87	019° 00′ E
WPT M	40° 00′ S	MP	2607.64	055° 00′ E
	d.lat 03° 15′ S		DMP 247.77	d.long 036° 00′ E
	(195′)			(2160′)

tan co $= d.long/DMP = 2160′/247.77 = 8.717762441$

Co $= S 83°.45629729 E$

Distance $= d.lat/cos co = 195′/cos 83°.45629729 = $ **1711′.1**

Leg 3

cos P3 $= tan lat B ÷ tan lat V2$

$= tan 34° 38′ ÷ tan 40° = 0.823159436$

P3 $= 34° 35′.9 W$

Long of point $= 138° 23′ E \sim 34° 35′.9 W = 103° 47′.1 E$

d.long leg 3 $= 103° 47′.1 E \sim 055° 00′$

E $= 48° 47′.1 (× 60) = 2927′.1$

Distance (dep) $= d.long × cos lat = 2927′.1 × cos 40°$

$= $ **2242′.3**

Leg 4

cos BV2 $= sin lat B ÷ sin lat V2$

$= sin 34° 38′ ÷ sin 40° = 0.884152901$

BV2 $= 27°.85254331 (× 60) = 1671′.2$

Distance $= 1671′.2$

Total distance $= 174′.2 + 1711′.1 + 2242′.3 + 1671′.2$

$= 5798′.8 = $ **5799′**

Author's Note:
This chapter has covered the calculations involved in sailings, along with some practical hints. It is very important to practice and learn these calculations. The results of calculations and plotting are an essential element of planning a route.

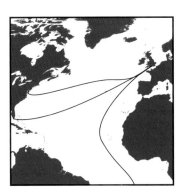

Ocean Routeing

4

Ocean routeing is part of passage planning but, as it is more complex, it demands special consideration. For an ocean passage the entire expanse of the ocean lies in front of the mariner. There are climactic patterns as well as day-to-day changes in the weather. There are ocean currents and wind-driven currents, navigational hazards and distance, all of these and other factors must be considered when an ocean route is being selected.

4.1 Use of Charts and Publications

As both climatic patterns and ocean current circulation are uniform most of the time, the general recommendations for ocean routeing can be followed. A number of charts, publications and associated materials can be specifically used for the ocean route.

4.1.1 Ocean Passages for the World

Ocean Passages of the World is published by the UKHO and contains information on planning ocean passages, oceanography and currents. It provides recommended routes and distances between the principal ports of the world, these are shown as diagrams and chartlets for power vessels and sailing ships. Power vessels are divided into two categories:

Full powered	Able to maintain a sea-going speed above 15 knots.
Low powered	Having a sea-going speed of not more than 15 knots

Generally, the routes are for power vessels with a moderate draught, using a value of 12 m. The routes for low-powered vessels are also shown where appropriate. Routes for sailing vessels should also be referred to when routes for low powered vessels are being considered.

Routes are given reference numbers and are based on principal ports and selected waypoints. Distances are provided with a reasonable level of accuracy. Details of winds, weather, currents, ice and other hazards that might be encountered are included. Some of this information is in chart format.

There are areas where routes are different on the eastbound and westbound directions. There are also different choices available for routes in the same direction, between the same ports or waypoints. In Figure 4.1, a chartlet (diagram 6.105 on page 132) from Ocean Passages for the World has been reproduced. This diagram shows the eastbound routes as 6.105 and 6.106 and a number of derivatives of these routes, eg 6.105.1, 6.105.1(a), 6.105.1(b). Route 6.107 and its variations are the westbound routes between the same ports.

The routes are between Cape Town and the ports on the West and South coast of Australia. The reasons for the choices are:

6.105.1

Going across the Agulhas current takes advantage of the east-going Southern Ocean current and westerly winds, yet keeps the ship out of the influence of the extreme winds South of 40°S. It is the Summer Zone from 16 October to 15 April, otherwise it is mainly through the Winter Zone. Example 3.15 in Chapter 3 was based on this route, but with a changed Zone.

6.105.2

Going across the Agulhas current is the shortest route, but it takes the ship into boisterous winds to the South. The route takes advantage of the east-going Southern Ocean current and the westerly winds.

6.105.3

The longest route of all in the 6.105 range. Initially, against the Agulhas current and not taking advantage of the east-going Southern Ocean current and westerly winds. But it avoids the strong winds and associated heavy seas of the Southern Ocean. Regardless of the time of year, it is within the Summer Zone.

6.107

A long Westbound route that avoids the east-going Southern Ocean current and westerly winds. This route keeps the vessel out of the influence of the extreme

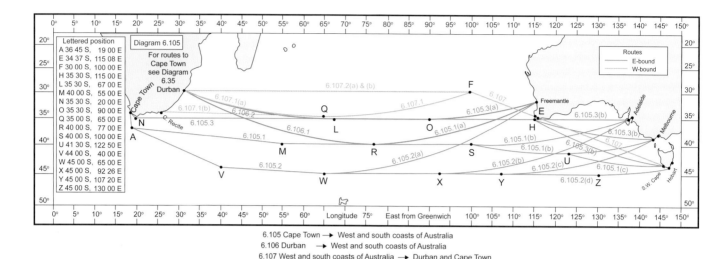

6.105 Cape Town → West and south coasts of Australia
6.106 Durban → West and south coasts of Australia
6.107 West and south coasts of Australia → Durban and Cape Town

Figure 4.1 Chartlet from ocean passages of the world © British crown copyright, 2006

winds and associated heavy seas and also keeps it well within the Summer Load Line Zone. For Cape Town, full advantage is taken of the Agulhas current when on the coast.

4.1.1.1 Multiple Routes

Multiple routes may be recommended for several reasons:

- In certain parts of the world where winds blow consistently in one direction during a season and the reverse direction during another, eg SW and NE Monsoon of the Northern parts of the Indian Ocean. The currents may also change direction and location of flow axis requiring a ship to take up routes at different locations
- strong winds set up strong currents in the same general direction as the wind. This may result in a ship experiencing strong sets
- strong winds can also create poor visibility due to dust and haze gathering from adjacent landmasses and driving spray from waves. A reduction in visibility in different seasons will require ships, for safety, to pass at various distances
- different depths around hazards may mean that they might have to be passed from different directions based on the direction of the wind and current
- the principal ocean currents usually flow in easterly and westerly directions, based on the direction of travel the ship might be able to take advantage of favourable currents and avoid adverse currents
- in different zones, winds blow from different directions at various strengths, ships should avoid adverse winds and take advantage of favourable ones
- depressions and TRS are another reason for a recommended direction of travel.

4.1.2 Charts

4.1.2.1 Routeing Charts

These are provided by the UKHO for five areas covering the oceans of the world. Some other hydrographic services provide their own ocean routeing charts. A chart is provided for every month of the year for each of the areas. The title of the chart, boundaries and inset plans indicate the area of coverage. The publication date is at the bottom and the last minor-correction date and other information is at the bottom left, outside the margin. A key of symbols and instructions are also given on the chart.

There are several inset windows that provide the following information:

- Percentage frequency of wind at Beaufort force 7 and higher is enclosed by green contours. Some selected TRS tracks for the month in past years are indicated by red arrows
- the frequency of low visibility percentage of less than 5 nm is in green contours and the percentage frequency of fog with a visibility of less than 0.5 nm is in red contours
- mean air temperature °F in green contours and mean air pressure mb in red contours
- mean sea temperature °F in green contours and Dew point temperature °F in red contours.

Shipping routes and distances are indicated as solid lines with arrows pointing in the direction of the route. A single arrow indicates that the route should be used one way TO, arrows in both directions indicate that it can be used in both directions, TO and FROM. A straight line indicates a rhumb line route and a curved line indicates a Great Circle route. Distances are stated between ports or waypoints.

Load Line zone boundaries are shown with:

- Effective dates
- parallels of latitude and meridian values
- latitude and longitude values at the change in boundary direction.

Zones are colour-coded: [Tropical-Green] [Summer-Pink] [Winter-Blue]

Date line information is provided on Pacific Ocean charts only.

Ocean currents are shown as green arrows in the direction of predominant ocean currents. The rates are stated at the tail of the arrow. > ½ indicates that the rate is over half a knot but less than 1 knot. < ½ indicates the rate is less than half a knot.

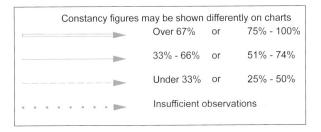

Figure 4.2 Predominant current arrows on routeing charts

Extreme iceberg limits and maximum pack ice limits are shown in red.

Figure 4.3 Iceberg and pack ice limits on routeing charts

Wind information is in red and is presented in a wind rose format, Figure 4.4, generally at 5° of latitude and longitude, with more on some coastal regions. The frequency is shown in a scale on the charts, it is 2 inches to 100%. Wind strength is indicated by the arrow length. From the arrow head to the circle, the frequency is 5%.

The wind direction is indicated by the arrow's direction. Arrows fly with the wind. The thickness and style of the arrow indicates the force of the wind.

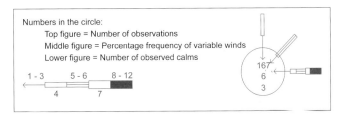

Figure 4.4 Wind rose with wind force arrow

4.1.2.2 Gnomonic Charts

On gnomonic charts, Great Circle tracks appear as straight lines. When plotting Great Circle tracks, they can be used to determine the maximum latitude to be reached and the proximity to hazards. Composite Great Circle routes can also be plotted to obtain a general idea about the longitudes where a track joins and leaves the limiting latitude. In both cases waypoints can be selected for transfer to Mercator charts.

4.1.2.3 Ocean Charts

These are the 4000 Series of charts that cover the oceans' areas. The Catalogue of Admiralty Charts and Publications can be used to select the appropriate ocean charts. The charts are based on limited information and may not contain every hazard. But known hazards, such as islands and rocks, are included. Scan the chart carefully before plotting a course on an ocean chart.

> **Author's Note:**
> When crossing oceans, it is important to plot courses on the charts as it allows the chart to be scanned for hazards. It is poor practice to steer to a GPS waypoint without having a course on an ocean chart.

Limit the use of Mercator plotting sheets to navigation related plots. They are not for plotting positions or courses.

4.1.2.4 Load Line Zone Chart

These provide the limits of the International Load Line Zones. When used with gnomonic and ocean charts, they allow a legal passage to be planned that complies with load line zones. The dates of seasonal zones must be checked carefully. A copy of the load line zone chart is included in the Ocean Passages of the World, the boundaries are also shown on routeing charts.

4.1.3 Current Charts

4.1.3.1 Vector Mean Current Chart

The mean vectors indicate the overall movement of water at the point of observation, which is at mid-length of the vector. The arrow represents the long term displacement of water, indicated by the direction and thickness of the arrow. The vector mean current is the result of all components of the observations considered for a given area. The components are differences of north/south and east/west movements.

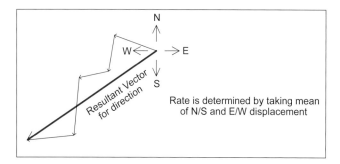

Figure 4.5 Resultant direction

The charts are used to indicate general circulation. In addition, they can be:

- Used to find the average drift of objects over a long period of time:
  - drifting ships or other derelicts
  - survival craft for search and rescue purposes
  - iceberg movement.
- they are also used to find the overall movement of water over a given period, for example the speed of a current in miles-per-day.

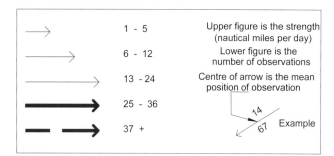

Figure 4.6 Vector mean current

4.1.3.2 Predominant Current Chart

This format is used to indicate currents on ocean routeing charts. The arrow points in the appropriate direction and the main body of the arrow indicates the change of direction in that locality. The rate may be indicated at the tail, either as a whole figure or as a fraction.

The constancy is represented by the thickness of the arrow.

- High constancy, when a large percentage (over 75% or 67%) of observations confirm the water movement in the indicated direction
- low constancy, where a small percentage (less than 50% or 33%) of observations confirm water movement in the indicated direction, shows variability in rate and direction.

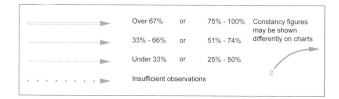

Figure 4.7 Predominant current arrows

The predominant direction is established by examining the number of occasions the current sets within a 90° sector of the compass, eg between north to east. The sector is rotated by 15° so that data of 24 sectors is available. The sector with the maximum number of observations provides the predominant current's direction. It indicates the current most likely to be experienced at an expressed point of interest and will be most useful to navigators. It would be used for:

- Passage planning/routeing
- the direction of the most-frequent currents in an area (approximate only)
- the current values in knots, these can be converted to nautical miles-per day.

4.1.3.3 Current Rose Chart

These charts provide data on the variation of ocean currents at the point of observation or interest. Information is presented in the form of a current rose. It is based on all observations recorded at 0.5 knots or more. The data is presented in 16 divisions of the compass and may present either amalgamated or further sub-divided directions. The length of the arrow is determined by calculating an average rate based on the percentage frequency of all observed figures in that direction. For passage planning and routeing purposes, these are used to determine the variation likely to be experienced in the currents in a given locality.

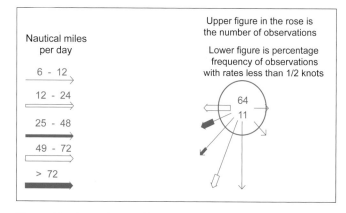

Figure 4.8 Current rose with current rate arrows

4.2 Choice of Routes

Safety is the most important consideration in routeing. However, in addition to safety, several other factors must be considered. In particular, there are economic and commercial constraints. The ship and her cargo are expensive property and a poor insurance claim record and liability claims should be avoided.

4.2.1 Operator Considerations

The company concerns can be summarised as:

- A good weather route can help to avoid wear and tear and also ensure the safety of the vessel. This will also reduce the risk of damage to the ship and her cargo. Maintenance costs and insurance claims will be minimised
- engines that are run at the optimum cost effective speed, a route that minimises fuel consumption is economical
- passenger comfort is important and is only possible if the route avoids heavy weather
- a ship can only proceed to ice areas where strength and classification allow it
- due to commercial considerations, the owners generally want to spend the least amount of time on passage, requiring the ship's speed on passage to be the maximum. However, berth availability, weather conditions, ie fog or heavy seas, and fuel consumption may determine a more optimum speed
- the reputation of owners or operators may be affected if an incident attracts adverse publicity.

4.2.1.1 Commercial Questions

Commercial managers work within a number of parameters:

- The company policy on routeing, these are the basis of instructions to the ship
- freight against fuel and running costs 1: The passage of the ship through different load line zones? How much extra cargo can be lifted if the vessel has to follow a longer passage to keep within a desired zone?
- freight against fuel and running costs 2: How much extra fuel will be consumed to achieve comfort on a longer fair weather route?
- C/P: can the ship proceed at the agreed speed as determined by the C/P and can the ship reach port within Laytime Cancellation (LAYCAN)?
- expert advice: what are the costs and benefits of shore routeing?
- damage or delay: will the cost of insurance claims or repair bills on a least time route exceed the claims for a delay on a fair weather route?

4.2.2 Master's Considerations

The Master can select from a choice of ocean routes. These routes may be based on several factors.

4.2.2.1 General Factors

- Departure and landfall positions
- shortest distance
- load line
- cargo restrictions
- navigational hazards
- weather – wind, visibility, etc
- ice limits/TRS zones.

4.2.2.2 Constant Factors

- Displacement of the ship
- draught of the ship
- engine power of the ship
- ports to be called at
- least depth/shallow water along the route
- hazards along the route
- land, islands or reefs along the route
- load line zones
- tidal heights and times
- currents of the ocean
- climatic conditions
- ice limits
- cargo and/or passenger care requirements/ instructions.

4.2.2.3 Variable Factors

- Present and forecast weather, that affects, or may affect, the sea state and swell may require a reduction of speed or damage might be caused
- effects of reduced visibility on speed of progress (safe speed)
- navigational warnings or reports
- war zones
- piracy attacks or other hostile activities

4.2.2.4 Facsimile Charts

The facsimile receiver can provide the ship with significant weather-related information that can be used for routeing decisions. These are the common types of facsimile charts that are transmitted for ships to use:

- Surface weather analysis is a synoptic chart that provides weather patterns for a specific time, based on observations made a few hours before transmission
- surface weather prognosis is a 24 or 36 hour outlook of expected future weather
- extended surface prognosis provides projected weather for 2 to 5 days

- satellite weather images provide an indication of any disturbances through cloud cover and the TRS view from space
- ice charts show the limits of pack ice and any known iceberg locations
- sea temperature charts provide surface temperature contours and forecasts for a specified period
- wave analysis charts provide contours of wave heights and direction of movement, based on a synopsis made a few hours before transmission
- wave prognosis charts forecast wave contours with heights and direction of movement.

All of these can influence routeing decisions and, in particular, the wave analysis and prognosis charts help estimate the ship's speed from the ship's performance curves. Provided the information was obtained on a regular basis, a knowledgeable Master should have no difficulty in taking routeing decisions.

4.2.3 Weather Routeing - Shore-Based

Forecasters and routeing experts use these technical developments to provide routeing advice to ships:

- Weather satellites
- extensive databases on oceanographic and meteorological conditions
- weather and wave modelling on computers
- an extensive knowledge of the ship's behaviour in varying circumstances
- better communications.

Services are provided by a number of government agencies and private establishments.

4.2.3.1 Circumstances for Weather Routeing

Weather routeing is most effective in the following circumstances:

- Length of Voyage: if the voyage is long and at least 1,500 nm, on shorter routes it may not be beneficial and/or possible to take the necessary avoiding actions
- sea-room available: the ship is in navigationally unrestricted waters, so there is sufficient sea-room for an advisory to be followed and the course can be changed as required
- direction of travel: there are more chances of encountering variable weather, head winds and sea on a west bound passage than going east
- expected weather: weather in the area is uncertain, rather than areas where weather is constant, eg in trade wind zones the weather is almost constant
- changing weather pattern: rapidly changing weather patterns are expected and where extremes of weather can be encountered, eg depressions or storms

- ship and cargo: certain types require special measures.

4.2.3.2 Types of Routeing

These form the basis of the aimed level of service provided by the routeing service:

- 'Constant speed' is often a C/P requirement and, if not maintained, may incur a financial penalty, it usually applies to bulk carriers or tankers on time charter
- 'least time' is used to keep the passage time to a minimum and is the preferred choice for large ships carrying liquid bulk cargoes, large parcels or dry bulk cargoes. This routeing may be based on Great Circles or its derivatives. These routes may incorporate a fuel saving option
- 'least damage' is preferred for vessels carrying cargo that is liable to be damaged by the movement of the vessel in heavy sea, eg Ro-Ro ships carrying expensive cars
- 'least time and least damage' is intended for keeping both damage and financial claims low and is preferred by most users of shore based routeing
- 'fuel saving' is based on the weather in general and in specific environmental factors, including ocean currents, where the ship may not necessarily sail the shortest route in circumstances where the current and weather are adverse. This is traditionally applied to bulk carriers, but recently many operators and ships are taking this option due to fuel costs.

Some vessels may have special requirements:

- Deep water route
- ice free route
- all weather route, eg passenger ships.

4.2.3.3 Considerations for Advice

The considerations of a routeing service when advising ships, are:

- Safety of the vessel, passengers, crew and cargo
- the dangers from ice, fog and storms
- speed and past performance of the vessel
- classification of vessel
- company and charterer's preferences
- Master's experience and preference
- present weather
- forecast weather for time of the voyage
- proximity to hazards
- endurance and bunker capacity
- economics of cargo and operations
- prognosis charts of wave heights
- recommendations from Ocean Passages for the World and routeing charts.

4.2.3.4 Routeing Procedure

The service may be contracted for a single voyage, period of time charter, for a ship throughout or for the entire fleet. The contract is usually made by the company, but at times it may be made by the Master.

4.2.3.4.1 Request for Service On Contract

Once a vessel contracts for service, the routeing service requires some basic information for entering into their database. The service must be advised of the company's preferences, the vessel's particulars and performance under different conditions, ie the speed of the ship at different draught or displacement conditions. They will also need the ship's trial manoeuvre data, as well as data from log books and observations, the time since drydocking and performance curves. The details of the method of obtaining the service and information that will be required when this is done are available in ALRS Vol 3.

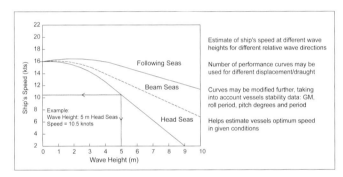

Figure 4.9   Performance curves for head, beam and following seas

4.2.3.4.2 Subsequent Information

Before sailing:

- Ship's particulars - name, call sign, contact details
- port of departure
- port of destination
- date and time of departure
- condition of the vessel – loaded/ballast, draught, freeboard, summer displacement
- type of cargo - weather sensitive/dangerous – angle of repose, high density cargo
- vessel's required ETA, if any
- vessel's speed – C/P requirement
- weather and sea conditions to be avoided
- other requirements – maintenance, passenger comfort
- vessel's meteorological equipment (if the vessel is a meteorological observation station).

While on passage, noon position reports are sent from the vessel with these details:

- Date/Time UTC
- name of the vessel/call sign

- position
- course and speed (daily average and present speed)
- meteorological conditions being experienced (pressure, wind and swell)
- ETA based on present/predicted average speed.

4.2.3.4.3 Routeing Advice

- Before sailing, the provisional route will be sent to the ship
- at the time of sailing, when the Master advises the routeing service of the time of departure, the route will be confirmed or updated if necessary. Weather reports are sent to the ship and updated every 48 hours
- the vessel updates its position to the routeing service every 24 hours or earlier if required. Routeing advice is received every 48 hours or earlier, as necessary.

4.2.3.4.4 Voyage Assessment

Shore weather routeing is based on information regarding the ship, the actual weather and the forecast weather conditions. Once the voyage is complete, Voyage Assessment Information is provided by the routeing service to the vessel or its owners.

Preliminary Voyage Analysis

This is a descriptive account of the route, explaining the reasons for the choice of the advised route and including a summary of the relevant weather conditions. It compares the estimated average speed with the performance speed of the vessel using direct routeing.

Voyage Abstract

It notes the vessel's noon positions along the route, the weather experienced and provides estimates of how the weather and currents affected the vessel's progress.

Routeing Chart

This is a plot of the vessel's noon positions and the weather experienced.

Hindcast Charts

These are provided on request and compare the weather and progress along the advised route with what was likely to have been experienced along an appropriate alternative route. The comparison shows how much time the ship may have saved by following the advised route.

Voyage Analysis

This can be provided on request for any voyage, whether it has been routed by the service or not. It is designed to be used for bunker or speed claims and is similar to a Voyage Abstract.

Routeing Summaries

This is a seasonal summary of the routes followed by a client's vessel(s) and is produced on request. It assists in assessing the benefits of using the service.

4.2.3.5 Least Time Track

One of the essential elements of any routeing is the development of Least Time Track. Using experience and the available information on board, it can be produced by the navigator. The information required by the navigator for constructing a Least Time Track is the ship's performance curves with different relative wave directions and how the waves and swell will affect speed with a change in wave height. A wave prognosis chart is also required.

A Least Time Track can be built from the guidance shown in Figure 4.10:

- From the departure position, several tracks towards the general direction of destination are generated at approximately 15° intervals
- the tracks are drawn on a transparent overlay and placed over a prognosis chart to analyse the conditions that will be encountered by the vessel during the voyage on the above tracks

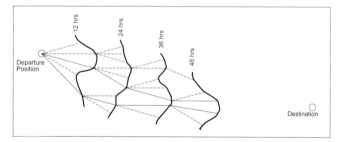

Figure 4.10 Construction of times fronts for Least Time Track

- after studying the prognostic wave height charts and the vessel's performance curves, plot the estimated 12 hour run distance on each of the tracks
- these positions are joined together to form a line known as The Time Front – bad tracks are discarded
- from each of the several positions on the time front, tracks are drawn at 15° intervals and the estimated 12 hour run is plotted again
- this procedure is repeated twice more at intervals of 12 hours. This allows a 48 hours contour to be drawn up
- the position on the 48 hours contour nearest to the vessel's destination is the point that the Master is advised to route by

- after 12 hours, the ship's actual position is marked on the chart and the exercise is repeated
- when estimating distance and speed on the projected tracks, an allowance is made for fog, ice, storms, wind, currents, wave heights and swell and other navigational hazards that are expected to be encountered, in accordance with the forecast.

4.2.3.6 Advantages of Weather Routeing

Routeing advice from the shore is based on strategic decisions by well experienced professionals who have at their disposal extensive databases of oceanographic and meteorological information. However, the ship's Master may make decisions based on the present weather and near-future expectations.

Routeing advice can be useful towards:

- Safety as the ship keeps clear of extreme weather conditions reducing the probability of severe catastrophic damage
- reduction in ship's hull metal fatigue
- reduction in ship and cargo damage fewer emergency repairs
- reduction in machinery wear and tear, extending ship-operating life
- saving in fuel consumption and costs leading to lower operating costs
- saving of time providing lower operating costs
- better scheduling of port operations and routine dry docking meaning no lost passage time
- passenger and crew comfort, enhancing the efficiency and health of the crew and the well-being of the passengers
- scheduled maintenance
- reductions in insurance premiums due to a reduction in claims
- reduction in litigation due to a reduction of claims against ships.

4.2.3.7 Disadvantages of Weather Routeing

- Routeing advice is for guidance only and the final responsibility rests with the Master. Therefore, the Master must consider the advice carefully before using it to select the vessel's route
- it is possible that, even with routeing advice, the ship will be unable to avoid the worst weather on the strategic route. Better average weather would have been possible on the more traditional optimum route
- as a result of poor strategic planning, the advice may take the ship towards an impossible position with no possibility of any better options

- the Master and the rest of the bridge team must spend time on extra reports and communicating with the routeing service
- in certain parts of the world where the weather remains fair, it can be an unnecessary expense.

4.2.3.8 Shipboard Weather Routeing

The Master can choose a route from the shortest, quickest, one at a constant speed or based on the weather. Information on the weather being experienced will also dictate routeing. A route may be an optimum route based on a favourable current, distance and climatic conditions. The weather forecasts can be used to strategically modify the route further, reducing the risk of damage to the ship and her cargo.

The Master can obtain the forecast weather and make use of the ship's performance curves to prepare the weather route on board. Advantages of shipboard weather routeing include:

- Master has up to date knowledge of the weather and sea state that is being experienced
- Master can make a judgement of the changes to weather over a period of time
- Master understands the ship's behaviour in different sea conditions
- shore based service provides advice based on forecast weather, whereas the ship can make a decision based on a combination of actual and forecast conditions
- weather information can be obtained from several sources to compare forecasts and actual conditions, the internet allows access to information to detect the incoming weather as soon as possible
- shipboard routeing allows navigating officers to gain experience of routeing and develop their skills
- costs of shore based routeing can be saved
- Master can use discretion and override the advisory, suggesting there is no point in paying for the service in the first place.

4.3 Oceanographic and Climatic Data

It is not necessary for a navigator to learn the oceanographic and climatic data of the entire world, but he should know how to find the data and use it to its full advantage. He must appreciate that the conditions being experienced at a given time may not be the same as the information in the published data. The variation may be due to differences in weather conditions from the stated climatic conditions, seasonal changes and either extra or insufficient heating of the landmasses and sea. The navigator must always be ready for any deviation from the norm and take corrective action in time to keep the ship away from danger. Variations may affect the performance of the ship and the navigator

should be ready to adjust the plan to accommodate these differences and minimise waste. The following sections provide a brief summary of the general oceanographic and climatic data of the main frequented ocean areas by using brief text notes, simple maps and bullet points in a tabulated format. As January and July represent the extremes of climatic data and its effects on the ocean currents, these are the maps that have been provided. The maps are only approximate and may not show all the islands or exact coastlines.

4.3.1 Ocean Currents and Climatic Data

4.3.1.1 Currents in the North Atlantic

The North Equatorial Current originates northward of the Cape Verde Islands and flows almost due west at an average rate of 0.7 knots. This current goes through the Antilles and enters the Gulf of Mexico. The South Equatorial Current originates off the west coast of Africa, south of the Gulf of Guinea and has a generally westerly flow at an average rate of 0.6 knots, although it may reach more than 2.5 knots off the east coast of South America, where it divides in two, flowing north and east of Brazil. The northern branch mainly turns around from May to November to form the Equatorial Counter Current, while some water goes past Guyana. Water entering the Gulf of Mexico exits in the form of Florida Current and becomes the Gulf Stream going NNE to NE at 3 to 3.5 knots. The remnants of the Gulf Stream and water from the St Lawrence and the Labrador Current, form the North Atlantic Current, going east. The North Atlantic Current splits to form the Azores Current, Portugal Current and the Canary Current going S to SE and, in part to NE to form the Irminger Current. The Irminger turns counter-clockwise on to the east coast of Greenland to form the East Greenland Current, it then continues to the west coast of Greenland forming the West Greenland Current. Part of the North Atlantic Current that reaches the North Sea splits into two. A small amount of water flows south past the Thames Estuary and the rest flows north as the Norwegian Current.

South of about 10°N, currents show a seasonal variation. Between the west-flowing North and South Equatorial Currents, the Equatorial Counter Current flows East only during May to November. In northern winter, there is no Equatorial Counter Current and the water generally emerges with an extension of the Guinea Current. When gales have been blowing SW to W, a set of up to 1.5 knots may be expected towards the entrance to the English Channel from the west. The current at the NW of the Bay of Biscay is SE to S, forming part of the Portugal Current. A branch enters the bay and goes west along the north coast of Spain. Where the gales have been blowing from W to NW, east-going scts may be experienced on the north coast of Spain.

4.3.1.2 North Atlantic Weather

SUMMER (MAY - SEPTEMBER)	WINTER (NOVEMBER - MARCH)
ITCZ: • The ITCZ remains N of the equator throughout the year • This is an area of calm and light variable winds, also called the Equatorial trough and Doldrums • Visibility is very good except in rain	ITCZ: • The ITCZ remains N of the equator throughout the year • This is an area of calm and light variable winds, also called the Equatorial trough and Doldrums • Visibility is very good except in rain
MONSOON • Area affected is off the African coast between Cameroon and Senegal • The monsoon during the summer is the SW monsoon • Cloudy weather, heavy rainfall • During April and May, severe squalls, violent thunderstorms during summer • Winds are SW'ly	MONSOON • Area affected is off the African coast between Cameroon and Senegal • The monsoon during the winter is the NE monsoon • Winds are dry and light N'ly over Liberia and Mauritania and S and W in the Gulf of Guinea • Weather generally fine, moderate visibility due to haze • During October and November, severe squalls, violent thunderstorms
NE TRADES: • The NE trade winds extend from the ITCZ and up to 30°N • The normal wind force is 4, but may increase to 7 or decrease to 2 • In the NE trade winds area, fair weather, little rain, small amount of clouds • Haze occurs frequently • Visibility is good except in rain	NE TRADES: • The NE trade winds extend from the ITCZ and up to 30°N • The normal wind force is 4, but may increase to 7 or decrease to 2 • In the Gulf of Mexico the phenomenon of very strong or gale force winds occur called the Northers • In the NE trade winds area, fair weather, little rain, small amount of clouds • Haze occurs frequently • Visibility is good except in rain
VARIABLES OR HORSE LATITUDES: • Light or variable winds area extends from NE trade wind N limit to 32°N • The predominant wind is between N and NE • Hurricanes occur in the W part of the Atlantic Ocean • Areas affected: Caribbean Sea, Gulf of Mexico, Florida, Bahamas and Bermuda • They occur from May to December • Greatest frequency is from Aug to October	VARIABLES OR HORSE LATITUDES: • Light or variable winds area extends from NE trade wind N limit to 28°N • The predominant wind is between N and NE • Hurricanes occur in the W part of the Atlantic Ocean • Areas affected: Caribbean Sea, Gulf of Mexico, Florida, Bahamas and Bermuda • They occur from May to December
WESTERLIES: • Area affected N part of Atlantic Ocean • Unsettled weather as a result of continuous passage of depression in E to NE direction • July is the quietest month • In July the strongest area remains SW of Iceland • The frequency of winds of force 7 is only about 7 days a month • Overcast skies, rain or snow, large clouds	WESTERLIES: • Area affected N part of Atlantic Ocean • Unsettled weather as a result of continuous passage of depression in E or NE direction • There is a high frequency of strong winds/gales especially in winter • The stormiest belt extends roughly from the vicinity of Newfoundland to the channel between Iceland and Forear • Stormy winds of force 7 or over can be expected 16-20 days per month in January

FOG AND VISIBILITY:	ICE:
<ul><li>The area E and S of Newfoundland is most affected by fog</li><li>Fog is very prevalent in spring and early summer</li><li>It is experienced more than 10 days per month.</li></ul>	<ul><li>Iceberg limits are reduced and frozen into pack ice</li><li>Ice information service is available from coast radio stations (Refer ALRS)</li><li>International ice patrol is operated by USCG (details in ALRS and Sailing directions)</li><li>Ice advisory service is operated by Canadian coastguard (Refer to Sailing Directions, ALRS, Ice Navigation in Canadian waters).</li></ul>

4.3.1.3 Currents in the South Atlantic

The Benguela Current sets NW on the SW coast of Africa. The South Equatorial Current is fed by the Benguela Current and the Guinea Current. The branch of South Equatorial Current going SSW on the east coast of South America is the Brazil Current.

The Falkland Current flows N to NNE on the east coast of Argentina and Uruguay. It meets the Brazil current and they both turn east to form the very slow-moving South Atlantic Current.

The Southern Ocean Current flows E to ENE from 55°S south of Cape Horn to 40°S, close to south coast of Africa.

4.3.1.4 South Atlantic Weather

SUMMER (NOVEMBER - MARCH)	WINTER (MAY - SEPTEMBER)
There is no ITCZ and hence no TRS	There is no ITCZ and hence no TRS
SE TRADES:<ul><li>The SE trade winds extend from equator to 30°S</li><li>Average wind force is 2 to 3</li><li>Slight to moderate swell</li></ul>	SE TRADES:<ul><li>The SE trade winds extend from equator to 20°S</li><li>Average wind force is 2 to 3</li></ul>
VARIABLES:<ul><li>S limit of SE trades to 31°S</li><li>Slight to moderate swell</li></ul>	VARIABLES:<ul><li>S limit of SE trades to 26°S</li></ul>
WESTERLIES OR ROARING FORTIES:<ul><li>W'ly winds predominate S of 35°S</li><li>There is continuous passage of depressions from W to E, hence the direction and strength of the wind varies</li><li>Depressions move from Cabo de Hornes to S. Georgia and then along 50°S</li><li>Gales are very prevalent S of 40° S from mid summer onwards</li><li>Wind force 7 prevails 7 - 9 days a month</li><li>S of 43°S and E of 40°W the frequency rises to about 15 days per month</li><li>Fog is common in summer and is associated with winds from warm latitudes</li><li>40°S to 50°S mainly moderate but often heavy swell</li><li>50°S to 60°S heavy swell, strong winds, abnormal waves (In the vicinity of shoal waters – Gough Is.)</li></ul>	WESTERLIES OR ROARING FORTIES:<ul><li>W'ly winds predominate S of 35°S</li><li>There is continuous passage of depressions from W to E, hence the direction and strength of the wind varies</li><li>Depressions move from Cabo de Hornes to S. Georgia and then along 50°S</li><li>Gales are very prevalent S of 40° S from mid summer onwards</li><li>Wind force 7 prevails 7 - 9 days a month</li><li>S of 43°S and E 40°W the frequency rises to about 15 days per month</li><li>In winter this frequency is S of a line joining Falkland Islands and Cape of Good Hope</li><li>40°S to 50°S mainly moderate but often heavy swell</li><li>50°S to 60°S heavy swell, strong winds, abnormal waves (In the vicinity of shoal waters – Gough Is.)</li></ul>

ICE:	ICE:
• The approx mean limits of pack ice are indicated on routeing charts, climatic chart and U.S. Marine climatic atlas • The main shipping routes of the S. Hemisphere are not affected by pack ice but its presence prevents the use of GC track between Cape of Good Hope and Cabo de Harnos especially in winter (Mar/Apr) • Icebergs are of immense size and are most likely to be encountered in the lower latitudes. They have been sighted as far as 31°S off the coast of S. America (Argentina, Brazil) • The normal iceberg limits are 35°S.	• The approx mean limits of pack ice are indicated on routeing charts, climatic chart and U.S. Marine climatic atlas • The main shipping routes of the S. Hemisphere are not affected by pack ice but its presence prevents the use of GC track between Cape of Good Hope and Cabo de Harnos especially in winter (Mar/Apr) • Icebergs are of immense size and are most likely to be encountered in the lower latitudes. They have been sighted as far as 31°S off the coast of S. America (Argentina, Brazil) • The normal iceberg limits are 35°S.

4.3.1.5 Currents in the North Indian Ocean during Summer (SW Monsoon)

The Equatorial Jet between 2°N to 2°S goes east and appears twice during the transition periods between the monsoon seasons. There is a clockwise flow on the coastal regions of the Arabian Sea and the Bay of Bengal to clear the water that has been pushed by the SW monsoon. The Somali Current flows in a NE direction at high rates averaging 3 knots with a maximum of 8 knots. At times, the actual Somali Current differs from its general trend. During June, this current usually sets up another clockwise flow, between 2°N and 6°N and south of Suqutra, as it leaves the coast of Africa. This usually happens into July as well. Late July and August see a change as the Somali Current turns at about 10°N. General easterly sets occur in the open waters of the Arabian Sea and the Bay of Bengal. During June, the Equatorial Jet gradually ceases and a weak westerly set replaces it. In later parts of September, the next phase of Equatorial Jet may begin to set.

4.3.1.6 Currents in the North Indian Ocean during Winter (NE Monsoon)

General westerly sets occur in the open waters of the Arabian Sea and the Bay of Bengal. The Equatorial Jet usually continues east up to late December, then is replaced by a broad westerly flow in January which continues up to March. The coastal currents change direction:

• Anti-clockwise in December and January
• clockwise in February and March. Early February in Bay of Bengal and end of March for the Arabian Sea.

There is a SW flow off the coast of Somalia south of about 8°N and to the north it sets NE. The NE flow shifts to about 4°N in March. During the northern winter, the North Equatorial Current flows west.

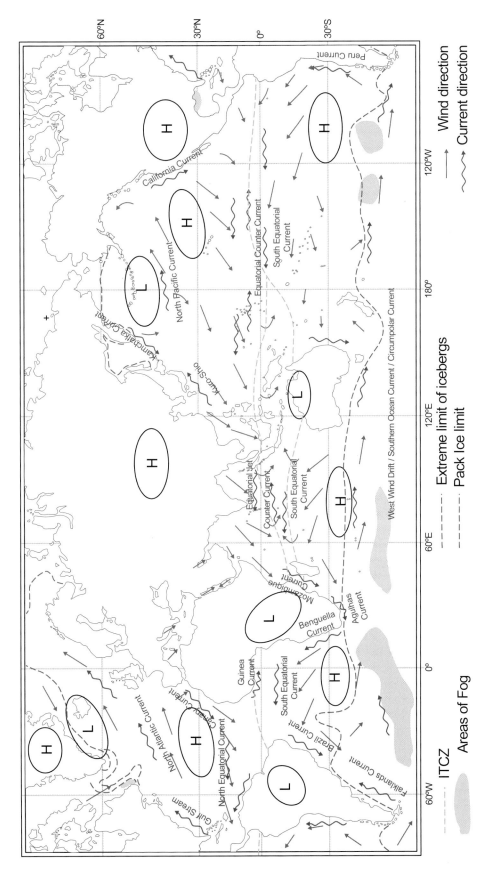

Figure 4.11   Currents, ice and met conditions - January

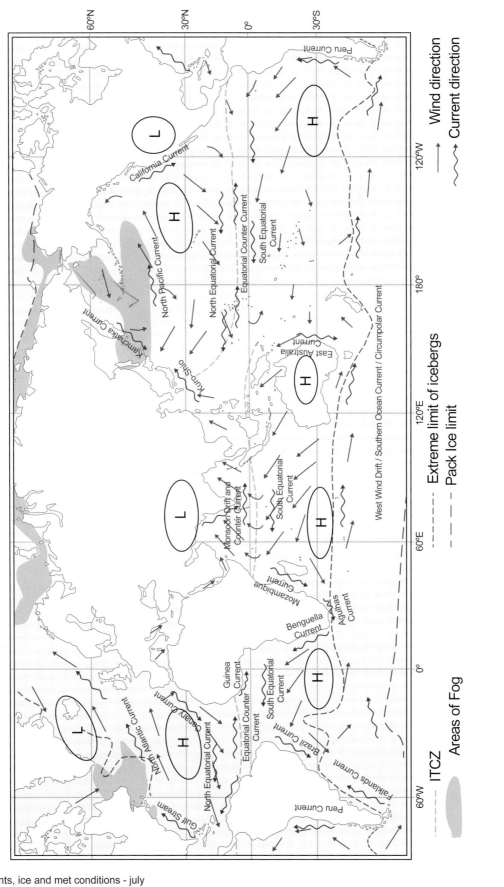

Figure 4.12 Currents, ice and met conditions - july

4.3.1.7 Currents in the South Indian Ocean

The South Equatorial Current of the Indian Ocean runs west well south of the equator when compared to similar currents in the Atlantic and Pacific Oceans. To the north of the South Equatorial Current, an east-going Equatorial Counter current, 0.5 to 1 knot – sets during the NE monsoon season, especially in the west parts of the Indian Ocean. This Counter current merges into the Equatorial Jet, at 1 to 2 knots, at the start and end of the NE monsoon.

The South Equatorial Current splits twice. Once when a small branch flows along the east coast of Madagascar and second, at the African east coast. Some water branches N into the East African Coast Current and the other forms the SSW flow in the Mozambique Channel as the Mozambique Current. The SSW flow on the east and west sides of Madagascar join to form the Agulhas Current, averaging 2 to 3 knots with a maximum of 5 knots. Part of the Agulhas Current helps to form the Benguela Current and a small part turns to flow east with the Southern Ocean Current.

During autumn and winter on the west coast of Australia, sets off the coast are south and turn south east off Cape Leeuwin. During spring and summer, some coastal eddy and some northerly flow (N of 33°S) is present. To the west of 113°E, there is a tendency for a N to NW set that joins the South Equatorial Current. When this N to NW current is more constant, it is termed the West Australian Current.

4.3.1.8 Indian Ocean Weather

SUMMER (MAY - SEPTEMBER) (S. winter)	WINTER (NOVEMBER - MARCH) (S. summer)
NORTH INDIAN OCEAN	NORTH INDIAN OCEAN
<ul><li>SW monsoon prevails</li><li>Period June to September</li><li>In the Arabian Sea TRS season is May/Jun/Jul/Oct/Nov</li><li>In Bay Of Bengal TRS season is May-November</li><li>North Equatorial current is absent</li><li>Equatorial Counter Current is absent</li><li>Both are replaced by Indian SW monsoon current flowing W, all to the N of Equator</li><li>Strength of winds averages force 6 – 7, about 10 days a month, the worst area is Suqutra</li><li>In the Arabian Sea the wind force is 4 – 6 and above force 7, 5 to 10 days per month</li><li>The Bay of Bengal wind force is 4 – 5 and reaches force 7, 5 to 10 days in July</li><li>Cloudy and unsettled weather with heavy rainfall</li><li>Good visibility except in rain</li><li>Visibility reduced in Apr/May due to dust haze</li><li>Inter-monsoon season prevails in April/May</li><li>The swell is governed by the prevalent monsoon</li></ul>	<ul><li>NE monsoon prevails</li><li>Period November to March</li><li>North Equatorial Current is replaced by NE Monsoon Current flowing west</li><li>Equatorial and South Equatorial Currents are also present</li><li>Wind force 3 - 4, direction N and NE</li><li>Weather in the Arabian Sea and Bay of Bengal is generally fine</li><li>Inter-monsoon season prevails in October</li><li>Good weather</li><li>Visibility is reduced due to rain in winter</li><li>The swell is governed by the prevalent monsoon</li></ul>
SOUTH INDIAN OCEAN	SOUTH INDIAN OCEAN
<ul><li>ITCZ is S of equator</li><li>TRS season is Nov – April</li><li>Tropical storms are known as cyclones. In the Australian area they are called hurricanes</li><li>Weather as that of Doldrums, Calm weather, light variable winds, heavy shower, squalls, thunder storms</li><li>NW monsoon prevails (NE monsoon in N. Hemisphere)</li><li>Wind of light force, except in TRS</li><li>Cloudy unsettled weather</li><li>Good visibility, except in rain</li></ul>	<ul><li>ITCZ is S of equator</li><li>TRS season is Nov – April</li><li>Tropical storms are known as cyclones. In the Australian area they are called hurricanes</li><li>Weather as that of Doldrums, Calm weather, light variable winds, heavy shower, squalls, thunder storms</li><li>NW monsoon prevails (NE monsoon in N. Hemisphere)</li></ul>

	• Wind light force, except in TRS • Cloudy unsettled weather • Good visibility, except in rain NW monsoon prevails (NE monsoon in N. Hemisphere) • Winds of light force, except in TRS • Cloudy unsettled weather • Good visibility, except in rain
SE TRADES: • Extends from equatorial trough to 30°S • Force 3 - 4	SE TRADES: • Extends from equatorial trough to 27°S • Force 4 - 5
VARIABLES: • Extends between S limit of SE trade winds and 35°S • Light and variable winds • Fair weather	VARIABLES: • Extends between S limit of SE trade winds and 30°S • Light and variable winds • Fair weather
WESTERLIES: • Extends between S limit of variables and N Limit of Polar easterlies • Winds are westerly and depend on east moving gales • The centre of most of these depressions pass S of 50°S • Wind force 7 is experienced for >6-12 days per month S of 40°S • Weather is variable, overcast skies, rain or snow associated with fronts of east moving depressions	WESTERLIES: • Extends between S limit of variables and N Limit of Polar easterlies • Winds are westerly and depend on east moving gales • The centre of most of these depressions pass S of 50°S • Gales are prevalent in winter where the wind force 7 is prevalent 12-16 days per month • Weather is variable, overcast skies, rain or snow associated with fronts of east moving depressions
ICE: • Greatest extent of pack ice is from Aug-Sept and runs from about 55°S 000° to 58°S 050°E, 60°S 110°E • The GC routes between S. Africa and Australia are obstructed • Icebergs mean limit reaches farthest N between 20°E and 70°E in Nov and Dec when it runs from 44°S in the longitude of Cape Agulhas.	ICE: • The GC routes between South Africa and Australia are obstructed • Icebergs mean limit everywhere S of 50°S.

4.3.1.9 Currents in the North Pacific Ocean

The North Equatorial Current flows westward in the general area of the NE Trades. The South Equatorial Current also flows westward in the area of SE Trades. Between the two is the weaker east going North Equatorial Counter current, at around 5°N to 7°N.

The North Equatorial Current curves towards the Philippines and Taiwan, where it deflects further north to become Kuroshio, also known as Japan Current, that moves NE. The Tsushima Current flows NE along the west coast of Japan. Water from Kuroshio curves east and widens between the Aleutians and the Hawaiian Islands. This is known as the North Pacific Current. As the North Pacific Current approaches the west coast of North America, it turns SE to become the California Current. During the winter, the Davidson Current flows northerly inside of the California Current. The Aleutian Current flows east and the Alaska Current flows north along the coast of Alaska. The Kamchatka Current flows SW along the Russian coast to the north of Japan.

4.3.1.10 Currents in the South Pacific

The Southern Ocean Current flows easterly around latitude 45°S. The Peru Current flows N to NW and feeds into the South Equatorial Current, which is west-going at the equator. The East Australian Current flows S along the coast. From Australia to New Zealand, it is called the Tasman Front and on the east coast of New Zealand, it becomes the East Auckland Current.

4.3.1.11 North Pacific Weather

- The ITCZ remains permanently N of equator at Longitude E of 160°W
- To the W of 160°W it lies in the S. hemisphere from about Nov or Dec until Apr or May
- In the Northern summer it is virtually non-existent W of 150°E
- NE trade winds blow on the equatorial side from 30°N
- Wind force 3 - 4 but often freshens to 5 - 6
- NE monsoon begins generally about September in the north and close to the equator around September
- In the summer of the N hemisphere the SW monsoon is present in the Western parts
- Fog is prevalent during summer off Japanese/Chinese coast and off California
- The foggy season reaches its maximum in April off Hong Kong, in the Japan Sea the fog is about 3 - 4 days per month and 5 -7 days per month off Northern Honshu
- After July the fog incidents drop sharply
- Wind force is 3 - 4 in South China Sea and force 3 elsewhere
- TRS is prevalent in summer when winds may reach force 7 and above
- These are known as Typhoons in the Western part and Hurricanes in the Eastern part
- The areas affected by Typhoon are Caroline Islands, Mariana Islands, Philippines, S China Sea near the coast of China and Taiwan, China Sea and Japan
- TRS activity is between June and October
- September is the month of greatest frequency of TRS
- The visibility along the Chinese coast is reduced by sea fog
- Variable belt is from 25°N to 30°N in winter and 35° - 40°N in summer, light and moderate winds are prevalent
- Winds in summer are generally light and rarely reach force 7 unless associated with tropical storm
- At the height of winter season in January, wind forces reach 7 or above in the areas N of 40°N
- The weather varies considerably in the westerlies during summer and winter
- N of 40°N there is a continuous passage of depressions from the vicinity of China and Japan in a NE direction towards the Aleutian Islands and south of Alaska
- Strong winds and gales are very frequent E of Japan, S of Aleutian and Alaska Peninsula where the wind force reaches force 7 or above more than 12 days a month
- Visibility is reduced by rain and snow
- In summer, depressions are less frequent, much less intense and their tracks are further North than in winter
- Polar easterlies, in winter since most depressions travel South of Aleutian Islands, the winds in the Bering Sea are mostly easterly.

4.3.1.12 South Pacific Ocean Weather

- ITCZ remains North of Equator throughout the year E of 160°W
- There is slight haze around east coast of Australia reducing the visibility to 8-15 nm
- To the W of 160°W it lies in the S hemisphere from about Nov or Dec until Apr or May
- Weather is typical of ITCZ, calm, light variable wind and fine weather alternate with squalls, heavy rain and thunderstorms
- Tropical storm area is W of 155°W and S of 8°-10°S
- The storm period is from December to April
- Greatest frequency of storms is from January to March, but storms are not unknown at other times
- Over the open oceans weather is fair with occasional showers
- Skies are about half covered with small cumulus clouds
- The SE trade wind limit is from equator to 20°S
- The average strength of the trade winds is about force 4, but often strengthens to about force 6
- There is a High on 30°S, W off Chile, 20°-30°S is an area of variable winds; areas east and west of High are also variable zones
- Winds of force 7 or more may be experienced for 1 to 4 days per month in variable zone between 30° and 40°S
- Cloudy weather with overcast skies is common when approaching coast of South America
- Fog and mist are common towards the coast of S America over the cold waters of Peru Current but rarely occur elsewhere.

4.3.1.13 Example Outline of Weather (For Route in Example 3.15)

The ship will initially encounter SE Trades generally Force 4 and occasionally Force 6. As latitude increases, up to 40°S, the winds will become variable and moderate in strength. Winds up to Force 7 might be experienced for up to four days a month. As the ship approaches the coast of S America, the winds will tend to be more Southerly.

In the variable belt between 20° to 40°S, the weather depends on the passage of anti-cyclones moving Easterly. The amounts of clouds and rainfall will be variable. When at the southern most sector of the route, cloud cover will generally be heavy with periods of rain/snow. Visibility will be poor if Northerly winds are encountered. Cloud cover decreases as the latitude decreases.

Cloud cover will increase again when it gets closer to the coast of S America, where Fog and mist may also be encountered.

4.4 General Hazards to be Found on an Ocean Passage

This is a brief summary of some of the hazards that may be encountered on an ocean passage.

- Sparse hydrographic information, some hazards may still be uncharted
- there may be lot of islands at short distances in the archipelagic waters
- some islands may be unlit, as a result they are not visible during darkness
- some islands may be very low and may not be visible at reasonable distances or picked up by radar at safe distances
- fishing craft in the vicinity of coasts and small islands. They may have no lights, inadequate lights or be improperly marked
- leisure crafts may be present in the vicinity of a coast, small islands and at times, even in the open seas
- cruise ships may pass very close to islands or coast, they may emerge suddenly having been obscured by landmarks
- some charts may be based on very old surveys
- some charts may be very old and have an inadequate scale
- the discrepancy between charted and actual positions, derived from modern navigation systems or celestial observations, may be very large. No data is available for correcting such positions

- cross currents, especially in vicinity of islands, can set a ship towards danger. Some of these currents may be very strong
- traffic may cause concerns, especially when crossing regular shipping lanes (across or going head-on) in frequent-shipping lanes
- force of wind in areas where gale force or stronger winds are likely
- tropical revolving storms. Ships at times on certain headings may encounter the same TRS twice, both before and after re-curvature
- large waves and a heavy swell
- areas where abnormal waves or Tsunamis may occur
- visibility affected by rain, falling snow, fog, sand storms and haze
- cloudy conditions or poor visibility may prevent celestial observations
- thunderstorms, sudden squalls and water spouts
- icebergs and other forms of ice
- areas of offshore activity and survey
- absence of adequate areas for choosing a suitable landfall position
- armed attacks, piracy and armed robbery and other security concerns
- possibility of debris falling following a satellite launch.

It must be appreciated that this list is generic and that the actual hazards on a passage may not include all these items. For example, there is no ice in the Caribbean Sea or other low latitudes. Similarly, there are no TRS or issues with unlit islands in the South Atlantic.

> **Author's Note:**
> Do not include irrelevant points like these in passage plans as their presence undermines the value of the input effort.

4.4.1 Recap of Factors for Choice of Routes

The shortest route is not always the quickest. The following factors should be taken into account when choosing a route:

- Distances by various routes
- recommendations from Ocean Passages of the World
- load line zones
- proximity to navigational hazards, including dangers, ice, offshore activity and hostile activity
- availability and consumption of bunkers, along with intermediate bunkering ports
- prevailing weather conditions, particularly the presence of storms or depressions

- climatic conditions, including general wind circulation and state of the sea
- favourable or adverse currents
- type of cargo
- advice and recommendations by routeing services
- the Charterer's instructions
- company preferences or limiting factors, including insurance policy warranty limits
- time available
- position-fixing reliability
- damage likely to be sustained
- maintenance work planned during the voyage
- comfort of crew and passengers
- the points where stores and bunkers are to be replenished
- the amount of traffic likely to be encountered
- draught at various stages of the voyage.

EXAMPLE 4.1:

A vessel has the option of three routes for an ocean passage as can be seen in the table below. Here we can see the effect of distance, wind and current on passage time:

Distance	3130	3220	3450
Steaming time	8d 3h 38m**	8d 9h 15m	8d 23h 38m
Current	Against 2 kts**	Against 1 kt	Favourable 0.5 kt
Current time factor	+ 24h 27m**	+ 12h 35m	- 6h 44m
Wind effect on speed	Against 0.5 kt	Against 0.5 (50%)	Against 0.5 (15%)
Wind time factor	+ 6h 7m	+ 3h 9m	+ 1h 1m
Time on passage	9d 10h 12m	9d 0h 59m	8d 17h 55m

Time lost due to current calculation: 8d 3h 38 m × 2 knots = 391´.27 ÷ 16 knots **= 24h 27m

The time on passage provides an indication of the optimum choice. In addition, fog and swell may also adversely affect the progress. Other factors should also be considered when deciding the route.

Author's Note:
Modern ship designs and high costs of construction, expensive cargo, ever increasing liability payments, increased costs of fuel, costs and timeout for repairs, unnecessary waiting times, intense competition and heightened media interest all put pressure on the Master and the ship's operators to demonstrate a performance level where there appears to be little room for error. Using efficient methods of planning a proposed transit before and during the voyage, plus a careful study of all the elements, particularly weather, provides an opportunity for the optimum conditions to be used to best advantage, ensuring safety and with reasonable operating costs.

5

Bridge Procedures

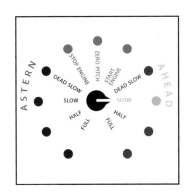

To achieve consistency and minimise accidents, it is important that all mariners follow similar procedures. Proper training and the availability of written procedures ensures that operations are carried out safely and consistently. In addition, applying some basic principles of management can help to create an environment that is mutually supportive and efficient.

5.1 Bridge Organisation

General principles of safe manning should be used to establish levels that are appropriate to any ship. At all times, ships must be navigated safely and in compliance with the International Regulations for Preventing Collisions at Sea.

The need to maintain a proper lookout should determine the basic composition of the navigational watch. There are several circumstances and conditions that may influence the actual watchkeeping arrangements and bridge manning levels at any time.

Effective bridge team organisation will manage all the available resources and promote good communication and teamwork. Efficient bridge resource and team management should eliminate the risk that an error on the part of one person results in a dangerous situation.

5.1.1 Navigational Watch Composition

The bridge team may vary in composition, depending on the navigational situation and the human resources that are available. At various stages of the passage, these may include:

- Master
- OOW
- Helmsman
- Lookout(s)
- Additional officer
- Pilot.

There will be circumstances when the Master is required on the bridge, due to:

- Passage planning requirements

- the Master's watch instructions
- standing orders under developing circumstances
- the OOW thinks the Master's presence is essential.

In this case, control remains with the OOW until the Master expressly takes command, which should always be logged. The OOW will now take the supportive role, but remains responsible for the actions of the watch members. There will be occasions when an additional officer will be summoned to the bridge to double-up the watch. Situations that demand the presence of an additional officer on the bridge might be a combination of:

- Restricted visibility
- heavy traffic
- navigation through congested waters.

For prolonged periods of time in these conditions, even the Master will require relief and a rota should be established where the Master and the junior navigation officer share one watch and the senior and junior navigation officers share the other. There may be certain high-risk situations when the Master and two watch officers are required on the bridge at the same time.

In such circumstances, the team members roles must be clearly defined. In most cases, these will be set by company policy, but they may also vary with the individual Master or practice on the ship and prevailing circumstances. In each case, it is imperative that all members of the team fully understand their role to avoid either overlapping or ignoring certain functions.

5.1.1.1 Factors for Navigational Watch Composition

When determining the adequacy of the navigational watch for ensuring proper lookout and execution of other routine bridge related duties, the Master should take account of the following:

- The size of the ship and the field of vision available from the coning position
- the bridge configuration that might hinder detection by sound or vision
- state of visibility, state of sea and weather condition
- traffic density and other activities at sea in the vicinity of the ship's track

- traffic separation or routeing schemes and the attention required in these
- the fitness for duty
- experience of each OOW
- familiarity of each OOW with the ship's equipment, procedures and manoeuvring characteristics
- rudder and propeller control and manoeuvring characteristics
- activities taking place on the bridge, for example, communication and the availability of additional help
- the operational status of bridge instruments and controls, including alarms, level of automation
- knowledge of, and the Master's confidence in, the professional competence of the ship's officers and crew
- additional workload caused by the nature of the ship's functions, including immediate operating requirements and anticipated manoeuvres
- any other relevant standard, procedure or guidance related to watchkeeping arrangements and fitness for duty.

When deciding on the composition of the bridge watch, which may include appropriately qualified ratings, the following must be considered:

- The bridge must not be left unattended at any time
- daylight/darkness, visibility and weather conditions
- need for the OOW to carry out additional duties in proximity to navigational hazards
- use and operational condition of navigational aids, including radar or electronic position-indicating devices, and any other equipment that affects the ship's safe navigation
- if the ship is fitted with operational autopilot
- the need to perform radio duties
- unattended machinery space (UMS) controls, alarms and indicators provided on the bridge, procedures for their use and any limitations they may have
- any unusual demands on the navigational watch that may arise due to special operational circumstances.

5.1.1.2 Change in Watch Levels

Circumstances change during the voyage and it may be necessary to review the manning levels of a navigational watch. The following factors can be categorised as a change in circumstances, (but the list is not exhaustive).

- Prevailing traffic conditions
- prevailing weather conditions
- the nature of the waters where the ship is navigating
- fatigue levels and workload on the bridge
- changes to the operational status of the bridge equipment
- emergency situations
- activities the ship is involved in.

5.1.1.3 Sole Lookout

In open sea conditions or when well away from dangers during daytime, the OOW may be the only person responsible for navigation. Although the lookout may be employed on other bridge-related duties at this time, he can be summoned when required by the OOW.

In these situations the vessel is to be steered by autopilot. This is permitted under the STCW Code. If this is to be practised on any vessel, the SMS should give clear guidance. The Master's standing orders should also clarify the precise procedure that is to be followed. The following guidance is also required:

- The circumstances where sole lookout watchkeeping can commence
- how sole lookout watchkeeping should be supported
- the circumstances when sole lookout watchkeeping must be suspended
- the Master should be satisfied with the following conditions on each occasion before sole lookout watchkeeping may commence
- that the OOW has had sufficient rest before standing his watch
- that the OOW confirms it is well within their capacity to maintain a proper lookout and remain in full control of the prevailing circumstances
- that the OOW is aware of the backup assistance that has been designated for the bridge and who should be called for assistance
- that all designated backup personnel are aware of response times, limitations on their movements and can hear the alarms or communications from the bridge. There should be two-way radio contact between the bridge and one of the designated personnel
- that all essential equipment and alarms on the bridge are fully functional, especially the bridge watchkeeping alarm.

This is an example of a guide to watch-composition in varying conditions:

Open sea – Day:	OOW on bridge, lookout on call and in close proximity to the bridge and with a radio. The Master on call
Open sea – Night:	OOW and lookout on bridge. The Master on call
Coast – light traffic:	OOW and lookout on bridge. The Master on call
Coast – heavy traffic:	OOW, lookout and helmsman on bridge. The Master where required
Congested waters:	The Master and 3rd Officer or the Chief Officer and 2nd Officer,

| Restricted visibility: | plus lookout and helmsman on the bridge (6 hour watches, if for a prolonged period) Master and 3rd Officer or the Chief Officer and 2nd Officer, the lookouts and helmsman on the bridge (6 hour watches, if for a prolonged period). |
| Restricted visibility and Congested waters: | Master and two watchkeeping officers, two lookouts and helmsman on the bridge. |

For example, the following are the main responsibilities of the individuals who form the bridge team in the last situation above:

MASTER

The Master is in command and observes the overall situation. He ensures that the bridge team is properly rested and that all the bridge equipment is operating satisfactorily. The Master delegates collision and navigation duties to the specific OOW but maintains an awareness of the situation. If the situation becomes complex and cannot be handled by the designated OOW, the Master can intervene and take immediate action to resolve the situation.

OOW 1

One of the OOWs will be responsible for navigation. The OOW will take charge of one of the radars operating in "ground stabilised mode". He will plot the position of the ship as per specified intervals and will monitor the track-keeping through continuous monitoring techniques, eg Parallel Indexing. The OOW also monitors the set and UKC, and also keeps the other OOW advised of the searoom available for any collision avoidance manoeuvres. The OOW alerts the lookouts of important objects that should be looked for and reported, as well as advising the helmsman of the course to be steered.

OOW 2

The other OOW monitors traffic movements around the ship and takes charge of Collision Avoidance. This OOW operates the second radar on "sea stabilised mode" and performs long range scanning in order to be aware of any potential developments. He will advise the lookouts of the traffics specific directions. The OOW responsible for navigation will be kept advised of any likely collision avoidance manoeuvres to be undertaken. This OOW will also keep a check on VHF and AIS regarding traffic and will also be responsible for making reports to VTS, etc.

LOOKOUTS

The lookouts will listen and watch for traffic and navigational marks, as well as any unusual occurrences around the ship, including distress signals. The lookouts will report promptly to the designated OOW.

HELMSMAN

Steers the course as advised by the OOW and advises if it is difficult to maintain course or the steering becomes erratic.

5.1.2 Engineering Watch

STCW Code stipulates the criteria for decisions on composition of the engineering watch:

- Type of ship
- type and condition of the machinery
- adequate supervision at all times of machinery that affects the safe operation of the ship
- qualifications and experience of the engineering watch personnel
- maintaining the normal ship's operations
- safety of ship, life, cargo, environment and port
- special modes of operation dictated by conditions including weather, shallow water, emergency conditions, contaminated waters, ice, damage containment or combating pollution
- observance of international, national and local regulations.

The Master must ensure that adequate watches are maintained in the engine room. This is achieved by advising the Chief Engineer of the prevailing circumstances and conditions and any factors that may affect the safety of the ship. Circumstances that demand manoeuvring the engine on standby (SBE) will require extra and expert help in the engine room. Any manning constraints in the engine department should be kept in mind when demanding watchkeeping in the engine room. However, the ship's safety comes first and foremost.

The following is a guide to watch arrangements for machinery spaces:

| Open sea | UMS | – engineers on routine maintenance and attending to alarms |
| Coast – Light traffic | UMS | – engineers on routine maintenance and attending to alarms |

Coast – Heavy traffic	Engine watch	– duty engineer in control/engine room
Restricted visibility	SBE	– duty engineer in control/engine room
Approach channels	SBE	– senior engineer, junior engineer
Pilotage waters	SBE	– senior engineer, junior engineer

The bridge team should keep the engine room informed of any change in circumstances that will require a change in machinery status or an SBE for manoeuvring. This notice time may be specified in the SMS or, if not, it should be agreed between the Master and Chief Engineer, based on engine specifications, level of automation and manning levels in the engine room.

For SBE, the engineers will:

- Change the main engine from heavy fuel oil to diesel oil
- keep the starting-air bottles topped up
- have the start air compressor running
- have sufficient generators to provide a power supply for all machinery that is running and required to be started at short notice
- check lines and valves to ensure smooth and uneventful manoeuvring
- ensure enough purified fuel is available in service tanks
- standby at the engine control and telegraph to await the bridge's instructions for running the engine.

The bridge team may not have advanced warning of any emergencies or difficult conditions developing. If they do, the bridge should advise the engine room of the required changes as soon as possible.

The OOW should keep the engine room and duty engineer informed of any developments. Communications between the bridge and engine room should include, but not be limited to:

- Synchronisation of clocks
- testing controls
- ETA and ETD - and any changes to these times
- exact times when the SBE is required for ending the sea passage
- requirements of any services, eg running pumps, power for deck machinery
- the development of emergencies
- time to anchoring or berthing

- the ship entering or leaving a special area and the distance from land for pollution prevention purposes
- any deviations from normal plans, eg the pilot's boarding time.

In case of UMS operations, if the engineers are required to enter the machinery space to attend to alarms, the bridge must be notified. The 'dead man alarm' should be activated immediately on arrival in the machinery space and should be reset within the specified intervals. Failure to do so may result in a search for the engineer inside the machinery space.

5.1.3 Fitness for Watch and Rest Periods

The STCW Code advises governments that a maximum blood alcohol level of 0.08% should be set for ship's personnel during watchkeeping and to prohibit alcohol being consumed within 4 hours of starting a watch. Some companies, flag state administrations and port states may exercise more stringent policies. The STCW Code has laid down regulations for mandatory rest periods for members of the bridge team to prevent fatigue.

The STCW Code has stipulated that:

- *Rest periods of at least 10 hours in any 24-hour period are required*
- *77 hours in any 7 day period*
- *The hours of rest may be divided into no more than two periods, one of which shall be at least 6 hours, and the intervals between consecutive periods of rest shall not exceed 14 hours*
- *The requirements of rest periods need not be maintained in the case of an emergency or in other overriding operational conditions.*
- *Exceptions may be allowed provided that the rest period is not less than 70 hours in a 7 day period. Exceptions from weekly rest period shall not be allowed for more than two consecutive weeks. The intervals between two periods of exceptions on board shall not be less than twice the duration of the exception.*
- *The prescribed hours of rest may be divided into more than three periods one of which shall be at least 6 hours, and neither of the other two periods shall be less than one hour. Intervals between consecutive periods of rest shall not exceed 14 hours. Exceptions shall not extend beyond two 24 hour periods in any 7 day period*
- *Exceptions shall take into account the guidance regarding prevention of fatigue.*

No more than 0.05% alcohol level in the blood, 0.25 mg/l alcohol in the breath or a quantity of alcohol leading to such an alcohol concentration must not be exceeded by Masters, officers and other seafarers while performing designated safety, security and environmental duties.

5.2 Keeping Watch

Watches will be conducted based on the following principles:

- There must be proper arrangements for watchkeeping personnel in accordance with the situation
- any limitations in qualifications or the fitness of individuals must be taken into account when appointing watchkeeping personnel
- understanding the individual roles, responsibility and team roles of the watch keeping personnel will be established
- Master and officer of the watch will maintain a proper watch, making the most effective use of the available resources, including information, equipment, installations and other personnel
- watchkeepers must understand the functions, limitations and operations of equipment and installations and must also be familiar with handling them
- watchkeepers must understand information from each station, equipment and installations and know how to deal with it
- information from the stations, equipment and installations should be shared by all the watchkeepers
- watchkeepers must maintain communications and exchange information in any situation
- watchkeepers must notify the Master/officer in charge of the watch immediately if there is any doubt about the action to take in the interest of safety.

The officer in charge of the bridge watch and those supporting the watch should be aware of the SMS procedures, layout of the bridge and use of equipment.

5.2.1 Familiarisation with Bridge Equipment

The OOW should fully understand how to operate the following equipment:

- Bridge and deck lighting
- emergency arrangements in the event of a main power failure
- navigation and signal lights, including searchlights, signalling lamps and Morse light, sound signalling apparatus and whistles
- bridge watchkeeping alarm
- fog bell and gong system

- safety equipment, including LSA equipment, pyrotechnics, EPIRB and SART, bridge fire detection panels
- general and fire alarm signalling arrangements
- emergency pump, ventilation, water-tight door controls and internal ship communications facilities, including portable radios
- emergency hand powered or wind up phone system
- public address system
- external communication equipment, including RT, DSC, INMARSAT and AIS
- alarm systems on the bridge
- echo sounder, electronic navigational position fixing systems gyro compass/repeaters, magnetic compass, off-course alarm
- radar, including ARPA
- speed/distance recorder, VDR
- steering gear, including manual, auto-pilot, emergency changeover and testing arrangements
- engine and thruster controls
- IBS functions (if fitted) and automatic track-keeping system (if fitted) (Chapter 14.2)
- ECDIS and electronic charts (if fitted) (Chapter 14.1)
- location and operation of ancillary bridge equipment, eg binoculars, signalling flags and meteorological equipment
- stowage of charts and hydrographic publications.

5.2.1.1 Steering Gear Tests

After a prolonged use of the autopilot, and before entering coastal waters, the steering gear should be tested at all of the manual steering positions on the bridge. In coastal and congested waters more than one steering gear power unit should be used when these units are capable of simultaneous operation. Twelve hours before departure, check and test the steering gear, including the operation of:

- The main steering gear
- the auxiliary steering gear
- the remote steering control systems
- the main steering position on the bridge
- the emergency power supply
- the rudder angle indicators in relation to actual rudder position
- the remote steering gear control system power failure alarms
- the steering gear power unit failure alarms
- automatic isolating arrangements and other automatic equipment.

Similar checks and tests should be carried out before arrival. The checks and tests should include:

- The full rudder movement (according to the steering gear specifications)

- the timing of rudder movement from hardover-to-hardover, to ensure compliance with the requirement
- a visual inspection of the steering gear and its connecting linkage
- the operation of the means of communication between the steering gear compartment and the bridge/engine room control
- gyro repeater in the steering gear compartment is synchronised with the master gyro.

5.2.1.2 Changeover Procedures

The change-over from automatic to manual or vice-versa should be done by either the Master or OOW. If not, they should supervise the change. All officers concerned with the operation or maintenance of the steering gear should be familiar with the change-over procedures. Instructions for changing-over from automatic to manual steering and vice-versa, should be posted at the steering control position on the bridge.

5.2.1.3 Emergency Steering Drills

Emergency steering drills should take place at least every three months and 24 hours before entering US Waters. They must include direct control from the steering gear compartment, communications procedures with the bridge and, where applicable, the operation of alternative power supplies. As many deck officers, cadets and ratings as possible who are responsible for steering should take part in these drills. The dates of when these checks and tests are conducted and the date and details of the emergency steering drills that are carried out must be recorded in the official logbook.

5.2.1.4 Auto Pilot Regulations

- Automatic pilot should not be used in coastal or estuarial waters unless a change-over can take place within 30 seconds
- hand steering should be engaged once every watch
- if the ship is being steered on automatic pilot, a qualified helmsman should be available to the OOW. The helmsman may be engaged on duties in the immediate vicinity of the bridge so that the OOW can summon him at any moment
- the change-over from automatic to manual steering should take place under the Master or OOW's supervision. Instructions for change-over should be displayed at (or near) the steering console.

(US Regulation: If the ship is being steered by automatic pilot and the hand-steering wheel is turned, an alarm should sound).

5.2.2 Keeping the Watch

The OOW is the Master's representative and is responsible at all times for the ship's safe navigation and for complying with the International Regulations for Preventing Collisions at Sea. As the Master's representative, the OOW is in charge of the bridge and the bridge team for that watch until properly relieved by the Master or another watchkeeping officer. The OOW should ensure that bridge watch manning levels are safe at all times for the prevailing circumstances and conditions, in compliance with shipboard operational procedures and the Master's standing orders. Procedures for handing over the watch and calling for support on the bridge should be in place and understood by the OOW.

5.2.2.1 Duties of the OOW

In order to maintain a safe navigational watch, the OOW will perform watchkeeping, navigation and GMDSS radio watchkeeping duties, including:

- Maintaining a lookout
- general surveillance of the ship
- monitoring the progress of the ship and fixing position
- collision avoidance in compliance with the International Regulations for Preventing Collisions at Sea
- recording bridge activities
- making periodic checks on the navigational equipment in use.

The navigational duties of the OOW are based on the need to execute the passage plan safely and to monitor the progress of the ship against that plan.

Under GMDSS, the OOW will be responsible for maintaining a continuous radio watch at sea. During distress incidents, one of the qualified radio personnel should be designated to have the primary responsibility for radio communications. On passenger ships, that person will have no other duties during a distress situation.

The OOW must understand the means and best practices for controlling the speed and direction of the ship, the handling characteristics and stopping distances.

Helm, engines and sound signalling apparatus are at the OOW's disposal and there should be no hesitation to use them at any time. The OOW must also be fully conversant with the shipboard obligations regarding pollution prevention, reporting and emergency situations. The OOW should know the location of all of the safety equipment on the bridge and how to operate that equipment.

In certain circumstances, there will be a helmsman in addition to the lookout.

Note: a helmsman is not a lookout. It is the responsibility of the OOW to ensure that the vessel is being steered safely and efficiently. The OOW must also ensure that the helm orders are clearly understood and complied with as required.

5.2.2.2 Factors for Composition of Navigational Watch

As per STCW Code, the master shall take into account:

- *Visibility, weather and state of the sea*
- *Traffic density and other activities occurring in the area in which the vessel is navigating*
- *The attention necessary when navigating in or near traffic separation schemes or other routeing measures*
- *Additional workload caused by the nature of the ship's functions, immediate operating requirements and anticipated manoeuvres*
- *Fitness for duty of any crew members on call who are assigned as members of the watch*
- *Knowledge of, and confidence in, the professional competence of the ship's officers and crew*
- *Experience of each officer of the navigational watch, and the familiarity of that officer with the ship's equipment, procedures and manoeuvring capability*
- *Activities taking place on board the ship at any particular time, including radio communication activities, and the availability of assistance to be summoned immediately to the bridge when necessary*
- *Operational status of bridge instrumentation and controls, including alarm systems*
- *Rudder and propeller control and ship manoeuvring characteristics*
- *Size of the ship and the field of vision available from the conning position*
- *Configuration of the bridge, to the extent such configuration might inhibit a member of the watch from detecting by sight or hearing of external development*
- *Any other relevant standard, procedure or guidance relating to watchkeeping arrangements and fitness for duty which has been adopted by the organization.*

5.2.2.3 Watch Arrangements

The following factors should be considered as per the STCW Code when deciding on the composition of the bridge watch:

- *At no time shall the bridge be left unattended*
- *Weather conditions, visibility and whether there is daylight or darkness*

- *Proximity of navigational hazards which may make it necessary for the OOW to carry out additional navigational duties*
- *Use and operational condition of navigational aids such as ECDIS, radar or electronic position indicating devices and any other equipment affecting the safe navigation of the ship*
- *Whether the ship is fitted with automatic steering*
- *Whether there are radio duties to be performed*
- *UMS controls, alarms and indicators provided on the bridge, procedures for their use and their limitations*
- *Any unusual demands on the navigational watch that may arise as a result of special operational circumstances.*

5.2.2.4 Changing Over the Watch

The OOW should not hand over the watch if there is any reason to believe that the relieving officer is unfit, or is temporarily unable, to carry out watchkeeping duties effectively. If there is any doubt, the OOW should call the Master. Reasons for unfitness for duty could be due to illness, the effect of drink, drugs or fatigue.

- Before taking over the watch, the relieving officer must be satisfied about the:
  - Master's night orders or standing instructions relating to navigation and operations
  - ship's position, course, speed and draught
  - prevailing and predicted tides, currents, weather, visibility and the effect these have on the course and speed
- procedures for using the main engines to manoeuvre when the main engines are on bridge control
- navigational situation:
  - operational condition of all navigation and safety equipment being used or likely to be used during the watch
  - gyro and magnetic compass errors
  - presence and movement of ships that are in sight or are known to be in the area
  - conditions and hazards likely to be encountered during the watch
  - possible effects of heel, trim, water density and squat on UKC.

The relieving officer should also be satisfied that all other members of the bridge team for the new watch are fit for duty, particularly with regards to their adjustment to night vision.

If a manoeuvre or other action to avoid a hazard is taking place when the OOW is being relieved, handover should be deferred until that action has been completed.

5.2.2.5 Calling the Master

In accordance with standing orders or special instructions and STCW, the OOW should notify the Master if unsure of the appropriate action for the safety of the ship. Guidance on specific circumstances for calling the Master or other back-up support should be given in the SMS, supported by standing orders and bridge orders as appropriate.

The Master should always be notified in these circumstances:

- If the movement of other ships or traffic conditions are causing concern
- if difficulties are experienced in maintaining the course
- if restricted visibility is encountered or expected
- when making landfall
- when a distress signal or unusual warning is received
- on failure to sight land, a navigational mark or obtaining soundings by the expected time
- if land or a navigational mark is sighted unexpectedly or there is a change in soundings
- on breakdown of the engine(s), propulsion machinery remote control, steering gear or any other essential navigational equipment, alarm or indicator
- if the radio equipment malfunctions
- if there is doubt about the risk of weather damage during heavy weather
- if the ship meets any hazard to navigation, such as ice or a derelict ship
- in any other emergency or position of doubt.

The OOW will continue to be responsible for the watch, despite the Master being present on the bridge, until informed specifically that the Master has assumed that responsibility and that this is mutually understood. The Master taking control on the bridge should be recorded in the logbook.

5.2.3 General Watchkeeping

5.2.3.1 Maintaining a Look-Out

The bridge team on watch must give their full attention to lookout duties. In compliance with the International Regulations for Preventing Collisions at Sea and general watchkeeping standards, a proper lookout must be maintained at all times to serve the purposes of:

- A continuous state of vigilance by sight and hearing and by all other available means to detect traffic or structures in the vicinity
- watching for any significant change in the operating environment, including weather, sea state, signs of shoals or shallow waters
- appraisal of a situation and the risk of a collision, stranding and other dangers to navigation

- detection of ships or aircraft in distress, shipwrecked persons, wrecks, debris and hazards to safe navigation.

On ships with fully enclosed bridges, sound reception equipment should be continuously in operation and should be correctly adjusted to ensure that all audible sounds on the open deck can be clearly heard on the bridge.

The OOW must ensure that the mariner assigned to watchkeeping duties:

- Has been given instructions in keeping lookout
- knows what is expected of a lookout
- knows how and what observations to report
- is suitably dressed and protected from the weather
- is complying with the working hours legislation and that frequent relief is possible.

A lookout must give their full attention to keeping a proper lookout, no other duties should be carried out or assigned that may interfere with this task.

A helmsman and lookout have separate duties, the helmsman must not be considered to be the lookout when they are steering the ship, unless the ship is small and there is an unobstructed view from the steering position.

5.2.3.2 Sole Lookout

Under the STCW Code, the OOW can be the sole lookout in daylight provided that, *"the situation has been carefully assessed and it has been established without doubt that it is safe to operate with a sole lookout".*

All relevant factors should be taken into account, including but not limited to:

- State of weather
- visibility
- traffic density
- proximity of dangers to navigation
- the attention required when navigating in or near traffic separation schemes.

When deemed necessary, assistance should be summoned immediately to the bridge. If sole lookout watchkeeping practices are to be followed, the SMS should include clear guidance on how they should operate.

5.2.3.3 General Surveillance

If circumstances and navigational safety allows, the OOW should endeavour to maintain general surveillance of the deck and cargo during the watch.

The OOW must maintain a high level of general awareness about the ship and its routine, ie day-to-day operations. This may include maintaining a general watch over the ship's decks to monitor, where possible, people working on deck and any cargo or cargo handling equipment. The OOW may have to carry out this surveillance before the watch, especially when there is heavy weather. Special watchkeeping arrangements may be appropriate in waters where it is thought there is a risk of piracy or armed attack.

Whenever work is being carried out on deck in the vicinity of the radar antennae, radio aerials and sound signalling apparatus, the OOW should be particularly observant and should post appropriate warning notices on the equipment controls. If possible, disconnect the power supply to that equipment. If these items of equipment have to be used, the work should stop.

5.2.3.4 Recording Bridge Activities

A formal record of navigational activities and incidents, that are important to the safety of navigation and are part of passage plan execution, should be kept in the appropriate logbooks.

Paper records from course recorders, echo sounders and NAVTEX receivers should be retained for the period stipulated in the SMS. These paper records should be dated and time-marked.

To allow the ship's actual track to be reconstructed at a later stage, sufficient information concerning the ship's position, course and speed should be recorded in the bridge logbook or using an approved electronic means. All positions marked on the navigational charts must also be retained until the end of the voyage. The Voyage Data Recorder (VDR) automatically records most of these, but the above practice confirms that the watch officers are performing their tasks efficiently.

5.2.3.5 Periodic Checks On Navigational Equipment

Operational checks on navigational equipment should be undertaken when preparing for sea and before port entry. After lengthy ocean passages and before entering restricted coastal waters, it is important to check that full engine and steering manoeuvrability is available. The OOW should undertake daily tests and checks on the bridge equipment, including the following:

- When the automatic pilot is in use, manual steering should be tested at least once every watch
- gyro and magnetic compass errors should be checked once every watch, where possible, and after any major course alteration

- compass and gyro repeaters should be synchronised. This procedure includes any repeaters mounted off the bridge, eg in the engine control room, or at the emergency steering position.

Checks on electronic equipment should both confirm that the piece of equipment is functioning properly and that it is successfully communicating to any bridge system that it is connected to. Built-in test facilities provide a useful health check on the functional state of the piece of equipment and should be used frequently. Electronic equipment systems should be checked to ensure that the configuration settings, important for correct interfacing between pieces of equipment, have not changed. To ensure adequate performance, information from electronic equipment should always be compared and verified against information from various independent sources.

Good practice also requires the OOW to check that orders are being correctly followed. For example, rudder angle and engine RPM indicators provide the OOW with an immediate check on whether the helm and engine movement orders are being followed.

5.2.3.6 Manoeuvring Data

The ship's manoeuvring data is contained on the Pilot Card and Wheelhouse Poster. Ships should also have a manoeuvring booklet, the OOW must be familiar with this data. On the Pilot Card, the ship's draught and any permanent or temporary idiosyncrasies that could affect manoeuvrability should be recorded. For example, a ship may have a tendency to steer to port at full speed and but steer to starboard at a slow speed.

To control the main engines effectively, the OOW should be familiar with their operation from the bridge and with operating the propeller mechanism. The OOW should also be aware of any limitations that the system may have, and appreciate that the type and configuration of the ship's engines could have implications when changing speed. Direct-drive diesel, diesel through gearbox/clutch, turbo-electric and gas turbine engines all have relatively quick responses to change, provided the engines are on stand-by. Geared turbines are less responsive.

5.3 Navigation

It is important that the OOW executes the passage plan as prepared and that the ship's progress is monitored and recorded, relative to that plan. If the OOW has to make a temporary deviation from the passage plan for any reason, he should return to the original plan as soon as it is safe to do so. At the first opportunity, the OOW should advise the Master of the actions that have been taken. The plan must be formally amended and a briefing made to the other members of the bridge team. In good practice, the amendment should have been available as a contingency plan.

The OOW for good navigational practice is expected to:

- Understand the capabilities and limitations of the systems and aids that are being used for navigation and that he will continually monitor their performance
- use the echo sounder to monitor any changes in water and contour depths
- when checking position fixes use dead reckoning (DR) techniques
- use independent sources of information when cross checking position fixes. This is very important when GPS, Loran-C or other electronic position fixing systems are being used as the main way to fix the ship's position
- use visual navigation aids as a support for electronic position fixing, ie landmarks that can be seen in coastal areas and celestial navigation in open water
- not become totally reliant on automated navigational equipment, including ECDIS, and not making proper use of the visually available navigational information.

Caution should be used when taking geographical positions from electronic position fixing systems, eg GPS, and then plotting the information onto a chart. The OOW should remember:

- If the chart datum is different to the datum used by the electronic position fixing system (usually WGS84), a datum shift must be applied to the position coordinates before being plotted on the chart. If there is an appreciable datum shift for a particular chart, a 'satellite derived position' note, that provides longitude and latitude datum shift values, will be visible on the chart
- charts that have very old survey source data, may not be very accurate in certain areas. If this occurs, the OOW should not totally rely on position fixing that uses electronic systems, he should use visual and navigational techniques, where possible, to maintain a safe distance away from land.

Generally, the most appropriate large scale chart on board should be used for navigation, the ship's position should be fixed at a planned frequency. The OOW should positively identify all the navigation marks before they are used. Visual and radar position fixing and monitoring techniques should be used when possible.

The OOW should be aware in coastal waters that ship routeing schemes and reporting systems, requiring reports made to the coast radio and vessel traffic system, may exist.

It is also important that there is knowledge about the ship's draught, stability conditions and manoeuvring characteristics. When a ship enters shallow water, squat may have a critical effect on the ship's manoeuvrability causing the draught to increase. Squat effect will vary in proportion to the square of the ship's speed, as a result it will reduce when the ship's speed reduces.

5.3.1 Anchoring

When approaching an anchorage, the passage and anchoring plan should be followed. The following should be taken into account when preparing the anchor plan:

- Reduce speed in ample time
- direction and strength of wind, current and/or tidal stream
- height of tide
- the tidal stream when manoeuvring at slow speeds
- that there is adequate sea room, particularly to seaward
- the depth of water, nature and type of seabed and the scope of cable required.

Before entering a restricted area and making the final approach:

- The engine room and anchor party should be informed of the time of anchoring
- anchors, lights/shapes and sound signalling appliances must be ready.

On anchoring, a fix should be made on the anchor let go position and the ship's swinging circle marked. The port authority or VTS should be informed of the anchor position. While at anchor, the OOW should:

- Determine and plot the ship's position on the appropriate chart. Take bearings of fixed navigational marks or readily identifiable shore objects to maintain a check on the anchor position and ensure that the ship does not drag its anchor
- make checks on the UKC
- use the GPS anchor alarm to check the position, particularly when using DGPS mode
- observe meteorological and tidal conditions and the sea state
- pay particular attention to the anchor position after a change of tide
- record any wind shift or change of weather
- ensure that the main engines and other machinery's state of readiness is in accordance with the Master's instructions
- a proper lookout must be maintained and ship inspection rounds made periodically, particularly if

the ship is anchored in waters where there is a risk of attack by pirates or armed robbers

- ensure that the ship exhibits the appropriate lights and shapes and that sound signals are made in accordance with all applicable regulations
- take measures to protect the environment from pollution caused by the ship, by complying with applicable pollution regulations
- notify the Master and take all counter measures if the ship drags its anchor
- immediately notify the Master if the sea conditions or visibility deteriorates.

5.3.2 Towing and Navigation

A vessel may be required to use tugs for various reasons. The tugs can be divided into two broad categories, ocean and harbour/coastal. These two categories can be subdivided further:

- Ocean towing ships in distress or in danger
- towing ships for delivery to repair facilities
- towing dumb lighters, barges, for cargo transport
- towing larger off shore installations, (rigs)
- harbour/coastal for ease of ship handling (pulling, pushing)
- escort services
- towage services into and out of harbour
- standby services
- supply and handling
- engagement in the event of a grounding or collision.

5.3.2.1 Factors Influencing Choice of Tugs

In harbour the port authority or terminal operator will provide tugs. The following should be considered:

- Size (displacement) and type of vessel requiring assistance
- sea room available for manoeuvring
- proximity of dangers
- bollard-pull of the tugs available
- manoeuvring/handling characteristics of the tugs available
- prevailing weather conditions
- effects of current or tidal stream
- windage area – loaded or in ballast/high sided (draught, freeboard).

In the event of ocean towage, the tug will be contracted by the owners/managers. The following questions should be considered:

- Size (displacement) and type of vessel that is to be towed
- length of voyage
- speed that towage is to take place (power)
- climatic and prevailing weather conditions

- power available on the towed vessel
- whether the towed vessel is to be manned
- can the towed vessel be steered
- can the towed vessel use her anchor
- proximity of dangers
- fuel capacity of the tug
- fire fighting capabilities of the tug
- handling capabilities of the tug.

5.3.2.2 Navigational Considerations

Harbour or coastal, the following points should be considered:

- Identity of the tugs
- communications (VHF channels and vocabulary)
- engagement position
- engines on standby
- readiness of ship's crew (deck party)
- location of securing tugs lines, tugs or ships lines
- speed and heading at the point of engagement
- possibility and awareness of interaction
- speed during the operation
- execution of planned manoeuvres
- possibility and awareness of girting
- sailing direction recommendations for the route that is to be followed
- signals and flags to be displayed
- command authority for the ship
- contingency planning
- area of operation
- route to be followed
- proximity of hazards
- UKC
- times of engagement and termination
- prevailing weather
- record keeping.

Ocean:

- Identity of the tug(s)
- communications - VHF channels
- rendezvous position. In the event of ocean towage, it is likely that the towed vessel would be disabled and will require the tug (s) to come to her)
- destination and any impending hazards
- any intermediate destinations for refuelling
- climate, prevailing and forecast weather
- proximity of hazards
- preparation and agreement of the passage plan
- recommendations laid down in the sailing directions
- advice and recommendations (tow is categorised as a low powered vessel) in the Ocean Passages for the World (shortest route may not be the quickest route)
- the speed of towing in different weather conditions
- contingency planning for emergencies/bad weather/ parting of tow line
- continuous radio contact between two vessels

- command authority (if the tow is unmanned all responsibility lies with the tug)
- possibility of steering the tow
- life saving appliances for the crew of tow
- agreement on direction and speed of commencement of towing operation (usually upwind)
- agreement on procedures to be followed while altering course (should be done in small steps, gradually)
- monitoring the strain on the towline (on long ocean passage, preferably some part of the towline should be in water)
- recommendations obtained from weather routeing services
- hazards (ice, fog, strong winds) on the route
- expected traffic
- allocations of duties
- readiness of anchors of tow in shallow waters
- record keeping.

5.3.2.3 Signals and Communications

Night: If the length of tow exceeds 200 m, the towing vessel will display 3 masthead lights in a vertical line. If the towing vessel is 50 m or more in length, another masthead light is required. The other lights are side lights, stern light and a towing light vertically above the stern light. The vessel being towed will display side lights and a stern light.

Day: If the length of tow exceeds 200 m, the towing vessel and vessel being towed will display a black diamond in a position where it can be seen most clearly. If the towing vessel is restricted in her ability to manoeuvre she will display red, white and red all round lights in a vertical line. During daytime, she will display a black ball, a diamond and a ball in a vertical line where they can be seen most clearly.

At night, a search light should be used to illuminate the towline.

A SECURITE message can be transmitted to inform shipping in the vicinity. It can also be used to keep the coast stations notified of progress.

In ocean towage, special attention should be paid at the start, during passage through shallow waters, coastal waters and at the termination. If the tow is in confined waters at the start, it is essential that harbour tugs are used for assistance until the ship is in clear waters and the ocean-going tug can then control the tow. The same routine may be followed at the termination if the ship is to proceed in confined waters. In confined waters, the length of the towline must be shorter as it should never drag along

the seabed. As the length reduces, strain will increase, so the speed should be eased to minimise the strain.

5.3.3 Collision Avoidance

This book does not discuss every regulation concerning collisions. The basic practices are given here and apply at all times in any scenario.

5.3.3.1 Signals

The OOW must always comply with the International Regulations for Preventing Collisions at Sea. Compliance not only applies to a vessels conduct under the steering and sailing rules, but also covers displaying the correct light, shape, sound and light signals. For example, a ship drifting off a port with her engines deliberately shut down is not a 'vessel not under command' (NUC) as defined by rule 3(f) of the COLREGS.

However, a ship drifting with her engines under repair is considered NUC. Caution should always be given when approaching other ships. Ships may not display the correct light or shape signals or, when approached from a certain direction, their signals may be badly positioned and obscured by the ship's structure.

5.3.3.2 Lookout

Lookout should be maintained by all available means, including sight and hearing. Radar, AIS and VHF are useful as support. VHF radio should not be used for collision avoidance purposes. Valuable time can be wasted trying to make contact, as positive identification may be difficult and once contact has been made, misunderstandings can arise. This should apply even when the identity is known through AIS. VHF calls for collision-avoidance should be avoided in restricted visibility. Any action should be based on COLREGS. A mutually-agreed solution that is contrary to COLREGS is NOT acceptable.

5.3.3.3 Safe Speed

In compliance with the International Regulations for Preventing Collisions at Sea, ships should proceed at a safe speed at all times. In restricted visibility, a safe speed may require a reduction in service speed to reduce the ship's stopping distance. Near ice, ships are specifically required to proceed at moderate speeds. Speed changes may be required to avoid a collision in circumstances where the ship is unable to alter course.

5.3.3.4 Risk of Collision

In clear weather, the risk of collision can be detected early by frequent compass bearings being taken of an approaching ship to ascertain whether or not the bearing is steady and if it is on a collision course.

Compass bearings eliminate the yaw of the ship's head. However, care must be taken when approaching very large ships, a ship under-tow or ships at close range. An appreciable bearing change may be evident under these circumstances but there may still be a risk of collision. In addition to a steady compass bearing, a reduction of range is also a significant factor for the risk of collision.

5.3.3.5 Time to Take Action

The time to take action is important. The rules suggest that it should be 'early' or in 'ample time'. There is no clear mention of the range or number of minutes before the risk of a collision or close-quarters situation when avoiding action should be taken. It depends on how close the ship and the rate it is closing at.

If the bearing of a vessel at 10´ is steady and the range is decreasing at 0´.5 per hour, there is no immediate risk of collision. But for the same ship on a steady bearing, if the range was decreasing 3´ in 5 minutes, the situation is different and immediate action must be taken. 'Ample time' also means that the Master or OOW has made a decision based on all the available information, rather than in haste or with incomplete information. The stand-on vessel should be in no doubt at any time about the intentions of the give-way vessel.

5.3.3.6 Large Enough

The action should not only be large enough and readily apparent to another ship observing, either visually or by radar, it should be executed by the appropriate use of the helm as well. A succession of small alterations should be avoided. A vessel planning to alter course by 60° and turning at the rate of 5° per minute is not making a large enough alteration to be readily apparent.

Another issue is relative plotting using a radar. When own vessel is altering course, relative plotting cannot be performed. Similarly, if own vessel has not been on a steady course and speed for the period of observation, another ship will not be able to calculate your course or speed accurately.

In general, early and positive action should always be taken when avoiding collisions. Once action has been taken, the OOW should always check to ensure it is having the desired effect.

5.3.3.7 Passage/Safe Passage

A ship's passage at a given time, can be described as the course being steered to maintain her charted track. Safe passage is based on the margins of safety, the ship must remain within these margins of safety after making an alteration to avoid another

ship. For example, a ship on a course of 040°T is on her passage. If the same ship has a safety margin of 3 miles on either side, and she can take action and still remain within the margin of safety, her safe passage is within the margins of safety.

This reasoning can also be used for ships within a TSS.

- A ship engaged in fishing is required to avoid impeding the passage of any ship following the traffic lane. The ship engaged in fishing is required to do so by allowing enough sea room for the ship within the lane to maintain her course, ie her passage
- a ship of less than 20 m in length, or a sailing vessel, is required to avoid impeding the safe passage of a power-driven ship following a lane. If the power-driven ship within the lane is able to take action and stay within the lane to maintain her safe passage, the ship of less than 20 m, or sailing vessel, may not have to take any action provided there is no risk of collision or a close quarters situation. However, if the power-driven ship within the lane has traffic around her and/or is in close proximity to other hazards and may not be able to alter course, then her present course is her safe passage and she should not be impeded.

In restricted visibility, a ship's conduct is specifically covered by the International Regulations for Preventing Collisions at Sea. In these conditions radar and in particular, automatic radar, plotting can be used effectively for assessing the risk of collision. The OOW should practice radar plotting and observation exercises in clear visibility whenever possible.

In sea areas where traffic flow is regulated, eg port approaches and traffic separation schemes, it may be possible to anticipate movements from certain ship types. In these circumstances, it is good practice to allow extra sea room, if it is safe to do so.

5.4 Use of Pilot

5.4.1 Reasons

Employing a marine pilot is of great assistance to the bridge team for the ship's safe navigation. Pilots may be employed for several reasons including:

- Required by law under local regulation
- local knowledge
- expertise in ship-handling and working with tugs
- to overcome language difficulties and communication problems during piloting with
  - shore authorities, VTS
  - tugs, mooring boats, mooring gangs

- pilots have up to date information about hazards and correct knowledge of local hydrographic details
- they are aware of the local laws and regulations and also any variations to international regulations
- they know the latest weather forecast and local weather conditions.

5.4.2 Initial Information Exchange

The ship is required to send some or all of this information to the pilotage or port authority before a pilot can be picked up. Details can be found in ALRS Vol 6.

- Ship identity: name, call sign, flag, agent, IMO number, ship type, cargo type, year built, last port
- communication info: fax, telex, VHF channel
- pilot boarding: ETA, freeboard, station
- ship particulars: draught, air draught, length, beam, displacement, DWT, GT, NT
- anchors and length of cable
- manoeuvring details at current condition: speeds, min. steerage speed, propeller, CPP, thrusters, rudder, hard over to hard over
- main engine: type, power, max no of engine starts, time from full ahead to full astern
- equipment defects.

The ship will require certain details from the pilotage or port authority. Some of this information will be available when making contact over the radio and some details will be provided by the pilot at the point of boarding.

- Name of the Pilotage Authority
- pilot boarding instructions: date, time, position, side, approach course and speed, ladder, height
- berth and tug details: prospects, intended berth, side alongside, transit time, tug engagement position, number, arrangement, total bollard pull
- local weather and sea conditions: tide, currents, forecast weather
- passage plan/emergency plan/abort point
- regulations
- traffic and ship movement
- communications and reports
- hazards/navigational warnings.

5.4.3 Navigation With a Pilot on Board

Once the pilot has arrived on the bridge, he assumes the conduct of the vessel's navigation after the necessary information exchange. The pilot has specialised knowledge of navigating in local waters and will advise the bridge team on navigating the ship. It is important that the pilot and the Master's responsibilities are agreed and clearly understood.

The presence of a pilot does not relieve the Master or the OOW of their duties and obligations for the safety of the ship. Both should be prepared to exercise their responsibility in keeping the ship away from danger.

5.4.3.1 Master/Pilot Information Exchange on Boarding

When the pilot is on board, the preliminary pilotage passage plan prepared in advance by the ship should be discussed and agreed by the pilot and bridge team. There should be sufficient time and sea room to allow this to happen safely. Where a lack of time or sea room prevent the plan from being discussed in detail, the main points should be covered immediately and the remainder discussed as soon as it is safe to do so. On a long pilotage passage, it may be appropriate to review and update the plan in stages.

Immediately on arrival the following information should be given to the pilot:

- Current control particulars of the vessel, including position, course, speed, engine telegraph setting
- completed Pilot Card, including the ship's particulars, vessel's draught and displacement, air draught, manoeuvring characteristics, anchor details, bulbous bow, bow thrusters, type of anchors and number of shackles on each, etc
- defects, if any, with relation to any bridge equipment and any machinery
- intended passage plan to the berth
- current status of the composition of the bridge team and individuals responsibilities. The electronic aids to navigation and their settings and controls especially the ones to be used by the pilot.

The Pilot should provide the Master with:

- His passage plan, including mooring plan
- berthing details as to number of tugs, estimated time the tugs will be deployed, where berthing either the post of starboard side, tide/current information, weather conditions, areas where speed alterations may be required
- any new hazards affecting navigation, eg UKC, shoals, new wrecks, special operations being carried out, dredging, cable laying, maintenance of buoys
- any on-coming traffic likely to be encountered especially dredgers, RAM vessels, deep draught vessels
- any new local regulations/laws effecting the vessel (any new reporting requirements).

The passage plan should be discussed and agreed with the Pilot, including:

- Radio and reporting points
- bridge manning
- use of tugs
- berthing/anchoring
- expected traffic
- change of pilot (if required)
- crew for stations or standby
- fenders.

5.4.4 Responsibilities

5.4.4.1 The Master

- In command of the vessel and responsible for overall safety
- must ascertain the credentials of the Pilot
- must inform the Pilot of the ship's current status
- discuss and agree the passage plan with the Pilot
- ensures that the Pilot is informed of all essential and critical data regarding the ship's manoeuvring and any peculiarities
- monitors the advice of the Pilot and over-rides his actions, if required, to ensure the ship's safety
- ensure safe navigation of the ship at all times, including UKC
- ensures adequate manning arrangements for the entire operation
- ensures that all personnel are well rested/fit for performing their duties safely, including the Pilot
- ensures all navigational aids and machinery are operational.

5.4.4.2 OOW

- Assists the Master and Pilot with the safe navigation of the ship
- is the Master's representative and will continuously monitor the ship's progress as agreed in the passage plan
- ensures the Pilot's instructions are carried out efficiently
- clarifies any doubts with the Pilot and advises the Master immediately
- monitors the performance of the helmsman and ensures that the bridge equipment and engine status are in accordance with the Pilot's advice
- liaises with deck and engine room personnel to arrange for relief
- supervises the boarding and disembarkation of the Pilot
- keeps the engine room and deck team informed of progress
- makes appropriate reports to VTS and the port authorities

- continuously monitors the vessel's position/UKC and ensures that the ship is proceeding in safe waters at all times. Any deviation should be brought to the attention of the Master and Pilot immediately.

5.4.4.3 Pilot

- On boarding, he must present his documents/identity card to the Master
- obtains the ship's course and engine status from the Master and ensures that the ship is on safe track
- discusses and agrees the passage plan, ie the tugs, lines, berthing side to, berth number
- obtains all essential and critical data regarding the vessel's manoeuvring and her machinery/equipment. Ensures the pilot card is received, then checks the ship's manoeuvring characteristics
- provides the Master with all information about the pilotage period
- advises the Master of any special requirements of the local laws/harbour authorities that will affect navigation
- informs the Master of the local weather and tidal conditions and their possible effects on navigation.

5.4.5 Monitoring the Pilotage

The ship's safe progress along the planned tracks should be closely monitored at all times. This will include regularly fixing the position of the ship, particularly after each course alteration, and monitoring UKC.

Verbal orders from the Pilot must be checked to confirm that they have been carried out correctly. This will include monitoring both the rudder angle and the RPM indicators when the helm and engine orders are given.

Communication between the Pilot and bridge team should be conducted in English, except where local regulations allow otherwise.

If the Master leaves the bridge, the OOW should always seek clarification from the Pilot if he has any doubt about the Pilot's actions or intentions. If a satisfactory explanation is not given, the OOW should notify the Master immediately and take whatever action is necessary before the Master arrives. Whenever there is any disagreement with the Pilot decisions, the cause of concern should always be made clear to the Pilot and an explanation sought.

The OOW should bear in mind that during pilotage, the ship must be properly secured for sea. Excessive use of deck lighting at night may cause visibility interference.

If for any reason the Pilot is incapacitated while the vessel is in compulsory pilotage waters, or the Master considers that the Pilot is not fit or competent, the following should be taken:

- The Master advises the Pilot positively about the concern and assumes control of the ship
  - the Master should call the Pilotage/Port authority and request a replacement Pilot
  - if it is a compulsory Pilotage area, the ship must not proceed any further
  - the Master will investigate the safe-anchorage option and anchor the vessel
  - if this is not possible, the ship must be held in a safe location until the replacement Pilot arrives
  - relevant entries should be made in the log book
- the Master should keep the relevant authorities informed of the events and seek advice for further action.

Personnel

- If the Master is not on the bridge, make sure he is informed
- engage hand steering and post a helmsman
- post additional lookouts.

Equipment

- Sound appropriate fog signals
- switch on navigation lights
- keep on radars at peak performance and commence systematic plotting of all targets in the vicinity.

Navigation

- Plot positions frequently.

5.4.6 Information on the Pilot Card

• SHIP'S PARTICULARS: • Name • Call sign • DWT • Draught • Displacement • Year built • LOA • Breadth • Anchor chain Port and Starboard; number of shackles • Bulbous bow • Air draught • Bow to bridge distance • Bridge to astern distance	• ENGINE PARTICULARS: • Type of engines • Max power • Speed • Manoeuvring characteristics for each RPM from full ahead to full astern for loaded and ballast condition • Time limit astern • Full ahead to full astern • Maximum number of consecutive starts • Minimum rpm and speed • Critical RPM • Astern power
• STEERING PARTICULARS: • Type of rudder • Maximum angle • Time for hard over to hard over • Rudder angle for neutral effects • Thrusters – Bow and Stern – KW and HP	• CHECKLIST FOR BRIDGE EQUIPMENT: • A list of all bridge equipment • Number of steering motors in operation • Gyro error

5.5 Procedures

The following are some of the essential standard procedures:

5.5.1 Restricted Visibility

Engine

- SBE
- advise engine room of restricted visibility and that it is to be manned until further notice
- reduce to safe speed.

Navigation on Coast

- Obtain a visual fix before entering restricted visibility
- employ parallel indexing techniques
- run the echo sounder.

Deck

- Have anchors ready for letting go
- close all watertight doors and hatches
- order silence on deck.

Bridge

- Open bridge wing doors
- run both steering motors
- keep a check on all bridge equipment
- radar-plotting for collision avoidance should be on water-track speed
- do not use VHF/AIS data for collision avoidance
- comply with the provisions of COLREGs, in particular Rule 19
- notify the Master if CPA of 2 miles with any target cannot be achieved
- bridge manning to meet the manning levels/for restricted visibility.

5.5.1.1 Engine Failure

- Inform the Master
- exhibit "NUC" signals
- if in shallow water, prepare for anchoring
- make use of headway and steer vessel towards safety, using the rudder and bow thruster to best advantage
- commence sound signalling
- if appropriate, broadcast URGENCY message to ships in the vicinity and the port authority. If drifting onto a lee shore, send DISTRESS
- in harbour, call tugs immediately if they are not already alongside
- plot and record the position of the ship
- note existing current, tidal stream, wind and weather
- estimate the time available before the ship stands in danger
- ask the Chief Engineer about the problem and for progress on restoring power
- notify the company.

5.5.1.2 Steering Gear Failure

- Inform the Master and engine room
- engage emergency steering
- use bow thrusters
- exhibit "not under command" signals
- if in shallow water, prepare for anchoring
- manoeuvre engine to take off the way, if required
- commence sound signalling
- if appropriate, broadcast URGENCY message to ships in the vicinity and port authority. If drifting onto a lee shore, send DISTRESS
- in harbour, call tugs immediately, if they are not already alongside
- plot and record the position of vessel
- note existing current, tidal stream, wind and weather
- estimate the time available before the ship stands in danger
- ask the Chief Engineer about the problem and for progress on restoring power
- notify the company.

5.5.1.3 Extreme Weather Conditions

At Sea

- Refer to the SMS Checklist and relevant procedures
- notify the Master, all department heads and crew
- secure all moveable objects for heavy weather
- secure accommodation and close all ports and deadlights
- close all weather-deck openings
- plot the position of the ship
- ensure the ship's stability is adequate, and that the ship is adequately ballasted
- adjust the course and speed as necessary
- rig lifelines and hand ropes where necessary
- obtain weather reports and forecasts from multiple sources
- make hourly entries of the observed weather in the logbook
- if required, make obligatory reports to other ships in the vicinity and the nearest CRS
- unless the ship is stopped, avoid having the wind/seas abeam to prevent synchronous rolling and the possibility of the cargo shifting
- steer with the wind at about 45° on the bow. The alternative heading is with the wind at about 45° on the quarter.

When in or approaching port or coastal waters, additional actions include:

- Enquire if the port is open or closed
- if the port is closed, proceed towards a sheltered anchorage
- if alongside, consider proceeding to sea. However, as a minimum, double-up the moorings and raise the gangway/accommodation ladder, let go one anchor under-foot
- if necessary, stop cargo operations.

At Anchor, additional actions

- Heave up the anchor and put to sea, or pay out more cable or consider coming to an open moor
- use the engine to reduce the strain on the cable(s).

5.5.1.4 Navigating around a Strong Current/Tidal Stream

In areas where strong currents or tidal streams are encountered, the following bridge procedures should be followed:

- Use the largest scale corrected charts
- work out tidal stream and/or current information and update the passage plan
- determine the gyro error and deviation for the ship's head

- operate the radar at the appropriate range to detect suitable navigational marks
- use parallel indexing to continuously monitor the track keeping and set tendency
- plot the ship's position at specified intervals
- plot positions using different methods, mainly visual
- plot DR and EP after every fix and determine the safe waters that are available
- observe the wind and its effect on track keeping
- engage hand steering and post lookouts.

5.5.1.5 Navigating around Shoals and Reefs

In areas where shoals and reefs are encountered, the following additional bridge procedures should be followed:

- Work out the height of tide and UKC available and update the passage plan accordingly.

5.5.2 Malfunction of Navigational Equipment

Position-fixing Systems

- Inform the Master and the Electro Technical Officer (ETO)
- if operational, use a secondary method to plot positions
- in coastal waters, use visual means to plot positions
- use the echo sounder
- if visibility is bad in coastal waters, increase the distance from the coastline or other obstructions
- in open waters, obtain positions by celestial observations
- reduce speed if necessary
- call and notify the ship-reporting system.

Gyro

- Inform the Master and the ETO
- inform the engine room
- engage hand-steering and steer by magnetic compass
- establish a rota for hand-steering
- once on each watch, and after every course alteration, calculate the compass error
- consider the effect of gyro failure on other navigation aids.

5.5.3 Piracy

Precautions before entry

- Brief all crew on the procedure to be followed in the event of an attack
- seal all entrances and areas as detailed in the ISPS recommendation
- test all internal and external communication facilities and ensure they are ready for use
- ensure all deck areas are well lit

- test the search light and the Aldis lamp and make them ready for use
- fire hoses should be rigged up, charged and ready for use around the vessel
- set up an anti-piracy patrol. Provide hand-held radios for contact with the bridge
- man the engine room. Standby engines (SBE), engines at full speed and ready for manoeuvring
- double the bridge watches and post additional lookouts to monitor the vessel's position continuously
- maintain a good listening watch on the radio for any reports of piracy
- if a suspicious craft approaches the vessel, immediately inform the Master and commence evasive manoeuvres. Inform the shore authorities and other shipping in the vicinity.

Precautions at anchor or alongside

- Maintain strict access controls at all gangways and access points
- place rat-guards on mooring ropes
- seal fairleads and hawse pipes
- at night, switch on all upper deck lights and rig extra lights near the ship's stern and the sides to illuminate dark areas. Use powerful search lights
- lock all upper deck lockers and lock access to accommodation and technical areas
- arm upper deck patrols with night sticks. Maintain patrols during the hours of darkness.

Precautions When Underway

- Consider passage through pirate-prone areas in daylight
- the ship must proceed at the maximum safe speed
- maintain a good radar and visual watch
- give a wide berth to small stationary objects or boats, especially if they are unlit at night
- at night, switch on all upper deck lights and rig extra lights near the ship's stern and sides to illuminate dark areas. Use powerful search lights
- lock all upper deck lockers and lock access to the accommodation and technical areas
- maintain upper deck patrols during the hours of darkness.

Horn of Africa and West Africa Piracy Threat

Somali and West African Pirates pose the greatest piracy threat today. Several initiatives have been taken to counteract the threat and/or eliminate it completely. The EU, in cooperation with Fairplay (Lloyd's Register), has established a web-based resource for ships to receive the latest alerts and to be able to register their ships before transiting high risk regions in the area.

In addition, the EU Naval Force (EUNAVFOR) Anti-Piracy Operation off the Somali coast uses the military forces at its disposal and cooperates with other states operating in the region, to provide protection to all ships operating in the Gulf of Aden. This is providing the best results to ships operating in the Internationally Recommended Transit Corridor due to the coordination of surface units, airplanes and helicopters.

The Commander of US Naval Central Command has also established a Maritime Security Patrol Area for international assistance to discourage attacks on commercial vessels transiting the Gulf of Aden within the Transit Area.

Shipowners can also take their own action by employing armed security personnel when transiting or navigating around the Gulf of Aden and the Somali coastal waters. Industry is working on measures to address West Africa piracy threats.

5.5.4 Pre-Departure Procedures

The exact procedures that should be followed before departure varies with the ship type and her trading pattern. However, the following basic procedures will apply for every type of ship.

The following are the significant pre-departure checks:

- Watertight integrity of the vessel
- readiness of the ship's machinery and gear
- availability of bunkers and stores for the voyage
- controls testing. Any defects should be rectified
- crew availability and readiness
- security of cargo and stores
- booking of pilot and tugs
- draught and freeboard
- tidal data, particularly of high water
- ship stability
- obtain NAVAREA, coastal and local warnings as well as the weather forecast
- passage plan finalised and bridge preparation. Carry out a set-up of the navigational equipment
- crew and passenger lists
- positive reporting by concerned departments regarding readiness
- searches for stowaways, terrorist devices and contraband
- port clearance.

5.5.5 Pre-Arrival Procedures

The exact procedures to be followed before arrival varies with the ship type and her trading pattern. However, the following basic procedures will apply for every type of ship.

The following are the significant pre-arrival checks:

- Readiness of the ship's machinery and gear
- controls testing. Any defects should be rectified
- anchors cleared and ready for use, mooring ropes on deck
- obtain coastal and local warnings and a local weather forecast
- set up NAVTEX for the appropriate station
- notice to the engine room and crew at appropriate stages
- book the pilot
- obtain berthing details and prospects
- arrival-draught calculation
- tidal data, particularly of high water
- ship stability
- passage plan finalised and bridge preparation. Carry out set-up of navigational equipment
- crew and passenger lists
- declaration for health, customs and immigration
- positive reporting by concerned departments regarding readiness
- searches for stowaways, terrorist devices and contraband.

These procedures are explained fully in the SMS. Detailed checklists will be available on board to ensure that full procedures are followed, nothing has been omitted and that no short cuts are being taken. On board the ship, it is the Master's responsibility to ensure that all the requirements are complied with. Responsibility will be delegated to the heads of departments and key individuals on board the ship. These heads and key individuals are responsible for making reports on the readiness and state of the ship to the Master.

It is understood that most shipboard operations are sequential and inter-related. Additionally, trading plans are generally known in advance. The Master and ship's staff may plan pro-actively for the oncoming voyage and instruct Management and the Operational staff who, in turn, can advise the support staff.

5.6 Navigational Risk Assessment

Risk refers to the harm, or the possibility of harm, that may be caused by a hazard. Risk assessment offers a planned foundation for the careful study of potential hazards to ensure that sufficient precautions are taken to reduce the risk and, where possible, prevent it. The significance of each hazard should be considered and decide if sufficient precautions were taken to manage the risk. These five steps should be used to assess a risk:

- Identify the hazards
- consider the potential harm

- evaluate the risks. Establish if existing precautions are sufficient
- record all findings and measures of control
- review the assessment and, if the risks are still not controlled, revise the plan until a satisfactory conclusion is reached.

The Navigation Officer will identify the hazards and assist in preparing contingencies. Once the hazards have been identified use control measures to manage risks so accidents can be avoided. Risks can be divided into five zones:

Trivial Risks – Risks deemed unimportant. Action to reduce the risk is not normally required.

Tolerable Risks – Risks that can be tolerated/accepted without any possible harm but they should be monitored to maintain control. For example, transiting a narrow passage during the day compared to a night transit in the same area.

Moderate Risks – Additional resources are required to achieve substantial control of the potential risk, with a possibility of an increase in cost. For example posting a helmsman.

Substantial Risks – Risks that are unacceptable and must be reduced at any cost. For example, in restricted visibility, reduction of speed and doubling watchkeepers on the bridge.

Intolerable Risks – Risks that cannot be controlled or reduced due to the level of severity and the non-availability of resources. Under these conditions, the passage cannot continue. For example, when a ship meets very severe weather and has to seek shelter.

An example risk assessment is provided, it should be noted that in this example the risk level has been re-assessed with the indicated control measures in place. If the control measures are not implemented, the risk assessment would not be valid and the risk level will vary. Some companies provide generic risk assessments for most general hazards. However, the risks of every case must be re-assessed and ensure that control measures are in place.

5.6.1 Example Risk Assessment

PASSAGE PLANNING RISK ASSESSMENT

Risk Assessment Number ....

For Passage from .... to ....

On Voyage from .... to ....

Date: .... Assessed by: ....

Hazard: Failure of GPS when passing at close proximity to One Fathom Bank Light in the Malacca Strait

Risk: Unable to use ECDIS due to unavailability of GPS position, track control may not prevent vessel from running aground.

Risk Assessment:

Severity of Hazard				Likelihood of Harm			Risk Level
☑	5	Very High			5	Very Likely	
	4	High	✕		4	Likely	
	3	Moderate		☑	3	Quite Possible	5 × 3 = 15
	2	Slight			2	Possible	
	1	Nil			1	Unlikely	

Control Measures:

- Do not use GPS as the primary source of position fixing.
- Ship's auto pilot not on 'track control'.
- Both radars switched on – one used solely for position fixing.
- Parallel Indexing in use with reference to One Fathom Bank Lighthouse.
- Calculate set and rate and apply as required.
- Position fixing interval to reduce to 5 minutes.
- Engines on Stand-by for immediate manoeuvring.

Re-assessment of Risks with Control Measures:

Severity of Hazard				Likelihood of Harm			Risk Level
	5	Very High			5	Very Likely	
	4	High	×		4	Likely	
	3	Moderate		☑	3	Quite Possible	2 × 3 = 6
☑	2	Slight			2	Possible	
	1	Nil			1	Unlikely	

Level	Rating	Action
1 – 5	Trivial	No further action required
6 – 10	Tolerable	Monitoring required to ensure that the controls are maintained
11 – 15	Moderate	Efforts to reduce risks required with attention to allocation of resources and amount of time required for reducing risk
16 – 20	Substantial	Ship cannot proceed on passage without reducing the risk. Allocation of resources and time can increase to very high amount but ship may proceed on voyage once risks have been reduces
21 – 25	Intolerable	Passage cannot be continued even with unlimited resources

5.7 Hydrographic and Port Information

The present day Hydrographic data is gathered through surveys carried out by the Royal Navy, surveying organisations, foreign hydrographic authorities, observation stations, lighthouse authorities and exploration companies. In addition, reports made by mariners and leisure sailors are valuable as the voyages undertaken by these individuals are higher in number and in more varied locations.

It is important that reports are made of any differences between the charted or stated information and what is actually observed. There are some natural changes that are taking place, as well as new developments bringing about changes. Additionally, confirmation of positions and other remarks on the old publications are also valuable.

When the report is sent depends on the authority of the charts or the publications being used. If using BA/UKHO charts and publications, the report should be sent to the UK Hydrographic Office. The law of the coastal state may have to be taken into account.

It is important to note that certain observations require an immediate report to be made by radio as the information may be of special navigational significance to mariners, eg reduced depth, sighting of a sinking vessel in shallow areas, navigational aids out of position, etc. Such radio reports should be made to all ships in the vicinity and to the nearest coast station.

5.7.1 Hydrographic Information

5.7.1.1 Report

Report the information on form H.102 – HYDROGRAPHIC NOTE. The following information is required:

- The name of the ship or sender, along with the address
- contact information: telephone/fax/telex/email particulars
- general locality
- subject
- position in latitude and longitude
- BA Chart(s) affected, along with date of its edition
- position fixing system used, along with the datum set
- latest weekly edition of Notice to Mariners held

- ENCs affected
- latest update disk held
- publications affected, along with edition number and date of the latest supplement and reference number, eg the Light List No
- details
- replacement copy of chart number
- signature of observer/reporter.

5.7.1.2 Details

What, where, when and how are important aspects of any observation. In case of soundings:

- The make, name and type of the echo sounder
- the echo sounder trace, annotated with date/time of the fix
- the number of revolutions per minute
- depth observed
- speed of sound in sea water
- if the soundings have been corrected
- setting of scale zero and whether depth was below keel or from sea surface
- draught
- time, which is very important for applying tidal data to the observation.

In the case of charted details, the alteration should be shown in red on the largest scale chart. Positions should be plotted on the largest scale chart, and a plotting sheet prepared to a suitable scale or on an ocean plotting sheet. Forward a cutting of the chart with the alterations. For positions:

- Geographical: latitude and longitude
- astronomical: names, times, altitudes of heavenly bodies, prevailing conditions
- visual fixes: time and simultaneous observations by horizontal sextant angle, compass bearings, ranges and any corrections applied

- GPS: datum, position shift on chart applied or not, make and model of receiver and PDOP, GDOP, HDOP values
- other electronic systems: time, full details and if any errors have been applied.

5.7.2 Port Information

The form H102a must be forwarded, together with form H102, containing the following details:

- Name of the port
- general remarks: principal activities and trade, latest population figures and date, number of ships or tonnage handled per year, copy of port handbook, if available
- anchorages: designation, depth, holding ground and shelter afforded
- pilotage: authority for request, embarkation position, regulations
- directions: entry and berthing information, tidal streams, navaids
- tugs: number of tugs available, max HP (Bollard Pull)
- wharves: name, number, or position, length, depth, ht. above chart datum, facilities available
- cargo handling: containers, lighters, ro-ro
- cranes: brief details and maximum capacity
- repairs: hull, machinery and under water. Docking or slipping facilities, size of vessels handled
- rescue and distress: salvage, lifeboat, coastguard
- supplies: fuel, fresh water, provisions
- services: medical, de-ratting, consuls, ship chandlers
- communications: road, rail, air services, nearest airport, port radio and information service with frequencies and hours of operating
- port authority: contact details, designations
- small craft facilities
- views: photographs of significant features.

6 Radar Navigation

From its early beginnings, radar has undergone significant technological development. However, the basics remain the same and it continues to be a valuable aid for monitoring navigation, collision avoidance, security and surveillance, provided its limitations are fully understood. Radar has accuracy, it can provide a Range to within 30m or 1% of the range scale being used whichever is greater, and Bearing to within 1°. This chapter looks at the value of radar, considers its limitations and discusses different displays.

6.1 Radar Displays

Radar displays are categorised according to the motion they generate and the stabilisation input. The motion can be either relative or true. Stabilisation is subdivided into course and speed. In the next section, a comparison is made, using sketches and a tabular list of advantages (left) against the disadvantages of radar (right).

6.1.1 Relative Motion

This display provides an immediate indication of the risk of collision or the Closest Point of Approach (CPA). The display usually originates from the centre, but off centre operation is possible with head-up and north-up modes. Fixed objects generate echo movement in a direction that is reciprocal to the ship's ground track.

Regardless of heading stabilisation, an echo blur or smear, will occur because of the relative motion of the echoes.

Head-up (Course-up, unstabilised) keeps the heading marker at 0° and the picture turns around it. This makes it unsuitable for narrow waters with frequent course changes.

Advantage	Disadvantage
Direct comparison with visual. Relative bearing provides quick indication of bearing of target relative to ship's head	*Must check course for True bearings. Echoes 'Blur' (smear) when altering course or yawing. Not possible to detect others relative motion when own heading is changing*

Course-up (stabilised) the picture has stabilised and the heading marker points mostly upwards. When yawing, the picture remains still, but the heading marker moves. The system is reset to bring the course-up after an alteration of course.

Advantage	Disadvantage
Direct comparison with visual mostly, with provision of obtaining true bearings. No blur or smear due to change of heading	*The heading marker rotates when yawing or changing course, causing orientation problems for some users*

North-up (stabilised) keeps the picture still and the heading marker shifts due to change of course or yawing.

Advantage	Disadvantage
Direct comparison with chart. No smear due to own ship's head movement. Increased bearing accuracy. Actual relative movement of echoes can be detected by bearings and ranges of after-glow as long as it remains	*No direct comparison with visual and some individuals may find problems with orientation*

6.1.2 True Motion

There is no effect on echoes when 'own ship' alters course. Discontinuity may occur when the centre spot is reset as this operation may occur at an awkward time. Plan the picture shift carefully, especially once the ship has settled on a new leg of the passage. When dealing with close-quarter or risk-of-collision situations, picture shifts should be performed at an appropriate time and not left to the last moment. True motion allows for a distinction between moving, fixed and stationary targets. Targets closing on a steady bearing are not immediately apparent. Errors in heading and speed input may cause a false movement to appear. Adjustments to remove the effects of wind, current or tidal stream are difficult to determine. Early warning is available due to the increased ahead-range capability, and there is no centring error.

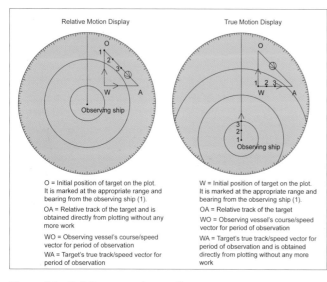

Figure 6.1 Relative versus true motion

Sea-stabilised (North-up)

Advantage	Disadvantage
Indicates course of all contacts through the water. Set and drift obtained at a glance by observation of fixed contacts. True alterations of course and speed of echoes displayed immediately	*Errors in compass and speed input cause false movement to appear on display*

Ground-stabilised (North-up)

Advantage	Disadvantage
Separation of stationary and moving targets. Useful in pilotage waters as ground speed displayed for targets	*Does not indicate the course and speed of ships through the water*

6.1.3 Interpretation of Vectors and Trails

On true motion, four targets have been used in Figures 6.3 and 6.3A to illustrate the difference in vectors and trails with sea and ground stabilised modes, the tidal stream is 090°T × 3 Kts.

0 – Own ship (000°T × 6 Kts)
1 – Fixed isolated beacon
2 – Target ship (180°T × 6 Kts)
3 – Target ship (245°T × 9 Kts)
4 – Target ship (Stopped in the water)

There is no change in relative vectors with sea or ground stabilised speed inputs. However, the true vectors and trails change when the input changes between sea and ground speed.

The input speed will cause a change in the speed and heading output of the targets, which affects the aspect. To emphasise this point, the true vectors for 'own ship' and target 3 are produced in Figure 6.2 As can be seen, the sea stabilised mode displays the true vector without any error, but the ground stabilised mode has caused an error in the true vectors, resulting in an incorrect aspect.

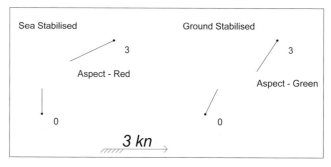

Figure 6.2 Sea stabilised vectors

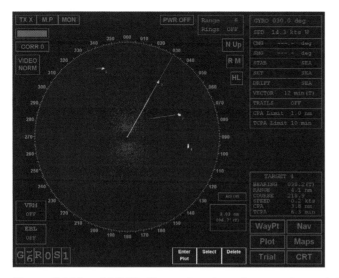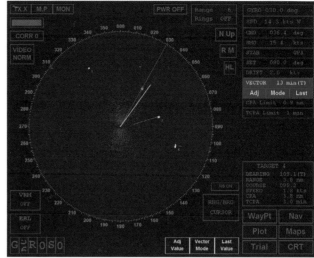

Figures 6.3.1A and 6.3.1B True vectors shown for sea and ground stabilised mode - Note the clearly visible inaccuracy in aspect

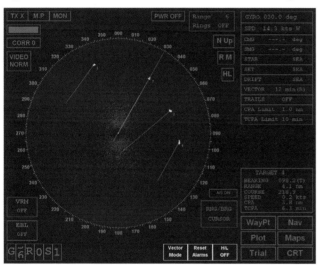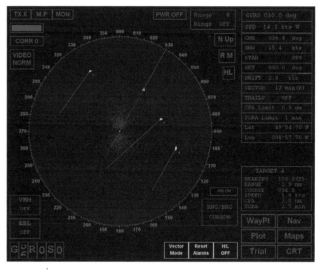

Figures 6.3.2A and 6.3.2B Relative vectors for sea and ground stabilised mode - there is no change in vectors

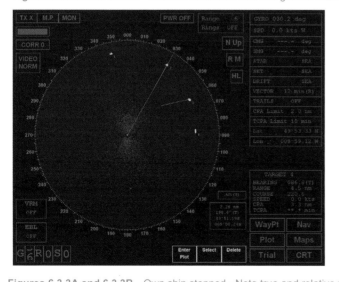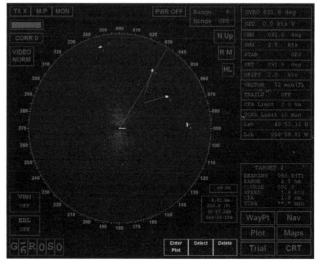

Figures 6.3.3A and 6.3.3B Own ship stopped - Note true and relative vectors in sea and ground stabilisation

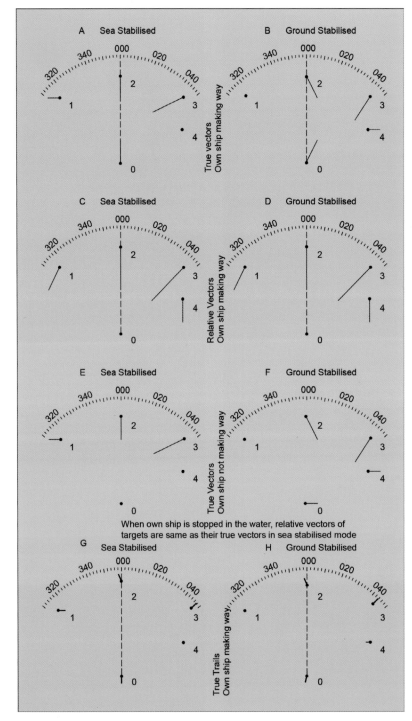

Figure 6.3A   Vector diagram for various ground and sea stabilised states

Key notes:

- Relative vectors do not change with speed input, the CPA information is correct, within limitations, and is independent of the input
- sea-stabilised or water-track mode provides the correct aspect, but with ground-stabilised or ground-track mode the aspect could be wrong. The correct aspect may be required to take a decision on a collision-avoidance manoeuvre

- sea-stabilised mode does not indicate whether 'own ship' is being set, but ground-stabilised mode gives a quick indication of how 'own ship' is setting. This implies that sea-stabilised mode should be used for collision-avoidance and ground-stabilised for navigation
- in open sea, if one radar is used off-centre, the other should be centred.

6.2 Plotting

Radar plotting is generally used to report on the radar contacts. Plotting can be carried out manually on a plotting sheet, either by using the reflection plotter or electronically. Regardless of the medium used, good results are produced through a combination of the basic methods being applied correctly and the skills of the operator. Navigators should practice plotting skills in clear weather when monitoring can be carried out by another means, such as on visual, results can be checked against reality or radar simulations, as with trial manoeuvres.

There are a few basic rules that the navigator must follow. Plotting tools (equipment) must be available at all times and ready for immediate use. Even basic tasks like keeping pencils or china graph crayons sharpened are essential. Compare the clocks and avoid any adjustments as they can cause confusion about the current time.

The navigator should select equal time-intervals between observations. For example, intervals of 3, 6, 10, 12 or 15 minutes are convenient fractions of an hour and lead to sensible arithmetic manipulation. The plotting interval selected should be appropriate to the range scale in use, the speed of 'own vessel' and the approach rates of the target vessels.

The targets should be marked on the plotter with an accurate cross or a fine point. Do not use a large blob. Electronic markers should be used when available. The

targets should be given designators at this stage. This approach is very helpful when observing several targets simultaneously. For plotting purposes, the actual ranges and bearings should be picked up from these marks. This avoids errors that may be introduced, either due to inaccurate timing or through a change of sequence to the observation and plotting of the targets.

6.2.1 Procedure and Terminology

The basic plot in Example 6.1 demonstrates the vectors and terminology used for relative plotting, along with some aspects of the procedure.

Example 6.1

A vessel heading 320° T at 21.5 knots, observes another vessel on the radar. These observations were made:

0900	*020°T*	*10′.0*
0906	*025°T*	*8′.1*
0912	*032°.5 T*	*6′.4*

Compile a radar report for 0912.

Solution and Comments

Plot the heading line of the observing ship and mark it with the course and speed of 320° T × 21.5 Kts. Plot the three bearings and ranges. The first one should be labelled 'O' and the final as 'A'. Make a note of the times of each observation next to the relevant mark. When observations are made on head-up display, the relative bearings may have to be converted to true bearings.

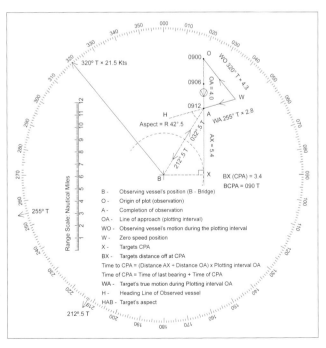

Figure 6.4 Plot for use with example 6.1

Draw a line of best fit through these points. This is the 'OA' line, the line of relative approach, and run it past the centre of the plotting sheet or display. Mark an arrow in the direction 'O' to 'A' and circle it. In actual practice, during real time plotting and before proceeding further, the points should be seen to fall closely on this line and that they are not scattered unduly. Look to see if the points are a similar distance apart. If the distances are uneven for an equal time interval, or the points are asymmetric, it could indicate that either the observed target is in the process of changing course and/or speed or that there are errors with the observations.

The 'OA' line provides information on the risk of collision. If this line passes through the middle of the sheet, the observed vessel is on a collision course. If it does not pass through the middle, as in this example, the distance that it passes from the middle should be determined. This is done by drawing a line perpendicular to the 'OA' line, which passes through the middle of the plot 'B'. The perpendicular meets the 'OA' line at point 'X', which is the CPA. Distance 'BX' is the distance off at the CPA, which is 3′.4. An arc also indicates the CPA distance.

The direction of line 'BX' indicates the bearing of the CPA.

The time of relative approach can also be measured along the 'OA' line. Distances 'OA' and 'AX' should be measured and, in this instance, are found to be 4′.0 and 5′.4.

'OA' is the approach distance covered during the plotting interval.

Time to CPA = (AX ÷ OA) × Plotting interval
= (5.4 ÷ 4.0) × 12 = 16.2 or 16 minutes
Time of CPA = 0912 + 0016 = 0928

Plot 'WO', usually referred to as 'way of own', in the direction of the observing ship's course, to join at 'O'. Mark a single arrow on this line in the direction of 'W' to 'O'. This is the motion line of 'own vessel' and equals:

WO = (Speed of observing ship ÷ 60 minutes) × plotting interval minutes
WO = (21.5 ÷ 60) × 12 = 4′.3.

During the actual plotting, 'WO' could be produced and plotted once the first plot has been marked in order to complete the vector triangle with minimum delay. Similarly, the plot should be labelled at an early stage, so that the rest of the bridge team can understand the plot and interpret it.

After plotting 'WO', join 'W' to 'A' to produce line 'WA' which is the true track of the observed ship, usually referred to as 'way of another'. Mark a single arrow on this line in the direction 'W' to 'A'. The direction of 'WA' indicates the course or track of the observed vessel (255° T) and its length is indicative of the speed.

Speed of observed ship = (WA ÷ Plotting interval in minutes) × 60 minutes.
Speed = (2′.8 ÷ 12) × 60 = **14 Kts**

The final stage is the aspect. This is the relative bearing of the observing vessel from the target vessel, or angle on the bow of the target vessel. It is expressed from 0° to 180° Red or Green, depending on whether the observing vessel is on the Port or Starboard side of the target vessel. It is worked out as the difference between the Target's true course and the reciprocal of the last observed bearing. Reciprocal of last observed bearing 032°.5 T is 212°.5 T

Aspect = **255°T ~ 212°.5 T = Red 42°.5** (always obtain the shorter angle)

It can be worked out from the azimuth ring on the plotting sheet when course and bearings are marked during measurement.

6.2.2 Report

Most navigators believe that the report is based upon six items: course, speed, CPA, TCPA, Bearing of Closest Point of Approach (BCPA) and aspect. Although these are usually the outcomes of the plot, they do not necessarily provide all the pertinent information about the target. For a full report or analysis of the situation, the following items should be reported:

- Time of the report
- target identifier or designator (when tracking a number of targets)
- target's last observed true bearing
- bearing steady, closing (drawing forward) or opening (drawing aft)
- target's last observed range
- range steady, decreasing or increasing
- distance of the target's CPA
- bearing of the target at CPA (true or relative)
- 'Time to' and 'Time of' the CPA
- calculated true track/course of the target
- calculated speed of the target
- target's aspect
- where applicable, general comments about overtaking or crossing, which side to which side.

For Example 6.1, the full report would read:

- 0912
- Bearing 032°.5T
- Opening (drawing aft)
- Range 6′.4, decreasing
- CPA 3′.4, bearing 090°T in 16 minutes at 0928
- Course/track 255°T
- Speed 14 Kts
- Aspect Red 42°.5.

Information can be presented in tabular format, especially when plotting multiple targets.

6.2.3 Current or Tidal Stream/Other Relations Between 'O', 'A' and 'W'

The four plots in Figure 6.5 illustrate the following issues:

Plot 1: The observing vessel is making way and the plot includes only the observations made during the plotting interval. There is no tidal stream. Note that for "A", 'O' and 'A' are at the same point.

Plot 2: There is no tidal stream and the observing vessel is making way. 'WO' is applied to both the targets "A" and "B". For "A", the 'WO' and 'WA' are in line, indicating that the target is moving on the same course and speed as the observing vessel. In case of "B", 'W' and 'A' fall on the same point, indicating a zero 'WA', which means that the target is stationary.

Plot 3: There is no tidal stream and the observing vessel is not making way, so 'WO' is zero. "A" is seen to be moving and "B" is stationary. For "B", 'O' and 'A' remain at the same point. Since 'WO' is zero, the relative approach of "A" is its true track as well. 'OA' = 'WA'.

Plot 4: The observing vessel is making way and the tidal stream is setting West. The plot of "A" is normal, while the distance between observing vessel and "B" is gradually increasing. "B" is known to be stationary. A fixed stationary object cannot be moving 'WA', so the vector 'AW' is the tidal stream, indicated by three arrow heads. The direction 'AW' is the set indicated as °T. The length of 'AW' is the drift experienced by the observing vessel during the plotting interval and is measured in nautical miles. It is used to work out the rate of tidal stream.

Rate of Tidal Stream = (Drift ÷ Plotting interval in minutes) × 60 minutes.

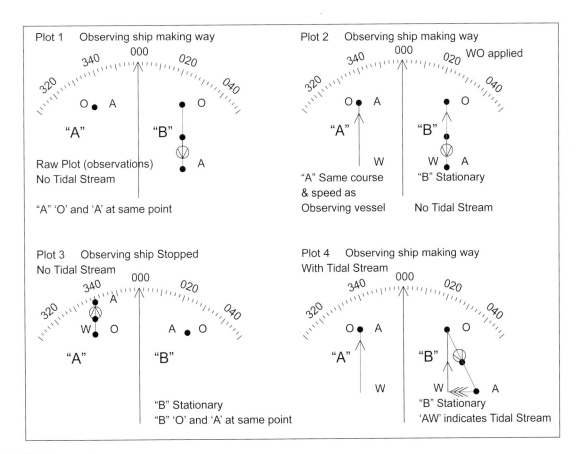

Figure 6.5 Tidal stream plots

6.2.4 Alteration by Observed Vessel

The navigator must spot a change in the direction and length of WA.

Example 6.2

A vessel steering 350°T at 15 knots, observes two targets on radar as follows:

0900	A - 006°T	× 10´.4	B - 305°T	× 10´.6
0910	A - 017°T	× 8´.5	B - 303°T	× 8´.5
0920	A - 032.5°T	× 7´.1	B - 301°	× 6´.4

If "A" is known to be a light vessel, compile a radar report for 0920.

Observation of "B" continued as follows:

0930	292.5°T × 5´.0
0940	259°T × 3´.3
0950	211°T × 3´.8

What action has been taken by "B" between 0920 and 0930?

Solution and Comments

Follow the standard plotting procedure described earlier. For "A", 'AW' must indicate the tidal stream, as it is a stationary object.

For the observation of "B" from 0930 onwards, the labels have been changed to O1, W1 and A1. W1A1 should be examined for any change. The change in direction is an indicator of a change in course, the direction W1A1 is the new course. A change in length indicates a change of speed. Zero length of W1A1 would mean that the target has stopped.

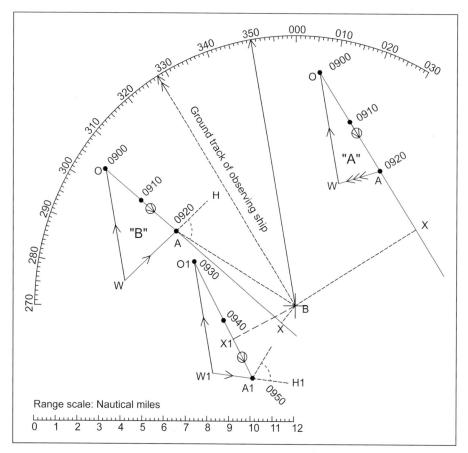

Figure 6.6   Plot for example 6.2

Report

	"A" at 0920	"B" at 0920	"B" at 0950
Bearing	032.5°T, opening	301°T, opening	211°T, opening
Range	7′.1, decreasing	6′.4, decreasing	3′.8, increasing
CPA	6′.4	1′	3′.2
BCPA	058°T	220°T	242°T
TCPA	12 minutes, 0932	30 minutes, 0950	Past 7 min, 0943
Course/Set	253°T	047°T	a/c 50° Stb, 097°T
Speed/Rate	5′.8	9.7 Kts	Reduced to 5.6 Kts
Aspect/Drift	1′.9	G 74°	R 66°

For "B" at 0950: in addition to new course/speed, all details have been added.

Note the 'past' TCPA and change of aspect to red. In Figure 6.7, the 'ground' track of the observing vessel has been marked. It is the reciprocal of the relative plot of the fixed stationary object, ie 328°T at a speed of 15.4 Kts, from length of OA. It can be used to obtain the ground track of target "B" and is illustrated in Figure 6.7.

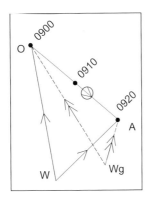

Figure 6.7   Second plot for example 6.2

6.2.5 Alteration By Observing Vessel

In this case, the change of course is indicated by a new direction of 'WO' and a change of speed is indicated by a change of length of 'WO'. Where the observing vessel stops, 'WO' will be zero. In case of stopping, what would be the resulting relative approach of the target?

In most theoretical problems, the alteration is often instantaneously effective (Example 6.3). However, in real life and in some problems, the alteration will have to allow for steadying on the new course or speed. This will involve the application of head reach of the observing vessel during the manoeuvre.

6.2.6 Head Reach

In reality, when a vessel commences a manoeuvre, the intended course or speed is not effective at once. There is usually a time interval between the commencement of the manoeuvre and its completion. During this period, the direction and/or length of the relative approach also changes. The distance travelled by a vessel in the direction of initial motion during a manoeuvre is called 'Head Reach'. The exact value can be determined from the manoeuvring characteristics of the vessel, its speed, loading condition, depth of water, sea state and the helm angle used.

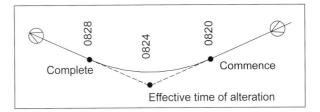

Figure 6.8   Effective time of alteration

It may not be possible to include all the above information in an exam-style problem. Usually, head reach distance and the time taken for the manoeuvre are included. For plotting purposes, the effective time to plot the new approach line of the manoeuvre is taken as the half way point. At that point of the manoeuvre, it is easier to plot a curved path (Example 6.6).

Another option is to plot the new approach from the position of the target vessel when the observing vessel has steadied on the new course/speed. In such cases, a bearing and distance of the target would be provided (Example 6.4).

Example 6.3

Using the information and initial observations given in Example 6.2, and assuming any alterations are instantaneously effective, find a single alteration of course to be made by the observing vessel at 0930, in order to pass the vessel "B" at a distance of 3 miles. What effect will this alteration have on target "A"? Find the earliest time that the observing vessel can resume its original course.

Solution and Comments

Draw the heading line of the observing vessel from the centre 'B' and label it 350°T @ 15 Kts. Plot the bearings and ranges of targets "A" and "B". Label the points and mark them with the times. Add the 'WO' line to complete the 'OAW' triangles. Extend the 'OA' lines for both. Mark the vectors with appropriate arrows.

The initial CPA of "B" was 1 mile on the port side. In order to pass it at 3 miles, the course should be altered to starboard. If visibility was restricted, avoid altering course to port for a vessel forward of the beam (Rule 19 d). Even when taking action in clear visibility, a power-driven vessel should avoid altering course to port for a power driven vessel on its own port side (Rule 17 c).

Using a radius of 3 miles and centred on the sheet, describe an arc towards the port side of the observing vessel. DO NOT use a full circle to make a decision against a single target, as you could easily turn the wrong way. Only use a circle when the decision concerns several targets.

Since a course alteration is required for 0930, it is important to determine these points for both the targets. Measure the length of the 'OA' vector for both separately; this is the approach for 20 minutes. Use half of this distance to obtain the 0930 position for the targets. (If in another problem, the time interval is not exactly half, use the appropriate fraction). Label it as 'A1'.

For target "B" (as 3 miles is required from it), draw a line A1X1 from A1 as a tangent to the arc drawn earlier. This is the required relative approach to pass "B" at 3 miles. With centre 'W' and a radius of 'WO', describe an arc to starboard of 'WO'. Draw a line parallel to A1X1 from 'A' backwards to intersect the arc from 'W' at the centre. Label the intersection point as 'O1'. Join 'W' to 'O1'. 'OWO1' is the alteration of course required to pass "B" at 3 miles, ie 25°. The new course is 350°T + 25° = 015°T.

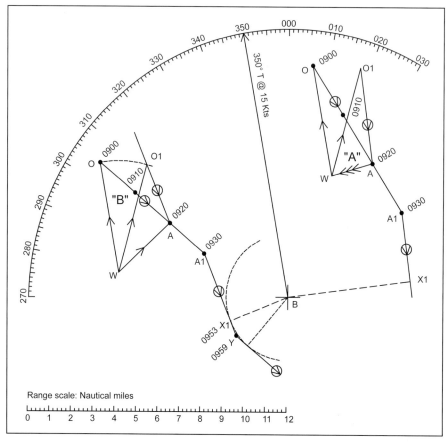

Figure 6.9 Plot for use with example 6.3

For effect on target "A", from point 'W', draw the new 'WO1' in direction 015°T at 15 kts. Join 'O1' to 'A' and obtain the new relative approach line for target "A". Draw a line parallel to 'O1A' from point 'A1' and run it past the CPA, 'X1'. For the time of course resumption, draw a line tangential (and parallel to the original 'OA') to the 3 mile arc, to intersect at 'Y' the new line of relative approach 'A1X1'. The point of intersection of these two lines, 'Y', marks the earliest time that the observing vessel may resume its original course. The time can be determined:

Time interval	= (A1Y ÷ O1A) × Plotting interval
	= (4′ ÷ 2′.8) × 20 = 28.57 minutes
	= 29 minutes
Time of resumption	= 1930 + 29 = **1959**

Example 6.4

A vessel steering 300°T at 18 Kts, observes a vessel on radar:

0800	340°T	9′
0810	340°T	7′
0820	340°T	5′

Compile a report for 0820. If the observing vessel alters course to 350°T, find the CPA information about the target if it was bearing 330°T × 3′.5 at 0830 when the observing vessel is steady on its new course.

If, in this situation, a decision was taken to reduce the speed instead, what speed should the observing vessel reduce to in order to get the same result?

Solution and Comments
Report:

- 0820
- Brg 340°T, steady
- Range 5′, decreasing
- CPA 0′.0
- BCPA 340°T
- TCPA in 25 minutes at 0845
- Course 259°T, Speed 11.7 Kts, Aspect Red 99°

After completion of the basic plot and compilation of the report:

With 'W' as centre and 'WO' as the radius, describe an arc to starboard of 'O'. From 'W' draw a line in the direction of 350°T to reach the arc drawn. Call this intersection point 'O1'. Join 'O1' to 'A'. This is the new relative approach of the target after observing that the vessel has altered course. O1'c' is so labelled to indicate its relation to course change.

Plot the bearing and range for 0830. From this point, draw a line parallel to 'O1A' and run it past the CPA. Obtain the CPA information based on this new approach. CPA 2′.8; BCPA 292°.5T; TCPA in 9 minutes at 0839.

For a possible speed reduction, the point where the new 'O1A' line intersects 'WO' has been labelled O1's', to indicate its relation to speed change. Measure the length 'W' to O1's'. This is the distance to be travelled in 20 minutes if speed is reduced. This distance can be converted into speed = **9.9 Kts.**

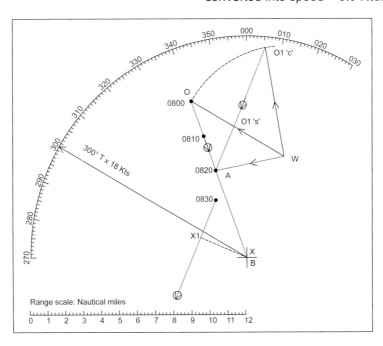

Figure 6.10 Plot for example 6.4

Example 6.5

A vessel steering 300°T × 18 Kts observed a vessel at 0800, 0810 and 0820 on a bearing of 340°T, ranges 9´, 7´ and 5´. The observing vessel's course was altered 50° to starboard at 0820 and was steady on the new course at 0828. Find the new CPA information and the target's bearing and range at 0828.

Solution and Comments

The observing vessel experiences head reach between 0820 and 0828, giving 0824 as the effective time, ie 4 minutes after commencement. Using 4 minutes, a new Zero speed point should be determined and labelled 'W1', ie 'WO' is for 20 minutes and 'W1O' is for 24 minutes – method A. From 'W1' draw a line parallel to 'WA' to intersect the 'OA' line. Label this point 'A1'. Using 'W1' as centre and 'W1O' as the radius, draw

an arc to starboard of 'WO'. From 'W1', draw a line in the direction 350°T. Where this line meets the arc is 'O1'. Join 'O1' to 'A1' and extend it past the CPA. Using 'O1A1' as the approach speed, determine 0828 position: 322°.5T × 3´.3; CPA 2´.8; BCPA 292°.5T; TCPA 0832 (remember 'O1A1' is for 24 minutes).

Note: If a speed change was done, point O1's' should have been used. Having understood the principle, a simpler method can be used.

An alternative method, shown as B, is to determine 'A1' by marking the 0824 point 'A1' on the relative approach line. Produce 'O1A' as normal and transfer it to the 'A1' point to obtain the bearing and range at 0828 and the CPA information. Both methods are shown for comparison.

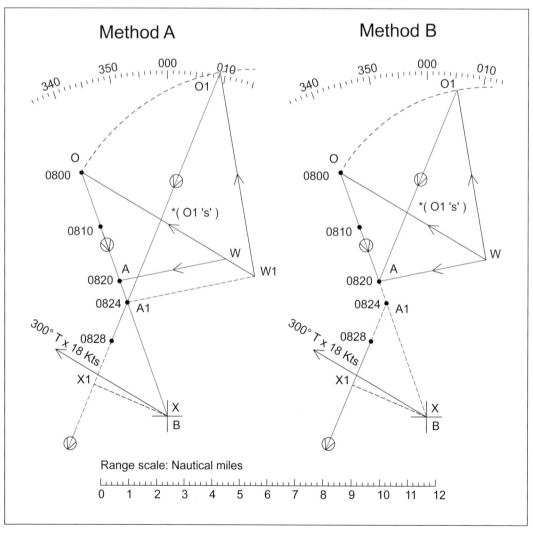

Figure 6.11 Plot for example 6.5

Example 6.6

A vessel on a course of 020°T at 10 Kts, observes a target on the radar:

0700	*300°T*	*10´.5*
0706	*301°T*	*8´.9*
0712	*302°T*	*7´.3*

If the observing vessel takes 10 minutes to stop and has a head reach of 1´.4, while maintaining the same heading, find the latest time to stop the engines so that the target will pass 2´.5 ahead of the observing vessel.

Solution and Comments

Draw the heading line, 3 observations and complete the OAW triangle. On the heading line, mark 'X1'. 'BX1' is 2´.5, the distance ahead that the target should pass.

Method C: Through 'X1', draw a line parallel to 'WA' and intersecting 'OA' extended. From any point, 'Y', on this line, draw a line in the direction of the observing vessel's course and equal to head reach, 'YZ'. If 'Z' falls on the intersection of 'OA' and 'YX1', call it point 'A1'. Otherwise draw a line parallel to 'YX1' through 'Z' and where it intersects the 'OA' line should be the point 'A1'. (Note 'Y1A1' and 'X1Z1' are 1´.4). 'A1' is the point

where the target should be when the observing vessel stops the engine. Work out the distance that the target will travel in 10 minutes and mark this distance from 'Y1' in the direction of the target's course to 'A2'. When the target reaches 'A2', the observing vessel would be stopped.

Method D: Having understood the principle, a simpler method can be used. Plot the heading line, the observations and complete the 'OAW' triangle. From 'W', measure the head reach of 1´.4 in the direction of the observing vessel's heading to 'O1'. Also, from 'W', measure the distance that the target would cover in 10 minutes and mark the point 'A1' on the 'WA' line. Join 'O1A1' as the relative approach while the observing vessel is stopping.

Mark 'X1' at 2´.5 from the centre and mark 'Z1' at 1´.4 from 'X1'. From 'Z1' draw a line parallel to the 'WA' to intersect line 'OA' extended. The point of intersection is 'O2'. At 'O2', draw a line equal in length and parallel to 'O1A1' to obtain point 'A2'. From 'A2', draw a line parallel to 'WA'. This line should pass 'X1'.

Using the relative approach 'OA', the time of stopping engines is calculated as 0721.

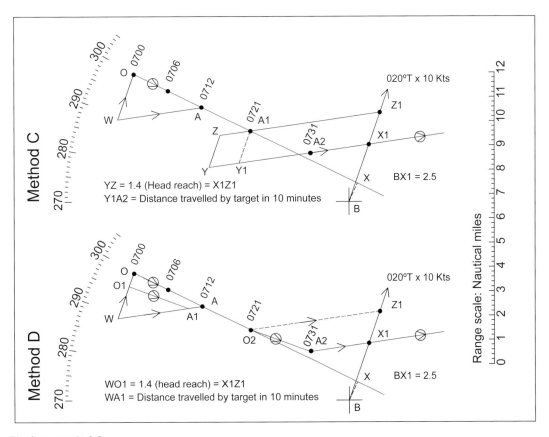

Figure 6.12 Plot for example 6.6

6.3 Collision Avoidance

The navigator can put the radar to good use through the important stages of collision avoidance. The combination of the suitable set up of the radar and the interaction with the navigator that makes it a valuable aid to navigation.

Detect: The influencing factors are:

- Range scale in use
- pulse length
- brilliance
- gain
- tuning
- sea and rain clutter controls
- blind and shadow sectors
- headlands and other obstructions in the vicinity.

Optimum set up and skilful observations ensure that the radar detects as expected, within its inherent limitations. Long range scanning should be used at appropriate intervals for early warning.

Prioritise: When the number of detected objects are small, they can all be tracked. But as the number increases, a navigator should examine and select target echoes for plotting. The degree of threat posed by the selected echoes should help to rank them for tracking. Most automatic aids have a limitation on the number of echoes that can be tracked at a given time.

Track: The Navigator should plot the tracks of the selected echoes. When plotting manually, and depending on the level of threat and the time available, the report may have to be restricted to the nearest approach information only.

ROR: The relevant paragraphs of the ROR should be considered to decide on the responsibility between vessels and the avoiding action that should to be taken. Aspect and relative location of the target vessel would be required for ROR application. Justification for the choice of action is heavily dependent on the mention and application of the relevant paragraphs of the Rules. The relevant application would be considered in the examples used.

Plan: The action to be taken by 'own vessel' should be planned and plotted. A trial manoeuvre may be used, when available, to plan the change required and to establish the appropriate time to take avoiding action. The effect of the intended action on other target echoes in the vicinity should also be examined.

Execute – Manoeuvre: The movements of all threatening echoes during the manoeuvre should be monitored carefully.

Monitor: Plotting should be resumed once the manoeuvre is completed. The vessel's return to her original status, or further avoiding action, should be considered, particularly when in the vicinity of other navigational hazards.

The following examples have been added to discuss the application of the ROR and some practical aspects that need to be considered while solving such problems.

Example 6.7
A vessel steering 045°T at 10 Kts, in conditions of restricted visibility, plots a number of echoes on the radar on a 12 mile scale between 1109 to 1127 hours. Analyse the situation at 1127. Also, determine a single alteration of course or speed at 1133, so as to pass at not less than 2 miles from all targets, assuming that any alteration is instantaneously effective. (OA lines provided on the plot)

Solution and Comments
The 'OAW' triangles should be completed and the 'OA' lines extended to the CPA to analyse the situation at 1127.

As it is restricted visibility, the requirements of Rule 19 apply. There are close quarters situations with targets "A", "B" and "C" but none with "D". Since "A", "B" and "C" are forward of the beam, the observing vessel should avoid altering course to port. "D" is abaft the starboard beam. But, as there is no close-quarters with it, alteration towards it is not a concern unless the action engaged it in another close-quarters. In more complicated problems, a simple table can be used to list the possible options:

Targets	Existing risk of collision or close-quarters	Alteration to starboard	Alteration to port	Slow/Stop
"A"	Yes	Yes	No	Yes
"B"	Yes	Yes	No	Yes
"C"	Yes	Yes	No	Yes
"D"	No	Yes	Yes	No

The action that is not in contravention (Yes for all targets) is usually the option. Additionally, aspects of Rule 8 should also be considered. These are the actions as per the rules:

- Positive
- in ample time
- with due regard to good seamanship
- large enough to be readily apparent
- a succession of small alterations to be avoided, alteration of course being more effective
- not engaging in close-quarters with other vessels.

Considering the above, an alteration of course to starboard would be the preferred choice, providing that the desired CPA is achievable.

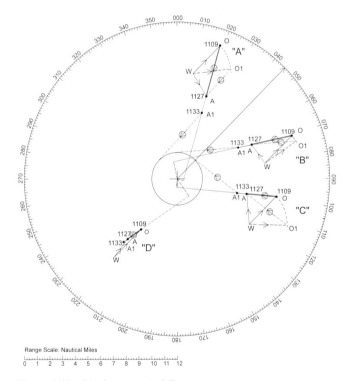

Figure 6.13 Plot for example 6.7

To determine the alteration, draw a circle of 2′ radius from the centre. Using the respective relative approach separately for each target, work out the point 'A1' where

the targets would be at 1133, ie 6 minutes from 1127. From 'A1', draw tangents to the 2′ circle towards the port, as the course is to be altered to starboard. No tangent has been drawn for "D".

Draw the new relative approach lines backwards at point 'A' for each target. With 'W' as centre and 'WO' as radius, describe arcs to starboard of 'WO' to cut the new approach lines. The intersection is point 'O1'. Join 'W' to 'O1' to determine the course alterations required. The courses worked out for "A", "B" and "C" respectively are 083°T, 055.5°T and 092°T. The largest would be chosen. If an observing vessel steers this course, "A" and "B" would pass at a larger distance. If in doubt, always check. Similarly the effect of alteration on "D" should also be checked.

Analysis:
Target "A" is forward of the beam on the port bow crossing from port to starboard with a CPA of 0′.5 and will be at CPA in 30 minutes. "A" has two more ships, in addition to own ship, forward of the beam on close quarters. It is unlikely that "A" will attempt to alter course to port. In terms of own action, it is better to alter course to starboard for "A" as per 19(d) as "A" is forward of the beam on close quarters.

Target "B" is forward of the beam on the starboard bow crossing from starboard to port with a CPA of 1′.3 and will be at CPA in 35 minutes. "B" has vessel "C", in addition to own ship, forward of the beam on close quarters and "A" abaft the beam on the port side. It is unlikely that "B" will attempt to alter course to port. In terms of own action, it is better to alter course to starboard for "B" as per 19(d) as "A" is forward of the beam on close quarters.

Target "C" is forward of the beam on the starboard bow crossing from starboard to port with a CPA of 0′.7 and will be at CPA in 44 minutes. "C" has two more vessels, in addition to own ship, forward of the beam on close quarters. It is unlikely that "C" will attempt to alter course to port. In terms of own action, it is better to alter course to starboard for "C" as per 19(d) as "C" is forward of the beam on close quarters.

Report	"A"	"B"	"C"	"D"
Bearing	020°T closing slowly	076°T closing slowly	102°T opening slowly	220°T opening
Range	6′.7 decreasing	6′.4 decreasing	5′.6 decreasing	6′.0 increasing
CPA	0′.5	1′.3	0′.7	1′.6
BCPA	106°T	348°T	185°T	145.5°T
TCPA	30 m, at 1157	35 m, at 1202	44 m, at 1211	Past 80 m
Course	149°T	324°T	355.5°T	037.5°T
Speed	6.7 Kts	6 Kts	7.7 Kts	6 Kts
Aspect	G 51°	R 78°	R 73.5°	G 2.5°
Remarks	Crossing P - S	Crossing S - P	Crossing S - P	Overtaken by observing vessel

Target "D" is abaft the beam on the starboard quarter and has been overtaken. "D" is unlikely to take any action, but must watch out for a possible course alteration to starboard by "A". No action is required by own vessel in terms of "D".

If the question required the report after altering course, then the chosen course must be applied to all targets to obtain the new relative approaches.

Example 6.8
A vessel navigating in restricted visibility within a lane of a traffic separation scheme, steering 225°T at 12 Kts, observes several echoes on the radar on a 12 mile

scale from 1530 to 1545 ('OA' lines are provided on the plot, for target "B", 'O' and 'A' are at the same point). After completing the plot, analyse the situation as it exists at 1545.

The Master decides to disengage from the present situation. Determine the alteration of course and/or speed required at 1550 to clear the situation, assuming that any alteration is instantaneously effective. State the reasons for the action taken by the observing vessel.

Solution and Comments
The 'OAW' triangles should be completed and 'OA' lines extended to CPA to analyse the situation at 1545.

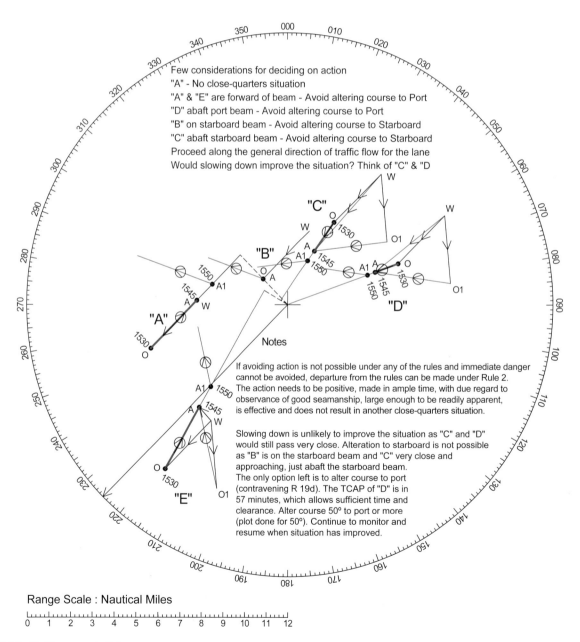

Few considerations for deciding on action
"A" - No close-quarters situation
"A" & "E" are forward of beam - Avoid altering course to Port
"D" abaft port beam - Avoid altering course to Port
"B" on starboard beam - Avoid altering course to Starboard
"C" abaft starboard beam - Avoid altering course to Starboard
Proceed along the general direction of traffic flow for the lane
Would slowing down improve the situation? Think of "C" & "D

Notes

If avoiding action is not possible under any of the rules and immediate danger cannot be avoided, departure from the rules can be made under Rule 2. The action needs to be positive, made in ample time, with due regard to observance of good seamanship, large enough to be readily apparent, is effective and does not result in another close-quarters situation.

Slowing down is unlikely to improve the situation as "C" and "D" would still pass very close. Alteration to starboard is not possible as "B" is on the starboard beam and "C" very close and approaching, just abaft the starboard beam. The only option left is to alter course to port (contravening R 19d). The TCAP of "D" is in 57 minutes, which allows sufficient time and clearance. Alter course 50° to port or more (plot done for 50°). Continue to monitor and resume when situation has improved.

Range Scale : Nautical Miles

0 1 2 3 4 5 6 7 8 9 10 11 12

Figure 6.14 Plot for example 6.8

Report	"A"	"B"	"C"	"D"
Bearing	020°T closing slowly	076°T closing slowly	102°T opening slowly	220°T opening
Range	6´.7 decreasing	6´.4 decreasing	5´.6 decreasing	6´.0 increasing
CPA	0´.5	1´.3	0´.7	1´.6
BCPA	106°T	348°T	185°T	145.5°T
TCPA	30 m, at 1157	35 m, at 1202	44 m, at 1211	Past 80 m
Course	149°T	324°T	355.5°T	037.5°T
Speed	6.7 Kts	6 Kts	7.7 Kts	6 Kts
Aspect	G 51°	R 78°	R 73.5°	G 2.5°
Remarks	Crossing P - S	Crossing S - P	Crossing S - P	Overtaken by observing vessel

As the vessel is in a TSS, in addition to Rules 8 and 19, the requirements of Rule 10 must also be considered. The vessel should proceed in the general direction of traffic flow for that lane. This implies that slowing down may be considered a viable option in similar situations if the result is passing at a safe distance. In this example, slowing down is a poor option. Similarly, altering course to starboard is a poor choice due to the presence of "B" and "C".

Altering course to port has been chosen after careful consideration of Rule 19(d), and importantly the times to CPA, as "D" has a TCPA in 57 minutes, and the action satisfies the considerations of Rule 8. The considerations and reasons have been listed on the plot. A table could also be prepared to list the possible choices. "C" and "D" will pass at 1´.8 from the observing vessel and "E" at 4´.2.

The example must not be used to suggest or recommend a departure from the rules, but to instil in the navigators mind the ability to consider all options to ensure the ship's safety. With regard to plotting, as the example did not require a minimum distance for passing, a single action has been used for all vessels. The course alteration has been worked out mentally just by observation of the targets and the threat they pose. This is a skill that the navigator should develop with knowledge and experience.

The working for O1 points for "A" and "B" have not been shown in order to keep the plot clear, although the new relative approach lines have been plotted. This is due to prioritising the other three targets for tracking, as they pose the main threat. Exam solutions would require all the workings to be shown.

Example 6.9
While making landfall, the observing ship encounters restricted visibility and is proceeding on a course of 060°T at 10 knots. Several targets are observed and tracked on radar from 0612 to 0630 (OA lines provided). Target "D" is a small island.

- *Analyse the situation as it exists at 0630 and determine the set and drift*
- *assuming that any alteration is instantaneously effective, determine the course of action at 0639 ensuring that none of the targets has a CPA of less than 1´.5*
- *determine the new CPA of "D" once action has been taken*
- *comment on the situation after 0639 and suggest further action if any is required with reasons.*

Solution and Comments
The 'OAW' triangles should be completed and 'OA' lines extended to the CPA to analyse the situation at 0630. In addition to collision avoidance, general navigational safety must also be considered as the ship is in vicinity of the coast and is being set towards it.

From analysis of the reasons listed on the plot, the observing ship should stop engines at 0639 in order to pass all targets at more than 1´.5.m. After stopping, "D" would have a CPA of 2´.8, BCPA 095°T, TCPA in 114 minutes at 0824.

After stopping, monitoring should continue. When "B" is forward of the beam, after 0651, resume speed. At this stage, "A" will cross 2´ ahead, "B" will continue well clear, "C" will converge and pass ahead at 2´.5 after 29 minutes at 0720.

Report	"A"	"B"	"C"	"D"
Bearing	125°T steady	212°T closing	034°T closing	042°T opening
Range	8´.2 decreasing	4´.6 decreasing	3´.5 decreasing	6´.7 decreasing
CPA	0´.0	1´.3	0´.2	1´.0
BCPA	125°T	139°T	120°T	321°T
TCPA	53 m, at 0723	32 m, at 0702	57 m, at 0727	35 m, at 0705
Course	005°.5T	053°T	075°T	Set 005°T
Speed	10.4 Kts	18.3 Kts	7.1 Kts	Rate 2.2 Kts
Aspect	R 60°.5	R 19°	G 139°	Drift 0´.7
Remarks	Crossing	Overtaking & converging	Being overtaken	Vessel setting towards land

Whereas "D" will pass at 0´.7 only. In order to increase the distance from the island "D", the observing ship should alter course to starboard by approximately 40°. For clarity, the section around "C" and "D" has been enlarged and can be seen in Figure 6.16 has been blown up below.

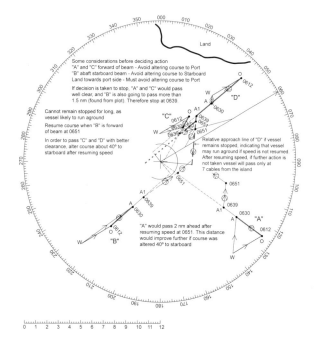

Figure 6.15   Plot for example 6.9

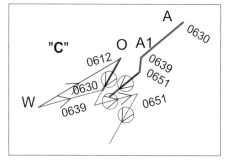

Figure 6.16   Second plot for example 6.9

6.3.1 Use of Trial Manoeuvre

When using ARPA, the change of course or speed required for passing other ships safely can be determined by using the trial manoeuvre function. Different makes of ARPA may show the results in different styles. The inputs required are:

- Planned course change (xx° port or starboard)
- planned speed change
- time delay (time after which action would be taken).

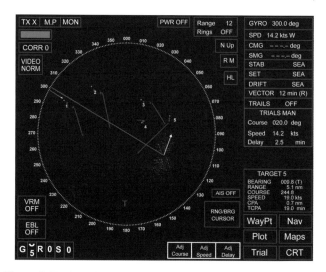

Figure 6.17   Use of trial manoeuvre

While the ARPA is displaying trial manoeuvre results, the letter "T" or word "TRIAL" would be visible on the PPI, indicating to the navigator that this is not reality. On most units, the trial manoeuvre function can be turned on and off. On others, the trial manoeuvre can only be turned off at the end of the time delay. The Required course alteration could be determined for a single ship using EBL on ARPAs with PAD (predicted area of danger). The EBL should be aligned with the desired edge of the PAD for the side to pass. The true bearing obtained gives the course required for passing the other ship at the desired safe distance, ie CPA. The size of PAD can be increased or decreased with the CPA selection. The edges of a PAD indicate the CPA selected.

6.4 Common Plotting Errors and Penalties (UK Examining Board)

During the UK Exams, main errors in initial plotting of target echoes and/or the incorrect plotting of the initial course and distance run of 'own vessel', making the target vessel's initial courses and speed wrong, are treated as serious errors in principle (P) – 50% of the marks are deducted

The following are clerical errors (C) – 10% of the marks are deducted:

- Times not given on target echoes positions
- recognised arrows not used on vector triangle
- recognised lettering not used on vector triangle.

The above are very minor omissions but are costly during exams. Minor errors in calculation may also be treated as C.

The following are clerical/principle errors (CP) – 30% of the marks are deducted:

- Wrong use of scale, especially when attempting to enlarge the area of plot
- using both sides of the plotting sheet with an incorrect scale.

The following may be marked as CP or P depending on the plotting approach demonstrated and how serious the resulting error is:

- Joining individual echoes of a target clearly on a steady course, which gives small alterations of course for the target
- unity or imprecise drawing
- not showing recognised construction for predicted alterations of course/speed of own vessel
- not showing recognised construction for alterations of course/speed of target vessel(s).

Errors that indicate a lack of understanding may be treated more seriously.

6.5 Use for Navigation

Radar is a very effective aid to navigation as it provides the range and bearings of objects detected within the range scale. Apart from plotting position, it can be effectively used to continuously monitor the ship's progress in coastal waters.

6.5.1 Parallel Indexing

As a ship moves on its intended track, fixed objects in the vicinity will appear to be moving in the reciprocal direction of its motion (ground track). This technique provides the radar observer with real-time, instant information on the ship's lateral position, relative to the planned track. The information is essential in restricted waters where there is a lot of traffic congestion, as frequent course changes that need to be made can only be done if the ship is operating within its planned margins of safety. For these reasons it is particularly useful during restricted visibility. Provided that the passage plan has been prepared diligently, parallel indexing provides confidence to the bridge team about the ship's continued progress in safe waters. There are at least two methods that can be used for PI.

6.5.1.1 "Cross Index Range" (CIR) Method – Straight Index Line

This is based on the lateral distance of the planned track from a selected object. It can be employed at all times when using PI. Having identified all of the hazards, marked the limiting danger lines and tracks, a suitable charted object should be selected. A line parallel to the planned track should be drawn on the inner edge of the selected object and not through it. Maximum "margins of safety" (MOS) should be marked either side, or the side with off-lying dangers. Perpendicular distance should be measured from the track to this line. This distance is the CIR. Distances should also be measured for the MOS.

In Figure 6.18, CIR is 4′.0, MOS port 2′.0 and MOS starboard 3′.0 from track. MOS port is 2′.0 (4 – 2) and MOS starboard is 7′.0 (3 + 4) from the Index line. The MOS port distance is treated as the "not less than" (NLT) distance from the danger and MOS starboard as the "not more than" (NMT) distance from the index line.

The three lines should be marked on the radar screen as index line and MOS lines, either electronically or on the plotter using VRM and cursor. Most modern radars can produce index lines directly without using VRM. To proceed safely, the selected object should remain on the track index line and never outside the NLT and NMT lines. VRM can also be set to monitor. This method can also be used for course alterations. The CIR for the present and next track should be measured off of a selected object. It is preferable to use a single object in this case. The index lines and, if required, the MOS lines, should be marked.

For wheel over, measure the perpendicular distance between the wheel over mark and the next track (025°T) index (2′.0). Mark this on the radar. When the

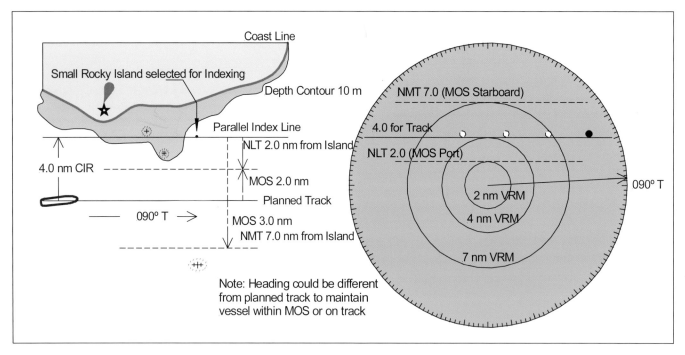

Figure 6.18 Planning for PI

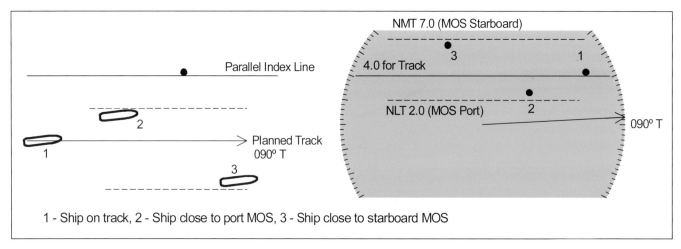

1 - Ship on track, 2 - Ship close to port MOS, 3 - Ship close to starboard MOS

Figure 6.19 3 Positions of ship and relative radar

echo of the selected object reaches the wheel over index, point "1", the planned helm should be applied. On completion of the turn, the ship would be on the planned track, with the echo on the next track index (point "2").

6.5.1.2 Bearing and Range Method – Straight Index Lines

Figure 6.21 illustrates the 'bearing and range method' being used. The "bearing and range" from the way point and the wheel over mark should be determined.

The bearing and range from the way point should be marked on the radar display in reverse. From this

point, "2", the index lines for the 090°T track and the reciprocal of 025°T should be marked. Initially, the echo of the selected object would be on the 090° index. As it reaches point "1", planned helm should be applied and the echo would steady up on the 025° index line once the ship has steadied on the new heading. Course corrections may be required to maintain track.

6.5.1.3 Bearing and Range Method – Curved Index Lines

Turns within narrow or congested waters are critical and require good monitoring, which can also be achieved through PI techniques. This can be performed in two

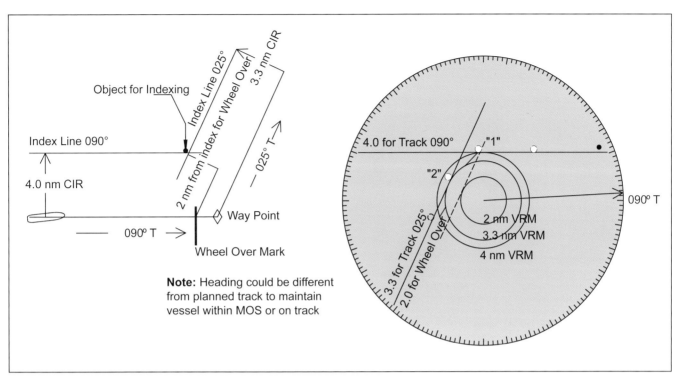

Figure 6.20 Planning for course alteration

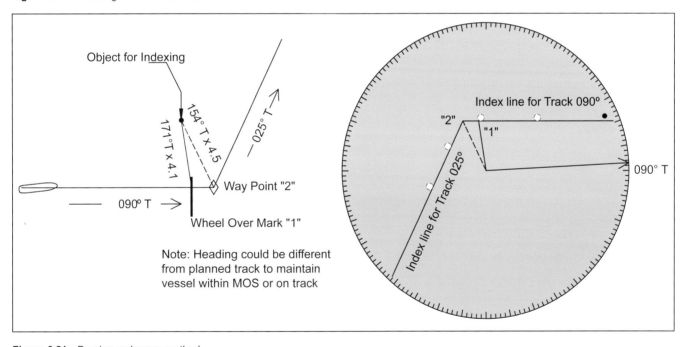

Figure 6.21 Bearing and range method

ways. Where it is just an alteration between two tracks, as seen in Figure 6.22, the curve can be plotted first on the chart, using the manoeuvring information on the turning circles of the ship. A suitable object on the inside of the curve should be selected and ranges and bearings for different changes of heading from this object should be plotted. This information can then be transferred to the radar.

This method of planning can be used to decide if the ship can make the turn without, for example, the assistance of tug(s).

Alternatively, the ship may be navigating through a narrow channel, making frequent course changes and executing curves of differing curvature, using different helm, shown in Figure 6.23. In these cases, the intended position of the ship within the channel should be marked, which depending on the channel, may take the form of a curve. On this curve, points at about 1 to 3 cables should be selected. Bearings and ranges of these points from an object conveniently fixed for indexing should be measured for transfer to radar. This object should be on or close to the centre of curvature of the curve. A table can be prepared listing the range and bearing of the selected object, along with the helm and engine orders that are planned to execute the manoeuvre.

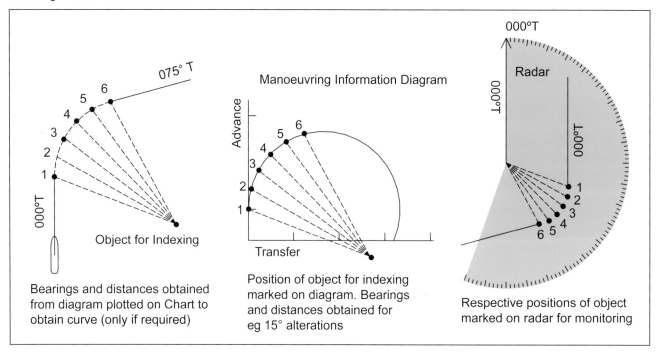

Bearings and distances obtained from diagram plotted on Chart to obtain curve (only if required)

Position of object for indexing marked on diagram. Bearings and distances obtained for eg 15° alterations

Respective positions of object marked on radar for monitoring

Figure 6.22 Planning and monitoring during course alteration

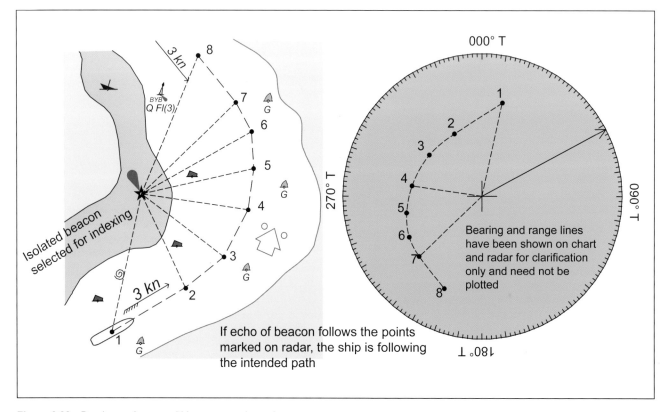

If echo of beacon follows the points marked on radar, the ship is following the intended path

Bearing and range lines have been shown on chart and radar for clarification only and need not be plotted

Figure 6.23 Bearing and range within a narrow channel

6.5.1.4 Zero CIR – Narrow Channel Technique

This method makes use of ground stabilised input and relative vectors, and is used in areas where channels are well marked with beacons or buoys. A single line parallel to the track of the ship is drawn or marked on the radar, through the point of origin, to act as the intended ground track of the ship. Relative vectors or trails should be selected to detect the cross track tendency. As long as the relative vectors or trails are parallel to the index line, the ships ground track will be in line with the intended track. The distance of channel markings can be determined from the origin, indicating the way the ship is setting. VRM can also be used to monitor distances from the channel markings. Actual headings may be different to make adjustments. VRM can also be used with the CIR method to check safe distances if the bridge team have decided not to use the NLT or NMT lines.

6.5.2 Use of Nav Lines

Most radar and ARPA units include the added functions of mapping and/or nav-lines. These functions can be used for channel keeping or track keeping within the margin of safety in congested waters. The maps or nav-lines can be created electronically. The operator selects a fixed object to ground reference the ARPA. The monitoring is performed and the bridge team can plan for any course correction or course change.

The object selected for reference should preferably, be an isolated fixed object, eg a very small island, a beacon in the water, etc. Where a selected object carries a RACON, it is possible that the ARPA might track the RACON signature of the reference target. If this happens, the nav-lines could move off the channel reference and the bridge team should choose a different navigational aid for reference and redraw the nav-lines.

On some units it is possible to fix the position of nav-lines with respect to the ship. These lines can then be used in a traditional parallel indexing manner.

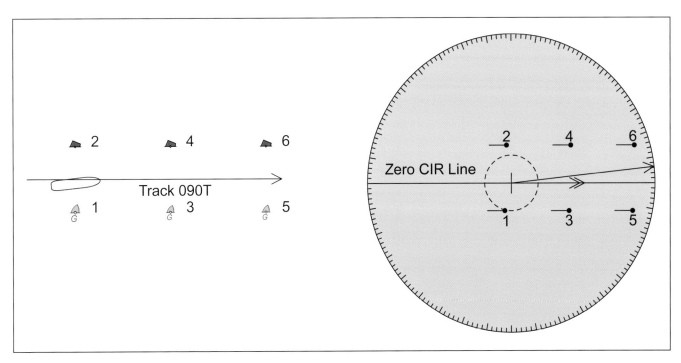

Figure 6.24   Zero CIR within a narrow channel

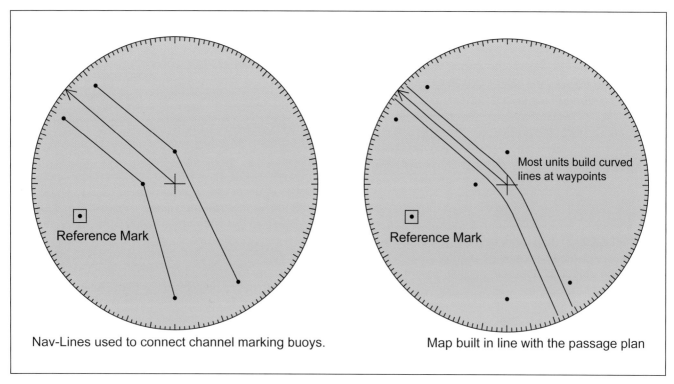

Figure 6.25   Use of nav-lines and mapping

6.5.3 Precautions With Parallel Indexing

To effectively use parallel indexing to monitor the ship's progress, once a plan has been carefully prepared the following precautions must be observed:

- The radar should be set up properly, presenting a picture of good quality and displaying the required echoes effectively. Control settings should allow for the optimum picture
- suppressing controls, like rain and sea control, should be minimised and they should be turned off when not required. The time base must be accurately centred
- the radar should be checked for range, bearing, heading marker and picture rotate accuracy
- the compass error must be known and the heading marker carefully aligned
- the choice of navigational set up depends on the area of operation. North-up relative motion is preferable in coastal waters, whereas North-up true motion would be a good choice in narrow channel
- the selected object should produce a good radar echo. Preferred choices would be steep sided, radar conspicuous marks, eg headlands, isolated rocks, isolated beacons and navigational marks with RACON. Objects should be selected on both sides of the ship's track to minimise errors in range plotting, mark identification and radar linearity errors. Low lying objects and coast line should not

be used, eg sand dunes, tidal low coast lines, etc. Objects should be correctly identified
- the selected object should not be obscured from the radar scanner by the presence of other objects
- consideration should be given to the radar's blind and shadow sectors and the length of time the selected object is likely to remain within these sectors
- range scale is an important factor, particularly when it has to be changed. On older conventional radars with reflection plotters, any change of range scale during parallel indexing would create a major work load for the navigator. Most modern radars allow index lines to shift with a change of range scale. However, not all modern radars perform in such a way. Navigators need to know the limitations and peculiarities of their own radars. Check the VRM and range rings
- too many index lines clutter the display. At any given time, not more than two sets should be on the radar display, one currently in use and the other for immediate use after the present set
- parallel indexing does not relieve the navigator of the responsibility to plot positions at predetermined intervals.

6.5.4 Landfall

Radar should be used with caution when used for landfall. Under normal conditions, radar pulses travel in a straight line. This implies that the radar can detect objects far beyond its horizon, provided that the object is at an elevation that can be negotiated by the radar. The maximum range that radar can detect to will depend on the height of scanner and height of the object. The maximum range "R" can be determined by the following formula:

$R = 2.23 (\sqrt{h} + \sqrt{H})$ sea miles (where heights are in metres)
$R = 1.23 (\sqrt{h} + \sqrt{H})$ sea miles (where heights are in feet)

A ship fitted with a radar scanner 35 m above sea level can detect a 450 m high peak at a range of 60.5 miles. The formulae can be transposed to determine the height of the object "H" that can be detected at a given range.

$H = 0.201 (R - 2.23 \sqrt{h})^2$ (heights in metres)
$H = 0.661 (R - 1.23 \sqrt{h})^2$ (heights in feet)

In addition to using radar for planning distance, when coast or peaks are raised on the radar, the mariner should also work out the maximum distance where the lighthouse will be raised as well as the passing on contours of the sounding.

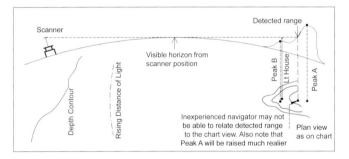

Figure 6.26 Visible radar horizon

If the height of a radar scanner is 35 m and it generates an echo at 44 miles, the height of the object generating the echo is 190.8 m. When plotting a fix at longer ranges using radar, the ranges are unlikely to cut at the actual position of the ship and give only a general indication of the area where the ship is. In such cases, radar bearings of any peaks that have been detected should also be plotted.

It is important to remember that radar will not necessarily detect an object with poor radar reflection properties even when it is within the detection range. Similarly, maximum detection range, in addition to heights, is dependent on the power and performance of the radar, reflective properties of the object, and the atmospheric and sea conditions.

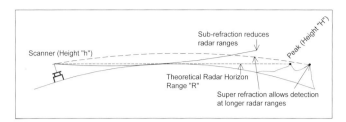

Figure 6.27 Theoretical radar horizon

6.5.5 Position Fixing

The best radar fix can be obtained through two or more ranges. Ranges ahead and astern should be measured first, followed by beam, as the distances ahead and astern will change more rapidly than those abeam. This keeps measurement time delay error to a minimum. Range should be measured from the near side of the displayed echo or RACON, ie the variable range marker VRM should not overlap the displayed echo. Other errors may be present in range.

These may be index errors, which can be caused by time delays or the radar set. If it is known, the range index error should be available to the navigator for application to the ranges measured. Some design factors like oscillator frequency, linearity in radar range rings and non-synchronisation between VRM and fixed rings cause errors in older designs. Range setting should be optimum, eg the range of an object at 2´.5 should be measured at 3´ scale and not 6´. Reflecting the properties of different objects and the height of tide may cause errors in range.

Bearing accuracy on radar is affected by horizontal beam width, using a longer scale than necessary, heading marker errors, alignment of radar antenna, antenna motor, gyro or transmitting compass error and squint, which is experienced in scanners fed from the end, the error occurs due to the change in frequency of oscillator.

Older radars may have centring and parallax errors associated with the cursor. Bearings should be taken through the middle of an isolated object, as well as RACON, to eliminate beam width error. When taking the bearing of a headland, it should be from the edge and a half beam-width should be applied.

6.6 Radar Detection and Interpretation

The ability of navigators to interpret the displayed picture on a radar depends on their understanding of the characteristics of radar propagation, the capabilities of the radar, the reflecting properties of different radar targets, and the navigator's ability to analyse the chart and compare the displayed picture to it.

6.6.1 Characteristics of Propagation

The pulses of energy that form the radar beam will be displayed as lobe-shaped patterns of radiation. The energy is concentrated along the axis of the beam. To enhance detection and improve accuracy, the radar beam has specified horizontal and vertical beam widths, these are referenced to arbitrary selected power limits.

The main lobe of the radar beam is composed of several separate lobes. As the wave passes an obstruction, it experiences bending. This is called diffraction and slightly illuminate will the region behind an obstruction or target. The radar beam of lower frequency radar will usually illuminate more of the shadow region behind an obstruction than a radar of a higher frequency.

Radar beam energy also experiences absorption and scattering as it passes through the atmosphere. This phenomenon is called attenuation, it causes a decrease in echo strength. It is greater at higher frequencies.

Radio/radar waves usually travel in line of sight. This implies that the detection range of radar is dependent on power output and height ($r = 2.23\sqrt{h}$ [m]). Atmospheric density gradients bend radar rays as they travel to and from a target. This is called 'refraction' and it has an effect on detection range.

Super-refraction is a phenomenon where rays are bent downwards more than normal, causing longer radar ranges. It occurs when air, having flown over a warm land mass, moves over a relatively cold sea. This mainly happens in temperate and tropical zones. A moderate degree of super-refraction is present over the sea.

Sub-refraction is a phenomenon where the radar radiation does not bend down sufficiently, or will even bend upwards, causing shorter radar ranges. It may occur at high latitudes when a cold air mass flows over a warmer surface, eg wind blowing over open water after having passed over ice. Detection ranges may be reduced to the point where at times contacts visible to the eye are not displayed on the radar.

6.6.2 Reflective Properties

The reflected radar pulses will depend on how many pulses are absorbed by the substance that they strike on. Common substances, in descending order of reflection are metal, stone, water, clay, wood or vegetation (trees).

The shape and aspect of the object are also important. Figure 6.28 illustrates the basics of reflection from various surfaces and different aspects. Size is also an influencing factor, a larger ship produces a stronger echo than a small one at the same distance.

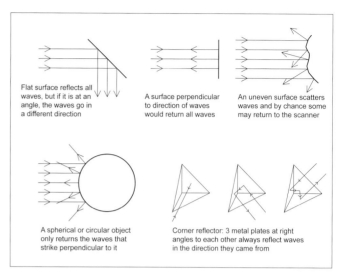

Figure 6.28   Reflective properties

6.6.3 Interpretation

Landmasses are generally recognisable by the steady brilliance of the relatively large areas displayed on the radar screen. Land generally matches the chart at a smaller scale, but all the features may not be easily recognisable. There may be some distortion due to beam width and pulse length. The following points need to be considered for the respective features:

- Lagoons and inland lakes would usually appear as blank areas
- long chains of islands or coral atolls may produce long lines of echoes, especially when the radar beam is perpendicular to the line of islands
- low islands usually produce small echoes
- land rising in a gradual manner produces a steadily glowing area on the display
- small hills and valleys produce patchy signals (radar shadow effects)
- smooth clear beaches and sand pits do not normally appear on the display beyond 2 miles approximately
- sand dunes covered with vegetation, that are far back on a low smooth beach, produce an apparent line on the display that matches the dunes rather than the actual shore line
- marshes and mud flats reflect radar pulses a little better than a sand pit. Weak echoes produced during low tide disappear at high tide
- some sizable features of landmass may be obscured due to other features blocking the pulses (radar shadow)
- objects close to the shore may merge with the picture of shore line (due to pulse length)

- land appears to be spread in bearing (due to beam width)
- one or more rocks above the surface or waves breaking over reefs may appear on the display.

6.6.4 Icebergs and Ice Fields

The absence of any returns from ice on the display does not mean there is no ice. Echoes produced depend on the inclination of the reflecting surface, the size and range. In calm seas, all sorts should be detected. Growlers may appear at a few miles in calm conditions, but may remain unnoticed with any sea running.

Clutter will suppress small ice fragments. Depending on the size, icebergs can be detected conveniently at: 4 to 15 miles for bergybits, 10 to 40 miles for medium sized icebergs and 14 to 48 miles for large icebergs.

Concentrated hummocked ice can be detected at approximately 3 miles. Smooth ice fields may be distinguished from the open sea when some sea is running, as they do not produce any return, as opposed to when the sea is running due to wind.

Ridges will show clearly and shadow areas behind ridges can be mistaken for open water. Large floes in the midst of brash ice will show on radar. A lead through static ice will not show unless it is at least 0.25 miles wide.

Areas of open water and smooth floes will look very similar. In ice, the filed edge of a smooth floe is prominent, which is not the case for open water.

6.6.5 Unwanted Echoes

In order to avoid confusion and unnecessary alterations, the navigator should be able to recognise the various unwanted echoes that may appear on the radar display.

6.6.5.1 Indirect Echoes

Indirect echoes are caused by a reflection of the main lobe of a radar beam from a part of the ship's structure, eg the funnel or masts. When it occurs, the echo returns from an actual target through the indirect radar wave path.

The main characteristics that identify indirect echoes are as follows:

- Indirect echoes appear on the same range as direct echoes
- indirect echoes usually occur in shadow sectors
- indirect echoes appear on substantially constant bearing, even when the true bearing of the target changes significantly
- the shapes of indirect echoes may indicate they are not direct. Movement of indirect echoes are usually abnormal.

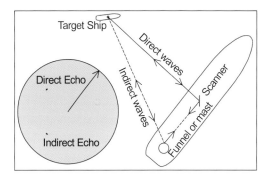

Figure 6.29   Indirect echo

6.6.5.2 Side-lobe Effects

A series of echoes are produced on each side of the main lobe echo at the same range as the latter, in semicircles or even full circles. This effect only occurs at shorter ranges, due to the low energy of side lobes, and can be eliminated or minimised by gain or anti-clutter controls. Slotted wave guide arrays have largely eliminated such problems.

6.6.5.3 Multiple Echoes

These may occur when a strong echo is received from another ship at close range, usually abeam, and is caused by waves bouncing between the observing and target ships. A second, third or more echoes may be observed on the radar display at double, triple or other multiples of the actual range of the radar contact.

6.6.5.4 Second Trace Echo

These are received from contacts at an actual range greater than the radar range setting. This type of echo

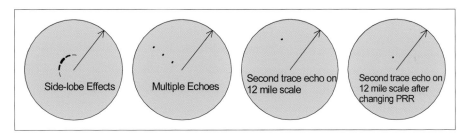

Figure 6.30   Multiple echoes

appears on the radar at the correct bearing, but not at the actual range, and is caused by the pulse arriving after the following pulse has been transmitted. These can be recognised by a change in position after a change of pulse repetition rate, a hazy, streaky or distorted shape or erratic movements on plotting. They occur in conditions of abnormal refraction, particularly super-refraction.

6.6.5.5 Interference and Spoking

Electronic interference occurs when another radar is operating in the area at the same frequency. Interference may appear as a large number of bright dots on the display, as curved dotted lines from the centre to the edge, or randomly scattered. They are distinguished easily as they do not appear in the same place during successive sweeps of the scanner. The effects are usually greater at longer radar range settings. Controls are available to suppress the interference.

Spoking appears as a number of radial lines or spokes. Lines are straight and may appear all around or in a confined sector. If in a sector, it can be distinguished from a Ramark signal of similar appearance through its steady relative bearing. Spoking is the result of a lack of maintenance or a need for adjustment.

6.6.5.6 Blind and Shadow Sectors

Parts of the ship's structure, eg funnels, masts and cranes, may reduce the intensity of the radar beam or block it completely. The blind sector will appear where the angle subtended at the antenna by the obstruction is more than a few degrees, whereas a shadow sector will appear where there is less reduction in the intensity of the radar beam beyond the obstruction. Within a shadow sector, while small targets at close range may not be detected, larger targets may be. Diagrams for blind and shadow sectors of each radar should be available on the bridge. The diagram can be prepared by swinging the ship in the vicinity of a small target, eg a buoy, at short range, and observing on radar.

6.6.5.7 Overhead Cables

The echo appears as a single echo at right angles to the cable and may sometimes be incorrectly identified as a ship on a steady bearing. Any avoiding action would result in the echo remaining on a steady bearing and moving to the same side of channel as the observing ship.

> *Author's Note:*
> *Radar is a continuously developing technology. Most modern radars have additional features to assist navigation. Data, eg maps and parallel indexing plans, can be stored for retrieval at the time of use and for future referencing. However, it is the knowledge of its basic principles, set up and the skilful interpretation of display, that makes it the valuable aid to navigation that it is meant to be.*

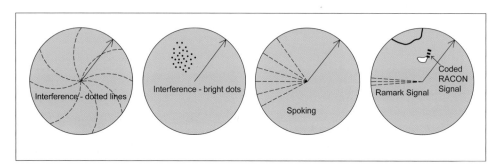

Figure 6.31   Interference and spoking

7

Extreme Weather and Navigation

Some areas or circumstances require special measures to be adopted for the ship's safe navigation. It is to be expected that a mariner will not always be warned about all hazards or dangers in good time. This chapter covers the aspects of navigation that are associated with such hazards.

7.1 Tropical Revolving Storms (TRS)

Figure 7.1 Satellite picture of a tropical revolving storm (TRS)

Unlike normal storms, a TRS is deceptively small in size and the weather experienced a few hundred miles from the centre may be beautiful. Because of this, the weather can deteriorate rapidly as the storm approaches. Without experiencing this type of storm, it is difficult to imagine the violence of a fully developed TRS.

With the increasing use of satellites for meteorological observations, the warnings about these storms location has improved significantly. However, the mariner must have a good understanding in order to properly read the signs of an approaching TRS, so that any changes can be monitored and to take avoiding action.

7.1.1 Description

7.1.1.1 Characteristics of a TRS

Tropical storms are intense depressions of approximately 500 miles in diameter that develop in tropical latitudes.

Due to the steep pressure gradient, very high and violent winds are caused, generating phenomenal seas that are usually high and confused.

Wind blows around the centre, in a spiral flow inwards going anticlockwise in the Northern hemisphere and clockwise in the Southern hemisphere. The TRS usually re-curves, as it reaches a maximum westerly longitude, making it different from an ordinary storm. The centre of the storm is called the eye, and is where the pressure is lowest. Typical wind forces associated with the storm, depending on the pressure, pressure gradient and diameter of the storm, are:

- 200-250 nm Force 6
- 100-200 miles Gale Force
- 80 miles Hurricane Force
- 5-50 miles Close to Eye, much higher 100 kn to 175 kn.

7.1.1.2 Categories of Storms

- Tropical depression winds of Force 7 or less
- tropical storm winds of Force 8 and 9
- severe tropical storm winds of Force 10 and 11
- TRS winds of Force 12 and above.

In the USA and other parts of the world, the Saffir-Simpson Scale is used to grade Hurricanes.

Strength	Wind Speed (Knots)	Pressure (hPa)
Category 1	64 – 82	> 980
Category 2	83 – 95	965 – 979
Category 3	96 – 113	945 – 964
Category 4	114 – 135	920 – 946
Category 5	> 135	< 919

Table 7.1 Saffir-simpson scale for hurricane classification

7.1.1.3 Areas of Formation

TRS predominantly form in six areas and are identified with different names:

- North Atlantic   Hurricane
- North Pacific (Eastern)   Hurricane

- North Pacific (Western) — Typhoon
- North Indian Ocean — Cyclonic Storm
- South Indian Ocean — Cyclone
- Southwest Pacific and Australian Areas — Cyclone

(In North and NW Australia there is a different version known as willy-willy or whirly-whirly).

TRS only develop over oceans and usually originate near the seasonal location of the ITCZ, usually between 5° – 15° N, in the early and late parts of the storm season, 10° and 25° N at the height of the season, and 5° – 18° S. TRS are most frequent in a hemisphere during the late summer and early autumn. However, in reality, no month is entirely safe and storms can occur at any time.

varies with the distance from the storm centre, the pressure gradient and the storm's rate of approach.

Dangerous semicircle: This lies on the side of the path towards the usual direction of re-curvature, ie to the right hand semicircle in the N and the left hand in the S. Away from the equator before re-curvature and towards the equator after recurvature.

Naming of Dangerous Semi-Circle: It is called 'dangerous' because:

- Wind will usually blow the ship forward of and towards the path of the storm
- re-curvature will decrease the distance from the centre
- isobars are likely to be tighter on this side causing stronger winds, the apparent wind will be more due to the storm's movement.

Area	Jan	Feb	Mar	Apr	May	Jun	Jul	Aug	Sep	Oct	Nov	Dec
N Atlantic					░	▓	▓	▓	▓	▓	▓	░
NE Pacific					▓	▓	▓	▓	▓	▓	░	
NW Pacific				░	▓	▓	▓	▓	▓	▓	▓	
Arabian Sea				▓	▓	▓				░	▓	▓ ░
Bay of Bengal			░	▓	▓	▓						
S Indian Ocean	▓	▓	▓	▓	░						░	▓
Australia W, NW, N, Q	▓	▓	▓	▓							░	▓
Oceania	▓	▓	▓	▓	░						░	▓

Greatest Activity ▓   Start/Finish of season ▓   Early/Late season ░

Table 7.2   Storm seasons

7.1.1.4 Definitions

Track is the line that the storm centre has already moved over. Path is the direction that the storm centre is moving in. The storm may continue on a straight line path, re-curve, or follow erratic movement and proceed in a loop. Vertex is the furthest westerly point reached by the storm centre. The storm generally re-curves at the vertex. Pressure continues to drop forward of the Trough line and increases behind it. The centre of a storm is called the eye and includes the eye wall and its associated phenomenon. Vortex is used to identify the central calm of the storm. The wind blows at an angle to the isobars, and is called the angle of in-draught, which

Dangerous quadrant: The advance quadrant of the dangerous semi-circle is known as the dangerous quadrant, as it lies ahead of the centre. The three reasons already listed for the dangerous semi-circle apply more strongly to this sector of the storm. In the dangerous quadrant, if the ship is lying towards the dangerous semi-circle and forward of the trough line, the natural movement of the storm will decrease the distance between the storm and ship, ie the storm will close in very rapidly with the normal movement of the storm.

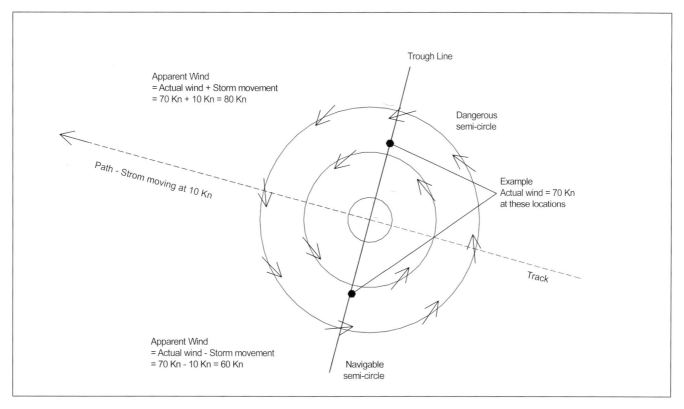

Figure 7.2   Apparent wind

Navigable semicircle: This lies on the left hand side of the path in the N and the right hand side in the S, towards the equator before re-curvature and away from the equator after re-curvature. A ship situated in this semi-circle will tend to be pushed behind the centre and the re-curvature of the storm will increase the distance from the centre. Apparent wind due to the storm moving will be less.

7.1.1.5 Movement

During the early stages the storm moves at about 10 knots and, as latitude increases it moves at about 15 knots. After re-curvature, the storm moves at 20 to 25 knots, attaining a speed of 40 knots in higher latitudes. Where the movement of storm is erratic, the speed of progress is seldom above 10 knots. In the northern hemisphere TRS move between 275° and 350°, when they re-curve at about 25° N and at 30° N they are moving NE. In the southern hemisphere they move between WSW and SSW, re-curve between 15° and 20° S and then follow a SE path. It is assumed that a storm will not generally travel towards the equator and if it is in a lower latitude than 20° the storm's path is unlikely to have an easterly component.

7.1.2 Shipboard Detection and Location of TRS

Early warning about the presence of a TRS is vital if appropriate action to ensure the ship's safety is to be taken. Detection and tracking is helped greatly by weather satellites and the reports sent by the authorities from ashore. Details are broadcast at frequent and regular intervals from weather centres. However, it is still very difficult to pinpoint their centre at all times and to predict their path. In order to decide an appropriate action, the mariner must have knowledge of the:

- Position or bearing of the storm centre
- path of the storm.

On board a ship, the mariner can detect the presence of a TRS and gain knowledge of its location and movement in several ways. These are categorised as:

- Visual observations
- instrument observations
- reports.

7.1.2.1 Precursory Signs

When a mariner is in or around an area where storms are likely, extra care should be taken. The weather should be observed all the time and an hourly log made of the observations. Weather reports and forecasts should be obtained from several sources.

7.1.2.1.1 Visual Observations (Visible signs)

Swell: The first visible indicator in deep open waters is an exceptionally long swell approaching from the general direction of the storm's point of origin. The swell moves at a reasonably high speed and may be detected at a distance of up to a thousand miles. The swell will be apparent before the barometer begins to fall. The direction of the swell may change in shallow waters. The direction that the swell approaches from is the historical direction of the storm, as the storm will have moved on in the time it has taken the swell to get to the observers position, however the difference in direction is small.

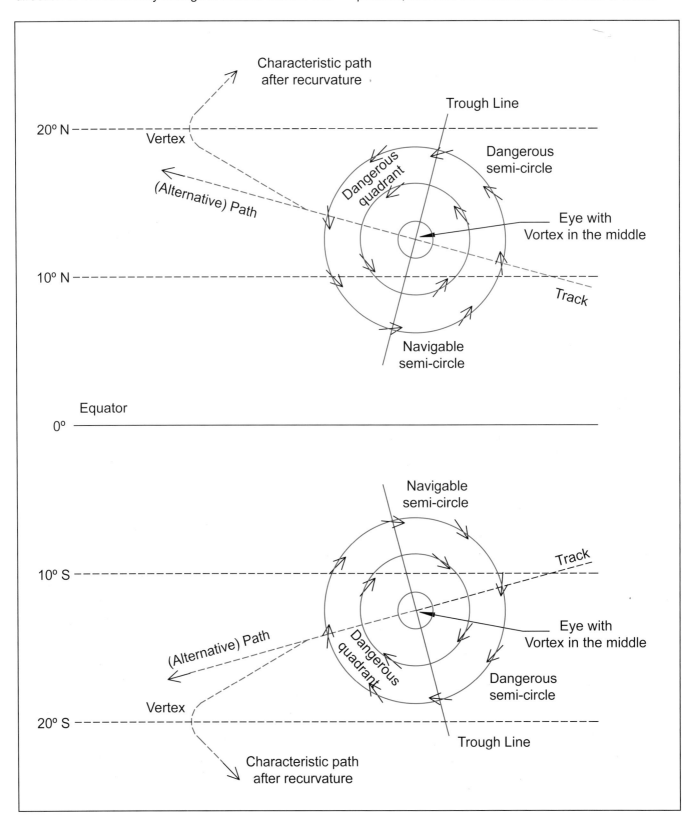

Figure 7.3 Elements and Paths of a TRS

Wind: This is the next sign. In areas where a TRS develops, the trade wind pattern is the predominant wind pattern. The presence of a TRS in a region changes the wind, its force and direction will be different to the predominant trade wind in the region.

Clouds: A large number of cirrus clouds followed by altostratus and broken cumulus or scud may indicate that a storm is approaching. The point where cirrus clouds converge, when they first appear, indicates the direction of the storm centre. If this point remains steady, the storm is approaching the observer's position. However, if this point shifts slowly in any direction, it indicates that the storm will pass to that side of the observer. The storm is mainly formed of a dark mass of cumulonimbus (Cb) clouds. The centre of this mass indicates the storm's direction. When the dense low clouds are overhead, their movement can provide an indication of the storm centre. The clouds move along the isobars and the centre is 90° to the direction that the clouds are moving in.

7.1.2.1.2 Instrument Observations

Pressure: All readings should be corrected for instrument/index error, height, latitude, temperature and diurnal variation. Readings must be taken and recorded every hour. The following apply in all cases:

- Corrected barometer reading 3 mb/hPa or more below the mean for the time of the year – suspicion is aroused
- corrected barometer reading 5 mb/hPa or more below the mean for the time of the year – little doubt about the existence of a storm in the vicinity
- in both the above cases diurnal variation will be masked to a degree but will still be evident
- cessation in diurnal variation, as if the barometer was malfunctioning, will occur when the pressure falls 10 hPa below average
- a change of pressure also indicates the ship's location relative to the storm. If the pressure is falling, the ship is forward of the trough line or is closing in towards the storm, if it is increasing, the ship is abaft the trough line or moving away from the storm.

Radar: Radar that are able to operate at long range, eg 96 nm or 120 nm, may display exactly where the eye of the storm is. As there is a lot of rain within these distances from the centre of the storm, the observation of individual echo returns, moving tangentially around the eye, can be spotted. If the position of the eye of the storm can be seen on the radar, the storm is already very close and the mariner should have already observed other signs of the storm.

7.1.2.2 Reports and Warnings (see Chapter 11)

The radio, NAVTEX, SafetyNET and facsimile messages provide reports about the location and movement of storms. The reports are based on the most up to date information available to the meteorological service who have produced the report. Compulsory reports are made by Masters of ships that encounter a TRS. It is important to note that any change since receiving such information should not be considered as part of the reports available to the mariner. It is more important for the mariner to make on board observations concerning knowledge of the location and movement of the storm.

7.1.3 Actions on Board Vessel

7.1.3.1 Prior to Detection

Vessels transiting or trading in areas prone to TRS activity, particularly during the TRS season, should establish routines for obtaining regular weather reports and facsimile charts. The OOW should note and record the weather every hour, particularly the pressure. The passage plans should allow for contingency actions and alternative routes at various stages to avoid storms, depending on where they develop. A risk assessment should be carried out and recorded as part of planning.

Before departing from any port within or transiting TRS prone areas, the Master should ensure that the ship is well supplied as delays may be likely if a TRS is encountered. Procedures from the company SMS, flag state and SOLAS must be followed. Weather reports should also be obtained while the vessel is in port.

7.1.3.2 Storm Detected/Reported

The first priority for any Master is the safety of own vessel. Before taking any decisions, the Master should establish:

- Position or bearing of the storm
- location of the ship relative to the storm (semi-circle)
- movement of the storm
- sea room available and the proximity to hazards.

'Buys Ballots' law can be used to determine the bearing of the storm centre. Wind generally blows in line with the isobars and has an angle of in-draught. The centre of the storm will be from 100° to 125° to the right of an observer facing the wind in the north, left if in the south, when the storm is approximately 200 miles away. As a rule, the closer an observer is to the centre the angle of approach will near 90°, especially forward of the storm. The angle varies with the pressure gradient, the rate of progress of the storm and whether the observer is ahead or abaft the storm. The wind direction during

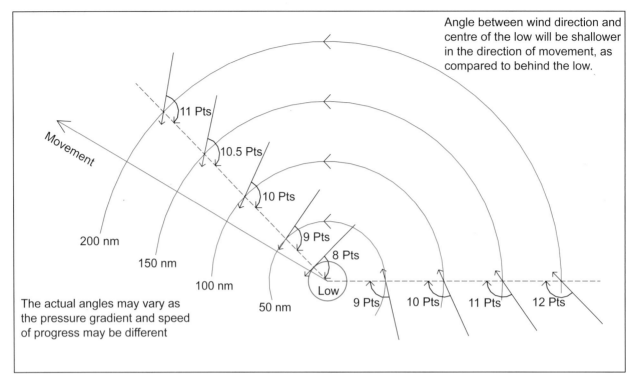

Figure 7.4 Approximate Relationship of Wind Direction and Storm Centre in N Hemisphere

a squall should not be used for this purpose. In the southern hemisphere, left is used instead of right.

The distance from the storm centre can be estimated by referring to the wind force being experienced at the point of observation. This information, coupled with two bearings taken 2-3 hours apart, should help to estimate the storm's path. Allowance should be made for the ship moving between observations. The wind changing direction is an indicator of the ship's location relative to the storm centre and movement.

Wind Shift	Veering	Steady	Backing
Northern Hemisphere	Dangerous semi-circle	Path of the storm	Navigable semi-circle
Southern Hemisphere	Navigable semi-circle	Path of the storm	Dangerous semi-circle

Table 7.3 Wind shift and ship location relative to TRS centre

Bearing of swell direction should also be used to determine the storm bearing. Wind shift will indicate to the mariner the ship's location in relation to the storm. A change of pressure indicates whether the ship is forward or aft of trough line.

An approximate indication of the storm's path can be obtained by taking another bearing 2-3 hours after the first observation, an allowance for the ship's movement during this time should be made. The speed the wind shifts at indicates how close or further away the mariner is from the path of the storm. If the wind is veering or backing slowly, the ship is close to the path of the storm, if the wind is veering or backing significantly, the ship is clear of the storm's path. Latitude should also be considered to determine if storm is moving westward or has recurved (or started to recurve) N–NE, or S–SE.

If a ship in the northern hemisphere at 15° N observes force 6 wind from NNE which is veering slowly, with a falling barometer, swell from SE, the centre of the storm would be between 'SE by E' and 'SE by S' at about 200 – 250 nm. As the pressure is falling, the ship is forward of the trough line.

It is important to remember that storms can be located in any direction during the season in the area of occurrence, and may be encountered during or after re-curvature. In Figures 7.6 and 7.7, latitude and wind shift are used to illustrate different scenarios.

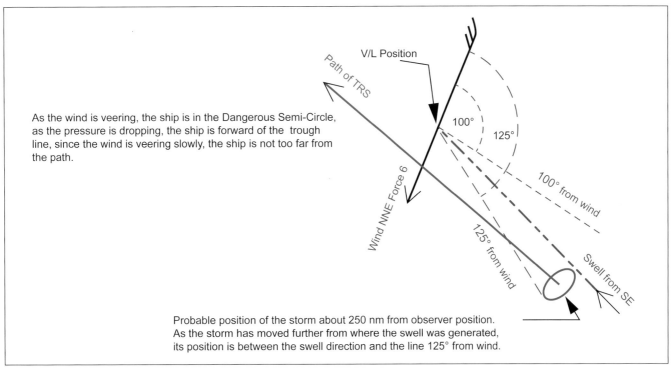

As the wind is veering, the ship is in the Dangerous Semi-Circle, as the pressure is dropping, the ship is forward of the trough line, since the wind is veering slowly, the ship is not too far from the path.

Probable position of the storm about 250 nm from observer position. As the storm has moved further from where the swell was generated, its position is between the swell direction and the line 125° from wind.

Figure 7.5   Location and path of storm based on wind direction, swell and wind shift

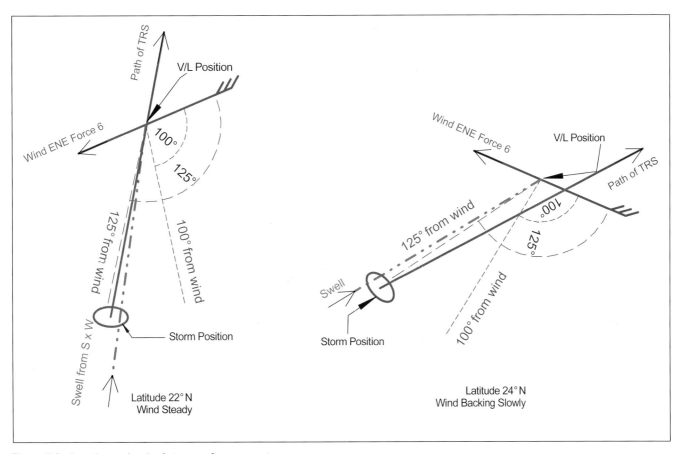

Figure 7.6   Location and path of storm – after re-curvature

The safety and security of the ship should be ensured along with a good check on stability. The Master should make an 'Obligatory' report. If a TRS is suspected nearby, SOLAS requires the Master to report the following, by all available means, to other ships in the vicinity and the nearest coast station:

- Position of the storm with the UTC and date
- position, true course and speed of the ship
- true barometric pressure
- pressure change in the previous 3 hours
- direction and force of the wind
- state of the sea
- height and direction of swell.

A report should be sent to the owners, charterers and agents.

A bridge routine should be established during TRS encounters, as per the SMS procedures and contingency plans. An hourly log of the weather should be maintained, along with any observation notes about the TRS. Up to date weather information should be obtained regularly. The position of the storm and its projected movement should be plotted on the chart, as follows:

- A circle equal to the storm radius should be constructed, centred at the storm's position
- tangents at 40° to the forecast path should be constructed either side of the storm
- 12 or 24 hours × speed of the storm provides the imminent danger area segment
- 24 or 48 hours × speed of the storm provides the probable danger area segment
- 12 and 24 hours if the storm is moving rapidly, 24 and 48 hours for slow moving storms.

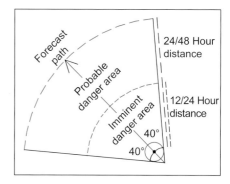

Figure 7.8 Plotting TRS and danger areas

Where, through basic observations, it is not possible to ascertain the position of the storm and the ship's location in relation to it, the ship should "heave to" either stopped, or at steerage way with wind on the bow.

7.1.4 Avoiding Actions

Every situation must be resolved on an individual basis, taking into account the relevant facts. However, if the recommendations are followed, the ship's safety can always be ensured. The risk assessment should involve a review of the hazards, the precautions to be taken and the advantages of any action when compared to its alternatives.

Attempts should be made to keep the ship in open waters with plenty of sea room in order to take avoiding action and, where practicable, the ship should never be taken into waters with restricted sea room. If a storm is moving slowly, a ship can easily outpace it if it is ahead of it and overtake if behind. Faster ships can overtake a TRS when it is moving at normal speeds in tropical

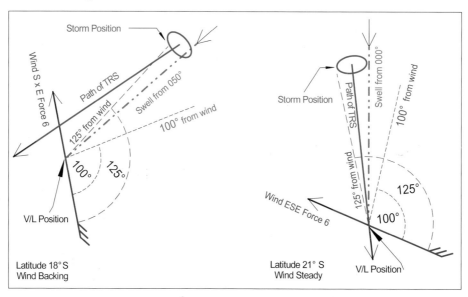

Figure 7.7 Location and path of storm – southern hemisphere

latitudes. In likely areas, frequent barometer readings should be made and recorded. If it is definite that the ship is behind the storm, or even in the navigable semi-circle, it will be enough to alter the course away from the centre, keeping in mind the tendency of a TRS to curve N and NE in the northern hemisphere and S and SE in the southern hemisphere.

Considering the available information and its analysis, the course of action should be decided. Three general principles apply:

1   A ship can pass the storm from any direction if it is able to pass at a distance of over 300 nm
2   An attempt should be made to remain outside a distance of 250 nm from the storm centre. When the ship is already at a safe distance from the storm, the course to steer can be determined by plotting and should be based on an analysis of the situation and risk assessment. In this case, the ship should keep clear of the imminent area of danger and try best to avoid the probable area of danger.
3   If it is not possible to pass at a distance of more than 250 nm, the actions recommended in The Mariners Handbook and outlined below should be followed, every effort should be made to pass the storm at a minimum distance of 80 nm.

7.1.4.1 At Sea – Unable to pass at over 250 nm

In the Northern hemisphere:

The veering wind indicates that the ship is in the dangerous semi-circle. The ship should adjust course and proceed at all available speed, with wind 10° to 45° on the starboard bow depending on that speed. As the wind veers, the ship should alter course to starboard

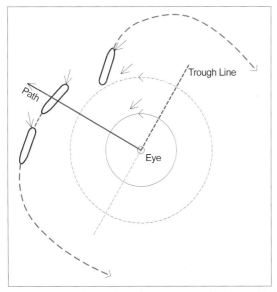

Figure 7.9   Diagrammatic effect of actions to avoid a storm in N hemisphere

and get behind the storm. Backing wind indicates that the ship is in the navigable semi-circle. The ship should bring wind on to the starboard quarter and proceed with all available speed, turning to port as the wind backs.

A steady or nearly steady wind direction indicates that the vessel is either in, or very nearly in, the path of the storm. She should bring the wind well on to the starboard quarter and proceed with all available speed. When well within the navigable semicircle, keep the wind on the starboard quarter and proceed with all available speed, turning to port as the wind backs.

With the wind on the bow the ship will roll and pitch.

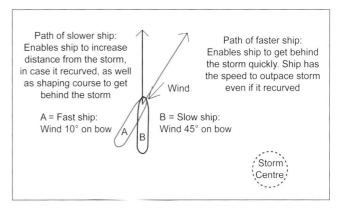

Figure 7.10   Speed of ship and positioning of wind on the bow

In certain situations, when a ship takes action as if it were in a dangerous quadrant and then experiences a wind shift indicating that the storm has recurved, the ship's course must be adjusted in line with the action required if the ship was in a navigable semi-circle. It must be noted that significant dangers will be experienced by the ship when altering course so that the wind is on the quarter from the bow. It is likely that the ship would make the turn with the wind moving from bow-beam-quarter. This is a dangerous manoeuvre in extreme conditions, the ship risks heavy rolling while passing the wind on the beam.

In every case, the ship should continue to observe the wind shift. This allows the mariner to assess whether the storm is continuing on its original path or has started to recurve. For example, if a ship takes action to avoid the storm, eg in a Dangerous Semi-circle, observes the wind and determines that it has steadied up, it means that the storm has been recurving and currently the ship is on the storm's path. If the wind then starts to back (northern hemisphere) or veer (southern hemisphere), the vessel is located in the Navigable Semi-circle and the storm has fully recurved. In these situations when a ship finds itself on path of the storm or in the Navigable Semi-circle, the ship should take appropriate action with the wind on the respective quarter.

		Dangerous semi-circle	On path, or nearly in the path of the storm	Navigable semi-circle
North	Observation	Wind veering	Wind steady	Wind backing
	Action	Wind 10°-45° on starboard bow, depending on speed of the ship. Proceed with all speed, observe the wind, as the wind veers alter course to starboard and shape a course to proceed behind the storm	Wind well on starboard quarter and proceed with all available speed towards the navigable semi-circle	Wind on starboard quarter, with all available speed. Alter course to port as wind backs
South	Observation	Wind backing	Wind steady	Wind veering
	Action	Wind 10°-45° on port bow, depending on the speed of the ship. Proceed with all speed, observe the wind, as the wind backs alter course to port and shape a course to proceed behind the storm	Wind well on port quarter and proceed with all available speed towards navigable semi-circle	Wind on port quarter, with all available speed. Alter course to starboard as wind veers
		Dropping pressure or wind increase (freshening) indicates that the ship is forward of the trough line		

Table 7.4   Summary of observations and actions to avoid a TRS

7.1.4.2 At Sea – Able to pass over 250 nm

Example 7.1

A TRS is moving at 305° T at 16 knots and is estimated to be 160°T at 200′ from a ship with a speed of 10 knots in the present conditions. Find:

- The course to steer to pass at maximum distance from the storm centre

- the minimum distance that the ship will pass the storm on this course.

Solution and Comments

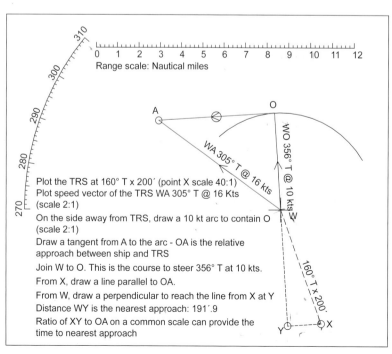

Plot the TRS at 160° T x 200′ (point X scale 40:1)
Plot speed vector of the TRS WA 305° T @ 16 Kts (scale 2:1)
On the side away from TRS, draw a 10 kt arc to contain O (scale 2:1)
Draw a tangent from A to the arc - OA is the relative approach between ship and TRS
Join W to O. This is the course to steer 356° T at 10 kts.
From X, draw a line parallel to OA.
From W, draw a perpendicular to reach the line from X at Y
Distance WY is the nearest approach: 191′.9
Ratio of XY to OA on a common scale can provide the time to nearest approach

Figure 7.11   Plot for example 7.1

7.1.4.3 Proximity to Land

A ship may often be close to land and might need to transit a strait or channel when there is a storm. Common examples are Taiwan Strait, Philippines, Mozambique Channel, Caribbean Sea and waters to the North of Australia. For example, a ship that is to the north of Taiwan and is intending to transit the Taiwan Strait may have to deviate from the passage plan in order to avoid a TRS that is heading for the coast of China. The navigator must consider all the options before deciding on the most appropriate course of action. The safety of the ship and crew will take priority. The options should be plotted for reference and measurements.

Scenario 1: A ship in the Caribbean on a course of 112° T, receives a report of a Hurricane ESE of its present position, a storm is located south of the Dominican Republic moving in a WNW direction.

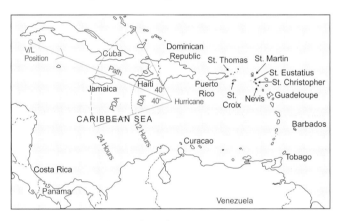

Figure 7.12   Scenario 1 – chart view

The ship is currently outside the storm field and the weather is what would normally be encountered in tropical waters at that time of year. There may also be a swell from the ESE.

As the storm approaches, the following changes can be expected, assuming that the ship does not take any action:

Wind: At present probably NE force 4 to 5
On entering the storm field, wind is likely to back towards N x W and then start to freshen
As the wind begins to increase, it will veer slowly and then steady up as the ship is in line with the path of the storm
At the end of 24 hours, the wind will be well above hurricane force from the NNE
If the ship enters the Eye of the Storm, there will be no wind there, however on re-passing the eye very strong winds from the opposite direction will be experienced

Pressure: Diurnal variation will be on a downward trend until the pressure is approximately 10 mb below the average for the time of year, eventually it will become completely masked when the ship is approximately 120 nm from the storm
The barometer will show a steady decline after seizure of diurnal variation
Afterwards the barometer will fall sharply

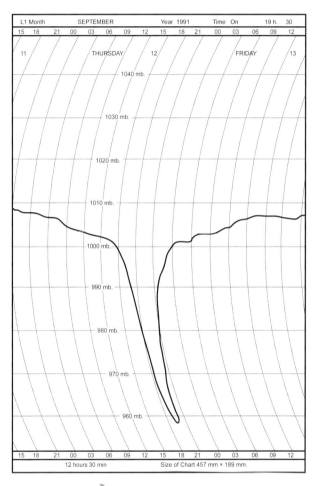

Figure 7.13   Barograph copy

Sea State: Initially waves will be small but they will build rapidly as the ship enters the storm and approaches the eye

Visibility: Initially this will be good but as the storm approaches the cloud layer will start to descend. As the ship moves into the rain bands surrounding the storm visibility will decrease rapidly. Once the wind is force 8 and above, sea spray will reduce visibility further.

Once it is known how the weather will change, the mariner must carry out a risk assessment based on several options. For example:

1 Vessel could slow down/heave-to and monitor the storm over the next few hours to see if the storm starts to recurve. If this happens, the ship will remain in the navigable semi-circle and can proceed on a reduced speed through the Caribbean until it is clear of the storm field. However, if the storm does not recurve, the ship will have lost valuable time and the storm will have closed in. This will put the ship in rough seas and the options for further action are limited with limited searoom.

2 The ship could turn to the south, proceed at full speed and make for the coast. The ship would still probably be in the storm field if the storm continues on its path. In addition, the ship may find itself within or close to shoals to the south. There is also a danger that the storm may start to move directly to the west and put the ship in danger. This may put the ship in a dangerous semi-circle if the storm starts to move directly west.

3 The ship may head in a WNW direction and make for open and deeper waters in the Gulf of Mexico and ride out the effects of the storm.

4 The ship could alter course towards N or NE and look for shelter or hurricane anchorage on the south coast of Cuba. However, if the storm keeps to its current path, the ship is very close to its path and would find itself in a dangerous situation even in a sheltered location.

The best solution is one that keeps the ship clear of the storm.

Scenario 2: A ship intends to pass through Taiwan Strait and is presently to NNE of the strait. A typhoon is reported to SW at about 500 nm, and is moving WNW.

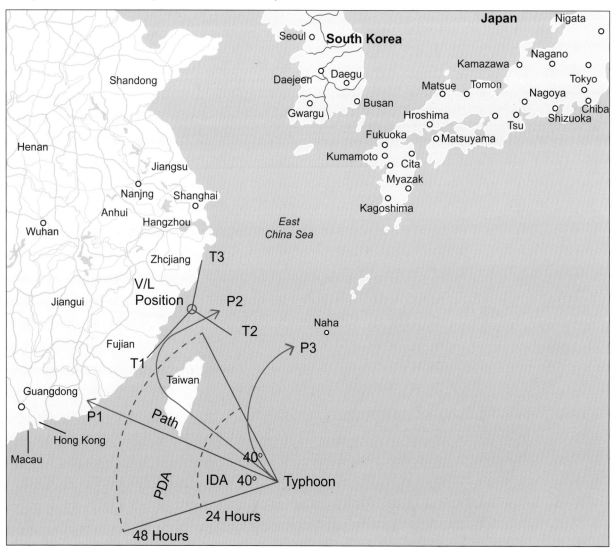

Figure 7.14   Scenario 2 – likely paths of TRS and ship tracks

The paths of the TRS should be in line with the extreme historic tracks followed by TRS' in that region. It must be remembered that TRS movement may not follow the historic pattern and regular monitoring must be carried out. There is an alternative and more structured approach, that can be taken for risk assessment. The Master must consider the following as part of risk assessment when making decisions about routes:

1 The position of the vessel relative to the storm (semi-circle).
2 Severity of weather along the option tracks.
3 The minimum distance that the ship passes the storm centre.
4 The likelihood of the storm changing its direction and catching up with the ship.
5 Proximity to navigational hazards.
6 Freedom of movement.
7 Any change in steaming distance.
8 Steaming time.
9 The possibility of the ship being caught up by the storm.
10 The possibility of damage.

Table 7.5 shows that there are dangers involved with both T1 and T2. The choice should be T3, as it is hazard free and only involves increased distance and steaming time. Be aware that in addition to the three possible paths, the storm may also move in any direction between P1 and WSW.

	T1	T2	T3
1	Dangerous semi-circle	Navigable semi-circle	Navigable semi-circle
2	Severe within Strait F 10- >12	Severe in open sea F 8-12	Winds F 5-6
3	Perhaps very close	May be small or large	Large
4	Yes – even without re-curving	Yes – if it re- curved early	No
5	Within Strait	Close to islands	Open sea or coast
6	Little	Significant	Sufficient
7	None	Increase of about 400´	Increase over 600´
8	Increased as speed lost - TRS	Due to distance and TRS	Due to distance
9	Yes	Yes	No
10	Severe	High	None

Table 7.5   Summary of evaluation criteria for route choice

Wind Shift Observed

Scenario 3: A ship is SW of Mauritius and is on a NE'ly course. The ship receives report of a Cyclone to NNE about 250 nm off. The current weather observations are:

Wind	SE x S Force 6 and Backing
Swell	Long swell from NNE
Pressure	5 hPa below average and still falling

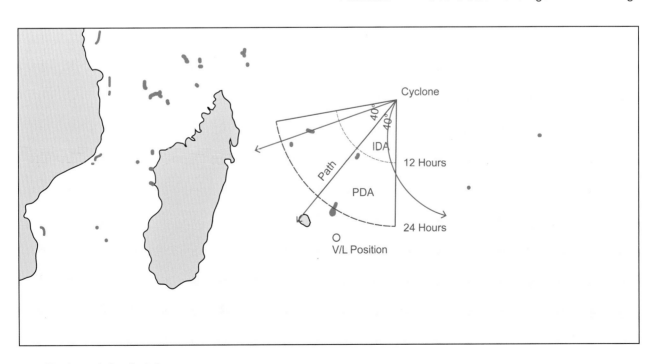

Figure 7.15   Scenario 3 – chart view

Weather report and on board observations are in line. Possible paths of the storm:

- Storm continues on present path
- storm starts to move west
- storm experiences immediate or delayed re-curvature

Based on risk assessment, it should be clear that the ship cannot avoid the storm at a distance of over 250 nm, the actions recommended in The Mariners Handbook should be taken.

The ship should adjust course so that the wind is 10° to 45° on the port bow and proceed with all speed. The ship should continue to observe the wind and as the wind backs, alter course to port and proceed behind the storm.

Observations should continue. After a few hours if the wind has steadied, it indicates that the storm has started to recurve and is heading for the ship's current position. If the wind begins to veer, the storm has re-curved and the ship is now in the navigable semi-circle. The course should be adjusted so that the wind is on the port quarter proceeding in the navigable semi-circle with all available speed, observations should continue and the course should be altered to starboard as the wind veers.

7.1.4.4 In Harbour or at Anchor

An immediate risk assessment should be carried out.

For a ship in port, the best choice is to proceed to sea as soon as possible, particularly when the storm is some distance away.

For a ship at anchor, the best choice is to heave up anchor and proceed to open waters. If there is not enough time or there are technical difficulties forcing the ship to stay at anchor, the following should be done:

- Both anchors should be used in an open mooring with an angle of about 30° to 40° between cables
- use increased scope of cable – pay out as much as possible
- engines ran ahead, depending on wind force, to reduce strain on the cable.

For a ship in port or at anchor the options available are to:

- Stay in port if already in port
- proceed to a storm anchorage
- proceed to sea.

The selected action will depend on how far from the port or anchorage the TRS is going to pass, the severity of hazards, the likelihood of precautions failing or the comparative advantages. The three general choices are considered separately:

Port

Advantages: If the ship is secured and there is no sea running, the decision to stay in port is a safe option, especially if the ship is well up river or where the storm is going to pass well clear.

In cases of extreme emergency, lives can be saved by moving to shelters ashore.

Some assistance from the authorities is possible.

Precautions: Moorings should be doubled/trebled up.

Reports on the storm's movement should be received regularly.

Security of the ship's gear, sufficient ballast and adequate stability should be ensured.

Stop cargo operations.

The engine should be kept on immediate readiness.

Tugs should be ordered to standby.

Let go outboard anchor on short stay.

Hazards: If a storm passes over the port, the ship is likely to surge alongside and land heavily on the berth, or other structures on the berth.

Authorities may close the port and order all vessels to leave. The vessels may not be fully prepared and there may not be sufficient tugs or pilots to handle all vessels in time.

Damage may be caused by the ship's bottom making contact with the seabed.

The ship is immediately in peril if moorings break or fail.

Negative storm surge and up-swelling of water onshore may cause smaller ships to end up 'out of channel' and on land.

As the storm approaches, the tugs may not remain on station and it is probably too late to move to sea.

Storm Anchor

Advantages: The selected storm anchorage is likely to be well sheltered and with adequate depth.

The swell and sea in confined waters may not be very high.

Precautions: Routine observations, analysis of the situation and recording of findings.

Reports should be received regularly.

The security of the ship and its stability should be ensured.

If required, the decision to move out to sea must be taken at an early stage. Both anchors should be laid out in an open mooring on a long scope.

The engine should be used ahead to ease the strain on the anchor cables and prevent the anchor dragging or the cables breaking.

Hazards: Other ships at the anchorage may make contact with own ship and anchor cables may foul.

Other ships may drag anchor and drift on to own ship.

Reduced chance of receiving assistance at anchorage when a storm is overhead.

If a ship is not sufficiently ballasted, secured or has inadequate stability, she may encounter serious problems.

Insufficient power or any defects may cause problems.

During the passage of a storm, if a ship drags her anchors, it may be difficult to find a way out from the anchorage to the sea.

In shallow waters, damage may be experienced due to excessive rolling and pitching and the ship's bottom making contact with the seabed.

Sea

Advantages: The ship is not dependent on the availability of services including tugs or a pilot for manoeuvring.

Freedom of movement provides the advantage of being able to clear away from an approaching storm.

Precautions: Routine observations, analysis of the situation and recording findings.

Reports should be received regularly and transmitted as needed.

Security and stability of the ship should be ensured.

If a ship is at port or an anchorage, the decision to move out to sea must be taken at an early stage.

Freedom of movement must be maintained.

Hazards: It may not be possible to receive any assistance at sea and if the ship is lost to sea, there is little chance of the individuals on board surviving.

If the ship is not sufficiently ballasted or secured, or has inadequate stability, serious problems may be encountered. When a ship is caught on a lee shore, with restricted sea room, she may run aground, with serious consequences for safety of life.

Insufficient power or any defects may hamper manoeuvring.

There is a possibility of running out of fuel if there are insufficient reserves.

In shallow waters, damage may be experienced due to excessive rolling and pitching and the ship's bottom making contact with the seabed.

7.1.5 Bridge Procedures – Summary

- Refer to Master's Standing Orders, Company SMS procedure and check lists on TRS
- make regular observations of the weather – especially the wind, swell, pressure and cloud, these observations should be logged every hour
- receive weather reports and forecasts from different stations covering the area
- keep a listening watch on international calling frequencies for warnings from other ships
- if experiencing storm conditions or in the vicinity of a storm, transmit an Obligatory Report
- post lookouts and be vigilant with observations of weather, sea and surroundings
- on observing precursory signs, determine the probable position of the storm and plot it on to a chart
- on receiving storm report/warning, plot the position of the storm on the chart
- determine any imminent and probable areas of danger
- make a PA announcement and inform all crew
- brief the department heads and request reports of securing the ship
- carry out a risk assessment
- determine the course of action to follow so that the storm can be avoided by the maximum possible distance
- engage hand steering
- ease speed of engine, unless required to proceed at full speed based on the required action
- make sure that the ship's stability is adequate, also eliminate any free surfaces by filling or emptying slack tanks based on the ship's stability and stresses
- if in ballast take on additional heavy weather ballast
- close and batten down all hatches and openings
- secure all loose objects and check/take additional lashings on cargo and anchors
- rig lifelines on deck

- follow Permit to Work system – no one to proceed on deck without permission
- explore contingency/storm shelter anchorage if required.

7.2 Planning for and Information on Ice

Ice is a concern for navigators who will encounter it as it affects several aspects of navigation:

- Appearance of features and landmarks
- electronic aids to navigation
- radar detection
- celestial navigation
- DR
- operation of compasses and logs
- establishment and maintenance of aids to navigation
- ship handling.

This section does not cover the issues related to ice formation, but discusses the problems associated with its detection, navigation in its vicinity and working in regions where it is present.

Figure 7.16   Iceberg

7.2.1 Sources of Information

Knowledge of the presence, position and movement of ice is important when planning for resources and navigational procedures. The sources of information include:

- Mariner's handbook
- ocean passages for the world
- ALRS
- sailing directions
- ice charts
- routeing charts
- weather facsimile charts
- ocean routeing services
- weather and ice reports

- NAVTEX and SafetyNET ice reports (see Chapter 11)
- international ice patrol
- US Coastguard, US Navy Ocean Office, Canadian Ice Reconnaissance Aircraft Facsimile Service, Baltic Ice Service
- Port Authorities, Pilots and Pilotage Authorities
- ocean weather ships
- ships departing from the area
- previous experience and knowledge of the individuals on board
- previous records on board if the vessel has already been to the area.

7.2.1.2 ICE Reporting

Mariner is required to interpret ice information that is received on board. WMO and Canadian ice service have developed relevant codes and procedures for coding of ice information for quick reference.

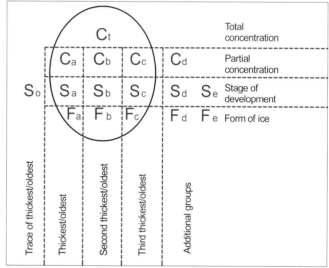

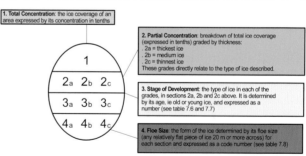

Figure 7.17   Egg code diagram for the position of total and partial ice concentration and ice form

Concentration	Symbol
Ice free	
Less than one tenth	0
1/10	1
2/10	2
3/10	3
4/10	4
5/10	5
6/10	6
7/10	7
8/10	8
9/10	9
More than 9/10 less than 10/10	9+
10/10	10
Undetermined or unknown	x

Table 7.6   Total concentration of ice (C)

Number from WMO Sea Ice Nomenclature	Concentration		Symbol
	No stage of development	-	0
2.1	New ice	-	1
2.2	Nilas, ice rind	< 10 cm	2
2.4	Young ice	10-30 cm	3
2.4.1	Grey ice	10-15 cm	4
2.4.2	Grey-white ice	15-30 cm	5
2.5	First-year ice	30-200 cm	6
2.5.1	Thin first-year ice	30-70 cm	7
2.5.1.1	Thin first-year ice, first stage	30-50 cm	8
2.5.1.2	Thin first-year ice, second stage	50-70 cm	9
2.5.2	Medium first-year ice	70-120 cm	1•
2.5.3	Thick first-year ice	> 120 cm	4•
2.6	Old ice		7•
2.6.1	Second year ice		8•
2.6.2	Multi-year ice		9•
10.4	Ice of land origin		Δ•
	Undetermined or unknown		x

Table 7.7   Stage of development and thickness (S)

Element	Floe size	Symbol
Pancake ice	-	0
Small ice cake, brash ice	< 2 m	1
Ice cake	2-20 m	2
Small floe	20-100 m	3
Medium floe	100-500 m	4
Big floe	500 m-2 km	5
Vast floe	2-10 km	6
Giant floe	> 10 km	7
Fast ice	-	8
Icebergs, growlers or floebergs	-	9
Undetermined or unknown	-	x

Table 7.8 Form of ice (F)

Chart Item   Explanation

Ice free: no ice present

Open water: ice concentration less than 1/10. A large area of freely navigable water, where sea ice is present in concentrations less than 1/10.

Very open ice: ice concentration 1-3/10. Floating ice where the concentration is 1/10 to 3/10 and water preponderates over ice.

Open ice: ice concentration 4-6/10. Floating ice where the concentration is 4/10 to 6/10, with many leads and polynyas, the floes are generally not in contact with another.

Close ice: ice concentration 7-8/10. Floating ice where the concentration is 7/10 to 8/10, composed of floes mostly in contact.

Very close ice: ice concentration 9/10 to 10/10.

Fast ice: Sea ice that forms and remains fast along the coast, where it is attached to the shore or between shoals. Vertical fluctuation may be observed during changes of sea-level. Fast ice may be formed in situ from sea water or by freezing of drift ice to the shore, it may extend a few meters or several hundred kilometres from the coast.

Ice shelf.

New, close or very close ice with ice concentration 7/10 -10/10, but thickness less than 10 cm.

Nilas, ice concentration 9-10/10. Grey ice, mainly on leads. A thin elastic crust of ice, bends easily on waves, swell and under pressure, thrusting in pattern of interlocking "fingers" (finger rafting). Has a matt surface and is up to 10 cm in thickness.

Table 7.9 Total concentration colour code standard

Chart Item   Explanation

Ice-free: no ice present.

Open water: ice concentration less than 1/10. A large area of freely navigable water, where sea ice is present in concentrations of less than 1/10.

Very open ice: ice concentration 1-3/10. Floating ice where the concentration is 1/10 to 3/10 and water preponderates over ice.

Open ice: ice concentration 4-6/10. Floating ice where the concentration is 4/10 to 6/10, with many leads and polynyas, the floes are generally not in contact with each other.

Close ice: ice concentration 7-8/10. Floating ice where the concentration is 7/10 to 8/10, composed of floes mostly in contact.

Very close ice: ice concentration 9/10 to less than 10/10.

Undefined ice

????

New ice: A general term for recently formed ice. These types of ice are composed of ice crystals, which are only weakly frozen together.

Level ice: Sea ice that has not been affected by deformation.

Fast ice: Sea ice that forms and remains fast along the coast, where it is attached to the shore or between shoals. Vertical fluctuation may be observed during changes of sea-level. Fast ice may be formed in situ from sea water or by drift ice freezing to the shore, it may extend a few meters or several hundred kilometres from the coast.

 Ridged or hummocked ice (f = number of ridges/nautical mile). Ice piled haphazardly one piece over another forming ridges or walls.

 Rafted ice (C = concentration). Type of deformed ice, it is created by one piece of ice overriding another.

 Ice edge or ice boundary. The demarcation at any given time between the open water and sea ice of any kind, whether fast or drifting (cf. ice boundary). It may be termed compacted or diffuse (cf. ice boundary).

 Fracture: Any break or rupture through very close ice, compact ice, consolidated ice, fast ice or a single floe resulting from deformation processes. Fractures may contain brash ice and/or be covered with nil as and/or young ice. Length may vary from a few meters to many kilometres.

 Lead: Any fracture or passage-way through sea ice that is navigable by surface vessels.

 Water temperature isotherm, °C

 Thickness measured in cm

Table 7.10 WMO symbols for ice charts

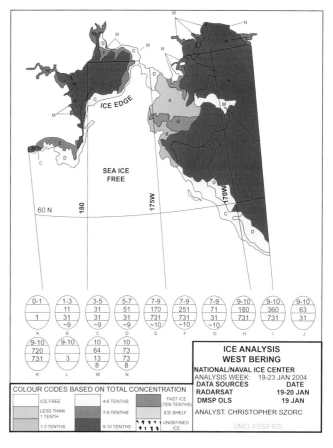

Figure 7.18 Sample ice chart of the bering sea

7.2.2 Readiness of the Vessel

A ship that is expected to operate or proceed in ice must be prepared for hazards. The following list of requirements provides a general guide:

- Appropriate ice classification and notation
- proper and detailed procedures and checklists formalised for ice operations as part of SMS
- the main engine and steering gear should be reliable and well maintained
- operational navigation and communication equipment should be in good order
- operational radars should be capable of peak performance
- the vessel must be adequately ballasted and trimmed to have the propeller fully immersed in water. Trim should not be excessive
- the ballast and fresh water tanks should not be more than 90% full
- good search lights
- international Code of Signals and communication procedures
- fenders
- towlines
- defrosters on bridge windows

- where available, tinted screens should be used on the wheelhouse windows, due to bright sunlight
- accommodation heating
- anti-skid salt/grit
- personnel provided with protective and cold weather gear
- personnel provided with equipment for abandonment in ice conditions
- additional crew employed for relief and work in extreme conditions
- navigational publications for ice regions and the latest reports
- adequate reserves of stores and bunkers
- bunker tank heating must be operational at all times
- if the vessel has steam mooring winches, the steam must be left warming through on deck
- if the vessel is a liquefied gas carrier, deck spray lines should be drained
- on chemical tankers and liquefied gas carriers, lines to decontamination showers should be drained
- on tankers fitted with pressure vacuum breakers, ensure Glycol is added
- on tankers, activate the deck seal heating coils
- in the lifeboats, check that the water tanks are no more than 90% full. If the water is in packets, it should be moved to a warm location in close proximity to the embarkation position
- apply cold weather lubricants to wires and machinery
- ensure that the low level sea chest is operational and that there are heating and compressed air arrangements at the sea chest
- use canvases to protect ropes and wires on mooring drums
- ensure there is sufficient equipment on board to remove ice or snow when necessary.

7.3 Navigation in Ice Areas

All ice is dangerous, particularly as it is likely that if there is ice in the area where a ship is operating, it is not uncommon for there to be more ice nearby. Ice may cause physical damage to the ship's structure and can pose operational problems. Several of these problems can directly affect the safe navigation of the ship.

7.3.1 Master's Duties

When ice is reported on or near their track, SOLAS requires every ship's Master to proceed at a moderate speed at night or to alter course in order to pass well clear of the danger area. On meeting dangerous ice, the Master is obliged under SOLAS to send a report to other ships in the vicinity and also to the nearest coast station.

7.3.1.1 Contents of the Obligatory Report

- Type of ice
- position of the ice
- UTC and date of observation.

7.3.2 Effects of Ice and Snow Presence on Navigation

7.3.2.1 Electronic Aids to Navigation

If the antennas are completely covered with ice or snow they may not detect any signal, collapse under the weight of ice, or malfunction due to a short-circuit as the terminals are covered with ice and snow. The movement of the scanners may be obstructed or might be completely covered under ice or snow. GPS and other electronic aids can be used for positions once errors have been applied.

The echo sounder trace may be lost due to ice under the ship or because of hull noises. Noise may also generate a false echo. The pressure (Pitot) tube or impeller type speed logs may have to be retrieved to prevent them from being damaged by any ice passing under the hull.

An impact with ice, frequent changes of course and speed will introduce errors to the gyro compass. These types of errors may be slow to settle.

7.3.2.2 Use of Charts/Landmarks/Topography

The navigational chart provides the coastal features without any ice or snow. The appearance of landmarks that are covered with ice or snow will change significantly, although many inlets and points may bear a marked resemblance to the charted features. The pack-ice limit can be mistaken for coastline when observed either visually or by radar.

Headlands where icebergs have grounded will also be longer and more extended than the actual headland. It is likely that there will be substantial errors in position when using snow covered headlands for radar ranges or bearings, visual bearings, clearing bearings or as clearing marks. In these circumstances the position must be checked using a different method.

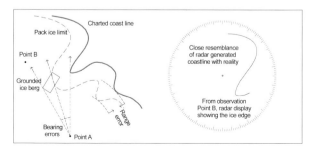

Figure 7.19 Effect of ice presence on bearings and ranges

Figure 7.20   The same headland in different conditions of visibility

7.3.2.3 Lighthouses and Beacons

Detecting or identifying lighthouses or beacons during daylight can become difficult, as snow or ice hides the identification features or, in extreme cases, the entire structure. During the night, the light's range of visibility may be impaired due to ice or snow on or around the lens.

7.3.2.4 Sectored Lights

Frost or ice on the lens of sectored lights is liable to significantly change their visibility sectors. Some may not perceive danger unless they see a light in the colour that suggests danger. The sectors may be unreliable but, if the lighthouse or beacon is correctly identified, it can still be used to take bearings. These should be used with extreme caution and under these circumstances the mariner should also confirm the position of the vessel using another method.

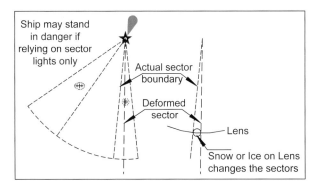

Figure 7.21   Changes of sector due to ice

7.3.2.5 Floating Navigational Aids

The force of the ice is liable to set floating navigational aids adrift, they may part from their moorings or simply drag them. They might be hidden under ice or snow or not be on station, as they are sometimes removed by authorities during the ice season. The mariner should be cautious using them, even after confirming their position when ice is affecting the floating aids.

7.3.2.6 Celestial Navigation

False horizons are often observed on ice because of refraction or a mirage. Sights may not be possible where the horizon is covered with ice or snow. In these circumstances reverse angle sights of bodies above 60° in altitude can be considered in the vicinity of ice shelves (see 8.6.3 and Figure 8.11). Another option is when the horizon is covered with ice, the height of ice over the horizon can be subtracted from the height of eye (maximum error being 4′). Sextants with artificial horizons can also be used.

It should be noted that it is possible to navigate in the vicinity of ice during the summer months, provided the ice has melted sufficiently to allow access. At that time, the days are long and the nights are short. This means that star sights in the morning or evening twilight will have a small gap between them during night and a long gap during the day. The reverse may be true during the winter seasons, where days are short and nights very long. During day time, observations of the sun can provide single position lines and running fixes must be plotted. Accurate DR is the key to satisfactory positions when transferring position lines for a running fix.

7.3.2.7 Radar Use

Radar must be operated at peak operational efficiency, although there will still be limitations. When there is no echo on the display, it does not mean that there is no ice. Echo return depends on the inclination of the reflecting surface, its size and distance. In a calm sea, different types of ice should be detectable. Sea or rain clutter will suppress small ice fragments. Snow sleet and rain-storms will impair detection (also see 6.6.4). One radar should be operated continuously, mainly on the 6 mile range, with frequent long range scanning for the early detection of larger ice pieces afloat. Figures 7.22 and 7.23 illustrates where, based on the settings currently in use on radar, the radar has not been able to detect the ice edge.

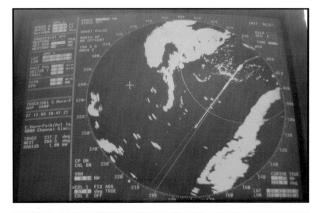

Figure 7.22 Radar image and corresponding chart view

Figure 7.23 Direct view of the area shown in figure 7.22

7.3.2.8 Maintaining DR

When working around ice, frequent course and speed changes are required to maintain progress and to avoid ice. It may not be practical to maintain an accurate log for reckoning. The course and speed changes will not be instantly effective, it will be a long process to allow for head reach when changing course and speed. In addition, any impact with the ice may cause the ship to shear off its heading and change speed, which may be hard to allow for. The introduction of a gyro error due to the sudden course and speed changes is difficult to anticipate as it would remain unknown for a while.

7.3.3 Signs of Drift Ice

Drift ice is usually unexpected. An early warning of ice assists in being prepared. Visual detection can only happen within the geometric detection range, provided that visibility is good and there is ample light. Radar detection also has limitations. However, there are signs that may indicate ice being present in the vicinity. Ice blink appears as a glare, well before ice is sighted. It appears as:

- Whitish or yellowish haze during a clear daylight
- whitish glare during the day, with overcast sky or low clouds
- white patches in fog.

The gradual lessening of an ordinary swell or the abrupt smoothing of the sea indicates that there is ice windward. Isolated fragments of ice are also noticeable downwind or downstream of ice. There may be a thick band of fog over the edge of drift ice.

The presence of marine life is another indicator of ice being in the vicinity. In the Arctic, walrus, seals and birds can be seen and around the Antarctic, Antarctic Petrel and Snow Petrel are noticeable.

A temperature of +1°C away from a cold current indicates an ice edge 150 miles off, or 100 miles if the wind is blowing off the ice. At -0.5°C ice is assumed to be no more than 50 miles off.

7.3.4 Signs of Open Water

In addition to detecting ice, the mariner should also endeavour to find open water. Distinguishable dark streaks on the underside of the clouds indicate the direction of leads or open water, dark bands on a cloud at a high altitude indicates small patches of open water. Dark spots in fog may appear where open water is at a shorter distance. Additionally, the sound of a surge in ice or a noticeable increase in swell indicates open water.

7.3.5 Icebergs

Radars or any of the signs should not be completely relied on, as there are no foolproof methods to indicate the proximity of an iceberg. In general, if the ship is far from land, the absence of sea in a fresh breeze indicates an iceberg windward. Similarly, the presence of growlers or smaller pieces of brash ice also indicate that there is probably an iceberg windward. The sound of seas breaking far from land, or a thunderous sound when icebergs calve, ice cracks or ice falls into the sea are also useful indicators. The iceberg may appear as a luminous white mass in fog when the sun is shining. During the night, sighting icebergs varies, as follows:

- On a clear night, with no moon, icebergs are visible at 1 - 2 miles as black or white objects
- they are easy to see when moonlight is behind the observer
- in a cloudy sky and with intermittent moonlight they are difficult to see
- cumulus or Cb clouds can create false impressions of icebergs at night.

Changes in air or sea temperature, or the echoes of a whistle or siren, cannot be relied on for detecting an iceberg.

7.3.6 Ice Accretion

Severe ice accretion may occur on ships that are experiencing sub-freezing air temperatures in association with strong winds. It is the precipitation and moisture in the air or sea water, in the form of spray, that freezes on the ships structure. The conditions are difficult to forecast and as they exist within a large air mass, it is not always possible to avoid them within the time that warnings are received. Ships do not move very fast and are unlikely to clear the area of ice accretion by the time warnings are received.

Figure 7.24   Ice accretion on a ship

7.3.6.1 Actions to Ensure Safety

The following actions are possible options available to a mariner in these conditions:

- Steer towards warmer conditions or seek shelter
- head into the wind at minimum speed to reduce spray
- if the weather does not allow the vessel to head into the wind, run before the wind at minimum speed to maintain steerage.

If all fails and ice is building up on the ship's structure, the last resort is to physically remove it as the adverse effects of a mass of ice to stability might be sufficient to capsize the vessel.

It should be noted that in rough weather conditions, it is not easy to head into wind or run before the wind. While heading into wind, the ship will pitch heavily, along with slamming of forefoot and shipping seas. Some ships may also experience parametric rolling, while running before the wind, the ship is in danger of experiencing pooping and surfing, the ship may also easily broach and find it difficult to maintain its heading. There are also greater chances of parametric rolling.

7.3.6.2 Obligatory Report

On encountering air temperatures that are below freezing and associated with gale force winds and are causing severe ice accumulation on ships, the Master under SOLAS must send a report to ships in the vicinity and the nearest coast station, stating that ice is accumulating and include:

- Air and sea temperatures
- force and direction of wind
- position of the ship
- UTC and date of observation.

7.4 Operating in Ice

The basic rules are:

- Keep moving, even if very slowly
- try to work with the ice movement and not against it
- excessive speed leads to damage.

7.4.1 Factors to be Considered Before Entering Ice

The vessel should not enter ice if an alternative route is available. Full attention should be given to the type of ice, time of year, weather conditions and the area of operation. It is also important that the ship has ice classification and, if necessary that, icebreakers are available for assistance. The hull, machinery, steering gear and critical equipment must be in a good state and the ship should have sufficient bunkers and stores. Manoeuvring characteristics of the ship, the draught in relation to the available depth of water, how well the propeller tips and rudder are immersed, along with the experience of the Master and officers are all important considerations. Section 7.2.2 should be referred to for more details on a ship's readiness. A proper passage plan based on the most up to date reports on the ice, open water and leads should be prepared.

7.4.2 Ship Handling in or Near Ice

7.4.2.1 Factors Dictating Entry

It is preferable to enter during daylight hours only. Entry or navigation at night, or in reduced visibility, should be avoided. If forced to proceed, good searchlights are essential.

Where practical, entry should be planned from leeward as the ice is likely to be less compacted and there would be less wave action. Entry should be attempted at right angles, at a reduced speed and at one of the bights.

7.4.2.2 Proceeding

The engine must be ready for immediate manoeuvre at all times. Once a ship is in ice, the speed should be increased to maintain headway and control. A ship that is proceeding very slowly is likely to become beset, however, a ship proceeding very fast risks damage. Use should be made of leads through the ice. The rudder should be amidships when going astern. If ice goes under the hull, engine revolutions should be reduced immediately.

7.4.2.3 Anchoring

Anchoring should be avoided in heavy concentrations of ice. Anchors should be weighed if it is likely that the wind will move the ice on to the ship, as the anchor and cable will be strained by the full force of moving ice. The anchor-party and windlass should be on immediate notice, with the engine on stop and ready to run if required.

7.4.2.4 A Ship Beset in Ice

The hull of a ship that is stuck in ice can be crushed. A ship beset in ice is at the mercy of ice movement. The engine should be kept turning slowly so that the propeller is kept clear. Icebreaker assistance should be requested immediately. An icebreaker will clear the ship by clearing ice from her sides and her intended course. Where icebreaker assistance is not available, attempts should be made to free the ship by going full ahead, then full astern and using maximum rudder one way then another. As the ship begins to move ahead, the rudder should be put amidships. The ship can be freed by changing trim and heel, by internal transfers of fuel, etc.

Use of anchors can help to move the ship by:

- Laying anchors towards each beam on the ice and attempting to move the bow
- by placing an anchor on ice astern and using the engine astern, to move the ship astern.

Remember: "MAINTAIN FREEDOM OF MOVEMENT"

7.5 Working with Ice Breakers

Figure 7.25   Ice breaker

The Master of an icebreaker will direct any escorting operation. Icebreakers may make use of aerial reconnaissance to find the position of leads and open water. Escorted vessels should:

- Establish the starting position of the escorting service
- amend the ETA if necessary
- maintain a continuous radio watch
- follow the route ordered
- proceed at the speed ordered
- always follow the path cleared by the icebreaker
- have towing gear rigged at all times
- the OOW should know the signals for icebreaker assistance in ICS
- acknowledge and execute icebreaker signals promptly
- if the icebreaker stops in an emergency, the escorted ship should stop immediately by either going astern on engine or ramming into the ice.

If the icebreaker is proceeding rapidly, the channel will be wider than its beam and fragments of ice will be left in the channel. This can slow down a following ship or may cause a block. The Master of the icebreaker will decide on the minimum and maximum distances from the icebreaker. The minimum distance is the stopping distance and the maximum depends on the ice conditions to keep the channel open. The distance may have to be reduced to a few metres if the channel is likely to close. The icebreaker can also decide to tow. It can tow at a short or long stay and usually connects the towline well forward on her deck. The icebreaker may request the engine of the ship being towed to be run at a particular speed.

7.5.1 Working in Convoys

The Master of the icebreaker will order the sequence and distance between the ships, which should be carefully maintained. If the speed is reduced, the ship astern must be informed immediately. The ship ahead and astern, as well as the ice, must be carefully watched. Light and sound signals must be repeated promptly by ships in the column, both in turn and sequence.

7.6 Navigation in High Latitudes

In addition to problems relating to ice and snow, navigation in high latitudes requires particular care due to the convergence of the globe at the poles and the scarcity of navigational information. High latitude factors do not necessarily apply to ice navigation.

7.6.1 Concept of Time

As time zones meet on the poles, local time has little significance. The normal phenomenon of day and night are not noticed as there may be very long days, nights and periods of twilight.

7.6.2 Charts and Bearings

Charts are based largely on aerial photography. Soundings, topography and navigational information are sparse in most polar-regions. The geographical position of features may be unreliable and any errors in their positions will become considerable as the distances increase.

Most regions are covered by gnomonic charts. Bearings (visual or radar) must be treated as Great Circles, unless they are of nearby objects. Half-convergency should be applied where bearings have to be plotted on Mercator charts.

7.6.3 Meridians and Parallels

Meridians converge at the poles and the perimeter of parallels reduces considerably (cosine of 90° = 0). Excessive longitudinal curvature renders meridians and parallels impractical to use as navigational references. The only significance of this is for plotting positions derived from electronic systems, such as GPS.

7.6.4 Dead Reckoning (DR)

It is good navigational practice to keep careful observation of the course, speed and time, in order to maintain a large-scale plot of the ship's track. As supporting data for estimated positions, eg information on tides and current, is not widely available it will be difficult to maintain an accurate reckoning of the ship's progress. Every opportunity to fix the ship's position should be taken. Systems like GPS etc, have reduced the need for DR, but it should be maintained as continued signals from GPS satellites may not be guaranteed.

7.6.5 Use of Compasses

At or near (85°) the geographical poles, the gyrocompass will become useless as it loses all of its directive force. The gyro is generally reliable up to a latitude of approximately 70°. At the magnetic poles, the magnetic compass becomes useless as it loses all of its directive force. Impact with ice and frequent changes of course and speed introduce errors that are slow to settle. Frequent comparisons of the gyro and magnetic compass should be made and logged and azimuths taken regularly.

7.6.6 Electronic and Radio Aids

GPS provides global coverage and, if a receiver is fitted, it can be relied on after making an allowance for errors. Other position fixing systems can be relied on where available, after making an allowance for errors. A radar that is set up correctly and at peak performance can be very useful for detection purposes.

7.6.7 Celestial Navigation

Accurate celestial observations cannot be relied on due to the long days and nights and the extensive periods of cloud cover. The following points are important (see also 8.6.1 and 8.6.3):

- The sun rises once in six months at a pole
- the sun sets once in six months at a pole
- the sun's maximum altitude will be 23° 27' at a pole
- the moon rises once a month at a pole
- the planets rise once each sidereal year at a pole
- stars with a declination of more than 23° 27' in the opposite hemisphere will never rise at a pole
- all bodies will have an upper and lower meridian transit (passage)
- the best fix is from the stars
- star observations may not be possible with the sun just below the horizon, during daylight or when there is total darkness (prolonged nights)
- observations at low altitudes may have to be made (10° may be the best altitude)
- during daylight, the sun may be the only body visible, clouds usually hide it for much of the navigational season.

The results of sights are usually good but abnormal conditions should be looked into, eg sub or super refraction. Transferred position lines will give a fix with questionable accuracy due to DR inaccuracies.

> **Author's note**
> At times, even with knowledge about an existing hazard, progress must be made as the hazard is unlikely to disappear, additional safeguards are required to be taken to ensure safety. Proper navigation practices include safeguards that ensure safety of life, environment and property.

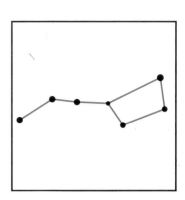

8 Celestial Navigation

The positions and motion of heavenly bodies are predictable. As the positions of these bodies can be referenced to the earth, the heavenly bodies can be used for navigational purposes.

8.1 The Celestial Sphere

An imaginary sphere, with the earth at its centre and an infinite radius is called the celestial sphere. Its reference marks are linked to the earth or the terrestrial sphere. Projection of the plane of the equator to the celestial sphere forms the celestial equator. It is also referred to as the equinoctial.

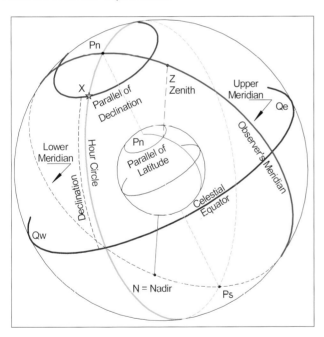

Figure 8.1 Celestial sphere and components

The celestial meridian is formed by projecting the plane of the terrestrial meridian on to the celestial sphere. The celestial meridians are arcs of Great Circles passing through poles of the celestial sphere. If a line from the centre of the earth is drawn through the position of the observer, it reaches the celestial sphere at a point called the zenith, ie a point that is vertically overhead the observer. The point on the opposite side to your zenith on the celestial sphere is called the nadir.

The part of celestial meridian that contains the zenith is called the upper celestial meridian or upper branch, the one containing the nadir is the lower celestial meridian or lower branch.

A Great Circle that passes through a point, or any heavenly body on the celestial sphere, as well as through the celestial poles, is termed the hour circle. It moves with the body or point as the celestial sphere rotates about the earth, whereas the celestial meridian remains fixed with respect to the earth. A circle parallel to the celestial equator and passing through the body is called the parallel of declination.

8.1.1 Celestial Co-Ordinates

As latitude and longitude indicate a position on the terrestrial sphere, their celestial equivalents are the declination and hour angle. The declination of a body is the arc of the hour circle or angle at the centre of the earth between the equinoctial or celestial equator and the parallel of declination through the body. It is measured 0° to 90° north or south of the celestial equator. The angular distance between the parallel of the declination and the celestial pole is called the polar distance and is 90° plus or minus the declination, depending on the pole being used. The declination of a few bodies changes significantly, eg the sun, moon and planets. For this reason the hourly values of the declination of these bodies are noted in the nautical almanac. The declination of stars will change very slowly, if at all, so it is noted only once every three days in the almanac for the selected stars.

Using North celestial pole:
(for example, declination 34° 20′ N and 34° 20′ S)

$$\text{Polar distance} = 90° − 34° \ 20′ \ N = 55° \ 40′$$
$$\text{Polar distance} = 90° + 34° \ 20′ \ S = 124° \ 20′$$

The local hour angle (LHA) is the arc of the equinoctial or the angle at the celestial pole, measured westwards between the observer's meridian and the hour circle through the body. Due to the rotation of the earth on its axis and revolution around the sun, the hour angle of the bodies changes quite frequently. As there are numerous heavenly bodies, the hour angle data for each would require a huge publication. Two further references are used to minimise hour angle data. For the sun, moon, planets and the First Point of Aries, hourly data is noted with reference to the Greenwich meridian, whereas for stars the data is noted with reference to the First Point of Aries every three days. The Greenwich hour angle (GHA) of a body is the arc of the equinoctial, or the angle at the celestial pole, measured westward from the Greenwich meridian to the hour circle through the body. Sidereal hour angle (SHA) of a body is the arc of the equinoctial, or the angle at the celestial pole, measured westward from the hour circle through the First Point of Aries to the hour circle through the body.

For LHA:

| Longitude East | GHA Least |
| Longitude West | GHA Best |

GHA	=	145° 30´	145° 30´
Longitude	=	030° 15´ E	030° 15´ W
LHA	=	175° 45´	115° 15°

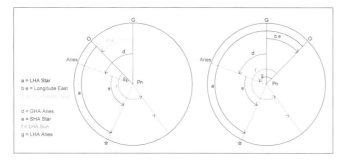

a = LHA Star
b e = Longitude East

d = GHA Aries
e = SHA Star
f = LHA Sun
g = LHA Aries

Figure 8.2 Longitude, GHA, SHA and LHA

Example 8.1 (geographical position)
Find the geographical position of Venus on 4th May 2006, at 06h 28m 15s GMT.
Solution, using the Nautical Almanac

GMT (Date/Time)		4-5-06/06 28 15
Declination	00° 55´.1 S	0600
d Corrⁿ	− 0´.5	Decreasing 1.0
Latitude	**00° 54´.6 S**	
GHA	310° 35´.0	0600
Increment	7° 03´.8	28m 15s
v Corrⁿ/SHA	- 0´.1	-0.2
Sub total	317° 38´.7	
(360° -)		- 360°
Longitude	**042° 21´.3 E**	

8.2 Horizons and Altitudes

As the celestial sphere referred to is the centre of the earth, the horizon can be used as a reference point for navigational purposes. There are several different horizons and they are all perpendicular to the line between the zenith and nadir. The visible horizon is the line where the earth and sky appear to meet. It is also referred to as the apparent horizon. It varies with the height of the observer's eye above the sea and the refraction. The sensible horizon is an imaginary line through the observer's eye and the geoidal horizon is the line that is tangent to the earth at the observer's position. The celestial, or rational, horizon is the line through the centre of the earth and is the reference horizon for the celestial calculations.

The celestial horizon in the reference system is the primary Great Circle. There may be other Great Circles called vertical circles, that are perpendicular to the celestial horizon and passing through the zenith and nadir. The arc of vertical circle through the body, between the celestial horizon and the zenith, is 90°. The arc between the celestial horizon and the body is the true altitude and the arc between the body and the zenith is the zenith distance. The zenith distance of a body is 90° minus the true altitude, where the body is above the celestial horizon. When the body is below the celestial horizon, it can be 90° plus the true altitude.

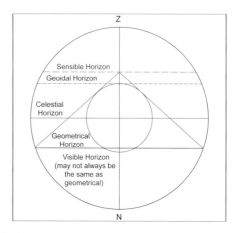

Figure 8.3 Horizons

Example 8.2
If the sextant altitude of Jupiter was 35° 37´.4, find the true altitude if the index error is 1´.8 off the arc and the height of eye was 14.2 m:
Using total correction table A2.
Using table A4 if pressure was 1020 mb and temperature was - 4°C.

Solution and Comments
From table A4 for 1020 mb and -4°C the zone letter is D. For D and an apparent altitude of 35°, the additional correction is -0´.1.

	Table A2	Table A4
Sextant altitude	35° 37´.4	35° 37´.4
Index error	+ 1´.8	+ 1´.8
Observed altitude	35° 39´.2	35° 39´.2
Dip	- 6´.6	- 6´.6
Apparent altitude	35° 32´.6	35° 32´.6
Total Correction	-1´.4	-1´.4
Sub total	35° 31´.2	35° 31´.2
Additional correction (Table A4)		- 0´.1
True altitude	35° 31´.2	35° 31´.1

The celestial horizon is above the visible horizon for any elevation above the surface. A body above the visible horizon and below the celestial horizon can be observed, ie a body with a negative altitude and a zenith distance greater than 90°.

8.3 Meridian Passage

Over the period of a day, a heavenly body will pass the observer's meridian. The meridian passage occurs when the body is on the observer's meridian. At meridian passage, P, Z and X are in line on the observer's meridian. If the body is on the observer's upper meridian, it is called the upper transit or the upper meridian passage. At this moment, the LHA of the body is 0° and the bearing will be true north or south of the observer.

There are times that a body can be observed when it is on the observer's lower meridian. The only bodies that can be observed at lower transit are the circumpolar bodies. For a body to be circumpolar for the observer, the latitude and declination must be of the same names. The lower meridian passage is also termed lower transit. At this moment, the LHA is 180° and the bearing is always 0° if the observer is in the northern hemisphere, the bearing is 180° if the observer is in the southern hemisphere.

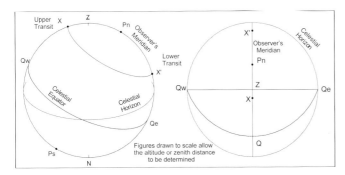

Figure 8.4 Meridian passage on plane of observers meridian and plane of celestial horizon

Example 8.3
Find the zone (+0500) time of meridian passage of Capella in 072° 42´ W on 4th May 2006.

Solution

LHA Capella	360° 00´.0	
SHA Capella	280° 43´.1	
LHA Aries	79° 16´.9	
Longitude	W 072° 42´.0	
GHA Aries	151° 58´.9	
Nearest whole hours (GHA)	147° 31´.3	19 00 00

Difference (increment table)	4° 27´.6	17 47
GMT of merpass		19 17 47
Zone + 0500 (to be subtracted)		05 00 00
Zone time merpass Capella		14 17 47

In problems involving a large East longitude, it is better to determine the approximate GMT first, in order to use the correct date.

Example 8.4
On 19th June 2006 in longitude 158° 30´ E, determine the precise zone (-1000) time of meridian passage of Venus.

Solution and Comments

LMT merpass Venus	09 41 (June 19)
Longitude 158° 30´ E	10 34
Approx GMT merpass Venus	23 07 (June 18)

LHA Venus	000° 00´.0	
Longitude	E 158° 30´.0	
GHA Venus	201° 30´.0	
Nearest whole hours (GHA)	199° 57´.0	(18th) 23 00 00
v Corrn	(- 0.5)	0´.1
Difference (increment table)	1° 33´.0	06 11
GMT of merpass		(18th) 23 06 11
Zone - 1000 (to be added)		10 00 00
Zone time merpass Venus		(19th) 09 06 11

At the meridian passage, if the sextant altitude of the body is observed and corrected, the true observed altitude can be used to determine the observer's latitude after applying the declination. It is advisable to draw a sketch, similar to the one in Figure 8.4, to determine Latitude. Only four variations are possible:

- Latitude > Declination (both same names and upper meridian passage)
  Latitude = Declination – True Altitude + 90°

- Latitude < Declination (both same names and upper meridian passage)
  Latitude = Declination + True Altitude – 90°

- Latitude and Declination contrary names (upper meridian passage)
  Latitude = 90° – True altitude – Declination

- Regardless of the names and values of latitude and declination (lower meridian passage)
  Latitude = 90° + True Altitude – Declination

8.3.1 Time of Observation for Meridian Passage

A body is on the meridian when it is true north or south of the observer. In cases when a body is at a very high altitude, or close to zenith, the accurate bearing is not always possible.

A body can be observed by using a sextant and, as it reaches maximum altitude or minimum altitude in the case of lower transit, it is assumed that it is on the observer's meridian. The meridian passage of a body does not necessarily occur at the maximum altitude in the case of upper transit or minimum altitude in the case of lower transit. This may be the case when there is a large northerly or southerly component in the observer's movement. Change in the declination of the body may also introduce a small error. It is preferable to start to observe for a meridian passage close to the calculated time.

Example 8.5
On 19th June 2006 in DR Position 36° 28´.5N 039° 46´.5W, calculate the setting for the sextant to observe the sun's lower limb at meridian passage if the index error of the sextant is 1´.5 on the arc and the height of eye is 20 m. State the bearing of the sun.

Solution and Comments
From the LMT of the meridian passage, the GMT would be worked out by applying the longitude in time (LIT). Having obtained the true altitude, all altitude corrections are applied in reverse to obtain the sextant altitude, working upwards from the true altitude.

Almanac data Altitude correction

Almanac data		Altitude correction	
LMT merpass	12 01 00	Sextant Alt	76° 50´.9
LIT	+ 02 39 06	IE	– 1´.5
GMT merpass	14 40 06	Observed Alt	76° 49´.4
		Dip	– 7´.9
Declination	N 23° 25´.7	Apparent Alt	76° 41´.5

d Corrⁿ		0.0	T Corrⁿ	+ 15´.7
Declination		N 23° 25´.7	True Alt	76° 57´.2
Latitude		N 36° 28´.5	Bearing	180° T
TA = D – L + 90°				
True Altitude		76° 57´.2		

8.4 Azimuths and Amplitudes

8.4.1 Azimuth

An Azimuth is the horizontal direction of a point or body on the celestial sphere and is the arc of the celestial horizon, or an angle at the zenith, from the north or south point of the celestial horizon. It can be measured clockwise from 0° to 360° from the north point, 0° to 90° clockwise or anticlockwise from the north or south points of the celestial horizon.

This is based on time that, if known exactly, allows accurate calculation, provided no errors have been introduced. It is preferable to select bodies that are between 30° and 60° in altitude. At very high altitudes, the azimuth of the celestial body will change rapidly, resulting in observation errors.

Example 8.6
On 20th June 2006, at 07h 35m 25s GMT, in DR 63° 38´.5N 027° 26´.5W, the sun was observed to bear 077°G. Find the gyro error.

Solution and Comments

Date	20 June 2006	A = tan lat ÷ tan LHA	N 0.139649488
GMT	07 35 25	B = tan dec ÷ sin LHA	N 0.434555223
GHA Sun	284° 37´.7	C = A ± B	N 0.574184711
Increment	8° 51´.3	tan Az = 1 ÷ (C x cos lat)	3.922666329
Sub-total	293° 29´.0	Az	75°.7
Longitude	W 027° 26´.5	True Bearing	N 75°.7 E
LHA Sun	266° 02´.5		075°.7
Declination	N 23° 26´.1	Gyro Bearing	077°
d Corrⁿ	0´.1	Gyro Error	**1°.3 H**
Declination	N 23° 26´.2		

Note: *If calculating of A or B results in a minus sign, it should be ignored and A and B should be named as stated in the rules.*

8.4.2 Amplitude

Amplitude is the arc between the observed body on its celestial horizon and the point where the celestial horizon intersects the celestial equator. The zenith distance at an amplitude observation is 90°, therefore Napier's rules can be applied when calculating the amplitude angle. It is named north or south depending on the name of the declination and east or west, depending on whether the body is rising or setting.

The formula is:

sin Amplitude = sin Declination ÷ cos Latitude

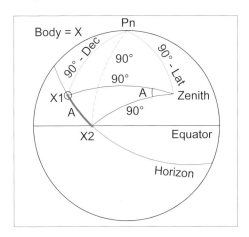

Figure 8.5 Amplitude reference

Example 8.7

On 20th June 2006, the observation of the rising sun gave a gyro bearing of 026°.5G in DR Position 63° 30′.5N 027° 02′.5W. Find the gyro error.

Solution and Comments

Date	20 June 2006	sin Declination	0.39770844
Lat 63° 30′.5 N		cos Latitude	0.446067645
LMT for 19th	02 09	sin Amplitude	0.891587733
LMT for 22nd	02 09	Amplitude	63°.07
LMT Sunrise 62°	02 09		E 63°.1 N
Increment	− 27	True Bearing	N 26°.9 E
LMT 63° 30′.5 N	01 42		026°.9
LIT	01 48	Gyro Bearing	026°.5
GMT	03 30	Gyro Error	**0°.4 L**
Declination	23° 26′.1		
d Corrn	0.0		
Declination	23° 26′.1		

Amplitude observations are usually taken for the sun or moon rising or setting. In the case of the sun, the moment of observation is when the lower limb of the sun is half a diameter above the visible horizon. At this position the sun is at the celestial horizon and the time is that of the theoretical sunrise or sunset. The zenith distance of a body is 90°. In the case of the moon, the moment of observation is when the upper limb of the moon is nearly on the visible horizon.

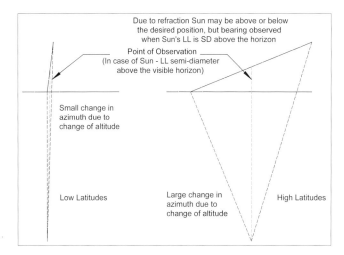

Figure 8.6 Amplitude, high and low latitudes

At high latitudes, when there is a small change in altitude there is a significant change in azimuth. If the refraction on the day or the position of observation was abnormal then, at the time of theoretical rising or setting, the body may be above or below the desired position. The problem is accentuated further in higher latitudes, where the body sets or rises at a shallow angle to the horizon. Due to abnormal refraction, the body may be apparently lifted above the actual position or may be depressed below the actual position. The observer would not be able to spot the difference and would take the bearing when, for example the sun was half the diameter above the visible horizon. This would cause an error in the observed bearing. Due to this, the error obtained in higher latitudes using the amplitude method may be less reliable when compared to the error obtained by the azimuth method.

If Examples 8.6 and 8.7 relate to the same ship with the gyro error obtained on the same day, at this high latitude the results of the azimuth observation would be more reliable when compared to amplitude observation.

8.5 Astronomical Position Lines

8.5.1 Navigational Triangle

This is the spherical triangle formed by the arcs of the following Great Circles:

- Celestial meridian through the observer
- Hour Circle through the body
- Vertical Circle through the zenith and the body.

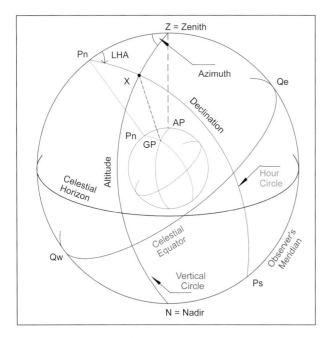

Figure 8.7 Triangle on plane of observers meridian

The three points of the triangle are P, Z and X for the celestial pole, zenith and the body respectively. The terrestrial equivalents are the geographical pole, the observer's assumed position and the geographical position of the body. The navigational triangle can help solve several navigational problems.

- Where latitude, declination and hour angle are known, altitude and the azimuth can be determined
- the identification of a body can be made possible by working out the declination and hour angle where latitude, altitude and the azimuth are known
- where the hour angle, declination and altitude are known the azimuth can be calculated.

The astronomical position line is part of a small circle, which has the body "X" as its centre and passes through the zenith "Z". As the solution of the navigational triangle is based on the observer's assumed position, the intercept distance is derived as the difference between the true and calculated altitudes, ie the zenith distance, and the position line also runs perpendicular to the azimuth of the heavenly body.

The following assumptions are made when plotting astronomical position lines:

- The true bearing of the geographical position of the heavenly body is the same at all points in the vicinity of the assumed position (DR or EP) and the observed position
- the position line is part of a small circle, that is plotted as a straight, or rhumb, line and coincides

with the arc of the observed position circle on the chart. The direction of the intercept is part of a Great Circle forming the true bearing to or from the body and is plotted as a straight (rhumb) line
- when several position lines are to be plotted for a common time of position, these position lines are run onwards or backwards.

There are a few methods for determining the position lines, two examples follow.

8.5.1.1 Intercept Method (Marq St Hilaire)

In this method, the calculated zenith distance and the azimuth are worked out from the observer's DR (assumed position). The calculated zenith distance (CZD) is compared with true zenith distance (TZD) to determine the intercept. The position line is plotted perpendicular to the azimuth from the intercept terminal point. The intercept is plotted towards or away, depending on whether the TZD is less than or more than the CZD.

TZD less than CZD:	Intercept Towards (True Tiny Towards)
TZD more than CZD:	Intercept Away
True Altitude less than Calculated Altitude:	Intercept Away
True Altitude more than Calculated Altitude:	Intercept Towards

Cosine method can be used for the zenith distance:

$\cos ZX = \cos PZ \cos PX + \sin PZ \sin PX \cos ZPX$ or

$\cos ZX = \sin Lat \sin Dec +/- \cos Lat \cos Dec \cos LHA$

8.5.1.2 Longitude By Chronometer

This method provides a calculated longitude through the DR latitude for plotting the position line. The plotting is simplified as no intercept is involved. The method is not suitable for a body approaching the meridian as a large displacement of longitude may be generated due to small errors. The calculation involves working out the LHA, which provides the calculated longitude:

LHA – GHA = East Longitude
GHA – LHA = West Longitude

$$\cos LHA = \frac{\sin True\ Altitude - (\sin Dec \times \sin Lat)}{\cos Dec \times \cos Lat}$$

Calculations involving longitude by chronometer have been added to the Example 8.8 solution.

Example 8.8

At 0825 on 06th May 2006, in DR Posn 34° 58´.0 N 146° 03´.0 E, the sextant altitude of the Sun's lower limb was 39° 42´.3 when the chronometer showed 10h 42m 06s.

The chronometer has no error. Find the intercept and direction of the position line if the index error is 2´.1 on the arc and the height of eye is 15.4m.

Solution and Comments

DR Latitude		N 34° 58´.0	Date and Z T		06 May'06 0825
DR Longitude		E 146° 03´.0	Zone	- 10	10
			Greenwich date		05 May'06 2225
Body		Sun's LL			
C T		22 42 06			
C E		00			
GMT		22 42 06			
Almanac data					
Tabulated GHA		150° 50´.0			
Increment		10° 31´.5			
v Corrⁿ	SHA		**Long by Chron Results**		
GHA		161° 21´.5	GHA		161° 21´.5
Longitude		E 146° 03´.0	cos LHA		0.60824428
- 360° ?			Calculated LHA		052° 32´.2
LHA		307° 24´.5			307° 27´.8
Declination		N 16° 24´.8			
d Corrⁿ	+ 0.7	0´.5			
Declination		N 16° 25´.3			
cos ZX		0.639540222			
CZD		50° 14´.5	**Calc Longitude**		**E 146° 06´.3**
Altitude					
Sext Alt		39° 42´.3			
IE		- 2´.1			
Obs Alt		39° 40´.2			
Dip		- 6´.9			
App Alt		39° 33´.3			
T Corrⁿ		+ 14´.8			
True Alt		39° 48´.1			
TZD		50° 11´.9			
Intercept		**2´.6 T**			
Azimuth					
A		S 0.534847663			
B		N 0.371040178			
C		S 0.163807484			
tan Az		7.44946243			
True Az		S82°.4E			
		097°.6 T			
P/L		**007°.6/197°.6**			

8.6 Fix by Celestial Observations

To obtain a fix at least two position lines are required. Using celestial bodies, these position lines can be based on observing the sun, moon, stars or planets. During daylight, when the sun is above the horizon, it is rare to see a celestial body other than the moon by the naked eye, and this is only when it is above the horizon. However, when Venus is not fixed by the sun, its altitude and bearing can be precomputed and observed during the day. If the moon is not visible, and the sun is the only body visible, a running fix must be used to fix the ship's position.

The following combinations are possible:

Sun – run – Sun
Sun – run – Meridian Altitude of sun
Meridian Altitude of sun – run – Sun
Sun – run – Moon or Moon – run – Sun
Sun – run – Star/Planet
Star/Planet – run – Sun (stars/planets during twilight only)

At night the horizon is not distinct enough to obtain the altitudes required for working out sights, the only exception being within three days of the Full Moon. As stars and planets are not visible by the naked eye during the day, and at night the horizon is not visible, sights of stars and planets can only be taken when both are distinct, ie during twilight.

The twilights are categorised as (when sun is):

Civil: Sunset to 6° below the horizon
Nautical: Sun 6° to 12° below the horizon
Astronomical: Sun 12° to 18° below the horizon

Total darkness occurs when the sun is 18° or more below the horizon. The best time for observation is at the beginning of nautical twilight in the evening and the end of nautical twilight in the morning. As several bodies may have to be observed, a time window should be allowed when sun is between 3° and 9° below the horizon, ie half way between the period of civil twilight to or from, half way between periods of nautical twilight. Similar to the circumpolar concept, in certain latitudes twilight may also last all night, allowing sights to be observed more frequently.

8.6.1 Planning Sights

8.6.1.1 Selection of Heavenly Bodies

For a fix to be reliable, the selection of stars and planets requires consideration. The following points should be considered when planning a morning or evening sight:

- Using a star chart or globe, the stars and planets to be used should be determined

- three or more stars and/or planets should be selected. In case of there being a partly cloudy sky, select an additional four standby stars
- the stars/planets selected should give the best cuts for position lines. At least two should be about 90° apart in the azimuth. In general, the bodies should never be less than 30° apart in the azimuth.

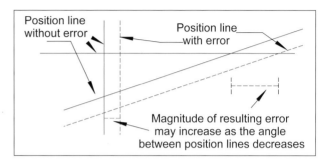

Figure 8.8 Errors due to small angles between position lines

- The best combination is four stars 90° apart within an azimuth. These combinations will have stars on opposite horizons, or all round the horizon. Opposite horizons will eliminate any abnormal refraction error
- star close to north or south azimuth points confirms the latitude well
- star close to east or west azimuth points confirms the longitude well
- choosing stars with an altitude of around 45°, or between 20° and 70°, though 30° to 60° would be a better choice.
- preferably, all stars should be on the same altitude, especially those on opposite horizons to each other. The refraction is in layers and, if the stars happen to be within similar layers to each other, abnormal refraction can be cancelled out.

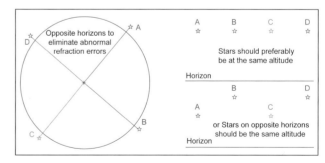

Figure 8.9 Azimuth and altitude of stars/planets

Planning should assist in identifying stars or planets and should also help to reduce the time loss between observations. The following should be considered:

- Make a general sketch of the approximate altitudes and bearings of the chosen stars relative to the ship's head, for identification. A sextant can be set to these altitudes to scan the horizon in the direction of the star for detection

- make a note of the weather and the direction where the horizon is likely to be clearest
- care must be taken while making observations in order to make use of the clearest horizon
- start taking sights from the eastern horizon first and then the west. In the morning the eastern stars will fade away first and, in the evening the eastern horizon will become indistinct first
- observe stars as early as possible at evening twilight and as late as possible at morning twilight to make use of clearest horizon
- in the morning start with the faintest star as it will not remain visible for long
- in the evening start with the brightest star as it will be seen first and the best horizon will be available
- choose stars that are clear of the ships rigging or exhaust gases when observing altitude.

General precautions for sights taken at any time of the day are as follows:

- In clear weather take observations from the highest convenient position to take advantage of the clear distant horizon. This avoids errors caused by high waves obscuring the horizon and parallax
- always swing the sextant a few degrees to each side of the vertical plane as the body is brought to the horizon. Adjustments to the altitude should then be made by micrometer, until it just touches the horizon
- when possible, check the sextant for side error before taking sights
- when possible, take the index error before and after sights
- when observing the sun, use sufficiently strong shades to avoid being dazzled
- if the identity of a body is uncertain after taking altitude, take its bearing
- when the ship is rolling heavily, observations should be taken from close to the centre line of the vessel to minimise errors due to changing DIP
- in the tropics, it is best to place the sextant outside, in its box, 15 minutes before use so it can warm up. This will stop condensation forming as it would if taken from an air conditioned bridge to a warm/humid bridge wing.

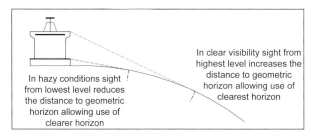

Figure 8.10 Observation points on ship in different conditions

8.6.2 Sights in Hazy Conditions

- In haze or mist, take observations from the lowest convenient position as this will reduce the distance to the horizon where it is likely to be clearer
- with an indistinct, cloudy or hazy sun, align the middle of the disk with the horizon instead of UL or LL. (Altitude corrections, less than for SD, must be applied separately)
- when possible, take observations of a heavenly body in sets of three or five at approximately equal time intervals
- when the horizon is poor, it is essential to take several altitudes of each body and to set the sextant to a given increase or decrease between each observation. If time intervals are not equal, sights should be either discarded or used with extreme caution.

8.6.3 Abnormal Refraction

Opposite horizons
A pair of stars on opposite sides of the horizon, almost 180° apart in azimuth, should be observed in order to cancel out the effect of refraction. When the two position lines are plotted, the linear or angular distance between them should be halved. A second pair 90° different in azimuth from the first pair should be observed and plotted in the same manner as the first pair. Example 8.11 illustrates this point.

Reverse angle sight
A body at an altitude higher than 60° should be observed twice, once with the normal observation of least altitude and once with the reverse observation (180° - least altitude) on the opposite horizon. (NB: A sextant can only measure angles up to 120°. 180° - >60° = <120°). The two altitudes, corrected for index error, should be added and their sum subtracted from 180°. The resulting difference is the sum of dip and refraction in both directions, and is twice the value of dip and refraction when the abnormal refraction is believed to be the same in both directions.

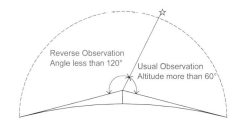

Figure 8.11 Reverse angle sight

Application of corrections
Nautical almanac table A4 for a range of temperature and pressure conditions temperatures and at different apparent altitudes.

Norie's tables provide separate correction tables for pressure and temperature against apparent altitude.

Example 8.9

On 5th May 2006, during the morning twilight, a ship in position 26° 05′ S, 150° 00′ W, needs to verify their position by observing the stars, after several days of the GPS receiver not working. Select the most suitable stars to be confident in verifying the ship's position.

Solution and Comments:

The time of Civil Twilight must be calculated first.

Civil Twilight LMT (20° S)	0554
Increment (6° 05′)	+ 0006
LMT (26° 05′ S)	0600
Long in Time (150° W)	+ 1000
GMT Civil Twilight	1600

Next, LHA of Aries must be calculated.

GHA Aries (1600) 05 May	103° 23′.0
Increment (00 min)	0
GHA (1600)	103° 23′.0
360° +	463° 23′.0
Longitude	150° 00′ W
LHA	313° 23′.0

Using the nearest whole number of LHA Aries degrees and latitude, stars can be obtained from the Sight Reduction Table, see Figure 8.12.

	DENEB	Enif	◆FOMALHAUT	ACHERNAR	◆ RIGIL KENT	ANTARES	◆ VEGA
300	18 03 008	45 59 039	50 40 106	24 31 144	27 21 213	43 15 257	22 23 343
301	18 10 007	46 32 038	51 32 106	25 03 144	26 52 213	42 23 257	22 06 342
302	18 16 006	47 04 036	52 24 105	25 35 143	26 23 213	41 30 257	21 49 341
303	18 22 006	47 36 035	53 16 105	26 07 143	25 54 212	40 38 256	21 31 340
304	18 27 005	48 06 034	54 08 105	26 39 143	25 25 212	39 45 256	21 13 340
305	18 31 004	48 36 033	55 00 105	27 12 143	24 56 212	38 53 256	20 54 339
306	18 34 003	49 04 031	55 52 105	27 44 143	24 27 212	38 01 256	20 34 338
307	18 37 003	49 32 030	56 44 105	28 16 143	23 59 212	37 08 255	20 14 337
308	18 39 002	49 58 029	57 36 105	28 49 143	23 30 212	36 16 255	19 52 337
309	18 40 001	50 23 027	58 28 105	29 21 143	23 02 212	35 24 255	19 31 336
310	18 41 000	50 47 026	59 20 105	29 54 143	22 33 212	34 32 255	19 08 335
311	18 41 000	51 10 024	60 12 105	30 26 143	22 05 212	33 40 254	18 45 334
312	18 40 359	51 32 023	61 05 105	30 59 143	21 36 212	32 48 254	18 22 334
313	18 39 358	51 52 021	61 57 105	31 31 143	21 08 211	31 56 254	17 57 333
314	18 37 357	52 11 020	62 49 105	32 04 143	20 40 211	31 05 253	17 33 332
	Alpheratz	◆ Diphda	ACHERNAR	◆ RIGIL KENT	ANTARES	◆ ALTAIR	DENEB
315	18 38 043	37 48 093	32 36 143	20 12 211	30 13 253	51 19 332	18 34 357
316	19 15 042	38 42 093	33 09 143	19 44 211	29 22 253	50 53 331	18 30 356
317	19 50 041	39 36 092	33 41 143	19 17 211	28 30 253	50 26 329	18 26 355
318	20 26 041	40 29 092	34 14 143	18 49 211	27 39 252	49 58 328	18 21 354
319	21 00 040	41 23 092	34 46 143	18 22 210	26 47 252	49 29 327	18 16 354

Figure 8.12   Extract of sight reduction table

Stars Available:

Star	Altitude (Hc)	Azimuth (Zn)
DENEB	18° 39′	358°
ENIF	51° 52′	021°
◆FOMALHAUT	61° 57′	105°
ACHERNAR	31° 31′	143°
◆RIGIL KENT	21° 08′	211°
ANTARES	31° 56′	254°
◆VEGA	17° 57′	333°

A◆ shape before the name of a star indicates that it is the most suitable for a three star fix, as they are well spread over the horizon.

In order to choose the best stars and plan the sight, it is best to draw a sketch of the horizon, indicating the azimuth and altitude of the stars on it.

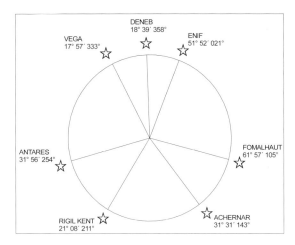

Figure 8.13   Sketch of horizon with stars for sight

Usually stars on opposite horizons can be selected for a high confidence fix. Considering the choice, an alternative approach is shown below.

- Vega and Achernar are stars on almost opposite horizons, they are actually 170° apart, to eliminate abnormal refraction
- secondly, Enif and Fomalhaut are stars that are almost perpendicular, they are actually 84° apart, enabling a good angle of intersection of the position lines.

The resulting position and position lines are shown in Example 8.15.

8.6.4 Plotting Sights

All of the position lines required for plotting a fix using stars and planets cannot be observed together at the same time. There will be a small time lapse between one observation and the next. The time between the first and last observation may be significant. Therefore, it is important to run the position lines obtained by the stars and planets around a common time for which the position is required. The following examples demonstrate this effectively. In addition, the examples cover the various planning and analysis aspects of the stellar/planetary fixes.

Example 8.10

A ship steering 247°T at 16 knots obtained the following intercepts using the 0615 DR Posn 21° 12′ N, 154° 35′ E for all sights:

	Time	Bearing	True Altitude	Intercept
Star A	0610	269°T	56° 55′	1′.2 Towards
Star B	0617	330°T	31° 42′	2′.3 Towards
Star C	0625	153°T	34° 11′	2′.3 Away
Star D	0635	095°T	59° 50′	7′.4 Away

Plot these observations to find the ship's position for 0615 hrs.

Solution and Comments

In general, the position should be run from the ITP, but in the case of stars when several position lines must be plotted, it is advisable to allow the run on the ship's track instead of the ITP. Before plotting, it is important to decide the run-on or run-back for each position line. For a running fix, the position lines obtained before the time of the position are run forward (Run-on) and the ones obtained after the time of the position are run backward (Run-back). Follow a tabular approach and always write the time of the star after the time of fix and obtain the arithmetic difference between the times and follow sign, + run-on, - run-back. As the position is required for 0615:

Star	Position Time	Star Time	Time Interval	Run Distance
Star A	0615	0610	+5 minutes	1′.33 Run-on
Star B	0615	0617	-2 minutes	0′.53 Run-back
Star C	0615	0625	-10 minutes	2′.67 Run-back
Star D	0615	0635	-20 minutes	5′.33 Run-back

Remember that the runs are for the common time of position and not necessarily from the DR.

By observation, it can be seen that the pairs of stars A and D, B and C are on opposite horizons. The angles between their position lines have been halved. The fix is selected as the point at the intersection of the bisector lines.

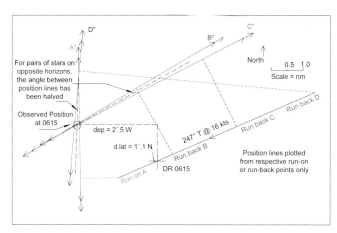

Figure 8.14 Plot for example 8.10

From the plot:

d.lat	= 1′.1 N	departure = 2′.5 W
mean lat	= DR lat + ½ d.lat	= 21° 12′ N + 0′.55 N
	= 21° 12′.55 N	
d.long	= dep/cos mean lat	= 2′.5/cos 21° 12′.55
	= 2′.7 W	

	DR lat	21° 12′.0 N		long	154° 35′.0 E
	d.lat	1′.1 N		d.long	2′.7 W
Position 0615		**21° 13′.1 N**			**154° 32′.3 E**

Reliability of Position

If it is necessary to comment on the reliability of an observed position, the following should be argued?

- Number of stars
- azimuth between stars, 90°, but not less than 30°
- opposite horizons
- altitude 45°, or between 30° and 60°, or 20° and 70°
- altitude of stars is the same or at least the same for stars on opposite horizons
- resulting angle of cut between the bisector lines.

Example 8.11

A ship steering 125°T at 20 knots observes the following stars:

	Time	Bearing	True Altitude	Intercept
Star A	0539	284°T	52° 45′	2′.1 Towards
Star B	0548	264°T	31° 42′	1′.3 Towards
Star C	0600	045°T	44° 16′	3′.9 Away
Star D	0609	169°T	34° 28′	9′.9 Towards

The 0545 DR position 38° 32′ S, 124° 25′ W was used for all intercepts. Find the ship's position at 0600 hrs.

Solution and Comments

As the position is required for 0600 and all intercepts have been worked from the same DR, Star C would be plotted at DR and the other stars will be run as per their times of observation:

Star	Position Time	Star Time	Time Interval	Run Distance
Star A	0600	0539	+21 minutes	7′.0 Run-on
Star B	0600	0548	+12 minutes	4′.0 Run-on
Star C	0600	0600	0	0′.0 (at DR)
Star D	0600	0609	-9 minutes	3′.0 Run-back

After working on Example 8.9, at first glance, it may appear to an inexperienced navigator that stars A and B are on opposite horizons. This would lead to a serious error as the navigator may halve the angle between the two stars. For opposite horizons, the azimuth must be considered and not the angle between position lines. In this case, stars B and D are almost at a right angle and stars A and C have angles of 65° and 56° with star D. Similarly, stars A and C have an angle of 59° between them. The position has been plotted close to the intersection of B and D, with an allowance made for A and C. The actual intersection between the position lines of A, B and C is not the observed position. Remember that a position line should not be discarded as it is not exactly at an intersection of the others. In this case position line D has the best angles of cut with all the other position lines.

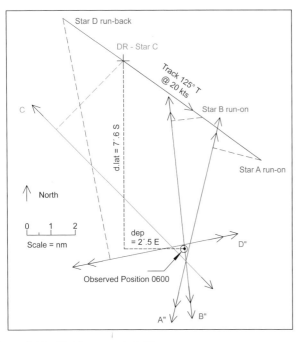

Figure 8.15 Plot for example 8.11

From the plot:

d.lat	= 7´.6 S	departure	= 2´.5 E
mean lat	= DR lat + ½ d.lat	= 38° 32´ S + 3´.8 S	
	= 38° 35´.8 S		
d.long	= dep/cos mean lat	= 2´.5/cos 38° 35´.8	
	= 3´.2 E		

	DR lat	38° 32´.0 S	long	124° 25´.0 W
	d.lat	7´.6 S	d.long	3´.2 E
Position 0600		**38° 39´.6 S**		**124° 21´.8 W**

Example 8.12

A ship in DR Posn 43° 52´ N 135° 32´ W, steaming on a course of 255°T at 15 knots observes the sun bearing 121°T at 0935 (+0900) on 05th May 2006. An intercept of 4´ towards was obtained. Index error is 1´.5 off the arc and height of eye is 16.5 m. Calculate:

- *GMT of the meridian passage of the sun*
- *the setting on the sextant to observe the Sun's lower limb at the meridian passage*
- *the position of the ship at the meridian passage of the Sun when the sextant altitude is 62° 36´.*

Solution and Comments

As the ship is proceeding, the longitude for the meridian passage must be determined first. This can be done by using either the approximation or iteration method. The calculation is shown on the following table. Using the results, the plot is:

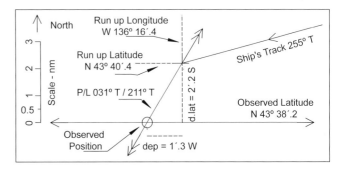

Figure 8.16 Plot for example 8.12

The accuracy of the above position depends heavily on the course maintained by the vessel and the distance covered, apart from general errors, which are discussed later in this chapter. If all the errors were taken care of the fix would be reliable, as observed latitude at the meridian passage is very reliable and the position lines cut at an angle of 59°.

DR Latitude	N 43° 52′.0	Date and Z T		05 May'06 0935
DR Longitude	W 135° 32′.0	Zone	+9	0900
Course/Speed	255°T/15 kts	Greenwich date		05 May'06 1835
For ITP				
d.lat	4 x cos 59°	= 2′.1 S		
dep	4 x sin 59°	= 3′.4 E		
mean lat	lat ~ ½ dl.lat	= 43° 50′.95		
d.long	dep/cos m lat	= 4′.7 E		
ITP	N 43° 49′.9	W 135° 27′.3		
1st Approx		**1st run up posn**		Course = S75°W
LMT merpass	11 57	d.lat		9′.3 S
LIT (135° 27′.3)	09 02	dep		34′.8 W
GMT	20 59	mean lat (from ITP)		43° 45′.25
Initial GMT	18 35	d.long		48′.2 W
Run	02 24	1st run up Lat		N 43° 40′.6
Speed	15	1st run up Long		W 136° 15′.5
Distance Run	36′			
2nd Approx		**2nd run up posn**		
LMT merpass	11 57	d.lat		9′.5 S
LIT (136° 15′.5)	09 05	dep		35′.5 W
GMT merpass	**21 02**	mean lat (from ITP)		43° 45′.15
Initial GMT	18 35	d.long		49′.1 W
Run	02 27	2nd run up Lat		N 43° 40′.4
Speed	15	2nd run up Long		W 136° 16′.4
Distance Run	36′.75			
		Altitude		
Declination 2100	N 16° 24′.1	Sext Alt		62° 36′.0
d Corr[n] + 0.7	0.0	IE		+ 1′.5
Declination	N 16° 24′.1	Obs Alt		62° 37′.5
		Dip		- 7′.1
Setting sextant		App Alt		62° 30′.4
Lat N 43° 40′.4		T Corr[n]		+ 15′.5
TA = D – L + 90°	62° 43′.7	True Alt		62° 45′.9
		L = D – TA + 90°		N 43° 38′.2
Sext Alt	**62° 33′.8**	From Plot		
IE	+ 1′.5	dep		1′.3 W
Obs Alt	62° 35′.3	mean lat		43° 39′.3
Dip	- 7′.1	d.long		1′.8 W
App Alt	62° 28′.2			
T Corr[n]	+ 15′.5	For T bearing of		121° T
True Alt	62° 43′.7	Position Line =		031° T/211° T
(working back)		**Observed Posn**		
		Latitude		**N 43° 38′.2**
		Longitude		**W 136° 18′.2**

8.6.5 Errors in Astronomical Position Lines

The position lines may be worked out or plotted with error(s). The following are the general errors that may affect the accuracy of the position lines:

- The sextant altitude of a heavenly body should be corrected for index error, dip, refraction, semi-diameter and parallax. Even then, the resulting true altitude may be incorrect due to a combination of observation errors and incorrect values of dip and refraction. The resulting error becomes part of the position line when it is plotted
- the error in the time may be due to:
  - an incorrect reading of the chronometer
  - an incorrect error
  - an error being applied incorrectly.

An error in time will result in an error in the hour angle. This will lead to an error in the calculated altitude and the intercept, so the position line will be incorrect. The position line may have an error in longitude by 1′ of longitude for every 4 seconds of time error. This error in distance would be greater at the equator than at the poles. Such an error would be zero when the body is on the observer's meridian.

The method of working sights may cause an error in the calculated altitude, affecting the intercept in the same way that an error in the observed altitude affects it. There are two reasons for this error. There is the accumulative and unavoidable error caused by the addition and rounding-off of the quantities taken from the almanac. There is also an error in the method used to resolve the astronomical triangle. The second error arises as the calculations may be simplified by working to only a few decimal places, the error will vary depending on the method being used.

When time has elapsed between two observations of heavenly bodies, the first position line may be incorrectly transferred for various reasons, including:

- The course laid down on the chart or plotting sheet may be different to the course made good or the course being steered is inaccurate
- inaccuracy of the speed made good, which is then passed on to the transferred position lines
- due to the rhumb line itself, the azimuth and intercept should range with the transfer.

8.6.6 Cocked Hat

Three astronomical position lines are unlikely to pass through the same point due to the errors mentioned above. Each position line is displaced parallel to its actual location and a cocked hat is formed. The errors may be equal in magnitude and a sign for each position line, termed the common equal error, eg index error. In this case mathematical construction techniques can be used to resolve the cocked hat.

Unless the separate errors are known, the true observed position cannot be found. However, if all the errors are assumed to be equal in magnitude and sign, as they would be if, for example, the only source of error lay in an inaccurate value of the index error, then simple constructions to find the fix can be applied.

The construction examples are for two conditions:

- All bodies contained within 180° of azimuth
- all bodies spread over the horizon – containing azimuth more than 180° regardless of whether the intercepts are towards, away or a mix of both.

When errors are random, the mathematical construction cannot be applied. The only option is to derive the most likely position, the explanation for this is not covered in this book. It should be remembered that in this type of case the most likely position will be inside the Cocked Hat, with a probability of 25%.

In the constructions below, the position lines are displaced either towards the body or away from the body. It is essential to displace all the position lines in the same direction, ie either all towards or all away. Additionally, all the offset distances should be the same, eg 1′ or 2′. It is not necessary to apply the exact error. By applying a known offset, a trend in error is introduced, which will assist in resolving the cocked hat.

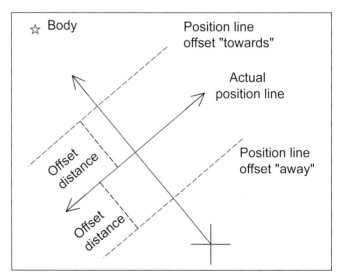

Figure 8.17 Position line offset

Construction for azimuth covering more than 180°

In this case the bodies are well spread over the horizon. All position lines are offset 1′ AWAY. Bisectors are drawn through the intersection of the actual position lines and the respective intersection of the offset position lines. The point where the bisectors meet is the observed position. The position in this case is within the actual Cocked Hat. The result would have been the same if position lines were offset TOWARDS.

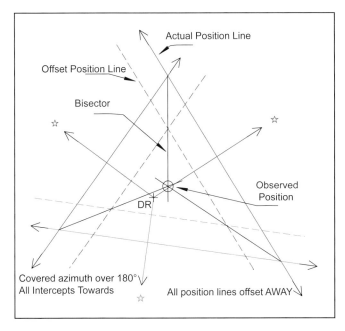

Figure 8.18   Observed position within actual cocked hat

Construction for azimuths covering less than 180°

In this case the bodies are on one side of the horizon. All position lines are offset 1′ AWAY.

Bisectors are drawn through the intersection of the actual position lines and the respective intersection of the offset position lines. The point where the bisectors meet is the observed position. The position in this case is outside the actual Cocked Hat. The result would have been the same if the position lines were offset TOWARDS.

By observing the angle contained within azimuth, mariners can determine where the position could be in case a cocked hat results after plotting.

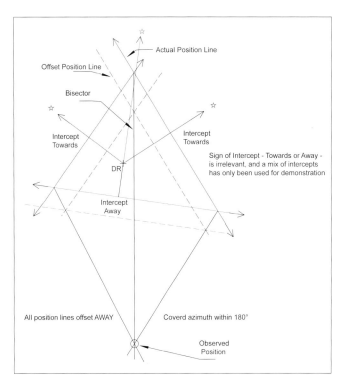

Figure 8.19   Observed position outside actual cocked hat

Alternate method

It is not essential to carry out elaborate construction. All that is required is the bisection of the angles at the intersection of the position lines in the appropriate direction. Instead of offsetting the position lines, the angles at TOWARDS or AWAY direction can be bisected.

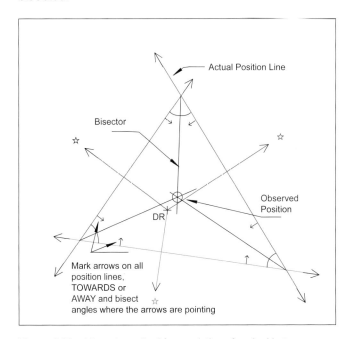

Figure 8.20   Alternate method for resolution of cocked hat

This section demonstrates the importance of taking star sights all round the horizon if possible.

It is very important to realise that the above constructions are valid only when the errors in the zenith distances obtained from the sextant observations are equal in magnitude and sign, as they are when the index error is incorrect or applied the wrong way. This implies that when there are systematic errors in the position lines, these errors can be resolved by construction techniques. On the other hand if there are random errors in the position lines, such errors cannot be resolved by construction alone. The constructions can be made whether or not other errors are taken into consideration and may give a false sense of accuracy. No reliance should be placed on such constructions unless it is known that the total errors in each intercept are equal in magnitude and sign.

Example 8.13
At 1920 hrs, a ship in DR Posn 25° 30′ S, 073° 42′ E, on a course of 230°T at 22 knots, makes the following observations:

	Time	True Alt	Azimuth	Intercept
Star A	1950	25° 48′	282°T	2′.5 T
Star B	1945	41° 13′	140°T	0′.6 A
Star C	1935	38° 42′	350°T	4′.5 A

The same DR was used for all intercepts. Determine the most probable position at 1935, if there was doubt about the accuracy of the index error.

Solution and Comments
The runs for the three stars from 1935 are as follows:

Star	Position Time	Star Time	Time Interval	Run Distance
Star A	1935	1950	= -15 minutes	= 5′.5 run-back
Star B	1935	1945	= -10 minutes	= 3′.67 run-back
Star C	1935	1935	= 0	= 0

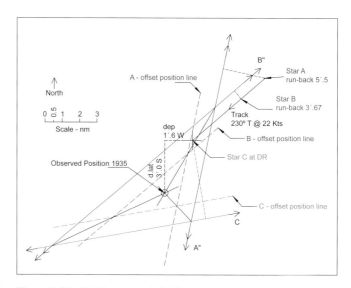

Figure 8.21 Plot for example 8.13

From the plot:

d.lat	= 3′.0 S	departure	= 1′.6 W
mean lat	= DR lat + ½ d.lat	= 25° 30′ S + 1′.5 S	
	= 25° 31′.5 S		
d.long	= dep/cos mean lat	= 1′.6/cos 25° 31′.5	
	= 1′.8 W		

DR lat	25° 30′.0 S	long	073° 42′.0 E
d.lat	3′.0 S	d.long	1′.8 W
Position 1935	**25° 33′.0 N**		**073° 40′.2 E**

8.6.7 Polaris

It is important to discuss Polaris, also known as α Ursæ Minoris, separately. Polaris is not exactly at the north celestial pole and describes a small circle of approximately 1° radius. If it was at the north celestial pole, its true altitude would provide the latitude of the observer in the northern hemisphere and its bearing would provide reference to the true north.

Example 8.14
On 5th May 2006 at 0330 (GMT 05h 29m 42s), in DR 48° 46′N 023° 12′W, Polaris was observed at a sextant altitude of 48° 36′. Determine the position line and the latitude through which to draw the position line on the observer's meridian. The index error is 0′.7 off the arc, height of eye is 15.7 m, course 090°T and speed 18 knots.

Solution

DR Latitude	N 48° 46´.0	Date and Z T		05 May'06 0330
DR Longitude	W 023° 12´.0	Zone	+2	0200
Course/Speed	090°T/18 kts	Greenwich date		05 May'06 0530
GMT	05 29 42	**Altitude**		
GHA Aries	297° 55´.9	Sext Alt		48° 36´.0
Increment	7° 26´.7	IE		+ 0´.7
Sub-total	305° 22´.6	Obs Alt		48° 36´.7
Longitude	W 023° 12´.0	Dip		- 7´.0
- 360° ?		App Alt		48° 29´.7
LHA Aries	282° 10´.6	T Corr^n		- 0´.9
		True Alt		48° 28´.8
		a_0		1° 18´.6
		a_1		0´.6
		a_2		0´.4
Azimuth	001°.0 T			-1° 00´.0
Position line	091° T ~ 271° T	Latitude		N 48° 48´.4

It must be remembered that the latitude obtained is not the latitude of the observer and is only a point on the observer's meridian through which to plot the position line.

8.6.8 Sight Reduction Tables

In addition to determining suitable stars for observations, sight reduction tables can also be used for rapid sight working, as an alternative to using Marq St Hilaire's techniques.

In this method, a whole degree of latitude is used and longitudes are adjusted to obtain a whole degree of LHA Aries. This latitude and the new longitude acts as the assumed position for plotting stars.

Example 8.15

On 5th May 2006, a ship steering 270°T at 18 knots observes the following stars:

Star	Time	Sextant Altitude
Fomalhaut	*16 00 02*	*62° 19´.5*
Achernar	*16 01 58*	*32° 00´.9*
Enif	*16 03 52*	*52° 29´.9*
Vega	*16 05 57*	*17° 30´.4*

The DR position 26° 05´ S, 150° 00´ W was used for all calculations. Using the Sight Reduction Table, determine the position at GMT1600 hrs, ie 2.0 on the arc, Height of Eye 11.5 m.

Solution and Comments

	FOMALHAUT	ACHERNAR	ENIF	VEGA
GMT	16 00 02	16 01 58	16 03 55	16 05 57
Tabulated GHA	103° 23´.0	103° 23´.0	103° 23´.0	103° 23´.0
Increment	00´.5	29´.6	58´.9	1° 29´.5
GHA Aries	103° 23´.5	103° 52´.6	104° 21´.9	104° 52´.5
360° +	463° 23´.5	463° 52´.6	464° 21´.9	464° 52´.5
Longitude	W 150° 23´.5	150° 52´.6	150° 21´.9	150° 52´.5
LHA	313° 00´.0	313° 00´.0	314° 00´.0	314° 00´.0
Sext Alt	62° 19´.5	32° 00´.9	52° 29´.9	17° 30´.4
IE (2´.0 On)	- 2´.0	- 2´.0	- 2´.0	- 2´.0
Obs Alt	62° 17´.5	31° 58´.9	52° 27´.9	17° 28´.4
Dip (11.5 m)	- 6´.0	- 6´.0	- 6´.0	- 6´.0
App Alt	62° 11´.5	31° 52´.9	52° 21´.9	17° 22´.4
T Corr[n]	- 0´.5	- 1´.6	- 0´.7	- 3´.1
True Alt	62° 11´.0	31° 51´.3	52° 21´.2	17° 19´.3
Using Latitude 26° S and LHA Aries of 313° and 314° for respective stars:				
Calculated Alt	61° 57´.0	31° 31´.0	52° 11´.0	17° 33´.0
True Altitude	62° 11´.0	31° 51´.3	52° 21´.2	17° 19´.3
Intercept	**14´.0 T**	**20´.3 T**	**10´.2 T**	**13´.7 A**
Since we are working with T. Alt, rule for naming intercept is reversed to: True Big - Towards				
Azimuth	105° T	143° T	020° T	332° T
P/L	**195°/015°**	**233°/053°**	**290°/110°**	**242°/062°**
Rounded Off GMT	1600	1602	1604	1606
Run Time	00	- 02	- 04	- 06
Run Distance	0´	0´.6 back	1´.2 Back	1´.8 Back

Note: Run distances have been applied to longitude points for plotting stars. Do not be concerned about the magnitude of intercepts before plotting.

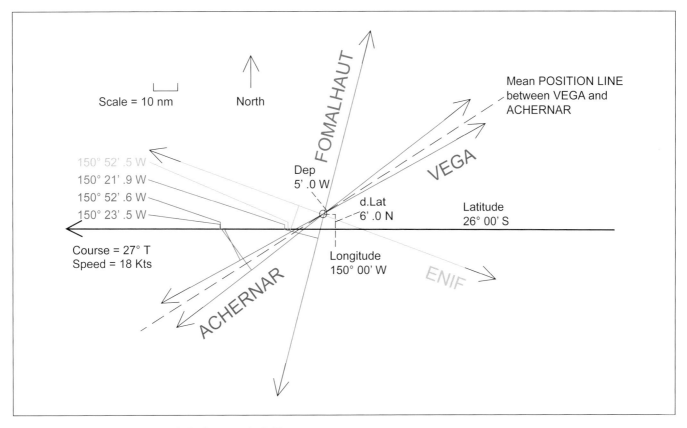

Figure 8.22   Resultant position and plot for example 8.15

From the plot:

d.lat	= 4´.0 N	departure	= 6´.0 W
mean lat	= DR lat + ½ d.lat	= 26° 05´ S + 2´.5 N	
	= 26° 02´.5 S		
d.long	= dep/cos mean lat	= 6´.0/cos 26° 02´.5	
	= 6´.7 W		

DR lat	26° 05´.0 S	long	150° 00´.0 W
d.lat	6´.0 N	d.long	6´.7 W
Position 1600	**25° 59´.0 S**		**150° 06´.7 W**

8.7 NAVPAC

NavPac provides navigators and astronomers with simple and efficient methods for calculating the position of the sun, moon, navigational planets and stars over several years with the aid of a pocket calculator, personal computer or laptop.

The software package NavPac runs on a windows PC or one that is compatible, it allows navigators to compute their position at sea. The manual is included on the CD-ROM, it also includes part of the Admiralty Manual of Navigation (Volume 2). There are functions for calculating the rise and set times of celestial objects and for determining the altitude and azimuths of navigational objects.

Author's Note
Satisfaction about the electronic navigational aids performance can be obtained through frequent cross checks using celestial navigation methods. This way the navigator remains in practice and is able to find out where the ship is, or how the equipment is performing, without having to look at a fancy box every time. It is possible, though not likely, that the electronic aids to navigation will fail, or be switched off. As an element of risk assessment, the preparedness to deal with any situation is an important step towards overcoming or tackling the problem itself. In the event of failure or malfunction of electronic aids to navigation, the basic practices of celestial navigation will have to be improvised. The integrity of modern aids to navigation is not at question, but the confidence gained to navigate without them is a primary skill.

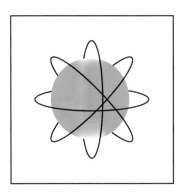

Electronic Navigation Aids

Recent decades have seen great advances in the techniques of navigation, largely due to technological development, especially in the fields of space and electronic computers. While it is essential to stay up to date with developments, the basic principles of marine navigation remain unchanged. Care must be taken to set up the navigational aids (navaids) properly, operate them correctly, apply any relevant errors and to plot positions accurately. This chapter covers the principles of operation and the precautions that should be taken during navigational use.

9.1 Satellite Navigation Systems

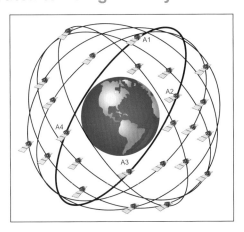

Figure 9.1   GPS orbits – 6 orbits with 4 satellites each

9.1.1 Global Positioning System (GPS)

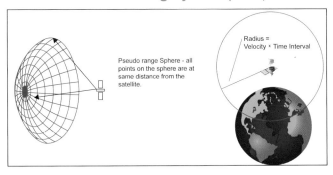

Figure 9.2   Section of pseudo-range sphere

GPS is based on the distance measured between satellites in orbit by a receiver. These distances are range spheres that intersect at the receiver for calculating the position. The receiver measures the propagation time of the satellite signals being received. The ranges measured are not true, but are pseudo ranges as they contain the receiver clock offset error. The receiver processor can resolve the three range equations to remove the effects of receiver clock offset and provide a 2-D fix, or it can resolve four pseudo-range equations to provide a 3-D fix. The systems, GPS and others, in current use or planned for the future are based on the measurement of time it takes for a radio signal to travel from a satellite to a receiver (Distance = Velocity × Time). These systems provide precise position, velocity and time information.

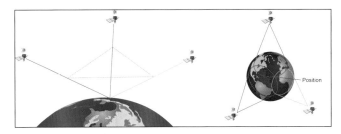

Figure 9.3   Three satellites produce 3 spheres for a 2D position

9.1.1.1 Frequencies and Codes

All transmissions from GPS satellites are on pseudo-random noise sequence modulated frequencies, L1, L2, etc. In the past, GPS satellites transmitted on two frequencies, L1 = 1575.42 MHz and L2 = 1227.60 MHz, but modernisation plans have allowed a third frequency to be used from 2005, L5 = 1176.45 MHz. Satellites transmitting the full range of L2 and L5 signals will be fully operational by 2011 and 2015. The basic reason for using two frequencies was that dual frequency receivers can correct for the effects of atmospheric refraction. L1 is less affected by ionospheric refraction error than L2 or L5 and it is anticipated that it will remain the most important civil frequency.

GPS can provide a Standard Positioning Service (SPS) or a Precise Positioning Service (PPS). SPS is based on the Coarse Acquisition (C/A) Code. Presently the C/A code is being transmitted on the L1 frequency, but plans are in place to also transmit it on the L2 frequency in order to provide a second civil signal. PPS is based on the Precise (P) Code, which is transmitted on both L1 and L2 frequencies. It is reserved for military use. Additionally, Y code has been developed separately from the C/A code for broadcast on a regional basis.

Over the next few years, the number of navigation signals will increase from three to seven. The C/A code can be received by all types of receivers, whereas the P code is encrypted for reception only by specific receivers. All codes carry a navigation message containing satellite ephemeris data, atmospheric propagation correction data and satellite clock bias. The new signals will have substantially better characteristics, including a pilot carrier, much longer codes, use of forward error correction and a more flexible message structure with much better resolution.

The system is designed to provide a minimum of four satellites above 9.5° elevation anywhere in the world. In most locations there are more than four satellites in view, the receiver can then select the four with the best GDOP (see 9.1.9.4) for the most accurate position.

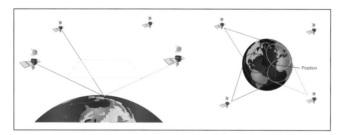

Figure 9.4   4 ranges for a 3-D fix

9.1.1.2 GPS Architecture

The system comprises of:

- A Master control station – this has equipment and facilities that are required for satellite monitoring, telemetry, tracking, commanding, controlling, uploading and navigation message generation
- monitoring stations – these passively track the satellites, accumulate ranging data from the satellites and relay to the Master station
- ground antennas – which are used for transmitting and receiving satellite control information
- satellite constellation
- receiver units – these can vary greatly in function and design, depending on their purpose.

9.1.2 GLONASS

This system is planned and controlled by the Russian Federation and is quite similar to the GPS. However,

there are some differences. It is based on the Earth Centred Earth Fixed co-ordinates as opposed to the Keplerian parameters used for GPS. The system architecture is also similar to GPS.

9.1.2.1 Frequencies and Codes

GLONASS satellites transmit on two carrier frequencies, L1 and L2, each satellite transmits on different frequencies. L1 ranges from 1602.5625 MHz to 1615.5 MHz with increments of 0.5625 MHz. L2 ranges from 1246.4375 MHz to 1256.5 MHz with increments of 0.4375 MHz. Each frequency transmitted by the satellites is modulated by one or both of the precise or coarse acquisition (C/A) codes.

The GLONASS administration plans to reduce the bandwidth utilisation. The satellites in the same plane and separated by 180° transmit on the same frequency.

9.1.3 Galileo

GPS and GLONASS are controlled by the governments of two 'super powers'. The systems can be switched off fully or selectively without warning to users, leading to dependency concerns. The European Union programme, known as Galileo, is designed to overcome many of these concerns and it is part of the second phase of the evolution of global navigation satellite systems, it is part of GNSS-2.

Galileo is planned to be independent from, but fully compatible with, GPS and GLONASS. The accuracy of each is compared in Table 9.1. Commercial service is claimed to offer an accuracy of 1 m for global use and better than 10 cm for local use, using locally augmented signals similar to DGPS. Galileo was expected to be fully operational in 2014, but delays have been experienced. Five positioning services are planned:

Open	The basic level for mass market applications (Free)
Commercial	Available for commercial and professional applications
Public Regulated	For government applications with high continuity characteristics
Safety of Life	Restricted access, certified service for safety critical applications, eg for passenger safety – air, rail, other transport, etc.
Search and Rescue	Global service to pinpoint the location of distress messages (evolution of COSPAS/SARSAT) (Free)

9.1.3.1 Galileo System Architecture

The core system comprises:

- A navigation control and constellation management centre
- a constellation of medium earth orbit satellites
- an up-link service network
- an integrity monitoring service network
- communication links to services.

The system will be linked to local and regional user components, operational services systems, the COSPAS-SARSAT ground segment, navigational users, communication links and other external complementary systems. Galileo is open to international partnerships outside of the European Union. The system is also being considered for navigation related communications and may eventually replace COSPAS-SARSAT.

9.1.4 Beidou Satellite Navigation System

Beidou was initially working on a test constellation and now the functional second constellation is being assembled. It is already providing services to Asia-Pacific customers and when fully developed with 35 satellites, it will be able to provide positioning services to global users.

9.1.5 Satellite System Comparison

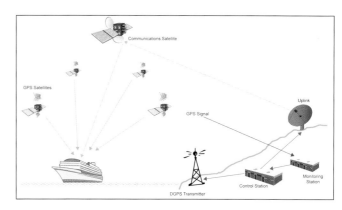

Figure 9.5 DGPS and augmented system components

A number of land based stations, equipped with a GPS receiver, have been set up at critical locations. As these reference stations are at fixed positions, the errors or differences in the received signals can be calculated. There are several ways that the differences can be recorded, but the preferred method is the pseudo-range differential as it can be worked out separately for each of the satellites in view. The pseudo-range differential is transmitted to receivers in the locality on MF (285 – 325 kHz) in RCTM SC104 format. This is

Satellite Navigation System Comparison			
	GPS	GLONASS	GALILEO
Coverage	Global	Global	Global
Availability	Continuous[1]	Continuous[1]	Guaranteed 99.8% of the time
Satellites	24 + 3	24 + 3 [2, 3]	27 + 3 [2]
Orbit inclination	55º	64.8º	56º
Altitude km	20,200	19,100	23,222
Orbit time	11h 58m	11h 15m	13h
Orbital planes	6, with 4 satellites each	3, with 8 satellites each	3, with 9 satellites each
Preferred use	Low to middle latitudes	High latitudes	Up to 75º Latitude
Accuracy Single Fq	22 m	8 to 33 m	10 m
Accuracy Dual Fq	1 to 5 m [2]	5 to 10 m	1 m
Control	Defence	Defence	Civil
Service	User's risk	User's risk	Guaranteed

[1] Subject to change without warning　　[2] When fully operational. Systems still under development　　[3] Currently the system is experiencing delays

Table 9.1　Satellite navigation system comparison GPS GLONASS GALILEO

9.1.6 Differential GPS

Satellite navigation systems has changed navigational practices and a lot of reliance is placed on them. In certain areas, such as harbours and approaches, the accuracy available was not adequate. To achieve a high level of accuracy, differential GPS was introduced.

an industry standard for encoding DGPS corrections. Users wishing to receive the DGPS service must have equipment that can receive MF transmissions from the local beacon, as well as the GPS receiver capable of incorporating encoded DGPS corrections. Some of these stations are commercial and require the receiver to have a special encryption decoding receiver unit. The general range of DGPS service is 200´, although some beacons are operating at longer ranges up to 300´. DGPS systems covering a large area using geostationary satellites are also available. The standard of accuracy is of the PPS. After discontinuity of selective availability (SA), accuracy figures of 2 to 5 m are being claimed. After SA there is a question mark on the number of users requiring DGPS service, although the system is still very attractive to users requiring high precision, eg DP, survey, dredging, etc. One advantage of DGPS is that it provides independent monitoring of the satellites.

9.1.7 Combined System – GNSS 1 (Global Navigation Satellite System)

GPS and GLONASS constellations have features that, if combined, can make up for the limitations of one another. A unit capable of receiving signals from both systems can make use of increased numbers of satellites, and can offer a number of added advantages:

- In higher latitudes, sufficient satellites at a good elevation would be available.

This is not possible using GPS alone

- A faster acquisition time can be achieved as more satellites are visible at any given time and location
- a decrease in PDOP parameter
- as the GLONASS P code is not yet encrypted, civilian users can enjoy accuracy equivalent to GPS Y code.

When Galileo becomes operational, plans are that it will integrate with GPS and GLONASS, while working independently of both systems, to form GNSS 2.

9.1.8 Augmentation Systems

These improve the use of the GPS and GLONASS through:

- Improved accuracy resulting in reliability
- integrity
- availability and continuity.

Regional arrangements, in the form of overlay systems are in place. The overlay stations provide a network of ground stations that detect and relay interpolative corrections through geostationary satellites (INMARSAT). A number of satellite based augmentation systems (SBAS) are in use; the three significant ones are:

WAAS American Wide Area Augmentation System
EGNOS European Geostationary Navigation Overlay System

MSAS Japanese Multi-functional transport satellite (MTSAT) – based Augmentation System

9.1.8.1 SBAS Functioning

The signals from GPS or GPS/GLONASS satellites are received at many widely spaced reference stations. The reference station locations are precisely surveyed so that any errors in the received signals can be detected. The GPS /GLONASS information collected by the reference stations is forwarded to the Master stations, via a terrestrial communications network, where the augmentation messages are generated. The messages contain information that allows GPS and GLONASS receivers to remove errors in the direct signals, significantly increasing location accuracy and reliability. The augmentation messages are sent from the Master station(s), via uplink stations, to be transmitted to geostationary communications satellites. The geostationary satellites broadcast the augmentation messages on a GPS/GLONASS like signal. The receiver processes the augmentation message as part of the exercise to estimate the position by applying corrections directly to the signal received.

9.1.8.2 WAAS

The Wide Area Augmentation System (WAAS) is a GPS based navigation system that provides precision guidance capability for the USA and some parts of neighbouring countries. WAAS specified accuracy is 7.6 m, but provides accuracy of up to 2-3 m for horizontal use. Further improvements are being made to achieve an accuracy of 1 m. WAAS can notify receivers within 6 seconds of any potential problems with the GPS system. WAAS was designed for aviation use and is not optimised for surface use. It can be used, with caution, in the maritime environment but it should not be relied on for safety-critical maritime navigation.

9.1.8.3 EGNOS

This is a GPS and GLONASS based system covering Europe and will provide accuracy of 5 m or less. In addition to basic ranging corrections, EGNOS will provide wide area differential corrections and an integrity monitoring service. EGNOS is also intended to work with Galileo when it becomes operational. Like WAAS, it targets the aviation field. In the maritime field it improves available accuracy where DGPS is not available.

9.1.8.4 MSAS

This system covers most of the Asia-Pacific region with an accuracy of within 5 m or less since 2005.

Other systems SDCM (Russia) and GAGAN (India) also exist.

9.1.9 Comparison of DGPS and SBAS

SBAS signals are transmitted on an L-band radio frequency which travels in line of sight only. The SBAS signal can be blocked behind obstructions. DGPS transmits on MF (285 – 325 kHz), the ground wave that can wrap around objects and arrive at the receiver position within the coverage area. DGPS only covers a small region of about 200′ radius (some beacons up to 300′), whereas SBAS can cover a large area. DGPS is designed for marine safety-critical navigation applications.

9.1.10 Factors Affecting Satellite Derived Positions

9.1.10.1 Satellite Clock Bias Error

Very small discrepancies in the accuracy within the satellite's atomic clocks can result in travel time measurement errors, causing a degradation of about 1.5 m in the final calculated position. For radio waves, a time difference of 1 µs (microsecond) equals 300 m in terms of distance.

9.1.10.2 Relativity Error

Time is compressed the closer one is to the earth's centre of mass. The satellite time is therefore different to a user who is closer to the earth's centre.

9.1.10.3 Positional Error

Monitoring satellites takes place at specific periods. Between these periods, small errors in the position of the satellite can lead to a range error of approximately 2.5 m.

9.1.10.4 GDOP (Geometric Dilution of Precision)

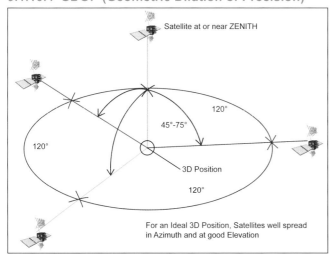

Satellite at or near ZENITH

120°

45°-75°

120°

120°

3D Position

120°

For an Ideal 3D Position, Satellites well spread in Azimuth and at good Elevation

Figure 9.6 Best GDOP for 3D position

GDOP is an indicator of reliability of the position, rather than the accuracy. It depends on the geometry of the satellites relative to the receiver and measures the spread of satellites around the receiver. The best combination would be to have one in a position overhead of the receiver and three spread at 120° on the horizon (Figure 9.6).

Satellites at low elevation produce a poor vertical position and can affect the determination of altitude. The VDOP (vertical) describes the effect of satellite geometry on altitude calculations. Satellites that are widely spaced cause different intersecting positions crossing almost at right angles and the HDOP (horizontal) describes the effect of this on position errors (latitude and longitude). An HDOP <3 is a good working figure. VDOP and HDOP combine to determine PDOP (position). Refer to Figure 9.4 for spread of satellites. PDOP combined with TDOP (time) results in GDOP. Good quality receivers have a built-in ability to determine the combination of the satellites in view providing the best possible calculated result, although user override is permitted.

9.1.10.5 Selective Availability

The intentional degradation of GPS satellite constellation was controlled by the US Department of Defence to limit the accuracy for non-US military users. This is so that hostile interests cannot use accurate positional data. Degradation was introduced by adding random noise into the clock data of the satellite. This practice has now been discontinued by the US, today a selective denial of GPS signals on a regional basis is employed. The new generation GPS III satellites do not even have (SA) capability.

9.1.10.6 Atmosphere and Ionosphere

Ionosphere is the part of the atmosphere that contains a high density of ions and exists at 70 to 80 km above the earth's surface. An error, in the form of a delay, may occur when the signal path from the satellite to the receiver passes through it. These delays are predictable. The delays are worked out using complex mathematical models, but the model used often sets one GPS receiver apart from another. It may cause range errors up to 5 m.

Troposphere is the lower part of the atmosphere that lies between the ground and 9-16 km above it. This layer contains the greatest mass of air, as well as all the water vapour. Within this region, weather systems cause complex and substantial pressure, temperature, humidity and density changes to occur. As these conditions are variable, the delays cannot be predicted with any degree of accuracy. These conditions usually account for a range error up to 1 m. The error can be minimised by calculating the relative speeds of two different signals from the same satellite.

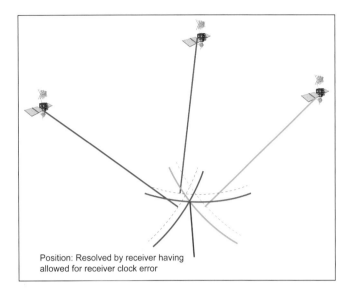

Position: Resolved by receiver having allowed for receiver clock error

Figure 9.7   Resolution of pseudorandom noise errors

9.1.10.7 Solar Activity

Large scale eruptions on the sun can lead to adverse effects on the transmission of the GPS signal, it may range from a negligible amount to total loss. Changes in the sun's magnetic field blow out a large part of sun's outer atmosphere. The earth is generally well protected to deflect this type of magnetic material. However, some may penetrate the atmosphere and can induce enhanced currents and particle streams that may cause tracking failure for satellites as well as power failures in general.

9.1.10.8 Multi-Path

It is likely that the receiver will pick up signals reflected from surfaces in its vicinity. These signals will not have followed a straight line path and will have bounced from one or more surfaces. These signals can cause confusion in calculations at the receiver due to the delayed reception compared to the direct signal. It is difficult to detect the effect using ordinary receivers but good quality receivers using signal rejection techniques can minimise the error.

The resultant combination of some of the above errors may limit the accuracy of the calculated horizontal position for the signal frequency GPS receivers to approximately 22 m for 95% of the time which is the equivalent of 2drms (two-distance root mean squared).

9.1.11 Precautions for Navigation

- All operators must be fully conversant with the manufacturer's instructions regarding the set up and use of the receiver unit
- all operators must be properly familiarised with, and trained on, using the equipment before working with it

- system limitations must be known and it must be understood that the displayed position is not necessarily the ship's actual position. If there are no errors, the position is that of the receiver antenna. If errors exist, the position is not of the antenna, but is within a circle of probability and contains the antenna within this circle
- errors are generally applied automatically, but if not the operator should make allowances and decide on the level of reliance to be placed on the output data
- warnings received about any problems with the systems in use must be taken into consideration and brought to the attention of the bridge team
- set up should be appropriate for the passage plan in use, setting the safety margins for the relevant stages of the passage plan. Where required, the antenna height must be entered correctly and adjusted for any changes on passage
- GDOP should be checked regularly. Most receivers select satellites automatically, but override is possible and where better satellites are available, the same should be tracked for position purposes
- differences between the chart datum and WGS 84 must be applied, as per the notes on the chart
- position monitoring must include the use of primary and secondary systems
- when the charts being used are based on older survey data, the charted positions may be significantly out from the actual positions, with no reference to the corrections to be applied between the satellite derived positions and charted positions. In such cases, an attempt should be made to obtain the range and bearing of charted objects and they should be applied on the chart for position fixing. A log should be maintained of satellite positions. Any variation in satellite based positions should be reported to the UKHO
- transferring positions between charts should not simply be by latitude and longitude, but also by range and bearing from a common charted mark
- a good check should be kept on the receiver and all alarms should be followed-up
- regular cross checks with other systems and thorough celestial observations must be carried out. The operator must know the limitations of the systems that are being used for cross checking purposes
- if a receiver shifts to DR mode, all watchkeeping officers must be made aware and positions should be plotted from other sources
- plot positions at the agreed fix frequency and check the distances run and course made good
- keep a separate check on the DR and estimated position after every fix, based on courses and speed, taking into account the expected set and drift

- cross track error and arrival alarms should be checked regularly, especially when approaching waypoints
- track adjustments should not be made too frequently unless in congested waters
- where other integrated bridge equipment requires satellite navigation data, ensure that the reliance and accuracy required from other equipment is not greater than the base data that is provided.

9.1.12 Satellite System Vulnerabilities

The use of satellite systems are likely to be affected by various external influences.

9.1.12.1 Human Factors

Over-reliance on any system is poor practice. Any system output is only as accurate as the data put in and the interpretation of the results.

9.1.12.2 Intentional Interference

Intentional interference is likely to be meant for longer periods. The most obvious is the complete denial by an administration. External influences may attempt to jam the system or spoof it through counterfeit signals. Physical damage can be caused to the satellites or the ground segment, leaving the system crippled for longer periods.

9.1.12.3 Unintentional Interference

Unintentional interference generally only lasts a short time. Some radio frequencies are likely to interfere with the satellite signals, making them useless for as long as the influence of the external frequency remains. In the recent past an active television antenna had the ability to transmit on GPS frequency. The high powered military radar fitted on warships has been known to severely affect the commercial GPS set on a merchant vessel. Satellite system testing may leave the signals unusable during the test period. It is also likely that the system will be affected by the frequency spectrum being congested. Solar magnetic particles may cause problems with the signals and ground segment control.

9.2 Hyperbolic Systems

Several hyperbolic systems based on signals coming from terrestrial stations on land have been used recently. Presently, LORAN-C and a similar Russian system CHAYKA with limited coverage, is still available for marine navigation. Numerous older systems are now obsolete.

9.2.1 LORAN-C (Long Range Navigation system)

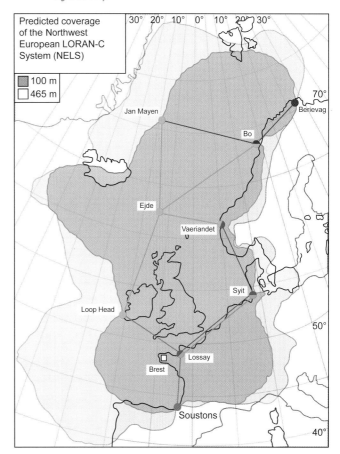

Figure 9.8   NW Europe E-LORAN chain

LORAN-C is a hyperbolic position fixing system. It uses a low frequency of 100 kHz and transmits pulses. The system has a ground wave range of 800´ to 1,200´. However, high accuracy useful range is only 300´ or so from the transmitting stations in the vicinity of the base line.

9.2.1.1 Principle

A hyperbola is a line or curve joining all points that are an equal difference of distance between two fixed points. LORAN-C uses the speed of a radio signal to calculate the difference of distance from the transmitting station.

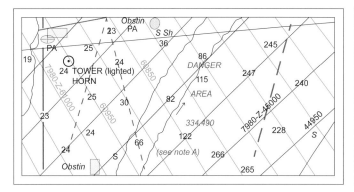
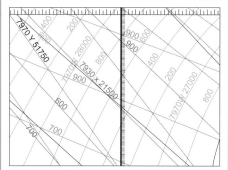

Figure 9.9 Sections of LORAN-C charts – navigation (L) and plotting (R)

At the time of these systems being developed, the absolute accuracy of the clocks that could be economically made available on ships, as well as other moving vehicles, was inadequate. The hyperbolic system uses two stations for each position line, which makes it possible to accurately measure the time difference between receiving the two separate signals. Figure 9.3 shows two stations that simultaneously send a radio pulse. The pulse arrives at the Line of Position (LOP) with a time difference of 2,000 µs (microseconds). All the points with a 2,000 µs form a position line, known as a hyperbolic line.

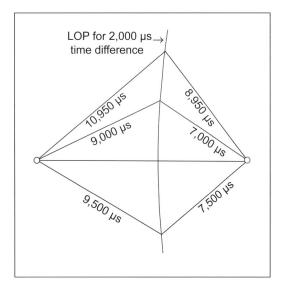

Figure 9.10 Hyperbolic LOP

9.2.1.3 System Composition

LORAN-C functions through chains of stations. Within each chain there is a Master station and two, three or four slave stations. Adjacent chains may share slave stations. The slave stations are identified as W, X, Y and Z. Transmissions within each chain are in sequence starting with the Master station transmission followed by the W, X, Y and Z.

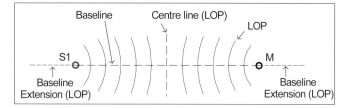

Figure 9.11 Lattice terminology

As all LORAN-C stations transmit on the same frequency of 100 kHz, a method must be incorporated to identify the relevant chains. This is achieved by introducing a specified interval between the successive transmissions of each Master station within a chain. This is known as the Group Repetition Interval (GRI) and is unique for an individual chain. The GRI should be such that transmissions from each station within the group are accommodated and it avoids Cross Rate Interference (CRI) with other chains. The total GRI divided by one hundred provides the chain's designator. This means that the Sylt chain with GRI 749,900 µs covering parts of NW Europe is designated 7499.

Once the signal from the Master station reaches the first slave, it waits for an interval known as the Secondary Coding Delay. The total time between the Master and slave station transmissions is called the 'emission delay'.

Emission Delay = signal travel time along base line + secondary coding delay.

This waiting period or delay ensures that the pulses arrive in the correct sequence anywhere within the coverage of the chain. The sequence is Master pulses first, followed by slave W, followed by slave X, followed by slave Y and finally slave Z. The sequence is only repeated after all stations within the chain have transmitted. The system includes monitoring stations that keep a check on the integrity of the chains.

9.2.1.4 LORAN C Pulse

The signal is transmitted in the form of pulses and not as continuous waves. This has the advantage of:

- Lower power output requirement
- better signal identification
- precise timing of signals
- better comparison for time difference measurements.

The Master station transmits a block of eight plus one (nine) pulses and each slave transmits a block of eight pulses. The ninth pulse is used to identify the Master station. The interval between transmissions of individual pulses within the group of eight is 1,000 µs. The Master ninth pulse is transmitted after 2,000 µs of the Master eighth pulse.

The pulse has a length of 300 µs. It is in the shape of an envelope that exhibits a steep rise to maximum amplitude within 65 µs. The time difference between the arrival of signals from two stations is determined by matching the eight pulses. The eight matches provide a better average and better signal to noise ratio at the receiver compared to those produced by a single pulse transmitted at high power. The measurements are a "coarse time difference measurement", which is achieved by matching pulse envelopes and then "fine time difference measurement", made by matching the phase of 100 kHz carrier within the envelope.

The receiver is programmed to detect the 3rd cycle of the carrier frequency of each pulse. This is done for two reasons. At this stage the pulse has built up sufficient signal strength for it to be detected. The leading edge of the pulse is not a good choice as it may be deformed.

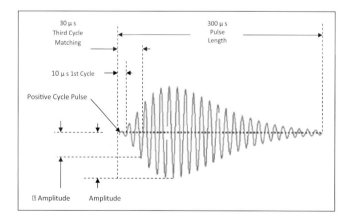

Figure 9.12   LORAN-C pulse

The second reason is that it is early enough in the pulse to ensure that the receiver is matching the ground-wave and not the sky-wave. The earliest a sky-wave can reach a receiver is 35 µs after the ground-wave. This

way the receiver would have carried out the matching in advance of the sky-wave's arrival.

The arrival of sky-waves may be as late as 1,000 µs. Another feature of the pulse that is used to eliminate sky-wave is the 'Phase Coding '. The phase of the carrier signal is changed systematically from pulse to pulse. On receipt, sky-wave pulses would be out of phase with simultaneously received ground-wave pulses and will be rejected. The phase coding also provides further assistance with identification of Master and slave station pulses.

9.2.1.5 LORAN C Charts and Receivers

Some nautical charts have LOPs overlaid on them. The LOP might be designated 7,980-X-15,750. 7,980 is the chain GRI designator, X indicates that it is the "Master - Slave X" LOP and the time difference is 15,750 µs. Interpolation must be performed when plotting positions between two LOPs. These LOPs are colour coded and can be identified by the colour symbols at the bottom left hand corner of the chart, outside of the margin.

Most modern receivers determine and display the latitude and longitude of the receiver position. Required corrections (see 9.2.1.6) can be incorporated in the receiver memory and are applied automatically. Care should be taken to set the notch filters correctly and to not set the notch filter on 100 kHz frequency.

9.2.1.6 Errors

Any errors or problems with a slave station are indicated by a blink of its first two pulses. The pulses are kept off for 3.6 seconds and on for 0.4 second. The Master station pulses are not blinked. Problems with LORAN-C system are notified through navigational warnings (NAVTEX "H", see 11.1.6.1 and 11.2.1). Terrestrial radio signals are characterised as having varying accuracy depending on the time of day, time of year and, at longer ranges, interference from sky-waves. The conductivity of terrain over which the LORAN-C signal passes dictates the velocity. Additional Secondary Factor (ASF) corrections are provided to take account of velocity errors. These are available on LORAN lattice charts, as well as tabulated in US HO publication No 221. When plotting positions on lattice charts that incorporate such corrections, care should be taken not to apply tabulated corrections before plotting.

A small angle between LOPs can deteriorate the quality of a fix. Assuming that the LOP error is constant, the position uncertainty varies inversely by the sine of the angle between the two position lines. Similarly, using stations close to the baseline extension can have the same effect.

9.2.1.7 Accuracy

LORAN-C is designed to provide an accuracy of 0.25 to 1 nm when receiving ground-waves close to the baseline and centreline. This figure gets worse during night, at extended distances from the stations, during twilight or when ground waves are being tracked; accuracy reduces to around 2 nm when within skywave coverage area. The journey of the signal over land or sea and the time it spends over land can lower the accuracy. Similarly, any signal attenuation may affect accuracy. The receiver processor's capability will also affect results.

9.2.2 Eurofix

Since the current satellite navigation systems do not guarantee availability, it is important to consider back-up systems.

GPS, LORAN-C and DGPS integration allows differential satellite corrections to be sent to receivers as time modulated signal information on the LORAN-C signal, without affecting the navigation function of LORAN-C. Both LORAN-C and satellite frequencies are received by a combined receiver. The user can operate in any mode:

- DGPS
- GPS
- LORAN C
- integrated function where LORAN-C position is a rough check on GPS and the user is not reliant on external warnings of satellite or LORAN-C failure.

A fix can be computed using the three systems, and each system checks the integrity of the other systems. The system is also expected to integrate with Galileo, once it is ready. The Eurofix system has the advantage of feeding satellite problems to the user on terrestrial frequencies, based on observations at a land based station nearby.

9.3 Echo Sounder

An echo sounder works on the principle of measuring the time taken by a sound pulse to return from the seabed. As the velocity of sound in sea water is known, the time can be translated into distance. As the sound pulse has to travel the same distance twice – ship to seabed to ship – the depth will be half this distance, the echo sounders automatically halve it before it is displayed. In order to obtain reliable depths, the echo sounder should be carefully adjusted and the relevant errors should be taken into account and applied correctly. There is also a possibility of false echoes or traces.

The sound pulse is generated by a transducer fitted in the ships bottom. Some ships' transducers transmit and receive, while others have separate transducers for transmission and reception. Where transmission and reception transducers are different, the vertical depth must be determined using tables provided to the ship. When the echo sounder operates, its transmissions are picked up straight away by the receiving transducer. This signal makes a mark on the recording paper in the form of a transmission line and is the benchmark for depths below the keel. With some echo sounders, the line may have to be adjusted to match the depth of the transducer or to allow for the draught of the ship in order to obtain the total depth. Draught adjustment may be made as a number setting on digital display type devices.

The distance travelled in a given time depends on the speed. The salinity, temperature and pressure of sea water can all change the speed of sound through it. Generally, a figure of 1,500 m/sec is applied as the standard velocity of sound in sea water. Regardless of the actual conditions, this value should allow depths to be determined to +/- 5% of true depths. Corrections can be obtained from correction tables for accurate results. On some devices, the speed of the motor controlling the stylus belt may be adjusted to allow for speed of sound.

9.3.1 False Echoes

An echo sounder may display traces showing the incorrect depth for a number of reasons:

- Layers of water having different speeds of sound through them
- sub-marine springs of water at different density
- shoals of fish
- seaweed
- faults
- artificial noises
- tidal streams or eddies causing turbulence when making contact with solid particles in suspension
- side echoes from objects not exactly below the vessel.

9.3.1.1 Double Echo

Some sounders may display an echo at twice the actual depth. This is caused by the returning echo bouncing off the hull, back to seabed and then being received by the transducer. It is always weaker than the true echo and fades out first when sensitivity is decreased.

9.3.1.2 Multiple Echoes

It is possible that the transmission pulse may be reflected several times between the seabed and the surface of the sea or ship's bottom, even in depths of several hundred metres. Every reflection received by the transducer causes a trace, although they can be eliminated by reducing the sensitivity.

9.3.1.3 Round the Clock Echoes

If the returning echo is not received until after the stylus has completed one or more of its cycles, false readings may be obtained. The stylus re-passes the transmission line and another pulse has been transmitted. A sounding of, for example, 20 m may appear as 20 m, 320 m or 620 m on a sounder that has its scale divided. These echoes can be identified as being weaker than the true echoes, or having a feathery appearance or pass through the transmission line.

9.3.2 Usability

An echo sounder can be used effectively:

- For warning when approaching a reducing depth or shoal waters, as the trace will show a steady decline in the depth
- determining when a line of contour is passed. This effectively acts as a position line – provided the chart is reliable

- to cross check the recorded depth at a plotted position, against the depth expected from the chart
- for observing changes to depths and reporting to the hydrographic authorities
- to check depth at a grounded location
- to check for approaching islands or shoals in an ocean area, or when making landfall
- but may not be effective in ocean areas where the depth is thousands of meters.

Author's Note
Navigation systems have developed significantly over recent years and continue to evolve. The equipment must be set up correctly to obtain the best results. The data provided by these systems is generally of a very high quality, but the limitations and inherent errors must be appreciated and applied correctly. In order to gain full confidence, the integrity of systems should be established with cross checks. Remember we all trust what we see through our eyes, but we should be able to trust something else when we are not able to see things in the vicinity for some reasons.

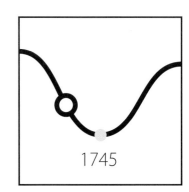
Tides and Tidal Streams

Tides are defined as the periodic motion of the sea caused by changes in the forces of attraction of the moon and sun on the rotating earth. This movement of water is the vertical rise or fall of the water level, that is normally accompanied by a horizontal movement of water called a tidal stream or tidal current.

Tides and tidal streams are an important element of voyage planning and play a significant part in navigational safety. In addition to tides, the rise or fall of water levels can also be caused by weather, seismic events or other natural forces. Similarly, the tidal streams are additional to river or channel flows, flood waters, etc.

10.1 Causes of Tides

There are two main causes of tides:

- Gravitational forces of the moon and sun on the earth
- centrifugal forces on the earth caused by the earth's revolution around the common centres of gravity of the earth-moon and earth-sun systems.

The earth-moon system rotates around one common centre of gravity and the earth-sun system rotates around another. The common centre of gravity is called the barycentre. The earth-moon and earth-sun systems have a different barycentre. The earth describes a very small ellipse and the moon describes a larger ellipse about the earth-moon barycentre.

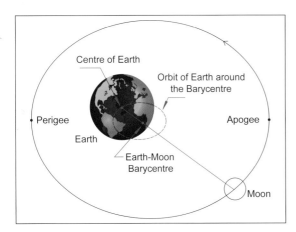

Figure 10.1   Earth-moon system

If there is no force of gravity, the centrifugal force would cause the earth to break away from the sun and move in a straight line into space. Similarly, due to gravity, the moon is in orbit around the earth and not breaking away. The gravity keeps them from moving off and the centrifugal forces keep them from crashing into each other.

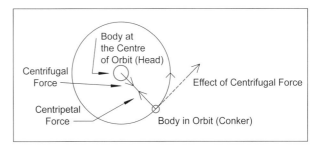

Figure 10.2   Orbital forces

According to the universal law of gravity, the force of gravity FG is proportional to the product of the mass of the bodies and inversely proportional to the square of the distance between their centres. m1 and m2 represent the masses of the two bodies and d is the distance between their centres.

$$F_G = G \, (m_1 \times m_2) \div d^2 \; (G = \text{Gravitational constant})$$

As the earth-moon distance is considerably less than the earth-sun distance, the moon has the largest effect on the tides. The sun's effect is approximately 45% that of the moon's.

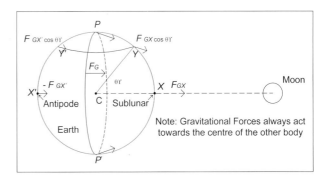

Figure 10.3   Earth-moon gravitational forces at various points on the earth

The force of gravity between the earth and the moon acts on all of the earth and everything on it, including water. Assume that at any given time, the moon is above a point X on the earth's surface. This point is called the sub-lunar point. If the line from the moon to X ran through to the other side of the earth, it would emerge at the point X′, which is called the antipode. The distance XX′ equals the earth's diameter. A plane perpendicular to this line, through the centre of the earth, divides the earth into two halves, forming the Great Circle PP′ on the surface of the earth.

The distance from the moon at all points on PP′ to the centre of the earth may be considered the same, implying that the gravitational pull at all points on PP′ and the centre of the earth are the same, ie FG. The point X is nearer to the moon compared to PP′ and the centre of the earth, the gravitational pull here is more than at the centre of the earth, FGX. For the same reasons the gravitational pull is less at X′ and has a negative comparative value - FGX′. Another way to term this negative value is that it applies in the opposite direction to the moon. An alternative explanation for the tide raising force is that it is the difference between the force of gravity and the centrifugal force. The centripetal force between two bodies is always uniform at any of the points.

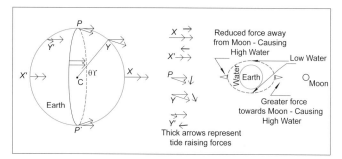

Figure 10.4   Tide raising forces at various points on the earth

At some point Y on the earth's surface away from X, X′ and PP′, the gravitational pull will be less than at X and more than at PP′. If Y is at an angle of θ° from the line XX′, the force at Y is equal to FGX cos θ°. For the same reasons, the gravitational pull at Y′ will be FGX′ cos θ°.

The gravitational pull at Y and Y′ can be resolved into its horizontal and vertical components FGXH and FGXV. The vertical component is only a small proportion of the earth's gravity. The actual tide that is causing force is the horizontal component which causes the water to move across the earth and pile up at X and X′.

10.2 Variation in Tides

The tide raising forces depend on several factors, including:

- The mass of the earth, moon and sun
- the distance of the moon and sun's centre from the earth's centre
- the size of the earth relative to its distance from the moon and from the sun
- the angle between the moon and sun, as measured at the earth's centre.

10.2.1 Rotation of the Earth

High water occurs shortly after the moon's upper and lower transit. The delay is due to the earth's rotation effect as the GHA of the moon changes. The earth rotates in approximately 24h and 50m relative to the moon. An observer on the earth would experience two high waters at an interval of 12h 25m and two low waters, also at an interval of 12h 25m. These are known as semi-diurnal tides. The earth rotates to the east and the moon moves relatively to the west. Similarly, the occurrence of tides also moves westwards.

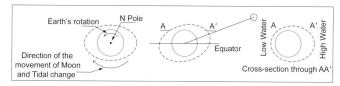

Figure 10.5   Earth's rotation effect and declination effect

10.2.2 Declination of the Moon

A diurnal tide will have one high and one low water every lunar day. This is affected by the declination of the moon.

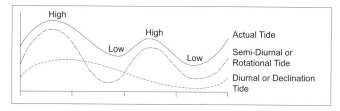

Figure 10.6   Diurnal and semi diurnal effect in tides

The actual tide is the sum of the semi-diurnal, consisting of two high and two low tides in one day, and diurnal tides. The usual effect is for the two high waters to be of a different height.

10.2.3 Distance of the Moon

The moon rotates around the earth in approximately 27½ days. When the moon is closest to the earth, ie at perigee, the tide-raising force is at its maximum and when the moon is furthest from the earth, ie at apogee, the tide raising force is at its weakest.

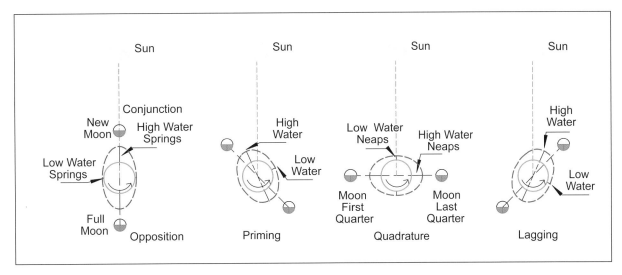

Figure 10.7   Springs, Priming, Neaps and Lagging

10.2.4 Earth-Sun System

This tide-raising system, has a tide raising force of approximately 45% that of the earth-moon system. A solar day is 24 hours in duration and causes two high waters 12 hours apart, with two low waters in between. The change in the sun's declination is very slow and has a slow changing effect on the solar tide. Similarly, the distance of the sun from the earth is not constant, but as it is so large it causes a very small force of about 3% of the total.

10.2.5 Spring Tides

When the moon is in conjunction or in opposition with the sun, ie twice every lunar month at new moon or full moon, the lunar and solar tidal forces are in line, causing high tides to be higher than average and low tides to be lower than average. The combined tide-raising effect of the sun and moon will be further pronounced when declination is the same.

10.2.6 Neap Tides

When the moon is in quadrature with the sun, ie twice every lunar month at 1st quarter or 3rd quarter, the lunar and solar tidal forces are at right angles, causing high tides to be lower than average and low tides to be higher than average.

10.2.7 Priming and Lagging

High waters due to lunar tides are caused at intervals of 12h 25m and those due to solar tides at 12h intervals. The effect of the sun and moon together alter the intervals between successive high and low waters.

When the moon is between new and first quarter, and between full and last quarter, the tide is said to prime

and the high tide during this period will occur before the moon's transit of the meridian. When the moon is between first quarter and full, and between last quarter and new, the tide is said to lag, the high tide during this period will occur after the moon's transit of the meridian.

10.2.8 Land Effect

The tide may be further modified by the shape of land. The average daily range in areas not affected by the shape of land is approximately 2 metres at spring tides and 1 metre on average. The configuration of the land and sea in the area where predictions have been made has a large influence on both the heights and times of tide. An estuary that is wide at the opening to the sea and narrow at the other end, eg the Bristol Channel, causes the tide to heap up as the land squeezes the tidal heap into a smaller space, resulting in very high tides being experienced, eg those at Avonmouth. Similarly, the dimensions of the Bay of Fundy in Western Nova Scotia cause synchronisation of the tidal movements and the moon's rotation resulting in the highest tides on the earth.

Another area of significance is a small inlet to a much larger area. The Straits of Gibraltar are narrow and allow relatively little water to flow into the Mediterranean Sea. The small amount of water that does flow in has a very small effect on the height of the tides in the Mediterranean Sea.

10.2.9 Distance from the Pacific Ocean

The Pacific Ocean, because of its size, has a significant effect on worldwide tides. The further away that a place is from the Pacific, the later the spring tides will be, depending on the date of the new or full moon. In European waters, spring tides usually occur two days after a new and full moon.

10.2.10 Meteorological Conditions

Seasonal meteorological conditions are predictable and seasonal corrections are listed in the tidal difference pages of the tide tables. When there is low pressure, there is an increase in height in all states of tides and when the pressure is high, there will be a reduction in height in all states of tides. A fall of 30 hPa will cause an increase of up to 30 cm in the height of water in all states of the tide.

Daily variations in weather cannot be predicted when a tide table is being complied. The wind has a variable effect on tidal times and heights. Strong onshore and offshore winds, or a significantly unusual pressure, may cause the water level to be higher or lower than predicted. Similarly, storm surges can be experienced with tropical revolving storms.

Excessive rainfall usually results in rivers flooding and the resulting water levels can be predicted. Melting snow will also have similar effect. In contrast, a lack of rainfall reduces the water flow in rivers, which means that the water level remains lower.

10.3 Tidal Definitions

Tidal change occurs twice a day in most places. The tide will rise until it reaches its maximum level called high water or high tide, it will then fall to a minimum level called a low water or low tide. Chart datum or sounding datum is the level that soundings and drying heights on the chart and heights in the tide tables, are referred to. The chart datum is generally referred to as MLWS. In some areas of the world, it is the level of the lowest astronomical tide (LAT). Under average meteorological conditions and any combination of astronomical conditions, it is the lowest level that tides are expected to fall. Due to changes in sea level, chart datum is subject to re-examination from time to time. A long period of observation for tides is 18.6 years, although some administrations use 19 years.

Mean Sea Level (MSL) – the average level of the sea surface over a long period of time, or the average level that would exist without tides.

Charted Depth – the actual depth of water at a place without applying the height of tide, it is also the vertical distance downwards from the chart datum to the seabed.

Drying height – the vertical distance from the chart datum upwards, to any surface that has a vertical height between the chart datum and the MHWS.

The Height of Objects – on metric charts it is measured in metres above MHWS. Examples of these heights include the height of the focal plane

of lighthouses, mountains, towers, and any other height that is of significance to the navigator. Vertical clearances like clearance under bridges and clearance under overhead cables are referred to as HAT.

The Height of Tide – the height of water above the chart datum at any given moment.

The depth of water – equal to the charted depth plus the height of the tide.

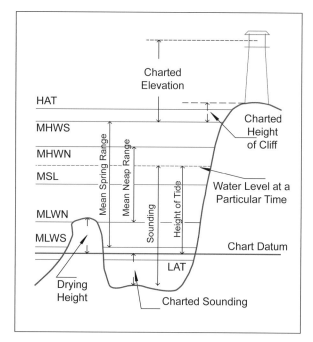

Figure 10.8   Tide levels, heights and ranges

A Spring tide – occurs when the moon is new or full, ie the moon is in conjunction with the sun and earth or in opposition to the sun and earth.

A Neap tide – occurs twice each month, when the moon is at the first or third quarter, ie it is in quadrature with the sun and earth. Some high water spring tides are higher than others. Mean High Water Springs (MHWS) is the average value for high water springs found by taking two consecutive highest tides from each fortnightly tide cycle over a long period or taken over a whole year when the average declination of the moon is at 23½°.

Some high water neap tides are lower than others. Mean High Water Neaps (MHWN) is the average value for high water neaps, it is found by taking two consecutive lowest high water neap tides every fortnight tide cycle over a long period, or taken over a whole year when the average declination of the moon is 23½°.

Some low water neap tides are higher than others. Mean Low Water Neaps (MLWN) is the average value for low water neaps, and is found by taking the two consecutive highest low water neap tides every fortnight tide cycle over a long period, or taken over a whole year when the average declination of the moon is 23½°.

Some low water spring tides are lower than others. Mean Low Water Springs (MLWS) is the average value for low water springs found by taking the two consecutive lowest tides each fortnightly tide cycle over a long period, or taken over a whole year when the average declination of the moon is 23½°.

Mean Higher High Water (MHHW) is the average higher height of the high waters of each tidal day over a long period of time.

Mean Lower High Water (MLHW) is the average lower height of the high waters of each tidal day over a long period of time.

Mean Higher Low Water (MHLW) is the average higher height of the low waters of each tidal day over a long period of time.

Mean Lower Low Water (MLLW) is the average lower height of low waters of each tidal day over a long period of time.

Mean High Water (MHW) is the average height of all high waters over a long period at a given place.

Mean Low Water (MLW) is the average height of all low waters over a long period at a given place.

Mean Tidal Level (MTL) is the average of the heights of MHWS, MHWN, MLWN and MLWS.

MHWS, MHWN, MLWN and MLWS vary from year to year in approximately an 18.6 year cycle, these levels are calculated at from least a year's predictions. They are also adjusted for long period variations to provide values that are the average over the whole cycle.

Highest Astronomical Tide (HAT) and Lowest Astronomical Tide (LAT) The highest and lowest levels respectively that can be predicted to occur under average meteorological conditions and under any combination of astronomical conditions. These levels will not be reached every year, it should also be noted that HAT and LAT are not the extreme levels that can be reached, eg storm surges may cause considerably higher or lower levels. HAT and LAT are determined by an inspection being carried out after several years, ideally the full Metonic Cycle of 19 years. A Metonic cycle is a period that is close to 19 years, it is a multiple of solar years and lunar years – and counts 6,940 days.

Mean Spring Range is the difference between MHWS and MLWS.

Range is the difference in height between consecutive high and low waters, ie between one high water and the next low water, or between a low water and the next high water. The value of range may change from tide to tide. Daily Range is the range experienced on any one day.

Spring Range is the tides range during the spring tides.

Neap Range is the range of tide during the neap tides.

Mean Spring Range is the difference between MHWS and MLWS.

Mean Neap Range is the difference between MHWN and MLWN.

Mean High Water Interval (MHWI) is the mean time interval between the moon's meridian passage over Greenwich and the time of the next high water at the place concerned.

10.4 Underkeel Clearance and Air Draught

Most voyages at sea must be through shallow water at some point. The navigator must ensure that adequate clearance is maintained under the keel at all times. In some parts of the world, especially port areas, harbours, rivers, canals and certain offshore areas, the authorities lay down the minimum under-keel allowance. In all other cases, under-keel clearances should be determined by the mariner. Under-keel allowance is expressed as the depth below the keel of the ship when stationary.

The factors in deciding this allowance will depend on:

- Uncertainties in charted depth
- uncertainties in the vessel's draught, especially after a long passage
- squat at a given speed
- risk of negative tidal surges
- the vessel's course relative to the prevailing weather. This must be considered separately for each leg of the passage
- the vessel's movement in heavy weather. Pitching, heaving and rolling of the vessel will significantly reduce under-keel clearance
- possible alterations in depth since the last chart survey

- areas of offshore exploration. Pipelines on the seabed can reduce under-keel clearance by up to 2 metres. Slant drilling can also reduce under-keel clearance considerably
- areas of a mobile sea bottom, eg sand waves
- areas of volcanic activity
- the possibility of inaccuracies of offshore tidal predictions
- non-availability of tidal predictions in certain areas, especially in offshore regions
- the extent of the survey when determining deepwater routes
- variation in consumption and the resulting errors in draught
- inaccuracies in determination of the initial draught
- changes of trim or draught that are unknown to the mariner
- high or low pressure can cause a significant difference
- human error in calculating the tidal heights and times from published data and the skill with which it is related to chart datum
- the likelihood of new dangers developing in the area and a delay in notifying the mariner of this information.

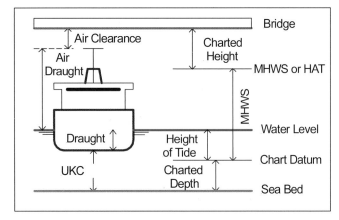

Figure 10.9 Draught and UKC

DRAUGHT + UNDER-KEEL ALLOWANCE = LEAST CHARTED DEPTH + HEIGHT OF TIDE

AIR DRAUGHT + AIR CLEARANCE = (HAT + CHARTED HEIGHT) – HEIGHT OF TIDE

Due to swells and the reliability of surveys, under-keel clearance required in offshore areas is likely to be greater than what is required in harbour areas.

Similarly, clearance above the highest point of the vessel may be important. Maintenance work being carried out on the underside of overhead objects will reduce the overhead clearance further.

10.5 Tidal Calculations

The basic principles of obtaining tidal heights are the same, regardless of the method being used. In the case of Tide Tables, the data for times and heights can be read off directly from the daily pages and the intermediate values can be obtained through graphs and calculations. In other cases, computer software is used to provide the predictions. The UKHO provides the 'TotalTide' CD and Easy Tide on the web. Other providers also use simple programmes to work out predictions, these are mainly based on harmonic constants. Harmonic constants from tide tables can be used directly to work out tides. Mariners are interested in the times and heights of high and low waters, as well as the time that the tide will be a certain height or the height of a tide at a certain time. Calculations may involve the standard or secondary port. The tides may be for European ports or Pacific Tide ports. For all cases, the calculation methods are explained using the following examples.

10.5.1 European Tides – Standard Port

Example 10.1
A ship drawing 9.0 m is unable to make the 1st high water on the 28th January 2006 at Greenock. She is required to pass over a shoal charted at 8.5 m with a UKC of 2.0 m. Find the latest time that she can pass the charted shoal with the required UKC during the 1st PM falling tide. Will the ship be able to pass over the shoal during the 1st PM falling tide with the required clearance if the ETA was 1400 hours local time?

Solution and Comments
1   The first stage is to determine the height of the tide using the equation:

DRAUGHT + UNDER-KEEL ALLOWANCE = LEAST CHARTED DEPTH + HEIGHT OF TIDE

9.0 + 2.0	= 8.5 + Height of Tide
Height of Tide	= (9.0 + 2.0) – 8.5 = 2.5 m

2   The next stage is to extract data from the tide tables. It is important that the correct port and date are referred to.

From ATT Vol 1, p 139, for 28th January 2006 at Greenock:

0426	0.8	
1135	3.3	1st HW is at 1135
1707	0.4	1st falling tide during PM is between 1135 and 1707
2353	3.2	

Range = 3.3 ~ 0.4 = 2.9 (Interpolation required between spring and neap curves, where applicable)

3   Reference should now be made to the spring and neap curves for the port. On the left hand side of the graph, mark the predicted height of HW along the top line at 3.3 m. Care should be taken to read the scale as some graphs have divisions of 1m while others have 2m. Similarly, mark LW along the bottom line at 0.4 m. Join the two marks.

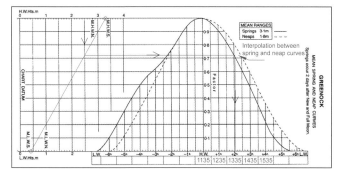

Figure 10.10   Graph for example 10.1
© British Crown Copyright, 2006

4   On the right hand side of the graph, note the predicted time of HW in the central box under HW. Add hourly incremental times in the boxes to the right.
5   Drop a line vertically from the 2.5 m mark to the diagonal line between HW and LW. At the intersection, draw a line horizontally to the spring and neap curves.
6   As the range is not the same as spring or neap, interpolation is required. The difference between the spring and neap range is 3.1 ~ 1.8 = 1.3. From spring range to current range the difference is 3.1 ~ 2.9 = 0.2. Therefore, the fraction required is 0.2/1.3 of the distance between spring and neap curves.
7   At this point, drop a vertical to reach the time scale. The middle of each box marks the time written in it. The small marks on the boxes are at 10 minute intervals.

From the tidal curve, the required time is +2h and 5 minutes after HW, ie, **1340 hours.**

As the tide is falling further, at 1400 the ship will not be able to pass over the shoal with the required clearance.

10.5.2 European Tides – Secondary Port

Example 10.2
On 27th April 2006 at 1530 local time, a ship with a draught of 4.0 m obtains a sounding of 2.5 m below the keel. Find the charted depth for this observation at Port Glasgow.

Solution and Comments
1   Charted depth can be determined using the equation:

DRAUGHT + UNDER-KEEL ALLOWANCE = LEAST CHARTED DEPTH + HEIGHT OF TIDE

4.0 + 2.5   = Charted Depth + Height of Tide

But first the height of tide has to be calculated for 1530.

2   Port Glasgow is a secondary port with Greenock being the standard port. The ATT reference numbers are:
404 Greenock
405 Port Glasgow

3   From ATT Vol 1, p 139, for 27th April 2006 at Greenock (In April, UK local time is BST and not GMT: 1530 local = 1430 GMT):

0503   (= 0603 BST)   0.2
1203   (= 1303 BST)   3.5
1727   (= 1827 BST)   - 0.1

The time in question (1430 GMT) falls between HW 1203 and LW 1727.

ATT Vol 1, Page 316				**SCOTLAND; WEST COAST**								
				TIME DIFFERENCES				HEIGHT DIFFERENCES (IN METRES)				ML
No.	Place	Lat.	Long.	High Water		Low Water		MHWS	MHWN	MLWN	MLWS	Z_o
		N	W	Zone UT(GMT)								m
				0000 and 1200	0600 and 1800	0000 and 1200	0600 and 1800					
404	**GREENOCK**	(see page 138)						3.4	2.8	1.0	0.3	
405	Port Glasgow	55 56	4 41	+0010	+0005	+0010	+0020	+0.2	+0.1	0.0	0.0	⊙
406	Bowling	55 56	4 29	+0020	+0010	+0030	+0055	+0.6	+0.5	+0.3	+0.1	⊙
406a	Clydebank (Rothesay Dock)	55 54	4 24	+0025	+0015	+0035	+0100	+1.0	+0.8	+0.5	+0.4	2.70
407	Glasgow	55 51	4 16	+0025	+0015	+0035	+0105	+1.3	+1.1	+0.7	+0.4	2.90

© British Crown Copyright, 2006

4   Data should now be extracted from ATT for the standard and secondary port differences, along with seasonal changes.

5   The height and time differences that are to be applied to the Greenock predictions for the Port Glasgow data should now be calculated. This may not seem like common sense, but the suggested format will help to avoid errors and speed up calculations.

For HW – Time difference:

Tabular time before	1203 is	1200: a
	Correction	= + 0010: c
Tabular time after	1203 is	1800: b
	Correction	= + 0005: d
Differences	(a – b) = -06h (-360 min): e	
	(c – d) = 5′: f	
Difference between	1200 and 1203	= -0h 03min (- 3′): g
Time correction for HW at 1203		= c – [(g × f) ÷ e]

= 10 - (3 × 5) ÷ - 360 = - 0.04 (negligible)   = 10′

For LW – Time difference:

Tabular time before	1727 is	1200: a
	Correction	= + 0010: c
Tabular time after	1727 is	1800: b
	Correction	= + 0020: d
Differences	a – b = -06h (-360 min): e	
	c – d	= - 10′: f
Difference between 1200 and 1727		= - 5h 27min (- 327′): g
Time correction for LW at 1727		= c – [(g × f) ÷ e]

= 10 – (- 327 × -10) ÷ - 360 = 10 + 9 (9′.08) = 19′

	HW	LW
	3.5	- 0.1
- Seasonal changes	- 0.1	- 0.1
	3.6	0.0 (These heights are to be used for interpolation)

For HW corrections:

Standard Port	MHWS – MHWN	= h
Secondary Port differences	MHWS – MHWN	= j
Standard Port	MHWS – Standard Port HW	= k

HW Correction = Secondary port MHWS Correction – [(h × j) ÷ k]

h = 3.4 – 2.8 = 0.6 j = 0.2 – 0.1 = 0.1 k = 3.4 – 3.6 = –0.2

HW Correction = 0.2 – [(0.6 × 0.1) ÷ - 0.2] = 0.23 = 0.2

For LW corrections:

Standard Port	MLWN – MLWS	= h
Secondary Port differences	MLWN – MLWS	= j
Standard Port	MLWN – Standard Port LW	= k

LW Correction = Secondary port MLWN Correction – [(h × j) ÷ k]

h = 1.0 – 0.3 = 0.7 j = 0.0 – 0.0 = 0.0 k = 1.0 – 0.0 = 1.0

LW Correction = 0.0 – [(0.7 × 0.0) ÷ 1.0] = 0.0

6   Using the calculations in Step 5, the times and heights of HW and LW are obtained as follows:

	HW	LW
Standard Port Times	1203	1727
Secondary Port Corrections	+ 0010	+ 0019
Secondary Port Times	1213	1746
Standard Port Heights	3.5	-0.1
Seasonal Correction (-)	-0.1	-0.1
	3.6	0.0 (-&-=+)
Secondary Port Correction	0.2	0.0
Secondary Port Heights	3.8	0.0 (un-corrected)
Seasonal Correction	-0.1	-0.1
Secondary Port Heights	3.7	-0.1

ATT Vol 1. Page 317				SEASONAL CHANGES IN MEAN LEVEL									
No	Jan. 1	Feb. 1	Mar. 1	Apr. 1	May 1	June 1	July 1	Aug. 1	Sep. 1	Oct. 1	Nov. 1	Dec. 1	Jan. 1
394 - 398	+0.1	0.0	-0.1	-0.1	-0.1	-0.1	0.0	0.0	0.0	0.0	+0.1	+0.1	+0.1
399 - 407	+0.2	+0.1	0.0	-0.1	-0.1	-0.1	-0.1	-0.1	0.0	0.0	+0.1	+0.2	+0.2
408 - 414a	+0.1	0.0	-0.1	-0.1	-0.1	-0.1	0.0	0.0	0.0	0.0	+0.1	+0.1	+0.1
415 - 444	0.0	0.0	0.0	-0.1	-0.1	0.0	0.0	0.0	0.0	0.0	+0.1	+0.1	0.0

Range = 3.5 ~ - 0.1 = 3.6 (since it is above the spring range, the spring curve would be used without any extrapolation)

7   Times and heights should now be marked on the Greenock graph, and height marks should be joined. (Notice -0.1 to the left of 0.0 mark)

8   From 1430, ie 27 minutes after 1403, draw a vertical line to the spring curve. At the intersection, draw a horizontal line to reach the heights diagonal line. At this intersection draw a vertical line to reach the scale. Read the height of tide 2.2 m.

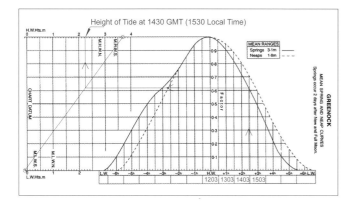

Figure 10.11   Graph for example 10.2
© British Crown Copyright, 2006

Total depth   = Draught + UKC   = **6.5 m**
Charted depth   = 6.5 – 2.2   = **4.3 m**

The tidal data is to one decimal place of a metre only. All fractions above the first decimal place are rounded off to the nearest decimetre, ie one decimal of a metre.

10.5.3   Pacific Tides – Standard Port

In most Pacific Tide ports, but not necessarily in the Pacific Ocean, the terminology used is different and different levels are referred to. The equivalents are:

MHWS   =   MHHW
MHWN   =   MLHW
MLWN   =   MHLW
MLWS   =   MLLW

Unlike European Tides, only one graph is provided for all ports, it will have three curves representing a time difference between the successive tides of 5h, 6h and 7h. If the difference in time falls between two successive curves, interpolation is carried out. If the time difference is less than 5h or more than 7h, curves cannot be used, as extrapolation cannot be carried out. In such cases the tides between HW and LW can only be worked out using harmonic constants.

Not all Pacific ports have two high and two low waters as some ports only have diurnal tides. For secondary ports, time differences take into account the time zone changes between the standard and secondary ports and do not need to be applied separately.

Example 10.3

A ship with an air draught of 59.5 m is ready to sail at 2000 hours on 4th January 2006 from Vancouver. Vancouver bridge has a charted height of 60 m. What is the earliest time that the ship will be able to pass underneath with a clearance of 2 m above the mast truck?

If the distance between the berth and the bridge is 9 miles, at what time must she sail in order to pass under the bridge with the required clearance if her average speed during the passage is 6 knots?

Solution and Comments

1   Height of tide can be determined using the following equation:

AIR DRAUGHT + AIR CLEARANCE = (MHHW or HAT + CHARTED HEIGHT) – HEIGHT OF TIDE

59.5 + 2.0 = (4.4 + 60) – Height of Tide
Height of Tide = (60.0 + 4.4) - (59.5 + 2.0) = 2.9 m
At tidal levels up to 2.9 m, the ship will be able to clear the bridge with the required clearance. At tidal levels higher than 2.9 m, the ship will not be able to clear the bridge with the required clearance.

2   Tidal data Vancouver: 4th and 5th January 2006 from ATT Vol 4, p 165

4th	0220	0.7	5th	0303	1.2
	0935	5.0		1010	5.0
	1554	2.8		1656	2.4
	2028	3.7		2154	3.4

As the ship is ready to sail at 2000, the tides to be taken into account are for 2028 on the 4th and 0303 on the 5th.

3   Time differences 2028 ~ 0303 = 6h 35m

Interpolation is required between 6 hour and 7 hour curves.

4   Mark the height and times on the graph and draw the required vertical and horizontal lines to determine the time when the tide will be 2.9 m.

From the graph, Figure 10.12, the time when the tide is at 2.9 m is 2301. At this time or afterwards the ship can pass under the bridge with the required clearance.

Steaming time from berth to bridge = 9/6 = 1h 30m
The ship should leave the berth at 2301 – 1h 30m = **2131** hours.

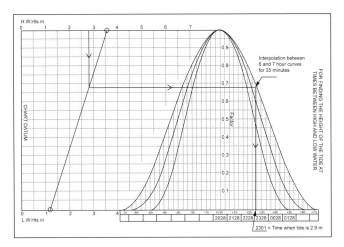

Figure 10.12 Graph for example 10.3
© *British Crown Copyright, 2006*

10.5.4 Pacific Tides – Secondary Port

Example 10.4

A fully loaded ship with a draught of 5.0 m has grounded on a shoal charted at 2.2 m at San Mateo Bridge, California on 8th February 2006 at 0600 local time. If the ship has a TPC of 18 t, find the minimum amount of cargo to tranship if the ship is to refloat by HW the next day.

Solution and Comments

1 First stage is to determine the height of tide using the equation:
DRAUGHT + UNDER-KEEL ALLOWANCE = LEAST CHARTED DEPTH + HEIGHT OF TIDE

$$5.0 + 0.0 = 2.2 + \text{Height of Tide}$$
Height of Tide $= (5.0 + 0.0) - 2.2 = 2.8$ m

2 Tidal data:

Standard Port data	HHW	LLW	MHHW	MLHW	MHLW	MLLW
9305 San Francisco			1.7	1.4	0.7	0.0
Secondary Port data						
9307a San Mateo Bridge	+0044	+0111	+0.6	+ 0.5	+ 0.1	0.0
Seasonal Changes:	9305 and 9307a			Negligible		

San Francisco (Golden gate) tides for day after grounding:

9th	0232	1.0
	0827	1.8
	1543	-0.1
	2257	1.5

The tides to consider are 0232 and 0827

3 Time and height differences:
Time differences are applied directly

	LW	HW
	0232	0827
	+ 0044	+ 0111
	0316	0938

Height Differences:
An alternate method of obtaining corrections has been used (Figure 10.13).
Corrections obtained are 0.6 m for HW and 0.1 m for LW.

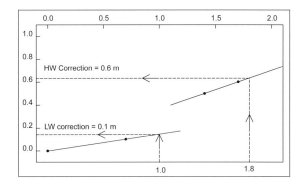

Figure 10.13 Graph for example 10.4

Standard Port Heights	1.0	1.8
Seasonal Correction (-)	Negligible	Negligible
	1.0	1.8
Secondary Port Correction	0.1	0.6
Secondary Port Heights	1.1	2.4 (un-corrected)
Seasonal Correction	Negligible	Negligible
Secondary Port Heights	1.1	2.4
Required height of tide		= 2.8 m
Available height of tide at 0938 on the 9th		= 2.4 m
Change of sinkage required		= 0.4 m
Cargo to tranship		= 0.4 m × 100 cm × 18 t = 720t

In order to float off, the ship should tranship more than **720 tonnes of cargo.**

10.5.5 Tidal Window on Passage

Deep draught vessels can only transit certain parts of the world at certain times, when the height of the tide is adequate to allow passage with a safe under-keel allowance. Planning is important to maximise the cargo and proceed with the minimum wastage of time. The mariner needs to plan the draught working backwards and then calculate the window of opportunity for the transit through the critical depth areas.

	Value (m)	Comments
HW from data range	05.78	*For the standard port near the offshore area*
Co-tidal Factor to be applied	00.83	*For the point of least depth*
Tidal Height in area	04.80	*Least depth*
Least Charted Depth	23.00	
Depth of Water in Area	27.80	
Required UKC	03.50	*As planned for this leg of passage*
Maximum Possible Draught	24.30	
Passage Consumption	00.12	*Up to the point under consideration*
Draught at Departure	24.42	

Table 10.1 Calculation of draught allowing for critical depth points

Permissible draughts should be determined for all critical areas with reduced depth. The next stage is to determine the ETA at these points and work out the tides around the ETA.

For example, for a ship requiring a height of tide of 3.5 m, the tidal window for the transit through the point of interest is as follows.

It can be seen, from the calculations in Table 10.2, that the ship must adjust the ETA to 0122 hours on the 13-1-06, by adjusting speed.

	Date	Time	Height	ETA 12-1-06 : 2200 hours
LW	12-1-06	2135	1.2	*Corrected for offshore area*
HW	13-1-06	0355	4.8	*Corrected for offshore area*
LW	13-1-06	0907	1.7	*Corrected for offshore area*
Rising Duration		6h 20m		*For Pacific Tides*
Range			3.6	*For European Tides*
Falling Duration		5h 12m		*For Pacific Tides*
Range			3.1	*For European Tides*
From Graph				*See Figure 10.17*
Interval Before HW		2h 33m		*From graph*
Interval After HW		2h 21m		*From graph*
Earliest Transit time	13-1-06	0122	3.5	
Latest Transit time	13-1-06	0616	3.5	

Table 10.2 Tidal window calculation

As several times and heights will have to be determined on a long passage that has various critical depths, the calculations in Table 10.2 could be done using a computer programme.

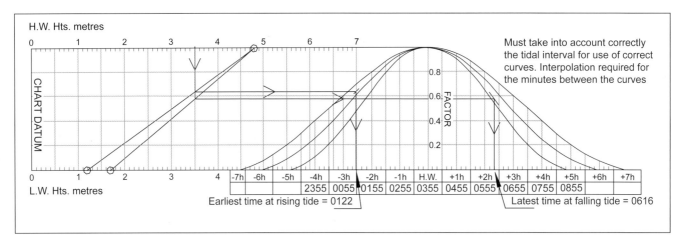

Figure 10.14 Graph for tidal window

10.5.6 Offshore Tides

In order to determine the height of tides in certain areas of navigational significance, co-tidal and co-range charts can be used. These charts show lines of equal time and range of tides. Co-tidal lines are drawn through points of equal MHWI. The co-range lines are drawn through points of equal MSR.

Several co-tidal and co-range charts are available for offshore areas of navigational significance. Additionally, such charts are also added in a smaller scale on passage planning guide charts, eg 5500, 5502. A section of BA 5502 can be seen in Figure 10.15, and contains an example of the calculation of tides in offshore regions. For point "X" marked on the chart, and using standard port "Klang":

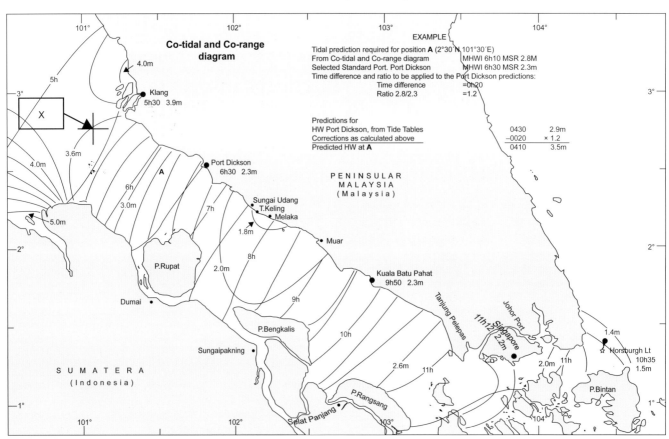

Figure 10.15 Co-tidal co-range chartlet from BA 5502
© British Crown Copyright, 2006

		MHWI		MSR
Point "X"		5h 25		3.6m
Klang		5h 30		3.9m
Time difference	= - 0h 05		Ratio 3.6/3.9	= 0.92
Prediction for Klang	1345			3.7m
Corrections		- 0005		× 0.92
Predicted tide at "X"	1340			3.4m

Procedure for use of co-tidal co-range charts:

- Plot position on the co-tidal co-range chart
- note Mean High Water Interval (MHWI) at position (interpolate between curves visually)
- note the Mean Spring Range (MSR) at position (interpolate between curves visually)
- note MSR and MHWI for a standard port
- subtract MHWI of standard port from the one for own position
- apply this time difference to standard port predicted times to obtain HW and LW times at position
- divide MSR at position by MSR of standard port to obtain the factor for height adjustment
- multiply standard port predicted heights with the factor to obtain HW and LW heights at position.

10.5.7 Tide Computations

Computer software is increasingly being used to provide tidal predictions.

UKHO provides 'TotalTide' on CD and 'Easy Tide' on the web. Other providers also use simple programs for tidal calculations.

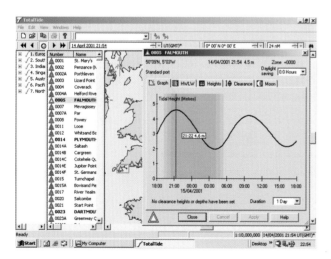

Figure 10.16   Tidal predictions displayed by total tide
© British Crown Copyright, 2006

By using approved websites on mobile devices like phones and tablets, tidal information can be accessed by using suitable APPS. While the information provided by APPS is generally fine, it must be noted that that most of the APPS are not approved by a hydrographic authority.

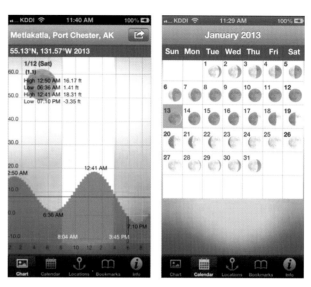

Figure 10.17   Tidal predictions displayed by a free APP

10.5.8 Neaping Situations

While operations are carefully planned, it may occasionally be possible for the ship to be unable to use the tidal opportunity and may be faced with a neaping situation, where the required height to tide only occurs after a few days gap.

Example 10.5
On 20 March 2006, a ship with a maximum draught of 12 m is required to pass a point in a channel at Greenock with a charted depth of 11.0 m. The ship must maintain a UKC of 1 m, and an allowance for squat equal to 10% of draught must be made. If the steaming time from the berth to the point of least depth is 30 minutes, find the latest time that the ship must leave its berth on 20 March 2006.

If due to technical problems, the ship is unable to sail on the 20th March, find the earliest time that she can sail out with the required clearance without having to discharge any cargo.

Solution and Comments

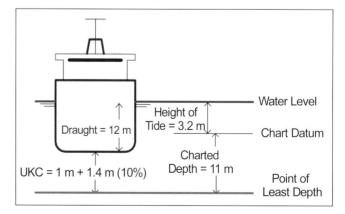

Figure 10.18   Levels and heights for example 10.5

Draught	=	12.0 m
UKC	=	1.0 m
Squat allowance	=	1.2 m
Required Depth	=	14.2 m
Charted Depth	=	11.0 m
Required Height of Tide	=	3.2 m

Tabulated Tidal Information

20 March 2006

Times	Heights
0325	3.1
0853	0.4
1540	3.2
2108	0.4

By inspection it can be seen that the required height of tide is available at 1540.

As the ship will require 30 minutes to reach the point with 11.0 m depth, she must leave berth by:

1540 – 30 minutes = **1510**

If the ship is unable to sail on 20th, Tidal Data for subsequent Dates:

21		22		23		24	
0356	3.0	0429	2.9	0513	2.7	0004	1.0
0937	0.6	1032	0.7	1141	0.9	0626	2.6
1617	3.1	1700	2.9	1758	2.7	1303	0.9
2156	0.8	2254	0.9			1926	2.6
25		26		27			
0126	1.1	0254	1.0	0356	0.7		
0837	2.6	1001	2.9	1054	3.2		
1437	0.7	1541	0.4	1628	0.1		
2124	2.7	2237	2.9	2329	3.1		

On inspection it can be seen that the required height of tide of 3.2 m will occur on 27th March 2006 at 1054. This means that the ship would be able to sail out at:

1054 – 30 minutes = **1024**

Note: In the above example the required height of tide is the maximum that occurs on the 20th and 27th March. Where the required height of the tide was less than the tabulated values, tidal curve must be used to determine the exact time that the required height of tide will occur.

10.6 Tidal Streams

The horizontal movement of water due to tide raising forces is referred to as the tidal stream. These streams are generally predictable. The interval where there is no or little horizontal movement of water, due to tide raising forces, is called slack water. Set is the direction that the water flows towards. Rate is the hourly speed of the water's movement in knots. Drift is the movement in nautical miles over a period of time.

Tidal stream data refers to the uppermost 10 m layer of the sea. Streams at depths below this layer may not always be the same. This could have an effect on ships with a deep draught or those engaged in underwater operations.

10.6.1 Rotary Streams

In offshore areas the tidal stream flows continuously in a rotary cycle as there is no restriction on the direction of flow. Rotation is caused by the earth's rotation, it is clockwise in the northern hemisphere and anticlockwise in the southern hemisphere, unless modified by local conditions. The hypothetical data related to the Tidal diamond "D" is rotary and can be represented with a current ellipse.

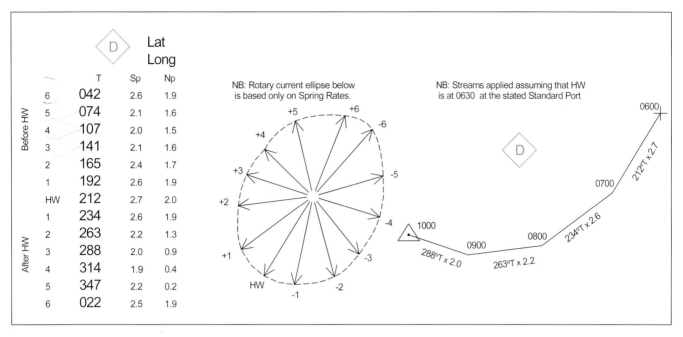

Figure 10.19   Example of a rotary tidal stream

The rates can be interpolated, but for general use the rates can be applied from 30 minutes before to 30 minutes after a stated data value. In Figure 10.18, at 0600 hrs a ship is stopped in close proximity to tidal diamond "D" and drifts up to 1000 hrs, which is the time the estimated position has been plotted. The rate of flow usually varies and achieves two maximums in almost opposite directions with two minimums almost in between.

10.6.2 Rectilinear Streams

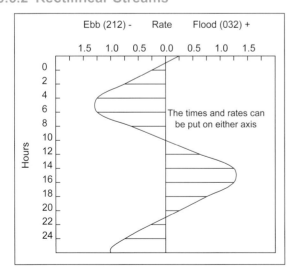

Figure 10.20   Rectilin tidal stream

This type of tidal stream will reverse due to restrictions within a river, channel or estuary which only has two directions, separated by slack periods or slack water at each reversal (both high and low water). The rate varies in each direction from zero at slack water to a maximum flow around mid-flood or mid-ebb. The movement of a tidal stream before high water, ie towards shore or upstream, is called the flood tide as it causes water to rush in and pile up in a certain region. Similarly, the movement of water before low water, ie away from shore or downstream, is called the ebb. The maximum rate of tidal stream in each direction is called the strength of flood or ebb. The permanent current in rivers or channels is included in such tidal stream data.

10.6.3 Tidal Stream Data

Tidal stream data only refers to the geographical point it is stated for and at times it may not be valid at even a small distance away from it. This is because the rates of flow are not uniform in a particular area. For example, the flow is maximum in the middle of a channel and almost zero at the edge of the same channel. But in the case of a bend, the rate is maximum at the outer edge and minimum or zero at the inner edge of the bend. The maximum flow is usually in the deepest part of the channel.

Similar to tidal heights, the tidal streams have diurnal and semi-diurnal components. The rates are related to the range of the tide and the times of slack water are related, but not necessarily identical, to the times of high and low water at the nearest standard port.

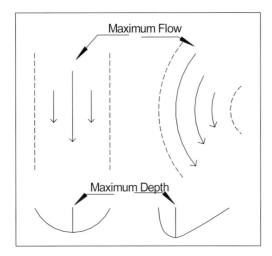

Figure 10.21 Flow at various parts of a channel

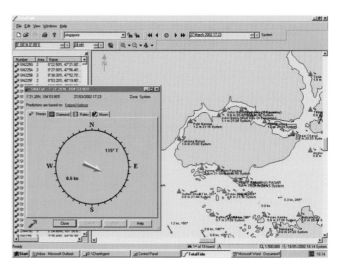

Figure 10.22 Tidal stream displayed by total tide
© British Crown Copyright, 2006

With semi-diurnal tides, there is no requirement for daily predictions. The data is related to a standard port and may be published on the navigational chart. The rates are provided for spring and neap tides. Interpolation must be performed for rates other than springs and neaps. At places where the diurnal inequality is large, this procedure cannot be used. Daily predictions are provided for certain important areas that have a large diurnal inequality. Tidal stream atlases cover a wide area and relates relating the data to a nearby standard port.

10.6.4 Harmonic Constants

These can be used to calculate the rate at a given diamond or position. The data can also be input into computer programmes for working out the rate and direction at a given time.

10.6.5 Use of Software

TotalTide is a good example of software providing tidal stream. The information may be displayed in the form of vectors and data from the tidal diamond. The information can also be displayed on a compass rose type panel along with the rate.

Example 10.6
Using the data provided, determine the direction and rate of tidal stream at San Francisco Bay Entrance (Golden Gate) on 1st of March 2006 at 1300 California standard time and time when tidal stream is 245°T at 2 knots.

Solution and Comments
Data for the 1st of March 2006 has been boxed below. Using the data, the curve for the tidal stream will be produced. To enhance the curve, times outside of the desired window may be plotted.

Mark the slack times and the maximum flow times on the graph. The marks should be joined using a curve that is gently rounded off at the plotted marks. From 1300, draw a line horizontally to the curve. At the intersection, draw a vertical line to reach rate scale. Stream is 065°T at 1.7 knots.

From 2 knots on the 245° side, draw a vertical line to reach the hour scale. At the intersection, draw a horizontal line to reach the hour scale. The time is 1522.

UNITED STATES– SAN FRANCISCO BAY ENTRANCE (GOLDEN GATE)

LAT 37°49′N   LONG   122°30′W

TIDAL STREAM PREDICTIONS (RATES IN KNOTS)

TIME ZONE +0800   POSITIVE (+) DIRECTION 065 NEGATIVE (–) DIRECTION 245   YEAR **2006**

	JANUARY							FEBRUARY							MARCH						
	SLACK	MAXIMUM			SLACK	MAXIMUM			SLACK	MAXIMUM			SLACK	MAXIMUM			SLACK	MAXIMUM			SLACK	MAXIMUM
	Time	Time	Rate		Time	Time	Rate		Time	Time	Rate		Time	Time	Rate		Time	Time	Rate		Time	Time	Rate
1	0249	0453	-2.2	**16**	0307	0515	-1.9	**1**		0014	4.2	**16**		0002	2.9	**1**	0206	0450	-4.3	**16**	0153	0443	-3.7
	0745	1043	2.8		0826	1113	2.2		0332	0606	-3.5		0314	0555	-3.0		0814	1111	4.0		0816	1110	3.0
SU	1325	1700	-5.7	M	1358	1719	-4.3	W	0928	1220	3.3	TH	0922	1213	2.4	W	1415	1709	-4.7	TH	1418	1701	-3.3
	2056				2119				1517	1820	-4.5		1510	1808	-3.2		2042	2336	4.0		2023	2318	2.8

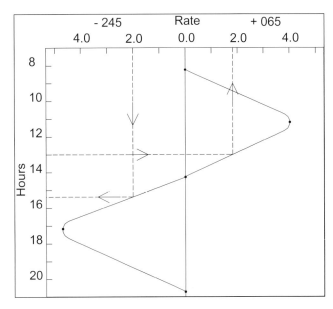

Figure 10.23 Graph for example 10.6

The tidal stream information should be carefully analysed and its effects taken into account when executing the passage. As a minimum, the required course and time of arrival calculations must be carried out. In extreme cases, where very strong tidal streams are experienced, ships should try to transit the area at slack water or during favourable tidal stream conditions only. If there was an extremely strong tidal stream, the ship may have to wait in clear waters or wait at anchor for favourable conditions or slack water.

11

RANGE	BRG	NAME
00.92	039.0	BASTO III
01.59	038.1	BREMER ROLAN
03.10	217.6	SALMO
04.17	272.0	BASTOE2
04.49	283.4	KNM CHRISTIA
04.50	288.3	*2576159
05.96	214.9	BRO.GLOBE
10.42	298.2	DROBAKSUND I
--.--	---.-	LORE D

LAT: 059° 24'32.22N
LON: 010° 37'30.66E ALARM
SOG: 015 COG: 074

Marine Communications

Good communications are vital for the success of a maritime venture. Instructions from operators and the authorities who are responsible for handling the ship must ensure that safety information is received by the ship in good time. With the recent advances in technology, communications at sea have improved significantly, in particular, the Global Maritime Distress and Safety System (GMDSS) have made improvements in maritime safety.

11.1 GMDSS

GMDSS provisions apply to cargo ships of 300 GT and over and ships carrying more than 12 passengers on international voyages. Under GMDSS, equipment carriage requirements are linked to the area of operation. The sea areas are designated as:

Sea Area A1
Area that is within radiotelephone coverage of at least one VHF coast station. The station must have continuous DSC availability. The limit of this area extends to approximately 20-50 nm offshore from the coast.

Sea Area A2
Area, excluding sea area A1, that is within the radiotelephone coverage of at least one MF coast station. This station must have continuous DSC availability. The limit of this area extends to approximately 150 nm offshore from the limit of sea area A1.

Sea Area A3
Area, excluding sea areas A1 and A2, within the coverage of an INMARSAT geostationary satellite, where continuous alerts are available. This area is within about 70°N to 70°S.

Sea Area A4
This area covers the polar-regions, where geostationary satellite coverage is not possible and it is outside the sea areas A1, A2 and A3.

Radio watchkeeping is automatic under GMDSS. When keeping watch, the OOW or Master must ensure that the on board equipment is in service and fully operational. The equipment should be correctly set up to perform all of the mandatory GMDSS functions. This can be achieved by carrying out regular checks and tests. Considering the operational needs of different circumstances, GMDSS must comply with the following functional requirements:

- The transmission of ship-to-shore radio distress alerts by at least two separate and independent means, each using a different radio service
- the reception of shore-to-ship radio distress alerts
- transmission and reception of ship-to-ship radio distress alerts
- transmission and reception of search and rescue co-ordinating radio communications
- transmission and reception of on-scene radio communications
- transmission and reception of locating signals
- transmission and reception of radio Maritime Safety Information (MSI)
- transmission and reception of general radio communications, linking with shore-based systems and networks
- transmission and reception of bridge-to-bridge radio communications.

In order to meet the above functional requirements in the appropriate sea areas, ships required to comply must be equipped as follows:

- VHF radio transceiver with DSC on Ch 70 and radiotelephony on channels 6, 13 and 16
- a radio receiver capable of continuous DSC watch on VHF channel 70
- search and rescue transponders (SART) operating in the 9 GHz band (ships 500 GT or over should have two and ships under 500 GT should have one)
- a satellite emergency position indicating radio beacon (EPIRB) which can be manually activated and float-free self-activation
- two-way hand held VHF radios (ships 500 GT or over and all passenger ships should have three and ships 300-500 GT should have two)
- a receiver with the capability to access NAVTEX broadcasts wherever the NAVTEX service is available

- receiving equipment with capability of receiving SafetyNET where the NAVTEX service is not available.

Individual sea areas have specific requirements under GMDSS.

Sea Area A1

- VHF RT apparatus
- float-free EPIRB – either DSC VHF channel 70 or satellite frequency
- initiating distress alert from a navigational position using DSC on VHF, HF or MF, by activating EPIRB manually or by Ship Earth Station.

Sea Areas A1 and A2

- MF RT on 2,182 kHz and DSC on 2,187.5 kHz
- radio equipment capable of continuous DSC watch on 2,187.5 kHz
- INMARSAT SES or general working radio communications in the MF band 1,605-4,000 kHz
- initiating distress alert by HF, by activating EPIRB manually or by INMARSAT SES.

Sea Areas A1, A2 and A3

- MF RT on 2,182 kHz and DSC on 2,187.5 kHz
- radio equipment capable of continuous DSC watch on 2,187.5 kHz
- INMARSAT A, B or C (class 2) SES Enhanced Group Call (EGC) or HF as required for sea area A4
- initiating distress alert by any two from within HF/DSC radio communications, by activating EPIRB manually or by INMARSAT A, B or C (class 2) SES.

Sea Area A4

- HF/MF transceiver within a band 1,605-27,500 kHz, using DSC, RT and direct printing
- radio equipment capable of selecting any safety and distress DSC frequency for band 4,000-27,500 kHz, maintaining DSC watch on 2,187.5, 8,414.5 kHz and at least one additional safety and distress DSC frequency within the band
- initiating distress alert from a navigational position through the Polar Orbiting System on 406 MHz.

11.1.1 INMARSAT

INMARSAT is an internationally owned co-operative providing mobile communications worldwide, excluding latitudes outside of 70° N and S. It was launched in 1979 to serve the maritime industry and has evolved to become a provider of global mobile satellite communications for commercial, distress and safety applications whether at sea, on land or in the air.

The INMARSAT satellite network supports, but is not limited to, the following key services for maritime users:

- Direct-dial telephone
- facsimile
- telex
- email
- data transmission.

The INMARSAT system makes use of its existing services on a priority basis providing for distress and safety communications. It eliminates the necessity for dedicated frequencies.

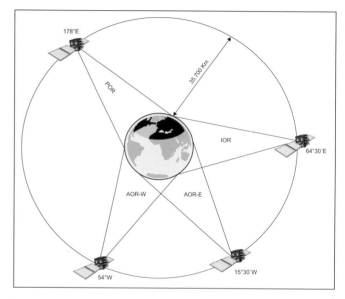

Figure 11.1   Plan view of the plane of equator with INMARSAT satellites

11.1.1.1 Satellites

INMARSAT has 4 geostationary satellites at an altitude of 35,700 km. Standard data services of up to 64 kbit/sec are provided. More modern I-3 satellites have a spot band facility that allows areas of heavy usage to be focussed on. I-4 satellites, available since 2004, have a much higher data rate capability at 432 kbits/sec, allowing full mobile provision for internet, multi-media and other advanced applications. INMARSAT satellites are configured in four coverage regions scanning up to 70° N or 70° S.

Detailed diagrams, providing coverage data as well as the azimuth and altitude of the satellite from within the coverage area, are available in the appropriate literature that is normally carried by ships.

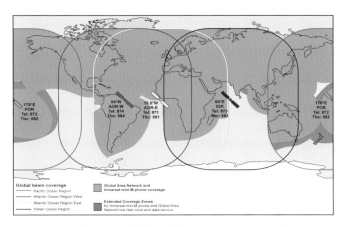

Figure 11.2 Coverage of INMARSAT satellites with permission of inmarsat

Figure 11.3 Mini-C

11.1.1.2 Tracking and Telemetry Control (TTC)

Satellites are controlled by 4 TTC stations, plus one back-up

11.1.1.3 Land Earth Stations (LES)

LES or Coast Earth Stations (CES) in the maritime world, known as ground earth stations (GES) in aeronautical circles, link INMARSAT's satellites with telecommunication networks.

11.1.1.4 Ship Earth Stations (SES)

SES or mobile earth stations, often referred to as mobile terminals, are the user terminals that connect to satellites, providing communications to the mobile end user. Several different mobile communications systems are offered by INMARSAT in order to provide users with a wide variety of mobile terminals and services. Each system uses a distinct INMARSAT Number series that allows the functionality to be recognised from the number allocated to specific terminals.

11.1.1.5 INMARSAT-B

This system extends the advantage of digital technology to mobile satellite communications. The digital system makes better use of satellite power and bandwidth at a much lower cost to users, while maintaining high quality reliable communications. INMARSAT -B also supports automatic, direct-dial telephone and fax, as well as telex. It is approved under GMDSS.

11.1.1.6 INMARSAT-C and mini-C

This is a small and light weight two way satellite communications system. It provides store-and-forward message or text communications at a data rate of 600 bits/sec, it also provides access to international telex/telex networks. It does not handle voice. INMARSAT-C terminals are able to receive multiple address messages (EGC).

11.1.1.7 INMARSAT-E

This is a safety only system and it provides global alerting for GMDSS to all ships and safety centres by picking up signals from EPIRBs.

11.1.1.8 INMARSAT Fleet 77

Fleet 77 service allows for call prioritisation to 4 levels and real-time, hierarchical two-way call pre-emption with high system availability. The 4 levels of priority are:

Distress	:	(P3) INMARSAT Priority 3
Urgency	:	(P2) INMARSAT Priority 2
Safety	:	(P1) INMARSAT Priority 1
General/Routine	:	(P0) INMARSAT Priority 0

The traffic originated by RCCs or other Search and Rescue authorities (see Chapter 12) have appropriate access for communications in both ship-to-shore and shore-to-ship directions. The system also meets the commercial needs of voice, fax, email and data. In addition, there are certain non-GMDSS systems available under INMARSAT.

11.1.2 Digital Selective Calling (DSC)

In order to make the initial contact between two stations, or groups of stations, the automatic calling system DSC is used. DSC works on dedicated radio frequencies, which are available in all bands, ie VHF, MF and HF for short, medium and long ranges.

The transmitting station sends a short message to the receiving station(s). The receivers display the information on a screen and activate an alarm. The information on the display indicates the purpose of the call and the mode of further communications. For urgency and safety, the transmitting station should:

- Announce the message
- transmit the message

The receiving ships, when the message is addressed to more than one ship, should not acknowledge receipt of the DSC call but should tune in to the appropriate RTF frequency for the message. Depending on the frequency used for the DSC alert, the receiver must take some basic actions. These actions, in the form of flow charts, must be displayed close to the DSC equipment.

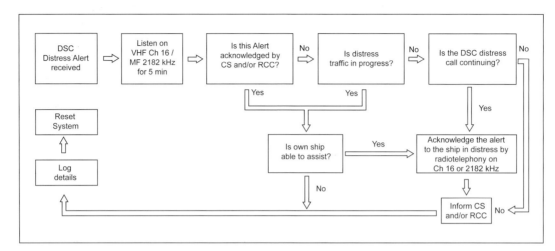

Figure 11.4   Actions by ships on receipt of VHF/MF DCS distress alert

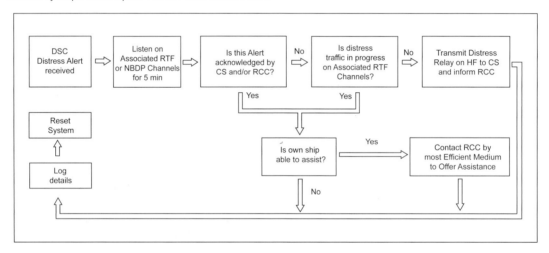

Figure 11.5   Actions by ships on receipt of HF DSC alert

11.1.3 SART

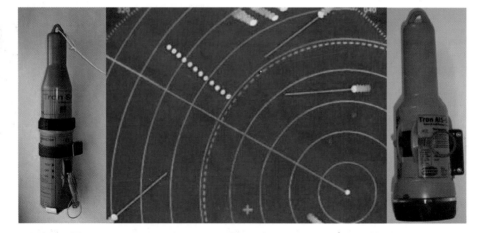

Figure 11.6   SART and radar display showing 12 distinct blips

Under GMDSS, a simple way to locate either a ship in distress or their survival craft, is to use SART – Search and Rescue Radar ·Transponder.

- SART operates in the 9 GHz band
- X-band (3 cm) radar can interrogate when the SART is switched on within the line of sight (usually 8 nm)
- a line as a 12 blip code appears on the radar display, outwards from the SART position along its line of bearing
- spacing between each pair of blips will be 0.64 nm, the radar should be operated within the 6 to 12 nm range scales to distinguish SART from other possible contacts
- at ranges of approximately 12 nm, the first blip may be 0.64 beyond its position
- when the search unit is close to being within 1 nm of the SART, the blips will start to change into wide arcs
- the blips change to concentric circles as the search units close in and are almost on the SART
- SART indicates to operators when it is being interrogated by radar
- visual or audible indication confirms that SART is being correctly operated
- the battery should allow SART to be in stand-by mode for 96 hours, followed by 8 hours of transmission when being interrogated by radar
- radar control settings should be optimum to raise small echoes at sea.

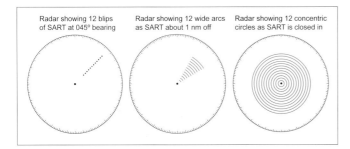

Figure 11.7   SART signature display on radar PPI

11.1.3.1 SART Detection ranges

- The IMO recommendation is to mount the SART at least 1 m above sea level
- with scanner heights of 15 m, a SART 1 m above sea level should be detected at 5 nm
- air units at an altitude of 3,000 ft (914.4 m) can detect a SART up to 40 nm.

11.1.3.2 EPIRB

An Emergency Position Indicating Radio Beacon can alert shore stations when a signal that is transmitted by it is received by satellite under INMARSAT EPIRB-E and COSPAS-SARSAT. Satellites can detect alerts from sea (EPIRB), land (PLB – personal locator beacon) and air (ELT - emergency locating transmitter).

11.1.3.3 COSPAS -SAR SAT

Full global coverage is possible with the COSPAS-SARSAT system. It has two components – LEOSAR and GEOSAR. The LEO Search and Rescue segment uses 4 satellites on polar orbits, which are low earth orbit satellites (LEOSAR), at an altitude of about 850 km. LEOSAR satellites can also pick up weaker signals. The EPIRBs under this system transmit on 406 MHz. Aircraft ELTs also include a homing signal on 121.5 MHz.

Figure 11.8   EPIRBs

The orbital period of the satellite is approximately 100 minutes and it sweeps a track about 4,000 km wide over the earth. Although the system provides global coverage, it is not continuous. For an alert to be detected, a satellite must be in view. For the satellite to download data to a receiving station, the satellite must be in view of the ground station.

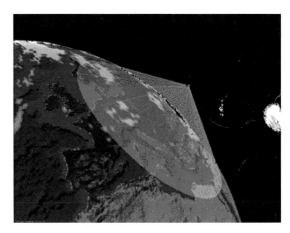

Figure 11.9   COSPAS SARSAT coverage cone

The satellites are able to calculate the position of the alert by using the Doppler frequency shift as the satellite moves past the transmitting beacon. This calculation results in two possible positions on either side of the satellite orbit resulting in ambiguity. The next satellite pass may resolve this ambiguity. The shore station receiving the satellite positions might also be able to resolve the ambiguity if a marine EPIRB alert results in one position being over sea and another over land, if there have been more reports on the same alert from other sources, or if two satellites have picked up the alert. In some cases, a significant delay is likely before the position can be confirmed.

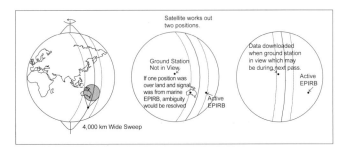

Figure 11.10   COSPAS-SARSAT satellite sweep and detection

GEOSAR uses 5 geostationary satellites. The coverage is limited to between 70° N and 70° S. The satellites cannot work out the position of the alert (the same as with INMARSAT EPIRB-E). Modern EPIRBs are able to transmit the position which can be entered manually or by GPS input, the GEOSAR satellites can then relay it. This segment cannot cover sea area A4. It has the advantage of directing the alert to RCCs without delay.

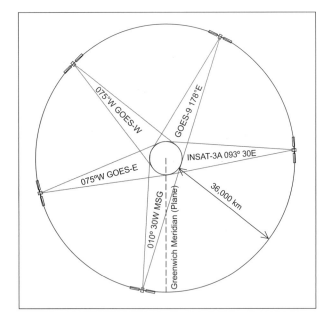

Figure 11.11   Plan view of the plane of equator with GEOSAR satellites

11.1.3.4 L-BAND

L-Band satellite EPIRBs make use of the 4 INMARSAT geostationary satellites. The EPIRB operates at L-band (1.6 GHz). The satellites cannot work out the position of the alert. Modern EPIRBs are able to transmit the position from a GPS input. Some L-Band EPIRBs have the added feature of SART for homing using X-band radar.

For sea area A1, a VHF EPIRB can be used. This portable unit transmits a DSC distress alert on VHF, which indicates "EPIRB emission" in place and the nature of the distress. The unit then transmits the SART signal, which can be homed in on by search units using 3 cm (X-band) radar, making electronic detection possible. EPIRBs should be float-free and are usually mounted in exposed locations. It is not uncommon for the unit to fall off into the sea accidentally, causing it to transmit. It can also be accidentally turned on when it is moved for testing, servicing or battery replacement. The ship's officers should be aware of this possibility, care and vigilance should be given or unnecessary search and rescue actions might be initiated due to false alerts. Modern devices are available that can detect whether an EPIRB has been activated in the ship's vicinity and if it belongs to own ship. EPIRBs must be registered and if any details change in the future, eg name, ownership, etc the registration authorities must be notified.

11.1.4 Enhanced Group Calling (EGC)

The enhanced group call is a method that is used to address particular regions or all or specific ships.

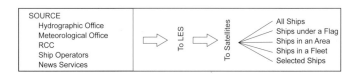

Figure 11.12   EGC message co-ordination

11.1.5 Maritime Safety Information (MSI)

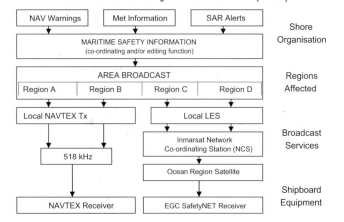

The following are the major categories of MSI for NAVTEX, AIS and SafetyNET:

- Navigational warnings
- meteorological warnings
- search and rescue information
- ice reports
- meteorological forecasts
- pilot service messages (excluding the United States)
- electronic navigation system messages (LORAN, GPS, DGPS, etc).

In order to ensure safe navigation, the navigator should receive an MSI message without any delay. This is one of the main objectives of GMDSS and is achieved in two ways, using SafetyNET and NAVTEX.

11.1.5.1 SafetyNET

SafetyNET is a service of the INMARSAT-C – EGC system. The SafetyNET service is designated by the IMO under GMDSS through which ships receive MSI. It makes use of an international direct-printing satellite based service. The information distributed includes:

- Distress alerts
- navigational warnings
- meteorological warnings
- forecasts
- other safety messages.

It is mandatory for all ships sailing outside NAVTEX coverage to be able to receive SafetyNET. Similarly, it is recommended for all administrations outside NAVTEX coverage. Messages can be originated by a registered information provider anywhere in the world and then broadcast to the appropriate ocean area through INMARSAT-C. A commercial service available under the EGC is FleetNET, which is used by ship operators to directly and privately contact the ships in their fleet.

11.1.5.2 NAVTEX

Figure 11.13   NAVTEX receiver

An international automated direct printing NAVTEX service for the notification of navigational and

meteorological warnings and also urgent safety information to ships has been made available. The main features are:

- It uses the Narrow Band Direct Printing (NBDP) principle
- it allows the automatic reception of maritime safety information (MSI)
- the system uses a single frequency of 518 kHz
- transmissions are from nominated stations within each NAVAREA/METAREA, on a time sharing basis to avoid mutual interference (see 11.2)
- the approximate range is 400 nm, although some stations have a longer range
- it forms an integral part of the GMDSS and is also a component of the WWNWS (see 11.2)
- the user may select messages from a single station in an area or from several different stations
- messages are usually transmitted in English and may be transmitted in additional languages to meet the requirements of the host governments.

National NAVTEX services may transmit on 490 kHz, 4209.5 kHz or another allocated frequency

- Messages are prioritised to dictate the timing of the first transmission of a new warning within NAVTEX:
  - VITAL - for immediate transmission (but avoiding interference to ongoing transmission)
  - IMPORTANT - for transmission at the next available period when no transmissions are being made
  - ROUTINE - at the next scheduled transmission period
- a NAVTEX receiver can select messages to be printed based on:
  - the technical code in the preamble of each message
  - whether the particular message has been already printed or not.

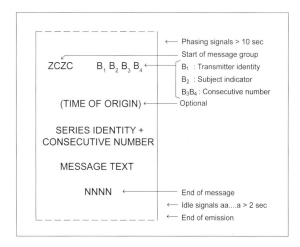

Figure 11.14   Standard format of NAVTEX messages

Transmitter Identification Character (B1)

Each transmitting station is allocated a single unique alphabetical identification character. Within each NAVAREA and METAREA, identification characters are allocated randomly. Consecutive characters are not allocated to adjacent stations. It is also guaranteed that there is sufficient distance between two stations that have been allocated the same character, so that the ship receiver is not within the range of both at the same time. The required station can be selected by choosing the appropriate alphabetical identifier on the NAVTEX receiver.

Subject Indicator Characters (B2)

Subject indicators that cannot be excluded from the reception list by the NAVTEX operator have been marked by *** in the list below and are also marked in bold.

A = Navigational Warnings *
B = Meteorological Warnings *
C = Ice Reports

D = **Search and Rescue information and pirate attack warnings ***
E = Meteorological Forecasts
F = Pilot Service Messages
G = AIS
H = LORAN Messages
I = Spare
J = SATNAV Messages
K = Other Electronic Navaid Messages
L = Navigations Warnings – additional to A *
V = Special services – allocation by the NAVTEX Panel
W = Special services – allocation by the NAVTEX Panel
X = Special services – allocation by the NAVTEX Panel
Y = Special services – allocation by the NAVTEX Panel
Z = No messages on hand
V, W, X and Y may be used for regional languages.

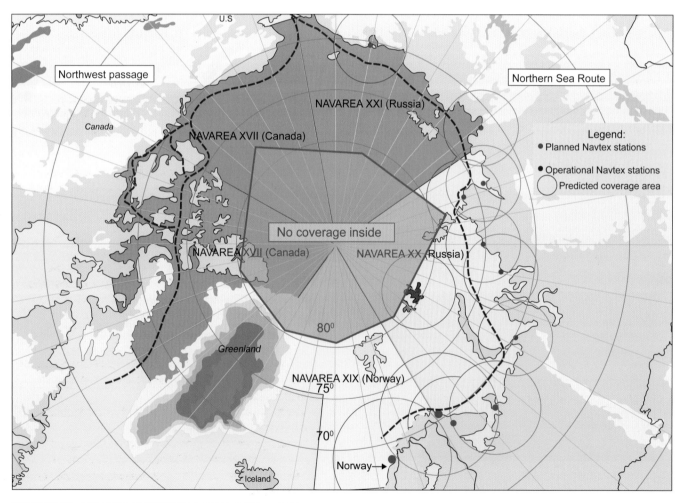

Figure 11.15 Inmarsat and NAVTEX coverage of NE passage

Message Numbering (B3B4)

A serial number between 01 and 99 is allocated to each subject group. It does not necessarily relate to serial numbers in other radio navigational warning systems. When the numbers reach 99, the numbers that are not being currently used are assigned, starting from 01. If there are more than 99 messages, the excess are allocated to other relevant message groups, eg from A to L.

11.1.6 Components of GMDSS

GMDSS has three components:

- LES - Land Earth Stations
- Space Segment
- MES - Mobile Earth Stations.

These perform the following summary functions.

11.1.6.1 Land Earth Stations

This segment is made up of the ground stations that participate in:

- Collecting of safety information, eg NAVAREA Coordinators, Meteorological Stations, MRCC, Coastguard
- processing, formatting and approval of information for transmission by the Coordinator
- transmitting the information to MES, eg INMARSAT ground stations, NAVTEX stations, VHF/MF stations for RT transmission, Port Controls, Coastguard, etc
- reception of MSI from ships at sea and communication to responsible coordinator
- transmission and receipt of distress alerts/ messages from ships at sea by DSC, RT, INMARSAT, NAVTEX (Tx only) etc
- processing alerts and location signals received by COSPAS-SARSAT through EPIRBs
- location of SART through coastguard stations
- transmission and reception of routine communications to and from ships.

11.1.6.2 Space Segment

This consists of INMARSAT, GEOSAR and COSPAS-SARSAT satellites for:

- Reception of 406 MHz EPIRB alerts and location signals through COSPAS-SARSAT satellites
- transmission and reception of MSI through INMARSAT
- transmission and reception of routine communications through INMARSAT.

11.1.6.3 Mobile Earth Stations

These ships, aircraft and drilling stations that comply with the GMDSS/SOLAS requirements:

- Observation, gathering and transmission of MSI
- reception of MSI
- transmission and reception of distress alerts/ messages by DSC, RT, INMARSAT, NAVTEX (Rx only)
- on scene distress communications
- communications between bridge and rescue craft.

11.1.7 Carriage Requirements for GMDSS

The main criteria for the carrying of equipment are the Sea Areas A1, A2, A3 and A3. Ship type (passenger) and ship size (300, 500 GT) have further criteria.

For example, a sea going vessel would carry:

- VHF RT
- VHF DSC
- NAVTEX
- EPIRB
- SART
- HAND HELD VHF
- MF RT
- MF DSC
- SAT-C or Fleet 77
- HF RT and DSC.

11.2 WWNWS

The International Hydrographic Service (IHO) and International Maritime Organization (IMO) have jointly established a World-Wide Navigational Warning Service (WWNWS). Its key features are:

- The world is divided into 21 regions known as NAVAREAs and are identified by roman numerals from I to XXI
- each NAVAREA has an Area Coordinator who is responsible for collating and issuing radio navigational warnings for the entire area. The coordinator also receives information from the National Coordinators of individual countries who want to notify items of navigational significance
- NAVAREA warnings refer to the area concerned, and part of the adjacent area, to cover 24 hours of steaming by a fast ship, ie about 700 nm
- at least two daily transmissions are necessary and schedules are prepared to avoid coinciding with ones of the adjacent areas
- warnings are consecutively numbered through the calendar year
- warnings are in English and can also be in one or more of the United Nations official languages
- warnings may be transmitted using radiotelephony, radiotelex, facsimile

- warnings are transmitted at specific times and are repeated in the broadcast immediately following the original transmission. Warnings can be repeated if it is considered necessary
- NAVAREA warnings address areas of information that ocean going mariners require for safe navigation, eg change in status of navigational aids information likely to affect navigational routes
- there are three main types of radio navigational warnings
  - NAVAREA warnings
  - coastal warnings
  - local warnings.

11.2.1 NAVAREA Warnings

The following are some common examples:

- Change or establish navigational aids, particularly when such a change could be misleading to shipping
- change of operational status or a malfunction/ casualty to lights, fog signals, buoys, etc that affect the main shipping lanes
- dangerous wrecks in or near the main shipping lanes, with relevant marking details given
- areas of search and rescue activity
- areas where anti-pollution operations are being carried out and whether the area is closed to shipping
- drifting mines
- large restricted tows in congested waters
- relay of information from MRCC about any ship, or aircraft over sea that is either reported missing or seriously overdue
- suspension or unexpected alteration of established routes
- newly discovered rocks, reefs, shoals, wrecks etc, likely to be a danger to shipping and where available, their marking details
- new offshore structures that have been established in or near shipping lanes or movement of offshore installations near shipping lanes
- any laying of submarine cables or pipelines
- underwater operations, use of submersibles, towing of large submerged objects, etc that are considered a potential danger in or near shipping lanes
- any malfunction of a radio navigational warning that is of a significant level
- any special operations that might affect the safety of shipping, particularly over wider areas, eg naval exercise areas, missile firing, nuclear tests, space missions. In such cases the degree of hazard should be stated, if known, and the warning should remain in force until the time of the event's completion.

11.2.2 Coastal Warnings

- Coastal warnings cover a region or portion of the NAVAREA
- these are issued by the National Coordinator of the country of origin
- the information is usually broadcast over NAVTEX but may be broadcast by radiotelephony
- the area covered is from pilot ground or fairway buoy to the limit of the NAVTEX (usually 250 nm), unless it is between two regions and the limits are agreed
- coastal warnings cover the whole service/coverage area, unlike the NAVAREA warnings
- the broadcasts are at scheduled times or on receipt, depending on the urgency
- the messages are in English. Administrations may set up national services on different frequencies, which are outside of WWNWS
- coastal warnings often supplement the information in NAVAREA warnings
- coastal warnings cover similar topics to NAVAREA, the difference being that coastal shipping is likely to be affected.

11.2.3 Local Warnings

- These warnings are usually issued by the port, pilotage or coastguard authorities
- the information contained in these warnings is not normally required by ocean-going vessels and usually supplements coastal warnings
- local warnings cover inland waters up to pilot ground or fairway buoy.

Details of all Radio Navigational Warning systems are contained in the relevant ALRS. Information can also be obtained from the Annual Summary of Admiralty Notices to Mariners. Serial numbers of all NAVAREA I warnings and those issued during the week are reprinted in Section III of the Admiralty Weekly Notices to Mariners. It also lists the additional NAVAREA messages that have been received. The US also issues long-range warnings in the form of HYDROLANTs and HYDROPACs. Information about current warnings can be obtained from US Weekly Notices to Mariners. Information is also contained in Section III of Admiralty Weekly Notices to Mariners.

11.3 Weather Reports

The distribution of weather reports and forecasts is carried out in a similar way to navigational warnings. The world is divided into regions, the coastal radio stations provide meteorological information to mariners in their area of coverage and responsibility. For identification purposes and convenience, the areas are further subdivided into small regions. The weather reports are divided into three categories:

- Ocean
- coastal
- local.

Ocean weather reports cover offshore and ocean areas and are transmitted by designated stations at routine times. Similarly, facsimile transmissions are made at specified times. Coastal weather reports are also transmitted by designated stations and cover areas on the coast. Local reports are issued by port, VTS or coastguard authorities. NAVTEX is commonly used by ships to receive meteorological information. In addition, INMARSAT is increasingly used to obtain meteorological information when in an ocean area outside the range of NAVTEX. The weather facsimile receiver is still the most popular choice for receipt of weather information as information can be understood easily in map form. Conventional radio transmissions are also broadcast. Information may be obtained from the relevant ALRS Signals and the accompanying diagram booklets.

Ships encountering a TRS, ice, storm force winds or subfreezing air temperatures in association with gale force winds must make obligatory reports to the nearest CRS and to ships in the vicinity. This information should warn the mariner of meteorological dangers in the immediate area.

11.4 Ship Reporting Systems

Ship reporting systems are designed and operated to maximise the co-ordination of search and rescue for ships either in the immediate vicinity of or close to a distress incident. The most well known service is the Automated Mutual Assistance Vessel Rescue System (AMVER). There are several of other systems in operation in most areas of the world. Details are available in ALRS Vol 1.

11.4.1 AMVER Organisation

The AMVER system provides worldwide coverage and is operated by the US Coast Guard for the benefit of all ships regardless of nationality. Ships of 1,000 GT or over on a deep sea voyage may participate on a voluntary basis.

The operation is conducted through selected radio stations or INMARSAT, ships can despatch their reports using this. The service is free of charge only through designated stations. All UK stations, including the 'GOONHILLY' CES, charge for servicing AMVER messages.

The purpose of AMVER is to:

- Maximise efficiency in coordinating assistance in the case of search and rescue incidents
- have knowledge of the route being followed and the positions of both the assisting ships and ships that require assistance

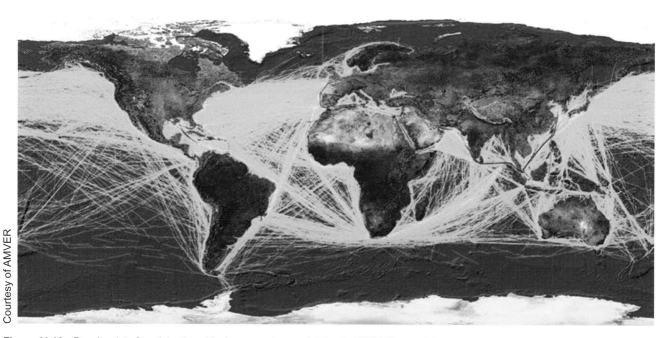

Courtesy of AMVER

Figure 11.16   Density plot of participating ships' voyage plans maintained at AMVER on a daily basis

- minimise the time between the incident and the initiation of search and rescue
- make best use of all available resources:
  - Vessel availability
  - medical facilities
  - on board resources
  - vessel details
  - the potential of an early arrival at the scene.

AMVER operates from the US Coastguard Operations Systems Centre in Martinsburg, West Virginia. The data is confidential and no details are disclosed apart from the particulars required for search and rescue operations. AMVER will usually initiate enquiries once a ship's report is 48 hours overdue. Participating ships are required to transmit several messages to the AMVER centres. The ships transmit these messages during normal communication schedules. Schedules are listed in ALRS Vol. 1, with details in the Annual Summary of Admiralty Notices to Mariners.

Ships send standard format messages. The following identifiers and lines are used:

A/ Vessel's name/radio call sign//
B/ Date and time (UTC)//
C/ Latitude/Longitude//
E/ Current course//
F/ Estimated average speed//
G/ Port of departure/Latitude/Longitude//
I/ Port of destination/Latitude/Longitude//
K/ Port name/Latitude/Longitude/Time of arrival//
L/ Route information//
M/ Current CRS or satellite number/next station, if any//
V/ On board medical resources//
X/ Up to 65 characters of amplifying comments//
Y/ For forwarding messages to JASREP or MAREP (on request)// (Y is required by US vessels only)
Z/ EOR (end of report) – for computer processing of messages//

The following reports are also required to be transmitted by participating vessels

11.4.1.1 Sailing Plan Report – AMVER/SP//

This plan can be transmitted days or weeks before the ships departure. It should contain the ship's name, call sign, time of departure, port of departure, port of destination, provisional ETA, proposed routeing track and any special resources on board. (Required: A, B, E, F, G, I, L, Z. Optional: M, V, X, Y).

11.4.1.2 Position Report – AMVER/PR//

This report should be despatched within 24 hours of departure and then within every 48 hours after that. It contains the ship's name, time and position (Lat/Long), port of destination and ETA. In addition, speed, present course and any other relevant comments can be added. (Required: A, B, C, E, F, Z. Optional: I. Strongly recommended M, X, Y).

11.4.1.3 Arrival Report – AMVER/FR//

This is usually sent on arrival, or just before arrival, at the port of destination. It contains the ship's name, call sign, arrival position or port and the time of arrival. (Required: A, K, Z. Optional: X, Y).

11.4.1.4 Deviation Report – AMVER/DR//

This is used to inform the AMVER centre of any changes to the passage plan. It contains details of the new track, course and any speed changes and revised ETA. (Required: A, B, C, E, F, Z. Optional: I, L). If a participating ship is in distress, the distress alert should be sent to RCC and not the AMVER co-ordinator.

11.4.2 AUSREP

The Australian Maritime Safety Authority operates the Australian Ship Reporting System (AUSREP) within the Australian Search and Rescue Area. Reporting is mandatory for all Australian ships when navigating within the designated area and for all foreign ships from arrival in their first Australian port until their departure from the last Australian port. The objectives of this reporting system are:

- To limit the time between the loss of a ship and the initiation of search and rescue action in cases where no distress signal is transmitted
- to limit the search area
- to provide up to date information on shipping in the event of a search and rescue incident developing.

Ships send reports under AUSREP to RCC AUSTRALIA as follows:

- If in port by INMARSAT -C, reverse charge telephone call or fax message
- at sea, using INMARSAT -C via POR or IOR satellites. These calls are free if the recommended procedures are followed – details are available in the ALRS Vol. 1.

The system requires the following messages to be transmitted.

11.4.2.1 Sailing Plan (SP) Report

This is transmitted either when entering the area or during the period up to two hours after departure from the port. It should contain:

- AUSREP SP
- Ship's name
- call sign
- port of departure or, if entering AUSREP area, the ship's position
- date and time (UTC) of departure or of position
- port of destination
- date and time of ETA (UTC). If leaving the area, the ETA at the boundary limits.
- intended route
- estimated speed of the ship
- a nominated daily reporting time (UTC)
- relevant remarks, such as intermediate port stops.

11.4.2.2 Position Report (PR)

This should be transmitted daily at the nominated time (UTC). It should contain:

- AUSREP PR
- the ship's name and call sign
- position, course and speed
- date and time (UTC) of the ship's position
- remarks such as changes in SP or nominated time
- the last PR should also confirm ETA or, if leaving the area, should include "FINAL REPORT".

11.4.2.3 Arrival Report (AR)

This should be transmitted once the ship is within two hours of steaming from the pilot station. It should contain:

- AUSREP AR
- ship's name
- call sign
- port of arrival
- date and time (UTC) of report.

Additional reports may be required concerning dangerous goods, harmful substances and maritime pollution.

11.4.2.4 Actions by RCC Australia

If a PR or FR is not received within 2 hours of the expected time, action is taken to ascertain the ship's whereabouts and the safety of the crew. The process will start with internal checks followed by attempts to contact the ship by INMARSAT or HF DSC. If a report is overdue by 6 hours, the RCC will broadcast a priority signal, requesting a REPORT IMMEDIATE. Operators and other ships should report any sightings and communications with the overdue ship. If the report

is 21 hours overdue, the signal will be upgraded to URGENCY. There are several other Ship Reporting Systems in existence. Details are available in ALRS Vol 1.

11.5 Ship Movement Report Systems

Ship movement reporting schemes operate in many areas of the world with different objectives. In some areas the main purpose is to enhance the safety of navigation, for example MAREP in the English Channel which is operated jointly by the UK and French administrations. Another similar service is in the St. Lawrence River, operated by the Canadian administration. Details are available in ALRS Vol 6.

11.5.1 MAREP

MAREP is a voluntary system that applies to ships requiring special attention. This includes:

- Merchant ships over 300 GT
- ships not under command or at anchor within the TSS or inshore traffic zone
- ships restricted in their ability to manoeuvre
- ships with defective navigation equipment.

Ships are required to keep a listening watch on designated frequencies and make the following reports, depending on their particular circumstances, prefixed with "MAREP":

- POSREP
  - position report for ships with no defects
- DEFREP
  - report from ships with defects or restricted in their ability to manoeuvre
- CHANGEREP
  - a report made to amend information included in any previous report(s).

The report includes the following, preceded by phonetics of the letters:
  A   Name and call sign of the ship
  B   Date and time (UTC)
  C   Latitude/Longitude
  D   True bearing and distance from a recognised landmark
  E   True course
  F   Speed
  G   Last port of call
  I   Destination
  M   VHF channels being monitored
  O   Maximum draught
  P   Type and quantity of cargo
  Q   Defects
  X   Other useful information.

11.5.2 SURNAV

This system aims to monitor the movement and condition of ships navigating in the approaches to the French coast that are carrying hydrocarbons, dangerous or noxious substances. The regions covered are the French coast of the North Sea, the English Channel and the Atlantic Ocean. The reports must be made at appropriate stages of the ship's voyage to four of the Regional Surveillance and Rescue Operations Centres (CROSS) on the French coast.

11.6 Radio Medical Advice

Very few merchant ships have a doctor or physician on board and while the ships' senior officers possess Medical Care on Board Ship qualifications, some medical problems are beyond their training and capabilities. For this reason, it is possible to seek medical advice by radio and several countries provide this. Details are available in ALRS Vol 1. Unless otherwise stated, there is usually no charge for the messages sent or for the advice received.

11.6.1 International Radio Medical Centre (C.I.R.M.)

This service is free of charge and is available to ships of any nationality, 24 hours a day. If required, the service arranges for a patient to be evacuated in coordination with the area MRCC.

11.7 Other Reports

- Piracy and armed robbery
  - a report should be made through RCC to law enforcement agencies and coastal state authorities. In the case of any on board casualty, a report should also be sent to the ship's maritime administration
  - the International Maritime Bureau (IMB), based in Kuala Lumpur, is the world's focal point as an information centre for acts of piracy and armed robbery
- alien smuggling
  - under an IMO resolution on alien smuggling, reports are co-ordinated by the USCG
- quarantine reports from ships at sea
  - several countries have specific reporting requirements, including ballast water management
- pollution reports
  - several countries have specific reporting requirements.

Details of the above are available in ALRS Vol 1.

11.8 Automatic Identification System (AIS)

Carriage of an AIS has been made mandatory by the IMO in the revised SOLAS Chapter V. There are various reasons for the development and implementation of AIS systems for marine use. The interested parties are:

- The mariner at sea
- administrations and authorities
- commercial organisations.

It is necessary for mariners to be able to identify ships reliably and effectively for collision avoidance purposes. This is to:

- Avoid VHF calls requesting identification and intention
- identify any vessel contravening the collision avoidance regulations and standing-on
- eliminate errors in making collision avoidance arrangements with the wrong ship.

However, these practices are not recommended. The coastal states monitor marine activities and ship movement in order to exercise control and law enforcement. The areas of major concern driving this monitoring activity are:

- Safety at sea
- ship traffic management
- pollution monitoring and control
- maritime security
- trafficking of illicit materials and crime at sea
- conservation of natural resources.

Physical sighting and identification demands a lot of resources. There are other areas of operation that benefit significantly from AIS, but these are only possible if information is made available in a timely manner. In particular, and for reasons of both safety and commerce, this applies to:

- Ship operators
- port authorities
- pilotage services.

AIS allows identification without reliance on voice communications. The IMO adopted the Universal AIS (UAIS) as an aid to safety of navigation. Other objectives included efficient navigation, improvement to the protection of the marine environment and to aid the effective operation of VTS.

11.8.1 Carriage Requirements

The IMO has set clear implementation dates for carriage requirements for AIS. All ships of 300 GT and above on international voyages, cargo ships of 500 GT and above not engaged on international voyages and all passenger ships must be fitted with AIS as follows:

- All ships constructed on or after 1st July 2002

- all ships on international voyages that were constructed before 1st July 2003:
  - all passenger ships and tankers, not later than 1st July 2003
    - all ships above 50,000 GT and above other than tankers, not later than 1st July 2004
    - all ships of 10,000 GT and above but less than 50,000 GT, other than tankers, not later than 1st July 2005
    - all ships of 3,000 GT and above but less than 10,000 GT, other than tankers, not later than 1st July 2006
    - all ships of 300 GT and above but less than 3,000 GT, other than tankers, not later than 1st July 2007
- ships requiring AIS that are not engaged on international voyages but were constructed before 1st July 2002 and not later than 1st July 2008.

11.8.2 Equipment

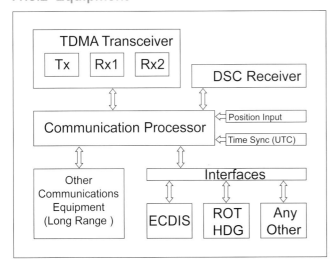

Figure 11.17 AIS shipboard unit block diagram

The shipboard AIS unit has two dedicated VHF receivers and one transmitter. The ITU has two dedicated frequencies allocated for transmission. These frequencies may not be available in all parts of the world:

- 161.975 MHz
- 162.025 MHz

The transponder may also be equipped with a positioning device (normally GPS). An alternative is to connect the AIS to an external GPS/DGPS device on board the ship. Both serve the purpose of supplying 'own ship's' position, as well as time synchronisation. Interfaces are available to a number of devices on the bridge.

VHF DSC allows polling by competent authorities, or at the request of other ships, whereas long range communications equipment is mainly linked with commercial interests. The equipment is connected to a power source, an antenna, and a variety of shipboard equipment or integrated navigation equipment.

11.8.3 Operating Principle

The AIS function is based on VHF radio transponders within the VHF maritime mobile band. It uses a Self-Organised Time Division Multiple Access system (SOTDMA), which is based on the concept of a time frame of one minute. The time frame is synchronised to UTC, divided into 2,250 slots with each slot equalling 22.67 milliseconds (ms). A transmission speed of 9.6 kbps is adopted, which allows sufficient time for 256 bits per time-slot to be transferred.

The AIS unit makes it possible on board to monitor other ships by using a shipboard transponder system. Ships equipped with AIS are required to transmit continually on designated frequencies. The range of the AIS is equal to the VHF horizon of the antenna on board the ship. Each ship is at the centre of an 'own communication cell'. At the start of a passage, or when entering a different area, the ship's AIS equipment captures a vacant slot for transmitting data. AIS stations continuously synchronise with other stations within the detection range. When a ship's AIS unit makes initial contact with another ship, it takes up an unoccupied time-slot and automatically reserves the future time slot for the next contact. This selection will depend on the ship's status and the standards of scheduled reporting (see 11.8.5). The size of a ship's communication cell will adjust to the traffic density. In a case where slot capacity is running out, the equipment discards the targets at greater ranges and assigns the slots to priority targets. When a vessel changes its slot assignment, the AIS unit advises of both the new location and the timeout for that location. This allows new stations, and those that suddenly appear within the radio range close to other vessels, to be received. The system has sufficient capacity to allow nearly 100% throughput, for ships within 8 to 10 nm of each other in a ship-to-ship mode. The operating modes dictate the process of occupying time-slots.

11.8.4 Operating Modes

- Continuous autonomous mode:
  - ship-to-ship, generally for identification and collision avoidance
  - for use in all areas
- assigned mode:
  - ○ can be set up by a competent authority for operation within their specific area
  - is used for monitoring traffic
  - allows control of data transmission intervals and/or time slots
    - ○ allows the authority to change the VHF channels used to avoid interference from adjacent areas
- polling mode:
  - this is the controlled mode where data transmission is in response to interrogation from a competent authority of a littoral state (a state at, or in the vicinity of, the shore)

- the design of AIS allows polling through VHF DSC. The information that is displayed is illustrated in Figure 11.18.

| MMSI Number |
| Ship's Name |
| Type |
| COG - - - SOG - -.- |
| Time DD MM YYYY HR:MN:SC |

Figure 11.18   DSC polled data displayed on screen of receiver

11.8.5 AIS Data Messages

The information broadcast by AIS equipment is sorted into three independent reports. The reports are transmitted at set schedules, using 12.5 watts of power.

Report Type and Description	Information	Reporting schedule		
Static Data It is pre-programmed on installation or on change of ship particulars, eg sale, renamed, alterations	• MMSI number • ship's name and call sign • IMO number • length and beam • location of antenna • ship's type	Updated every 6 minutes		
Voyage Related Data It is input every new voyage before or at commencement	• draught • cargo information • destination and ETA • other relevant information	Updated every 6 minutes		
Dynamic Data It is automatically derived from ship's interfaces	• MMSI number • time • ship's position and accuracy • course over ground • speed over ground • gyro heading and rate of turn • navigational status (as per Collision Regulations 1972, as amended)	Updated depending on the ships speed and navigational status		
		Status/Speed		time
		• At anchor • 0 – 14 knots • 0 – 14 knots & changing course • 14 – 23 knots • 14 – 23 knots & changing course • 23 + knots • 23 + knots & changing course		3 min 10 sec 3.3 sec 6 sec 2 sec 2 sec 2 sec

11.8.6 Additional Messages

AIS equipment has the ability to transmit and receive short safety related messages, it is also an additional way to transmit MSI. These messages can either be addressed to a specified destination using MMSI, or broadcast to all AIS fitted ships in the area. The message should be as short as possible and can include up to 160 six-bit characters. These messages should be relevant to the safety of navigation (light status, derelict or iceberg sighting, etc) and can either be a fixed format, or as text messages. The receiving operator may be required to acknowledge the message.

The Aid to Navigation Message provides information on:

- The location and identification of hazards
- matters of a meteorological or oceanographic nature of interest to the mariner
- marks used for navigation
- the operational status of navigational aids
- the location and identification of specific geographical reference points, along with meteorological and hydrographic data at that site, the identity, dimensions and position of offshore structures in the form of pseudo aids to navigation message.

A Route Plan Message (or Advice of VTS Waypoints) is used by a VTS centre to advise ships of the routeing instructions in the particular area. The message either includes up to 12 advised waypoints, or can be a text description of the route. A recommended turning radius may be included for each waypoint.

11.8.7 AIS Types

ITU recommendation M.1371-1 describes two types of AIS.

Class A: Shipborne mobile equipment meeting the IMO AIS carriage requirement for vessels.

Class B: Shipborne mobile equipment providing facilities not necessarily in accord with the IMO AIS carriage requirements. Class B is nearly identical to Class A, however Class B equipment:

- Does not transmit the vessel's IMO number or call sign
- does not transmit destination and ETA
- does not transmit navigational status
- does not transmit rate of turn information

- does not transmit draught
- has a reporting rate less than Class A
- is only required to receive, not transmit, text safety messages
- is only required to receive, not transmit, application identifiers.

11.8.8 Data Entry

An AIS unit should be fitted with a minimum keyboard and display (MKD), which can be used to input static information. After installation, static information on the ship is entered into the AIS shipboard equipment. This must be tested as several incidents have been recorded where incorrect set up on installation has left ships transmitting incorrect data. The MKD can be used to input:

- Voyage related information
- safety related messages
- a change of mode of response to long-range (LR)
- the setting to automatic or manual response to LR interrogations, with indication of interrogation and means of acknowledgement.

The MKD can be used to control the AIS channel switching, operational frequencies and power setting.

11.8.9 Display of AIS Information

Information can be displayed on MKD or a dedicated dynamic display interfaced with AIS:

- AIS display should provide at least three lines of 16 alphanumeric characters, which is enough to obtain the target ship's identity and position
- the minimum display should provide no less than three lines of data, consisting of bearing, range and name of the selected ship
- the minimum keyboard and display indicates:
  - alarm conditions
  - the means to display, view and acknowledge alarms
  - selected alarms that can be acknowledged
- data can be viewed by scrolling horizontally, but the bearing and range cannot be scrolled
- all the ships in contact with the AIS can be seen by vertically scrolling
- 'own ship' position should be displayed continually where it is from an AIS integral GPS
- a dedicated dynamic display should:
  - display the unit's operational status
  - display target information.

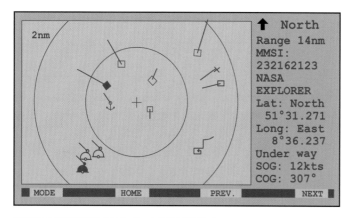

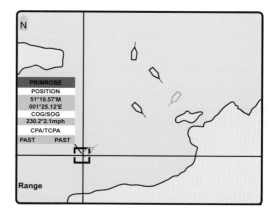

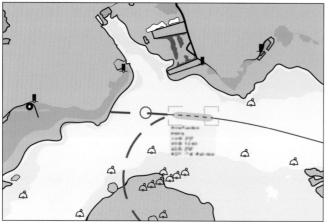

Figure 11.19   AIS – Different displays, including overlay on ECDIS

The AIS should be integrated to one of the existing graphical displays on the bridge or to a dedicated graphical display. It is best if the display is on radar/ARPA, ECDIS or in any other graphical format.

11.8.10 Graphic/Radar Display

The Graphic display should provide the following information:

- Vessel position
- course and speed over ground
- heading and rate of turn
- positional information, displayed relative to the observing ship.

The operator should be aware of the active display mode and whether it is radar or AIS. They must also be aware of the dangers of overloading the screen. Technologically advanced equipment is able to display the projected positions of a ship during manoeuvres by using AIS information. The projection is usually displayed in a large scale window and can be used by VTS, the pilot and any AIS equipped ship.

11.8.10.1 Targets On Radar

- Where AIS information is graphically displayed on radar, the radar echoes should not be masked, obscured or degraded
- target data that is derived from radar or AIS should be clearly distinguishable
- the source of any target data should be clearly indicated, whether it originates from a radar or AIS
- where an AIS target is marked for data display, the operator may still be able to access data about the targets from other sources.

11.8.10.2 VTS Information

Vessels with AIS can view all VTS-held radar targets (as pseudo-targets) and AIS targets, as well as those on their own radar, using approved "VTS foot-printing" or "radar target broadcasting".

11.8.10.3 Pilot Usage

On ships that do not have AIS fitted, the pilot may carry a workstation that is combined with a portable AIS. The pilot pack contains GPS/DGPS, AIS, heading sensor (optional) and a workstation.

11.8.10.4 AIS Target Categories

1. A sleeping target is shown as an acute angled isosceles triangle, with its apex pointing as the heading. It is termed sleeping because the target is seen as outside the avoidance consideration.

2. An activated target is specified as such when the target moves into the avoidance consideration. Three vectors are added at this stage:

   - A dashed line from triangle apex for heading
   - a short vector, from the end of heading vector, to indicate the rate of turn
   - a plain line indicating course and speed over ground.

3. A selected target is one where the CPA and TCPA have been calculated and made available as an alpha-numeric window. At this stage the triangle changes to a rectangle.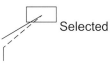

4. A dangerous target is one that passes the pre-set CPA and TCPA limits. The rectangle changes to an equilateral triangle and an alarm is initiated.

5. A lost target is shown as a diamond using two back to back equilateral triangles.

11.8.10.5 AIS Operational Requirements

- The AIS should operate in autonomous and continuous mode and provide information automatically and continuously without further involvement of ship's personnel
- if the Master decides that, the continued operation of the AIS compromises the ship's security, whether at sea or in port, the AIS can be switched off. It should be reactivated as soon as the danger has been eliminated
- during some cargo handling operations, it may be necessary to either switch off or reduce the transmission power of the AIS
- if a sensor is not installed or fails to provide data, the AIS should automatically transmit the "not available" data value
- the static and voyage-related information should remain stored while the AIS is switched off.

11.8.11 National Arrangements

In accordance with SOLAS Chapter V, appropriately equipped shore-based stations should be able to automatically receive standard information that is transmitted by the ship's AIS.

The MCA has established an AIS network of base station transponders that are able to automatically receive all message types and, in particular, AIS messages on Ship Static and Voyage related data, scheduled at six minute intervals. The automated procedure allows suitably equipped ships to be identified and tracked without further intervention from the ship's bridge team or the coastguard personnel.

In addition, AIS stations using the TDMA have been established at several lighthouses around the UK, broadcasting the Base Station Message that provides identity and location. Another category of station transmits the Aid to Navigation Message and Addressed Safety Related Messages.

11.8.12 International Arrangements

Administrations can use AIS to gather evidence about incidents that lead to collisions and pollution, which can subsequently be used for prosecution purposes. By using long range communication equipment, AIS information can be transmitted to services that collate and provide information to the relevant interested parties. This avoids the need for costly routine reports. Private establishments are currently publishing AIS information about 'ships in port' on the web, posing serious security risks, particularly to high profile ships. This misuse of AIS data causes concern amongst the maritime community. The IMO strongly recommends that AIS information should not be made available on the worldwide web and national authorities are required to prevent this type of information being posted.

11.8.13 AIS and Collision Avoidance

Using AIS should ensure the improvement of navigational safety worldwide because of the improved situation awareness and the near elimination of VHF R/T traffic. This should reduce the workload, with significant benefits to bridge watchkeepers and VTS operators. Doubts about the identity of ships in an area and uncertainty about their actions can be eliminated. The AIS display negates certain radar limitations by:

- Detecting targets within sea and rain clutter
- detecting targets within radar blind and shadow sectors

- detecting targets behind islands, capes, round bends, in rivers etc
- eliminating line of sight detection only.

An AIS will receive course and speed alterations in less time than it takes ARPA to compute. AIS shows the course alteration virtually from the moment the wheel is put over or when the ship started to change speed. AIS display also eliminates the danger from target swap with another ship, floating aids to navigation, headlands, small islands or bridges.

It should be noted that AIS collision avoidance data is based on the course and speed over the ground of the 'own ship' and the target ship. As discussed under radar navigation (see 6.1.3 and Figure 6.3), this method may provide incorrect information related to target aspect. Care should be taken when relying on collision avoidance data from AIS sources. Information obtained from radar plotting is based on data measured by 'own ship' radar and provides an accurate relative approach, which is one of the most important factors in determining the risk of collision and the avoiding action that must be taken.

11.8.14 Issues with AIS

- All information required by shore authorities may not be available on all models, so additional reporting might be required
- small ships and warships may not be fitted with an AIS, so they cannot be tracked. Similarly, ships that have switched off AIS or are experiencing an equipment breakdown may not be tracked
- the datum used by the position fixing system could be different to GPS and might result in a discrepancy with radar targets
- because of the above limitations the actual situation may not be the same as indicated on the AIS
- faulty AIS input results in faulty information
- the pilot connector socket, along with the power source, should be available at a convenient location
- the quality and reliability of position information from targets depends on the system in use on board the target ships
- using VHF to discuss actions with approaching ships, based on AIS information, does not remove the danger of agreeing action with the wrong ship. Collision avoidance manoeuvres should be in line with the IRPCS.

11.9 Long Range Information and Tracking (LRIT)

As per SOLAS-V (19-1), from January 2008, the following types of ships on international voyages must be able to transmit long range ship identification, date and time of transmission at regular intervals:

- Passenger ships and high speed craft carrying passengers
- cargo ships and high speed craft over 300 GT
- mobile offshore drilling rigs.

The primary purpose of the regulation is to improve on maritime security, search and rescue and marine environment protection.

All ships at Security Level 1 that are required to comply must automatically transmit a report every six hours. At higher Security Levels transmissions will be more frequent. The frequency of the transmissions may have to be increased on the demand of flag or coastal State. Generally, there are no direct costs to the ship, however a number of flag States charge an annual fee for the service.

In terms of system requirements:

- LRIT Data centre
- LRIT data distribution plan (by Flag state in consultation with ship owners/application service provider)
- shipboard transmitting equipment
- application service provider
- communications service provider.

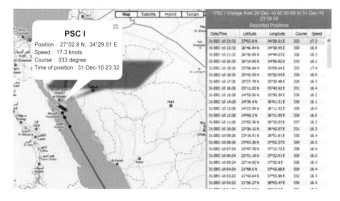

Figure 11.20   LRIT data display created by service provider (Source: plain sailing, UK)

The on board equipment of ships must be able to:

- Automatically transmit the ship's LRIT information, without human intervention, at six hourly intervals, to a LRIT Data Centre
- be configured remotely to transmit LRIT information at intervals other than six hourly
- transmit LRIT information following receipt of a polling command
- interface with the ship's GNSS, or have an internal positioning capability

- supply energy from the main and emergency power supply.

The LRIT equipment must be compliant with IMO recommendations and must also be tested for electromagnetic capability.

Author's Note
Communication technology continues to develop quickly and there is no shortage of new developments and equipment. The mariner must be aware of how to use the on board equipment and to correctly apply the information obtained. Safety of a marine venture depends on the timely transmission, receipt and correct application of information. The bridge team must be aware of the most suitable way to obtain information at all times.

12

Search and Rescue at Sea

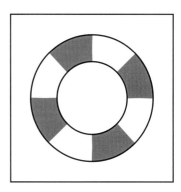

Maritime emergencies are unique as they may occur at distances where shore assistance is not always possible or readily available. The centuries old tradition of mariners helping fellow mariners in the hour of need is still the back bone of many rescue efforts at sea. SOLAS 1974 imposes an obligation on Masters to provide assistance to those who are in need of assistance at sea, whenever they can do so.

The International Convention on Maritime Search and Rescue establishes international practice for search and rescue, it has developed an International Aeronautical and Maritime Search and Rescue Manual (IAMSAR) in the following three volumes:

- Volume I Organisation and Management (for administrations)
- Volume II Mission Co-ordination (for Rescue Coordination Centre (RCC) Personnel)
- Volume III Mobile Facilities (for Ships, Aircraft, and Coastal Radio Station (CRS) Personnel).

Each volume of the IAMSAR and Rescue Manual is drafted with specific search and rescue system duties in mind and is intended to be used either as a stand-alone document, or in conjunction with the other two volumes. A mariner at sea is mainly concerned with the Mobile Facilities volume (Vol. III). This volume is intended to be carried aboard rescue units, aircraft and ships to help with the performance of a search and rescue on scene coordinator function or with aspects of search and rescue that pertain to their own emergencies. It contains an overview, listing the responsibilities and obligations to assist:

- Rendering assistance
- on-scene co-ordination
- on-board emergencies.

Search and rescue incidents are the result of units or individuals in distress or urgency or when vessels or aircraft are reported missing or overdue. Participants are likely to learn of the incident through GMDSS communications or audio/visual signals. It is likely that several units may be involved in search and rescue, indicating the need for co-ordination.

12.1 Search and Rescue Co-Ordination

Universally, the search and rescue system has three general levels of co-ordination:

- Search and rescue co-ordinators (SCs)
- search and rescue mission co-ordinator (SMCs)
- on-scene co-ordinator (OSCs).

In addition, some co-ordination is possible through ship reporting systems, AMVER and aircraft reporting system.

SCs are the top-level managers associated with a search and rescue system. Each state will normally have one or more designated person or agency. Each search and rescue operation is carried out under the guidance of an SMC. This function exists only for the duration of a specific search and rescue incident and is normally performed by the RCC chief or designee. The SMC guides a search and rescue operation until a rescue has been effected or it becomes apparent that further efforts would not be productive. The SMC should be well trained in all search and rescue processes and be thoroughly familiar with the applicable search and rescue plans. The main responsibilities of the SMC are to:

- Gather information about distress situations
- develop accurate and workable search and rescue action plans
- dispatch and co-ordinate the resources to carry out search and rescue missions.

12.1.1 On-Scene Co-Ordination

The Master or officer in charge of the facilities involved in the response and the region of the search and rescue incident will provide on-scene co-ordination. In most oceanic and coastal regions, ships will normally be available, depending on the density of shipping. In remote regions, search and rescue aircraft may not always be available to participate. When two or more search and rescue units are participating in the same mission, one person on-scene may be required to co-ordinate activities.

12.1.1.1 Designation of On Scene Co-ordinator (OSC)

The SMC usually designates an OSC, who may be in charge of:

- A Search and Rescue Unit (SRU), ship or aircraft participating in the search
- a nearby facility in a position to handle OSC duties.

Designation of OSC:

- The SMC should designate an OSC
- if this is not practiced or not yet done, the units involved should designate an OSC by mutual agreement. This should be done at an early stage, preferably before arriving in the area
- until an OSC has been designated, the person in charge of the first unit to arrive at the scene should normally assume the OSC role. The SMC may arrange for that person to be relieved.

The responsibility that is delegated to the OSC by the SMC depends on the communications and capabilities of the personnel manning the unit. Generally, the poorer the communications, the more authority the OSC will need. It is often possible to deploy shore based search and rescue units in a coastal incident. The area MRCC/CS will automatically take up the role of the SMC. Very little authority will be delegated to the OSC.

Ocean incidents are out of the range of shore-based units and are well away from land. An RCC covering the ocean area, will most probably coordinate the search and rescue activity. The bulk of the coordination work will be delegated to the nominated OSC, a lot of delegated authority comes with the nomination.

12.1.1.2 Factors for Designating the OSC

At this stage the role is coordination, which relies on:

- The experience and training of the ship's Master and officers
- the communication facilities of the ship, including language
- number of qualified staff on board able to assist with coordination
- the amount of time the ships can spend at the scene
- location/proximity of the ship with relation to the search and rescue area
- the nature of work being carried out and the work load.

12.1.1.3 Duties of the OSC

The duties of an OSC will include the following:

- Coordination of all search and rescue operations for facilities on-scene and shore

- obtaining the search action plan or rescue plan from the SMC. Alternatively, prepare the plan if it is not otherwise available
- modification of the search action or rescue plan as the situation on-scene dictates, in consultation with, or providing advice to, the SMC
- coordination of all on-scene communications
- monitoring of the performance of other participating facilities, ensuring that operations are conducted safely while paying particular attention to maintaining safe operations across all facilities, both surface and air
- making periodic situation reports (SITREPs) to the SMC. The reports should include, but not be limited to:
  - weather and sea conditions
  - the results of the search to date
  - any actions taken
  - any future plans or recommendations
- maintenance of a detailed record of the operation:
  - on-scene arrival and departure times of search and rescue facilities, other ships and aircraft engaged in the operation
  - areas searched
  - track spacing used
  - sightings and leads reported
  - actions taken
  - results obtained
- advising the SMC when to release facilities that are no longer required
- requesting additional SMC assistance where necessary (eg for medical evacuation)
- reporting the number and names of survivors to the SMC, providing the SMC with the identity of units with survivors on board along with the details of the survivors in each unit, destination of the unit and its ETA.

12.2 Search and Rescue Communications

12.2.1 Initial Communications

Depending on the frequency used, the mode of communication and global location, the receiving unit should acknowledge the distress call. For example, a unit in area A3 that receives a distress call on VHF RT on Ch 16, would acknowledge immediately. The unit will allow a few minutes for the coast station to acknowledge first for the same signal in area A1. Where RT has been used, the receiving unit should log (note) the call, particularly the position. The officer of the watch in receipt of the distress message must notify the Master immediately. On receiving the distress call, the receiving unit should maintain a continuous listening watch on 2182 kHz, VHF Ch 16, other GMDSS equipment and 121.5 MHz (for aircraft distress). The purpose is to determine whether other units or stations have acknowledged and whether a RCC has been alerted. If not, the receiving unit should transmit a Distress Relay to the units in the vicinity and the RCC covering the area. Once a decision has been made to assist, the following information should be transmitted to the distressed craft, (or coast station where there is no further contact with the distressed craft):

- Own ship's identity
- own ship's position
- own ship's speed and ETA to the distressed craft's reported site
- distressed craft's true bearing and distance from own ship.

A coast station will take up the role of SMC and an OSC will be nominated. The OSC should coordinate communications on scene and ensure that reliable communications are maintained.

- Search and rescue facilities normally report to the OSC on an assigned frequency
- if a frequency shift is carried out, instructions should be given about what to do if intended communications cannot be re-established on the new frequency
- all search and rescue facilities should maintain a continuous watch on distress frequencies.

12.2.2 Information on Distressed Unit

Most incidents involving search and rescue are initiated by a radio distress, urgency message or alerts from EPIRB. The basic information to be transmitted in a distress message should include:

- Distress identifier (MAYDAY)
- identity (name or call sign)
- position
- nature of distress
- type of assistance required
- number of persons at risk
- additional information
  - weather in the immediate vicinity
  - number and type of survival craft carried, and the type and number that are being launched
  - number of victims
  - the distressed craft's course or speed
  - type of craft, and the cargo being carried
  - type of location aids available and deployed
  - has the parent craft been abandoned or is it about to be abandoned
  - has the parent craft sunk
  - any other pertinent information that might facilitate the rescue.

The distress message should contain most of this information. However, reports indicate that in times of distress the information is usually incomplete and ships/persons seldom transmit a standard distress message due to panic. Detailed information should be obtained about the casualty if communication is still possible. Contact should also be maintained throughout if possible. Alternatively, a reasonable amount of information can usually be obtained from the owners or managers, the flag State administration or ship reporting service.

Position
This is normally transmitted as latitude and longitude up to 2 or 3 decimal places. However, decimal places, or the fact that it is a lat/long, does not confirm its accuracy. It is important to know whether it is a fix, an EP or a DR. If it is a fix, what is it based on? Perhaps it is a DGPS fix with an accuracy of a few centimetres, or a fix using a LORAN-C system 1,200 miles from the chain. Can the observer relate it to a landmark as a bearing and distance? Another important fact about a position is the time. Is it the current position? Is it the last known position? All this information will assist the responding ships or coordinator to establish an accurate datum.

12.2.3 Information on Other Units

Basic information should be obtained from other units:

- Identity of crafts
- position of crafts
- estimated time of arrival (ETA) of crafts at the scene of the incident
- number of crew
- experience of the Master and crew with search and rescue
- navigational appliances fitted and their accuracy
- communication facilities
- medical (doctor, hospital and first aid) facilities
- lifting appliances
- life saving appliances
- size of the craft
- type of the craft
- draught of the craft
- freeboard
- manoeuvring restrictions/capabilities
- length of time that a craft can stay to participate in the search and rescue
- type and quantity of cargo carried
- destination.

The above information will help the SMC to decide on the best unit to coordinate the activity on scene, those that can easily participate in the search if required and the best choice for the rescue units.

12.3 On board Preparation

This preparation will depend on the emergency organisation on board the ship, whether the Master has been nominated as the OSC and any instructions from the SMC. Some aspects of seamanship have been added as the command position will have to order the same.

Participating ships should establish a traffic coordinating system among themselves. A ship responding to a search and rescue incident should make preparations on board. It is best to raise the alarm to muster all concerned, ie emergency, engine room, back up and first aid parties. Additional officer(s) and lookouts should be summoned to the bridge. There should be two-way communications between the bridge and all parties involved on board. After deciding to proceed, the course should be adjusted and the engine room should be advised to make good all available speed and be ready for manoeuvring in the vicinity of the search and rescue area.

Bridge/Navigation

- Brief and advise watch officers and lookouts
- up-to-date weather information for the route and the distress position
- determine datum and update as necessary (see 12.4.1)
- operate radar(s) especially X band, 3 cm
- call or designate a communications officer
- make sure binoculars are available
- plot the position of 'own ship' frequently to maintain the quickest route to the scene. Make course adjustments as necessary
- plot the positions of other ships attending the distress call
- consider using search or deck lights during the hours of darkness.

Communications

- Monitor all distress frequencies
- try to maintain continuous contact with the ship in distress
- update CRS/RCC with any developments and obtain current information from the service
- have copies of the International Code of Signals available
- locate the daylight signalling lamp, search lights, flashlights, hand held VHF radios and loud hailer
- establish communications with emergency/deck (rescue) team.

Engine Room

- Advise to maintain maximum possible speed
- advise when the engine(s) are to be on stand-by and ready for manoeuvring

- order other services in good time, eg fire pump, power for deck machinery, etc.

Deck

- Prepare rescue boat (and lifeboat if required) for launching, subject to weather condition
- have a liferaft ready (without inflating it) and consider using it, if required, as a boarding station
- rig scrambling nets on both sides of the ship
- rig rope ladders on both sides of the ship
- rig boat ropes on both sides of the ship
- have life jackets and life buoys in readiness
- have heaving lines, rescue quoits, line throwing apparatus and messenger ropes in readiness
- rig man ropes on both sides
- provide survival/immersion suits for the crew of the rescue boat or those who may be required to enter the water
- get ready the boat and grappling hooks, hatchets, rescue baskets and litters and fire fighting equipment
- check cargo lifting appliances (crane, derrick, gantry, etc) on each side of the ship, with cargo net and spreaders for recovery of survivors.

Medical Assistance (made ready)

- Stretchers
- blankets
- medical supplies, first aid kits, resuscitator and medicines
- dry clothing
- food and hot drinks
- hospital
- shelter.

12.4 Search Planning

Careful planning is the key to a successful search and rescue operation. The plan is prepared in several stages and each stage requires information. Generally, the SMC will prepare a search action plan and pass it to the OSC. If the plan is not available, the OSC should develop one. Most well-run coastguards and rescue services use computer programmes for developing the plan. However, the basic principles of both remain the same and it is essential to know:

- The most probable position of the casualty to begin the search
- the size of the search area
- what type of search patterns will be used and the spacing to use in the search area
- the type of search target(s) and the number of available search and rescue units.

12.4.1 Datum

The first stage in every search and rescue incident is establishing a geographical reference or DATUM for starting the search. This depends on:

- The reported position
- the time of the incident
- any bearings or sightings
- the time interval between the incident and arrival of search and rescue facilities
- the size, type and condition of the search object
- the estimated surface movements of the distressed craft or survival craft, depending on drift.

Drift is caused by wind and water movement and is based on:

- Leeway caused downwind, due to wind
- total water current, comprising of two components, ie current/tidal stream and wind driven current.

For the purpose of planning, assume that the distress signal was sent stating the distress ships position for 1000 and that the first unit will take 2 hours to arrive on-scene. Assumed rates are stated on the sketch. Working out a wind-driven current involves a complicated calculation. If the datum has not been provided by the SMC, and the OSC has to work it out on board, the wind driven current could be ignored, as the OSC may not have the appropriate facilities data and experience to work it out.

The time interval is the interval between the incident time, or last computed datum, and the start of search time. This emphasises the need to work out the ETA as precisely as possible.

If the search is for a liferaft, without a drogue and the wind is force 5, leeway is 1.35 kts downwind.

Note: These are estimates and the actual values may vary. Some ships carry drift predictions for different vessels at sea, but it must be understood that these are estimations only and the actual result under the given circumstances may be different.

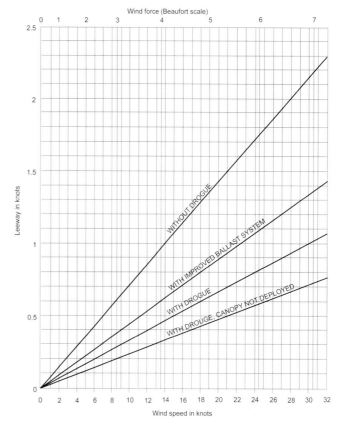

Figure 12.2   Liferaft leeway   (Source IAMSAR Vol III, page 3-17)

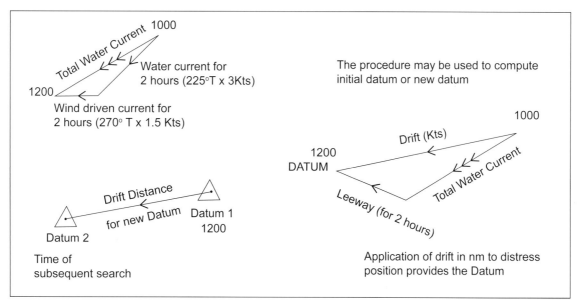

Figure 12.1   Drift distance calculations

12.4.2 Search Area

The underlying and driving principle used to calculate the search area is simple, detection cannot be compromised. If there are several units available, the area can be shared among them and they can each search a comparatively smaller area. If there is a single unit, it should never attempt to search an area that is larger than is reasonable to have searched normally in the time given. The calculation of the search area, therefore, depends on several factors.

12.4.2.1 Track Spacing (S)

In order to search effectively, units must cover the search area following designated tracks. The distance between adjacent tracks is called track spacing. The IAMSAR manual provides tables for recommended track spacing based on meteorological visibility. Track spacing depends on:

- The size of the search object
- the type of search object
- meteorological visibility
- the sea state/ condition
- time of the day (day/night/twilight)
- the position of the sun
- the effectiveness of the observers (height, etc)
- the number of assisting craft.

Track spacing may have to be altered if any of the above conditions vary during the course of the search. The tabulated track spacing may have to be adjusted for weather correction factors, which are also provided in the IAMSAR.

	Meteorological visibility (nautical miles)				
Search Object	**3**	**5**	**10**	**15**	**20**
Person in water	0.4	0.5	0.6	0.7	0.7
4-person liferaft	2.3	3.2	4.2	4.9	5.5
6-person liferaft	2.5	3.6	5.0	6.2	6.9
15-person liferaft	2.6	4.0	5.1	6.4	7.3
25-person liferaft	2.7	4.2	**5.2**	6.5	7.5
Boat < 5 m (17 ft)	1.1	1.4	1.9	2.1	2.3
Boat 7 m (23 ft)	2.0	2.9	4.3	5.2	5.8
Boat 12 m (40 ft)	2.8	4.5	7.6	9.4	11.6
Boat 24 m (79 ft)	3.2	5.6	10.7	14.7	18.1

Table 12.1   Recommended track spacing for merchant vessels (IAMSAR)

Weather Winds km/h (kts or seas m (ft)	Search object	
	Person in water	**Liferaft**
Winds 0 – 28 km/h (0-15 kt) or seas 0 – 1 m (0 – 3 ft)	1.0	1.0
Winds 28 – 46 k/h (15 – 25 kt) or seas 1 – 1.5 m (3 – 5 ft)	0.5	**0.9**
Winds > 46 km/h (>25 kt) or seas >1.5 m (>5 ft)	0.25	0.6

Table 12.2   Weather correction factors for all types of search units (IAMSAR)

Track spacing (S) = Recommendation × Weather correction factor searching for a 25 person liferaft, where wind is 20 kt and visibility is 10 nm, the track spacing to be used is = 5.2 × 0.9 = 4.7 nm.

12.4.2.2 Search Speed (V)

When carrying out a parallel track search jointly (in a co-ordinated manner), all units should proceed at the same speed, as advised by OSC. This speed will normally be the maximum speed of the slowest ship participating in the search. For safety reasons, eg reduced visibility, a safer reduced speed may be ordered by the OSC.

12.4.2.3 Immediate Search Area (A)

If a search must begin immediately, assume R = 10 nm Draw circle of 10 nm radius and close box with tangents Datum

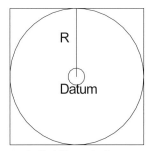

Initial Search Area

This area should be used if search units are in the immediate vicinity and arrive on scene very rapidly to begin the search.

12.4.2.4 Calculated Search Area (A)

When there is available time for the computation, the area is:

A = Track space (S) × Search speed (V) × Time (T)

A ship with a speed of 14 knots and planning to search for 2 hours for the 25 person liferaft, can search an area = 4.7 × 14 × 2 = 131.6 nm²

Where more than one unit is available, the individual areas can be added to obtain the total area that can be searched:

$A_t = A_1 + A_2 + etc$

But if the search speed is the same:

$A_t = N \times A$ (where N is the number of units)

In this case the search radius:

$R = \sqrt{(A_t)}/2$ (half the square root of Area)

For a 131.6 nm² area:

$R = \sqrt{(131.6)}/2 = 5.7$ nm

12.4.3 Search Patterns

12.4.3.1 Expanding Square Search

- All course alterations are 90°
- the first two legs will be of same length 'S', which is the track space
  - legs 3 and 4 will be a length of 2S
  - legs 5 and 6 will be a length of 3S
  - legs 7 and 8 will be a length of 4S
  - and so on until the area is fully searched
- the commence search point (CSP) is always the datum position.

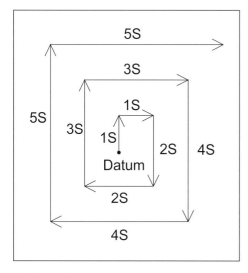

Figure 12.3   Expanding square search

An expanding square can only be used by a single ship and is often appropriate for ships or small boats to use when searching either for people in the water or for other search objects with little or no leeway. It is most effective when the location of the search object is known within relatively close limits. Generally, accurate

navigation is required. To enhance visual referencing at sea the first leg is usually oriented directly into the wind if some sea is running, to minimise navigational errors.

12.4.3.2 Sector Search

This is used to search a circular area centred at the datum and can only be used by one craft at a time in a certain location. A suitable marker may be dropped at the datum and used as a reference point.

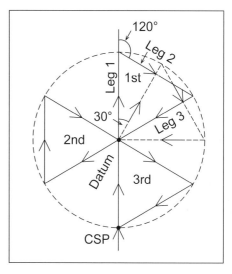

Figure 12.4   Sector search

An aircraft and a ship may be used to perform independent sector searches of the same area.

- CSP is where the search unit enters the area
- sectors are marked from datum as 1st, 2nd, 3rd and the course alterations are 120°
- after an initial search, the pattern is oriented 30° in the direction of turn.

A sector search is most effective when the position of the search object is accurately known and the search area is small. Typically, this might be after a man overboard incident as part of the immediate action in searching for the person when the lookouts have lost sight of the person in the water. For a man overboard incident, the search legs should be defined in terms of time rather than distance, eg 2 minutes on each leg will allow the initial search to be completed in 18 minutes (2 × 3 × 3 = 18).

12.4.3.3 Creeping Line Search, Co-ordinated

In this case, an OSC must be present to give direction to and provide communications to the participating craft. The aircraft will do most of the searching while the ship steams along a course at a speed specified by the OSC, so the aircraft can use it as a navigational checkpoint and for rescue.

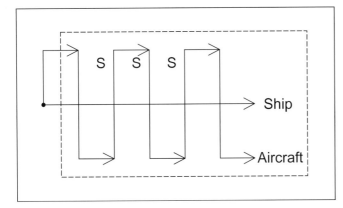

Figure 12.5   Creeping line search

The CSP is where the ship or aircraft enters the area that is to be searched. The aircraft, as it passes over the ship, can make corrections to stay on the track of the search pattern. This search pattern provides a higher probability of detection compared to a single aircraft searching alone. Ship speed varies according to the speed of the aircraft and the size of the area that is to be searched.

12.4.3.4 Parallel Sweep (Track) Search

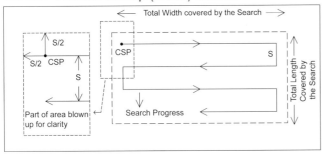

Figure 12.6   Parallel sweep (track) search

This pattern makes use of search legs that are parallel to each other and is used when a large area has to be searched and the location of the survivors is uncertain. The area may be assigned to individual search units on-scene at the same time, once it has been divided into smaller sub-areas. The CSP for each ship is S/2 inwards from the edge of the area. All turns and outermost legs are planned at no more than S/2 inwards of the edges. When the search pattern is being used by more than one unit in a coordinated search, the search speed is the maximum speed of the slowest ship, unless a different speed has been ordered. This pattern has a few variations. It may be used by:

- A single ship (Figure 12.6)
- a number of ships within individual allocated areas (Figure 12.7)
- a number of ships searching in a co-ordinated manner (Figure 12.8).

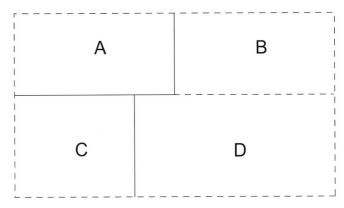

Figure 12.7   Sub-divided areas (search)

NB: It must be remembered that a coordinated search can only begin once all of the participating units are present at the scene.

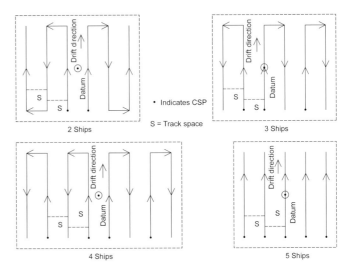

Figure 12.8   Parallel track search

12.4.4 Practical Application

The available or calculated drift rates are only estimates and may not match the actual situation. There may be errors in the transmitted position of the distressed vessel (eg DR or position based on a less accurate system, etc). A longer time interval will cause more pronounced errors. For example, a survival craft or ship may not drift exactly down wind. It may drift in several of directions due to 'sail' and 'flag' effects.

For the following example, the assumptions are:

- The distress ship position for 0900 GMT (position source unknown)
- abandoned in a 15 person liferaft, without drogue
- visibility 5 nm
- current 135°T × 3 kts
- wind, N'ly 21 kts
- a wind driven current in SSE direction at 1 kt

- initial search interval of 1.5 hour
    - 6 participating ships are approaching:
        - "A" from NW in 1 h 30 min, speed 18 kts
        - "B" from E in 1 h 50 min, speed 24 kts
        - "C" from SE in 2 h 10 min, speed 12 kts
        - "D" from S in 2 h 25 min, 25 kts
        - "E" from SW in 2 h 10 min, 18 kts.

Datum: Ship "A" will be the first to arrive. For Figure 12.9, the liferaft leeway will be 1.5 kts.

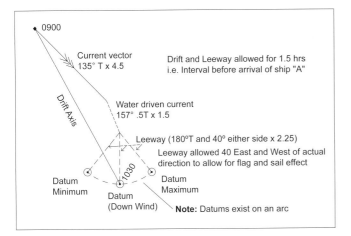

Figure 12.9 Drift calculations

Track spacing:
From Table 12.1, a 15 person liferaft in 5 nm visibility requires a track spacing of 4.0 nm.

From Table 12.2, the weather correction factor is 0.9. Therefore, the track spacing that should be applied is

$$= 4.0 \times 0.9 \qquad = 3.6 \text{ nm}$$

Area: Ship "A" can search $= 3.6 \times 18 \times 1.5 = 97.2 \text{ nm}^2$

Radius: $\qquad = \sqrt{97.2/2} \qquad = 4.9 \text{ nm}$

If there is uncertainty about the position of the distressed unit and a significant amount of time has elapsed since the incident, the wind effect on the search object may be different. For this reason, the minimum and maximum datum points of the down wind datum have been established, simply by allowing leeway vectors 40° from the down wind direction.

There may be several other factors that introduce errors into the calculations. Search planners allow for these factors and work out the maximum allowable error radius for each of the three datum points. These radii are used to draw error circles from the three datum points. The search area is then obtained by enclosing the error circles in the smallest possible rectangle.

In fact there may be several datum points on the arc between the downwind and the two extreme datum points.

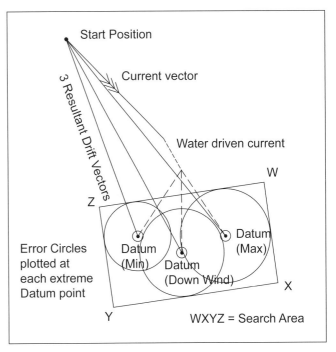

Figure 12.10 Search areas

Orientation of the search area should be in line with the drift axis. This would cause the search and search patterns to be oriented to the drift axis. It is less likely that a search object will be missed when searching along the drift axis.

The search area should be sub-divided and allocated to individual units. Ship "A" should reach Datum (or CSP) and commence an expanding square search. As the other units arrive, they should commence a parallel sweep search within their allocated area. In this case all of the units should search at their maximum speed. Figures 12.10 and 12.11 are not to scale and are provided to clarify the concept. The above plan helps with the maximum use of the available resources and completion of a search in the minimum possible time. In reality, all situations are likely to be different, but the application of basic principles will help to plan effectively. To maximise the use of available resources, ships can be grouped for a search according to similar speeds, a group of fast ships will cover more area than a mixture of fast and slow ships in a coordinated search. To reduce the time element, the OSC may give directions to a ship or group of ships to begin searching an area close by, before they formally arrive on-scene.

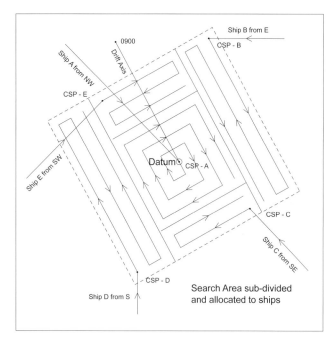

Figure 12.11 Search area sub-divisions

12.4.5 Records

- A summary of communications relating to distress, urgency and safety traffic
- a reference to important service incidents.

A record of every distress signal or message that a ship, aircraft or person is in distress at sea, observed or received, should be entered. When a Master receives a distress signal at sea, or information from any source that a ship or aircraft is in distress, but is unable or considers it unreasonable or unnecessary to go to the assistance of the persons in distress, a statement should be made of his reasons for not going to the assistance of those persons in the OLB.

12.4.6 Radar Use

If the position of the incident is not reliably known and there are no search and rescue aircraft available, a radar search may be effective when several ships are available to assist. No prescribed pattern has been provided, but the ships can search the area, keeping abreast of each other in a loose line fashion and maintaining a track spacing between them of the expected detection range multiplied by 1.5.

12.4.7 Aircraft Assistance

Aircraft participating in search and rescue activity can be very useful. They are much faster, compared with surface craft and can search larger areas in a shorter period of time. Due to their altitude they have a longer visible horizon. This is another aid when searching

larger areas in less time although it depends on the visibility levels and the size of the search object.

Once the search object is located, helicopters can carry out the rescue, the number of people that can be lifted will depend on the type and available capacity of the helicopter. Fixed wing aircraft can drop supplies and messages to survivors. They can also guide ships to the rescue point.

12.4.8 Conclusion of the Search

12.4.8.1 Successful

It is vital that all survivors are accounted for. Once the distressed craft or survivors have been sighted, and if the detecting ship is unable to carry out the rescue, the OSC should assess the best method to use and the most suitably equipped craft on the scene directed for rescue. However, at times the detecting ship may have to make an effort to carry out the rescue when more suitably equipped craft are not available.

The information on the survivors and the incident should be relayed promptly to the SMC once the survivors have been debriefed and questioned on:

- The ship or aircraft in distress, and the number of people on board
- whether survivors or survival craft have been seen.

When all rescuing action is complete, the OSC should immediately inform all search facilities that the search has been terminated. The OSC should inform the SMC of the conclusion of the search and provide the following details:

- Names, destinations and ETA of ships with survivors, along with the identities and number of survivors in each
- physical condition of the survivors and whether medical assistance is required
- the state of the distressed craft and whether it is a hazard to navigation, if so its position should be communicated.

12.4.8.2 Unsuccessful

The search should be continued until all reasonable hope of effecting a rescue has passed. An important factor will be the possible survival time under the current circumstances. The OSC may have to make the decision on whether or not to terminate an unsuccessful search. The factors to consider when terminating a search are:

- The probability of survivors in the search area
- the probability of detecting the search object

- the remaining time that the search facilities can remain on scene
- the probability of survivors still being alive.

After consultation with other craft and land-based authorities, the OSC may terminate the active search, advise assisting craft to proceed on passage and inform the land based authority. The coast station should transmit an URGENCY message to all ships in the area asking them to continue to keep a lookout. For coastal incidents, the OSC should consult with land based authorities about the termination of the search.

12.5 Rendezvous

Mariners or specialist agencies at sea may be required to rendezvous with another ship or ships (units), intercept them for operational reasons, or provide assistance. Practical use and experiences vary as some mariners may never rendezvous during their entire career at sea, but they should be prepared for such an operation. All navigating personnel, especially at management level, are normally tested on rendezvous during certificate of competency examinations, as any unit may be called on to assist when required.

Due to the urgency associated with most of these operations, it is essential to rendezvous or intercept in the shortest time. Other than for saving lives at sea or intercepting for special purposes, units participating in routine operations should rendezvous at the earliest time to conserve fuel, save time and maintain commercial deadlines.

Where possible, both units should set course for each other and proceed at best speed. However, most problems or operations are not that simple, and often one unit will be on a steady course and speed, with the other setting the course to rendezvous. In the case of search and rescue and other emergencies, the approach will be at the unit's best speed under the circumstances, or at the speed required to rendezvous at an agreed time. However, in some operations, a unit may be required to determine its speed in order to rendezvous at a required time. There is more than one method of carrying out the plots. Calculations may also be used to obtain course and/or speed. The methods used to determine the course and speed required will vary with the operational requirements. There may be situations when the assisting unit is required to rendezvous at the earliest time possible. In other cases, the rendezvous may have to be planned for a predetermined time, such as sunrise. Each of these methods will be discussed separately. The problems may be to find the course, speed, time and position of the rendezvous:

- With one unit maintaining course and speed
- with wind and/or current
- with one unit altering course and/or speed, the other making the approach
- when taking up station with another unit on a steady course speed
- when changing station and working with another unit
- to rendezvous at a specific time with one unit maintaining course and speed.

The unit requiring assistance may maintain its course and speed either due to the weather or because it may be heading for a port of refuge. The assisting unit will have to adopt a different approach if the unit requiring assistance is able to make way, or is required to make way through the water. If the unit requiring assistance is not making way through the water, the rendezvous will be a matter of setting course for the position where the unit requiring assistance has stopped or is drifting to. Plotting can be carried out using a radar plotting sheet, which most mariners prefer, graph paper or even a plain sheet. Some may prefer to calculate it instead. Before beginning the plot, prepare a mental picture as to how the plot will develop so that the problem or requirement can be fully understood. Choosing an appropriate scale is always the first step, unless the distances involved happen to be within the scale of the plotting sheet. When using graph or plain paper, either a portrait or landscape layout must be chosen.

From the problem, it can be determined whether the plot would develop more on a North/South or East/West axis. With the former, portrait would be the preferred choice, and landscape as a preferred choice for the latter. Where graph paper or a plain sheet is used, North should be marked clearly on the paper, along with the scale used for plotting. The choice of scale should be given careful consideration. The larger the scale, the better the result. Similarly, a plotting interval may have to be decided to allow a reasonable sized plot to be formed, to aid clarity and accuracy.

12.5.1 Plotting Method

Plotting can be done using either relative or true motion. True motion should be used when wind and/or current are affecting the units involved in the operation. For the majority of the problems, however, relative plotting can be used. Rendezvous is, in reality, a meeting of two units at sea meaning they will meet on a steady bearing. This steady bearing, in terms of radar plotting, is the relative approach, represented by the OA vector, or line. If the WOA triangle was constructed, OA would represent the relative approach, WO the course/speed of the unit maintaining course and speed, which is usually plotted at the centre of the sheet, and WA would provide the course and speed required to rendezvous. The rendezvous is based on the maintenance of a steady bearing between the vessels. The position of both of the vessels for a common time must be known. A worked example explains the method for determining the approach course.

Example 12.1

Vessel "X" receives a call for assistance from vessel "Y" at 0800 hours. Vessel "Y" has a fire on board and is bearing 220° T × 48 nautical miles from vessel "X". Vessel "Y" is steaming at 12 knots on a course of 270° T, due to an easterly wind. If the maximum speed of "X" is 24 knots, what course must it set in order to rendezvous at the earliest time? What is the ETA of "X" at the rendezvous position?

Solution and comments

On a plotting sheet or graph paper, plot "X" and "Y" relative to each other, using an appropriate scale. For the adjacent sketch, a scale of 1:6 has been used, ie 8 miles on the sheet = 48′ (8 × 6). This scale should be used throughout.

If using a radar plotting sheet, plot vessel "Y" at the centre (point A′) and then vessel "X", so that "Y" is 220°T × 48' from "X". "Y" is moving at a steady course of 270°T at 12 knots.

Choose the position of vessel "X" as point "O" for the OAW triangle. Choose a plotting interval. For this first plot, one hour has been used.

Produce "WO" and link it to "O", so that "WO" is 270° T and 12 miles (2 miles on plot). 12′ represents the distance travelled by "Y" in one hour.

Using a distance of 24 miles, ie the distance travelled by "X" in one hour, draw an arc from "W" on the "OA" line. Join "W" to "A". Determine the direction of "WA".

"WA" is the course to steer by "X" in order to rendezvous with "Y" at the earliest time. From the plot, the course is 242°T.

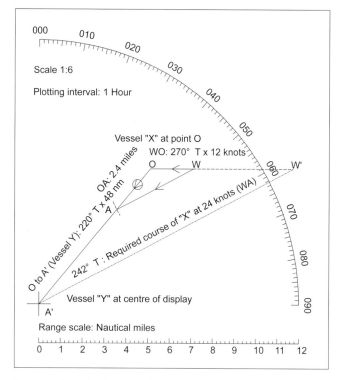

Figure 12.12 Plot for example 12.1

The time of rendezvous can be best determined by using the relative approach speed "OA". From the plot distance "OA" is 14′.4. The total distance of OA′ is 48′.0. The distance OA is covered in one hour, so total time can be determined:

Time to R/V = (OA′ ÷ OA) × Plotting interval

= (48 ÷ 14.4) × 1   = 3 hours 20 minutes

0800 + Time to R/V = ETA at Rendezvous
0800 + 0320   = **1120**

In some cases the geographical position of the two vessels may be known, rather than the bearing and distance. The following example demonstrates the steps involved in solving such a problem.

Example 12.2

On 08 May at 1300 local time, 'own ship' is in position at 37° 41′N, 157° 00′.5E and has a maximum speed of 18 knots. A distress call is received from a ship on fire at position 38° 37′N, 156° 30′.0 E, making for a landfall position of 36° 32′N, 141° 40′E at 10 knots. Find the following:

- *The course of the ship in distress*
- *the course to steer to rendezvous at the earliest time*
- *the ETA of rendezvous*
- *the position of rendezvous*

- *the time when both ships will be close to being within 2 miles of each other*
- *calculate the daylight remaining to provide assistance.*

Solution and comments

Identify 'own ship' as "X", the ship requiring assistance as "Y", and the landfall position as "Z".

Initially Mercator sailing must be used to calculate the course of the vessel in distress Y to Z.

"Y" Lat	38°	37′ N	MP 2500.80	Long	156°	30′ E
"Z" Lat	36°	32′ N	MP 2343.74	Long	141°	40′ E
d.Lat	2	05′ S	DMP 157.06		14°	50′ W
					(or 890′ W)	

$$\text{Tan Co} = \text{d.Long/DMP} = 890/157.06$$
$$= 5.66662422$$

Course of Y $= S\ 80°\ W = 260°\ T$

The principles of plane sailing can be used to find out the bearing and distance between both ships. The positions described above can be plotted directly on a Mercator chart. Using a Mercator chart avoids the need to calculate the mean latitude and the conversion of departure to d.long, or vice versa. For this example, we will work from a plotting sheet or graph paper and will use plane sailing techniques.

Calculate the bearing and distance from X to Y.

"X" Lat	37°	41′ N	Long	157°	00′.5 E
"Y" Lat	38°	37′ N	Long	156°	30′.0 E
d.lat		56′ N	d.long	0°	30.5′ W

Use mean latitude to convert d.long into departure.

M Lat   38° 09′ N

Dep = d.long × Cos Mean Lat = 30′.5 × Cos 38° 09′
= 24′.0 W

To find bearing of Y from X:

$$\text{Tan } \theta = \text{Dep} \div \text{d.lat} = 24 \div 56 = 0.428305104$$
$$\theta = 23°.18 \text{ Bearing} = N\ 23°\ W = 337°\ T$$

Distance = d.lat ÷ Cos θ = 56 ÷ Cos 23°.18   = 60′.9

Select a suitable scale that fits easily on to the plotting sheet or graph paper. The scale should be as large as possible to ensure greater accuracy. A scale of 1:4 has been used in this instance.

Using a bearing of 337° T and a distance of 60′.9, "X" and "Y" can be plotted relative to each other on a plotting sheet or graph paper. Departure and d.lat can be used directly to plot "X" and "Y" on graph paper, but it is preferable to confirm the positions using range and bearing. For better accuracy a plotting interval of 2 hours has been used. If graph paper or a plain sheet is used, a portrait orientation is preferable.

The position of ship "Y" is represented by A and ship "X" as O. At "O" draw 'WO' in the direction of the course of B, 260° T. Measure off 20 miles (10 knots × 2 hrs). WO is 260° T × 20′.

Using a compass (or dividers) measure 36 (18 knots × 2 hrs) miles and with "W" as centre, draw an arc to cut OA′ at point "A", so that WA = 36 nautical miles. The direction of WA is the course to be steered by vessel "X" in order to rendezvous with "Y" at the earliest time. (304°T from plot)

To determine time of rendezvous, measure OA. (25′.7)

Time to R/V   = (OA′ ÷ OA) × Plotting interval
= (60.9 ÷ 25′.7) × 2   = 4 h 44 m
Time of R/V   = 1300 + Time to R/V (1300 + 0444)
                                          = **1744**

The position of rendezvous can be determined by applying run to either of the two vessels from their start position. Their course and distance can be used to obtain d.lat and Departure. If we run vessel "Y" to the rendezvous position, it should travel a distance of 47′.4 (10 knots × 4h 44m) on a course of 260° T.

d.lat   = Dist × Cos θ = 47′.4 × Cos 260° = 8.2′ S
Dep   = Dist × Sin θ   = 47′.4 × Sin 260°   = 46′.7 W

For Latitude: Lat Y ± d.lat = Lat R/V (38° 37′ N – 8.2′S)
                                          = **38° 28′.8N**

Find Mean Lat and convert departure into d.long

Mean Lat   = Lat Y ± ½ d.lat = 38° 37′ N – 4′.1 S
                  = 38° 32′.9 N
d.long   = Dep ÷ Cos Mean Lat (46′.7 ÷ Cos 38° 32′.9)
                  = 59′.7 W

Long Y ± d.long = Long R/V (156° 30′ E – 0° 59′.7 W)
                                = **155° 30′.3 E**

In the above example, d.lat, Departure, the conversion of d.long into Departure and vice versa can be done using the traverse table.

When both vessels are at 2 miles, draw an arc of radius 2 miles from O and call it "A".

OA′ − OA″ = 58′.9

Time to 2 miles = (OA″ ÷ OA) × Plotting interval
= (58′.9 ÷ 25′.7) × 2   = 4 h 35 m
Time at 2 miles = 1300 + Time to 2 nm
(1300 + 0435)   = **1735**

Sunrise should now be calculated to determine the daylight remaining, using 8th May Almanac data.

LMT 35° N	1851	LMT 40° N	1901
Increment	0007		
LMT 38° 28′.8 N	1858		
LIT 155° 30′.3 E	1022		
GMT	0836		
Zone	1000		
Local Time SUNSET	1836		
Time of Rendezvous	1744		
Time Remaining	**0052**		

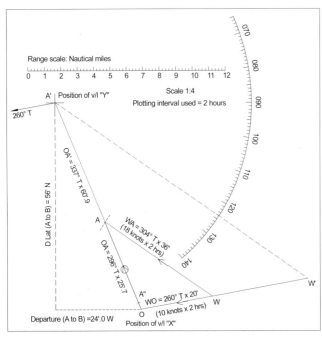

Figure 12.13   Plot for example 12.2

Because of the nature of the triangles in some of the plot, it is possible that the assisting vessel has two choices of course to the rendezvous. In such cases, the course that gives the earliest rendezvous should be steered.

Such a situation will usually arise when the course of the ship requiring assistance is converging on the assisting ship. On the adjacent diagram, the arc centred at W will cut OA′ at two different points. "A" should be selected as the point nearer to point A′ as the faster of the two possible approach speeds, ie OZ or OA, would be preferred. OA is greater, so the course to steer is WA and not WZ. (see Figure 12.14)

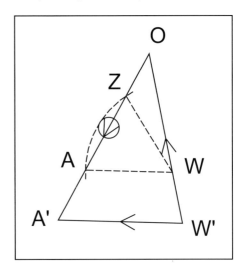

Figure 12.14   Two choices of course

12.5.2 Effect of Wind and Current

If wind is present, it will probably affect both units differently, depending on their windage area and displacement/draught. Units that are disabled, requiring assistance and at the mercy of the weather will be set by the wind. The unit providing assistance will have to counteract the leeway that has been caused by the wind in order to rendezvous in the least time.

The current will generally influence both units at the same rate, providing both units are in an area experiencing the same current. It should also be understood that current affects surface craft and not aeroplanes or helicopters. The following example demonstrate this.

Example 12.3
At 0900, a liferaft is bearing 100° T, at a distance of 55 miles from a ship. A northerly wind is causing the liferaft to drift at the rate of 3 knots. The ship is expecting a leeway of 6° due to wind. Find the course for the ship to steer by and the earliest time it will rendezvous with the liferaft. The maximum speed of the ship is 17 knots.

Solution and comments

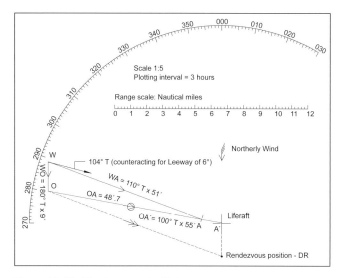

Figure 12.15 Plot for example 12.3

Using a suitable scale on a plotting sheet or graph paper, the ship and liferaft positions should be plotted relative to each other, using a bearing of 100° T and a distance of 55 miles. The liferaft should be at the centre, as its movement will remain steady.

From O, plot the liferaft's drift of 3 knots going south, as the wind is from the north. A suitable time interval should be selected, eg 3 hours to get a drift of 9′ [3 × 3], in order to plot a reasonable triangle for better accuracy. Project the liferaft's progress for calculated drift (9′) and call it point W. WO is 180° T × 9.

Use the ship's speed of 17 knots for the same time interval, ie 3 hours, and work out the distance to be travelled by the ship in 3 hours (3 × 17 = 51′). Measure a distance of 51′ on the compass, centred at point W, and draw an arc to cut OA′ at A. OA is the course to rendezvous with the liferaft. From the plot, the course obtained is 110° T.

As the ship will experience a leeway of 6° with a northerly wind, the course to steer will be:

110° T
- 006° Leeway
104°T (Course to steer)

Time of rendezvous = 0900 + [(OA′ ÷ OA) × plotting interval]

= 0900 + [(55 ÷ 48.7) × 3] = 0900 + 3h 23m = **1223 hrs**

Example 12.4

Using Example 12.3, find the EP of the rendezvous as the bearing and distance from the ship's start position at 0900, if a current of 155° T at 2.8 knots was setting throughout.

Solution and comments

In Example 12.3, if a current was setting 155° T at 2.8 knots throughout, both the units would experience similar current. In this type of case, the course to steer would not change. The total current would be applied to the R/V position to determine the actual position of rendezvous.

Time to R/V × set = Total Drift experienced
3h 23m × 2.8 knots = 9′.47 or 9′.5

This drift should be plotted in a direction of 155° T from the rendezvous DR to obtain the EP. From the plot, bearing and distance of the EP of the rendezvous from the ship's start position at 0900 is **116°T × 64′.7.** It should also be noted that the ground tracks in the examples 12.3 and 12.4 are different.

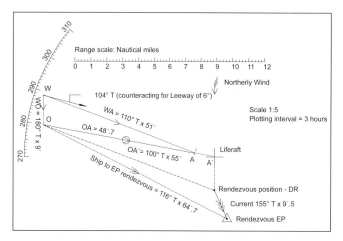

Figure 12.16 Plot for example 12.4

12.5.3 Rendezvous Involving Change of Course/Speed

It is likely that one of the units involved will be required to alter course and/or speed for operational reasons. To achieve a successful rendezvous, the final tentative track of the unit should be plotted after the alteration of course and/or speed and it should be projected backwards. The purpose is to determine the final relative approach between the units. For this to happen, it is important to assume that both units are on a steady bearing. An effective position (ghost position) will be used when determining the final relative approach. The following example addresses such a situation.

Example 12.5

At 1100, a vessel "X" with an injured seafarer on board is bearing 305° T, 48 miles from a large survey ship "Y", which has a doctor on board. The survey ship is presently steering 240° T at 9 knots. After 1 hour, the survey ship will alter course to 000° T and increase speed to 12 knots and then maintain it throughout. Find the course to steer by "X" in order to rendezvous as soon as possible with the survey ship, if the maximum speed is 15 knots. Determine the time of rendezvous.

Solution and comments

At 1100 hours, position A1 on the plot, survey ship "Y" is on a course of 240° T at 9 knots. After one hour, ie travelling 9 miles, it alters course to 000° T and increases speed to 12 knots at position A2. This change may not allow relative approach to be used.

Using a scale of 1:6, from the point of course and speed alteration, ie A2, the new course, 000° T at 12 knots, is projected to A3, as well as in a reciprocal direction at the new speed for 1 hour to point A′. The position derived from the reciprocal course and distance is the effective position of the survey ship for 1100, and is used for the relative approach. Some navigators refer to this type of position as the ghost position, as it is imaginary.

For plotting purposes, it is assumed that the survey ship is on a course of 000° T at 12 knots throughout and was at A′ at 1100. It is important to note that this assumption will only hold true if the rendezvous was to take place after the course/speed alteration. If it is to occur before the alteration, then the standard approach should be adopted. If there is any uncertainty a simple plot may help to determine the approximate time of rendezvous, which will be useful for deciding on the final approach. From the centre, plot the bearing and distance of the vessel "X", ie 305° T × 48′. This is shown as a pecked line on the plot and with the point O.

Join OA′. This is the effective relative approach between both the ships.

Draw WO at O, which is 000° T × 12′, as the plotting interval of one hour has been used and it is assumed that the survey ship is on a course of 000° T at 12 knots throughout.

Using W as the origin, mark A along the line OA′, so that WA is 15′, as the maximum speed of the ship "X" is 15 knots.

Direction of WA represents the course to steer by "X" to rendezvous at the earliest time. From the plot WA is **118°5 T**.

Time of rendezvous $= 1100 + [(OA' \div OA) \times \text{plotting interval}]$

$= 1100 + [(54.1 \div 24.1) \times 1]$

$= 1100 + 2h\ 15m = \textbf{1315 hrs}$

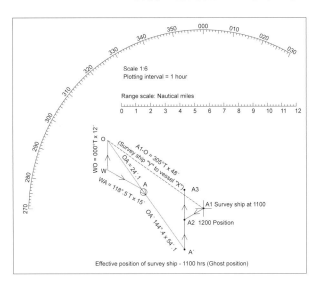

Figure 12.17 Plot for example 12.5

12.5.4 Station Keeping

Other than for direct rendezvous, units are also expected to know how to approach each other to provide assistance, receive or supply stores, participate in search and rescue, or for any other operational reasons. The aim is to position the unit as advised. Units may be required to reach a particular station or change an existing station for a new one. This positioning could be in the form of true or relative bearing and the distance from either of the units.

In such scenarios or problems, as the required station is related to one of the units in the form of a bearing and distance, it moves at the same course and speed as the unit it is related to. The movement of this point is the same as WO.

Example 12.6

Your vessel is engaged on Ministry of Defence assigned duties. At 0400 GMT, your ship has been ordered to come 2.5 miles to the port beam of an RFA vessel to receive stores by helicopter. The RFA ship is heading 350° T at 10 knots and is bearing 290° T from you at a distance of 22 miles. Your maximum speed is 15 knots. Find the following by plotting:

- *The course to steer to reach the advised station as early as possible*
- *the ETA at the station*
- *the distance that you expect to pass astern of the RFA vessel*
- *the CPA from the RFA.*

Solution and comments

Choose a suitable scale. For the example, plot 1:2 has been used. Plot the course of the RFA ship from the centre of the sheet.

Plot the bearing and distance between both ship as line O-RFA, with O representing your ship.

As you are expected to position yourself at 2´.5 miles to the port beam of the RFA ship (270° R × 2´.5), measure the distance 2´.5 miles to the port beam of the RFA ship at point A´. Join OA´. This is the relative approach as seen on the radar of the RFA. Your ship would be seen as moving along this line from the RFA.

The plotting interval used is 1 hour. At O, plot WO in direction of 350° T × 12´.

From W, mark 15´ along the line OA´ and identify it as A. Join WA. WA is the course to steer to reach 270° R × 2´.5 from the RFA. From the plot the course is 323°.5 T.

For ETA: Time to station (A´) = (OA´ ÷ OA) ×
Plotting interval
= (24.2 ÷ 7.5) × 1 = 3h 14m
ETA = 0400 + 0314 = **0714 GMT**

For distance astern:

- Draw a line reciprocal to the course of the RFA to meet the line OA´. Measure the distance of this line. From the plot, it is **1´.3.**

For CPA:

- Draw a line from the centre to be perpendicular to the OA´ and reaching OA´. Measure the distance of this line. This is the CPA and is **1´.1.**

Example 12.7

At 1600 hours, two ships are engaged on a parallel track search on a course of 160° T and a speed of 12 knots. The assisting ship is 2´ to the port beam of the On Scene Co-ordinator's (OSC) ship. Due to the improved conditions of visibility, the assisting ship is advised to take up a new station 6´ on the port beam of the OSC's ship.

Assuming that any alterations are instantly effective, find the course and speed of the assisting ship to take up new station at the earliest time, while maintaining the same relative bearing from the OSC 's ship. The maximum speed of the assisting ship is 15 knots. Find the time when the assisting ship would be on the advised station.

Solution and Comments

Plot the course of the OSC's ship, 160° T, from the centre of the plotting sheet. Considering the distances, the scale of the plotting sheet could be used directly and a smaller plotting interval of half an hour has been used.

Plot the port beam bearing for the OSC's ship, ie 270° R. On this line, mark distances of 2´ and 6´. The line has been marked solid and thick between these two distances. This is the relative approach (OA) as seen from the OSC's radar.

The point 2´ on the port beam is marked O and indicates the position of the assisting ship at 1600. The point 6´ on the port beam is identified as A´ and indicates the position where the assisting ship will take up the advised station.

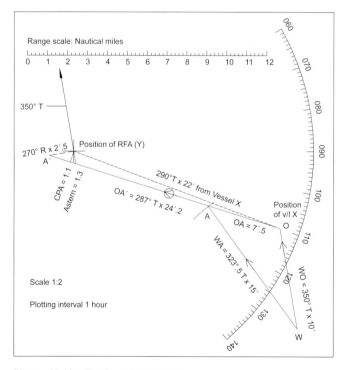

Figure 12.18 Plot for example 12.6

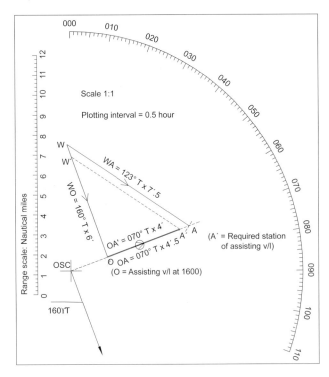

Figure 12.19 Plot for example 12.7

Choose WO of 6′ and plot it at O, so that WO is 160° T × 6′. With W as centre, mark the point A on the extended OA′ line. WA (7′.5 – half of the speed for half an hour plot) represents the course of the assisting ship to take up the advised station at the earliest time.

From the plot, the course is **123°T**, when the assisting ship is at its maximum speed of **15 knots.**

For time: Time to station = (OA′ ÷ OA) × Plot interval

= (4′ ÷ 4′.5) × 0.5

= 26m 40s   = 27m approx

Time at station   = 1600 + 0027   = **1627 hrs**

Example 12.8
Example 12.7 can be modified. The time statement might read, 'Find the time of alteration', so that the assisting ship is at the advised station at precisely 1630 hours.

The plot and calculations will remain as above, the only change would be the final step involving "Time at station".

Time at station   = 1630 − 0027   = **1603** hrs
(Note that the time taken to station is the same.)

Example 12.9
Example 12.7 can be modified further. 'Find the course and speed, such that the assisting vessel completes the manoeuvre in half an hour'.

Solution and Comments
Repeat the steps in Example 12.7 up to plotting the WO, so that WO = 160° T × 6′. Join W to A directly. As the assisting ship must complete the manoeuvre in half an hour and as the plot has been done with a plotting interval of half an hour, WA represents a run for half an hour.

Direction of WA represents the course and the length of WA (x 2, as the plot has been done for half an hour) represents the speed of the assisting ship to take up the advised station and to complete the manoeuvre in half an hour.

From the plot, the course is **126°T** and speed is 14.4 knots (7′.2 × 2). No calculation is required for time as the manoeuvre has been set as half an hour.

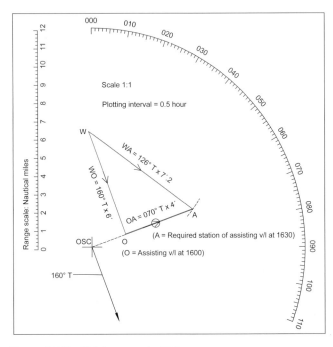

Figure 12.20 Plot for example 12.9

Example 12.10
At 1100 hours, two ships are engaged in a parallel track search on a course of 150° T at 10 knots, during a search and rescue operation. The assisting ship is 3′ on the port beam of the OSC's ship and has a maximum speed of 13 knots. The assisting ship is advised to shift station to a position 3′.5 due west of the OSC's ship with immediate effect. Find the course the assisting ship must take in order to complete the manoeuvre in the shortest time, assuming that any alteration is instantly effective. Find the time when the assisting ship:

- *Will be on the new station*
- *will be seen if visibility was 2 miles*
- *will be astern of the OSC's ship.*

What will the distance be when the assisting ship passes astern of the OSC's ship?

Solution and Comments

Draw the course of the OSC's ship at the centre. Plot the position of the assisting ship 3 miles to the port beam of the OSC's ship (270° R × 3´). Identify it as point O.

Plot point A´, 3´.5 due west of the OSC's ship. Join O to A´. OA´ is the relative approach as seen from the OSC's radar.

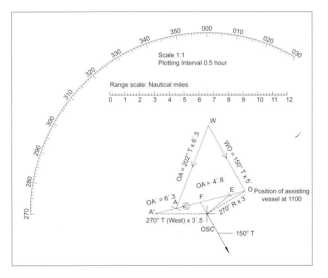

Figure 12.21 Plot for example 12.10

At O, plot WO, 150° T × 5´. As the OSC's ship is conducting a search at 10 knots, point O is moving at the same speed. A plotting interval of half an hour has been used.

From W, draw an arc on the line OA´ using 6´.5 as the radius (half of speed). Identify this point as A. Join W to A. WA is the course of the assisting ship at 13 knots to allow her to take up position at the advised station at the earliest time. From the plot the course is **202°T**.

Complete the other construction. From the centre, draw an arc along the line OA´, with 2´ as the radius, and identify this as point E. Draw the reciprocal of the heading line from the centre to meet the OA´. Identify this as point F. Measure OA´, OA, OE and OF. Also measure the distance of the centre to F.

These are OA´ = 6´.3, OA = 4´.8, OE = 1´.1, OF = 3´.1 and Centre-F = 0´.9

Times:

At new station = 1100 + [(OA´ ÷ OA) × 0.5] = 1100 + [(6.3 ÷ 4.8) × 0.5]

$$= 1100 + 0039 = \textbf{1139 hrs}$$

When visible = 1100 + [(OE ÷ OA) × 0.5] = 1100 + [(1.1 ÷ 4.8) × 0.5] = 1100 + 0007 = **1107 hrs**

When astern = 1100 + [(OF ÷ OA) × 0.5] = 1100 + [(3.1 ÷ 4.8) × 0.5] = 1100 + 0019 = **1119 hrs**

The distance when passing astern = **0´.9**

Example 12.11

Three ships, X, Y and Z, are engaged in a line abreast parallel track search on a course of 090° T at 10 knots, with a track spacing of 4´, during a search and rescue operation at 1200 hours. X is the northern most of all and is the OSC's ship, with Y in the middle and Z to the south. At 1230, due to visibility deteriorating to 2´.0, Z is advised to shift station to a new position, 2´.5 on the starboard quarter of X. If the maximum speed of Z is 13 knots, find the course required of Z in order to complete the manoeuvre in the shortest time, assuming any alteration is instantly effective.

Find the times when the ship Z will be on the new station.
Find the time and bearing when Z will sight ship Y, if visibility is 2´.0.

Solution and Comments

Plot the three ships, X, Y and Z as in the example statement.

The reader should now be able to complete the basic plot, mark the respective points O, A´, A and W, and determine the course to steer at 13 knots, which is 031°.5T.

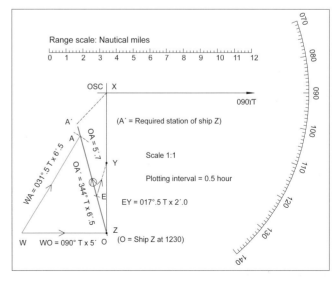

Figure 12.22 Plot for example 12.11

The required distances for time are OA′ = 6′.5, OA = 5′.7, OE = 2′.2

Times:

At new station = 1230 + [(OA′ ÷ OA) × 0.5] = 1230 + [(6.5 ÷ 5.7) × 0.5] = 1230 + 0034 = **1304 hrs**

When visible = 1230 + [(OE ÷ OA) × 0.5] = 1230 + [(2.2 ÷ 5.7) × 0.5] = 1230 + 0012 = **1242 hrs at a bearing of 017°.5 T**

12.5.5 Rendezvous at a Specific Time

In this type of problem, the assisting ship usually maintains course and speed, and the ship requiring assistance heads for a position, advised by the assisting ship at a determined time.

The usual examples for the determined time might be sunrise, civil twilight or one hour before sunrise.

Some navigators find these types of problems very complicated, although in reality, the work is rather simple.

Only the sunrise time and plane sailing are required to be worked out before the calculation can be performed in five steps:

1 Work out the time of sunrise for the ship required to maintain its course and speed, based on the position stated in the problem (1st approximation).
2 From sunrise, work out the time and distance it is required to run, and obtain the position reached.
3 Based on the new position, work out the refined time of the sunrise for the ship required to maintain course and speed (2nd approximation).
4 From the refined sunrise, work out the time and distance it is required to run, and obtain the refined position reached.
5 Between the other ships position and the position of the first ship at sunrise, work out the course distance and speed.

Example 12.12

At 0450 GMT on 19 June 2006, a tanker in position 39° 42′ N, 145° 06′ W has an injured seafarer requiring urgent medical attention on board.

At the same time a passenger ship in position 40° 00′ N, 148° 07′ W heading 076°T at 26 knots, has a doctor on board and has agreed to assist. This ship will maintain course and speed.

It has been agreed that the transfer will take place at sunrise next morning. Find the following:

- *GMT of sunrise*
- *rendezvous position*
- *the course and speed of the tanker in order to rendezvous at sunrise.*

Solution and Comments

The Local date should be confirmed first, in order to enter almanac for LMT sunrise:

GMT	June 19,	04 50	
LIT (148° 07′ W)		- 09 52	(to nearest minute only)
LMT	June 18,	18 58	The next local date is 19 June.

Step 1   1st Approximation

	h m	
LMT sunrise for 40° N (19-6-06)	04 31	
Increment	00 00	
LMT sunrise for 40° 00′ N	04 31	
Longitude in time (148° 07′ W) +	09 52	
GMT sunrise (1st approx)	**14 23**	based on position at 0450 GMT
Initial GMT	04 50	
Difference	**09 33**	
Speed	26 knots	
Distance to run	248′.3	

Step 2

For course 076°T and distance 248′.3, d.lat and Departure are:

d.lat = Cos Course × Distance = Cos 076° × 248′.3
 = 60′.1 N (1° 0′.1)
Dep = Sin Course × Distance = Sin 076° × 248′.3
 = 240′.9 E

Latitude	= Lat of Pass V/L ~ d.lat
	= 40° 00′ N ~ 01° 00′.1 N = 41° 00′.1 N
Mean Latitude	= 40° 30′.05 N
d.long	= Dep/Cos Mean Lat
	= 240′.9/Cos 40° 30′.05 N = 316′.8 E
	= 005° 16′.8 E
Longitude	= Long Pass V/L ~ d.long
	= 148° 07′ W ~ 005° 16′.8 E = 142° 50′.2 W

Step 3   2ⁿᵈ Approximation for a refined time of sunrise

LMT sunrise for 40° N	04 31
Increment for 01° 00´.1	-00 03
LMT sunrise for 41° 00´.1 N	04 28
Longitude in time (142° 50´.2 W)+	09 31
GMT sunrise (2ⁿᵈ Appx)	**13 59** based on 1ˢᵗ approximation of position

Initial GMT	04 50
Difference	09 09
Speed	26 knots
Distance to run	237´.9

Step 4

For course 076°T and distance 237´.9, d.lat and Departure are:

d.lat	= Cos Course × Distance	
	= Cos 076° × 237´.9	= 57´.6 N
Dep	= Sin Course × Distance	
	= Sin 076° × 237´.9	= 230´.8 E

Arrived latitude = Lat of Pass V/L ~ d.lat
= 40° 00´.0N ~ 57´.6 N   = **40° 57´.6 N**

Mean Latitude = 40° 28´.8 N

d.long	= Dep/Cos Mean Lat	
	= 230´.8/Cos 40° 28´.8 N	= 005° 03´.4 E
	= 303´.4 E	

Arrived Long = Long Pass V/L +/- d.long
= 148° 07´ ~ 005° 03´.4 E   = **143° 03´.6 W**

The tanker will have to head for the position of the passenger ship at sunrise (1359), ie 40 57´.6 N, 143 03´.6 W (Rendezvous position).

Step 5

Tanker's position at 0450 GMT	39° 42´ N	145° 06´ W
Passenger Vessel's position at Sunrise	40° 57´.6 N	143° 03´.6 W
d.lat	01° 15´.6 N d.long	002° 02´.4 E
	(75´.6)	(122´.4)

M Lat 40° 19´.8 N

Dep	= d.long × Cos M Lat = 122´.4 × Cos 40° 19´.8
	= 93´.3

Tan Course = Dep/d.lat = 93´.3/75´.6 = 1.23413 Course
= N 51° E

Distance = d.lat/Cos Course = 75´.6/Cos 51°
= 120.1 Nautical Miles

Speed = Distance/Time = 120.1/09 09 = 13.13 Knots

GMT Sunrise = **1359** Course = **N 51° E**
Speed = **13.1 Knots**
Rendezvous Position Lat = **40° 57´.6 N**
Long = **143° 03´.6 W**

Example 12.13

At 1835 GMT, 06 May 2006, a passenger ship steaming at 25 knots is in position 38° 24´N 052° 42´W following a Rhumb line for a landfall at 40° 43´N 074° 00´W. A seriously injured seafarer on a bulk carrier is to be transferred to the passenger ship, which has a doctor on board, at sunrise the next morning. The bulk carrier, at 1835 GMT, is in position 36° 48´N 058° 26´W.

- *Calculate the LMT sunrise for the passenger ship*
- *calculate the rendezvous position*
- *calculate the course and speed required of the bulk carrier in order to rendezvous successfully.*

Solution and comments

In this problem the course of the passenger ship is not stated and must be worked out using Mercator Sailing between its position at 1835 and landfall.

Position at 1835	38° 24´N	MP 2484.26	052° 42´W
Landfall position	40° 43´N	MP 2663.85	074° 00´W
	d.lat 02° 19´N	DMP 179.59	21° 18´W
	d.long (139´)		(1278)

Tan Co	= d.long/DMP	= 1278/179.59	= 7.116209
Course	= 82°	= N 82° W	= 278°T

Next, the Local date should be confirmed, in order to enter the almanac for LMT sunrise:

GMT	May	06,	18 35	
LIT (052° 42´W)			- 0331	(to nearest minute only)
LMT	May	06,	1504	The next local date is 07 May

Looking at the Nautical Almanac (HMSO) 2006, it can be seen that 07 May 2006 is not the middle of the three days. It may be required to interpolate between the times of sunrise for 05 May 2006 and 08 May 2006 as those are the middle days on the corresponding daily pages. The time of sunrise is required for Latitude 35°N and 40°N, so times are observed as follows:

	05 May	08 May	07 May
LMT for 35° N	0505	0503	= 0504
LMT for 40° N	0456	0452	= 0453

Step 1   1st Approximation

LMT sunrise for 35°N (07-5-06)		05 04
Increment for 3° 24′	-	00 07
LMT for 38° 24′N		04 57
Longitude in time (052° 42′W)	+	03 31
GMT 07 May based on position at 1835		2130 GMT
Initial GMT 06 May		18 35
Difference		13 53
Speed		x 25
Distance to run		347′.1

Step 2

For course N 82° W and distance 347′.1, d.lat and Departure are:

d.lat	= Cos Course × Distance = Cos 82° × 347′.1
	= 48′.3 N
Dep	= Sin Course × Distance = Sin 82° × 347′.1
	= 343′. 7 W

Latitude	= Lat of passenger ship ~ d.lat	
	= 38° 24′N ~ 48′.3 N	= 39° 12′.3 N

Mean Lat	= 38° 48′.15 N	
d.long	= Dep/Cos Mean Lat	
	= 343′.7/Cos 38° 48′.15 = 441′.0 = 7° 21′ W	
Longitude	= Long of passenger ship ~ d.long	
	= 052° 42′ W ~ 7° 21′ W	= 060° 03′ W

Step 3   2nd Approximation for a refined sunrise time

LMT sunrise 35° N (07-5-06)		05 04	
Increment 4° 12′.3	-	00 09	
LMT sunrise 39° 12′.3 N		04 55	
Longitude in time (060° 03′ W)	+	04 00	
GMT 7		08 55	based on 1st approximation position
Initial GMT 6		18 35	
Difference		14 20	
Speed		× 25	
Distance to run		358′.3	

Step 4

For course N 82° W and distance 358′.3 d.lat and Departure are:

d.lat	= Cos Course × Distance
	= Cos 82° × 358′.3 = 49′.9 N
Dep	= Sin Course × Distance
	= Sin 82° × 358′.3 = 354′.8 W

Arrived Latitude = Lat of passenger ship ~ d.lat

	= 38° 24′ N ~ 49′.9 N	= **39° 13′.9 N**
Mean Latitude	= 38° 48′.95 N	
d.long	= Dep/Cos Mean Lat	
	= 354′.8/Cos 38° 48′.95 = 455′.3 W	
	= 7° 35′.4 W	

Arrived Longitude = Long of passenger ship ~ d.long
= 052° 42′ W ~ 7° 35′.4 W = **060° 17′.4 W**

Step 5

The bulk carrier must head for the position of the passenger ship at sunrise (08 55), ie 39° 13′.9 N, 060° 17′.4 W.

Bulk carrier's position at 1835 GMT		36° 48′N		058° 26′W
Passenger ship's position at Sunrise		39° 13′.9 N		060° 17′.4 W
	d.lat	02° 25′.9 N	d.long	001° 51′.4 W
		(145′.9)		(111′.4)

Mean Lat = 38° 00′.95 N

Dep	= d.long × Cos Mean Lat	
	= 111′.4 × Cos 38° 00′.95 = 87′.8 W	
Tan Course	= Dep/d.lat	= 87′.8/145′.9 = 0.601782
		= 31°.038

Course = **N 31°W = 329°T**

Distance	= d.lat/Cos Course = 145′.9/Cos 31°.038
	= 170′.3
Speed	= Distance/Time = 170′.3/14 20 = 11.88 knots

LMT Sunrise = **07th 0855 GMT** Course = **329°T**
Speed = **11.9 kts**

Rendezvous position Lat = **39° 13′.9 N** Long = **060° 17′.4 W**

Example 12.14

A seriously injured seafarer on an oil tanker is to be transferred to a passenger ship with a doctor on board at sunrise.

At 0145 Zone Time, 06 May 2006, a tanker was in 35° 22′S 179° 32′W.

At the same time the passenger ship was in 35° 00′S 178° 30′E, on a course of 090°T, speed 27 knots. The passenger ship is to maintain its course and speed.

- *Calculate the time of sunrise for the passenger ship*
- *calculate the rendezvous position*
- *calculate the course and speed required for the oil tanker in order to rendezvous successfully.*

Solution and comments

This problem is complex, as the initial time given is the zone time. Looking at the longitude of both ships, it is evident that they are on either side of the 180° meridian, ie the International Date Line. This means that the ship in the eastern hemisphere (the passenger ship) will keep to Zone −1200 and the ship in the western hemisphere (the oil tanker), will be keeping to Zone +1200. They will both have a common GMT. GMT is determined by:

Zone Time 06 May 0145 (For oil tanker)
Zone   1200 (+) (as ship is in Western Hemisphere)
GMT   06 May 1345

It is necessary to interpolate between times for 05 May 2006 and 08 May 2006 as they are the middle days on the corresponding pages.

Sunrise is required for latitude 35° 00′ N for 07 May 2006, as the passenger ship, being in the eastern hemisphere, will be there on 06 May. The, times are observed as follows:

	05 May	08 May	Difference
LMT for 35° S	0639	0642	3 minutes for 3 days

(1 minute for 1 day)
LMT for 35° S   0641 on 07 May 2006 & 0640 on 06 May 2006

Step 1   1st Approximation

	h m	
LMT sunrise for 35° S (07 May)	06 41	
Longitude in time - (178° 32′E)	11 54	
GMT	06 18 47	based on position at 1345 GMT
Initial GMT	06 13 45	
Difference	**05 02**	
Speed	× 27	
Distance to run	135′.9	

Step 2

For course 090° T and distance 135′.9, d.lat and Departure are:

d.lat   = Nil (as ship going 090° T)
Dep   = Distance run   = 135′.9 E
Latitude   = 35° 00′ S (Mean Lat also = 35° 00′ S)
d.long   = Dep/Cos Mean Lat
          = 135′.9/Cos 35° = 165′.9 E = 2° 45′.9 E
Longitude = Long of passenger ship ~ d.long
          = 178° 30′ E + 2° 45′.9 E = 178° 44′.1 W
          (ie 360° − 181° 15′.9)

Step 3   2nd Approximation for a refined time of sunrise

As the passenger ship's new position is now in the western hemisphere, the LMT will be taken for 06 May 2006.

LMT sunrise 35° S (06 May)		06 40
Longitude in time (178° 44′.1 W)	+	11 55
GMT	06	18 35
Initial GMT	06	13 45
Difference		04 50
Speed		× 27
Distance to run		130′.5

Step 4

For course 090° T and distance 130′.5. d.lat and Departure are:

d.lat	= Nil	
Dep	= Distance	= 130′.5 E
Arrived Latitude	= Lat of passenger ship (course 090° T)	
	= **35° 00′S**	
Mean Latitude	= 35° 00′ S	
d.long	= Dep/Cos Mean Lat	
	= 130′.5/Cos 35° = 159′.3 E = 2° 39′.3 E	

Arrived Longitude = Long of passenger ship ~ d.long

= 178° 30′ E + 2° 39′.3 E = (360° − 181° 09′.3)

= **178° 50′.7 W**

Step 5

Tanker's position at 1345 GMT		35° 22′ S	179° 32′ W
Passenger Vessel's position at Sunrise		35° 00′ S	178° 50′.7 W
	d.lat	00° 22′ S d.long	0° 41′.3 W

Mean Lat	= 35° 11′.0 S
Dep	= d.long × Cos Mean Lat = 41′.3 × Cos 35° 11′ = 33′.75 W
Tan Course	= Dep/d.lat = 33.75/22 = 1.5343185 Course = 56°.9
Course	= **S 57°W = 237°T**
Distance	= d.lat/Cos Course = 22/Cos 56°.9 = 40′.3
Speed	= Distance/Time = 40′.3/04 50 = **8.33 knots**

Sunrise = **06th May 1835** Course = **237°T** Speed = **8.3 kts**
Rendezvous position Lat = **35° 00′ N** Long = **178° 50′.7 W**

12.6 Interception

Example 12.15

In conditions of restricted visibility, a support ship is steering a course of 130° T at 15 Kts. It has a radar contact, which is later confirmed as being a ship in distress, heading for a port of refuge. The radar observations are as follows:

Time	Bearing	Range
1310	220°	11′.8
1319	230°.5	9′.6
1328	247°	7′.8

The support ship is advised to intercept and escort to port, maintaining station 1 mile to the starboard beam of the distressed ship. Assuming that any alterations are instantaneously effective and the distressed ship maintains its course and speed, find:

- *The course to steer at a maximum speed of 20 Kts, at 1337 to intercept and take station 1 mile on the starboard beam of the distressed ship*
- *the time of taking station as advised*
- *the course and speed required to maintain station.*

Tidal stream is slack and the wind is calm throughout.

Solution and Comments

Considering the distances, the natural scale of the plotting sheet can be used.

Plot the support ship at the centre, A′.

Plot the observations and label them with the times, the first as O and the last as A. Join OA to obtain the relative approach of the distressed ship. Extend this line to the point A1, which represents the position of the distressed ship at 1337.Plot WO, 130° T at 15 Kts for 18 minutes (1310~1328), ie 4′.5. Join W to A to obtain the distressed ship's course and speed. This is 051° T × 4′.95, giving its speed as 16.5 Kts.

From the centre plot a point one mile on the starboard beam of the distressed vessel. This would be 051° + 90° = 141° T. Identify it as point A2. Join A2 to A1 and extend it beyond A1. This line is the required relative approach to take up the interception station.

A 15 minute time interval has been used to complete the rest of the plot. Draw a line 051° T × 4′.1 (16.5 × 15/60) as W2A2. With W2 as the centre and a radius of 5′ (20 × 15/60), draw an arc on the extended A1A2 line to obtain point O2. Join W2O2. This is the course that the support ship should steer at 20Kts to intercept and take station as advised.

Time of interception	= 1337 + [(A1A2 ÷ O2A2) × 15]
	= 1337 + [(6′.4 ÷ 8′) × 15]
= 1337 + 0012	= 1349 hours

The course and speed required to maintain station are the same as the course and speed of the distressed vessel, ie 051° T at 16.5 Kts.

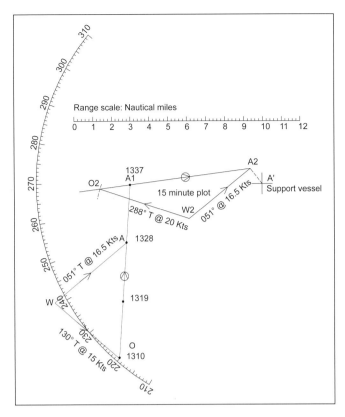

Figure 12.23   Plot for example 12.15

Example 12.16

A naval ship is patrolling on a course of 110° T, at a speed of 9 knots, and is in a position bearing 350° T, distance 5´.5, from a lighthouse in position 25° 32´ N, 057° 43´ E. The naval ship observes a ship on its radar as follows:

Time	Bearing (°T)	Range (nm)
1012	055	10.0
1024	036	8.3
1036	012	7.8

A decision is made to intercept this ship for investigation. Assuming that any alterations are instantaneously affective, and that the observed ship maintains its course and speed, find:

- *The course to steer from 1048 hours to intercept the observed ship using a maximum speed of 27 knots*
- *the ETA at the interception position*
- *the interception position relative to the lighthouse.*

The average estimated set of the tidal stream is 235° T at 3 knots for the naval ship and 250° T at 2 knots for the observed ship.

Solution and comments

Considering the distances involved, this plot can be completed on a radar plotting sheet, using its natural scale. This problem is best dealt with in five stages. These have been indicated on the plot.

1   Plot the lighthouse and the naval ship (A´) relative to each other. From the centre plot the lighthouse, so that the naval ship is bearing 350° T, at a distance of 5´.5 from the lighthouse.

2   Determine the naval ship position in relation to the lighthouse at 1048 and its ground track by applying the course/distance steered (110° T × 5´.4) and the tidal stream (235° T × 1´.8) experienced for 36 minutes (1012~1048). The reciprocal of the relative movement of the lighthouse is the ground track of the naval ship.

3   Plot the radar observations from 1012 to 1036. Draw a line through the same, OA, and extend to reach 1048, ie A1. This is the relative approach of the observed vessel. Apply the ground track of the naval ship (WO) to determine the water (WA2 = 274° T at 8.5 Kts) and ground (WA) track of the observed vessel. For this purpose, tidal stream 250° T at 2 knots would have to be applied for 24 minutes (0´.8).

4   From the naval ship position (A´) draw a line to run through and beyond the observed vessels position at 1048. This is the final approach line to intercept (A´O1). Using a plotting interval of half an hour, draw the observed vessels water track (W1A´ ie 4´.25) to join the centre. Apply the average drift being experienced by both vessels for a half-hour interval as W2W1 (250°T × 1´) and W2W3 (235° T × 1´.5).

With W3 as the centre and a radius of 13´.5 (½ of 27 Kts), draw an arc on the required interception line to obtain point O1. W3O1 is the course to be steered by the naval ship in order to intercept the observed vessel = 333° T.

A´O1 is the approach distance for half an hour. The ETA can be worked out:

ETA = 1048 + [(A´A1 ÷ A´O1) × 30] = 1048 + [(8´.7 ÷ 11´.4) × 30] = 1048 + 0023

ETA = 1111 hours

5   Apply for 23 minutes, the course to steer (333° T), distance (10´.35) and the tidal stream experienced by the naval ship (235° T × 1´.15) to the lighthouse position at 1048, in order to determine the position at 1111 hours. The range and bearing of centre from this point is the position of the naval ship relative to the lighthouse, at the interception time, ie 344°.5 T × 11´.9.

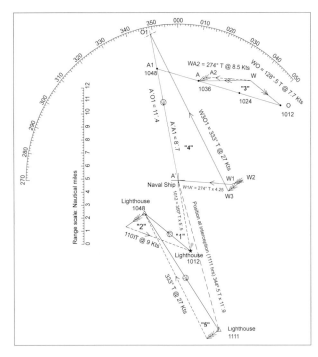

Figure 12.24 Plot for example 12.16

12.7 Rescue by Helicopter

Helicopters can be used for search and rescue at sea. Fixed-wing aircraft can be used to locate survivors and drop supplies, but cannot be used for practical rescue. The materials dropped might include liferafts, pumps, rations or communication equipment.

Helicopters have a limited range and can only be used in waters 200 to 550 miles from their base before having to refuel. Helicopters can either be civil or military.

12.7.1 Onboard Preparations

12.7.1.1 Bridge

Where possible, the ship must maintain a steady course as directed by the helicopter pilot. General guidance is based on the shipboard operating area. The helicopter usually approaches from the port side of the ship. The ship should maintain relative wind as follows, where the operating area is:

- Aft: 30° on the port bow
- midships: 30° on the port bow, or on either beam
- forward: 30° on the starboard quarter
- where this is not possible, the ship should remain stationery keeping its head into the wind. No attempt should be made to provide lee.

The sea area for operation should be selected carefully. It should be clear of navigational hazards and other shipping if possible, so that the ship has freedom of

movement. The course and speed can be agreed in advance with the helicopter pilot and attempts should be made to maintain this, avoiding any delay, as helicopter flying time depends on the fuel it carries.

Early communication with the helicopter is important. When requested, the ship should use methods to identify itself. Position, heading, ETA, name, description, colour, special features and transmitting a homing signal can help the helicopter pilot to identify the ship. Details of the area of operation and persons/equipment to be transferred are important. The helicopter pilot may be advised of relative wind by an air sock being displayed, international code flag, etc. Smoke and exhaust from the funnel indicates the same, the wind should be at least two points off the port bow. The ship should also display signals indicating its "restricted in ability to manoeuvre". All of the bridge team should be briefed before the operation. The ship must be under the Master's orders and he must ensure that all safety and operational standards are complied with before engagement. The engine should be on standby and hand steering should be engaged before operations begin. Position monitoring should be continuous, along with situation awareness to keep the ship in the safe and clear area of operation. Extreme care must be exercised when using line throwing apparatus or any pyrotechnics.

12.7.1.2 Deck

The winching or landing area should be cleared, the yellow marking should be enhanced and upper parts of any obstructions should be conspicuously painted. All aerials and stays in the area should be struck, if possible. Obstructions that cannot be lowered should be well illuminated at night. Rails, etc should be lowered or removed. All loose items should be removed from the area or secured firmly. The emergency and rescue party should be ready with the rescue boat, safety and fire fighting appliances.

12.7.2 Evacuation

A simple way to effect a rescue is for the helicopter to land on the distressed unit and take personnel on board. This has the advantage of speed, but is subject to a suitable landing station being available on board the distressed unit. Most units at sea lack this facility. However, large bulk carriers, oil tankers, container ships and some specialised ships have been operating with helicopter landing facilities for a while.

It is now a requirement for passenger ships, and Ro-Ro ships carrying passengers, to be equipped with a helicopter landing area. There may be other restrictions to a helicopter landing on a distressed unit, eg fire, poor stability, weather or its location.

If a landing is not possible, the rescue will have to be carried out by using a winch. The winching area is normally marked on the deck. Where and how to conduct operations will be at the pilot's discretion. The deck party should remain stationary and allow the helicopter to move to them. A winchman might be lowered with an additional strop, or only a strop at the end of the winch wire may be lowered. The survivor should put the strop under his/her arms and, after indicating that they are ready, should hold both arms against the side of their body. If the condition of the survivor does not allow a strop to be used, a stretcher and winchman will be lowered, the casualty will then be strapped into the stretcher. (A helicopter will not normally lift marine Neil-Robertson type stretchers directly. The winchman may choose to transfer the casualty into the helicopter's own stretcher, or place the casualty and the ship's stretcher into the helicopter's own stretcher for lifting).

12.7.3 Hi-Line Technique

If there are obstructions on the ship, in the form or masts or rigging, the helicopter pilot may resort to a highline technique as it may not be possible to lower the winchman and/or strop directly to the deck. A rope extension of the winch wire may be lowered to the ship and be handled by a member of the ship's crew. The slack is taken in as the helicopter pays out the winch wire. The extension rope should be coiled down onto the deck, clear of snags, it should not be made fast. The helicopter will descend after moving out to one side of the ship. As the descent is being made the ship's crew should continue to take in the slack. A winchman may be lowered with the strop. The earthing lead or winch hook should be allowed to touch the deck to disperse any static electricity before the wire is handled. After securing the casualty in the strop, the helicopter is signalled. The helicopter will hoist the winch wire. At this stage, the extension rope should be paid out with enough weight on it to keep it taut. Two strops may be lowered if more people are to be transferred, the end of the extension rope should be kept in hand if possible, (but not secured) to facilitate the recovery of the strop for the next lift.

Ships that have several obstructions on and around the decks, an alternative for transferring a casualty or casualties is by pre-transfer of the person(s) to the ship's boat and towing the boat astern on a long painter. The helicopter can then winch the person(s) from the boat.

Example 12.17

At 1600 a helicopter is at bearing 330° T, 90´ from a ship. The ship has been advised to steer 270° T at 14 knots and is being set 345° T at 3 knots by a current. The ground speed of the helicopter is 60 knots. What is the earliest time the ship can expect to rendezvous with the helicopter, and what will the EP be as a bearing and distance from the ship's position at 1600?

Solution and comments

In this example, the helicopter is making the approach and the ship will maintain its course and speed. The helicopter's position is O and the ship's position is A´. The current will only affect units floating in the water although the helicopter may be affected by wind.

Choose a suitable scale, 1:8 has been used for the example plot. Plot the ship's 1600 position at the centre and identify it as A´. From A´ measure 330° T × 90´. This is O and is the position of the helicopter. Join the two points as line OA´. This will be the relative approach line.

The ship's ground track must be determined. To achieve a more accurate ground track, a triangle of 3 hours has been constructed. Draw a line in the direction of 270°T × 42´ (14 knots × 3 hours). The end of this line has been identified as point A1. From A1, draw set and drift, ie 345° T × 9´ (3 kts × 3 hrs). The end of this vector is the point A2. Join A´ to A2 to obtain the ground track of the ship. Measure A´A2 and divide it by 3 to obtain the ground speed of the ship. This is 15.1 knots and is the distance A´A3.

Using a plotting interval of one hour, draw WO (281°.1 T × 15´.1) at point O. With W as the centre, draw an arc on the line OA´ and call it point A. WA is the course of the helicopter (and is its ground track). Measure the distance OA, which is 68´.8

Time of rendezvous = 1600 + [(OA´ ÷ OA) × plotting interval]
= 1600 + [(90´ ÷ 68´.8) × 1] = 1600 + 1h 18.5m = **1718** hours

To obtain EP, draw a line parallel to WA from point O and run it to the ship's ground track. Measure the distance from A to EP, which is 19´.7

Another method of finding the EP distance is by multiplying the ship's ground speed by the time to rendezvous, ie 15.1 knots × 1h 18.5m = 19´.7

Therefore, the EP rendezvous **is 281°1 T × 19´.7** from the ship's position at 1600.

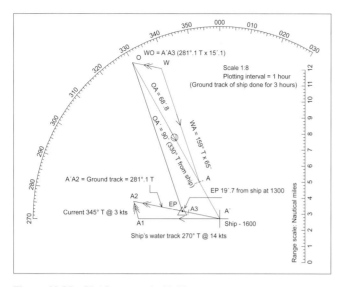

Figure 12.25 Plot for example 12.17

12.8 Search and Rescue Co-Operation Plans Aboard Passenger Ships

A plan for cooperation with the appropriate search and rescue services must be drawn up and carried by all passenger ships (Class I to Class VIA) using UK waters. International requirements also exist through SOLAS.

The plan must be agreed with the search and rescue service relevant to the ship's area(s) of operation. Ships that operate on inland waterways may have existing arrangements with the local search and rescue authorities eg the police, which are considered acceptable under the regulations. The plan must be available on board and it should be kept on the bridge.

The plan should contain:

- List of contents
- introduction
- description of a plan for cooperation.

The company

- Name and address
- contact list
  - 24 hr emergency initial, and alternative, contact arrangements
  - further communications arrangements (phone/fax, etc)
- chartlet(s) showing details of route(s) and service(s) together with boundaries of relevant SRR (search and rescue regions)
- liaison arrangements between the company and relevant RCCs
  - provision of incident information – checklist detailing persons, cargo and bunkers on board,

search and rescue facilities and any specialist support available at the time, etc
  - provision of liaison officer(s) – with access to supporting documentation concerning the company and the ship(s), eg copies of fire control and safety plans as required by the flag state.

The ship

- The basic details of the ship
  - MMSI, call sign, country of registry, type of ship, GT, LOA, maximum permitted draught (in m), service speed, maximum number of persons allowed on board and the number of crew normally carried
- communication equipment carried
- a general plan of the decks and a profile of the ship, including basic information on:
  - LSA, FFA, helicopter deck and winching area with approach sector
  - helicopter types that the deck is designed for
  - means on board intended to be used to rescue people from the sea or other vessels
  - a colour picture of the ship and whether the above details are transmittable by electronic means.

The RCCs

- SRRs along the route, a chartlet showing SRRs in the area(s) of the ship's operation
- search and rescue mission coordination (SMC), definition and summary of functions
- on-scene coordination (OSC), definition, selection criteria and summary of functions.

Search and rescue facilities

- RCC/ SCs along the route and their addresses
- communications: equipment, frequencies available, watch maintained and contact list (MMSIs, call signs, telephone, fax and telex numbers)
- general description and availability of designated search and rescue units (surface and air) and additional facilities along the route, such as fast rescue vessels, other vessels, heavy/light helicopters, long-range aircraft and fire fighting facilities
- communications plan
- search planning
- medical advice/assistance
- fire fighting, chemical hazards, etc
- shore reception arrangements
- informing next of kin
- suspension/termination of Search and Rescue action.

The plan should include details on media relations and periodic exercises.

12.9 Man Overboard

The loss of a person from the ship, or a ship's boat, requires the Master of the ship to take measures for their recovery. The sequence of actions depends on the time of notification of the bridge team, compared to the time of loss of the person. In cases where the watch officer witnesses the fall of the person, or has been notified immediately, the response is immediate.

12.9.1 In Open Waters

Initial actions that are to be taken simultaneously (immediate response, when a person is seen to fall overboard or an immediate report is made):

- Raise the general emergency alarm (sounding of three prolonged blasts also acts as an alarm)
- engage hand steering and shift helm hard over to the side that the person has fallen and commence Williamson's Turn
- release bridge wing buoy with "man overboard signal"
- note time and position. Press 'man overboard' key on position fixing device, or initiate auto waypoint, as appropriate
- put the engine onto immediate standby.

Specialised ships may be able to execute a single turn, to bring them back to the position where the person fell overboard, instead of using Williamson's Turn.

Subsequently:

- Post lookouts as high as possible and on all sides – keep the person in sight, use binoculars
- hoist flag "O"
- sound three prolonged blasts on the whistle (if not already done), and repeat at regular intervals in restricted visibility
- transmit a DISTRESS message to ships in the vicinity and shore authorities
- muster the rescue boat crew, emergency and backup team
- prepare the rescue boat for launching
- reduce speed
- establish communications with all teams using hand held VHF radios
- rig scrambling nets and rope ladders on both sides to aid recovery
- prepare stretcher, resuscitator, first aid kit and hospital
- proceed with the man overboard to leeward and stop the ship up wind for recovery.

If the man overboard is not sighted, the vessel should commence a "Sector Search" to locate the person. In this case the length of each sector leg should be based on time and not distance. For example, if a length of say 1 mile was selected, a full sector search would be 1 × 3 × 3 = 9 nm. Remember that a ship turning frequently by 120° will lose speed significantly. A ship capable of 16 knots may average about 9 knots in this type of situation. So a distance of 9 nm would be covered in an hour. The initial Williamson's Turn would take between 5 to 15 minutes depending on the size of the ship. Adding another hour to it could prove critical, particularly in very cold sea conditions. Considering this, if the leg was 2 minutes, 2 × 3 × 3 = 18 minutes would be the time taken for the search. It is important to appreciate that a person who falls overboard is unlikely to have drifted far and the search should be focused on the position where the person was seen to fall overboard.

When a person has been reported missing and has not been seen to fall overboard, the Master is still obliged to carry out a search to the last position where the person was positively seen on board. It is very important to establish that the person is in fact missing. A full ship search should be conducted. Witnesses who sighted the person positively should be questioned carefully to establish the full facts. On board preparations should be as above.

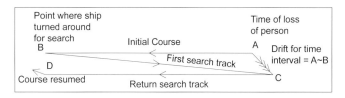

Figure 12.26 Man overboard

The ship should be turned around using a Scharnov Turn, as it is a delayed action and the distance lost would be less when compared to a Williamson's Turn. Once the ship that has lost the person has conducted an up and down search to the position where the last known sighting of the person overboard was, allowing for drift, it should resume its voyage. If the person is not found, the next port authorities must be notified. The company should also be advised to provide a replacement at the next port. If the search is unsuccessful, the CRS should be advised to transmit URGENCY messages to shipping in the area advising them to keep a sharp lookout for a person in the water and to report the sighting and effect a rescue.

12.9.2 In Port

All of the manoeuvres described above are relevant, but instead of turning hard over and commencing a Williamson's Turn, speed should be reduced and a rescue boat launched in addition to calling the port authority. If a person falls overboard during mooring operations, a port tug or mooring boat should be called to recover the person from the water.

12.9.3 Man Overboard Manoeuvres

12.9.3.1 Williamson's Turn

This is used as an 'immediate action manoeuvre' just after a person has fallen overboard:

- Helm immediately hard over to the side that the person fell. This has the advantage of pushing the stern away from the person in the water
- when the ship has turned 60° off the original heading, the helm should be shifted hard over to the other side. (Note: The course does not have to be changed 60° for every ship. Masters should determine the course change required during drills or other practice manoeuvres)
- when ship's heading is 20° short of the reciprocal heading, order helm amidships and steady up the ship on the reciprocal course. At the same time, a reduction of speed should be advised. (By this time, the ship will have lost a significant amount of its speed due to the turn. If propeller revolutions are not reduced, the ship would gain speed on a steady heading)
- at the final stages, the ship can be manoeuvred easily to create lee for the person in water
- there is a possibility that lookouts may lose sight of the person as they have to focus from one side to the other. For this reason, lookouts should be posted as high as possible and on all sides of the ship, in particular in the stern.

12.9.3.2 Scharnov Turn

This is used as a delayed action manoeuvre after the person has been reported missing for a while.

- Helm hard over to one side and when the ship has turned 240° off the original heading, the helm should be shifted hard over to the other side
- when the ship's heading is 20° short of the reciprocal heading, order the helm amidships and steady up the ship on the reciprocal course. At the same time, a reduction in speed should be advised
- this should never be used as an immediate action manoeuvre.

The Scharnov turn has the advantage of reducing distance lost during the manoeuvre. The Williamson's Turn has the advantage of bringing the ship back in

to its wake, to the position where the manoeuvre was begun.

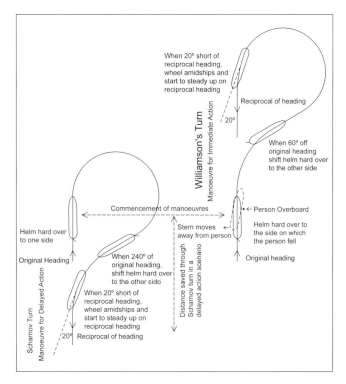

Figure 12.27   Scharnov and williamson turns

12.9.3.3 Single Turn

This is another option for an immediate action manoeuvre. Specialised units which can turn very rapidly should complete the turn that has been initiated by shifting the helm hard over to the side that the person has fallen. This should only be attempted on ships with a very small turning circle, and when the person overboard can be kept in view.

12.9.3.4 Single Delayed Turn

Used as a manoeuvre to turn a ship around, when:

- There has been a brief delay in reporting the person overboard
- due to operational reasons, the ship cannot begin the turn immediately, eg presence of navigational hazards
- when ship has nearly turned around, the heading should be steadied so that the ship is positioned upwind of the person in the water, so as to create lee.

Single turns are usually executed on the windward side when the person falls overboard on the lee side.

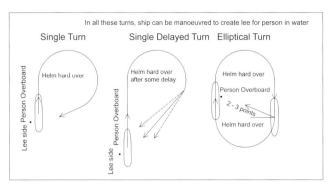

Figure 12.28 Turns

12.9.3.5 Elliptical Turn (Double Turn)

This can be used as an immediate action manoeuvre or when there is a brief delay in reporting the person overboard

- The turn is started by shifting the helm hard over to the side that the person fell and allowing the ship to turn 180°. At this stage the ship is steadied up on the reciprocal heading

- when the person is 2 to 3 points abaft the beam, the helm is shifted hard over on the same side again to bring the ship on to the original heading
- this turn has the advantage of keeping the person on the same side. It is also preferable for use in traffic separation schemes or other circumstances when the ship needs to avoid heading into opposing traffic, or there are navigational hazards in close proximity that will hinder the turn.

Author's Note
It is important to complete search and rescue operations in the shortest possible time to minimise the misery of those in distress. Making effective use of all available resources in a coordinated manner can expedite the operation and help bring it to a successful conclusion. The mariner needs to develop adequate skills to perform the expected tasks.

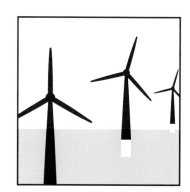

13

Offshore Installations and Navigation

13.1 Offshore Oil and Gas Installations

Navigation in the vicinity of offshore installations must be carefully considered. The Proximity of these installations to busy shipping lanes makes matters worse. Special care must be exercised if an approaching ship is engaged with offshore activities.

Offshore exploration in an area begins with a seismic survey. This can be done by towing an object at the end of a very long wire, caution must be exercised around them.

13.1.1 Rigs

Mobile rigs are used for drilling wells. Jack-up rigs can be used in depths down to approximately 120 m and are towed into the drilling position, where their steel legs are lowered to the seabed. The drilling platform is kept jacked-up clear of the water. Semi-submersible

rigs consist of a platform on columns that rise from a caisson submerged deep enough to avoid many of the effects of the sea and swell. These can be used in up to 1,700 m in an anchored mode. In dynamic positioning (DP) mode, they can be used in depths of more than 1,700 m. Drill ships are used in depths of less than 200 m by using an 8-point anchor system. With dynamic positioning, drilling can be done in depths between 2,000 m and 6,000 m below the seabed.

- Rigs are marked by illuminated name panels, lights, obstruction lights and fog signals. Flares burn at times to dispose of unwanted oil or gas
- mobile rigs on station are not charted
- buoys and other obstacles are often moored near rigs and anchors wires, chains and obstructions often extend as far as one mile
- a standby vessel and other small craft may be in attendance. Installations usually have a safety zone
- the rig should be given a wide berth

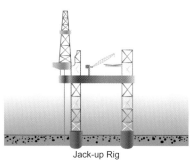

Jack-up Rig

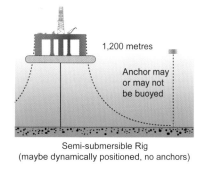

1,200 metres

Anchor may or may not be buoyed

Semi-submersible Rig
(maybe dynamically positioned, no anchors)

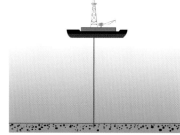

Drillship. (Dynamically positioned, no anchors)

Figure 13.1   Drilling Rigs

- during the course of development, large structures can be moved without notice. On some charts, such areas are designated development areas and their limits are shown. Mariners are strongly advised to keep outside of the development areas
- drilling could be done at an angle to the vertical, extending well beyond the base of the rig
- positions are given by radio navigational warnings or temporary notices, NAVTEX. In NAVAREA I these are published weekly in SafetyNET and reprinted in Section III of Admiralty Notices to Mariners.

13.1.2 Wells

Numerous wells could be drilled during a development. Some are sealed with cement below the seabed and abandoned, known as being plugged and abandoned. Wells required at a later date are termed as suspended wells. These usually extend 2 m to 6 m above the sea bed. In some cases, an extension could be 15 m above the seabed. Those in use are termed as production wells and may be protected by a 500 m exclusion zone.

Production wells, and in some cases, suspended wells, are marked by buoys or light-buoys. Wells are shown on charts as a danger circle.

Figure 13.2 Production wells

13.1.3 Platforms

Piled steel structures have legs drilled into the seabed. Concrete structures stay in position by gravity. Tension leg platforms consist of semi-submersible platforms secured by wires to flooded caissons on the seabed below, they are kept in tension by the platforms buoyancy.

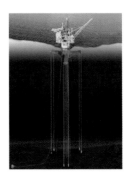

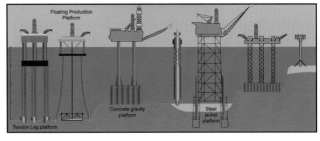

Concrete Production Platform

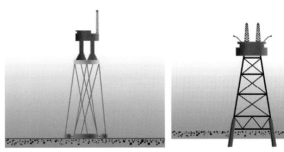

Tension Leg Platform   Steel Production Platform

Figure 13.3 Platforms

Several wells may be drilled from one rig. A template placed on the seabed below the rig is used to guide the drill. A template can be as much as 15 m above the seabed. Platforms may stand in singles or in complex structures connected by bridges or underwater cables.

Platforms are marked by:

- Illuminated name panels displaying the registered name, at least one panel should be visible from any direction

- a white light flashing Morse code (U) every 15 seconds. This should be visible 15 miles all round the horizon. Elevation should be 12 m to 30 m
- secondary lights with the same characteristics, but only visible for 10 miles. They are automatically brought into operation when the lights fail
- red lights, flashing Morse code (U) in unison with each other, every 15 seconds, visible at 2 miles, exhibited from the horizontal extremities of the structure that are not already marked by the main light or lights (obstruction lights)
- fog signals sounding Morse code (U) every 30 seconds, audible at a range of at least 2 miles.

In addition to the above list, the platform may also be burning gas.

Platforms are charted and may be mentioned in sailing directions. Drilling rigs or barges, that may be up to 1 mile from them, may not be charted. This ancillary equipment might be marked by buoys.

13.1.4 Mooring Systems (Single Point Moorings - SPM)

Catenary Anchor Leg Moorings (CALM) have a large buoy on the surface that does not turn when the ship swings to wind or tide. It is moored by 4 or more anchors which may lie up to 400 m from the buoy. Mooring hawsers and cargo hoses lead from the buoy through a turntable that is mounted on top.

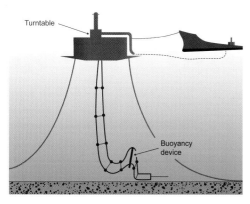

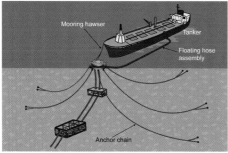

Figure 13.4   Catenary anchor leg mooring

A Single Anchor Leg Mooring (SALM) has a rigid frame with a buoyancy device at its upper end. Its lower end is secured on a large steel or concrete base resting on the seabed. The upper connects to a mooring buoy by a chain or wire span. Oil flows into the frame through a universal joint. The buoy can swing with the ship and it is likely to tilt in that direction. It is particularly suited to loading from deep water subsea wellheads.

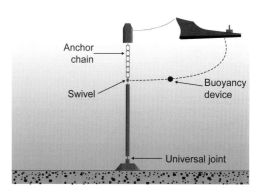

Figure 13.5   Single anchor leg mooring

A Single Anchor Leg Storage (SALS) is a SALM-type of mooring system that is permanently attached to the stem or stern of a storage tanker through a yoke and is supported by a buoyancy tank. Tankers secure to the storage tanker to load.

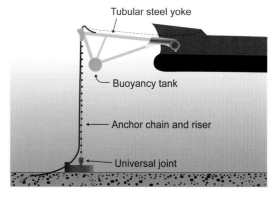

Figure 13.6   Single anchor leg storage system

A SPAR mooring is similar to ELSBM, but it has a larger floating structure which accounts for its storage capacity, allowing production to continue even in adverse weather. It is manned permanently.

An Exposed Location Single Buoy Mooring (ELSBM) is used in deep water where there is often bad weather, it has a large cylindrical floating structure, with a helicopter platform at the top. It has emergency accommodation and its anchors may lie up to half a mile from the structure.

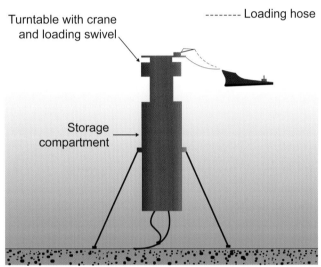

Figure 13.8   Spar buoy

An Articulated Loading Column (ALC) is a modification of SALM. The anchor span and buoyant frame or tube is replaced by a metal lattice tower, buoyant at one end and attached by a universal joint to a concrete-filled base on the seabed. In bad weather, a tower can be inclined at angles up to 20° from vertical. Mooring towers are not SPMs and are secured to the seabed, surmounted by a turntable, and used to moor ships.

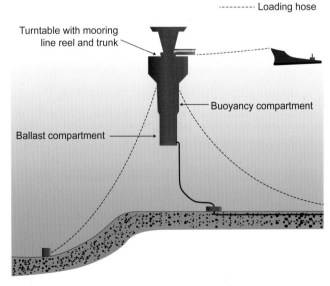

Figure 13.7   Exposed location single buoy mooring

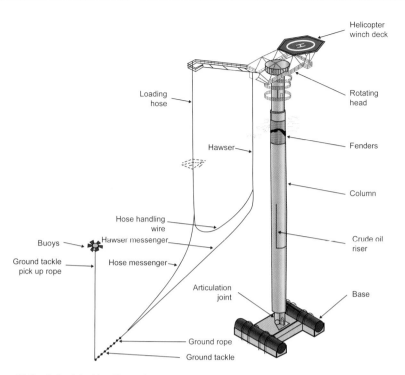
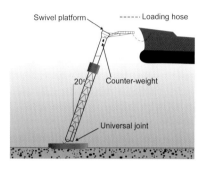

Figure 13.9 Articulated loading column

13.1.5 Submarine Pipelines

Laid on the seabed for the conveyance of oil, gas and water, they may extend many miles into the sea, be buried, trenched or stand up to 2 m above the seabed. Pipes that were originally buried can become exposed over time. Some pipes have joints or manifolds extending up to 10 m above the seabed. Anchoring and trawling should not be carried out in the vicinity of the pipelines. Pipes may contain dangerous, explosive substances. In addition to being a fire hazard, a ship could lose buoyancy due to gas leaking from a ruptured pipeline.

Figure 13.10 Submarine pipeline

13.1.6 Navigation in Offshore Areas

- Navigational warnings for towing large objects, rig movements, the establishment of or changes to areas of activity and seismic survey are usually provided. Charts with relevant warnings should be updated

- if a ship needs to transit the area, the passage plan should be prepared so that the ship is kept well clear of the safety zones, and within the safety fairways where available

- ships should stay clear of safety zones as marked on the chart or advised by warnings. A minimum safe distance of 500 m must be maintained in the absence of information on the safety zone. Safety zones and positions of structures + 500 m should be marked as no-go areas

- the passage plan notes should include warnings on reduced soundings and use of an echo sounder

- notes should also include details on identifying structures and warning on problems associated with identification. Alternative primary and secondary methods of monitoring, other than by using offshore structures, should be listed including the use of visual, radar and electronic systems

- maintain a sharp lookout in the area for the movement of support and supply ships and buoys, some may not be lit

- "No anchoring" should be marked clearly. Contingency plans should be based on emergency actions other than anchoring

- when in the area, mark the direction of set due to the current on the chart and update it with the direction of leeway (when in the area)

- the maximum speed possible, taking into consideration the manoeuvring characteristics of the ship and proximity to hazards, should be noted in the passage plan

- usual remarks, eg notices, hand steering, the Master's calls, doubling watches and lookouts should be entered in the passage plan.

> **Author's Note:**
> While the stipulated safety zone around an offshore platform is 500 m, it is better practice to chart courses 1'-2' off such platforms as an approach of 500 m will cause panic to the stand by vessel.

13.2 Offshore Renewable Energy Installations (OREI)

In order to minimise greenhouse gases and produce energy through renewable means, the wind, waves and tidal energy are all viable options. Wind turbine generators (wind farms) are well established in several sea areas around the world. In addition, a number of prototype and actual wave and tidal energy generating systems have also been established. As most of these structures exist at sea, they present new challenges to safe navigation. However, by accessing the relevant information and effective passage planning, these challenges can be overcome.

A mariner generally has three options:

- Avoid the OREI area completely
- navigate around the edge of the OREI
- in the case of a wind farm, navigate, with caution, through the wind farm area.

13.2.1 Offshore Wind Farms

The most rapidly increasing structures at sea and close to the shore are wind turbine generators (WTG). The WTG may be a single structure or in a group called a Wind Farm (WF). These installations do not have the status of the islands.

The structures are developed to keep the WTG at a certain distance above the sea level, some installations incorporate a separate anemometer mast. In shallow waters, they are based on a monopile structure erected from the seabed, others opt for a tripodpile structure. In deeper waters the WTG may be supported on top of a single or group floating structures.

Figure 13.11 WTG's

In a WF, a corner structure, or another significant point on the boundary of the WF, is called a Significant Peripheral Structure (SPS). On a large or extended WF, the distance between SPSs should not normally exceed 3 nm. If the distances are more than 3 nm, Intermediate Peripheral Structures (IPS) are introduced. The distance between IPSs or the nearest SPS should not exceed 2 nm.

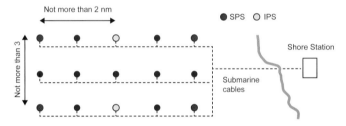

Figure 13.12 Plan for SPS and IPS with layout

Each WTG has a submarine cable that runs underground at the seabed and is connected to the shore based station, which usually houses the transformer(s).

13.2.1.1 Marking and Identification of WTG

Figure 13.13 Base of WTG tower

- During construction standard cardinal marks will be used around the area
- offshore the WTG should be marked so that it is conspicuous by day and night, consideration should

be given to the prevailing conditions of visibility and traffic in the area

- each WTG is given an identity number which must be illuminated with a low intensity hooded light. The ID number must be able to be seen at 3 m high and at a distance of 150 m
- in certain cases cardinal marks can be permanently placed adjacent to wind farms
- WTG towers and fins are painted matt white or light grey to blend in with the skyline
- the base of the WTG below the platform structure is either painted yellow or black and yellow bands
- single structures are marked according to the IALA Recommendation O-114 on the marking of offshore structures, with a white light flashing Morse code "U"
- the SPS must be marked with lights that are visible from all directions in the horizontal plane. These lights should be synchronised to display simultaneously an IALA "special mark" characteristic, flashing yellow, with a range of no less than 5 nm
- as a minimum, each SPS will show synchronised flashing characteristics. In some cases all SPSs may be synchronised
- selected IPS on the boundary of a wind farm between SPSs will be marked with flashing yellow lights which should be visible from all directions horizontally. The characteristics of these light areas differ from those displayed on the SPSs, and have a range of no less than 2 nm
- a red aircraft warning beacon at the top of the Nacelle
- the characteristics of the lights and marks will be displayed on the chart
- additional marking of the SPS and selected ISP as per IALA may include:
  - illuminating peripheral structures and all structures within the wind farm
  - racons, which may have the morse characteristic "U"
  - radar reflectors and radar target enhancers
  - AIS as an aid to navigation (as per IALA Recommendation A-126)
- aids to navigation on individual structures placed below the arc of the rotor blades, typically at the top of the yellow section
- where required on a wind farm, the typical range of a sound signal should be no less than 2 nm. Details of the sound signal will be given on the chart.

13.2.1.2 Emergency Procedures

A control station will have the remote control of all WTGs for each WF or individual WTG. Control is constantly manned. The national maritime administration (MCA in the UK) agrees safe shutdown procedures with the control room. These procedures are tested twice each year.

MRCC and the control station maintain a chart showing the GPS position and ID of every unit. MRCC and the control station also exchange contact numbers.

Each structure has an access ladder that allows the service or inspection personnel to climb to the platform, the access ladder can also be used as a refuge point. There is an access hatch above the platform. Each WTG also has a Nacelle hatch so that a SAR winchman can enter. The platform is positioned 15 m above the highest astronomical tide (HAT) and marks the start of turbine tower.

If there is a collision the MRCC is required to establish the ID of the WTG. Control is then advised of the WTG's ID and shutdown is initiated. This procedure is also tested twice every year.

Figure 13.14   A. turbine 90° to wind B. helicopter winchman C. boarding arrangement from sea

If a rescue is to be carried out by helicopter, the fin rotors are locked shut in position. The Nacelle is slewed 90° to bring the rotor axis in line with the wind. Once this is done a helicopter can safely approach the WTG Nacelle and carry out the rescue.

13.2.1.3 Navigational Considerations

- Each individual structure has an exclusion zone of 50 m and all ships, not involved with the structure, must respect these safety zones
- if there is adequate safe water it may be prudent when planning a larger ships voyage to set tracks at least 2 nm clear of WTG fields
- all wind farms will be charted by the hydrographic authorities either by a group of black wind turbine chart symbols, or an outer limit with an encircled black wind turbine symbol. The outer limit will be a black dashed line, or a magenta T - shaped dashed line if there are navigational or other restrictions in the area. The charting of the submarine cables associated with wind farms will depend on the chart scale. Mariners should pay attention to the notes on the chart that relate to the WF
- mariners should also note the hazards associated with anchoring or trawling near the submarine cables. All craft operating within a WF should avoid anchoring except in emergencies
- in planning a voyage mariners must appraise and assess all hazards and the associated risks. The proximity of wind farms and turbines should be included in this assessment
- WTGs are generally spaced 500 m or more apart depending on the size of the turbine. Small craft may be able to navigate safely within the WF area, whereas larger ships must keep well clear
- most of the WF that are operating or planned are located in relatively shallow water, eg on shoals or sand banks that are not accessible by larger ships. The next generation of WFs will be constructed in deeper water, where navigable channels in the area may restrict ships to a particular route that passes close to a WF boundary
- WTG structures may, over time, affect the depth of water in their vicinity. In dynamic seabed areas with strong tidal streams, changes in the scouring of the seabed may occur. This may result in unreliable depth information. Some WTGs have scour protection, these are boulders and/or concrete mattresses which are placed around their base
- WTG structures may obstruct tidal streams locally, creating eddies nearby, these are only likely to be significant very close to the structures
- ships involved in turbine maintenance and safety duties may be encountered within or around a WF. There may also be fishing vessels operating in the area. Mariners should be aware that the structures may occasionally obscure these small craft. This is particularly relevant at night. Large ships may also become obscured, for example if they are on the opposite side of a WF. A good lookout should therefore be maintained at all times

- in coastal areas shore marks may be obscured by WF structures. Mariners should be aware of this. In particular, the characteristics of lights at night may need to be carefully verified if the turbines temporarily mask them
- the ship's position should be plotted by using another method when a WF obscures coastal marks
- in or adjacent to larger WFs, there may be offshore electrical transformer stations present. These are similar in appearance to small offshore production platforms. Submarine cables link the turbines to this substation
- offshore WTGs are required to have their lowest point of rotor sweep at least 22 m above Mean High Water Springs. This provides ample clearance for the majority of small craft. Ships with a larger air draught should be careful
- a 10% reduction in wind velocity in the lee of a wind turbine can be expected. It is anticipated that this windshadow effect will be focused in a vertical air column up to heights of 15 m. The impact of the windshadow reduces with distance in the lee of a turbine. As the rotor wake interacts with the sea surface further shadow effects are predicted. The wind, having changed its flow through the rotors, is expected to recover downwind of the turbine. This results in windsheer as the wind back fills
- the downwind effect usually impacts proportionally to a ship's windage area and, for a sailing vessel the mast height. Mariners, particularly yachtsmen, must be aware of these effects. During the day normal visual clues should be noted and changes in leeway or balance of tidal stream to wind power anticipated. Visual clues are not so easily detected at night, due to this extra care should be taken
- ships must always proceed at safe a speed with due regard to Rule 6 of IRPCS'72 and operating in and around OREI. Requirements of Rule 19 along with Rule 6 should be applied in restricted visibility.

13.2.1.4 Navigation and Communications systems

- There is a minimal impact on Global Positioning Systems (GPS) receivers, VHF radio, cellular telephones and AIS. UHF and microwave systems suffer from the normal masking effect when turbines are in the line of transmissions
- mariners should be aware that not all ships are equipped with AIS
- under Rule 5 of IRPCS'72 Lookout, information from other sources should be taken into account which may include sound signals and VHF information, for example from a VTS, or AIS.

13.2.1.5 Radar use

- The WTGs produce strong radar echoes and are detected early
- at close range WTGs may produce multiple reflected and side lobe echoes that might mask the real targets. These develop at approximately 1.5 nm, the radar display will progressively deteriorate as the range closes

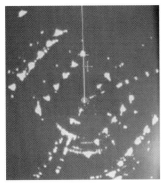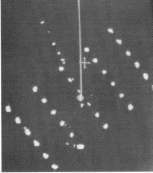

Figure 13.15 Radar displays from ship working within OREI field showing multiple and side lobe echoes

- there will be poor target definition when using long pulse
- small targets may only be identified when they are more than 300 m away from the WTG. However, the echo strength of a small target can fade on a 3 cm radar when close to WTG
- a 3 cm radar provides better target definition than a 10 cm one
- echoes of targets on a 10 cm radar may join up at distances of 0.6 nm
- target swap of echoes easily occurs on ARPA when a small target echo gets close to a WTG echo. This effect may even prevent small targets being acquired when they are moving close to a WTG
- when a shipping lane passes within this range it is likely that there will be interference along a line of WTGs. The target size of the turbine echo increases close to the turbine, consequently there will be a degradation of target definition and bearing discrimination. These effects are encountered on both 3 cm and 10 cm radars
- radar antennae that are unfavourably sited with regard to the ship's structure can enhance these effects, usually as indirect echoes
- careful adjustment of the gain or interference controls can suppress some of these spurious radar returns but there is a risk of losing targets with a small radar cross section, these may include buoys or small craft, particularly yachts or GRP constructed craft

- if these interfering echoes develop, the requirements of Rule 6 Safe speed are particularly applicable and must be observed with regard to the prevailing circumstances.

13.3 Offshore Wave and Tidal Energy Installations

These separate types of systems that use wave or tidal energy may not be clearly visible to the mariner.

13.3.1 Wave Energy Convertors (WECs)

WECs capture kinetic energy carried by waves and are likely to be located at or near the surface of an attachment or mooring point on the seabed. WECs can be visible or semi-submerged. Figure 13.16 is an image of a wave attenuator.

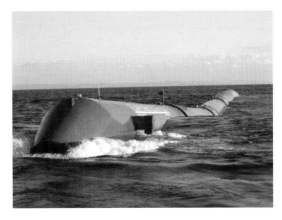

Figure 13.16 Wave attenuator

Other examples of wave energy generators include:

- Point absorber
- linear generator buoy
- oscillating wave surge converter
- oscillating water column
- overtopping device
- submerged pressure differential.

Other devices can also be used that may have unique and very different designs to the established types of technology.

13.3.2 Tidal Energy Convertors (TECs)

TECs capture potential energy from large bodies of water moving as the tides ebb and flow. TEC devices may be surface or sub surface structures incorporating a generator fixed or moored to the sea bed, capturing the potential energy present in the moving body of water associated with a tidal stream. Power takeoff is normally via cables to an electrical terminal.

Figure 13.17 Horizontal axis turbine

Other examples of tidal energy generators include:

- Horizontal axis turbine (enclosed blade tips)
- vertical axis turbine
- oscillating hydrofoil.

13.4 Visibility and Marking of Wave and Tidal Energy Installations

There are various methods that can be used to fix WECs and TECs to the seabed, they will affect visibility above the surface. Visibility will depend on the device type. Some installations are totally submerged while others may protrude slightly above the sea surface. Marking will be based on IALA Recommendation O-131 on the marking of offshore wave and tidal energy devices.

Wave and tidal energy extraction devices should be marked as a single unit or as a block or field as follows:

- When structures are fixed to the seabed and extend above the surface, they should be marked in accordance with the IALA recommendations O-117
- areas containing surface or sub-surface energy extraction devices, wave and/or tidal, should be marked using appropriate navigation buoys in accordance with the IALA Buoyage System, fitted with the corresponding top marks and lights
- in addition, active or passive radar reflectors, retro reflecting material, Racons and/or AIS transponders should be fitted as the level of traffic and degree of risk requires
- the boundaries of the wave and tidal energy extraction field should be marked by lit Navigational Lighted Buoys, so they are visible to mariners from all relevant directions in the horizontal plane, by day and at night. Taking the results of a risk assessment into account, lights should have a nominal range of at least 5 nm. The boundaries should normally be marked with the appropriate IALA Cardinal marks for northerly, easterly, southerly and westerly sides. In addition, depending on the shape and size of the field, intermediate lateral or special marks may need to be deployed

- in the case of a large or extended energy extraction field, the distance between navigation buoys marking the boundary should not normally exceed 3 nm
- individual wave and tidal energy devices within a field extending above the surface should be painted yellow above the waterline, taking into account environmental considerations. Depending on the boundary marking, individual devices within the field do not need to be marked. However, if they are marked, they should have flashing yellow lights so that they are visible to the mariner from all relevant directions in the horizontal plane. The flash sequence of the lights should be different to those displayed on the boundary lights with a range of no less than 2 nm
- AIS as an aid to navigation (IALA Recommendation A-126) on selected peripheral wave and/or tidal energy devices may be installed
- a single wave and/or tidal energy extraction structure, standing alone, extending above the surface should be painted black with red horizontal bands, and should be marked as an Isolated Danger as set out in the IALA Maritime Buoyage System
- if a single wave and/or tidal energy device is not visible above the surface but is considered a hazard to surface navigation, it should be marked by an IALA special mark yellow buoy with a yellow flashing light and a range of no less than 5 nm
- notices to Mariners should be issued to publicise the establishment of a wave and/or tidal energy device or field. The Notice to Mariners should include the marking, location and extent of these devices/fields
- it should also be noted that many tidal concepts have fast moving subsurface elements, eg whirling blades, these should be passed at a safe distance.

Author's Note
The requirement to find energy for the human race to use is ever more significant. Sea covers approximately 70% of the world's surface area, as a result it likely to have more energy resources within it. The elements of the wind, waves and flow of water can be used to generate energy. Some mariners work to survey, install and maintain such systems. All mariners must be fully aware of the effects such installations have on the safety of navigation, and should be able to adopt procedures to overcome any problems.

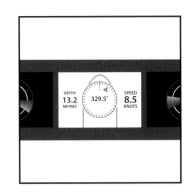

14

ECDIS and IBS

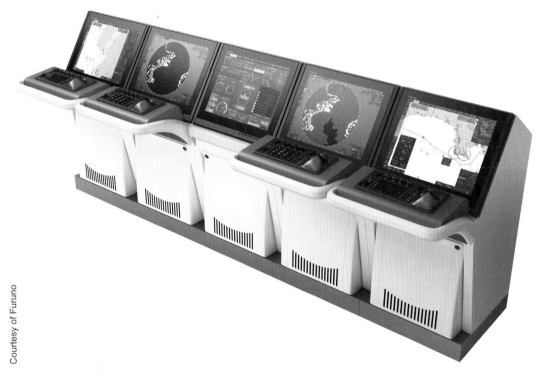

Figure 14.1   Bridge layout with IBS

14.1 ECDIS

An Electronic Chart Display and Information System (ECDIS) is an electronic chart system that meets IMO specifications for carrying charts, as per SOLAS Chapter V. The ECDIS system must be type approved to IEC61174. The ECDIS must also conform to A.817(19). MSC232(82).

Used correctly, ECDIS provides enhanced navigation through dynamic display of vessel position – past, present and future. It also ensures situation and spatial awareness when compared to using traditional paper charts. Many manufacturers provide ECDIS for marine use.

14.1.1 Requirements

Several requirements must be satisfied before a ship can start using ECDIS as its primary method of navigation:

- Installed ECDIS is type approved
- official data (ENC and/or RNC) is installed for the intended passage
- a back-up is available in the form of a second type approved ECDIS is available, or a full paper chart backup
- the Master and all watch officers have successfully completed the approved generic and type specific training
- in case of ENCs, only official charts are used
- in case of RNC, backup paper charts are available
- main and Uninterrupted Power Supply (UPS) is available
- any additional flag state requirements are satisfied.

Operators and Masters must ensure that in order to achieve the desired results by using ECDIS, standard shipboard procedures must be adopted. These may be part of SMS, Standing Orders and/or Checklists. There should be procedures for the following (but not necessarily limited to):

- Arrangements to ensure that up to date charts and data are always available
- arrangements to ensure that charts and data are properly maintained and corrected
- arrangements to monitor the correct operation and accuracy of all devices/sensors making an input to ECDIS by checking errors and accuracy, applying them and maintaining a proper log
- ensure that sensor inputs are properly configured and calibrated during ECDIS installation, if not there will be inherent errors in the system
- all bridge officers and the Master have successfully completed all the approved generic and type specific training
- procedures to perform Navigational Risk Assessment
- procedures to regularly check and test backup systems and an alternative power supply
- procedures to prevent over reliance on one system, there should be a regular cross check of position (GNSS input to ECDIS) using a different method

- procedures to configure ECDIS to suit the environment and conditions
- procedures to properly use the Safety Contour and Safety Depth values
- mariners ability to fix the ship's position using other techniques, eg Visual, Radar, Celestial and also to generate accurate DR and EP, in case the primary GNSS input fails
- readily available user guide in the form of a hard copy on the bridge, and the help files installed on the ECDIS.

ECDIS requires three mandatory sensor inputs:

- GNSS for continuous position fixing capability
- gyro for heading input
- speed log for speed and distance input.

In addition, other sensor inputs can enhance navigational capability:

- Additional GNSS
- additional gyro
- radar/ARPA (1 and 2)
- echo sounder
- AIS
- anemometer
- NAVTEX.

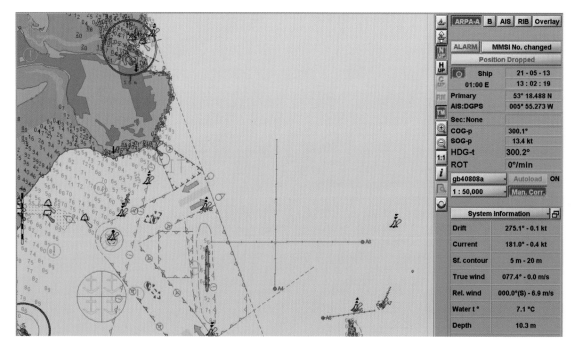

Figure 14.2   ECDIS with ARPA targets

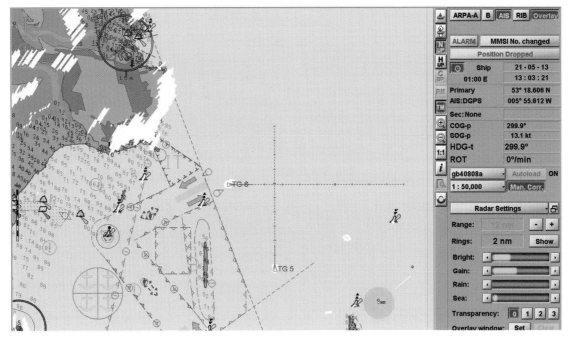

Figure 14.3 ECDIS with AIS overlay

14.1.1.1 Training

STCW, as amended, make ECDIS training mandatory:

Table A-II/1	Use of ECDIS to maintain safety of navigation
Table A-II/2	Maintain the safety of navigation by using ECDIS and associated navigation systems to assist command decision making
Table A-II/3	Plan and conduct a coastal passage and determine position, through the knowledge of and ability to use ECDIS (This only applies to certification as Master under 500 GT)

Generic training can be conducted through an approved flag State, 5 day generic ECDIS course, in accordance with IMO 1.27 Model ECDIS course.

Once training is completed all navigators should undertake Type Specific ECDIS training so that they are familiar with the equipment being used on their ship. All officers must be familiar with the specific equipment on board before taking responsibility for its use.

14.1.1.2 ENC

An Electronic Navigational Chart (ENC) of content, structure and format issued by a government authorised Hydrographic Office is used for ECDIS. The

ECDIS performance standards developed by the IMO and IHO for ENCs are:

- **S57** ENC Product Specification
- **S52** ENC Symbols.

ENCs conform to IHO specifications and, when used with a type-approved ECDIS system with adequate back-up arrangements, meet the SOLAS Chapter V chart carriage requirement. ENCs are vector charts and are compiled from a set of individual items or objects, arranged in layers from the database. A number of these layers can be added or removed by the operator. ENCs allow the interrogation of any object for the purpose of finding out more details about it.

An ENC can be displayed as a seamless chart. While using ECDIS, the change over from one chart to the other would generally be automatic, unless the navigator loads the chart manually. The navigator must be aware that on occasions ENC data may be from different suppliers and most ECDIS would handle overlaps within the same usage bands, but some ECDIS may handle and display data in a different way. In these circumstances there is a possibility that the data being displayed may not be updated to the same level, two chart cells may be displayed simultaneously.

The Hydrographic offices of individual governments are responsible for providing ENCs for their own coastal and inland waters, using up to date hydrographic information. Not all governments produce the required ENCs, a significant part of the earth is not at present covered by ENCs.

14.1.1.3 RNC

A Raster Navigational Chart (RNC) is a scanned version of the corresponding paper chart. RNC's can also be used with the ECDIS system when ENC's are not available and an appropriate folio of up to date paper charts are available. RNCs do not make full use of ECDIS system functionality as several of the functions related to route checking and monitoring cannot be performed. As the whole world is not covered by ENCs, Raster charts are likely to remain in use for some time.

14.1.2 Use of ECDIS

The navigator of a ship equipped with ECDIS can use it effectively for all stages of a passage if it is used correctly. Planning and monitoring can be performed on all makes of approved systems. ECDIS allows a route to be checked and verified when vector charts are being used.

In open sea/ocean, ECDIS is mainly used as a planning tool as well as for navigating out of sight of land as the primary means of navigation using GNSS. Integrity should be checked by using celestial observations and any other available systems. It is recommended that the Safety Frame/Anti Grounding Cone is set 15 minutes ahead and 0.2 nm to port and starboard.

In coastal waters, the primary source would remain GNSS. Radar Information Overlay (RIO), when it is available, should be used to monitor the coast line as detected by the optimum radar set-up. Position should also be fixed by using visual means and radar to verify accuracy of GNSS. DR and EP should also be projected. Continuous monitoring techniques like parallel indexing should also be used. It is recommended that the Safety Frame/Anti Grounding Cone is set 12 minutes ahead and 0.1 nm to port and starboard.

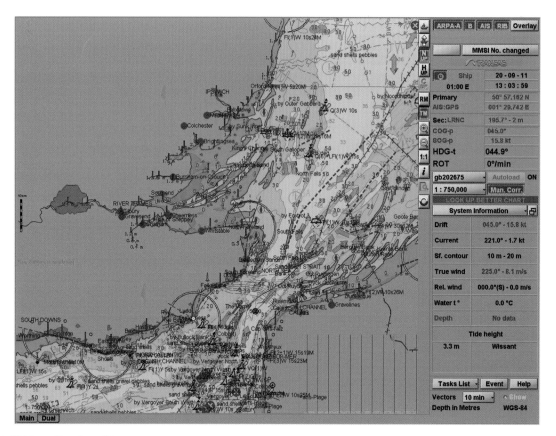

Figure 14.4   ENC small scale – all layers

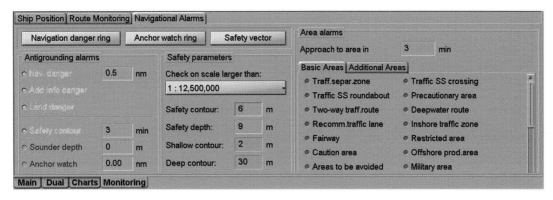

Figure 14.5 Safety contour and depth settings

In pilotage and confined waters, ECDIS should be used in conjunction with RIO to verify position input. When available, input should be switched to DGPS or an Augmented System. Regular cross checks with other visual and continuous monitoring techniques should be performed. It is recommended that the anti grounding cone is set 3 minutes ahead and 0.1 nm to port and starboard.

In restricted visibility, ECDIS should be used in conjunction with a dedicated Radar/ARPA display. Depending on the circumstances, an AIS overlay can also be used on ECDIS.

The navigator will set a safety depth to detect depths that are a danger to navigation. Care must be taken to ensure that the setting is configured correctly and not left at the default setting, usually 30 m. Safety contour is also set up to distinguish between safe and unsafe water. The safety contour is generated as a bold line on ECDIS. If the safety contour is dropped due to a change of chart showing the ship's current position, an alarm is generated and the system automatically sets the safety contour equal to a deeper available depth contour.

14.1.2.1 Manoeuvring Data

When commissioned, the ECDIS will receive the ship's manoeuvring data. But before passage planning can begin, the ship's exact condition for the intended voyage must be loaded. This helps the system, as it calculates the wheel-over distances and the curved path followed by the ship when it alters course. At the planning stage, the navigator uses the draught and air-draught of the ship to set the safe-depth/safe-height parameters for the current voyage. These may have to be changed for different stages of the voyage. For example, in open coastal waters, a larger margin may be allowed, while in narrow and pilotage waters only the safe margin should be used.

Approved systems set a safety guard zone around the ship. This is based on its physical characteristics plus half-of-beam ahead, astern and either side. The ship's time course vector over the ground is also displayed, based on the look-ahead time and current speed.

14.1.2.2 Position System Failure while using ECDIS - sample routine

The watchkeeping officers must ensure:

- The alarm is read to identify the failed sensor and acknowledge the alarm
- start to plot positions using visual and radar techniques
- select the secondary position fixing system, if one is not available select DR/EP mode, ensure that the gyro error is known and applied
- in coastal waters, use RIO to cross check position
- identify other navigational and communication equipment affected by the failed system
- inform the Master as soon as possible
- follow the checklist to rectify fault and call ETO
- modify the ship's route as required
- on restoration of Primary Fixing System, correlate with RIO and other techniques
- perform a route check
- inform the Master of the system resuming full and correct service.

14.1.2.3 Route Planning

The principles of voyage planning were discussed in Chapter 2, in this section routeing done on ECDIS is being considered. The following is a summary of generic route creation on ECDIS, navigators must ensure that they apply any additional requirements based on the specific system that is on their ship.

- Chart Autoload and Autoscale should be ON
- unload old routes, manual corrections and information to create a blank canvas

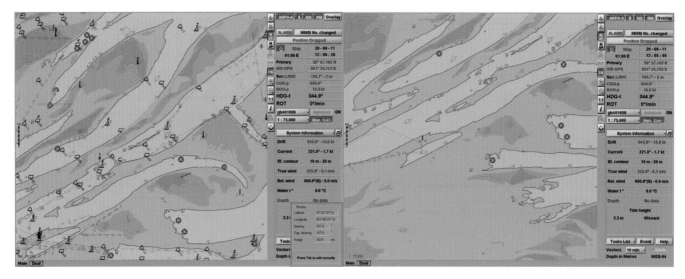

Figure 14.6 ENC standard layer (L) and base layer (R)

- standard or base display is used to reduce screen clutter
- switch to planning screen, use a scale so that the start and end positions are in the same frame
- selecting chart priority, use ENC or RNC
- select new route
- plot waypoints graphically or by data entry and name waypoints
- set route defaults to rhumb line or great circle and line properties to rhumb line or great circle
- set port and starboard XTD
- set safety depth and safety contour taking into consideration the maximum draught during voyage
- modify waypoints to allow for critical stages of the passage, and activate appropriate layers for the necessary safe information to be displayed
- amend the route further through reference to the source data diagram
- navigator should allow for appropriate XTD for various stages of the route for the environmental conditions, sea room availability, margins of safety and traffic density, etc
- check that arrival circles are set in line with wheel over points, if being used
- set helm angle and compare ECDIS generated turn radius with the ship's manoeuvring data to ensure it is realistic
- plan should be completed using all the relevant information from all sources, comparisons should be made to ensure that the plan looks realistic
- an ECDIS (working with ENCs) will recognise and warn of dangers on the planned track and will not save the route. To accept the route, the navigator must adjust the course, distance or waypoint

- an appropriate name should be given to the route and should be saved.

On an ECDIS, the route can be developed in two ways. In the first, you can either use a smaller display scale, or a small scale paper chart in case of RNC, to plan the route. In the second method, waypoints can be selected at intended alterations and the system can calculate the course and distances between them. The keypad should be used to enter waypoints, taking the numbers from the chart or by using the cursor to select the on-screen digits. The navigator has other options to establish a waypoint, eg ERBL, EBL or VRM.

You can change parameters for the XTD during the voyage. Settings are controlled either manually or automatically by the system:

- In automatic mode, the voyage plan safety zone = 2 × XTD, plus a ship width on either side of the track. This safety zone may bypass the waypoints and is only established around the track
- in manual setting, the navigator will define the port and starboard XTD limits.

Use the route-editing function in these circumstances:

- If a start or end waypoint has been created or added, check the newly created leg of the route for dangers to navigation
- where a waypoint in the middle of the route has been added or moved, check the route legs on either side and edit (if appropriate)
- where XTD has been altered without changing the waypoint position.

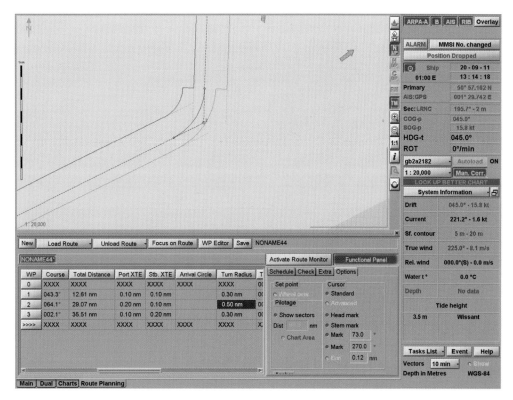

Figure 14.7   Wheel over at waypoint and XTD

14.1.2.4 Route Checking

Route check automatically checks for the presence of dangers to navigation against the set parameters within the XTD. Route checking should be performed:

- On completion of route planning
- by the Master before he/she approves the route
- on modification of a route
- after a system malfunction and restoration or GNSS position loss and restoration
- after charts have been updated.

It is only possible to detect dangers on the ENC and not the RNC. In addition the route check function will only detect certain dangers to navigation when these are located within the XTD. However, an RNC using a manual correction that has an associated danger, can be detected within the XTD.

It is useful to perform the check on a setting of the smallest scale ENC used for the route, when the check is being performed on chart scales specified by the operator.

14.1.2.4.1 Route Check - sample routine

- Configure the display so that all navigational dangers can be viewed
- select ENC as chart priority

- route check parameters should be configured correctly
- when the check is being performed on operator specified chart scales, ensure that the smallest scale ENC setting is used for the route
- confirm correct XTD for various/all legs of the passage is set correctly for the relevant factors
- make use of the Check Route Planning function to check the route
- visit each alarm generated and edit the route to achieve the desired safety
- after visiting and verifying all alarms, manually scroll along the full route on a 1:1 scale for checking
- apply any manual corrections as required
- apply any additional information required
- re-check ETD, ETA, distance and tidal information
- save the route
- print as required
- create and save backup
- Master to verify and confirm route
- make a record of the Master's approval
- upload the route and schedule into both/all ECDIS
- if required, pilotage notebook can be created
- if updates are installed before departure/execution, the route should be checked again, the Master should approve this route
- route should be made active prior to execution.

14.1.2.5 Safety Zones

When a safety zone violation occurs, an ECDIS working on ENCs triggers danger alarms for specified safety parameters, as well as a variety of other specific object types. The navigator can add danger areas and other features to the RNCs to obtain danger warnings. The ECDIS should have alarms for several events including:

- A Chart on a different datum than the positioning system
- chart data displayed overscale
- a larger scale chart available
- deviation from planned route
- exceeding cross track limits
- approach to waypoints or other critical stages
- ARPA or AIS target enters the Guard Zone
- failure of the position fixing system that is providing data
- the ship crossing a safety contour
- a system failure or malfunction.

It is possible to annotate the Electronic chart systems with messages in support of navigational activities. The navigator may add T&P notices, Master or pilot calls, etc. A large number of options are available and these vary with the system in use.

14.1.2.6 Execution

Before departure the voyage plan should be activated. It is important that the relevant panel or screen is displayed. The navigator should ensure the appropriate

configuration, eg safety depth, safety contour, anti-grounding cone, safety parameters. The ECDIS management cards should be kept updated and on location. A record should be maintained of all XTD used in case there is a deviation.

The navigator should follow the route and use look ahead for any voyage notes. The latest weather forecasts should be obtained and check whether the route will be adversely affected. Obtain current navigational warnings and plot the relevant information manually, check the route to see if it is affected. Perform checks to ensure that the ECDIS is correct, and perform position cross checks using various methods.

14.1.2.7 Monitoring

For monitoring purposes, the selected position fixing system integrated with the ECDIS allows the real time position of the ship to be displayed on the ECDIS. These features allow the following to be monitored:

- Heading Line
- COG Line
- heading vector
- XTE
- arrival circle
- turns
- waypoint names
- ARPA data on ship's motion parameters
- ARPA cursor
- target table
- predicted positions of the ship during the manoeuvre.

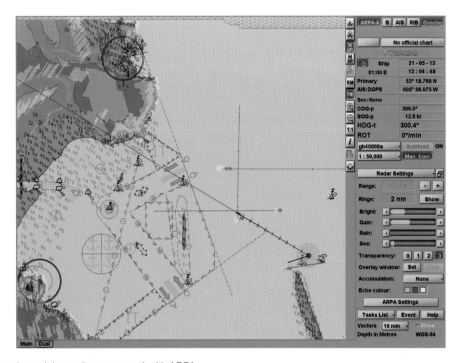

Figure 14.8   Radar overlay; minimum (transparency) with ARPA

Every navigator during the monitoring phase should check and confirm that the route is safe, they should also be aware of the nearest danger. The distance and time to the next waypoint should be known and the speed of approach should be calculated.

The navigator uses the various functions of the system to help monitor the voyage. The navigator should also be aware of any errors in the input sensors and ensure that the ECDIS is provided with the correct input. A cross check of position should be carried out using various systems. Use should be made of Visual, RIO, Parallel Indexing, Radar Ranges and Celestial Observations.

Features like EBRL, EBL and VRM are aids to monitoring. They allow visual or radar observations to confirm the integrity of the secondary systems and the overall monitoring process. The navigator may also overlay the radar/ARPA and AIS on ECDIS. The risk of information overload on the ECDIS is balanced by reducing the number of devices or displays that have to be monitored.

14.1.2.7.1 ECDIS Failure - sample routine

The watchkeeping officers must ensure the following is done:

- When a single ECDIS unit has failed, switch to or start using the second ECDIS unit
- inform the Master as soon as possible
- follow the checklist to rectify fault and call ETO
- if there is main power failure and both systems are running, they should switch to UPS. A controlled shutdown of one system should be carried out
- start the shut system in time before the first system UPS expires, then shutdown the first system
- when the system is restored after a power failure or uncontrolled shutdown, check that there is a power supply to all the ECDIS units and other systems that make an input to ECDIS, especially the primary position fixing system
- verify own vessel profile/shape is correct and is realistic for the scale being used on the display
- refer to bridge check cards and check all settings
- check correct route is loaded
- check correct scale is in use
- check correct primary position fixing system is selected
- check chart autoload is on
- check chart priority is correctly selected
- check anti grounding cone settings
- check safety depth is correct
- check safety contour is correct
- check units of measurement are correct
- check velocity vector is correct

- verify accuracy of primary position fixing system and determined position is correct
- verify heading/gyro input is correct and gyro error is determined
- verify that RIO is correct
- verify all corrections, particularly that manually input corrections are still in place
- carry out a route check
- perform alarm self test
- maintain a log of event.

14.1.2.8 ALARMS

An alarm requires the navigator to take action, whereas information is a notification and may not necessarily require action. The navigator should ensure that the audible alarm is on and it should be tested to verify that the alarm setting is correct. There are many types of alarms, some of the common ones are:

Route alarms

- Out of XTD
- WPT approach alarm
- out of schedule
- off leg course alarm
- end of route alarm.

Navigational alarms

- Anti grounding alarm
- safety contour
- navigational danger
- land danger
- aids to navigation
- off chart alarm
- primary/secondary divergence
- sounder alarm.

There are numerous other alerts, and the navigator should be familiar with them all.

14.1.3 Updating Electronic Charts

Ships use ENC and RNC under a license arrangement, which allows a chart specific permit to be used in the system. Only the most recent permits should be installed on ECDIS to ensure that the current editions of charts are being used. Permits are issued on CD or by email. This allows additional charts to be installed on ECDIS but to remain dormant. In case of an emergency or diversion, additional permits can be gained easily, allowing the required charts to be uploaded quickly.

ECDIS can be corrected manually or by adding corrections on a CD, corrections can also be accessed online and by email. Some versions have an online correction and update facility. The preferred set-up involves internet free ECDIS. ECDIS does not have virus protection, there must be procedures for scanning CD and flash drives for viruses before installing in to ECDIS.

Manual corrections are possible by using S-52 objects. Both ENC and RNC can have manual corrections applied. A log must be kept of all the corrections that are manually applied. Manual corrections are not necessarily removed following an update. The log will help in deleting any information that is no longer valid.

Notices to Mariners are issued in CD format on a weekly basis. The update also includes T&P Corrections. The corrections contained in the CD are cumulative. This means that if there is a back log, the most recent CD will apply all corrections to the ENCs and RNCs.

The navigator must be aware that the updating process can be lengthy and should ideally be done when the ship is alongside. If an update is required while underway, a risk assessment should be conducted, as there are significant safety implications including:

- Updating uses capacity of the system, therefore ECDIS may be diverted from the primary navigation task
- updating is only possible on some systems when safety monitoring is turned off
- following an update, all routes must be rechecked.

Taking the above into consideration, only one ECDIS should be corrected at a time. Once the update is complete, the navigator should be satisfied that the ECDIS is performing correctly, before updating the next ECDIS or synchronising through LAN.

After updating some checks should be carried out on random ENCs and RNCs to ensure that the corrections and new editions are done correctly. The CD must be kept secure and a proper log of the corrections should be maintained, along with maintaining the licenses and permits.

In addition to chart corrections and updates, the navigator should ensure that system and software updates are also installed, tested as per the manufacturers' instructions and logged.

14.1.4 Precautions During the Use of ECDIS

The navigator should always be aware of things going wrong, for this reason there should be a critical approach to everything, eg is this expected, is it making sense, is it looking right? The navigator should have full situational awareness as at times there is intense

pressure, on other occasions there may be little time to react at critical stages.

The three most important elements that must be understood when using ECDIS are the scale being used, the setting of the safety depth and safety contour. Some other commonly recurring interpretation issues are:

- What type of stabilisation is in use? Is there any confusion over orientation? What is the nature of the vectors being displayed? (head-up, north-up, course-up, relative, true, ground stabilised, etc)
- is the correct display mode being used? Is the display for planning, maintenance or navigation? What is the scale and what reference systems are in use?
- is the mariner aware that in auto track control, the observed position is being controlled and not the ship's actual position?
- how reliable is the primary position fixing source? (eg 95% probability of GPS accuracy).

The navigator should carry out regular checks using RIO and plotting fixes, the accuracy of the fixes must be checked before accepting the same. In addition, checks should be carried out and logged on the accuracy of primary and secondary positioning systems. This can be done by comparing the vessel track display history against fixes that the navigator plotted at specific times.

On a coastal passage, the navigator should specifically monitor the primary track against the secondary track at each check fix stage. Visual methods should be set as primary when navigating on the coast, subject to visibility and distance from the fixed marks. Alternatively, RIO should be set as primary. The interval between the check fixes should not be more than 30 minutes. However, an alignment check with the coastline using ROI should be done at intervals of no longer than 15 minutes.

On an ocean passage, primary and secondary ship tracks should be monitored at each check fix stage. The fixes should be checked using RIO when passing land or islands, as well as by celestial observations. The interval between check fixes should not be any longer than 30 minutes.

While plotting fixes that are being input specifically, the navigator should be aware that:

- Such fixes will not affect the ship's position if GNSS is set as the primary fixing system
- such fixes may not be displayed where track history or ship's track is not being displayed

- such fixes accepted by the navigator in DR/EP mode will determine the ship's position.

Back-up:

- The navigator should ensure that routes are properly backed-up
- manual corrections, logs and all relevant ECDIS data should be saved to disc to minimise the clutter on the hard disc. This also remains as data if there is an investigation.

The more recent versions of ECDIS system loads charts on to the hard drive of a computer. This is normally a stand-alone PC for ECDIS-use only. This PC must not be used for any other purpose. There are many documented instances of ECDIS failure where additional software for administration (or even games), have been loaded and used. Once the software is loaded, do not allow any other software to be loaded and back-up the PC with a suitable utility, such as Norton Ghost.

Load the ECDIS only PC with a portfolio of electronic charts, particularly those required for the voyage. They can be selected from an electronic catalogue

included on the ECDIS system and can be loaded either automatically or manually, at the discretion of the navigator. From the point it begins to load the charts, the system automatically displays the chart best suited to the view area. Automatic display allows the charts to be scrolled as the ship navigates from one chart area to another. Some systems only use the selected portfolio as a safety check on the voyage being planned and will ignore all other ECDIS system charts. The navigator must be certain that the selected charts are the current editions with up-to-date corrections applied.

- Navigators should be fully familiar and trained in using the equipment, as per the manufacturer's instructions
- the chart supply and correction arrangement should remain active
- the position displayed by the ECDIS system is only as good as that of the input system and over reliance should be avoided
- the position displayed should be cross checked using the monitoring tools of the ECDIS system, to confirm integrity of all systems
- unnecessary overlay of external data should be avoided.

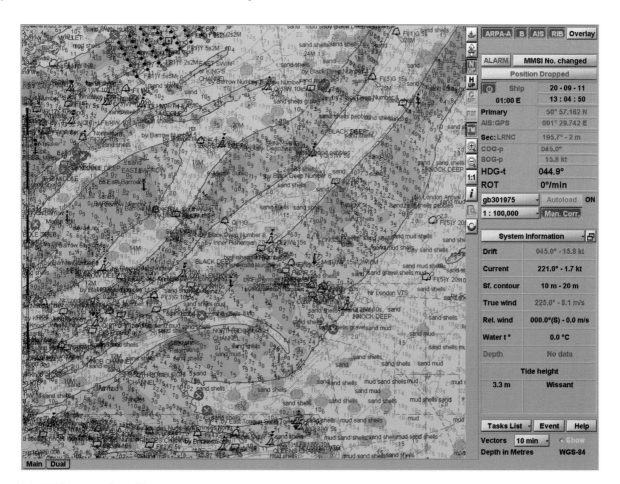

Figure 14.9 ENC large scale – all layers

The navigator must be aware of several issues when using ENCs:

- The symbols and colours used do not necessarily match across paper charts and ENCs. Colours are different for day and night displays
- when the scale of the chart is changed on an ECDIS system, the size of symbols will not change. This may cause problems when working on smaller scales as some objects from a lower layer may be hidden under objects on the upper layers
  - too many layers may hide data or clutter the display, especially on a smaller scale
  - de-layering may remove data that may be significant to safe navigation
  - objects or data could be hidden behind overlaid radar/ARPA or AIS data
  - the alarms will only activate against set parameters. If they have been set incorrectly, the alarms may not activate in time to take avoiding action.

The navigator must be aware of several key issues that make the RNC use different to the ENC:

- A Risk Assessment should be carried out every time RNCs are used
- an RNC can only be used in conjunction with an appropriate portfolio of up to date paper charts
- with RNC use, automatic alarms will not be triggered. Some user-inserted information can generate alarms, eg ship safety contour lines, clearing lines, danger areas, etc
- in congested waters, the accuracy of chart data may be less than the position-fixing system used for the ECDIS system
- the horizontal chart datum may be different to the position fixing system. The datum may also differ between RNCs
- RNCs are not seamless and the next chart usually has to be uploaded
- the RNC should be displayed on the scale of the paper chart. An increase or decrease in scale by excessive zooming in or zooming out can seriously degrade the quality of the display, as the size of charted features changes with the scale
- without selecting different scales, the look ahead capability may be limited. The determination of range and bearing of distant objects may be more difficult
- the colours displayed may not be the same as those on the paper charts and may be different for day and night displays, they may be difficult to view other than the Day Bright palette
- chart features cannot be removed or simplified to meet specific navigational situations

- interrogation of the charted features may not be possible and additional information about them cannot be obtained
- orientation of the display, other than chart-up/north-up, may make it difficult to interpret chart symbols and read text.

It is important to note that there are no spurious alarms in ECDIS and all alarms must be taken seriously. A list of alarms should be kept on the bridge, only the OOW should acknowledge alarms and warnings carefully assessing the nature and significance of the alarm, and take corrective action when required.

14.1.4.1 Taking Over The Navigational Watch - sample routine

The watchkeeping officers must ensure the following:

- Correct route is loaded in route monitoring
- correct display setting is shown
- chart in use is the most recent and corrected ENC or RNC
- review all voyage notes and check that quality of data is correct
- fix position on ECDIS using different techniques and confirm ECDIS is correct
- when operating in true motion, look ahead is correctly configured
- ECDIS bridge card/Check-Off Card are completed as the passage plan requires
- ECDIS management card is up to date
- safety depth and safety contour are correct as per ECDIS bridge card
- anti grounding cone is set as per the ECDIS bridge card/passage plan for the area of operation
- XTD is applied and displayed correctly
- velocity vector is configured correctly
- chart set to optimum scale
- secondary ECDIS also set up and operating as set above orders
- where ECDIS is in use
  - correct chart datum in use
  - paper back up chart is corrected and available for ready reference
  - chart notes are understood
  - source data diagram is understood.

14.1.4.2 Hazards Associated with ECDIS Use

Note these potential hazards with using an ECDIS:

- Next RNC chart is not available
- planned passage may cross or enter designated areas
- vessel's position between charts may not be the same

- accuracy of navigational information may be doubtful
- datum shift
- hardware failure
- software failure
- power failure
- failure to update charts
- input information failure (position, course, speed)
- virus infection of computer files
- competency of the ECDIS operator/OOW
- complacency/over reliance by the OOW.

14.2 Integrated Bridge Systems

IMO defines an IBS as a: "*combination of systems which are interconnected in order to allow centralized access to sensor information or command/control from workstations, with the aim of increasing safe and efficient ship's management by suitably qualified personnel.* Performance standards for integrated bridge systems were adopted by the IMO in 1996 Resolution MSC.64(67)."

The revised SOLAS Chapter V adopted in December 2000 says in **Regulation 19** paragraph 6: "*Integrated bridge systems shall be so arranged that failure of one sub-system is brought to immediate attention of the officer in charge of the navigational watch by audible and visual alarms, and does not cause failure to any other sub-system. In case of failure in one part of an integrated navigational system, it shall be possible to operate each other individual item of equipment or part of the system separately.*"

To reduce the time spent on data processing by the OOW, ships bridges are being automated at an increasing rate. The bridge team is also being provided with displays that allow for a quick evaluation of the navigation picture. The integrated bridge system

may be based on several different combinations of equipment and systems, these are designed for an individual ship's needs. Accessibility is an important issue. Some basic elements are:

- Computer processor and network
- chart arrangement
- display arrangements
- planning station
- radar and ARPA
- control system.

As per MSC 64(67), the IBS should provide functional integration ensuring the following requirements are met:

> *The functionality of IBS should ensure that its operation is at least as effective as for stand-alone equipment*
>
> *Continuously displayed information should be reduced to the minimum necessary for safe operation of the ship. Supplementary information should be readily accessible*
>
> *Where multifunctional displays and controls are used to perform functions necessary for safe operation of the ship they should be duplicated and interchangeable*
>
> *It should be possible to display the complete configuration, the available configuration and the configuration in use*
>
> *Each part to be integrated should provide details of its operational status, the latency and validity of essential information. A way should be provided within the IBS to make use of this information*
>
> *An alternative means of operation should be provided for essential functions*

Figure 14.10 Integrated bridge system
source – maritimusd.p.o

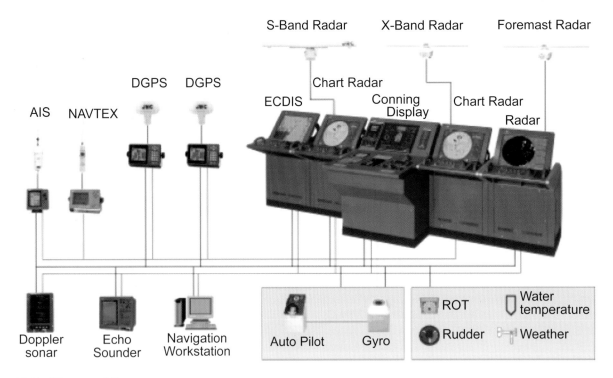

Figure 14.11 IBS connectivity
source: AWA marine – JRC IBS

An alternative source of essential information should be provided. The IBS should identify loss of either source

The source of information (sensor, result of calculation or manual input) should be displayed continuously or on request.

The most important element is the operator. The design of the system should provide intelligent options to the operator to minimise the workload and free up the bridge team. Fully integrated bridge systems can steer the ship on its planned route. It is very important to ensure that systems are maintained within the specifications and that any changes made during a service or refit will not adversely affect the integration. The integration should ensure that electronic signals are transmitted to at least the NMEA 0183 format, defining how data is to be transmitted from a navigational device. The standard allows the integrated use of different manufacturer's navigation devices and the design and manufacture of compatible modular marine electronic equipment.

The integrated bridge should be seen only as a mechanism to assist with decision making, and not one for making decisions.

Author's Note
ECDIS x 2 in compliance with SOLAS requirements now exempts a ship from carrying paper charts, unless RNCs are in use. When it is setup and used correctly, ECDIS provides enhanced navigation. It provides a real time display of position, as well as past and future positions. Knowledge of its abilities and limitations, as well as proper training and familiarisation will allow the mariner to use this aid to navigation effectively. Sample routines included in this chapter can also be used as standing orders.

These exercises are provided on each subject as an addition to those in the main text.

1   A ship with a service speed of 14 knots has to follow a great circle track from a position off Rio de la Plata 34° 55′S 055° 58′W (Zone +0400) to a position off Cape Town 33° 50′S 018° 20′E (Zone -0200). Additional distance on the coast is 158 nm. Find the:

   a. Distance on passage
   b. position of vertex
   c. distance along the meridian from Gough Island (40° 20′S 009° 55′W)
   d. ETA Cape Town if ship departed Rio on 5th May 2006 at 1400 local time.

Hint: Add the additional distance to the distance between the two positions. For ETA, convert to GMT, add steaming time and then convert to local time.

2   A vessel has to follow a great circle track from 33° 50′S 032° 20′E to 04° 10′N 101° 50′E. Find the:

   a. Distance between the two positions
   b. initial course
   c. final course
   d. position of vertex.

3   A vessel has to follow a great circle track from 38° 35′S 135° 44′E to 08° 50′S 118° 10′W. Find the:

   a. Distance between the two positions
   b. position of vertex
   c. latitudes where the track crosses 160°E, 180° and 160°W.

4   A vessel has to follow a composite great circle track from 40° 55′N 072° 50′ W to 44° 55′N 008° 20′W with a limiting latitude of 46° N. Find the:

   • Distance between the two positions initial course latitude where the track crosses the meridian of 055° 00′W.

Hint: For "c", apply 1st d.long to the initial longitude to obtain the meridian of vertex (latitude of vertex is the limiting latitude).

5   A ship is on a voyage from Singapore to the Panama Canal. The Master wishes to take advantage of the shortest possible route without contravening Load Line Rules. The ship is loaded to the Summer marks. 265 tonnes of fuel and water must be consumed, before the ship can enter the Winter zone at 35°N. The ship has a service speed of 16 knots and consumes 25 tonnes of fuel and water per day.

   Departure position 20° 00′N 121° 50′E
   Landfall position 20° 00′N 110° 00′W

Calculate the shortest legal distance on the passage if the additional distance on passage is 3641 nm. Calculate ETA Panama Canal (Balboa) (Zone +0500) if the ship departed Singapore (Zone -0800) on 3rd January 2006 at 1200 local time.

Hint: Add the additional distance to the distance between the two positions. For ETA, convert to GMT, add steaming time and then convert to local time. This way the date line will not affect the calculation.

6   At 1000 hrs, a ship is steering a course of 320°T at 10 knots in a TSS in conditions of restricted visibility. The ship's track is 1′ inwards of the outer edge of the TSS. On a 12′ range scale, the following radar observations were made over a period of 12 minutes:

	A	B	C
1000	010° T × 10′	135° T × 7′	170° T × 7′
1012	010° T × 6′.9	133° T × 5′	180° T × 4′.7

Compile a radar report for 1012.

The Master wishes to disengage from the present situation. Determine a single alteration of course or speed to disengage from the present situation, assuming that the alteration is effective instantly. Comment on the new situation and suggest further course of action.

7   At 1600 hrs, a ship steering a course of 280°T at 12 knots is approaching a narrow channel in conditions of restricted visibility. Target A is a headland. On a 12′ range scale, the following radar observations were made over a 15 minutes period:

	A	B	C
1600	290° T × 11′	280° T × 9′	130° T × 4′
1615	288° T × 8′	274° T × 5′	155° T × 1′.9

- Compile a radar report for 1615
- determine a single alteration of course or speed at 1620 to disengage from the present situation, assuming that the alteration is instantly effective
- comment on the new situation and suggest a further course of action.

8   A ship steering 165°T at 20 knots observes the following stars:

	Time	Bearing	Intercept
Star A	0545	200°T	1′.2 Towards
Star B	0551	105°T	1′.4 Away
Star C	0600	135°T	2′.6 Towards
Star D	0603	290°T	1′.3 Away

The DR position 22° 45′N, 064° 25′E was used for all intercepts.

Find the vessel's position at 0600 hrs.

9   At 1840 hrs, a ship in DR 22° 50′S, 070° 12′E, on a course of 325°T at 20 knots, makes the following observations:

	Time	Azimuth	Intercept
Star A	1826	210°T	3′.4 T
Star B	1835	260°T	1′.6 T
Star C	1841	340°T	6′.0 T

The DR was used for all intercepts.

Determine the observed position at 1835, as there was doubt that the index error had been applied the wrong way.

10   At 1625 GMT, 04 May 2006, a passenger ship is steering 180°T at 27 knots and is in position 21° 30′N 064° 40′E. A seriously injured seafarer on a bulk carrier is to be transferred to the passenger ship with a doctor on board at sunrise next morning. The bulk carrier at 1625 GMT is in position 18° 30′N 063° 56′E.

a.   Calculate the GMT sunrise for the passenger ship
b.   calculate the rendezvous position
c.   calculate the course and speed required of the bulk carrier in order to rendezvous successfully.

11   Three ships, X, Y and Z, are engaged in a line abreast (co-ordinated) a parallel track search on a course of 000° T at 12 knots, with a track spacing of 5′, during a search and rescue operation at 1400 hours. X is to the west, Y is in the middle and is the OSC's ship, with Z to the east of all. At 1430, due to the visibility deteriorating to 2′.0, Z is advised to shift station to a new position in the middle of tracks of X and Y, but to remain 2 miles behind.

If the maximum speed of Z is 15 knots, find the course required for Z in order to complete the manoeuvre in the shortest time, assuming any alteration is instantly effective.

Find the time when ship Z will be on the new station and its CPA with Y.

12   On 19th June 2006, at 1000 GMT a ship with a maximum speed of 18 knots, in 42° 30′N 020° 30′W, is required to rendezvous urgently with a ship bearing 190°T 60′ off, on a course of 260°T at 13 knots, in order to transfer an injured seafarer. Find:

a.   Course to steer
b.   the rendezvous position
c.   the daylight remaining to complete the operation.

Answers

1

a. 3746′ (158 + 3588′.1)
b. 40° 39′.1S 020° 21′.0W (Initial course S 67° 42′.2E)
c. 9′.2 (N of Gough Island, if required to report) (latitude 40° 10′.8S)
d. Steaming time = 3746/14 = 11d 03h 34m

Departure	May	05	1400
Zone (+0400)		+	0400
Departure GMT			1800
Steaming time		11	0334
Arrival GMT	May	16	2134
Zone (-0200)		+	0200
ETA local time	May	16	2334

2

a. 4533 (4532′.5)
b. N 75° E (74° 44′.5)
c. N 53° E (53° 28′.0)
d. 36° 44′.3S 006° 13′.9E

3

a. 5808′ (5808′.1)
b. 41° 38′.1S 161° 54′.1E (Initial course S 72° 57′.7E)
c. Latitudes 41° 37′.1S (160°E), 40° 11′.8S (180°), 34° 38′.5S (160°W)

4

a. 2780′ (1465′.5 + 652′.9 + 661′.1)
b. N 66° 49′.2E
c. 44° 57′.6 N (1st d.long = 33° 10′.5)

5

Distance to travel to consume 265t = 265/25
= 10.6d × 24h × 16kts = 4070′.4

Distance to limiting latitude	= 3203′.7
1st d.long	= 58° 40′.9
Distance along parallel of 35°N	= 866′.7 (4070′.4 − 3203′.7)
d.long for parallel sailing	= 17° 38′.0
Longitude where GC can be followed	= 161° 51′.1W
GC distance	= 2868′.3
Total distance	= 10580′ (4070′.4 + 2868′.3 + 3641′)

Steaming time = 10580/16 = 27d 13h 15m

Departure	Jan	03	1200
Zone (-0800)		-	0800
Departure GMT			0400
Steaming time		27	1315
Arrival GMT	Jan	30	1715
Zone (+0500)		-	0500
ETA local time	Jan	30	1215

6

Target	A	B	C
Bearing	010°T, steady	133°T, closing slowly	180°T, closing slowly
Range	6′.9, decreasing	5′, decreasing	4′.7, decreasing
CPA	0	0′.6	2′.2
TCPA	At 1039 in 27 m	At 1042 in 30 m	At 1032 in 20 m
BCPA	010°T	050°T	242°T
Course	230°T	320°T	326°T
Speed	11.5	20	22.2
Aspect	R40°	R07°	G34°
Comments	Crossing stbd to port, and TSS at right angles.	Overtaking, same course	Overtaking, converging slowly

Hint: In TSS speed reduction is a good choice, but this will not improve the situation with B. Alteration to port will result in a smaller CPA with C, ie developing a close quarters with C. Alteration to starboard will take the ship out of the TSS.

Alter course 60° to starboard to 020°T.

New CPA	2′.4	1′.6	3′.6
New TCPA	At 1032 in 15 m	At 1031 in 14 m	At 1023 in 6 m
New BCPA	306°T	200°T	210°T

The action may take the ship out of TSS. After 1032, adjust the course to rejoin the TSS at a small angle. (Join TSS at small angle from the side)

7

Target	A	B	C
Bearing	288°T, closing slowly	274°T, closing slowly	155°T, closing slowly
Range	8′, decreasing	5′, decreasing	1′.9, decreasing
CPA	1′.0	1′.2	1′.4
TCPA	At 1654 in 39 m	At 1633 in 18 m	At 1624 in 9 m
BCPA	205°.5T	200°T	197°.5T
Course	Set 021°T	128°T	284°T
Speed	Rate 3.4	4.6	21.2
Aspect	-	R34°	G51°
Comments		Crossing stbd to port	Overtaking, converging slowly

Hint: Should not alter course towards land, ie to starboard. Alteration to port is also a poor choice as vessel C will be at CPA in 9 minutes and is abaft the beam.

Stop at 1620. (Slowing down to steerage way may be considered, but the CPA with B will be less).

New CPA	7′.0	2′.3	1′.4
New TCPA	Past	At 1658 in 36 m	At 1621 in 1 m
New BCPA		288°.5T	214°T	194°T

The ship is setting 021°T in the direction of land. Resume speed when B is at CPA and adjust course to pass headland at a safe distance, allowing for the set.

8 Position at 0600 = 22° 39′.9N 064° 23′.7E
Hint: C from DR, D run-back, A and B run-on.
Stars B and D on opposite horizon. d.lat 5′.1 S, dep 1′.2W

9 Position at 1835 = 22° 49′S 070° 14′.1E (B-DR, A run-on, C run-back, azimuth <180°)

10 GMT: 5th May 2006 at 0113
R/V Position: 17° 32′.4N 064° 40′E (No change in longitude as course is 180°T)
Course: S 36° E Speed 8.1 kts (Dist 71′.2).

11 Course 305°T at 15 knots. Time 1507.CPA 1′.3.
Hint: Plot all the ships. Plot the new station for Z.
Join old Z (O) station to new Z (A′) station. Measure CPA with Y along OA′ line.

12

a. Course: 232°T
b. Position: 41° 15′N, 022° 38′.9W
c. Daylight remaining: 44 minutes (sunset = 1730 GMT, Time to R/V = 6h 46m)

ALMANAC
DATA 2006

A2 ALTITUDE CORRECTION TABLES 10°– 90° SUN, STARS, PLANETS

OCT. — MAR. SUN APR.— SEPT.

App. Alt.	Lower Limb	Upper Limb	App. Alt.	Lower Limb	Upper Limb
9 33			9 39		
	+ 10.8	− 21.5		+ 10.6	− 21.2
9 45			9 50		
	+ 10.9	− 21.4		+ 10.7	− 21.1
9 56			10 02		
	+ 11.0	− 21.3		+ 10.8	− 21.0
10 08			10 14		
	+ 11.1	− 21.2		+ 10.9	− 20.9
10 20			10 27		
	+ 11.2	− 21.1		+ 11.0	− 20.8
10 33			10 40		
	+ 11.3	− 21.0		+ 11.1	− 20.7
10 46			10 53		
	+ 11.4	− 20.9		+ 11.2	− 20.6
11 00			11 07		
	+ 11.5	− 20.8		+ 11.3	− 20.5
11 15			11 22		
	+ 11.6	− 20.7		+ 11.4	− 20.4
11 30			11 37		
	+ 11.7	− 20.6		+ 11.5	− 20.3
11 45			11 53		
	+ 11.8	− 20.5		+ 11.6	− 20.2
12 01			12 10		
	+ 11.9	− 20.4		+ 11.7	− 20.1
12 18			12 27		
	+ 12.0	− 20.3		+ 11.8	− 20.0
12 36			12 45		
	+ 12.1	− 20.2		+ 11.9	− 19.9
12 54			13 04		
	+ 12.2	− 20.1		+ 12.0	− 19.8
13 14			13 24		
	+ 12.3	− 20.0		+ 12.1	− 19.7
13 34			13 44		
	+ 12.4	− 19.9		+ 12.2	− 19.6
13 55			14 06		
	+ 12.5	19.8		+ 12.3	− 19.5
14 17			14 29		
	+ 12.6	− 19.7		+ 12.4	− 19.4
14 41			14 53		
	+ 12.7	− 19.6		+ 12.5	− 19.3
15 05			15 18		
	+ 12.8	− 19.5		+ 12.6	− 19.2
15 31			15 45		
	+ 12.9	− 19.4		+ 12.7	− 19.1
15 59			16 13		
	+ 13.0	− 19.3		+ 12.8	− 19.0
16 27			16 43		
	+ 13.1	− 19.2		+ 12.9	− 18.9
16 58			17 14		
	+ 13.2	− 19.1		+ 13.0	− 18.8
17 30			17 47		
	+ 13.3	− 19.0		+ 13.1	− 18.7
18 05			18 23		
	+ 13.4	− 18.9		+ 13.2	− 18.6
18 41			19 00		
	+ 13.5	− 18.8		+ 13.3	− 18.5
19 20			19 41		
	+ 13.6	− 18.7		+ 13.4	− 18.4
20 02			21 24		
	+ 13.7	− 18.6		+ 13.5	− 18.3
20 46			21 10		
	+ 13.8	− 18.5		+ 13.6	− 18.2
21 34			21 59		
	+ 13.9	− 18.4		+ 13.7	− 18.1
22 25			22 52		
	+ 14.0	− 18.3		+ 13.8	− 18.0
23 20			23 49		
	+ 14.1	− 18.2		+ 13.9	− 17.9
24 20			24 51		
	+ 14.2	− 18.1		+ 14.0	− 17.8
25 24			25 58		
	+ 14.3	− 18.0		+ 14.1	− 17.7
26 34			27 11		
	+ 14.4	− 17.9		+ 14.2	− 17.6
27 50			28 31		
	+ 14.5	− 17.8		+ 14.3	− 17.5
29 13			29 58		
	+ 14.6	− 17.7		+ 14.4	− 17.4
30 44			31 33		
	+ 14.7	− 17.6		+ 14.5	− 17.3
32 24			33 18		
	+ 14.8	− 17.5		+ 14.6	− 17.2
34 15			35 15		
	+ 14.9	− 17.4		+ 14.7	− 17.1
36 17			37 24		
	+ 15.0	− 17.3		+ 14.8	− 17.0
38 34			39 48		
	+ 15.1	− 17.2		+ 14.9	− 16.9
41 06			42 28		
	+ 15.2	− 17.1		+ 15.0	− 16.8
43 56			45 29		
	+ 15.3	− 17.0		+ 15.1	− 16.7
47 07			48 52		
	+ 15.4	− 16.9		+ 15.2	− 16.6
50 43			52 41		
	+ 15.5	− 16.8		+ 15.3	− 16.5
54 46			56 59		
	+ 15.6	− 16.7		+ 15.4	− 16.4
59 21			61 50		
	+ 15.7	− 16.6		+ 15.5	− 16.3
64 28			67 15		
	+ 15.8	− 16.5		+ 15.6	− 16.2
70 10			73 14		
	+ 15.9	− 16.4		+ 15.7	− 16.1
76 24			79 42		
	+ 16.0	− 16.3		+ 15.8	− 16.0
83 05			86 31		
	+ 16.1	− 16.2		+ 15.9	− 15.9
90 00			90 00		

STARS AND PLANETS

App. Alt.	Conⁿ
9 55	
	− 5.3
10 07	
	− 5.2
10 20	
	− 5.1
10 32	
	− 5.0
10 46	
	− 4.9
10 59	
	− 4.8
11 14	
	− 4.7
11 29	
	− 4.6
11 44	
	− 4.5
12 00	
	− 4.4
12 17	
	− 4.3
12 35	
	− 4.2
12 53	
	− 4.1
13 12	
	− 4.0
13 32	
	− 3.9
13 53	
	− 3.8
14 16	
	− 3.7
14 39	
	− 3.6
15 03	
	− 3.5
15 29	
	− 3.4
15 56	
	− 3.3
16 25	
	− 3.2
16 55	
	− 3.1
17 27	
	− 3.0
18 01	
	− 2.9
18 37	
	− 2.8
19 16	
	− 2.7
19 56	
	− 2.6
20 40	
	− 2.5
21 27	
	− 2.4
22 17	
	− 2.3
23 11	
	− 2.2
24 09	
	− 2.1
25 12	
	− 2.0
26 20	
	− 1.9
27 34	
	− 1.8
28 54	
	− 1.7
30 22	
	− 1.6
31 58	
	− 1.5
33 43	
	− 1.4
35 38	
	− 1.3
37 45	
	− 1.2
40 06	
	− 1.1
42 42	
	− 1.0
45 34	
	− 0.9
48 45	
	− 0.8
52 16	
	− 0.7
56 09	
	− 0.6
60 26	
	− 0.5
65 06	
	− 0.4
70 09	
	− 0.3
75 32	
	− 0.2
81 12	
	− 0.1
87 03	
	0.0
90 00	

Additional Corrⁿ

2006 VENUS

App. Alt. (°)	Additional Corrⁿ (')
Jan. 1 – Feb. 3	
0	
26	+ 0.5
46	+ 0.4
60	+ 0.3
73	+ 0.2
84	+ 0.1
Feb. 4–Feb. 18	
0	
29	+ 0.4
51	+ 0.3
68	+ 0.2
83	+ 0.1
Feb. 19–Mar. 13	
0	
34	+ 0.3
60	+ 0.2
80	+ 0.1
Mar. 14–May 2	
0	
41	+ 0.2
76	+ 0.1
May 3–Dec. 31	
0	
60	+ 0.1
Jan. 1–Jan. 23	
0	
41	+ 0.2
76	+ 0.1
Jan. 24–Dec. 31	
0	
60	+ 0.1

DIP

Ht. of Eye (m)	Corrⁿ	Ht. of Eye (ft.)
2.4		8.0
	− 2.8	
2.6		8.6
	− 2.9	
2.8		9.2
	− 3.0	
3.0		9.8
	− 3.1	
3.2		10.5
	− 3.2	
3.4		11.2
	− 3.3	
3.6		11.9
	− 3.4	
3.8		12.6
	− 3.5	
4.0		13.3
	− 3.6	
4.3		14.1
	− 3.7	
4.5		14.9
	− 3.8	
4.7		15.7
	− 3.9	
5.0		16.5
	− 4.0	
5.2		17.4
	− 4.1	
5.5		18.3
	− 4.2	
5.8		19.1
	− 4.3	
6.1		20.1
	− 4.4	
6.3		21.0
	− 4.5	
6.6		22.0
	− 4.6	
6.9		22.9
	− 4.7	
7.2		23.9
	− 4.8	
7.5		24.9
	− 4.9	
7.9		26.0
	− 5.0	
8.2		27.1
	− 5.1	
8.5		28.1
	− 5.2	
8.8		29.2
	− 5.3	
9.2		30.4
	− 5.4	
9.5		31.5
	− 5.5	
9.9		32.7
	− 5.6	
10.3		33.9
	− 5.7	
10.6		35.1
	− 5.8	
11.0		36.3
	− 5.9	
11.4		37.6
	− 6.0	
11.8		38.9
	− 6.1	
12.2		40.1
	− 6.2	
12.6		41.5
	− 6.3	
13.0		42.8
	− 6.4	
13.4		44.2
	− 6.5	
13.8		45.5
	− 6.6	
14.2		46.9
	− 6.7	
14.7		48.4
	− 6.8	
15.1		49.8
	− 6.9	
15.5		51.3
	− 7.0	
16.0		52.8
	− 7.1	
16.5		54.3
	− 7.2	
16.9		55.8
	− 7.3	
17.4		57.4
	− 7.4	
17.9		58.9
	− 7.5	
18.4		60.5
	− 7.6	
18.8		62.1
	− 7.7	
19.3		63.8
	− 7.8	
19.8		65.4
	− 7.9	
20.4		67.1
	− 8.0	
20.9		68.8
	− 8.1	
21.4		70.5

Ht. of Eye (m)	Corrⁿ (')
1.0 –	1.8
1.5 –	2.2
2.0 –	2.5
2.5 –	2.8
3.0 –	3.0
See table ←	
20 –	7.9
22 –	8.3
24 –	8.6
26 –	9.0
28 –	9.3
30 –	9.6
32 –	10.0
34 –	10.3
36 –	10.6
38 –	10.8
40 –	11.1
42 –	11.4
44 –	11.7
46 –	11.9
48 –	12.2

Ht. of Eye (ft.)	Corrⁿ (')
2 –	1.4
4 –	1.9
6 –	2.4
8 –	2.7
10 –	3.1
See table ←	
70 –	8.1
75 –	8.4
80 –	8.7
85	8.9
90 –	9.2
95 –	9.5
100 –	9.7
105 –	9.9
110 –	10.2
115 –	10.4
120 –	10.6
125 –	10.8
130 –	11.1
135 –	11.3
140 –	11.5
145 –	11.7
150 –	11.9
155 –	12.1

App. Alt. = Apparent altitude = Sextant altitude corrected for index error and dip.

ALTITUDE CORRECTION TABLES 0° – 10° SUN, STARS, PLANETS A3

App. Alt.	OCT. – MAR. SUN Lower Limb	Upper Limb	APR. – SEPT. Lower Limb	Upper Limb	STARS PLANETS
° ′	′	′	′	′	′
0 00	− 17.5	− 49.8	− 17.8	− 49.6	− 33.8
0 03	16.9	49.2	17.2	49.0	33.2
0 06	16.3	48.6	16.6	48.4	32.6
0 09	15.7	48.0	16.0	47.8	32.0
0 12	15.2	47.5	15.4	47.2	31.5
0 15	14.6	46.9	14.8	46.6	30.9
0 18	− 14.1	− 46.4	− 14.3	− 46.1	− 30.4
0 21	13.5	45.8	13.8	45.6	29.8
0 24	13.0	45.3	13.3	45.1	29.3
0 27	12.5	44.8	12.8	44.6	28.8
0 30	12.0	44.3	12.3	44.1	28.3
0 33	11.6	43.9	11.8	43.6	27.9
0 36	− 11.1	− 43.4	− 11.3	− 43.1	− 27.4
0 39	10.6	42.9	10.9	42.7	26.9
0 42	10.2	42.5	10.5	42.3	26.5
0 45	9.8	42.1	10.0	41.8	26.1
0 48	9.4	41.7	9.6	41.4	25.7
0 51	9.0	41.3	9.2	41.0	25.3
0 54	− 8.6	− 40.9	− 8.8	− 40.6	− 24.9
0 57	8.2	40.5	8.4	40.2	24.5
1 00	7.8	40.1	8.0	39.8	24.1
1 03	7.4	39.7	7.7	39.5	23.7
1 06	7.1	39.4	7.3	39.1	23.4
1 09	6.7	39.0	7.0	38.8	23.0
1 12	− 6.4	− 33.7	− 6.6	− 38.4	− 22.7
1 15	6.0	38.3	6.3	38.1	22.3
1 18	5.7	38.0	6.0	37.8	22.0
1 21	5.4	37.7	5.7	37.5	21.7
1 24	5.1	37.4	5.3	37.1	21.4
1 27	4.8	37.1	5.0	36.8	21.1
1 30	− 4.5	− 36.8	− 4.7	− 36.5	− 20.8
1 35	4.0	36.3	4.3	36.1	20.3
1 40	3.6	35.9	3.8	35.6	19.9
1 45	3.1	35.4	3.4	35.2	19.4
1 50	2.7	35.0	2.9	34.7	19.9
1 55	2.3	34.6	2.5	34.3	18.6
2 00	− 1.9	− 34.2	− 2.1	− 33.9	− 18.2
2 05	1.5	33.8	1.7	33.5	17.8
2 10	1.1	33.4	1.4	33.2	17.4
2 15	0.8	33.1	1.0	32.8	17.1
2 20	0.4	32.7	0.7	32.5	16.7
2 25	1.0	32.4	− 0.3	32.1	16.4
2 30	+ 0.2	− 32.1	0.0	− 31.8	− 16.1
2 35	0.5	31.8	0.3	31.5	15.8
2 40	0.8	31.5	0.6	31.2	15.4
2 45	1.1	31.2	0.9	30.9	15.2
2 50	1.4	30.4	1.2	30.6	14.9
2 55	1.7	30.6	1.4	30.4	14.6
3 00	+ 2.0	− 30.3	+ 1.7	− 30.1	− 14.3
3 05	2.2	30.1	2.0	29.8	14.1
3 10	2.5	29.8	2.2	29.6	13.8
3 15	2.7	29.6	2.5	29.3	13.6
3 20	2.9	29.4	2.7	29.1	13.4
3 25	3.2	29.1	2.9	28.9	13.1
3 30	+ 3.4	− 28.9	+ 3.1	− 28.7	− 12.9

App. Alt.	OCT. – MAR. SUN Lower Limb	Upper Limb	APR. – SEPT. Lower Limb	Upper Limb	STARS PLANETS
° ′	′	′	′	′	′
3 30	+ 3.4	− 28.9	+ 3.1	− 28.7	− 12.9
3 35	3.6	28.7	3.3	28.5	12.7
3 40	3.8	28.5	3.6	28.2	12.5
3 45	4.0	28.3	3.8	28.0	12.3
3 50	4.2	28.1	4.0	27.8	12.1
3 55	4.4	27.9	4.1	27.7	11.9
4 00	+ 4.6	− 27.7	+ 4.3	− 27.5	− 11.7
4 05	4.8	27.5	4.5	27.3	11.5
4 10	4.9	27.4	4.7	27.1	11.4
4 15	5.1	27.2	4.9	26.9	11.2
4 20	5.3	27.0	5.0	26.8	11.0
4 25	5.4	26.9	5.2	26.6	10.9
4 30	+ 5.6	− 26.7	+ 5.3	− 26.5	− 10.7
4 35	5.7	26.6	5.5	26.3	10.6
4 40	5.9	26.4	5.6	26.2	10.4
4 45	6.0	26.3	5.8	26.0	10.3
4 50	6.2	26.1	5.9	25.9	10.1
4 55	6.3	26.0	6.1	25.7	10.0
5 00	+ 6.4	− 25.9	+ 6.2	− 25.6	− 9.8
5 05	6.6	25.7	6.3	25.5	9.7
5 10	6.7	25.6	6.5	25.3	9.6
5 15	6.8	25.5	6.6	25.2	9.5
5 20	7.0	25.3	6.7	25.1	9.3
5 25	7.1	25.2	6.8	25.0	9.2
5 30	+ 7.2	− 25.1	+ 6.9	− 24.9	− 9.1
5 35	7.3	25.0	7.1	24.7	9.0
5 40	7.4	24.9	7.2	24.6	8.9
5 45	7.5	24.8	7.3	24.5	8.8
5 50	7.6	24.7	7.4	24.4	8.7
5 55	7.7	24.6	7.5	24.3	8.6
6 00	+ 7.8	− 24.5	+ 7.6	− 24.2	− 8.5
6 10	8.0	24.3	7.8	24.0	8.3
6 20	8.2	24.1	8.0	23.8	8.1
6 30	8.4	23.9	8.2	23.6	7.9
6 40	8.6	23.7	8.3	23.5	7.7
6 50	8.7	23.6	8.5	23.3	7.6
7 00	+ 8.9	− 23.4	+ 8.7	− 23.1	− 7.4
7 10	9.1	23.2	8.8	23.0	7.2
7 20	9.2	23.1	9.0	22.8	7.1
7 30	9.3	23.0	9.1	22.7	6.9
7 40	9.5	22.8	9.2	22.6	6.8
7 50	9.6	22.7	9.4	22.4	6.7
8 00	+ 9.7	− 22.6	+ 9.5	− 22.3	− 6.6
8 10	9.9	22.4	9.6	22.2	6.4
8 20	10.0	22.3	9.7	22.1	6.3
8 30	10.1	22.2	9.9	21.9	6.2
8 40	10.2	22.1	10.0	21.8	6.1
8 50	10.3	22.0	10.1	21.7	6.0
9 00	+ 10.4	− 21.9	+ 10.2	− 21.6	− 5.9
9 10	10.5	21.8	10.3	21.5	5.8
9 20	10.6	21.7	10.4	21.4	5.7
9 30	10.7	21.6	10.5	21.3	5.6
9 40	10.8	21.5	10.6	21.2	5.5
9 50	10.9	21.4	10.6	21.2	5.4
10 00	+ 11.0	− 21.3	+ 10.7	− 21.1	− 5.3

Additional corrects for temperature and pressure are given on the following page.
For bubble sextant observations ignore dip and use the star corrections for Sun, planets and stars.

A4 ALTITUDE CORRECTION TABLES – ADDITIONAL CORRECTIONS
ADDITIONAL REFRACTION CORRECTIONS FOR NON–STANDARD CONDITIONS

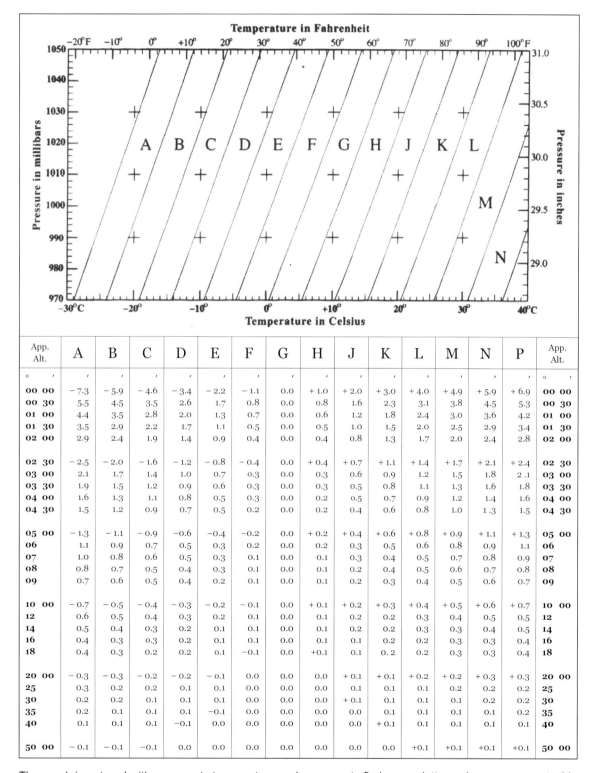

App. Alt.	A	B	C	D	E	F	G	H	J	K	L	M	N	P	App. Alt.
° ′	′	′	′	′	′	′	′	′	′	′	′	′	′	′	° ′
00 00	− 7.3	− 5.9	− 4.6	− 3.4	− 2.2	− 1.1	0.0	+ 1.0	+ 2.0	+ 3.0	+ 4.0	+ 4.9	+ 5.9	+ 6.9	00 00
00 30	5.5	4.5	3.5	2.6	1.7	0.8	0.0	0.8	1.6	2.3	3.1	3.8	4.5	5.3	00 30
01 00	4.4	3.5	2.8	2.0	1.3	0.7	0.0	0.6	1.2	1.8	2.4	3.0	3.6	4.2	01 00
01 30	3.5	2.9	2.2	1.7	1.1	0.5	0.0	0.5	1.0	1.5	2.0	2.5	2.9	3.4	01 30
02 00	2.9	2.4	1.9	1.4	0.9	0.4	0.0	0.4	0.8	1.3	1.7	2.0	2.4	2.8	02 00
02 30	− 2.5	− 2.0	− 1.6	− 1.2	− 0.8	− 0.4	0.0	+ 0.4	+ 0.7	+ 1.1	+ 1.4	+ 1.7	+ 2.1	+ 2.4	02 30
03 00	2.1	1.7	1.4	1.0	0.7	0.3	0.0	0.3	0.6	0.9	1.2	1.5	1.8	2.1	03 00
03 30	1.9	1.5	1.2	0.9	0.6	0.3	0.0	0.3	0.5	0.8	1.1	1.3	1.6	1.8	03 30
04 00	1.6	1.3	1.1	0.8	0.5	0.3	0.0	0.2	0.5	0.7	0.9	1.2	1.4	1.6	04 00
04 30	1.5	1.2	0.9	0.7	0.5	0.2	0.0	0.2	0.4	0.6	0.8	1.0	1.3	1.5	04 30
05 00	− 1.3	− 1.1	− 0.9	−0.6	−0.4	−0.2	0.0	+ 0.2	+ 0.4	+ 0.6	+ 0.8	+ 0.9	+ 1.1	+ 1.3	05 00
06	1.1	0.9	0.7	0.5	0.3	0.2	0.0	0.2	0.3	0.5	0.6	0.8	0.9	1.1	06
07	1.0	0.8	0.6	0.5	0.3	0.1	0.0	0.1	0.3	0.4	0.5	0.7	0.8	0.9	07
08	0.8	0.7	0.5	0.4	0.3	0.1	0.0	0.1	0.2	0.4	0.5	0.6	0.7	0.8	08
09	0.7	0.6	0.5	0.4	0.2	0.1	0.0	0.1	0.2	0.3	0.4	0.5	0.6	0.7	09
10 00	− 0.7	− 0.5	− 0.4	− 0.3	− 0.2	− 0.1	0.0	+ 0.1	+ 0.2	+ 0.3	+ 0.4	+ 0.5	+ 0.6	+ 0.7	10 00
12	0.6	0.5	0.4	0.3	0.2	0.1	0.0	0.1	0.2	0.2	0.3	0.4	0.5	0.5	12
14	0.5	0.4	0.3	0.2	0.1	0.1	0.0	0.1	0.2	0.2	0.3	0.3	0.4	0.5	14
16	0.4	0.3	0.3	0.2	0.1	0.1	0.0	0.1	0.1	0.2	0.2	0.3	0.3	0.4	16
18	0.4	0.3	0.2	0.2	0.1	−0.1	0.0	+0.1	0.1	0.2	0.2	0.3	0.3	0.4	18
20 00	− 0.3	− 0.3	− 0.2	− 0.2	− 0.1	0.0	0.0	0.0	+ 0.1	+ 0.1	+ 0.2	+ 0.2	+ 0.3	+ 0.3	20 00
25	0.3	0.2	0.2	0.1	0.1	0.0	0.0	0.0	0.1	0.1	0.1	0.2	0.2	0.2	25
30	0.2	0.2	0.1	0.1	0.1	0.0	0.0	0.0	+ 0.1	0.1	0.1	0.1	0.2	0.2	30
35	0.2	0.1	0.1	0.1	−0.1	0.0	0.0	0.0	0.0	0.1	0.1	0.1	0.1	0.2	35
40	0.1	0.1	0.1	−0.1	0.0	0.0	0.0	0.0	0.0	+ 0.1	0.1	0.1	0.1	0.1	40
50 00	− 0.1	− 0.1	−0.1	0.0	0.0	0.0	0.0	0.0	0.0	0.0	+0.1	+0.1	+0.1	+0.1	50 00

The graph is entered with arguments temperature and pressure to find a zone letter; using as arguments this zone letter and apparent altitude (sextant altitude corrected for index error and dip), a correction is taken from the table. This correction is to be applied to the sextant altitude in addition to the corrections for standard conditions (for the Sun, stars and planets from page A2–A3 and for the Moon from pages xxxiv and xxxv).

PLANETS, 2006
LOCAL MEAN TIME OF MERIDIAN PASSAGE

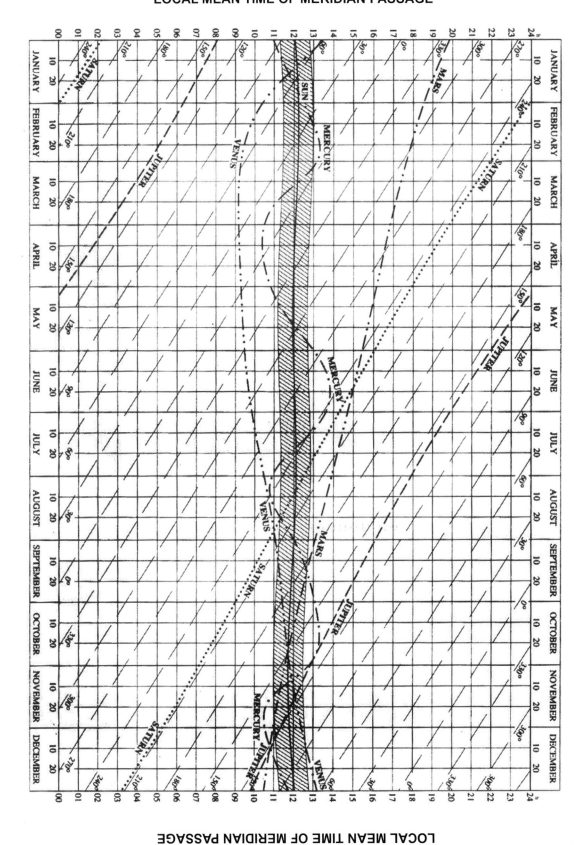

2006 MAY 4, 5, 6 (THURS., FRI., SAT.)

UT	ARIES GHA	VENUS −4.0 GHA	Dec	MARS +1.5 GHA	Dec	JUPITER −2.5 GHA	Dec	SATURN +0.3 GHA	Dec	STARS Name	SHA	Dec
4 00	221 44.5	220 36.0	S 1 01.2	118 56.0	N24 29.2	359 43.0	S14 47.2	94 05.9	N19 43.2	Acamar	315 22.8	S40 16.7
01	236 46.9	235 35.8	1 00.2	133 56.9	29.1	14 45.8	47.1	109 08.2	43.2	Achernar	335 31.1	S57 12.2
02	251 49.4	250 35.7	0 59.2	148 57.7	28.9	29 48.6	47.0	124 10.5	43.1	Acrux	173 15.4	S63 08.3
03	266 51.9	265 35.5	. . 58.2	163 58.6	. . 28.8	44 51.4	. . 46.9	139 12.9	. . 43.1	Adhara	255 17.1	S28 58.9
04	281 54.3	280 35.3	57.1	178 59.4	28.7	59 54.2	46.8	154 15.2	43.1	Aldebaran	290 56.1	N16 31.4
05	296 56.8	295 35.1	56.1	194 00.3	28.5	74 56.9	46.7	169 17.5	43.0			
06	311 59.2	310 35.0	S 0 55.1	209 01.1	N24 28.4	89 59.7	S14 46.6	184 19.9	N19 43.0	Alioth	166 24.7	N55 55.6
07	327 01.7	325 34.8	54.1	224 02.0	28.2	105 02.5	46.5	199 22.2	43.0	Alkaid	153 02.5	N49 16.9
08	342 04.2	340 34.6	53.1	239 02.8	28.1	120 05.3	46.4	214 24.5	42.9	Al Na'ir	27 50.6	S46 55.7
09	357 06.6	355 34.4	. . 52.1	254 03.7	. . 27.9	135 08.1	. . 46.3	229 26.9	. . 42.9	Alnilam	275 52.2	S 1 11.8
10	12 09.1	10 34.3	51.0	269 04.5	27.8	150 10.8	46.2	244 29.2	42.9	Alphard	218 01.5	S 8 41.2
11	27 11.6	25 34.1	50.0	284 05.4	27.7	165 13.6	46.2	259 31.5	42.9			
12	42 14.0	40 33.9	S 0 49.0	299 06.2	N24 27.5	180 16.4	S14 46.1	274 33.9	N19 42.8	Alphecca	126 15.3	N26 41.4
13	57 16.5	55 33.7	48.0	314 07.1	27.4	195 19.2	46.0	289 36.2	42.8	Alpheratz	357 49.6	N29 07.3
14	72 19.0	70 33.5	47.0	329 07.9	27.2	210 22.0	45.9	304 38.5	42.8	Altair	62 13.5	N 8 52.8
15	87 21.4	85 33.4	. . 45.9	344 08.8	. . 27.1	225 24.7	. . 45.8	319 40.9	. . 42.7	Ankaa	353 21.3	S42 16.2
16	102 23.9	100 33.2	44.9	359 09.6	26.9	240 27.5	45.7	334 43.2	42.7	Antares	112 32.8	S26 26.9
17	117 26.4	115 33.0	43.9	14 10.5	26.8	255 30.3	45.6	349 45.5	42.7			
18	132 28.8	130 32.8	S 0 42.9	29 11.4	N24 26.6	270 33.1	S14 45.5	4 47.9	N19 42.6	Arcturus	146 00.4	N19 08.8
19	147 31.3	145 32.7	41.9	44 12.2	26.5	285 35.9	45.4	19 50.2	42.6	Atria	107 39.2	S69 02.4
20	162 33.7	160 32.5	40.8	59 13.1	26.3	300 38.6	45.3	34 52.5	42.6	Avior	234 20.6	S59 32.0
21	177 36.2	175 32.3	. . 39.8	74 13.9	. . 26.2	315 41.4	. . 45.2	49 54.9	. . 42.6	Bellatrix	278 38.2	N 6 21.4
22	192 38.7	190 32.1	38.8	89 14.8	26.0	330 44.2	45.1	64 57.2	42.5	Betelgeuse	271 07.5	N 7 24.6
23	207 41.1	205 31.9	37.8	104 15.6	25.9	345 47.0	45.1	79 59.5	42.5			
5 00	222 43.6	220 31.8	S 0 36.8	119 16.5	N24 25.7	0 49.8	S14 45.0	95 01.9	N19 42.5	Canopus	263 59.0	S52 42.1
01	237 46.1	235 31.6	35.7	134 17.3	25.6	15 52.5	44.9	110 04.2	42.4	Capella	280 43.1	N46 00.4
02	252 48.5	250 31.4	34.7	149 18.2	25.4	30 55.3	44.8	125 06.5	42.4	Deneb	49 35.3	N45 17.8
03	267 51.0	265 31.2	. . 33.7	164 19.0	. . 25.3	45 58.1	. . 44.7	140 08.9	. . 42.4	Denebola	182 39.0	N14 32.2
04	282 53.5	280 31.1	32.7	179 19.9	25.1	61 00.9	44.6	155 11.2	42.3	Diphda	349 01.6	S17 57.1
05	297 55.9	295 30.9	31.6	194 20.7	25.0	76 03.7	44.5	170 13.5	42.3			
06	312 58.4	310 30.7	S 0 30.6	209 21.6	N24 24.8	91 06.4	S14 44.4	185 15.8	N19 42.3	Dubhe	193 57.7	N61 43.3
07	328 00.9	325 30.5	29.6	224 22.4	24.7	106 09.2	44.3	200 18.2	42.2	Elnath	278 19.9	N28 36.9
08	343 03.3	340 30.3	28.6	239 23.3	24.5	121 12.0	44.2	215 20.5	42.2	Eltanin	90 48.3	N51 28.9
09	358 05.8	355 30.2	. . 27.6	254 24.1	. . 24.4	136 14.8	. . 44.1	230 22.8	. . 42.2	Enif	33 52.6	N 9 54.0
10	13 08.2	10 30.0	26.5	269 25.0	24.2	151 17.6	44.0	245 25.2	42.2	Fomalhaut	15 30.1	S29 35.3
11	28 10.7	25 29.8	25.5	284 25.9	24.1	166 20.3	44.0	260 27.5	42.1			
12	43 13.2	40 29.6	S 0 24.5	299 26.7	N24 23.9	181 23.1	S14 43.9	275 29.8	N19 42.1	Gacrux	172 07.0	S57 09.2
13	58 15.6	55 29.4	23.5	314 27.6	23.8	196 25.9	43.8	290 32.2	42.1	Gienah	175 57.8	S17 34.8
14	73 18.1	70 29.3	22.4	329 28.4	23.6	211 28.7	43.7	305 34.5	42.0	Hadar	148 55.5	S60 24.4
15	88 20.6	85 29.1	. . 21.4	344 29.3	. . 23.5	226 31.5	. . 43.6	320 36.8	. . 42.0	Hamal	328 07.4	N23 29.5
16	103 23.0	100 28.9	20.4	359 30.1	23.3	241 34.2	43.5	335 39.1	42.0	Kaus Aust.	83 50.9	S34 23.0
17	118 25.5	115 28.7	19.4	14 31.0	23.2	256 37.0	43.4	350 41.5	41.9			
18	133 28.0	130 28.5	S 0 18.3	29 31.8	N24 23.0	271 39.8	S14 43.3	5 43.8	N19 41.9	Kochab	137 18.0	N74 07.7
19	148 30.4	145 28.4	17.3	44 32.7	22.9	286 42.6	43.2	20 46.1	41.9	Markab	13 44.1	N15 14.2
20	163 32.9	160 28.2	16.3	59 33.5	22.7	301 45.4	43.1	35 48.5	41.8	Menkar	314 21.2	N 4 06.9
21	178 35.3	175 28.0	. . 15.3	74 34.4	. . 22.6	316 48.1	. . 43.0	50 50.8	. . 41.8	Menkent	148 13.9	S36 24.3
22	193 37.8	190 27.8	14.2	89 35.2	22.4	331 50.9	42.9	65 53.1	41.8	Miaplacidus	221 41.3	S69 44.8
23	208 40.3	205 27.6	13.2	104 36.1	22.3	346 53.7	42.9	80 55.4	41.7			
6 00	223 42.7	220 27.5	S 0 12.2	119 36.9	N24 22.1	1 56.5	S14 42.8	95 57.8	N19 41.7	Mirfak	308 49.0	N49 53.1
01	238 45.2	235 27.3	11.2	134 37.8	21.9	16 59.3	42.7	111 00.1	41.7	Nunki	76 04.9	S26 17.4
02	253 47.7	250 27.1	10.1	149 38.7	21.8	32 02.0	42.6	126 02.4	41.6	Peacock	53 27.6	S56 42.8
03	268 50.1	265 26.9	. . 09.1	164 39.5	. . 21.6	47 04.8	. . 42.5	141 04.7	. . 41.6	Pollux	243 34.6	N28 00.8
04	283 52.6	280 26.7	08.1	179 40.4	21.5	62 07.6	42.4	156 07.1	41.6	Procyon	245 05.6	N 5 12.6
05	298 55.1	295 26.6	07.0	194 41.2	21.3	77 10.4	42.3	171 09.4	41.5			
06	313 57.5	310 26.4	S 0 06.0	209 42.1	N24 21.2	92 13.2	S14 42.2	186 11.7	N19 41.5	Rasalhague	96 11.3	N12 33.1
07	329 00.0	325 26.2	05.0	224 42.9	21.0	107 15.9	42.1	201 14.1	41.5	Regulus	207 49.3	N11 56.2
08	344 02.5	340 26.0	04.0	239 43.8	20.8	122 18.7	42.0	216 16.4	41.5	Rigel	281 17.7	S 8 11.7
09	359 04.9	355 25.8	. . 02.9	254 44.6	. . 20.7	137 21.5	. . 41.9	231 18.7	. . 41.4	Rigil Kent	139 59.0	S60 51.8
10	14 07.4	10 25.6	01.9	269 45.5	20.5	152 24.3	41.8	246 21.0	41.4	Sabik	102 18.6	S15 44.1
11	29 09.8	25 25.5	S 00.9	284 46.3	20.4	167 27.1	41.8	261 23.4	41.4			
12	44 12.3	40 25.3	N 0 00.2	299 47.2	N24 20.2	182 29.8	S14 41.7	276 25.7	N19 41.3	Schedar	349 47.7	N56 34.1
13	59 14.8	55 25.1	01.2	314 48.0	20.1	197 32.6	41.6	291 28.0	41.3	Shaula	96 29.1	S37 06.6
14	74 17.2	70 24.9	02.2	329 48.9	19.9	212 35.4	41.5	306 30.3	41.3	Sirius	258 38.8	S16 43.5
15	89 19.7	85 24.7	. . 03.2	344 49.7	. . 19.7	227 38.2	. . 41.4	321 32.7	. . 41.2	Spica	158 36.8	S11 11.8
16	104 22.2	100 24.6	04.3	359 50.6	19.6	242 41.0	41.3	336 35.0	41.2	Suhail	222 56.7	S43 27.7
17	119 24.6	115 24.4	05.3	14 51.5	19.4	257 43.7	41.2	351 37.3	41.2			
18	134 27.1	130 24.2	N 0 06.3	29 52.3	N24 19.3	272 46.5	S14 41.1	6 39.6	N19 41.1	Vega	80 42.5	N38 47.0
19	149 29.6	145 24.0	07.4	44 53.2	19.1	287 49.3	41.0	21 42.0	41.1	Zuben'ubi	137 11.3	S16 04.3
20	164 32.0	160 23.8	08.4	59 54.0	18.9	302 52.1	40.9	36 44.3	41.1			
21	179 34.5	175 23.6	. . 09.4	74 54.9	. . 18.8	317 54.9	. . 40.8	51 46.6	. . 41.0		SHA	Mer. Pass.
22	194 37.0	190 23.5	10.4	89 55.7	18.6	332 57.6	40.8	66 48.9	41.0	Venus	357 48.2	9 18
23	209 39.4	205 23.3	11.5	104 56.6	18.5	348 00.4	40.7	81 51.3	41.0	Mars	256 32.9	16 02
Mer. Pass.	9 07.6	v −0.2	d 1.0	v 0.9	d 0.2	v 2.8	d 0.1	v 2.3	d 0.0	Jupiter	138 06.2	23 52
										Saturn	232 18.3	17 37

2006 MAY 4, 5, 6 (THURS., FRI., SAT.)

UT	SUN GHA	SUN Dec	MOON GHA	v	MOON Dec	d	HP
d h	° '	° '	° '	'	° '	'	'
4 00	180 47.5	N15 51.8	98 38.3	11.0	N24 43.7	7.9	55.1
01	195 47.6	52.6	113 08.3	11.1	24 35.8	8.0	55.1
02	210 47.6	53.3	127 38.4	11.2	24 27.8	8.1	55.1
03	225 47.7	.. 54.0	142 08.6	11.3	24 19.7	8.2	55.0
04	240 47.8	54.7	156 38.9	11.4	24 11.5	8.3	55.0
05	255 47.8	55.5	171 09.3	11.4	24 03.2	8.5	55.0
06	270 47.9	N15 56.2	185 39.7	11.6	N23 54.7	8.5	55.0
07	285 47.9	56.9	200 10.3	11.7	23 46.2	8.7	55.0
08	300 48.0	57.6	214 41.0	11.8	23 37.5	8.7	54.9
09	315 48.1	.. 58.4	229 11.8	11.8	23 28.8	8.8	54.9
10	330 48.1	59.1	243 42.6	12.0	23 20.0	9.0	54.9
11	345 48.2	15 59.8	258 13.6	12.1	23 11.0	9.0	54.9
12	0 48.2	N16 00.5	272 44.7	12.1	N23 02.0	9.1	54.8
13	15 48.3	01.3	287 15.8	12.2	22 52.9	9.3	54.8
14	30 48.3	02.0	301 47.0	12.4	22 43.6	9.3	54.8
15	45 48.4	.. 02.7	316 18.4	12.4	22 34.3	9.4	54.8
16	60 48.5	03.4	330 49.8	12.5	22 24.9	9.5	54.8
17	75 48.5	04.1	345 21.3	12.6	22 15.4	9.6	54.6
18	90 48.6	N16 04.9	359 52.9	12.7	N22 05.8	9.7	51.7
19	105 48.6	05.6	14 24.6	12.8	21 56.1	9.8	54.7
20	120 48.7	06.3	28 56.4	12.9	21 46.3	9.8	54.7
21	135 48.7	.. 07.0	43 28.3	13.0	21 36.5	10.0	54.7
22	150 48.8	07.7	58 00.3	13.0	21 26.5	10.0	54.7
23	165 48.8	08.5	72 32.3	13.2	21 16.5	10.2	54.7
5 00	180 48.9	N16 09.2	87 04.5	13.2	N21 06.3	10.2	54.6
01	195 49.0	09.9	101 36.7	13.3	20 56.1	10.2	54.6
02	210 49.0	10.6	116 09.0	13.4	20 45.9	10.4	54.6
03	225 49.1	.. 11.3	130 41.4	13 5	20 35.5	10.5	54.6
04	240 49.1	12.0	145 13.9	13.6	20 25.0	10.5	54.6
05	255 49.2	12.8	159 46.5	13.6	20 14.5	10.6	54.6
06	270 49.2	N16 13.5	174 19.1	13.8	N20 03.9	10.7	54.5
07	285 49.3	14.2	188 51.9	13.8	19 53.2	10.7	54.5
08	300 49.3	14.9	203 24.7	13.9	19 42.5	10.9	54.5
09	315 49.4	.. 15.6	217 57.6	14.0	19 31.6	10.9	54.5
10	330 49.4	16.3	232 30.6	14.1	19 20.7	11.0	54.5
11	345 49.5	17.0	247 03.7	14.1	19 09.7	11.0	54.5
12	0 49.5	N16 17.7	261 36.8	14.2	N18 58.7	11.2	54.5
13	15 49.6	18.5	276 10.0	14.3	18 47.5	11.2	54.5
14	30 49.6	19.2	290 43.3	14.4	18 36.3	11.2	54.4
15	45 49.7	.. 19.9	305 16.7	14.4	18 25.1	11.4	54.4
16	60 49.7	20.0	319 50.1	14.6	18 13.7	11.4	54.4
17	75 49.8	21.3	334 23.7	14.6	18 02.3	11.4	54.4
18	90 49.8	N16 22.0	348 57.3	14.6	N17 50.9	11.6	54.4
19	105 49.9	22.7	3 30.9	14.7	17 39.3	11.6	54.4
20	120 49.9	23.4	18 04.7	14.8	17 27.7	11.7	54.4
21	135 50.0	.. 24.1	32 38.5	14.9	17 16.0	11.7	54.4
22	150 50.0	24.8	47 12.4	14.9	17 04.3	11.8	54.4
23	165 50.1	25.5	61 46 3	15.1	16 52.5	11.8	54.3
6 00	180 50.1	N16 26.2	76 20.4	15.1	N16 40.7	12.0	54.3
01	195 50.2	27.0	90 54.5	15.1	16 28.7	11.9	54.3
02	210 50.2	27.7	105 28.6	15.2	16 16.8	12.1	54.3
03	225 50.3	.. 28.4	120 02.8	15.3	16 04.7	12.1	54.3
04	240 50.3	29.1	134 37.1	15.4	15 52.6	12.1	54.3
05	255 50.4	29.8	149 11.5	15.4	15 40.5	12.2	54.3
06	270 50.4	N16 30.5	163 45.9	15.5	N15 28.3	12.3	54.3
07	285 50.5	31.2	178 20.4	15.5	15 16.0	12.3	54.3
08	300 50.5	31.9	192 54.9	15.6	15 03.7	12.4	54.3
09	315 50.6	.. 32.6	207 29.5	15.7	14 51.3	12.4	54.3
10	330 50.6	33.3	222 04.2	15.7	14 38.9	12.5	54.3
11	345 50.7	34.0	236 38.9	15.7	14 26.4	12.5	54.3
12	0 50.7	N16 34.7	251 13.6	15.9	N14 13.9	12.6	54.2
13	15 50.8	35.4	265 48.5	15.8	14 01.3	12.7	54.2
14	30 50.8	36.1	280 23.3	16.0	13 48.6	12.6	54.2
15	45 50.9	.. 36.8	294 58.3	16.0	13 36.0	12.8	54.2
16	60 50.9	37.5	309 33.3	16.0	13 23.2	12.8	54.2
17	75 50.9	38.2	324 08.3	16.1	13 10.4	12.8	54.2
18	90 51.0	N16 38.9	338 43.4	16.1	N12 57.6	12.9	54.2
19	105 51.0	39.6	353 18.5	16.2	12 44.7	12.9	54.2
20	120 51.1	40.3	7 53.7	16.2	12 31.8	12.9	54.2
21	135 51.1	.. 41.0	22 28.9	16.3	12 18.9	13.0	54.2
22	150 51.2	41.7	37 04.2	16.3	12 05.9	13.1	54.2
23	165 51.2	42.4	51 39.5	16.4	N11 52.8	13.1	54.2
	SD 15.9	d 0.7	SD 4.9		14.8		14.8

THURSDAY (d 4), FRIDAY (d 5), SATURDAY (d 6)

Lat.	Twilight Naut.	Twilight Civil	Sunrise	Moonrise 4	5	6	7
°	h m	h m	h m	h m	h m	h m	h m
N 72	////	////	01 16	☐	☐	09 37	11 59
N 70	////	////	02 08	☐	06 59	10 11	12 14
68	////	////	02 39	☐	08 21	10 34	12 25
66	////	01 30	03 02	06 10	08 58	10 53	12 34
64	////	02 07	03 21	07 26	09 25	11 07	12 42
62	////	02 33	03 35	08 02	09 45	11 20	12 49
60	01 20	02 52	03 48	08 27	10 01	11 30	12 55
N 58	01 54	03 08	03 58	08 47	10 15	11 39	13 00
56	02 17	03 22	04 08	09 04	10 27	11 47	13 05
54	02 36	03 34	04 16	09 18	10 37	11 54	13 08
52	02 51	03 44	04 23	09 30	10 46	12 00	13 12
50	03 04	03 53	04 30	09 41	10 54	12 06	13 15
45	03 30	04 11	04 44	10 04	11 12	12 18	13 22
N 40	03 50	04 26	04 56	10 22	11 26	12 28	13 28
35	04 05	04 38	05 05	10 37	11 37	12 36	13 33
30	04 18	04 48	05 14	10 50	11 48	12 43	13 37
20	04 38	05 05	05 29	11 12	12 05	12 56	13 45
N 10	04 54	05 19	05 41	11 31	12 21	13 07	13 52
0	05 07	05 32	05 53	11 49	12 35	13 18	13 58
S 10	05 18	05 43	06 05	12 07	12 49	13 28	14 04
20	05 28	05 54	06 17	12 26	13 04	13 39	14 11
30	05 38	06 06	06 31	12 48	13 22	13 51	14 18
35	05 43	06 13	06 39	13 00	13 32	13 59	14 23
40	05 48	06 20	06 49	13 15	13 43	14 07	14 28
45	05 53	06 28	06 59	13 32	13 56	14 16	14 33
S 50	05 59	06 38	07 12	13 53	14 13	14 27	14 40
52	06 01	06 42	07 18	14 03	14 20	14 33	14 43
54	06 04	06 47	07 25	14 15	14 29	14 38	14 46
56	06 07	06 52	07 32	14 28	14 38	14 45	14 50
58	06 10	06 57	07 41	14 43	14 45	14 52	14 54
S 60	06 13	07 03	07 50	15 00	15 01	15 00	14 59

Lat.	Sunset	Twilight Civil	Twilight Naut.	Moonset 4	5	6	7
°	h m	h m	h m	h m	h m	h m	h m
N 72	22 49	////	////	☐	☐	05 00	04 03
N 70	21 51	////	////	☐	06 06	04 24	03 47
68	21 18	////	////	☐	04 43	03 59	03 33
66	20 54	22 30	////	05 15	04 43	03 39	03 22
64	20 35	21 51	////	03 59	03 37	03 23	03 13
62	20 20	21 24	////	03 22	03 16	03 10	03 05
60	20 07	21 03	22 40	02 56	02 59	02 59	02 58
N 58	19 56	20 47	22 03	02 35	02 44	02 49	02 52
56	19 47	20 33	21 39	02 18	02 32	02 40	02 46
54	19 39	20 21	21 20	02 04	02 21	02 32	02 41
52	19 31	20 11	21 04	01 51	02 11	02 25	02 37
50	19 25	20 02	20 51	01 40	02 02	02 19	02 33
45	19 10	19 43	20 24	01 16	01 44	02 06	02 24
N 40	18 58	19 28	20 05	00 57	01 28	01 54	02 16
35	18 49	19 16	19 49	00 41	01 16	01 45	02 10
30	18 40	19 05	19 36	00 27	01 04	01 36	02 04
20	18 25	18 48	19 16	00 04	00 45	01 21	01 54
N 10	18 12	18 34	19 00	24 28	00 28	01 08	01 46
0	18 00	18 22	18 47	24 12	00 12	00 56	01 37
S 10	17 48	18 10	18 35	23 56	24 44	00 44	01 29
20	17 36	17 59	18 25	23 38	24 30	00 30	01 21
30	17 22	17 47	18 15	23 18	24 15	00 15	01 10
35	17 14	17 40	18 10	23 06	24 06	00 06	01 04
40	17 04	17 33	18 05	22 53	23 56	24 57	00 57
45	16 54	17 25	18 00	22 36	23 44	24 49	00 49
S 50	16 41	17 15	17 54	22 16	23 29	24 39	00 39
52	16 35	17 11	17 51	22 07	23 22	24 35	00 35
54	16 28	17 06	17 49	21 56	23 14	24 30	00 30
56	16 20	17 01	17 46	21 44	23 06	24 24	00 24
58	16 12	16 55	17 43	21 29	22 56	24 18	00 18
S 60	16 03	16 49	17 39	21 12	22 44	24 11	00 11

Day	SUN Eqn. of Time 00h	12h	Mer. Pass.	MOON Mer. Pass. Upper	Lower	Age	Phase
d	m s	m s	h m	h m	h m	d	%
4	03 10	03 13	11 57	18 00	05 37	07	43
5	03 15	03 18	11 57	18 46	06 23	08	53
6	03 20	03 23	11 57	19 28	07 7	09	62

2006 MAY 7, 8, 9 (SUN., MON., TUES.)

UT	ARIES GHA	VENUS GHA	VENUS Dec	MARS GHA	MARS Dec	JUPITER GHA	JUPITER Dec	SATURN GHA	SATURN Dec	STARS Name	SHA	Dec
		−3.9		+1.5		−2.5		+0.3				
7 00	224 41.9	220 23.1	N 0 12.5	119 57.4	N24 18.3	3 03.2	S14 40.6	96 53.6	N19 40.9	Acamar	315 22.8	S40 16.7
01	239 44.3	235 22.9	13.5	134 58.3	18.1	18 06.0	40.5	111 55.9	40.9	Achernar	335 31.1	S57 12.2
02	254 46.8	250 22.7	14.6	149 59.1	18.0	33 08.8	40.4	126 58.2	40.9	Acrux	173 15.4	S63 08.3
03	269 49.3	265 22.5	.. 15.6	165 00.0	.. 17.8	48 11.5	.. 40.3	142 00.5	.. 40.8	Adhara	255 17.1	S28 58.9
04	284 51.7	280 22.4	16.6	180 00.8	17.6	63 14.3	40.2	157 02.9	40.8	Aldebaran	290 56.1	N16 31.4
05	299 54.2	295 22.2	17.7	195 01.7	17.5	78 17.1	40.1	172 05.2	40.8			
06	314 56.7	310 22.0	N 0 18.7	210 02.5	N24 17.3	93 19.9	S14 40.0	187 07.5	N19 40.7	Alioth	166 24.7	N55 55.6
07	329 59.1	325 21.6	19.7	225 03.4	17.1	108 22.6	39.9	202 09.8	40.7	Alkaid	153 02.5	N49 16.9
S 08	345 01.6	340 21.6	20.8	240 04.3	17.0	123 25.4	39.8	217 12.2	40.7	Ai Na'ir	27 50.5	S46 55.7
U 09	0 04.1	355 21.4	.. 21.8	255 05.1	.. 16.8	138 28.2	.. 39.7	232 14.5	.. 40.6	Alnilam	275 52.3	S 1 11.8
N 10	15 06.5	10 21.3	22.8	270 06.0	16.7	153 31.0	39.7	247 16.8	40.6	Alphard	218 01.5	S 8 41.2
D 11	30 09.0	25 21.1	23.9	285 06.8	16.5	168 33.8	39.6	262 19.1	40.6			
A 12	45 11.4	40 20.9	N 0 24.9	300 07.7	N24 16.3	183 36.5	S14 39.5	277 21.4	N19 40.5	Alphecca	126 15.3	N26 41.4
Y 13	60 13.9	55 20.7	25.9	315 08.5	16.2	198 39.3	39.4	292 23.8	40.5	Alpheratz	357 49.6	N29 07.3
14	75 16.4	70 20.5	27.0	330 09.4	16.0	213 42.1	39.3	307 26.1	40.5	Altair	62 13.5	N 8 52.9
15	90 18.8	85 20.3	.. 28.0	345 10.2	.. 15.8	228 44.9	.. 39.2	322 28.4	.. 40.4	Ankaa	353 21.3	S42 16.2
16	105 21.3	100 20.1	29.0	0 11.1	15.7	243 47.7	39.1	337 30.7	40.4	Antares	112 32.7	S26 26.9
17	120 23.8	115 20.0	30.1	15 11.9	15.5	258 50.4	39.0	352 33.1	40.4			
18	135 26.2	130 19.8	N 0 31.1	30 12.8	N24 15.3	273 53.2	S14 38.9	7 35.4	N19 40.3	Arcturus	146 00.4	N19 08.8
19	150 28.7	145 19.6	31.1	45 13.6	15.2	288 56.0	38.8	22 37.7	40.3	Atria	107 39.2	S69 02.4
20	165 31.2	160 19.4	33.2	60 14.5	15.0	303 58.8	38.7	37 40.0	40.3	Avior	234 20.7	S59 32.0
21	180 33.6	175 19.2	.. 34.2	75 15.4	.. 14.8	319 01.6	.. 38.6	52 42.3	.. 40.2	Bellatrix	278 38.2	N 6 21.4
22	195 36.1	190 19.0	35.2	90 16.2	14.7	334 04.3	38.6	67 44.7	40.2	Betelgeuse	271 07.5	N 7 24.6
23	210 38.6	205 18.9	36.3	105 17.1	14.5	349 07.1	38.5	82 47.0	40.2			
8 00	225 41.0	220 18.7	N 0 37.3	120 17.9	N24 14.3	4 09.9	S14 38.4	97 49.3	N19 40.1	Canopus	263 59.0	S52 42.0
01	240 43.5	235 18.5	38.3	135 18.8	14.2	19 12.7	38.3	112 51.6	40.1	Capella	280 43.1	N46 00.4
02	255 45.9	250 18.3	39.4	150 19.6	14.0	34 15.4	38.2	127 53.9	40.1	Deneb	49 35.3	N45 17.8
03	270 48.4	265 18.1	.. 40.4	165 20.5	.. 13.8	49 18.2	.. 38.1	142 56.3	.. 40.0	Denebola	182 39.0	N14 32.2
04	285 50.9	280 17.9	41.4	180 21.3	13.6	64 21.0	38.0	157 58.6	40.0	Diphda	349 01.6	S17 57.1
05	300 53.3	295 17.7	42.5	195 22.2	13.5	79 23.8	37.9	17.3 00.9	40.0			
06	315 55.8	310 17.5	N 0 43.5	210 23.0	N24 13.2	94 26.5	S14 37.8	188 03.2	N19 39.9	Dubhe	193 57.7	N61 43.3
07	330 58.3	325 17.4	44.5	225 23.9	13.1	109 29.3	37.7	203 05.5	39.9	Elnath	278 20.0	N28 36.9
M 08	346 00.7	340 17.2	45.6	240 24.7	13.0	124 32.1	37.6	218 07.8	39.9	Eltanin	90 48.3	N51 28.9
O 09	1 03.2	355 17.0	.. 46.6	255 25.6	.. 12.8	139 34.9	.. 37.6	233 10.2	.. 39.8	Enif	33 52.6	N 9 54.0
N 10	16 05.7	10 16.8	47.6	270 26.5	12.6	154 37.7	37.5	248 12.5	39.8	Fomalhaut	15 30.1	S29 35.3
D 11	31 08.1	25 16.6	48.7	285 27.3	12.5	169 40.4	37.4	263 14.8	39.8			
A 12	46 10.6	40 16.4	N 0 49.7	300 28.2	N24 12.3	184 43.2	S14 37.3	278 17.1	N19 39.7	Gacrux	172 07.0	S57 09.2
Y 13	61 13.0	55 16.2	50.8	315 29.0	12.1	199 46.0	37.2	293 19.4	39.7	Gienah	175 57.8	S17 34.8
14	76 15.5	70 16.0	51.8	330 29.9	11.9	214 48.8	37.1	308 21.8	39.7	Hadar	148 55.5	S60 24.4
15	91 18.0	85 15.9	.. 52.8	345 30.7	.. 11.8	229 51.6	.. 37.0	323 24.1	.. 39.6	Hamal	328 07.4	N23 29.5
16	106 20.4	100 15.7	53.9	0 31.6	11.6	244 54.3	36.9	338 26.4	39.6	Kaus Aust.	83 50.9	S34 23.0
17	121 22.9	115 15.5	54.9	15 32.4	11.4	259 57.1	36.8	353 28.7	39.6			
18	136 25.4	130 15.3	N 0 55.9	30 33.3	N24 11.2	274 59.9	S14 36.7	8 31.0	N19 39.5	Kochab	137 18.0	N74 07.7
19	151 27.8	145 15.1	57.0	45 34.1	11.1	290 02.7	36.6	23 33.3	39.5	Markab	13 44.1	N15 14.2
20	166 30.3	160 14.9	58.0	60 35.0	10.9	305 05.5	36.6	38 35.7	39.4	Menkar	314 21.2	N 4 06.9
21	181 32.8	175 14.7	0 59.1	75 35.9	.. 10.7	320 08.2	.. 36.5	53 38.0	.. 39.4	Menkent	148 13.9	S36 24.3
22	196 35.2	190 14.5	1 00.1	90 36.7	10.6	335 11.0	36.4	68 40.3	39.4	Miaplacidus	221 41.3	S69 44.8
23	211 37.7	205 14.4	01.1	105 37.6	10.4	350 13.8	36.3	83 42.6	39.3			
9 00	226 40.2	220 14.2	N 1 02.2	120 38.4	N24 10.2	5 16.6	S14 36.2	98 44.9	N19 39.3	Mirfak	308 49.0	N49 53.1
01	241 42.6	235 14.0	03.2	135 39.3	10.0	20 19.3	36.1	113 47.2	39.3	Nunki	76 04.9	S26 17.4
02	256 45.1	250 13.8	04.2	150 40.1	09.9	35 22.1	36.0	128 49.5	39.2	Peacock	53 27.6	S56 42.8
03	271 47.5	265 13.6	.. 05.3	165 41.0	.. 09.7	50 24.9	.. 35.9	143 51.9	.. 39.2	Pollux	243 34.6	N28 00.8
04	286 50.0	280 13.4	06.3	180 41.8	09.5	65 27.7	35.8	158 54.2	39.2	Procyon	245 05.6	N 5 12.6
05	301 52.5	295 13.2	07.4	195 42.7	09.3	80 30.5	35.7	173 56.5	39.1			
06	316 54.9	310 13.0	N 1 08.4	210 43.5	N24 09.1	95 33.2	S14 35.6	188 58.8	N19 39.1	Rasalhague	96 11.3	N12 33.1
07	331 57.4	325 12.8	09.4	225 44.4	09.0	110 36.0	35.6	204 01.1	39.1	Regulus	207 49.3	N11 56.2
T 08	346 59.9	340 12.6	10.5	240 45.2	08.8	125 38.8	35.5	219 03.4	39.0	Rigel	281 17.7	S 8 11.6
U 09	2 02.3	355 12.5	.. 11.5	255 46.1	.. 08.6	140 41.6	.. 35.4	234 05.7	.. 39.0	Rigil Kent.	139 59.0	S60 51.8
E 10	17 04.8	10 12.3	12.6	270 47.0	08.4	155 44.3	35.3	249 08.1	39.0	Sabik	102 18.6	S15 44.1
S 11	32 07.3	25 12.1	13.6	285 47.8	08.3	170 47.1	35.2	264 10.4	38.9			
D 12	47 09.7	40 11.9	N 1 14.6	300 48.7	N24 08.1	185 49.9	S14 35.1	279 12.7	N19 38.9	Schedar	349 47.6	N56 34.1
A 13	62 12.2	55 11.7	15.7	315 49.5	07.9	200 52.7	35.0	294 15.0	38.9	Shaula	96 29.1	S37 06.6
Y 14	77 14.7	70 11.5	16.7	330 50.4	07.7	215 55.4	34.9	309 17.3	38.8	Sirius	258 38.8	S16 43.5
15	92 17.1	85 11.3	.. 17.7	345 51.2	.. 07.5	230 58.2	.. 34.8	324 19.6	.. 38.8	Spica	158 36.8	S11 11.8
16	107 19.6	100 11.1	18.8	0 52.1	07.4	246 01.0	34.7	339 21.9	38.7	Suhail	222 56.7	S43 27.7
17	122 22.0	115 10.9	19.8	15 52.9	07.2	261 03.8	34.6	354 24.3	38.7			
18	137 24.5	130 10.7	N 1 20.9	30 53.8	N24 07.0	276 06.6	S14 34.6	9 26.6	N19 38.7	Vega	80 42.5	N38 47.0
19	152 27.0	145 10.5	21.9	45 54.6	06.8	291 09.3	34.5	24 28.9	38.6	Zuben'ubi	137 11.3	S16 04.3
20	167 29.4	160 10.4	23.0	60 55.5	06.6	306 12.1	34.4	39 31.2	38.6			
21	182 31.9	175 10.2	.. 10.2	75 56.4	.. 06.5	321 14.9	.. 34.3	54 33.5	.. 38.6		SHA	Mer. Pass
22	197 34.4	190 10.0	25.0	90 57.2	06.3	336 17.7	34.2	69 35.8	38.5	Venus	354 37.6	9 19
23	212 36.8	205 09.8	26.1	105 58.1	06.1	351 20.4	34.1	84 38.1	38.5	Mars	254 36.9	15 58
Mer. Pass.	h m 8 55.8	v −0.2	d 1.0	v 0.9	d 0.2	v 2.8	d 0.1	v 2.3	d 0.0	Jupiter	138 28.9	23 39
										Saturn	232 08.3	17 26

2006 MAY 7, 8, 9 (SUN., MON., TUES.)

UT (d h)	SUN GHA	SUN Dec	MOON GHA	v	MOON Dec	d	HP
7 00	180 51.3	N16 43.0	66 14.9	16.4	N11 39.7	13.1	54.2
01	195 51.3	43.7	80 50.3	16.5	11 26.6	13.2	54.2
02	210 51.3	44.4	95 25.8	16.5	11 13.4	13.2	54.2
03	225 51.4	.. 45.1	110 01.3	16.5	11 00.2	13.3	54.2
04	240 51.4	45.8	124 36.8	16.6	10 46.9	13.3	54.2
05	255 51.5	46.5	139 12.4	16.6	10 33.6	13.3	54.2
06	270 51.5	N16 47.2	153 48.0	16.6	N10 20.3	13.4	54.2
07	285 51.6	47.9	168 23.6	16.7	10 06.9	13.4	54.2
08	300 51.6	48.6	182 59.3	16.7	9 53.5	13.4	54.2
09	315 51.6	.. 49.3	197 35.0	16.8	9 40.1	13.5	54.2
10	330 51.7	50.3	212 10.8	16.8	9 26.6	13.5	54.2
11	345 51.7	50.7	226 46.6	16.8	9 13.1	13.6	54.2
12	0 51.8	N16 51.3	241 22.4	16.8	N8 59.5	13.6	54.2
13	15 51.8	52.0	255 58.2	16.9	8 45.9	13.6	54.2
14	30 51.8	52.7	270 34.1	16.9	8 32.3	13.6	54.2
15	45 51.9	.. 53.4	285 10.0	16.9	8 18.7	13.7	54.2
16	60 51.9	54.1	299 45.9	17.0	8 05.0	13.7	54.2
17	75 52.0	54.8	314 21.9	17.0	7 51.3	13.7	54.2
18	90 52.0	N16 55.5	328 57.9	17.0	N7 37.6	13.8	54.2
19	105 52.0	56.1	343 33.9	17.0	7 23.8	13.8	54.2
20	120 52.1	56.8	358 09.9	17.0	7 10.0	13.8	54.2
21	135 52.1	.. 57.5	12 45.9	17.1	6 56.2	13.9	54.2
22	150 52.2	58.2	27 22.0	17.1	6 42.3	13.9	54.2
23	165 52.2	58.9	41 58.1	17.1	6 28.4	13.9	54.2
8 00	180 52.2	N16 59.6	56 34.2	17.1	N6 14.5	13.9	54.2
01	195 52.3	17 00.3	71 10.3	17.1	6 00.6	13.9	54.2
02	210 52.3	00.9	85 46.4	17.2	5 46.7	14.0	54.2
03	225 52.3	.. 01.6	100 22.6	17.1	5 32.7	14.0	54.3
04	240 52.4	02.3	114 58.7	17.2	5 18.7	14.1	54.3
05	255 52.4	03.0	129 34.9	17.2	5 04.6	14.0	54.3
06	270 52.5	N17 03.7	144 11.1	17.2	N4 50.6	14.1	54.3
07	285 52.5	04.3	158 47.3	17.2	4 36.5	14.0	54.3
08	300 52.5	05.0	173 23.5	17.2	4 22.5	14.2	54.3
09	315 52.6	.. 05.7	187 59.7	17.2	4 08.3	14.1	54.3
10	330 52.6	06.4	202 35.9	17.2	3 54.2	14.1	54.3
11	345 52.6	07.0	217 12.1	17.3	3 40.1	14.2	54.3
12	0 52.7	N17 07.7	231 48.4	17.2	N3 25.9	14.2	54.3
13	15 52.7	08.4	246 24.6	17.2	3 11.7	14.2	54.3
14	30 52.7	.. 09.1	261 00.8	17.3	2 57.5	14.2	54.3
15	45 52.8	09.7	275 37.1	17.2	2 43.3	14.2	54.3
16	60 52.8	10.4	290 13.3	17.2	2 29.1	14.2	54.3
17	75 52.8	11.1	304 49.5	17.3	2 14.9	14.3	54.4
18	90 52.9	N17 11.8	319 25.8	17.2	N2 00.6	14.2	54.4
19	105 52.9	12.4	334 02.0	17.2	1 46.4	14.3	54.4
20	120 52.9	13.1	348 38.2	17.2	1 32.1	14.3	54.4
21	135 53.0	.. 13.8	3 14.4	17.2	1 17.8	14.3	54.4
22	150 53.0	14.5	17 50.6	17.2	1 03.5	14.3	54.4
23	165 53.0	15.1	32 26.8	17.2	0 49.2	14.3	54.4
9 00	180 53.1	N17 15.8	47 03.0	17.2	N0 34.9	14.4	54.4
01	195 53.1	16.5	61 39.2	17.2	0 20.5	14.3	54.4
02	210 53.1	17.1	76 15.4	17.1	N0 06.2	14.3	54.4
03	225 53.2	.. 17.8	90 51.5	17.2	S0 08.1	14.4	54.5
04	240 53.2	18.5	105 27.7	17.1	0 22.5	14.4	54.5
05	255 53.2	19.2	120 03.8	17.1	0 36.9	14.3	54.5
06	270 53.3	N17 19.8	134 39.9	17.1	S0 51.2	14.4	54.5
07	285 53.3	20.5	149 16.0	17.1	1 05.6	14.3	54.5
08	300 53.3	21.2	163 52.1	17.1	1 19.9	14.4	54.5
09	315 53.3	.. 21.8	178 28.2	17.0	1 34.3	14.4	54.5
10	330 53.4	22.5	193 04.2	17.0	1 48.7	14.4	54.5
11	345 53.4	23.1	207 40.2	17.0	2 03.1	14.3	54.6
12	0 53.4	N17 23.8	222 16.2	17.0	S2 17.4	14.4	54.6
13	15 53.5	.. 24.5	236 52.2	16.9	2 31.8	14.4	54.6
14	30 53.5	25.1	251 28.1	16.9	2 46.2	14.4	54.6
15	45 53.5	25.8	266 04.0	16.9	3 00.6	14.4	54.6
16	60 53.5	26.5	280 39.9	16.9	3 14.9	14.4	54.6
17	75 53.6	27.1	295 15.8	16.8	3 29.3	14.3	54.6
18	90 53.6	N17 27.8	309 51.6	16.8	S3 43.6	14.4	54.6
19	105 53.6	28.5	324 27.4	16.8	3 58.0	14.4	54.7
20	120 53.7	29.1	339 03.2	16.7	4 12.4	14.3	54.7
21	135 53.7	.. 29.8	353 38.9	16.7	4 26.7	14.3	54.7
22	150 53.7	30.4	8 14.6	16.7	4 41.0	14.4	54.7
23	165 53.7	31.1	22 50.3	16.6	S4 55.4	14.3	54.7
	SD 15.9	d 0.7	SD 14.8			14.8	14.9

SUNDAY (7), MONDAY (8), TUESDAY (9)

Lat.	Twilight Naut.	Twilight Civil	Sunrise	Moonrise 7	8	9	10
N 72	////	////	00 29	11 59	14 01	15 59	18 05
N 70	////	////	01 47	12 14	14 05	15 54	17 49
68	////	////	02 25	12 25	14 08	15 50	17 36
66	////	01 05	02 51	12 34	14 11	15 47	17 26
64	////	01 52	03 10	12 42	14 13	15 44	17 18
62	////	02 21	03 27	12 49	14 15	15 42	17 11
60	00 58	02 43	03 40	12 55	14 17	15 40	17 04
N 58	01 40	03 00	03 51	13 00	14 19	15 38	16 59
56	02 07	03 14	04 01	13 04	14 20	15 36	16 54
54	02 27	03 27	04 10	13 08	14 21	15 35	16 50
52	02 44	03 38	04 18	13 12	14 22	15 33	16 46
50	02 58	03 47	04 25	13 15	14 23	15 32	16 43
45	03 25	04 07	04 40	13 22	14 26	15 30	16 35
N 40	03 46	04 22	04 52	13 28	14 28	15 27	16 29
35	04 02	04 35	05 03	13 33	14 29	15 26	16 23
30	04 15	04 46	05 12	13 37	14 31	15 24	16 19
20	04 36	05 04	05 27	13 45	14 33	15 21	16 11
N 10	04 53	05 18	05 41	13 52	14 35	15 19	16 04
0	05 06	05 31	05 53	13 58	14 37	15 17	15 57
S 10	05 19	05 43	06 05	14 04	14 39	15 14	15 50
20	05 29	05 55	06 18	14 11	14 42	15 12	15 44
30	05 40	06 08	06 33	14 18	14 44	15 09	15 36
35	05 45	06 15	06 42	14 23	14 45	15 08	15 31
40	05 50	06 23	06 52	14 28	14 47	15 06	15 26
45	05 56	06 32	07 03	14 33	14 49	15 04	15 21
S 50	06 03	06 42	07 17	14 40	14 51	15 02	15 14
52	06 06	06 46	07 23	14 43	14 53	15 01	15 10
54	06 09	06 51	07 30	14 46	14 52	15 00	15 07
56	06 12	06 57	07 38	14 50	14 53	14 59	15 03
58	06 15	07 03	07 47	14 54	14 56	14 57	14 59
S 60	06 19	07 10	07 57	14 59	14 57	14 56	14 54

Lat.	Sunset	Twilight Civil	Twilight Naut.	Moonset 7	8	9	10
N 72	☐	☐	☐	04 03	03 26	02 54	02 21
N 70	22 12	////	////	03 47	03 19	02 54	02 29
68	21 32	////	////	03 33	03 13	02 54	02 35
66	21 05	22 57	////	03 22	03 08	02 54	02 41
64	20 45	22 06	////	03 13	03 04	02 55	02 46
62	20 28	21 35	////	03 05	03 00	02 55	02 50
60	20 15	21 13	23 03	02 58	02 56	02 55	02 53
N 58	20 03	20 55	22 17	02 52	02 54	02 55	02 56
56	19 53	20 40	21 49	02 46	02 51	02 55	02 59
54	19 44	20 28	21 28	02 41	02 49	02 55	03 02
52	19 36	20 17	21 11	02 37	02 46	02 55	03 04
50	19 29	20 07	20 57	02 33	02 44	02 55	03 06
45	19 14	19 47	20 29	02 24	02 40	02 55	03 11
N 40	19 01	19 31	20 08	02 16	02 36	02 56	03 15
35	18 51	19 19	19 52	02 10	02 33	02 56	03 18
30	18 42	19 08	19 38	02 04	02 30	02 56	03 21
20	18 26	18 49	19 17	01 54	02 25	02 56	03 27
N 10	18 13	18 35	19 00	01 46	02 21	02 56	03 31
0	18 00	18 22	18 47	01 37	02 17	02 56	03 36
S 10	17 48	18 09	18 35	01 29	02 13	02 56	03 40
20	17 34	17 57	18 24	01 20	02 08	02 56	03 45
30	17 19	17 44	18 13	01 10	02 03	02 56	03 50
35	17 11	17 37	18 08	01 04	02 00	02 56	03 53
40	17 01	17 30	18 02	00 57	01 57	02 56	03 57
45	16 50	17 21	17 56	00 49	01 53	02 56	04 01
S 50	16 36	17 11	17 50	00 39	01 48	02 56	04 06
52	16 29	17 06	17 47	00 35	01 46	02 56	04 08
54	16 22	17 01	17 44	00 30	01 43	02 57	04 11
56	16 14	16 56	17 41	00 24	01 41	02 57	04 13
58	16 05	16 49	17 37	00 18	01 38	02 57	04 16
S 60	15 55	16 4	17 33	00 11	01 34	02 57	04 20

Day	SUN Eqn. of Time 00h	12h	Mer. Pass.	MOON Mer. Pass. Upper	Lower	Age	Phase
d	m s	m s	h m	h m	h m	d	%
7	03 25	03 27	11 57	20 08	07 48	10	71
8	03 29	03 31	11 56	20 47	08 27	11	79
9	03 32	03 34	11 56	21 26	09 06	12	86

2006 JUNE 18, 19, 20 (SUN., MON., TUES.)

UT	ARIES GHA	VENUS −3.8 GHA	VENUS Dec	MARS +1.8 GHA	MARS Dec	JUPITER −2.3 GHA	JUPITER Dec	SATURN +0.4 GHA	SATURN Dec	STARS Name	SHA	Dec
18 00	266 05.7	215 08.8	N16 43.0	134 41.7	N19 23.0	48 37.1	S13 30.2	134 43.2	N18 48.8	Acamar	315 22.6	S40 16.5
01	281 08.2	230 08.3	43.8	149 42.6	22.6	63 39.7	30.2	149 45.4	48.7	Achernar	335 30.8	S57 11.9
02	296 10.7	245 07.8	44.6	164 43.5	22.1	78 42.3	30.2	164 47.6	48.6	Acrux	173 15.7	S63 08.4
03	311 13.1	260 07.3 ..	45.4	179 44.4 ..	21.7	93 44.9 ..	30.1	179 49.8	48.6	Adhara	255 17.2	S28 58.8
04	326 15.6	275 06.7	46.2	194 45.3	21.3	108 47.5	30.1	194 52.0	48.5	Aldebaran	290 56.0	N16 31.4
05	341 18.1	290 06.2	47.0	209 46.2	20.9	123 50.1	30.1	209 54.1	48.4			
06	356 20.5	305 05.7	N16 47.8	224 47.1	N19 20.5	138 52.7	S13 30.0	224 56.3	N18 48.4	Alioth	166 25.0	W55 55.7
S 07	11 23.0	320 05.2	48.6	239 48.1	20.1	153 55.3	30.0	239 58.5	48.3	Alkaid	153 02.7	N49 17.0
U 08	26 25.4	335 04.7	49.4	254 49.0	19.7	168 57.9	30.0	255 00.7	48.2	Al Na'lf	27 50.1	S46 55.6
N 09	41 27.9	350 04.2 ..	50.2	269 49.9 ..	19.2	184 00.5 ..	30.0	270 02.9 ..	48.1	Alnilam	275 52.2	S 1 11.8
D 10	56 30.4	5 03.7	50.9	284 50.8	18.8	199 03.1	29.9	285 05.1	48.1	Alphard	218 01.6	S 8 41.2
A 11	71 32.8	20 03.2	51.7	299 51.7	18.4	214 05.7	29.9	300 07.3	48.0			
Y 12	86 35.3	35 02.7	N16 52.5	314 52.6	N19 18.0	229 08.3	S13 29.9	315 09.5	N18 47.9	Alphecca	126 15.2	N26 41.6
13	101 37.8	50 02.1	53.3	329 53.5	17.6	244 10.9	29.8	330 11.7	47.9	Alpheratz	357 49.3	N29 07.4
14	116 40.2	65 01.6	54.1	344 54.5	17.2	259 13.5	29.8	345 13.9	47.8	Altair	62 13.2	N 8 53.0
15	131 42.7	80 01.1 ..	54.9	359 55.4 ..	16.7	274 16.1 ..	29.8	0 16.1 ..	47.7	Ankaa	353 20.9	S42 16.0
16	146 45.2	95 00.6	55.7	14 56.3	16.3	289 18.7	29.7	15 18.3	47.7	Antares	112 32.6	S26 26.9
17	161 47.6	110 00.1	56.5	29 57.2	15.9	304 21.3	29.7	30 20.4	47.6			
18	176 50.1	124 59.6	N16 57.2	44 58.1	N19 15.5	319 23.9	S13 29.7	45 22.6	N18 47.5	Arcturus	146 00.4	N19 08.9
19	191 52.6	139 59.0	58.0	59 59.0	15.1	334 26.5	29.6	60 24.8	47.5	Atria	107 38.9	S69 02.5
20	206 55.0	154 58.5	58.8	75 00.0	14.6	349 29.0	29.6	75 27.0	47.4	Avior	234 21.0	S59 31.9
21	221 57.5	169 58.0	16 59.6	90 00.9 ..	14.2	4 31.6	29.6	90 29.2 ..	47.3	Bellatrix	278 38.2	N 6 21.4
22	236 59.9	184 57.5	17 00.4	105 01.8	13.8	19 34.2	29.5	105 31.4	47.2	Betelgeuse	271 07.5	N 7 24.6
23	252 02.4	199 57.0	01.1	120 02.7	13.4	34 36.8	29.5	120 33.6	47.2			
19 00	267 04.9	214 56.5	N17 01.9	135 03.6	N19 13.0	49 39.4	S13 29.5	135 35.8	N18 47.1	Canopus	263 59.1	S52 41.9
01	282 07.3	229 55.9	02.7	150 04.5	12.6	64 42.0	29.4	150 38.0	47.0	Capella	280 43.0	N46 00.3
02	297 09.8	244 55.4	03.5	165 05.4	12.1	79 44.6	29.4	165 40.2	47.0	Deneb	49 35.0	N45 17.9
03	312 12.3	259 54.9 ..	04.3	180 06.4 ..	11.7	94 47.2 ..	29.4	180 42.4 ..	46.9	Denebola	182 39.1	N14 32.2
04	327 14.7	274 54.4	05.0	195 07.3	11.3	109 49.8	29.4	195 44.5	46.8	Diphda	349 01.3	S17 57.0
05	342 17.2	289 53.9	05.8	210 08.2	10.9	124 52.4	29.3	210 46.7	46.8			
06	357 19.7	304 53.3	N17 06.6	225 09.1	N19 10.5	139 55.0	S13 29.3	225 48.9	N18 46.7	Dubhe	193 58.1	N61 43.3
M 07	12 22.1	319 52.8	07.4	240 10.0	10.0	154 57.6	29.3	240 51.1	46.6	Elnath	278 19.9	N28 36.9
O 08	27 24.6	334 52.3	08.1	255 10.9	09.6	170 00.2	29.2	255 53.3	46.6	Eltanin	90 48.1	N51 29.1
N 09	42 27.0	349 51.8 ..	08.9	270 11.9 ..	09.2	185 02.7 ..	29.2	270 55.5 ..	46.5	Enif	33 52.3	N 9 54.2
D 10	57 29.5	4 51.2	09.7	285 12.8	08.8	200 05.3	29.2	285 57.7	46.4	Fomalhaut	15 29.7	S29 35.2
A 11	72 32.0	19 50.7	10.5	300 13.7	08.3	215 07.9	29.1	300 59.9	46.3			
Y 12	87 34.4	34 50.2	N17 11.2	315 14.6	N19 07.9	230 10.5	S13 29.1	316 02.1	N18 46.3	Gacrux	172 07.2	S57 09.3
13	102 36.9	49 49.7	12.0	330 15.5	07.5	245 13.1	29.1	331 04.3	46.2	Gienah	175 57.9	S17 34.8
14	117 39.4	64 49.1	12.8	345 16.4	07.1	260 15.7	29.1	346 06.4	46.1	Hadar	148 55.6	S60 24.6
15	132 41.8	79 48.6 ..	13.6	0 17.4 ..	06.7	275 18.3 ..	29.0	1 08.6 ..	46.1	Hamal	328 07.2	N23 29.5
16	147 44.3	94 48.1	14.3	15 18.3	06.2	290 20.9	29.0	16 10.8	46.0	Kaus Aust.	83 50.6	S34 23 0
17	162 46.8	109 47.6	15.1	30 19.2	05.8	305 23.5	29.0	31 13.0	45.9			
18	177 49.2	124 47.0	N17 15.9	45 20.1	N19 05.4	320 26.1	S13 28.9	46 15.2	N18 45.9	Kochab	137 18.4	N74 07.9
19	192 51.7	139 46.5	16.6	60 21.0	05.0	335 28.6	28.9	61 17.4	45.8	Markab	13 43.7	N15 14.3
20	207 54.2	154 46.0	17.4	75 22.0	04.5	350 31.2	28.9	76 19.6	45.7	Menkar	314 21.0	N 4 07.0
21	222 56.6	169 45.4 ..	18.2	90 22.9 ..	04.1	5 33.8 ..	28.9	91 21.8 ..	45.6	Menkent	148 13.9	S36 24.3
22	237 59.1	184 44.9	18.9	105 23.8	03.7	20 36.4	28.8	106 24.0	45.6	Miaplacidus	221 41.9	S69 44.8
23	253 01.5	199 44.4	19.7	120 24.7	03.3	35 39.0	28.8	121 26.1	45.5			
20 00	268 04.0	214 43.8	N17 20.5	135 25.6	N19 02.8	50 41.6	S13 28.8	136 28.3	N18 45.4	Mirfak	308 48.7	N49 53.0
01	283 06.5	229 43.3	21.2	150 26.5	02.4	65 44.2	28.7	151 30.5	45.4	Nunki	76 04.6	S26 17.4
02	298 08.9	244 42.8	22.0	165 27.5	01.9	80 46.7	28.7	166 32.7	45.3	Peacock	53 27.1	S56 42.8
03	313 11.4	259 42.2 ..	22.7	180 28.4 ..	01.6	95 49.3 ..	28.7	181 34.9 ..	45.2	Pollux	243 34.6	N28 00.8
04	328 13.9	274 41.7	23.5	195 29.3	01.1	110 51.9	28 7	196 37.1	45.2	Procyon	245 05.7	N 5 12.6
05	343 16.3	289 41.2	24.3	210 30.2	00.7	125 54.5	28.6	211 39.3	45.1			
06	358 18.8	304 40.6	N17 25.0	225 31.1	N19 00.3	140 57.1	S13 28.6	226 41.5	N18 45.0	Rasalhague	96 11.1	N12 33.2
07	13 21.3	319 40.1	25.8	240 32.1	18 59.9	155 59.7	28.6	241 43.7	44.9	Regulus	207 49.4	N12 56.3
T 08	28 23.7	334 39.6	26.5	255 33.0	59.4	171 02.3	28.5	256 45.8	44.9	Rigel	281 17.6	S 8 11.5
U 09	43 26.2	349 39.0 ..	27.3	270 33.9 ..	59.0	186 04.8 ..	28.5	271 48.0 ..	44.8	Rigil Kent	139 59.0	S60 52.0
E 10	58 28.7	4 38.5	28.1	285 34.8	58.6	201 07.4	28.5	286 50.2	44.7	Sabik	102 18.4	S15 44,1
S 11	73 31.1	19 38.0	28.3	300 35.7	58.2	216 10.0	28.5	301 52.4	44.7			
D 12	88 33.6	34 37.4	N17 29.6	315 36.6	N18 57.7	231 12.6	S13 28.4	316 54.6	N18 44.6	Schedar	349 47.2	N56 34.1
A 13	103 36.0	49 36.9	30.3	330 37.6	57.3	246 15.2	28.4	331 56.8	44.5	Shaula	96 28.9	S37 06.6
Y 14	118 38.5	64 36.4	31.1	345 37.8	56.9	261 17.8	26.4	346 59.0	44.5	Sirius	258 38.9	S16 43.4
15	133 41.0	79 35.8 ..	31.8	0 39.4 ..	56.5	276 20.3 ..	28.3	2 01.2 ..	44.4	Spica	158 36.9	S16 11.8
16	148 43.4	94 35.3	32.6	15 40.3	56.0	291 22.9	28.3	17 03.3	44.3	Suhail	222 56.9	S43 27.6
17	163 45.9	109 34.7	33.3	30 41.2	55.6	306 25.5	28.3	32 05.5	44.2			
18	178 48.4	124 34.2	N17 34.1	45 42.2	N18 55.2	321 28.1	S13 28.3	47 07.7	N18 44.2	Vega	80 42.2	N38 47.2
19	193 50.8	139 33.7	34.8	60 43.1	54.7	336 30.7	28.2	62 09.9	44.1	Zuben'ubi	137 11.2	S16 04.3
20	208 53.3	154 33.1	35.6	75 44.0	54.3	351 33.2	28.2	77 12.1	44.1			
21	223 55.8	169 32.6 ..	36.3	90 44.9 ..	53.9	6 35.8 ..	28.2	92 14.3 ..	44.0		SHA	Mer. Pass.
22	238 58.2	184 32.0	37.1	105 45.8	53.5	21 38.4	28.2	107 16.5	43.9	Venus	307 51.6	9 41
23	254 00.7	199 31.5	37.8	120 46.8	53.0	36 41.0	28 1	122 18.7	43.8	Mars	227 58.7	14 59
										Jupiter	142 34.6	20 38
Mer. Pass.	6 10.7	v 0.5	d 0.8	v 2.6	d 0.0	v 2.6	d 0.0	v 2.2	d 0.1	Saturn	228 30.9	14 55

2006 JUNE 18, 19, 20 (SUN., MON., TUES.)

UT	SUN GHA	Dec	MOON GHA	v	Dec	d	HP
d h	° ′	° ′	° ′	′	° ′	′	′
18 00	179 45.2	N23 23.9	275 55.8	12.0	S 5 18.6	16.7	59.4
01	194 45.1	23.9	290 26.8	12.0	5 01.9	16.7	59.3
02	209 45.0	24.0	304 57.8	12.0	4 45.2	16.8	59.3
03	224 44.8	.. 24.1	319 28.8	12.1	4 28.4	16.7	59.3
04	239 44.7	24.1	333 59.9	12.2	4 11.7	16.8	59.3
05	254 44.6	24.2	348 31.1	12.1	3 54.9	16.8	59.3
06	269 44.4	N23 24.2	3 02.2	12.2	S 3 38.1	16.8	59.3
S 07	284 44.3	24.3	17 33.4	12.2	3 21.3	16.8	59.3
U 08	299 44.1	24.4	32 04.6	12.2	3 04.5	16.8	59.3
N 09	314 44.0	.. 24.4	46 35.8	12.3	2 47.7	16.9	59.3
D 10	329 43.9	24.5	61 07.1	12.2	2 30.8	16.8	59.3
11	344 43.7	24.5	75 38.3	12.3	2 14.0	16.9	59.3
A 12	359 43.6	N23 24.6	90 09.6	12.3	S 1 57.1	16.8	59.3
Y 13	14 43.5	24.6	104 40.9	12.3	1 40.3	16.9	59.3
14	29 43.3	24.7	119 12.2	12.4	1 23.4	16.9	59.3
15	44 43.2	.. 24.7	133 43.6	12.3	1 06.5	16.9	59.3
16	59 43.1	24.8	148 14.9	12.4	0 49.6	16.8	59.2
17	74 42.9	24.8	162 46.3	12.3	0 32.8	16.9	59.2
18	89 42.8	N23 24.9	177 17.6	12.4	S 0 15.9	16.9	59.2
19	104 42.6	24.9	191 49.0	12.4	N 0 01.0	16.8	59.2
20	119 42.5	25.0	206 20.4	12.4	0 17.8	16.9	59.2
21	134 42.4	.. 25.0	220 51.8	12.4	0 34.7	16.8	59.2
22	149 42.2	25.1	235 23.2	12.4	0 51.5	16.8	59.2
23	164 42.1	25.1	249 54.6	12.4	1 08.3	16.9	59.2
19 00	179 42.0	N23 25.1	264 26.0	12.4	N 1 25.2	16.8	59.2
01	194 41.8	25.2	278 57.4	12.4	1 42.0	16.8	59.2
02	209 41.7	25.2	293 28.8	12.5	1 58.8	16.8	59.2
03	224 41.6	.. 25.3	308 00.3	12.4	2 15.6	16.8	59.2
04	239 41.4	25.3	322 31.7	12.4	2 32.4	16.7	59.1
05	254 41.3	25.3	337 03.1	12.3	2 49.1	16.7	59.1
06	269 41.1	N23 25.4	351 34.4	12.4	N 3 05.8	16.8	59.1
M 07	284 41.0	25.4	6 05.8	12.4	3 22.6	16.7	59.1
O 08	299 40.9	25.5	20 37.2	12.4	3 39.3	16.6	59.1
N 09	314 40.7	.. 25.5	35 08.6	12.3	3 55.9	16.7	59.1
D 10	329 40.6	25.5	49 39.9	12.4	4 12.6	16.6	59.1
A 11	344 40.5	25.6	64 11.3	12.3	4 29.2	16.6	59.1
Y 12	359 40.3	N23 25.6	78 42.6	12.3	N 4 45.8	16.6	59.1
13	14 40.2	25.6	93 13.9	12.3	5 02.4	16.5	59.1
14	29 40.1	25.7	107 45.2	12.3	5 18.9	16.5	59.1
15	44 39.9	.. 25.7	122 16.5	12.3	5 35.4	16.5	59.0
16	59 39.8	25.7	136 47.8	12.2	5 51.9	16.4	59.0
17	74 39.6	25.8	151 19.0	12.2	6 08.3	16.4	59.0
18	89 39.5	N23 25.8	165 50.2	12.2	N 6 24.7	16.4	59.0
19	104 39.4	25.8	160 21.4	12.2	6 41.1	16.3	59.0
20	119 39.2	25.9	194 52.6	12.1	6 57.4	16.3	59.0
21	134 39.1	25.9	209 23.7	12.1	7 13.7	16.2	59.0
22	149 39.0	25.9	223 54.8	12.1	7 29.9	16.2	59.0
23	164 38.8	25.9	238 25.9	12.1	7 46.1	16.2	59.0
20 00	179 38.7	N23 26.0	252 57.0	12.0	N 8 02.3	16.1	58.9
01	194 38.6	26.0	267 28.0	12.0	8 18.4	16.1	58.9
02	209 38.4	26.0	281 59.0	12.0	8 34.5	16.0	58.9
03	224 38.3	.. 26.1	296 30.0	11.9	8 50.5	16.0	58.9
04	239 38.1	26.1	311 00.9	11.9	9 06.5	15.9	58.9
05	254 38.0	26.1	325 31.8	11.8	9 22.4	15.8	58.9
06	269 37.9	N23 26.1	340 02.6	11.9	N 9 38.2	15.8	58.9
T 07	284 37.7	26.1	354 33.5	11.7	9 54.0	15.8	58.9
U 08	299 37.6	26.2	9 04.2	11.8	10 09.8	15.7	58.8
E 09	314 37.5	.. 26.2	23 35.0	11.7	10 25.5	15.6	58.8
S 10	329 37.3	26.2	38 05.7	11.6	10 41.1	15.6	58.8
D 11	344 37.2	26.2	52 36.3	11.6	10 56.7	15.5	58.8
A 12	359 37.1	N23 26.2	67 06.9	11.6	N11 12.2	15.5	58.8
Y 13	14 36.9	26.3	81 37.5	11.5	11 27.7	15.4	58.8
14	29 36.8	26.3	96 08.0	11.5	11 43.1	15.3	58.8
15	44 36.6	.. 26.3	110 38.5	11.4	11 58.4	15.3	58.8
16	59 36.5	26.3	125 08.9	11.4	12 13.7	15.2	58.7
17	74 36.4	26.3	139 39.3	11.3	12 28.9	15.1	58.7
18	89 36.2	N23 26.3	154 09.6	11.3	N12 44.0	15.0	58.7
19	104 36.1	26.3	168 39.9	11.2	12 59.0	15.0	58.7
20	119 36.0	26.4	183 10.1	11.2	13 14.0	14.9	58.7
21	134 35.8	.. 26.4	197 40.3	11.1	13 28.9	14.9	58.7
22	149 35.7	26.4	212 10.4	11.1	13 43.8	14.7	58.7
23	164 35.5	26.4	226 40.5	11.0	N13 58.5	14.7	58.7
	SD 15.8	d 0.0	SD 16.2		16.1		16.0

Lat.	Twilight Naut.	Civil	Sunrise	Moonrise 18	19	20	21
°	h m	h m	h m	h m	h m	h m	h m
N 72	▢	▢	▢	00 44	{00 27 / 23 26}	22 37	▢
N 70	▢	▢	▢	00 37	{00 08 / 23 39}	23 03	21 53
68	▢	▢	▢	00 31	{00 10 / 23 48}	23 23	22 43
66	▢	▢	▢	00 26	{00 11 / 23 56}	23 39	23 15
64	////	////	01 31	00 22	00 12	{00 02 / 23 52}	23 39
62	////	////	02 09	00 18	00 13	00 08	{00 03 / 23 58}
60	////	00 49	02 35	00 15	00 14	00 13	00 12
N 58	////	01 40	02 56	00 12	00 14	00 17	00 21
56	////	02 10	03 13	00 09	00 15	00 21	00 28
54	00 45	02 32	03 27	00 07	00 16	00 25	00 35
52	01 32	02 50	03 39	00 05	00 16	00 28	00 41
50	02 00	03 06	03 50	00 03	00 17	00 31	00 47
45	02 46	03 35	04 13	24 18	00 18	00 37	00 58
N 40	03 16	03 58	04 31	24 19	00 19	00 42	01 08
35	03 39	04 16	04 46	24 19	00 19	00 47	01 17
30	03 58	04 31	04 59	24 20	00 20	00 51	01 24
20	04 27	04 56	05 21	24 21	00 21	00 59	01 37
N 10	04 50	05 17	05 40	24 23	00 23	01 05	01 49
0	05 09	05 35	05 58	24 24	00 24	01 11	02 00
S 10	05 25	05 52	06 15	24 25	00 25	01 17	02 11
20	05 42	06 10	06 34	24 26	00 26	01 24	02 23
30	05 59	06 28	06 55	24 27	00 27	01 32	02 36
35	06 07	06 39	07 07	24 28	00 28	01 36	02 44
40	06 17	06 51	07 21	24 29	00 29	01 41	02 54
45	06 27	07 04	07 38	24 30	00 30	01 47	03 04
S 50	06 39	07 21	07 59	24 32	00 32	01 54	03 17
52	06 44	07 28	08 09	24 32	00 32	01 57	03 24
54	06 50	07 36	08 20	24 33	00 33	02 01	03 30
56	06 56	07 45	08 33	24 34	00 34	02 05	03 38
58	07 03	07 56	08 48	24 35	00 35	02 10	03 47
S 60	07 10	08 07	09 05	24 36	00 36	02 15	03 57

Lat.	Sunset	Twilight Civil	Naut.	Moonset 18	19	20	21
°	h m	h m	h m	h m	h m	h m	h m
N 72	▢	▢	▢	11 31	13 53	16 27	
N 70	▢	▢	▢	11 34	13 45	16 04	19 00
68	▢	▢	▢	11 37	13 39	15 46	18 12
66	▢	▢	▢	11 39	13 34	15 32	17 41
64	22 32	////	////	11 41	13 29	15 21	17 19
62	21 54	////	////	11 42	13 26	15 11	17 01
60	21 27	23 14	////	11 44	13 22	15 03	16 46
N 58	21 07	22 23	////	11 45	13 20	14 55	16 33
56	20 50	21 53	////	11 46	13 17	14 49	16 23
54	20 36	21 30	23 18	11 47	13 15	14 43	16 13
52	20 23	21 12	22 31	11 48	13 13	14 38	16 05
50	20 12	20 57	22 03	11 48	13 11	14 34	15 57
45	19 50	20 27	21 17	11 50	13 07	14 24	15 42
N 40	19 32	20 05	20 46	11 52	13 03	14 16	15 29
35	19 17	19 46	20 23	11 53	13 01	14 09	15 18
30	19 04	19 31	20 05	11 54	12 58	14 02	15 08
20	18 42	19 06	19 35	11 56	12 54	13 52	14 52
N 10	18 23	18 46	19 13	11 57	12 50	13 43	14 37
0	18 05	18 28	18 54	11 59	12 46	13 34	14 24
S 10	17 48	18 10	18 37	12 00	12 42	13 25	14 11
20	17 29	17 53	18 21	12 02	12 39	13 16	13 57
30	17 08	17 34	18 04	12 03	12 34	13 06	13 41
35	16 55	17 24	17 55	12 04	12 32	13 00	13 31
40	16 41	17 12	17 46	12 05	12 29	12 53	13 19
45	16 24	16 58	17 35	12 06	12 26	12 46	13 08
S 50	16 04	16 42	17 24	12 08	12 22	12 36	12 54
52	15 54	16 35	17 18	12 08	12 20	12 32	12 47
54	15 42	16 26	17 13	12 09	12 18	12 27	12 39
56	15 30	16 17	17 06	12 10	12 16	12 22	12 30
58	15 15	16 07	17 00	12 11	12 13	12 16	12 21
S 60	14 57	15 55	16 52	12 12	12 11	12 10	12 10

Day	SUN Eqn. of Time 00ʰ	12ʰ	Mer. Pass	MOON Mer. Pass. Upper	Lower	Age	Phase
d	m s	m s	h m	h m	h m	d	%
18	00 59	01 05	12 01	05 47	18 11	22	51
19	01 12	01 18	12 01	06 35	18 59	23	40
20	01 25	01 32	12 02	07 22	19 47	24	29

2006 JUNE 21, 22, 23 (WED., THURS., FRI.)

UT	ARIES	VENUS −3.7		MARS +1.8		JUPITER −2.3		SATURN +0.4	
d h	GHA	GHA	Dec	GHA	Dec	GHA	Dec	GHA	Dec
21 00	269 03.1	214 31.0	N17 38.6	135 47.7	N18 52.6	51 43.6	S13 28.1	137 20.8	N18 43.7
01	284 05.6	229 30.4	39.3	150 48.6	52.2	66 46.1	28.1	152 23.0	43.7
02	299 08.1	244 29.9	40.1	165 49.5	51.7	81 48.7	28.1	167 25.2	43.6
03	314 10.5	259 29.3	.. 40.8	180 50.4	.. 51.3	96 51.3	.. 28.0	182 27.4	.. 43.5
04	329 13.0	274 28.8	41.6	195 51.4	50.9	111 53.9	28.0	197 29.6	43.5
05	344 15.5	289 28.2	42.3	210 52.3	50.5	126 56.5	28.0	212 31.8	43.4
06	359 17.9	304 27.7	N17 43.1	225 53.2	N18 50.0	141 59.0	S13 28.0	227 34.0	N18 43.3
07	14 20.4	319 27.1	43.8	240 54.1	49.6	157 01.6	27.9	242 36.1	43.3
08	29 22.9	334 26.6	44.5	255 55.0	49.2	172 04.2	27.9	257 38.3	43.2
W 09	44 25.3	349 26.0	.. 45.3	270 56.0	.. 48.7	187 06.8	.. 27.9	272 40.5	.. 43.1
E 10	59 27.8	4 25.5	46.0	285 56.9	48.3	202 09.3	27.9	287 42.7	43.0
D 11	74 30.3	19 24.9	46.8	300 57.8	47.9	217 11.9	27.8	302 44.9	43.0
N 12	89 32.7	34 24.4	N17 47.5	315 58.7	N18 47.4	232 14.5	S13 27.8	317 47.1	N18 42.9
E 13	104 35.2	49 23.8	48.2	330 59.6	47.0	247 17.1	27.8	332 49.3	42.8
S 14	119 37.6	64 23.3	49.0	346 00.6	46.6	262 19.6	27.8	347 51.4	42.8
D 15	134 40.1	79 22.7	.. 49.7	1 01.5	.. 46.1	277 22.2	.. 27.7	2 53.6	.. 42.7
A 16	149 42.6	94 22.2	50.4	16 02.4	45.7	292 24.8	27.7	17 55.8	42.6
Y 17	164 45.0	109 21.6	51.2	31 03.3	45.3	307 27.4	27.7	32 58.0	42.5
18	179 47.5	124 21.1	N17 51.9	46 04.3	N18 44.8	322 29.9	S13 27.7	48 00.2	N18 42.5
19	194 50.0	139 20.5	52.6	61 05.2	44.4	337 32.5	27.6	63 02.4	42.4
20	209 52.4	154 20.0	53.4	76 06.1	44.0	352 35.1	27.6	78 04.6	42.3
21	224 54.9	169 19.4	.. 54.1	91 07.0	.. 43.5	7 37.7	.. 27.6	93 06.7	.. 42.3
22	239 57.4	184 18.9	54.8	106 07.9	43.1	22 40.2	27.6	108 08.9	42.2
23	254 59.8	199 18.3	55.6	121 08.9	42.7	37 42.8	27.5	123 11.1	42.1
22 00	270 02.3	214 17.8	N17 56.3	136 09.8	N18 42.2	52 45.4	S13 27.5	138 13.3	N18 42.0
01	285 04.8	229 17.2	57.0	151 10.7	41.8	67 48.0	27.5	153 15.5	42.0
02	300 07.2	244 16.7	57.8	166 11.6	41.4	82 50.5	27.5	168 17.7	41.9
03	315 09.7	259 16.1	.. 58.5	181 12.5	.. 40.9	97 53.1	.. 27.4	183 19.8	.. 41.8
04	330 12.1	274 15.5	59.2	196 13.5	40.5	112 55.7	27.4	198 22.0	41.8
05	345 14.6	289 15.0	17 59.9	211 14.4	40.0	127 58.2	27.4	213 24.2	41.7
06	0 17.1	304 14.4	N18 00.7	226 15.3	N18 39.6	143 00.8	S13 27.4	228 26.4	N18 41.6
07	15 19.5	319 13.9	01.4	241 16.2	39.2	158 03.4	27.3	243 28.6	41.5
T 08	30 22.0	334 13.3	02.1	256 17.2	38.7	173 05.9	27.3	258 30.8	41.5
H 09	45 24.5	349 12.8	.. 02.8	271 18.1	.. 38.3	188 08.5	.. 27.3	273 33.0	.. 41.4
U 10	60 26.9	4 12.2	03.6	286 19.0	37.9	203 11.1	27.3	288 35.1	41.3
R 11	75 29.4	19 11.6	04.3	301 19.9	37.4	218 13.7	27.3	303 37.3	41.3
S 12	90 31.9	34 11.1	N18 05.0	316 20.9	N18 37.0	233 16.2	S13 27.2	318 39.5	N18 41.2
D 13	105 34.3	49 10.5	05.7	331 21.8	36.6	248 18.8	27.2	333 41.7	41.1
A 14	120 36.8	64 10.0	06.4	346 22.8	36.1	263 21.4	27.2	348 43.9	41.0
Y 15	135 39.3	79 09.4	.. 07.2	1 23.6	.. 35.7	278 23.9	.. 27.2	3 46.1	.. 41.0
16	150 41.7	94 08.8	07.9	16 24.5	35.2	293 26.5	27.1	18 48.2	40.9
17	165 44.2	109 08.3	08.6	31 25.5	34.8	308 29.1	27.1	33 50.4	40.8
18	180 46.6	124 07.7	N18 09.3	46 26.4	N18 34.4	323 31.6	S13 27.1	48 52.6	N18 40.8
19	195 49.1	139 07.1	10.0	61 27.3	33.9	338 34.2	27.1	63 54.8	40.7
20	210 51.6	154 06.6	10.8	76 28.2	33.5	353 36.8	27.0	78 57.0	40.6
21	225 54.0	169 06.0	.. 11.5	91 29.2	.. 33.1	8 39.3	.. 27.0	93 59.2	.. 40.5
22	240 56.5	184 05.4	12.2	106 30.1	32.6	23 41.9	27.0	109 01.3	40.5
23	255 59.0	199 04.9	12.9	121 31.0	32.2	38 44.5	27.0	124 03.5	40.4
23 00	271 01.4	214 04.3	N18 13.6	136 31.9	N18 31.7	53 47.0	S13 27.0	139 05.7	N18 40.3
01	286 03.9	229 03.7	14.3	151 32.9	31.3	68 49.6	26.9	154 07.9	40.3
02	301 06.4	244 03.2	15.0	166 33.8	30.9	83 52.2	26.9	169 10.1	40.2
03	316 08.8	259 02.6	.. 15.7	181 34.7	.. 30.4	98 54.7	.. 26.9	184 12.2	.. 40.1
04	331 11.3	274 02.0	16.4	196 35.6	30.0	113 57.3	26.9	199 14.4	40.0
05	346 13.7	289 01.5	17.2	211 36.6	29.5	128 59.8	26.9	214 16.6	40.0
06	1 16.2	304 00.9	N18 17.9	226 37.5	N18 29.1	144 02.4	S13 26.9	229 18.8	N18 39.9
07	16 18.7	319 00.3	18.6	241 38.4	28.6	159 05.0	26.8	244 21.0	39.8
08	31 21.1	333 59.8	19.3	256 39.3	28.2	174 07.5	26.8	259 23.2	39.7
F 09	46 23.6	348 59.2	.. 20.0	271 40.3	.. 27.8	189 10.1	.. 26.8	274 25.3	.. 39.7
R 10	61 26.1	3 58.6	20.7	286 41.2	27.3	204 12.7	26.8	289 27.5	39.6
I 11	76 28.5	18 58.0	21.4	301 42.1	26.9	219 15.2	26.7	304 29.7	39.5
D 12	91 31.0	33 57.5	N18 22.1	316 43.0	N18 26.4	234 17.8	S13 26.7	319 31.9	N18 39.5
A 13	106 33.5	48 56.9	22.8	331 44.0	26.0	249 20.3	26.7	334 34.1	39.4
Y 14	121 35.9	63 56.3	23.5	346 44.9	25.6	264 22.9	26.7	349 36.2	39.3
15	136 38.4	78 55.8	.. 24.2	1 45.8	.. 25.1	279 25.5	.. 26.7	4 38.4	.. 39.2
16	151 40.9	93 55.2	24.9	16 46.7	24.7	294 28.0	26.6	19 40.6	39.2
17	166 43.3	108 54.6	25.6	31 47.7	24.2	309 30.6	26.6	34 42.8	39.1
18	181 45.8	123 54.0	N18 26.3	46 48.6	N18 23.8	324 33.1	S13 26.6	49 45.0	N18 39.0
19	196 48.2	138 53.5	27.0	61 49.5	23.3	339 35.7	26.6	64 47.2	39.0
20	211 50.7	153 52.9	27.7	76 50.4	22.9	354 38.3	26.6	79 49.3	38.9
21	226 53.2	168 52.3	.. 28.4	91 51.4	.. 22.5	9 40.8	.. 26.5	94 51.5	.. 38.8
22	241 55.6	183 51.7	29.1	106 52.3	22.0	24 43.4	26.5	109 53.7	38.7
23	256 58.1	198 51.1	29.8	121 53.2	21.6	39 45.9	26.5	124 55.9	38.7
Mer. Pass.	h m 5 58.9	v 0.6	d 0.7	v 0.9	d 0.4	v 2.6	d 0.0	v 2.2	d 0.1

STARS

Name	SHA	Dec
Acamar	315 22.6	S40 16.5
Achernar	335 30.7	S57 11.9
Acrux	173 15.7	S63 08.4
Adhara	255 17.2	S28 58.8
Aldebaran	290 56.0	N16 31.4
Alioth	166 25.0	N55 57.7
Alkaid	153 02.7	N49 17.0
Al Na'ir	27 50.1	S46 55.6
Alnilam	275 52.2	S 1 11.7
Alphard	218 01.6	S 8 41.2
Alphecca	126 15.2	N26 41.6
Alpheratz	357 49.2	N29 07.4
Altair	62 13.2	N 8 53.0
Ankaa	353 20.9	S42 16.0
Antares	112 32.6	S26 26.9
Arcturus	146 00.4	N19 09.0
Atria	107 38.9	S69 02.6
Avior	234 21.0	S59 31.9
Bellatrix	278 38.2	N 6 21.4
Betelgeuse	271 07.5	N 7 24.6
Canopus	263 59.1	S52 41.8
Capella	280 43.0	N46 00.3
Deneb	49 34.9	N45 18.0
Denebola	182 39.1	N14 32.2
Diphda	349 01.3	S17 56.9
Dubhe	193 58.1	N61 43.3
Elnath	278 19.9	N28 36.9
Eltanin	90 48.1	N51 29.2
Enif	33 52.3	N 9 54.2
Fomalhaut	15 29.7	S29 35.1
Gacrux	172 07.2	S57 09.3
Gienah	175 57.9	S17 34.8
Hadar	148 55.6	S60 24.6
Hamal	328 07.1	N23 29.5
KausAust.	83 50.6	S34 23.0
Kochab	137 18.4	N74 07.9
Markab	13 43.7	N15 14.3
Menkar	314 21.0	N 4 07.0
Menkent	148 13.9	S36 24.3
Miaplacidus	221 41.9	S69 44.8
Mirfak	308 48.7	N49 53.0
Nunki	76 04.6	S26 17.4
Peacock	53 27.0	S56 42.8
Pollux	243 34.6	N28 00.8
Procyon	245 05.7	N 5 12.6
Rasalhague	96 11.1	N12 33.2
Regulus	207 49.4	N11 56.3
Rigel	281 17.6	S 8 11.5
Rigil Kent.	139 59.1	S60 52.0
Sabik	102 18.4	S15 44.1
Schedar	349 47.1	N56 34.1
Shaula	96 28.9	S37 06.6
Sirius	258 38.8	S16 43.4
Spica	158 36.9	S11 11.8
Suhail	222 56.9	S43 27.6
Vega	80 42.2	N38 47.2
Zuben'ubi	137 11.2	S16 04.3

	SHA	Mer. Pass.
	° '	h m
Venus	304 15.5	9 43
Mars	226 07.5	14 54
Jupiter	226 43.1	20 25
Saturn	228 11.0	14 45

2006 JUNE 21, 22, 23 (WED., THURS., FRI.)

	UT	SUN GHA	SUN Dec	MOON GHA	v	MOON Dec	d	HP
	d h	° ′	° ′	° ′	′	° ′	′	′
	21 00	179 35.4	N23 26.4	241 10.5	10.9	N14 13.2	14.6	58.6
	01	194 35.3	26.4	255 40.4	10.9	14 27.8	14.5	58.6
	02	209 35.1	26.4	270 10.3	10.8	14 42.3	14.4	58.6
	03	224 35.0	. . 26.4	284 40.1	10.8	14 56.7	14.4	58.6
	04	239 34.9	26.4	299 09.9	10.7	15 11.1	14.3	58.6
	05	254 .34.7	26.4	313 39.6	10.7	15 25.4	14.1	58.6
	06	269 34.6	N23 26.4	328 09.3	10.6	N15 39.5	14.1	58.5
	07	284 34.5	26.4	342 38.9	10.5	15 53.6	14.0	58.5
W	08	299 34.3	26.4	357 08.4	10.4	16 07.6	13.9	58.5
E	09	314 34.2	. . 26.4	11 37.8	10.4	16 21.5	13.9	58.5
D	10	329 34.0	26.5	26 07.2	10.4	16 35.4	13.7	58.5
N	11	344 33.9	26.5	40 36.6	10.3	16 49.1	13.6	58.5
E	12	359 33.8	N23 26.5	55 05.9	10.2	N17 02.7	13.6	58.5
S	13	14 33.6	26.5	69 35.1	10.1	17 16.3	13.4	58.4
D	14	29 33.5	26.5	84 04.2	10.1	17 29.7	13.3	58.4
A	15	44 33.4	. . 26.5	98 33.3	10.0	17 43.0	13.3	58.4
Y	16	59 33.2	26.4	113 02.3	9.9	17 56.3	13.1	58.4
	17	74 33.1	26.4	127 31.2	9.9	18 09.4	13.0	58.4
	18	89 33.0	N23 26.4	142 00.1	9.8	N18 22.4	13.0	58.4
	19	104 32.8	26.4	156 28.9	9.7	18 35.4	12.8	58.3
	20	119 32.7	26.4	170 57.6	9.7	18 48.2	12.7	58.3
	21	134 32.5	. . 26.4	185 26.3	9.6	19 00.9	12.6	58.3
	22	149 32.4	26.4	199 54.9	9.5	19 13.5	12.5	58.3
	23	164 32.3	26.4	214 23.4	9.5	19 26.0	12.4	58.3
	22 00	179 32.1	N23 26.4	228 51.9	9.4	N19 38.4	12.2	58.3
	01	194 32.0	26.4	243 20.3	9.3	19 50.6	12.2	58.2
	02	209 31.9	26.4	257 48.6	9.2	20 02.8	12.0	58.2
	03	224 31.7	. . 26.4	272 16.8	9.2	20 14.8	11.9	58.2
	04	239 31.6	26.4	286 45.0	9.1	20 26.7	11.8	58.2
	05	254 31.4	26.4	301 13.1	9.0	20 38.5	11.7	58.2
	06	269 31.3	N23 26.3	315 41.1	9.0	N20 50.2	11.6	58.2
	07	284 31.2	26.3	330 09.1	8.9	21 01.8	11.4	58.1
T	08	299 31.0	26.3	344 37.0	8.8	21 13.2	11.3	58.1
H	09	314 30.9	. . 26.3	359 04.8	8.8	21 24.5	11.2	58.1
U	10	329 30.8	26.3	13 32.6	8.7	21 35.7	11.1	58.1
R	11	344 30.6	26.3	28 00.3	8.6	21 46.8	10.9	58.1
S	12	359 30.5	N23 26.3	42 27.9	8.5	N21 57.7	10.8	58.1
D	13	14 30.4	26.2	56 55.4	8.5	22 08.5	10.7	58.0
A	14	29 30.2	26.2	71 22.9	8.4	22 19.2	10.5	58.0
Y	15	44 30.1	. . 26.2	85 50.3	8.3	22 29.7	10.4	58.0
	16	59 29.9	26.2	100 17.6	8.3	22 40.1	10.3	58.0
	17	74 29.8	26.2	114 44.9	8.2	22 50.4	10.2	58.0
	18	89 29.7	N23 26.1	129 12.1	8.1	N23 00.6	10.0	57.9
	19	104 29.5	26.1	143 39.2	8.0	23 10.6	9.8	57.9
	20	119 29.4	26.1	158 06.2	8.0	23 20.4	9.8	57.9
	21	134 29.3	. . 26.1	172 33.2	8.0	23 30.2	9.6	57.9
	22	149 29.1	26.0	187 00.2	7.8	23 39.8	9.4	57.9
	23	164 29.0	26.0	201 27.0	7.8	23 49.2	9.3	57.9
	23 00	179 28.9	N23 26.0	215 53.8	7.7	N23 58.5	9.2	57.8
	01	194 28.7	26.0	230 20.5	7.7	24 07.7	9.0	57.8
	02	209 28.6	25.9	244 47.2	7.6	24 16.7	8.8	57.8
	03	224 28.4	. . 25.9	259 13.8	7.6	24 25.5	8.8	57.8
	04	239 28.3	25.9	273 40.4	7.4	24 34.3	8.5	57.8
	05	254 28.2	25.9	288 06.8	7.5	24 42.8	8.5	57.7
	06	269 28.0	N23 25.8	302 33.3	7.3	N24 51.3	8.3	57.7
	07	284 27.9	25.8	316 59.6	7.3	24 59.6	8.1	57.7
	08	299 27.8	25.8	331 25.9	7.3	25 07.7	8.0	57.7
F	09	314 27.6	. . 25.7	345 52.2	7.2	25 15.7	7.8	57.7
R	10	329 27.5	25.7	0 18.4	7.1	25 23.5	7.6	57.6
I	11	344 27.4	25.7	14 44.5	7.1	25 31.1	7.6	57.6
D	12	359 27.2	N23 25.6	29 10.6	7.0	N25 38.7	7.3	57.6
A	13	14 27.1	25.6	43 36.6	7.0	25 46.0	7.2	57.6
Y	14	29 27.0	25.6	58 02.6	6.9	25 53.2	7.1	57.6
	15	44 26.8	. . 25.5	72 28.5	6.9	26 00.3	6.8	57.5
	16	59 26.7	25.5	86 54.4	6.8	26 07.1	6.8	57.5
	17	74 26.5	25.5	101 20.2	6.8	26 13.9	6.5	57.5
	18	89 26.4	N23 25.4	115 46.0	6.8	N26 20.4	6.4	57.5
	19	104 26.3	25.4	130 11.8	6.7	26 26.8	6.3	57.5
	20	119 26.1	25.3	144 37.5	6.6	26 33.1	6.1	57.4
	21	134 26.0	. . 25.3	159 03.1	6.6	26 39.2	5.9	57.4
	22	149 25.9	25.3	173 28.7	6.6	26 45.1	5.8	57.4
	23	164 25.7	25.2	187 54.3	6.6	N26 50.9	5.5	57.4
		SD 15.8	*d* 0.0	SD		15.9	15.8	15.7

Lat.	Twilight Naut.	Twilight Civil	Sunrise	Moonrise 21	Moonrise 22	Moonrise 23	Moonrise 24
°	h m	h m	h m	h m	h m	h m	h m
N 72	▭	▭	▭	▭	▭	▭	▭
N 70	▭	▭	▭	21 53	▭	▭	▭
68	▭	▭	▭	22 43	▭	▭	▭
66	▭	▭	▭	23 15	22 18	▭	▭
64	////	////	01 31	23 39	23 18	▭	▭
62	////	////	02 09	00 03 / 23 58	23 52	23 43	▭
60	////	00 49	02 36	00 12	00 13	00 17	00 27
N 58	////	01 40	02 56	00 21	00 27	00 37	00 56
56	////	02 11	03 13	00 28	00 38	00 54	01 18
54	00 45	02 33	03 28	00 35	00 49	01 08	01 37
52	01 32	02 51	03 40	00 41	00 58	01 20	01 52
50	02 00	03 06	03 51	00 47	01 06	01 31	02 06
45	02 46	03 36	04 13	00 58	01 23	01 54	02 34
N 40	03 17	03 59	04 31	01 08	01 38	02 13	02 56
35	03 40	04 17	04 47	01 17	01 50	02 29	03 14
30	03 59	04 32	05 00	01 24	02 01	02 42	03 30
20	04 28	04 57	05 22	01 37	02 19	03 06	03 57
N 10	04 50	05 18	05 41	01 49	02 36	03 26	04 20
0	05 10	05 36	05 58	02 00	02 51	03 45	04 42
S 10	05 27	05 53	06 16	02 11	03 07	04 05	05 04
20	05 43	06 10	06 34	02 23	03 23	04 25	05 27
30	05 59	06 29	06 56	02 36	03 43	04 49	05 55
35	06 08	06 40	07 08	02 44	03 54	05 04	06 11
40	06 17	06 52	07 22	02 54	04 07	05 20	06 30
45	06 28	07 05	07 39	03 03	04 23	05 40	06 53
S 50	06 40	07 21	08 00	03 17	04 42	06 05	07 23
52	06 45	07 29	08 10	03 24	04 51	06 17	07 37
54	06 51	07 37	08 21	03 30	05 01	06 31	07 54
56	06 57	07 46	08 34	03 38	05 13	06 48	08 15
58	07 04	07 56	08 48	03 47	05 27	07 07	08 40
S 60	07 11	08 08	09 06	03 57	05 43	07 32	09 16

Lat.	Sunset	Twilight Civil	Twilight Naut.	Moonset 21	Moonset 22	Moonset 23	Moonset 24
°	h m	h m	h m	h m	h m	h m	h m
N 72	▭	▭	▭	▭	▭	▭	▭
N 70	▭	▭	▭	19 00	▭	▭	▭
68	▭	▭	▭	18 12	▭	▭	▭
66	▭	▭	▭	17 41	20 29	▭	▭
64	22 33	////	////	17 19	19 31	▭	▭
62	21 54	////	////	17 01	18 58	21 03	▭
60	21 28	23 15	////	16 46	18 33	20 20	21 53
N 58	21 07	22 23	////	16 33	18 14	19 52	21 15
56	20 51	21 53	////	16 23	17 58	19 29	20 48
54	20 36	21 31	23 19	16 13	17 44	19 11	20 27
52	20 24	21 13	22 31	16 05	17 32	18 56	20 10
50	20 13	20 58	22 03	15 57	17 22	18 43	19 55
45	19 51	20 28	21 18	15 42	17 00	18 15	19 24
N 40	19 32	20 05	20 47	15 29	16 42	17 54	19 01
35	19 17	19 47	20 24	15 18	16 27	17 36	18 41
30	19 04	19 32	20 05	15 08	16 15	17 21	18 25
20	18 42	19 07	19 36	14 52	15 53	16 55	17 56
N 10	18 23	18 46	19 13	14 37	15 34	16 33	17 32
0	18 06	18 28	18 54	14 24	15 17	16 12	17 10
S 10	17 48	18 11	18 37	14 11	14 59	15 52	16 47
20	17 30	17 54	18 21	13 57	14 41	15 30	16 23
30	17 08	17 35	18 05	13 41	14 19	15 04	15 55
35	16 56	17 24	17 56	13 31	14 07	14 49	15 39
40	16 42	17 12	17 46	13 21	13 53	14 32	15 19
45	16 25	16 59	17 36	13 08	13 36	14 11	14 56
S 50	16 04	16 43	17 24	12 54	13 15	13 45	14 26
52	15 54	16 35	17 19	12 47	13 06	13 32	14 11
54	15 43	16 27	17 13	12 39	12 55	13 18	13 54
56	15 30	16 18	17 07	12 30	12 42	13 01	13 33
58	15 16	16 08	17 00	12 21	12 28	12 41	13 07
S 60	14 58	15 56	16 53	12 10	12 11	12 16	12 31

Day	SUN Eqn. of Time 00ʰ	SUN Eqn. of Time 12ʰ	SUN Mer. Pass.	MOON Mer. Pass. Upper	MOON Mer. Pass. Lower	MOON Age	Phase
d	m s	m s	h m	h m	h m	d %	
21	01 38	01 45	12 02	08 12	20 37	25 19	
22	01 51	01 58	12 02	09 04	21 31	26 11	
23	02 04	02 11	12 02	09 59	22 27	27 6	

STARS, 2006 JANUARY - JUNE

Mag	Name and Number		SHA							Declination						
			°	JAN. ′	FEB. ′	MAR. ′	APR. ′	MAY ′	JUNE ′	°	JAN. ′	FEB. ′	MAR. ′	APR. ′	MAY ′	JUNE ′
1.6	α Geminorum		246	14.9	14.8	14.9	15.0	15.2	15.2	N 31	52.6	52.6	52.6	52.7	52.6	52.6
3.3	σ Puppis		247	38.3	38.3	38.4	38.7	38.8	38.9	S 43	18.7	18.9	19.0	19.0	19.0	18.9
2.9	β Canis Minoris		248	07.5	07.5	07.6	07.7	07.8	07.8	N 8	16.7	16.7	16.6	16.6	16.7	16.7
2.4	η Canis Majoris		248	54.6	54.7	54.8	54.9	55.1	55.1	S 29	18.8	19.0	19.0	19.0	19.0	18.9
2.7	π Puppis		250	39.3	39.3	39.4	39.6	39.8	39.9	S 37	06.4	06.6	06.7	06.7	06.6	06.5
1.8	δ Canis Majoris		252	50.1	50.1	50.2	50.4	50.5	50.6	S 26	24.1	24.2	24.3	24.3	24.3	24.2
3.0	σ Canis Majoris		254	10.5	10.5	10.6	10.8	10.9	10.9	S 23	50.5	50.6	50.6	50.7	50.6	50.5
1.5	ε Canis Majoris	19	255	16.7	16.7	16.9	17.0	17.1	17.2	S 28	58.8	58.9	59.0	59.0	58.9	58.8
2.9	τ Puppis		257	28.2	28.3	28.5	28.8	29.0	29.4	S 50	37.3	37.4	37.5	37.5	37.4	37.3
−1.5	α Canis Majoris	18	258	38.5	38.5	38.6	38.7	38.8	38.9	S 16	43.4	43.5	43.6	43.6	43.5	43.4
1.9	γ Geminorum		260	28.8	28.8	28.9	29.0	29.1	29.1	N 16	23.7	23.7	23.7	23.7	23.7	23.7
−0.7	α Carinas	17	263	58.2	58.3	58.6	58.8	59.0	59.1	S 52	41.9	42.1	42.1	42.1	42.0	41.9
2.0	β Canis Majoris		264	15.2	15.2	15.4	15.5	15.6	15.6	S 17	57.5	57.6	57.6	57.6	57.6	57.5
2.6	θ Aurigae		269	57.6	57.7	57.8	58.0	58.0	58.0	N 37	12.9	13.0	13.0	13.0	12.9	12.9
1.9	β Aurigae		270	00.0	00.1	00.2	00.4	00.5	00.4	N 44	57.0	57.1	57.1	57.1	57.1	57.0
Var.‡	α Orionis	16	271	07.2	07.3	07.4	07.5	07.6	07.5	N 7	24.6	24.5	24.5	24.5	24.6	24.6
2.1	κ Orionis		272	59.1	59.1	59.2	59.4	59.4	59.4	S 9	40.0	40.1	40.1	40.1	40.0	39.9
1.9	ζ Orionis		274	43.8	43.8	43.9	44.1	44.1	44.1	S 1	56.3	56.4	56.4	56.4	56.3	56.2
2.6	α Columbae		275	01.6	01.7	01.9	02.1	02.2	02.2	S 34	04.3	04.4	04.4	04.4	04.3	04.1
3.0	ζ Tauri		275	29.6	29.7	29.8	29.9	30.0	29.9	N 21	08.9	08.9	08.9	08.9	08.9	08.9
1.7	ε Orionis	15	275	51.9	52.0	52.1	52.2	52.3	52.2	S 1	11.8	11.9	11.9	11.9	11.8	11.8
2.8	ι Ononis		276	03.8	03.8	04.0	04.1	04.1	04.1	S 5	54.3	54.4	54.4	54.4	54.3	54.2
2.6	α Leporis		276	44.7	44.8	44.9	45.1	45.2	45.1	S 17	49.1	49.1	49.2	49.1	49.1	49.0
2.2	δ Orionis		276	55.0	55.0	55.2	55.3	55.3	55.3	S 0	17.6	17.7	17.7	17.7	17.6	17.6
2.8	β Leporis		277	52.1	52.2	52.3	52.5	52.6	52.5	S 20	45.3	45.3	45.4	45.3	45.7	45.1
1.7	β Tauri	14	278	19.6	19.6	19.8	19.9	20.0	19.9	N 28	36.9	36.9	36.9	36.9	36.9	36.9
1.6	γ Orionis	13	278	37.9	38.0	38.1	38.2	38.2	38.2	N 6	21.4	21.4	21.4	21.4	21.4	21.4
0.1	α Aurigae	12	280	42.6	42.7	42.9	43.0	43.1	43.0	N 46	00.4	00.5	00.5	00.5	00.4	00.3
0.1	β Orionis	11	281	17.3	17.4	17.5	17.6	17.7	17.6	S 8	11.6	11.7	11.7	11.7	11.6	11.5
2.8	β Eridani		282	57.5	57.6	57.7	57.8	57.9	57.8	S 5	04.7	04.7	04.7	04.7	04.7	04.6
2.7	ι Aurigae		285	38.9	39.0	39.1	39.3	39.3	39.2	N 33	10.7	10.7	10.7	10.7	10.7	10.6
0.9	α Tauri	10	290	55.8	55.8	56.0	56.1	56.1	56.0	N 16	31.4	31.4	31.4	31.4	31.4	31.4
3.0	γ Eridani		300	25.1	25.2	25.3	25.4	25.4	25.3	S 13	29.5	29.5	29.5	29.5	29.4	29.3
2.9	ε Persei		300	25.9	26.0	26.2	26.3	26.3	26.1	N 40	01.9	01.9	01.9	01.8	01.8	01.7
2.9	ζ Peisei		301	22.1	22.2	22.4	22.5	22.5	22.3	N 31	54.3	54.3	54.3	54.2	54.2	54.2
2.9	η Tauri		303	02.2	02.3	02.4	02.5	02.5	02.3	N 24	07.6	07.6	07.6	07.5	07.5	07.5
1.8	α Persei	9	308	48.5	48.7	48.9	49.0	49.0	48.7	N 49	53.2	53.2	53.2	53.1	53.0	53.0
Var.§	β Persei		312	51.5	51.6	51.7	51.8	51.8	51.6	N 40	59.0	59.0	58.9	58.9	58.8	58.8
2.5	α Ceti	8	314	21.0	21.0	21.2	21.2	21.2	21.0	N 4	06.8	06.8	06.8	06.8	06.9	07.0
3.2	θ Eridani	7	315	22.4	22.6	22.7	22.8	22.8	22.7	S 40	17.0	17.0	17.0	16.8	16.7	16.5
2.0	α Ursae Minoris		320	19.8	32.0	42.3	47.9	45.7	37.4	N 89	17.8	17.8	17.8	17.6	17.5	17.4
3.0	β Trianguli		327	31.5	31.6	31.7	31.7	31.6	31.4	N 35	01.2	01.1	01.1	01.0	01.0	01.0
2.0	α Arietis	6	328	07.7	07.4	07.5	07.5	07.4	07.2	N 2	29.6	29.6	29.5	29.5	29.5	29.5
2.3	γ Andromedae		328	56.0	56.1	56.2	56.3	56.2	55.9	N 42	21.8	21.7	21.7	21.6	21.5	21.5
2.9	α Hydri		330	15.3	15.6	15.8	15.9	15.8	15.6	S 61	32.7	32.7	32.5	32.4	32.2	32.0
2.6	β Arietis		331	15.4	15.5	15.6	15.6	15.5	15.3	N 20	50.4	50.3	50.3	50.3	50.3	50.3
0.5	α Eridani	5	335	30.7	30.9	31.1	31.2	31.1	30.8	S 57	12.6	12.6	12.5	12.3	12.1	12.0
2.7	δ Cassiopeiae		338	27.0	27.3	27.4	27.5	27.3	26.9	N 60	16.3	16.3	16.2	16.0	15.9	15.9
2.1	β Andromedae		342	29.1	29.2	29.3	29.2	29.1	28.8	N 35	39.3	39.3	39.2	39.1	39.1	39.1
Var.||	γ Cassiopeiae		345	44.2	44.4	44.6	44.6	44.3	43.9	N 60	45.3	45.2	45.1	44.9	44.9	44.8
2.0	β Ceti	4	349	01.7	01.7	01.8	01.7	01.6	01.4	S 17	57.4	57.3	57.3	57.2	57.1	57.0
2.2	α Cassiopeiae	3	349	47.6	47.8	47.9	47.8	47.6	47.2	N 56	34.5	34.4	34.3	34.2	34.1	34.1
2.4	α phoenicis	2	353	21.3	21.4	21.4	21.4	21.2	20.9	S 42	16.6	16.6	16.5	16.3	16.2	16.0
2.8	β Hydri		353	28.9	29.4	29.6	29.6	29.2	28.5	S 77	13.5	13.4	13.3	13.1	12.9	12.7
2.8	γ Pegasi		356	37.0	37.0	37.0	37.0	36.8	36.6	N 15	13.1	13.0	13.0	13.0	13.0	13.1
2.3	β Cassiopeiae		357	37.9	38.1	38.2	38.1	37.8	37.4	N 59	11.2	11.1	11.0	10.9	10.8	10.8
2.1	α Andromedae		357	49.7	49.8	49.8	49.71	49.6	49.3	N 29	07.5	07.5	07.4	07.3	07.3	07.4

‡ 0.1 − 1.2   § 2.1 − 3.4 || Irregular variable; 2004 mag. 2.2

STARS, 2006 JULY - DECEMBER

Mag	Name and Number		SHA °	JULY '	AUG. '	SEPT. '	OCT. '	NOV. '	DEC. '	Declination °	JULY '	AUG. '	SEPT. '	OCT. '	NOV. '	DEC. '
1.6	Castor		246	15.1	15.0	14.8	14.5	14.2	14.0	N 31	52.6	52.5	52.5	52.4	52.4	52.4
3.3	σ Puppis		247	38.9	38.8	38.6	38.3	38.1	37.8	S 43	18.7	18.6	18.3	18.5	18.5	18.7
2.9	β Canis Minoris		248	07.7	07.6	07.4	07.2	06.9	06.7	N 8	16.7	16.8	16.8	16.7	16.7	16.6
2.4	η Canis Majoris		248	55.1	55.0	54.8	54.5	54.3	54.1	S 29	18.8	18.7	18.6	18.6	18.7	18.8
2.7	π Puppis		250	39.8	39.7	39.5	39.3	39.0	38.8	S 37	06.4	06.3	06.2	06.2	06.2	06.4
1.8	Wezen		252	50.5	50.4	50.2	50.0	49.7	49.5	S 26	24.0	23.9	23.9	23.9	23.9	24.1
3.0	o Canis Majoris		254	10.9	10.8	10.6	10.3	10.1	09.9	S 23	50.4	50.7	50.2	50.2	50.3	50.4
1.5	Adhara	19	255	17.1	17.0	16.8	16.6	16.3	16.1	S 28	58.7	58.6	58.3	58.3	58.6	58.7
2.9	τ Puppis		257	29.1	28.9	28.7	28.4	28.1	27.9	S 50	37.1	37.0	36.9	36.9	37.0	37.2
−1.5	Sirius	18	258	38.8	38.6	38.4	38.2	38.0	37.8	S 16	43.3	43.2	43.2	43.2	43.3	43.4
1.9	Alhena		260	29.0	28.8	28.6	28.3	28.1	27.9	N 16	23.8	23.8	23.8	23.8	23.7	23.7
−0.7	Canopus	17	263	59.1	58.9	58.6	58.3	58.0	57.9	S 52	41.7	41.6	41.5	41.5	41.6	41.8
2.0	Mirzam		264	15.5	15.3	15.1	14.9	14.7	14.5	S 17	57.4	57.3	57.2	57.2	57.3	57.4
2.6	θ Aurigae		269	57.9	57.6	57.3	57.1	56.8	56.6	N 37	12.9	12.8	12.8	12.8	12.8	12.9
1.9	Menkalinan		269	60.3	60.0	59.7	59.4	59.1	58.9	N 44	56.9	56.9	56.9	56.9	56.9	57.0
Var.‡	Betelgeuse	16	271	07.4	07.2	07.0	06.8	06.5	06.4	N 7	24.7	24.7	24.7	24.7	24.7	24.6
2.1	κ Ononis		272	59.3	59.1	58.9	58.7	58.5	58.3	S 9	39.8	39.8	39.7	39.7	39.8	39.9
1.9	Alnitak		274	43.9	43.8	43.3	43.3	43.1	43.0	S 1	56.2	56.1	56.1	56.1	56.1	56.2
2.6	Phact		275	02.0	01.9	01.6	01.4	01.2	01.0	S 34	04.0	03.9	03.8	03.8	03.9	04.1
3.0	ζ Tauri		275	29.8	29.6	29.3	29.1	28.8	28.7	N 21	08.9	08.9	08.9	08.9	08.9	08.9
1.7	Alnilam	15	275	52.1	51.9	51.7	51.5	51.3	51.1	S 1	11.7	11.6	11.6	11.6	11.6	11.7
2.8	ι Orionis		276	04.0	03.8	03.6	03.3	03.1	03.0	S 5	54.1	54.1	54.0	54.0	54.1	54.2
2.6	α Leporis		276	45.0	44.8	44.6	44.4	44.2	44.0	S 17	48.8	48.7	48.7	48.7	48.8	48.9
2.2	δ Orionis		276	55.2	55.0	54.7	54.5	54.3	54.2	S 0	17.5	17.4	17.4	17.4	17.4	17.5
2.8	β Leporis		277	52.4	52.2	52.0	51.8	51.6	51.4	S 20	45.0	44.9	44.9	44.9	45.0	45.1
1.7	Elnath	14	278	19.7	19.5	19.2	19.0	18.7	18.6	N 28	36.9	30.9	36.9	36.9	36.9	36.9
1.6	Bellatrix	13	278	38.0	37.8	37.6	37.4	37.2	37.1	N 6	21.5	21.5	21.6	21.6	21.5	21.5
0.1	Capella	12	280	42.8	42.5	42.2	41.9	41.6	41.4	N 46	00.3	00.3	00.3	00.3	00.4	00.4
0.1	Rigel	11	281	17.5	17.3	17.0	16.8	16.6	16.5	S 8	11.4	11.4	11.3	11.3	11.4	11.5
2.8	β Eridani		282	57.7	57.5	57.2	57.0	56.8	56.7	S 5	04.5	04.4	04.4	04.4	04.4	04.5
2.7	ι Aurigae		285	39.0	38.8	38.5	38.2	38.0	37.9	N 33	10.6	10.6	10.7	10.7	10.7	10.8
0.9	Aldebaran	10	290	55.8	55.6	55.3	55.1	54.9	54.8	N 16	31.4	31.5	31.5	31.6	31.6	31.7
3.0	γ Eridani		300	25.2	24.9	24.7	24.5	24.4	24.3	N 13	29.2	29.1	29.0	29.1	29.0	29.2
2.9	ε Persei		300	25.9	25.6	25.3	25.0	24.9	24.8	N 40	01.7	01.7	01.8	01.9	02.0	02.0
2.9	ζ Persei		301	22.1	21.8	21.5	21.3	21.2	21.1	N 31	54.2	54.2	54.3	54.3	54.4	54.4
2.9	Alcyone		303	02.1	01.9	01.6	01.4	01.2	01.2	N 24	07.6	07.6	07.7	07.7	07.8	07.8
1.8	Mirfak	9	308	48.5	48.1	47.8	47.5	47.3	47.7	N 49	53.0	53.0	53.1	53.2	53.3	53.4
Var.§	Algol		312	51.3	51.0	50.7	50.5	50.4	50.3	N 40	58.8	58.8	58.9	59.0	59.1	59.2
2.5	Menkar	8	314	20.8	20.6	20.3	20.2	20.1	20.0	N 4	07.0	07.1	07.2	07.2	07.2	07.1
3.2	Acamar	7	315	22.4	22.2	21.9	21.7	21.6	21.7	S 40	16.4	16.3	16.3	16.4	16.5	16.6
2.0	Polaris		319	85.0	70.7	57.8	49.0	45.5	49.6	N 89	17.3	17.4	17.5	17.6	17.8	18.0
3.0	β Trianguli		327	31.1	30.8	30.6	30.4	30.4	30.4	N 35	01.0	01.1	01.2	01.3	01.4	01.5
2.0	Hamal	6	328	07.0	06.7	06.5	06.3	06.3	06.3	N 23	29.6	29.7	29.8	29.8	29.9	29.9
2.3	Almak		328	55.6	55.3	55.1	54.9	54.8	54.9	N 42	21.5	21.6	21.8	21.9	22.0	22.1
2.9	α Hydri		330	15.2	14.8	14.5	14.3	14.3	14.5	S 61	31.9	31.9	31.9	32.0	32.2	32.3
2.6	Sheratan		331	15.0	14.8	14.6	14.4	14.4	14.4	N 20	50.4	50.5	50.6	50.6	50.7	50.7
0.5	Achernar	5	335	30.5	30.1	29.8	29.7	29.7	29.9	S 57	11.8	11.8	11.9	12.0	12.2	12.3
2.7	Ruchbah		338	26.5	26.1	25.8	25.6	25.6	25.7	N 60	15.9	16.0	16.2	16.4	16.5	16.6
2.1	Mirach		342	28.6	28.3	28.1	28.0	28.0	28.0	N 35	39.2	39.7	39.4	39.6	39.6	39.7
Var.‖	γ Cassiopeiae		345	43.5	43.2	42.9	42.8	42.8	43.0	N 60	44.9	45.0	45.2	45.4	45.3	45.6
2.0	Diphda	4	349	01.1	00.9	00.7	00.7	00.7	00.7	N 17	56.9	56.8	56.8	56.8	56.9	57.0
2.2	Schedar	3	349	46.9	46.5	46.3	46.2	46.3	46.4	S 56	34.2	34.3	34.5	34.6	34.8	34.8
2.4	Ankaa	2	353	20.6	20.4	20.2	20.2	20.2	20.3	N 42	15.9	15.9	16.0	16.1	16.2	16.3
2.8	β Hydri		353	27.7	26.9	26.5	26.4	26.8	27.4	S 77	12.7	12.7	12.9	13.0	13.1	13.2
2.8	Algenib		356	36.3	36.1	36.0	35.9	36.0	36.0	N 15	13.2	13.3	13.4	13.4	13.3	13.5
2.3	Caph		357	37.1	36.7	36.5	36.5	36.6	36.8	N 59	10.9	11.1	11.2	11.4	11.5	11.6
2.1	Alpheratz		357	49.0	48.8	48.7	48.6	48.7	48.8	N 29	07.5	07.6	07.8	07.9	07.9	07.9

‡ 0.1 – 1.2   § 2.1 – 3.4   ‖ Irregular variable; 2004 mag. 2.2

POLARIS (POLE STAR) TABLES, 2006
FOR DETERMINING LATITUDE FROM SEXTANT ALTITUDE AND FOR AZIMUTH

LHA ARIES	0° – 9°	10° – 19°	20° – 29°	30° – 39°	40° – 49°	50° – 59°	60° – 69°	70° – 79°	80° – 89°	90° – 99°	100° – 109°	110° – 119°
°	a_0	a_0	a_0	a_0	a_0	a_0	a_0	a_0	a_0	a_0	a_0	a_0
0	0 26.4	0 22.1	0 19.0	0 17.1	0 16.5	0 17.2	0 19.2	0 22.4	0 26.7	0 32.0	0 38.1	0 44.8
1	25.9	21.8	18.8	17.0	16.5	17.3	19.4	22.7	27.1	32.5	38.7	45.5
2	25.5	21.4	18.5	16.9	16.5	17.5	19.7	23.1	27.6	33.1	39.4	46.2
3	25.0	21.1	18.3	16.8	16.6	17.6	20.0	23.5	28.2	33.7	40.0	46.9
4	24.6	20.7	18.1	16.7	16.6	17.8	20.3	23.9	28.7	34.3	40.7	47.6
5	0 24.1	0 20.4	0 17.9	0 16.6	0 16.7	0 18.0	0 20.6	0 24.4	0 29.2	0 34.9	0 41.4	0 48.3
6	23.7	20.1	17.7	16.6	16.8	18.2	20.9	24.8	29.7	35.5	42.0	49.1
7	23.3	19.8	17.6	16.5	16.8	18.4	21.3	25.3	30.3	36.2	42.7	49.8
8	22.9	19.5	17.4	16.5	16.9	18.7	21.6	25.7	30.8	36.8	43.4	50.5
9	22.5	19.3	17.2	16.5	17.1	18.9	22.0	26.2	31.4	37.4	44.1	51.2
10	0 22.1	0 19.0	0 17.1	0 16.5	0 17.2	0 19.2	0 22.4	0 26.7	0 32.0	0 38.1	0 44.8	0 52.0
Lat. °	a_1	a_1	a_1	a_1	a_1	a_1	a_1	a_1	a_1	a_1	a_1	a_1
0	0.5	0.5	0.6	0.6	0.6	0.6	0.5	0.5	0.4	0.4	0.3	0.3
10	.5	.6	.6	.6	.6	.6	.6	.5	.5	.4	.4	.4
20	.5	.6	.6	.6	.6	.6	.6	.5	.5	.5	.4	.4
30	.5	.6	.6	.6	.6	.6	.6	.5	.5	.5	.5	.5
40	0.6	0.6	0.6	0.6	0.6	0.6	0.6	0.6	0.6	0.5	0.5	0.5
45	.6	.6	.6	.6	.6	.6	.6	.6	.6	.6	.6	.6
50	.6	.6	.6	.6	.6	.6	.6	.6	.6	.6	.6	.6
55	.6	.6	.6	.6	.6	.6	.6	.6	.6	.6	.7	.7
60	.6	.6	.6	.6	.6	.6	.6	.6	.7	.7	.7	.7
62	0.7	0.6	0.6	0.6	0.6	0.6	0.6	0.7	0.7	0.7	0.7	0.8
64	.7	.6	.6	.6	.6	.6	.6	.7	.7	.8	.8	.8
66	.7	.6	.6	.6	.6	.6	.7	.7	.7	.8	.8	.9
68	0.7	0.7	0.6	0.6	0.6	0.6	0.7	0.7	0.8	0.8	0.9	0.9
Month	a_2	a_2	a_2	a_2	a_2	a_2	a_2	a_2	a_2	a_2	a_2	a_2
Jan.	0.7	0.7	0.7	0.7	0.7	0.7	0.7	0.7	0.7	0.7	0.7	0.7
Feb.	.6	.7	.7	.7	.8	.8	.8	.8	.8	.8	.8	.8
Mar.	.5	.5	.6	.6	.7	.7	.8	.8	.9	.9	.9	.9
Apr.	0.3	0.4	0.4	0.5	0.6	0.6	0.7	0.8	0.8	0.9	0.9	0.9
May	.2	.3	.3	.4	.4	.5	.6	.6	.7	.8	.8	.9
June	.2	.2	.2	.3	.3	.4	.4	.5	.6	.6	.7	.8
July	0.2	0.2	0.2	0.2	0.3	0.3	0.3	0.4	0.4	0.5	0.5	0.6
Aug.	.4	.3	.3	.3	.3	.3	.3	.3	.3	.3	.4	.4
Sept.	.6	.5	.4	.4	.4	.3	.3	.3	.3	.3	.3	.3
Oct.	0.7	0.7	0.6	0.6	0.5	0.5	0.4	0.4	0.3	0.3	0.3	0.3
Nov.	0.9	0.9	0.8	.8	.7	.6	.6	.5	.4	.4	.3	.3
Dec.	1.0	1.0	1.0	0.9	0.9	0.8	0.7	0.6	0.6	0.5	0.4	0.3
Lat. °	AZIMUTH											
0	0.4	0.3	0.2	0.1	359.9	359.8	359.7	359.6	359.5	359.4	359.4	359.3
20	0.4	0.3	0.2	0.1	359.9	359.8	359.7	359.6	359.5	359.4	359.3	359.3
40	0.5	0.4	0.2	0.1	359.9	359.8	359.6	359.5	359.3	359.2	359.2	359.1
50	0.6	0.5	0.3	0.1	359.9	359.7	359.5	359.4	359.2	359.1	359.0	358.9
55	0.7	0.5	0.3	0.1	359.9	359.7	359.5	359.3	359.1	359.0	358.9	358.8
60	0.8	0.6	0.4	0.1	359.9	359.6	359.4	359.2	359.0	358.8	358.7	358.6
65	1.0	0.7	0.4	0.1	359.8	359.5	359.3	359.0	358.8	358.6	358.5	358.4

Latitude = Apparent altitude (corrected for refraction) $-1° + a_0 + a_1 + a_2$

The table is entered with LHA Aries to determine the column to be used; each column refers to a range of 10°. a_0 is taken, without interpolation, from the upper table with the units of LHA Aries in degrees as argument; a_1, a_2 are taken, without interpolation, from the second and third tables with arguments latitude and month respectively. a_0, a_1, a_2, are always positive. The final table gives the azimuth of *Polaris*.

POLARIS (POLE STAR) TABLES, 2006
FOR DETERMINING LATITUDE FROM SEXTANT ALTITUDE AND FOR AZIMUTH

LHA ARIES	120° – 129°	130° – 139°	140° – 149°	150° – 159°	160° – 169°	170° – 179°	180° – 189°	190° – 199°	120° – 129°	210° – 219°	220° – 229°	230° – 239°
°	a_0 ° ′	a_0 ° ′	a_0 ° ′	a_0 ° ′	a_0 ° ′	a_0 ° ′	a_0 ° ′	a_0 ° ′	a_0 ° ′	a_0 ° ′	a_0 ° ′	a_0 ° ′
0	0 52.0	0 59.3	1 06.7	1 13.7	1 20.4	1 26.3	1 31.5	1 35.6	1 38.7	1 40.5	1 41.1	1 40.4
1	52.7	1 00.1	07.4	14.4	21.0	26.9	31.9	36.0	38.9	40.6	41.1	40.3
2	53.4	00.8	08.1	15.1	21.6	27.4	32.4	36.3	39.1	40.7	41.1	40.1
3	54.2	01.5	08.8	15.8	22.2	28.0	32.8	36.6	39.3	40.8	41.0	40.0
4	54.9	02.3	09.5	16.5	22.8	28.5	33.2	37.0	39.5	40.9	41.0	39.8
5	0 55.6	1 03.0	1 10.2	1 17.1	1 23.4	1 29.0	1 33.7	1 37.3	1 39.7	1 41.0	1 40.9	1 39.6
6	56.4	03.7	10.9	17.8	24.0	29.5	34.1	37.6	39.9	41.0	40.8	39.4
7	57.1	04.5	11.6	18.4	24.6	30.0	34.5	37.9	40.1	41.1	40.8	39.2
8	57.8	05.2	12.3	19.1	25.2	30.5	34.9	38.1	40.2	41.1	40.7	39.0
9	58.6	05.9	13.0	19.7	25.8	31.0	35.2	38.4	40.4	41.1	40.6	38.8
10	0 59.3	1 06.7	1 13.7	1 20.4	1 26.3	1 31.5	1 35.6	1 38.7	1 40.5	1 41.1	1 40.4	1 38.5

Lat. °	a_1 ′	a_1 ′	a_1 ′	a_1 ′	a_1 ′	a_1 ′	a_1 ′	a_1 ′	a_1 ′	a_1 ′	a_1 ′	a_1 ′
0	0.3	0.3	0.3	0.3	0.4	0.4	0.5	0.5	0.6	0.6	0.6	0.6
10	.3	.3	.4	.4	.4	.5	.5	.6	.6	.6	.6	.6
20	.4	.4	.4	.4	.5	.5	.5	.6	.6	.6	.6	.6
30	.4	.4	.5	.5	.5	.5	.5	.6	.6	.6	.6	.6
40	0.5	0.5	0.5	0.5	0.5	0.6	0.6	0.6	0.6	0.6	0.6	0.6
45	.6	.6	.6	.6	.6	.6	.6	.6	.6	.6	.6	.6
50	.6	.6	.6	.6	.6	.6	.6	.6	.6	.6	.6	.6
55	.7	.7	.7	.7	.6	.6	.6	.6	.6	.6	.6	.6
60	.7	.7	.7	.7	.7	.7	.6	.6	.6	.6	.6	.6
62	0.8	0.8	0.8	0.7	0.7	0.7	0.7	0.6	0.6	0.6	0.6	0.6
64	.8	.8	.8	.8	.7	.7	.7	.6	.6	.6	.6	.6
66	.9	.9	.9	.8	.8	.7	.7	.6	.6	.6	.6	.6
68	0.9	0.9	0.9	0.9	0.8	0.8	0.7	0.7	0.6	0.6	0.6	0.6

Month	a_2 ′	a_2 ′	a_2 ′	a_2 ′	a_2 ′	a_2 ′	a_2 ′	a_2 ′	a_2 ′	a_2 ′	a_2 ′	a_2 ′
Jan.	0.6	0.6	0.6	0.6	0.6	0.5	0.5	0.5	0.5	0.5	0.5	0.5
Feb.	.8	.8	.7	.7	.7	.6	.6	.5	.5	.5	.4	.4
Mar.	0.9	0.9	0.9	0.9	.8	.8	.7	.7	.6	.6	.5	.5
Apr.	1.0	1.0	1.0	1.0	0.9	0.9	0.9	0.8	0.8	0.7	0.6	0.6
May	0.9	1.0	1.0	1.0	1.0	1.0	1.0	0.9	0.9	.8	.8	.7
June	.8	0.9	0.9	1.0	1.0	1.0	1.0	1.0	1.0	0.9	.9	.8
July	0.7	0.7	0.8	0.8	0.9	0.9	1.0	1.0	1.0	1.0	0.9	0.9
Aug.	.5	.6	.6	.7	.7	.8	0.8	0.9	0.9	0.9	.9	.9
Sept.	.3	.4	.4	.5	.5	.6	.6	.7	.8	.8	.8	.9
Oct.	0.3	0.3	0.3	0.3	0.4	0.4	0.5	0.5	0.6	0.6	0.7	0.7
Nov.	.2	.2	.2	.2	.2	.2	.3	.3	.4	.4	.5	.6
Dec.	0.3	0.2	0.2	0.2	0.2	0.2	0.2	0.2	0.2	0.3	0.3	0.4

Lat.						AZIMUTH						
°	°	°	°	°	°	°	°	°	°	°	°	°
0	359.3	359.3	359.3	359.4	359.4	359.5	359.6	359.7	359.8	359.9	0.1	0.2
20	359.3	359.3	359.3	359.3	359.4	359.5	359.6	359.7	359.8	359.9	0.1	0.2
40	359.1	359.1	359.1	359.2	359.3	359.4	359.5	359.6	359.8	359.9	0.1	0.2
50	358.9	358.9	358.9	359.0	359.1	359.2	359.4	359.5	359.7	359.9	0.1	0.3
55	358.8	358.8	358.8	358.9	359.0	359.1	359.3	359.5	359.7	359.9	0.1	0.3
60	358.6	358.6	358.6	358.7	358.9	359.0	359.2	359.4	359.6	359.9	0.1	0.4
65	358.3	358.3	358.4	358.5	358.7	358.8	359.1	359.3	359.6	359.9	0.1	0.4

ILLUSTRATION	From the daily pages:	°	′		°	′
On 2006 April 21 at 23ʰ 18ᵐ 56ˢ UT in longitude W 37° 14' the apparent altitude (corrected for refraction), H_0, of Polaris was 49° 31'.6	GHA Aries (23ʰ)	194	52.3	H_0	49	31.6
	Increment (18ᵐ 56ˢ)	4	44.8	a_0 (argument 162° 23')	1	21.8
	Longitude (west)	-37	14	a_1 (Lat 50° appox.)		0.6
				a_2 (April)		0.9
	LHA Aries	162	23			
				Sum -1° + Lat =	49	54.9

POLARIS (POLE STAR) TABLES, 2006

FOR DETERMINING LATITUDE FROM SEXTANT ALTITUDE AND FOR AZIMUTH

LHA ARIES	240° – 249°	250° – 259°	260° – 269°	270° – 279°	280° – 289°	290° – 299°	300° – 309°	310° – 319°	320° – 329°	330° – 339°	340° – 349°	350° – 359°
°	a_0 ° ′	a_0 ° ′	a_0 ° ′	a_0 ° ′	a_0 ° ′	a_0 ° ′	a_0 ° ′	a_0 ° ′	a_0 ° ′	a_0 ° ′	a_0 ° ′	a_0 ° ′
0	1 38.5	1 35.4	1 31.2	1 26.0	1 20.0	1 13.3	1 06.2	0 58.9	0 51.5	0 44.4	0 37.7	0 31.6
1	38.3	35.0	30.7	25.4	19.4	12.7	05.5	58.2	50.8	43.7	37.1	31.1
2	38.0	34.6	30.2	24.9	18.7	12.0	04.8	57.4	50.1	43.0	36.4	30.5
3	37.7	34.3	29.7	24.3	18.1	11.3	04.1	56.7	49.4	42.3	35.8	30.0
4	37.4	33.8	29.2	23.7	17.4	10.5	03.3	55.9	48.7	41.7	35.2	29.4
5	1 37.1	1 33.4	1 28.7	1 23.1	1 16.7	1 09.8	1 02.6	0 55.2	0 47.9	0 41.0	0 34.6	0 28.9
6	36.8	33.0	28.2	22.5	16.1	09.1	01.9	54.5	47.2	40.3	34.0	28.4
7	36.5	32.6	27.7	21.9	15.4	08.4	01.1	53.7	46.5	39.7	33.4	27.9
8	36.1	32.1	27.1	21.3	14.7	07.7	1 00.4	53.0	45.8	39.0	32.8	27.4
9	35.8	31.7	26.6	20.6	14.0	07.0	0 59.6	52.3	45.1	38.3	32.2	26.9
10	1 35.4	1 31.2	1 26.0	1 20.0	1 13.3	1 06.2	0 58.9	0 51.5	0 44.4	0 37.7	0 31.6	0 26.4

Lat. °	a_1 ′	a_1 ′	a_1 ′	a_1 ′	a_1 ′	a_1 ′	a_1 ′	a_1 ′	a_1 ′	a_1 ′	a_1 ′	a_1 ′
0	0.5	0.5	0.4	0.4	0.3	0.3	0.3	0.3	0.3	0.3	0.4	0.4
10	.6	.5	.5	.4	.4	.4	.3	.3	.4	.4	.4	.5
20	.6	.5	.5	.5	.4	.4	.4	.4	.4	.4	.5	.5
30	.6	.5	.5	.5	.5	.5	.4	.4	.5	.5	.5	.5
40	0.6	0.6	0.6	0.5	0.5	0.5	0.5	0.5	0.5	0.5	0.5	0.6
45	.6	.6	.6	.6	.6	.6	.6	.6	.6	.6	.6	.6
50	.6	.6	.6	.6	.6	.6	.6	.6	.6	.6	.6	.6
55	.6	.6	.6	.6	.7	.7	.7	.7	.7	.7	.6	.6
60	.6	.6	.7	.7	.7	.7	.7	.7	.7	.7	.7	.7
62	0.6	0.7	0.7	0.7	0.7	0.8	0.8	0.8	0.8	0.7	0.7	0.7
64	.6	.7	.7	.8	.8	.8	.8	.8	.8	.8	.7	.7
66	.7	.7	.7	.8	.8	.9	.9	.9	.9	.8	.8	.7
68	0.7	0.7	0.8	0.8	0.9	0.9	0.9	0.9	0.9	0.9	0.8	0.8

Month	a_2 ′	a_2 ′	a_2 ′	a_2 ′	a_2 ′	a_2 ′	a_2 ′	a_2 ′	a_2 ′	a_2 ′	a_2 ′	a_2 ′
Jan.	0.5	0.5	0.5	0.5	0.5	0.5	0.6	0.6	0.6	0.6	0.6	0.7
Feb.	.4	.4	.4	.4	.4	.4	.4	.4	.5	.5	.5	.6
Mar.	.4	.4	.3	.3	.3	.3	.3	.3	.3	.3	.4	.4
Apr.	0.5	0.4	0.4	0.3	0.3	0.3	0.2	0.2	0.2	0.2	0.3	0.3
May	.6	.6	.5	.4	.4	.3	.3	.2	.2	.2	.2	.2
June	.8	.7	.6	.6	.5	.4	.4	.3	.3	.2	.2	.2
July	0.9	0.8	0.8	0.7	0.7	0.6	0.5	0.5	0.4	0.4	0.3	0.3
Aug.	.9	.9	.9	.9	.8	.8	.7	.6	.6	.5	.5	.4
Sept.	.9	.9	.9	.9	.9	.9	.9	.8	.8	.7	.7	.6
Oct.	0.8	0.8	0.9	0.9	0.9	0.9	0.9	0.9	0.9	0.9	0.8	0.8
Nov.	.6	.7	.8	.8	.9	.9	1.0	1.0	1.0	1.0	1.0	1.0
Dec.	0.5	0.6	0.6	0.7	0.8	0.9	0.9	1.0	1.0	1.0	1.0	1.0

Lat. °	AZIMUTH °	°	°	°	°	°	°	°	°	°	°	°
0	0.3	0.4	0.5	0.6	0.6	0.7	0.7	0.7	0.7	0.6	0.6	0.5
20	0.3	0.4	0.5	0.6	0.7	0.7	0.7	0.7	0.7	0.7	0.6	0.5
40	0.4	0.5	0.6	0.8	0.8	0.9	0.9	0.9	0.9	0.8	0.8	0.7
50	0.5	0.6	0.8	0.9	1.0	1.1	1.1	1.1	1.1	1.0	0.9	0.8
55	0.5	0.7	0.9	1.0	1.1	1.2	1.2	1.2	1.2	1.1	1.0	0.9
60	0.6	0.8	1.0	1.1	1.3	1.4	1.4	1.4	1.4	1.3	1.2	1.0
65	0.6	0.9	1.2	1.4	1.5	1.6	1.7	1.7	1.6	1.5	1.4	1.2

Latitude = Apparent altitude (corrected for refraction) - 1° + a_0 + a_1 + a_2

The table is entered with LHA Aries to determine the column to be used; each column refers to a range of 10°. a_0 is taken, without interpolation, from the upper table with the units of LHA Aries in degrees as argument; a_1, a_2 are taken, without interpolation, from the second and third tables with arguments latitude and month respectively. a_0, a_1, a_2, are always positive. The final table gives the azimuth of *Polaris*.

CONVERSION OF ARC TO TIME

0°–59°			60°–119°			120°–179°			180°–239°			240°–299°			300°–359°				0′.00		0′.25		0′.50		0′.75	
°	h	m	°	h	m	°	h	m	°	h	m	°	h	m	°	h	m	°	m	s	m	s	m	s	m	s
0	0	00	60	4	00	120	8	00	180	12	00	240	16	00	300	20	00	0	0	00	0	01	0	02	0	03
1	0	04	61	4	04	121	8	04	181	12	04	241	16	04	301	20	04	1	0	04	0	05	0	06	0	07
2	0	08	62	4	08	122	8	08	182	12	08	242	16	08	302	20	08	2	0	08	0	09	0	10	0	11
3	0	12	63	4	12	123	8	12	183	12	12	243	16	12	303	20	12	3	0	12	0	13	0	14	0	15
4	0	16	64	4	16	124	8	16	184	12	16	244	16	16	304	20	16	4	0	16	0	17	0	18	0	19
5	0	20	65	4	20	125	8	20	185	12	20	245	16	20	305	20	20	5	0	20	0	21	0	22	0	23
6	0	24	66	4	24	126	8	24	186	12	24	246	16	24	306	20	24	6	0	24	0	25	0	26	0	27
7	0	28	67	4	28	127	8	28	187	12	28	247	16	28	307	20	28	7	0	28	0	29	0	30	0	31
8	0	32	68	4	32	128	8	32	188	12	32	248	16	32	308	20	32	8	0	32	0	33	0	34	0	35
9	0	36	69	4	36	129	8	36	189	12	36	249	16	36	309	20	36	9	0	36	0	37	0	38	0	39
10	0	40	70	4	40	130	8	40	190	12	40	250	16	40	310	20	40	10	0	40	0	41	0	42	0	43
11	0	44	71	4	44	131	8	44	191	12	44	251	16	44	311	20	44	11	0	44	0	45	0	46	0	47
12	0	48	72	4	48	132	8	48	192	12	48	252	16	48	312	20	48	12	0	48	0	49	0	50	0	51
13	0	52	73	4	52	133	8	52	193	12	52	253	16	52	313	20	52	13	0	52	0	53	0	54	0	55
14	0	56	74	4	56	134	8	56	194	12	56	254	16	56	314	20	56	14	0	56	0	57	0	58	0	59
15	1	00	75	5	00	135	9	00	195	13	00	255	17	00	315	21	00	15	1	00	1	01	1	02	1	03
16	1	04	76	5	04	136	9	04	196	13	04	256	17	04	316	21	04	16	1	04	1	05	1	06	1	07
17	1	08	77	5	08	137	9	08	197	13	08	257	17	08	317	21	08	17	1	08	1	09	1	10	1	11
18	1	12	78	5	12	138	9	12	198	13	12	258	17	12	318	21	12	18	1	12	1	13	1	14	1	15
19	1	16	79	5	16	139	9	16	199	13	16	259	17	16	319	21	16	19	1	16	1	17	1	18	1	19
20	1	20	80	5	20	140	9	20	200	13	20	260	17	20	320	21	20	20	1	20	1	21	1	22	1	23
21	1	24	81	5	24	141	9	24	201	13	24	261	17	24	321	21	24	21	1	24	1	25	1	26	1	27
22	1	28	82	5	28	142	9	28	202	13	28	262	17	28	322	21	28	22	1	28	1	29	1	30	1	31
23	1	32	83	5	32	143	9	32	203	13	32	263	17	32	323	21	32	23	1	32	1	33	1	34	1	35
24	1	36	84	5	36	144	9	36	204	13	36	264	17	36	324	21	36	24	1	36	1	37	1	38	1	39
25	1	40	85	5	40	145	9	40	205	13	40	265	17	40	325	21	40	25	1	40	1	41	1	42	1	43
26	1	44	86	5	44	146	9	44	206	13	44	266	17	44	326	21	44	26	1	44	1	45	1	46	1	47
27	1	48	87	5	48	147	9	48	207	13	48	267	17	48	327	21	48	27	1	48	1	49	1	50	1	51
28	1	52	88	5	52	148	9	52	208	13	52	268	17	52	328	21	52	28	1	52	1	53	1	54	1	55
29	1	56	89	5	56	149	9	56	209	13	56	269	17	56	329	21	56	29	1	56	1	57	1	58	1	59
30	2	00	90	6	00	150	10	00	210	14	00	270	18	00	330	22	00	30	2	00	2	01	2	02	2	03
31	2	04	91	6	04	151	10	04	211	14	04	271	18	04	331	22	04	31	2	04	2	05	2	06	2	07
32	2	08	92	6	08	152	10	08	212	14	08	272	18	08	332	22	08	32	2	08	2	09	2	10	2	11
33	2	12	93	6	12	153	10	12	213	14	12	273	18	12	333	22	12	33	2	12	2	13	2	14	2	15
34	2	16	94	6	16	154	10	16	214	14	16	274	18	16	334	22	16	34	2	16	2	17	2	18	2	19
35	2	20	95	6	20	155	10	20	215	14	20	275	18	20	335	22	20	35	2	20	2	21	2	22	2	23
36	2	24	96	6	24	156	10	24	216	14	24	276	18	24	336	22	24	36	2	24	2	25	2	26	2	27
37	2	28	97	6	28	157	10	28	217	14	28	277	18	28	337	22	28	37	2	28	2	29	2	30	2	31
38	2	32	98	6	32	158	10	32	218	14	32	278	18	32	338	22	32	38	2	32	2	33	2	34	2	35
39	2	36	99	6	36	159	10	36	219	14	36	279	18	36	339	22	36	39	2	36	2	37	2	38	2	39
40	2	40	100	6	40	160	10	40	220	14	40	280	18	40	340	22	40	40	2	40	2	41	2	42	2	43
41	2	44	101	6	44	161	10	44	221	14	44	281	18	44	341	22	44	41	2	44	2	45	2	46	2	47
42	2	48	102	6	48	162	10	48	222	14	48	282	18	48	342	22	48	42	2	48	2	49	2	50	2	51
43	2	52	103	6	52	163	10	52	223	14	52	283	18	52	343	22	52	43	2	52	2	53	2	54	2	55
44	2	56	104	6	56	164	10	56	224	14	56	284	18	56	344	22	56	44	2	56	2	57	2	58	2	59
45	3	00	105	7	00	165	11	00	225	15	00	285	19	00	345	23	00	45	3	00	3	01	3	02	3	03
46	3	04	106	7	04	166	11	04	226	15	04	286	19	04	346	23	04	46	3	04	3	05	3	06	3	07
47	3	08	107	7	08	167	11	08	227	15	08	287	19	08	347	23	08	47	3	08	3	09	3	10	3	11
48	3	12	108	7	12	168	11	12	228	15	12	288	19	12	348	23	12	48	3	12	3	13	3	14	3	15
49	3	16	109	7	16	169	11	16	229	15	16	289	19	16	349	23	16	49	3	16	3	17	3	18	3	19
50	3	20	110	7	20	170	11	20	230	15	20	290	19	20	350	23	20	50	3	20	3	21	3	22	3	23
51	3	24	111	7	24	171	11	24	231	15	24	291	19	24	351	23	24	51	3	24	3	25	3	26	3	27
52	3	28	112	7	28	172	11	28	232	15	28	292	19	28	352	23	28	52	3	28	3	29	3	30	3	31
53	3	32	113	7	32	173	11	32	233	15	32	293	19	32	353	23	32	53	3	32	3	33	3	34	3	35
54	3	36	114	7	36	174	11	36	234	15	36	294	19	36	354	23	36	54	3	36	3	37	3	38	3	39
55	3	40	115	7	40	175	11	40	235	15	40	295	19	40	355	23	40	55	3	40	3	41	3	42	3	43
56	3	44	116	7	44	176	11	44	236	15	44	296	19	44	356	23	44	56	3	44	3	45	3	46	3	47
57	3	48	117	7	48	177	11	48	237	15	48	297	19	48	357	23	48	57	3	48	3	49	3	50	3	51
58	3	52	118	7	52	178	11	52	238	15	52	298	19	52	358	23	52	58	3	52	3	53	3	54	3	55
59	3	56	119	7	56	179	11	56	239	15	56	299	19	56	359	23	56	59	3	56	3	57	3	58	3	59

The above table is for converting expressions in acr to their equivalent in time; its main use in ths Almanac is for the conversion of longitude for application to LMT (*added* if west, *subtacted* if east) to give UT or vice versa, particularly in the case of sunrise, sunset, etc.

INCREMENTS AND CORRECTIONS

0m ... **1m**

m 0	SUN PLANETS	ARIES	MOON	v or Corrⁿ d	v or Corrⁿ d	v or Corrⁿ d
s	° ′	° ′	° ′	′ ′	′ ′	′ ′
00	0 00.0	0 00.0	0 00.0	0.0 0.0	6.0 0.1	12.0 0.1
01	0 00.3	0 00.3	0 00.2	0.1 0.0	6.1 0.1	12.1 0.1
02	0 00.5	0 00.5	0 00.5	0.2 0.0	6.2 0.1	12.2 0.1
03	0 00.8	0 00.8	0 00.7	0.3 0.0	6.3 0.1	12.3 0.1
04	0 01.0	0 01.0	0 01.0	0.4 0.0	6.4 0.1	12.4 0.1
05	0 01.3	0 01.3	0 01.2	0.5 0.0	6.5 0.1	12.5 0.1
06	0 01.5	0 01.5	0 01.4	0.6 0.0	6.6 0.1	12.6 0.1
07	0 01.8	0 01.8	0 01.7	0.7 0.0	6.7 0.1	12.7 0.1
08	0 02.0	0 02.0	0 01.9	0.8 0.0	6.8 0.1	12.8 0.1
09	0 02.3	0 02.3	0 02.1	0.9 0.0	6.9 0.1	12.9 0.1
10	0 02.5	0 02.5	0 02.4	1.0 0.0	7.0 0.1	13.0 0.1
11	0 02.8	0 02.8	0 02.6	1.1 0.0	7.1 0.1	13.1 0.1
12	0 03.0	0 03.0	0 02.9	1.2 0.0	7.2 0.1	13.2 0.1
13	0 03.3	0 03.3	0 03.1	1.3 0.0	7.3 0.1	13.3 0.1
14	0 03.5	0 03.5	0 03.3	1.4 0.0	7.4 0.1	13.4 0.1
15	0 03.8	0 03.8	0 03.6	1.5 0.0	7.5 0.1	13.5 0.1
16	0 04.0	0 04.0	0 03.8	1.6 0.0	7.6 0.1	13.6 0.1
17	0 04.3	0 04.3	0 04.1	1.7 0.0	7.7 0.1	13.7 0.1
18	0 04.5	0 04.5	0 04.3	1.8 0.0	7.8 0.1	13.8 0.1
19	0 04.8	0 04.8	0 04.5	1.9 0.0	7.9 0.1	13.9 0.1
20	0 05.0	0 05.0	0 04.8	2.0 0.0	8.0 0.1	14.0 0.1
21	0 05.3	0 05.3	0 05.0	2.1 0.0	8.1 0.1	14.1 0.1
22	0 05.5	0 05.5	0 05.2	2.2 0.0	8.2 0.1	14.2 0.1
23	0 05.8	0 05.8	0 05.5	2.3 0.0	8.3 0.1	14.3 0.1
24	0 06.0	0 06.0	0 05.7	2.4 0.0	8.4 0.1	14.4 0.1
25	0 06.3	0 06.3	0 06.0	2.5 0.0	8.5 0.1	14.5 0.1
26	0 06.5	0 06.5	0 06.2	2.6 0.0	8.6 0.1	14.6 0.1
27	0 06.8	0 06.8	0 06.4	2.7 0.0	8.7 0.1	14.7 0.1
28	0 07.0	0 07.0	0 06.7	2.8 0.0	8.8 0.1	14.8 0.1
29	0 07.3	0 07.3	0 06.9	2.9 0.0	8.9 0.1	14.9 0.1
30	0 07.5	0 07.5	0 07.2	3.0 0.0	9.0 0.1	15.0 0.1
31	0 07.8	0 07.8	0 07.4	3.1 0.0	9.1 0.1	15.1 0.1
32	0 08.0	0 08.0	0 07.6	3.2 0.0	9.2 0.1	15.2 0.1
33	0 08.3	0 08.3	0 07.9	3.3 0.0	9.3 0.1	15.3 0.1
34	0 08.5	0 08.5	0 08.1	3.4 0.0	9.4 0.1	15.4 0.1
35	0 08.8	0 08.8	0 08.4	3.5 0.0	9.5 0.1	15.5 0.1
36	0 09.0	0 09.0	0 08.6	3.6 0.0	9.6 0.1	15.6 0.1
37	0 09.3	0 09.3	0 08.8	3.7 0.0	9.7 0.1	15.7 0.1
38	0 09.5	0 09.5	0 09.1	3.8 0.0	9.8 0.1	15.8 0.1
39	0 09.8	0 09.8	0 09.3	3.9 0.0	9.9 0.1	15.9 0.1
40	0 10.0	0 10.0	0 09.5	4.0 0.0	10.0 0.1	16.0 0.1
41	0 10.3	0 10.3	0 09.8	4.1 0.0	10.1 0.1	16.1 0.1
42	0 10.5	0 10.5	0 10.0	4.2 0.0	10.2 0.1	16.2 0.1
43	0 10.8	0 10.8	0 10.3	4.3 0.0	10.3 0.1	16.3 0.1
44	0 11.0	0 11.0	0 10.5	4.4 0.0	10.4 0.1	16.4 0.1
45	0 11.3	0 11.3	0 10.7	4.5 0.0	10.5 0.1	16.5 0.1
46	0 11.5	0 11.5	0 11.0	4.6 0.0	10.6 0.1	16.6 0.1
47	0 11.8	0 11.8	0 11.2	4.7 0.0	10.7 0.1	16.7 0.1
48	0 12.0	0 12.0	0 11.5	4.8 0.0	10.8 0.1	16.8 0.1
49	0 12.3	0 12.3	0 11.7	4.9 0.0	10.9 0.1	16.9 0.1
50	0 12.5	0 12.5	0 11.9	5.0 0.0	11.0 0.1	17.0 0.1
51	0 12.8	0 12.8	0 12.2	5.1 0.0	11.1 0.1	17.1 0.1
52	0 13.0	0 13.0	0 12.4	5.2 0.0	11.2 0.1	17.2 0.1
53	0 13.3	0 13.3	0 12.6	5.3 0.0	11.3 0.1	17.3 0.1
54	0 13.5	0 13.5	0 12.9	5.4 0.0	11.4 0.1	17.4 0.1
55	0 13.8	0 13.8	0 13.1	5.5 0.0	11.5 0.1	17.5 0.1
56	0 14.0	0 14.0	0 13.4	5.6 0.0	11.6 0.1	17.6 0.1
57	0 14.3	0 14.3	0 13.6	5.7 0.0	11.7 0.1	17.7 0.1
58	0 14.5	0 14.5	0 13.8	5.8 0.0	11.8 0.1	17.8 0.1
59	0 14.8	0 14.8	0 14.1	5.9 0.0	11.9 0.1	17.9 0.1
60	0 15.0	0 15.0	0 14.3	6.0 0.1	12.0 0.1	18.0 0.2

m 1	SUN PLANETS	ARIES	MOON	v or Corrⁿ d	v or Corrⁿ d	v or Corrⁿ d
s	° ′	° ′	° ′	′ ′	′ ′	′ ′
00	0 15.0	0 15.0	0 14.3	0.0 0.0	6.0 0.2	12.0 0.3
01	0 15.3	0 15.3	0 14.6	0.1 0.0	6.1 0.2	12.1 0.3
02	0 15.5	0 15.5	0 14.8	0.2 0.0	6.2 0.2	12.2 0.3
03	0 15.8	0 15.8	0 15.0	0.3 0.0	6.3 0.2	12.3 0.3
04	0 16.0	0 16.0	0 15.3	0.4 0.0	6.4 0.2	12.4 0.3
05	0 16.3	0 16.3	0 15.5	0.5 0.0	6.5 0.2	12.5 0.3
06	0 16.5	0 16.5	0 15.7	0.6 0.0	6.6 0.2	12.6 0.3
07	0 16.8	0 16.8	0 16.0	0.7 0.0	6.7 0.2	12.7 0.3
08	0 17.0	0 17.0	0 16.2	0.8 0.0	6.8 0.2	12.8 0.3
09	0 17.3	0 17.3	0 16.5	0.9 0.0	6.9 0.2	12.9 0.3
10	0 17.5	0 17.5	0 16.7	1.0 0.0	7.0 0.2	13.0 0.3
11	0 17.8	0 17.8	0 16.9	1.1 0.0	7.1 0.2	13.1 0.3
12	0 18.0	0 18.0	0 17.2	1.2 0.0	7.2 0.2	13.2 0.3
13	0 18.3	0 18.3	0 17.4	1.3 0.0	7.3 0.2	13.3 0.3
14	0 18.5	0 18.6	0 17.7	1.4 0.0	7.4 0.2	13.4 0.3
15	0 18.8	0 18.8	0 17.9	1.5 0.0	7.5 0.2	13.5 0.3
16	0 19.0	0 19.1	0 18.1	1.6 0.0	7.6 0.2	13.6 0.3
17	0 19.3	0 19.3	0 18.4	1.7 0.0	7.7 0.2	13.7 0.3
18	0 19.5	0 19.6	0 18.6	1.8 0.0	7.8 0.2	13.8 0.3
19	0 19.8	0 19.8	0 18.9	1.9 0.0	7.9 0.2	13.9 0.3
20	0 20.0	0 20.1	0 19.1	2.0 0.1	8.0 0.2	14.0 0.4
21	0 20.3	0 20.3	0 19.3	2.1 0.1	8.1 0.2	14.1 0.4
22	0 20.5	0 20.6	0 19.6	2.2 0.1	8.2 0.2	14.2 0.4
23	0 20.8	0 20.8	0 19.8	2.3 0.1	8.3 0.2	14.3 0.4
24	0 21.0	0 21.1	0 20.0	2.4 0.1	8.4 0.2	14.4 0.4
25	0 21.3	0 21.3	0 20.3	2.5 0.1	8.5 0.2	14.5 0.4
26	0 21.5	0 21.6	0 20.5	2.6 0.1	8.6 0.2	14.6 0.4
27	0 21.8	0 21.8	0 20.8	2.7 0.1	8.7 0.2	14.7 0.4
28	0 22.0	0 22.1	0 21.0	2.8 0.1	8.8 0.2	14.8 0.4
29	0 22.3	0 22.3	0 21.2	2.9 0.1	8.9 0.2	14.9 0.4
30	0 22.5	0 22.6	0 21.5	3.0 0.1	9.0 0.2	15.0 0.4
31	0 22.8	0 22.8	0 21.7	3.1 0.1	9.1 0.2	15.1 0.4
32	0 23.0	0 23.1	0 22.0	3.2 0.1	9.2 0.2	15.2 0.4
33	0 23.3	0 23.3	0 22.2	3.3 0.1	9.3 0.2	15.3 0.4
34	0 23.5	0 23.6	0 22.4	3.4 0.1	9.4 0.2	15.4 0.4
35	0 23.8	0 23.8	0 22.7	3.5 0.1	9.5 0.2	15.5 0.4
36	0 24.0	0 24.1	0 22.9	3.6 0.1	9.6 0.2	15.6 0.4
37	0 24.3	0 24.3	0 23.1	3.7 0.1	9.7 0.2	15.7 0.4
38	0 24.5	0 24.6	0 23.4	3.8 0.1	9.8 0.2	15.8 0.4
39	0 24.8	0 24.8	0 23.6	3.9 0.1	9.9 0.2	15.9 0.4
40	0 25.0	0 25.1	0 23.9	4.0 0.1	10.0 0.3	16.0 0.4
41	0 25.3	0 25.3	0 24.1	4.1 0.1	10.1 0.3	16.1 0.4
42	0 25.5	0 25.6	0 24.3	4.2 0.1	10.2 0.3	16.2 0.4
43	0 25.8	0 25.8	0 24.6	4.3 0.1	10.3 0.3	16.3 0.4
44	0 26.0	0 26.1	0 24.8	4.4 0.1	10.4 0.3	16.4 0.4
45	0 26.3	0 26.3	0 25.1	4.5 0.1	10.5 0.3	16.5 0.4
46	0 26.5	0 26.6	0 25.3	4.6 0.1	10.6 0.3	16.6 0.4
47	0 26.8	0 26.8	0 25.5	4.7 0.1	10.7 0.3	16.7 0.4
48	0 27.0	0 27.1	0 25.8	4.8 0.1	10.8 0.3	16.8 0.4
49	0 27.3	0 27.3	0 26.0	4.9 0.1	10.9 0.3	16.9 0.4
50	0 27.5	0 27.6	0 26.2	5.0 0.1	11.0 0.3	17.0 0.4
51	0 27.8	0 27.8	0 26.5	5.1 0.1	11.1 0.3	17.1 0.4
52	0 28.0	0 28.1	0 26.7	5.2 0.1	11.2 0.3	17.2 0.4
53	0 28.3	0 28.3	0 27.0	5.3 0.1	11.3 0.3	17.3 0.4
54	0 28.5	0 28.6	0 27.2	5.4 0.1	11.4 0.3	17.4 0.4
55	0 28.8	0 28.8	0 27.4	5.5 0.1	11.5 0.3	17.5 0.4
56	0 29.0	0 29.1	0 27.7	5.6 0.1	11.6 0.3	17.6 0.4
57	0 29.3	0 29.3	0 27.9	5.7 0.1	11.7 0.3	17.7 0.4
58	0 29.5	0 29.6	0 28.2	5.8 0.1	11.8 0.3	17.8 0.4
59	0 29.8	0 29.8	0 28.4	5.9 0.1	11.9 0.3	17.9 0.4
60	0 30.0	0 30.1	0 28.6	6.0 0.2	12.0 0.3	18.0 0.5

2m   INCREMENTS AND CORRECTIONS   3m

m 2	SUN PLANETS	ARIES	MOON	v or Corrⁿ d	v or Corrⁿ d	v or Corrⁿ d	m 3	SUN PLANETS	ARIES	MOON	v or Corrⁿ d	v or Corrⁿ d	v or Corrⁿ d
s	° ′	° ′	° ′	′ ′	′ ′	′ ′	s	° ′	° ′	° ′	′ ′	′ ′	′ ′
00	0 30.0	0 30.1	0 28.6	0.0 0.0	6.0 0.3	12.0 0.5	00	0 45.0	0 45.1	0 43.0	0.0 0.0	6.0 0.4	12.0 0.7
01	0 30.3	0 30.3	0 28.9	0.1 0.0	6.1 0.3	12.1 0.1	01	0 45.3	0 45.4	0 43.2	0.1 0.0	6.1 0.4	12.1 0.7
02	0 30.5	0 30.6	0 29.1	0.2 0.0	6.2 0.3	12.2 0.5	02	0 45.5	0 45.6	0 43.4	0.2 0.0	6.2 0.4	12.2 0.7
03	0 30.8	0 30.8	0 29.3	0.3 0.0	6.3 0.3	12.3 0.5	03	0 45.8	0 45.9	0 43.7	0.3 0.0	6.3 0.4	12.3 0.7
04	0 31.0	0 31.1	0 29.6	0.4 0.0	6.4 0.3	12.4 0.5	04	0 46.0	0 46.1	0 43.9	0.4 0.0	6.4 0.4	12.4 0.7
05	0 31.3	0 31.3	0 29.8	0.5 0.0	6.5 0.3	12.5 0.5	05	0 46.3	0 46.4	0 44.1	0.5 0.0	6.5 0.4	12.5 0.7
06	0 31.5	0 31.6	0 30.1	0.6 0.0	6.6 0.3	12.6 0.5	06	0 46.5	0 46.6	0 44.4	0.6 0.0	6.6 0.4	12.6 0.7
07	0 31.8	0 31.8	0 30.3	0.7 0.0	6.7 0.3	12.7 0.5	07	0 46.8	0 46.9	0 44.6	0.7 0.0	6.7 0.4	12.7 0.7
08	0 32.0	0 32.1	0 30.5	0.8 0.0	6.8 0.3	12.8 0.5	08	0 47.0	0 47.1	0 44.9	0.8 0.0	6.8 0.4	12.8 0.7
09	0 32.3	0 32.3	0 30.8	0.9 0.0	6.9 0.3	12.9 0.5	09	0 47.3	0 47.4	0 45.1	0.9 0.1	6.9 0.4	12.9 0.8
10	0 32.5	0 32.6	0 31.0	1.0 0.0	7.0 0.3	13.0 0.5	10	0 47.5	0 47.6	0 45.3	1.0 0.1	7.0 0.4	13.0 0.8
11	0 32.8	0 32.8	0 31.3	1.1 0.0	7.1 0.3	13.1 0.5	11	0 47.8	0 47.9	0 45.6	1.1 0.1	7.1 0.4	13.1 0.8
12	0 33.0	0 33.1	0 31.5	1.2 0.1	7.2 0.3	13.2 0.6	12	0 48.0	0 48.1	0 45.8	1.2 0.1	7.2 0.4	13.2 0.8
13	0 33.3	0 33.3	0 31.7	1.3 0.1	7.3 0.3	13.3 0.6	13	0 48.3	0 48.4	0 46.1	1.3 0.1	7.3 0.4	13.3 0.8
14	0 33.5	0 33.6	0 32.0	1.4 0.1	7.4 0.3	13.4 0.6	14	0 48.5	0 48.6	0 46.3	1.4 0.1	7.4 0.4	13.4 0.8
15	0 33.8	0 33.8	0 32.2	1.5 0.1	7.5 0.3	13.5 0.6	15	0 48.8	0 48.9	0 46.5	1.5 0.1	7.5 0.4	13.5 0.8
16	0 34.0	0 34.1	0 32.5	1.6 0.1	7.6 0.3	13.6 0.6	16	0 49.0	0 49.1	0 46.8	1.6 0.1	7.6 0.4	13.6 0.8
17	0 34.3	0 34.3	0 32.7	1.7 0.1	7.7 0.3	13.7 0.6	17	0 49.3	0 49.4	0 47.0	1.7 0.1	7.7 0.4	13.7 0.8
18	0 34.5	0 34.6	0 32.9	1.8 0.1	7.8 0.3	13.8 0.6	18	0 49.5	0 49.6	0 47.2	1.8 0.1	7.8 0.5	13.8 0.8
19	0 34.8	0 34.8	0 33.2	1.9 0.1	7.9 0.3	13.9 0.6	19	0 49.8	0 49.9	0 47.5	1.9 0.1	7.9 0.5	13.9 0.8
20	0 35.0	0 35.1	0 33.4	2.0 0.1	8.0 0.3	14.0 0.6	20	0 50.0	0 50.1	0 47.7	2.0 0.1	8.0 0.5	14.0 0.8
21	0 35.3	0 35.3	0 33.6	2.1 0.1	8.1 0.3	14.1 0.6	21	0 50.3	0 50.4	0 48.0	2.1 0.1	8.1 0.5	14.1 0.8
22	0 35.5	0 35.6	0 33.9	2.2 0.1	8.2 0.3	14.2 0.6	22	0 50.5	0 50.6	0 48.2	2.2 0.1	8.2 0.5	14.2 0.8
23	0 35.8	0 35.8	0 34.1	2.3 0.1	8.3 0.3	14.3 0.6	23	0 50.8	0 50.9	0 48.4	2.3 0.1	8.3 0.5	14.3 0.8
24	0 36.0	0 36.1	0 34.4	2.4 0.1	8.4 0.4	14.4 0.6	24	0 51.0	0 51.1	0 48.7	2.4 0.1	8.4 0.5	14.4 0.8
25	0 36.3	0 36.3	0 34.6	2.5 0.1	8.5 0.4	14.5 0.6	25	0 51.3	0 51.4	0 48.9	2.5 0.1	8.5 0.5	14.5 0.8
26	0 36.5	0 36.6	0 34.8	2.6 0.1	8.6 0.4	14.6 0.6	26	0 51.5	0 51.6	0 49.2	2.6 0.2	8.6 0.5	14.6 0.9
27	0 36.8	0 36.9	0 35.1	2.7 0.1	8.7 0.4	14.7 0.6	27	0 51.8	0 51.9	0 49.4	2.7 0.2	8.7 0.5	14.7 0.9
28	0 37.0	0 37.1	0 35.3	2.8 0.1	8.8 0.4	14.8 0.6	28	0 52.0	0 52.1	0 49.6	2.8 0.2	8.8 0.5	14.8 0.9
29	0 37.3	0 37.4	0 35.6	2.9 0.1	8.9 0.4	14.9 0.6	29	0 52.3	0 52.4	0 49.9	2.9 0.2	8.9 0.5	14.9 0.9
30	0 37.5	0 37.6	0 35.8	3.0 0.1	9.0 0.4	15.0 0.6	30	0 52.5	0 52.6	0 50.1	3.0 0.2	9.0 0.5	15.0 0.9
31	0 37.8	0 37.9	0 36.0	3.1 0.1	9.1 0.4	15.1 0.6	31	0 52.8	0 52.9	0 50.3	3.1 0.2	9.1 0.5	15.1 0.9
32	0 38.0	0 38.1	0 36.3	3.2 0.1	9.2 0.4	15.2 0.6	32	0 53.0	0 53.1	0 50.6	3.2 0.2	9.2 0.5	15.2 0.9
33	0 38.3	0 38.4	0 36.5	3.3 0.1	9.3 0.4	15.3 0.6	33	0 53.3	0 53.4	0 50.8	3.3 0.2	9.3 0.5	15.3 0.9
34	0 38.5	0 38.6	0 36.7	3.4 0.1	9.4 0.4	15.4 0.6	34	0 53.5	0 53.6	0 51.1	3.4 0.2	9.4 0.5	15.4 0.9
35	0 38.8	0 38.9	0 37.0	3.5 0.1	9.5 0.4	15.5 0.6	35	0 53.8	0 53.9	0 51.3	3.5 0.2	9.5 0.6	15.5 0.9
36	0 39.0	0 39.1	0 37.2	3.6 0.2	9.6 0.4	15.6 0.7	36	0 54.0	0 54.1	0 51.5	3.6 0.2	9.6 0.6	15.6 0.9
37	0 39.3	0 39.4	0 37.5	3.7 0.2	9.7 0.4	15.7 0.7	37	0 54.3	0 54.4	0 51.8	3.7 0.2	9.7 0.6	15.7 0.9
38	0 39.5	0 39.6	0 37.7	3.8 0.2	9.8 0.4	15.8 0.7	38	0 54.5	0 54.6	0 52.0	3.8 0.2	9.8 0.6	15.8 0.9
39	0 39.8	0 39.9	0 37.9	3.9 0.2	9.9 0.4	15.9 0.7	39	0 54.8	0 54.9	0 52.3	3.9 0.2	9.9 0.6	15.9 0.9
40	0 40.0	0 40.1	0 38.2	4.0 0.2	10.0 0.4	16.0 0.7	40	0 55.0	0 55.2	0 52.5	4.0 0.2	10.0 0.6	16.0 0.9
41	0 40.3	0 40.4	0 38.4	4.1 0.2	10.1 0.4	16.1 0.7	41	0 55.3	0 55.4	0 52.7	4.1 0.2	10.1 0.6	16.1 0.9
42	0 40.5	0 40.6	0 38.7	4.2 0.2	10.2 0.4	16.2 0.7	42	0 55.5	0 55.7	0 53.0	4.2 0.2	10.2 0.6	16.2 0.9
43	0 40.8	0 40.9	0 38.9	4.3 0.2	10.3 0.4	16.3 0.7	43	0 55.8	0 55.9	0 53.2	4.3 0.3	10.3 0.6	16.3 1.0
44	0 41.0	0 41.1	0 39.1	4.4 0.2	10.4 0.4	16.4 0.7	44	0 56.0	0 56.2	0 53.4	4.4 0.3	10.4 0.6	16.4 1.0
45	0 41.3	0 41.4	0 39.4	4.5 0.2	10.5 0.4	16.5 0.7	45	0 56.3	0 56.4	0 53.7	4.5 0.3	10.5 0.6	16.5 1.0
46	0 41.5	0 41.6	0 39.6	4.6 0.2	10.6 0.4	16.6 0.7	46	0 56.5	0 56.7	0 53.9	4.6 0.3	10.6 0.6	16.6 1.0
47	0 41.8	0 41.9	0 39.8	4.7 0.2	10.7 0.4	16.7 0.7	47	0 56.8	0 56.9	0 54.2	4.7 0.3	10.7 0.6	16.7 1.0
48	0 42.0	0 42.1	0 40.1	4.8 0.2	10.8 0.5	16.8 0.7	48	0 57.0	0 57.2	0 54.4	4.8 0.3	10.8 0.6	16.8 1.0
49	0 42.3	0 42.4	0 40.3	4.9 0.2	10.9 0.5	16.9 0.7	49	0 57.3	0 57.4	0 54.6	4.9 0.3	10.9 0.6	16.9 1.0
50	0 42.5	0 42.6	0 40.6	5.0 0.2	11.0 0.5	17.0 0.7	50	0 57.5	0 57.7	0 54.9	5.0 0.3	11.0 0.6	17.0 1.0
51	0 42.8	0 42.9	0 40.8	5.1 0.2	11.1 0.5	17.1 0.7	51	0 57.8	0 57.9	0 55.1	5.1 0.3	11.1 0.6	17.1 1.0
52	0 43.0	0 43.1	0 41.0	5.2 0.2	11.2 0.5	17.2 0.7	52	0 58.0	0 58.2	0 55.4	5.2 0.3	11.2 0.7	17.2 1.0
53	0 43.3	0 43.4	0 41.3	5.3 0.2	11.3 0.5	17.3 0.7	53	0 58.3	0 58.4	0 55.6	5.3 0.3	11.3 0.7	17.3 1.0
54	0 43.5	0 43.6	0 41.5	5.4 0.2	11.4 0.5	17.4 0.7	54	0 58.5	0 58.7	0 55.8	5.4 0.3	11.4 0.7	17.4 1.0
55	0 43.8	0 43.9	0 41.8	5.5 0.2	11.5 0.5	17.5 0.7	55	0 58.8	0 58.9	0 56.1	5.5 0.3	11.5 0.7	17.5 1.0
56	0 44.0	0 44.1	0 42.0	5.6 0.2	11.6 0.5	17.6 0.7	56	0 59.0	0 59.2	0 56.3	5.6 0.3	11.6 0.7	17.6 1.0
57	0 44.3	0 44.4	0 42.2	5.7 0.2	11.7 0.5	17.7 0.7	57	0 59.3	0 59.4	0 56.6	5.7 0.3	11.7 0.7	17.7 1.0
58	0 44.5	0 44.6	0 42.5	5.8 0.2	11.8 0.5	17.8 0.7	58	0 59.5	0 59.7	0 56.8	5.8 0.3	11.8 0.7	17.8 1.0
59	0 44.8	0 44.9	0 42.7	5.9 0.2	11.9 0.5	17.9 0.7	59	0 59.8	0 59.9	0 57.0	5.9 0.3	11.9 0.7	17.9 1.0
60	0 45.0	0 45.1	0 43.0	6.0 0.3	12.0 0.5	18.0 0.8	60	1 00.0	1 00.2	0 57.3	6.0 0.4	12.0 0.7	18.0 1.1

INCREMENTS AND CORRECTIONS

4m   **5m**

m 4 s	SUN PLANETS ° ′	ARIES ° ′	MOON ° ′	v or Corrn d ′ ′	v or Corrn d ′ ′	v or Corrn d ′ ′
00	1 00.0	1 00.2	0 57.3	0.0 0.0	6.0 0.5	12.0 0.9
01	1 00.3	1 00.4	0 57.5	0.1 0.0	6.1 0.5	12.1 0.9
02	1 00.5	1 00.7	0 57.7	0.2 0.0	6.2 0.5	12.2 0.9
03	1 00.8	1 00.9	0 58.0	0.3 0.0	6.3 0.5	12.3 0.9
04	1 01.0	1 01.2	0 58.2	0.4 0.0	6.4 0.5	12.4 0.9
05	1 01.3	1 01.4	0 58.5	0.5 0.0	6.5 0.5	12.5 0.9
06	1 01.5	1 01.7	0 58.7	0.6 0.0	6.6 0.5	12.6 0.9
07	1 01.8	1 01.9	0 58.9	0.7 0.1	6.7 0.5	12.7 1.0
08	1 02.0	1 02.2	0 59.2	0.8 0.1	6.8 0.5	12.8 1.0
09	1 02.3	1 02.4	0 59.4	0.9 0.1	6.9 0.5	12.9 1.0
10	1 02.5	1 02.7	0 59.7	1.0 0.1	7.0 0.5	13.0 1.0
11	1 02.8	1 02.9	0 59.9	1.1 0.1	7.1 0.5	13.1 1.0
12	1 03.0	1 03.2	1 00.1	1.2 0.1	7.2 0.5	13.2 1.0
13	1 03.3	1 03.4	1 00.4	1.3 0.1	7.3 0.5	13.3 1.0
14	1 03.5	1 03.7	1 00.6	1.4 0.1	7.4 0.6	13.4 1.0
15	1 03.8	1 03.9	1 00.8	1.5 0.1	7.5 0.6	13.5 1.0
16	1 04.0	1 04.2	1 01.1	1.6 0.1	7.6 0.6	13.6 1.0
17	1 04.3	1 04.4	1 01.3	1.7 0.1	7.7 0.6	13.7 1.0
18	1 04.5	1 04.7	1 01.6	1.8 0.1	7.8 0.6	13.8 1.0
19	1 04.8	1 04.9	1 01.8	1.9 0.1	7.9 0.6	13.9 1.0
20	1 05.0	1 05.2	1 02.0	2.0 0.2	8.0 0.6	14.0 1.1
21	1 05.3	1 05.4	1 02.3	2.1 0.2	8.1 0.6	14.1 1.1
22	1 05.5	1 05.7	1 02.5	2.2 0.2	8.2 0.6	14.2 1.1
23	1 05.8	1 05.9	1 02.8	2.3 0.2	8.3 0.6	14.3 1.1
24	1 06.0	1 06.2	1 03.0	2.4 0.2	8.4 0.6	14.4 1.1
25	1 06.3	1 06.4	1 03.2	2.5 0.2	8.5 0.6	14.5 1.1
26	1 06.5	1 06.7	1 03.5	2.6 0.2	8.6 0.6	14.6 1.1
27	1 06.8	1 06.9	1 03.7	2.7 0.2	8.7 0.7	14.7 1.1
28	1 07.0	1 07.2	1 03.9	2.8 0.2	8.8 0.7	14.8 1.1
29	1 07.3	1 07.4	1 04.2	2.9 0.2	8.9 0.7	14.9 1.1
30	1 07.5	1 07.7	1 04.4	3.0 0.2	9.0 0.7	15.0 1.1
31	1 07.8	1 07.9	1 04.7	3.1 0.2	9.1 0.7	15.1 1.1
32	1 08.0	1 08.2	1 04.9	3.2 0.2	9.2 0.7	15.2 1.1
33	1 08.3	1 08.4	1 05.1	3.3 0.2	9.3 0.7	15.3 1.1
34	1 08.5	1 08.7	1 05.4	3.4 0.3	9.4 0.7	15.4 1.2
35	1 08.8	1 08.9	1 05.6	3.5 0.3	9.5 0.7	15.5 1.2
36	1 09.0	1 09.2	1 05.9	3.6 0.3	9.6 0.7	15.6 1.2
37	1 09.3	1 09.4	1 06.1	3.7 0.3	9.7 0.7	15.7 1.2
38	1 09.5	1 09.7	1 06.3	3.8 0.3	9.8 0.7	15.8 1.2
39	1 09.8	1 09.9	1 06.6	3.9 0.3	9.9 0.7	15.9 1.2
40	1 10.0	1 10.2	1 06.8	4.0 0.3	10.0 0.8	16.0 1.2
41	1 10.3	1 10.4	1 07.0	4.1 0.3	10.1 0.8	16.1 1.2
42	1 10.5	1 10.7	1 07.3	4.2 0.3	10.2 0.8	16.2 1.2
43	1 10.8	1 10.9	1 07.5	4.3 0.3	10.3 0.8	16.3 1.2
44	1 11.0	1 11.2	1 07.8	4.4 0.3	10.4 0.8	16.4 1.2
45	1 11.3	1 11.4	1 08.0	4.5 0.3	10.5 0.8	16.5 1.2
46	1 11.5	1 11.7	1 08.2	4.6 0.3	10.6 0.8	16.6 1.2
47	1 11.8	1 11.9	1 08.5	4.7 0.4	10.7 0.8	16.7 1.3
48	1 12.0	1 12.2	1 08.7	4.8 0.4	10.8 0.8	16.8 1.3
49	1 12.3	1 12.4	1 09.0	4.9 0.4	10.9 0.8	16.9 1.3
50	1 12.5	1 12.7	1 09.2	5.0 0.4	11.0 0.8	17.0 1.3
51	1 12.8	1 12.9	1 09.4	5.1 0.4	11.1 0.8	17.1 1.3
52	1 13.0	1 13.2	1 09.7	5.2 0.4	11.2 0.8	17.2 1.3
53	1 13.3	1 13.5	1 09.9	5.3 0.4	11.3 0.8	17.3 1.3
54	1 13.5	1 13.7	1 10.2	5.4 0.4	11.4 0.9	17.4 1.3
55	1 13.8	1 14.0	1 10.4	5.5 0.4	11.5 0.9	17.5 1.3
56	1 14.0	1 14.2	1 10.6	5.6 0.4	11.6 0.9	17.6 1.3
57	1 14.3	1 14.5	1 10.9	5.7 0.4	11.7 0.9	17.7 1.3
58	1 14.5	1 14.7	1 11.1	5.8 0.4	11.8 0.9	17.8 1.3
59	1 14.8	1 15.0	1 11.3	5.9 0.4	11.9 0.9	17.9 1.3
60	1 15.0	1 15.2	1 11.6	6.0 0.5	12.0 0.9	18.0 1.4

m 5 s	SUN PLANETS ° ′	ARIES ° ′	MOON ° ′	v or Corrn d ′ ′	v or Corrn d ′ ′	v or Corrn d ′ ′
00	1 15.0	1 15.2	0 11.6	0.0 0.0	6.0 0.6	12.0 1.1
01	1 15.3	1 15.5	0 11.8	0.1 0.0	6.1 0.6	12.1 1.1
02	1 15.5	1 15.7	0 12.1	0.2 0.0	6.2 0.6	12.2 1.1
03	1 15.8	1 16.0	0 12.3	0.3 0.0	6.3 0.6	12.3 1.1
04	1 16.0	1 16.2	0 12.5	0.4 0.0	6.4 0.6	12.4 1.1
05	1 16.3	1 16.5	0 12.8	0.5 0.0	6.5 0.6	12.5 1.1
06	1 16.5	1 16.7	0 13.0	0.6 0.1	6.6 0.6	12.6 1.2
07	1 16.8	1 17.0	0 13.3	0.7 0.1	6.7 0.6	12.7 1.2
08	1 17.0	1 17.2	0 13.5	0.8 0.1	6.8 0.6	12.8 1.2
09	1 17.3	1 17.5	0 13.7	0.9 0.1	6.9 0.6	12.9 1.2
10	1 17.5	1 17.7	0 14.0	1.0 0.1	7.0 0.6	13.0 1.2
11	1 17.8	1 18.0	0 14.2	1.1 0.1	7.1 0.7	13.1 1.2
12	1 18.0	1 18.2	1 14.4	1.2 0.1	7.2 0.7	13.2 1.2
13	1 18.3	1 18.5	1 14.7	1.3 0.1	7.3 0.7	13.3 1.2
14	1 18.5	1 18.7	1 14.9	1.4 0.1	7.4 0.7	13.4 1.2
15	1 18.8	1 19.0	1 15.2	1.5 0.1	7.5 0.7	13.5 1.2
16	1 19.0	1 19.2	1 15.4	1.6 0.1	7.6 0.7	13.6 1.2
17	1 19.3	1 19.5	1 15.6	1.7 0.2	7.7 0.7	13.7 1.3
18	1 19.5	1 19.7	1 15.9	1.8 0.2	7.8 0.7	13.8 1.3
19	1 19.8	1 20.0	1 16.1	1.9 0.2	7.9 0.7	13.9 1.3
20	1 20.0	1 20.2	1 16.4	2.0 0.2	8.0 0.7	14.0 1.3
21	1 20.3	1 20.5	1 16.6	2.1 0.2	8.1 0.7	14.1 1.3
22	1 20.5	1 20.7	1 16.8	2.2 0.2	8.2 0.8	14.2 1.3
23	1 20.8	1 21.0	1 17.1	2.3 0.2	8.3 0.8	14.3 1.3
24	1 21.0	1 21.2	1 17.3	2.4 0.2	8.4 0.8	14.4 1.3
25	1 21.3	1 21.5	1 17.5	2.5 0.2	8.5 0.8	14.5 1.3
26	1 21.5	1 21.7	1 17.8	2.6 0.2	8.6 0.8	14.6 1.3
27	1 21.8	1 22.0	1 18.0	2.7 0.2	8.7 0.8	14.7 1.3
28	1 22.0	1 22.2	1 18.3	2.8 0.3	8.8 0.8	14.8 1.4
29	1 22.3	1 22.5	1 18.5	2.9 0.3	8.9 0.8	14.9 1.4
30	1 22.5	1 22.7	1 18.7	3.0 0.3	9.0 0.8	15.0 1.4
31	1 22.8	1 23.0	1 19.0	3.1 0.3	9.1 0.8	15.1 1.4
32	1 23.0	1 23.2	1 19.2	3.2 0.3	9.2 0.8	15.2 1.4
33	1 23.3	1 23.5	1 19.5	3.3 0.3	9.3 0.9	15.3 1.4
34	1 23.5	1 23.7	1 19.7	3.4 0.3	9.4 0.9	15.4 1.4
35	1 23.8	1 24.0	1 19.9	3.5 0.3	9.5 0.9	15.5 1.4
36	1 24.0	1 24.2	1 20.2	3.6 0.3	9.6 0.9	15.6 1.4
37	1 24.3	1 24.5	1 20.4	3.7 0.3	9.7 0.9	15.7 1.4
38	1 24.5	1 24.7	1 20.7	3.8 0.3	9.8 0.9	15.8 1.4
39	1 24.8	1 25.0	1 20.9	3.9 0.4	9.9 0.9	15.9 1.5
40	1 25.0	1 25.2	1 21.1	4.0 0.4	10.0 0.9	16.0 1.5
41	1 25.3	1 25.5	1 21.4	4.1 0.4	10.1 0.9	16.1 1.5
42	1 25.5	1 25.7	1 21.6	4.2 0.4	10.2 0.9	16.2 1.5
43	1 25.8	1 26.0	1 21.8	4.3 0.4	10.3 0.9	16.3 1.5
44	1 26.0	1 26.2	1 22.1	4.4 0.4	10.4 1.0	16.4 1.5
45	1 26.3	1 26.5	1 22.3	4.5 0.4	10.5 1.0	16.5 1.5
46	1 26.5	1 26.7	1 22.6	4.6 0.4	10.6 1.0	16.6 1.5
47	1 26.8	1 27.0	1 22.8	4.7 0.4	10.7 1.0	16.7 1.5
48	1 27.0	1 27.2	1 23.0	4.8 0.4	10.8 1.0	16.8 1.5
49	1 27.3	1 27.5	1 23.3	4.9 0.4	10.9 1.0	16.9 1.5
50	1 27.5	1 27.7	1 23.5	5.0 0.5	11.0 1.0	17.0 1.6
51	1 27.8	1 28.0	1 23.8	5.1 0.5	11.1 1.0	17.1 1.6
52	1 28.0	1 28.2	1 24.0	5.2 0.5	11.2 1.0	17.2 1.6
53	1 28.3	1 28.5	1 24.2	5.3 0.5	11.3 1.0	17.3 1.6
54	1 28.5	1 28.7	1 24.5	5.4 0.5	11.4 1.0	17.4 1.6
55	1 28.8	1 29.0	1 24.7	5.5 0.5	11.5 1.1	17.5 1.6
56	1 29.0	1 29.2	1 24.9	5.6 0.5	11.6 1.1	17.6 1.6
57	1 29.3	1 29.5	1 25.2	5.7 0.5	11.7 1.1	17.7 1.6
58	1 29.5	1 29.7	1 25.4	5.8 0.5	11.8 1.1	17.8 1.6
59	1 29.8	1 30.0	1 25.7	5.9 0.5	11.9 1.1	17.9 1.6
60	1 30.0	1 30.2	1 25.9	6.0 0.6	12.0 1.1	18.0 1.7

INCREMENTS AND CORRECTIONS

6m

m 6	SUN PLANETS	ARIES	MOON	v or Corrn d	v or Corrn d	v or Corrn d
s	° '	° '	° '	' '	' '	' '
00	1 30.0	1 30.2	1 25.9	0.0 0.0	6.0 0.7	12.0 1.3
01	1 30.3	1 30.5	1 26.1	0.1 0.0	6.1 0.7	12.1 1.3
02	1 30.5	1 30.7	1 26.4	0.2 0.0	6.2 0.7	12.2 1.3
03	1 30.8	1 31.0	1 26.6	0.3 0.0	6.3 0.7	12.3 1.3
04	1 31.0	1 31.2	1 26.9	0.4 0.0	6.4 0.7	12.4 1.3
05	1 31.3	1 31.5	1 27.1	0.5 0.1	6.5 0.7	12.5 1.4
06	1 31.5	1 31.8	1 27.3	0.6 0.1	6.6 0.7	12.6 1.4
07	1 31.8	1 32.0	1 27.6	0.7 0.1	6.7 0.7	12.7 1.4
08	1 32.0	1 32.3	1 27.8	0.8 0.1	6.8 0.7	12.8 1.4
09	1 32.3	1 32.5	1 28.0	0.9 0.1	6.9 0.7	12.9 1.4
10	1 32.5	1 32.8	1 28.3	1.0 0.1	7.0 0.8	13.0 1.4
11	1 32.8	1 33.0	1 28.5	1.1 0.1	7.1 0.8	13.1 1.4
12	1 33.0	1 33.3	1 28.8	1.2 0.1	7.2 0.8	13.2 1.4
13	1 33.3	1 33.5	1 29.0	1.3 0.1	7.3 0.8	13.3 1.4
14	1 33.5	1 33.8	1 29.2	1.4 0.2	7.4 0.8	13.4 1.5
15	1 33.8	1 34.0	1 29.5	1.5 0.2	7.5 0.8	13.5 1.5
16	1 34.0	1 34.3	1 29.7	1.6 0.2	7.6 0.8	13.6 1.5
17	1 34.3	1 34.5	1 30.0	1.7 0.2	7.7 0.8	13.7 1.5
18	1 34.5	1 34.8	1 30.2	1.8 0.2	7.8 0.8	13.8 1.5
19	1 34.8	1 35.0	1 30.4	1.9 0.2	7.9 0.9	13.9 1.5
20	1 35.0	1 35.3	1 30.7	2.0 0.2	8.0 0.9	14.0 1.5
21	1 35.3	1 35.5	1 30.9	2.1 0.2	8.1 0.9	14.1 1.5
22	1 35.5	1 35.8	1 31.1	2.2 0.2	8.2 0.9	14.2 1.5
23	1 35.8	1 36.0	1 31.4	2.3 0.2	8.3 0.9	14.3 1.5
24	1 36.0	1 36.3	1 31.6	2.4 0.3	8.4 0.9	14.4 1.6
25	1 36.3	1 36.5	1 31.9	2.5 0.3	8.5 0.9	14.5 1.6
26	1 36.5	1 36.8	1 32.1	2.6 0.3	8.6 0.9	14.6 1.6
27	1 36.8	1 37.0	1 32.3	2.7 0.3	8.7 0.9	14.7 1.6
28	1 37.0	1 37.3	1 32.6	2.8 0.3	8.8 1.0	14.8 1.6
29	1 37.3	1 37.5	1 32.8	2.9 0.3	8.9 1.0	14.9 1.6
30	1 37.5	1 37.8	1 33.1	3.0 0.3	9.0 1.0	15.0 1.6
31	1 37.8	1 38.0	1 33.3	3.1 0.3	9.1 1.0	15.1 1.6
32	1 38.0	1 38.3	1 33.5	3.2 0.3	9.2 1.0	15.2 1.6
33	1 38.3	1 38.5	1 33.8	3.3 0.4	9.3 1.0	15.3 1.7
34	1 38.5	1 38.8	1 34.0	3.4 0.4	9.4 1.0	15.4 1.7
35	1 38.8	1 39.0	1 34.3	3.5 0.4	9.5 1.0	15.5 1.7
36	1 39.0	1 39.3	1 34.5	3.6 0.4	9.6 1.0	15.6 1.7
37	1 39.3	1 39.5	1 34.7	3.7 0.4	9.7 1.1	15.7 1.7
38	1 39.5	1 39.8	1 35.0	3.8 0.4	9.8 1.1	15.8 1.7
39	1 39.8	1 40.0	1 35.2	3.9 0.4	9.9 1.1	15.9 1.7
40	1 40.0	1 40.3	1 35.4	4.0 0.4	10.0 1.1	16.0 1.7
41	1 40.3	1 40.5	1 35.7	4.1 0.4	10.1 1.1	16.1 1.7
42	1 40.5	1 40.8	1 35.9	4.2 0.5	10.2 1.1	16.2 1.8
43	1 40.8	1 41.0	1 36.2	4.3 0.5	10.3 1.1	16.3 1.8
44	1 41.0	1 41.3	1 36.4	4.4 0.5	10.4 1.1	16.4 1.8
45	1 41.3	1 41.5	1 36.6	4.5 0.5	10.5 1.1	16.5 1.8
46	1 41.5	1 41.8	1 36.9	4.6 0.5	10.6 1.1	16.6 1.8
47	1 41.8	1 42.0	1 37.1	4.7 0.5	10.7 1.2	16.7 1.8
48	1 42.0	1 42.3	1 37.4	4.8 0.5	10.8 1.2	16.8 1.8
49	1 42.3	1 42.5	1 37.6	4.9 0.5	10.9 1.2	16.9 1.8
50	1 42.5	1 42.8	1 37.8	5.0 0.5	11.0 1.2	17.0 1.8
51	1 42.8	1 43.0	1 38.1	5.1 0.6	11.1 1.2	17.1 1.9
52	1 43.0	1 43.3	1 38.3	5.2 0.6	11.2 1.2	17.2 1.9
53	1 43.3	1 43.5	1 38.5	5.3 0.6	11.3 1.2	17.3 1.9
54	1 43.5	1 43.8	1 38.8	5.4 0.6	11.4 1.2	17.4 1.9
55	1 43.8	1 44.0	1 39.0	5.5 0.6	11.5 1.2	17.5 1.9
56	1 44.0	1 44.3	1 39.3	5.6 0.6	11.6 1.3	17.6 1.9
57	1 44.3	1 44.5	1 39.5	5.7 0.6	11.7 1.3	17.7 1.9
58	1 44.5	1 44.8	1 39.7	5.8 0.6	11.8 1.3	17.8 1.9
59	1 44.8	1 45.0	1 40.0	5.9 0.6	11.9 1.3	17.9 1.9
60	1 45.0	1 45.3	1 40.2	6.0 0.7	12.0 1.3	18.0 2.0

7m

m 7	SUN PLANETS	ARIES	MOON	v or Corrn d	v or Corrn d	v or Corrn d
s	° '	° '	° '	' '	' '	' '
00	1 45.0	1 45.3	1 40.2	0.0 0.0	6.0 0.8	12.0 1.5
01	1 45.3	1 45.5	1 40.5	0.1 0.0	6.1 0.8	12.1 1.5
02	1 45.5	1 45.8	1 40.7	0.2 0.0	6.2 0.8	12.2 1.5
03	1 45.8	1 46.0	1 40.9	0.3 0.0	6.3 0.8	12.3 1.5
04	1 46.0	1 46.3	1 41.2	0.4 0.1	6.4 0.8	12.4 1.6
05	1 46.3	1 46.5	1 41.4	0.5 0.1	6.5 0.8	12.5 1.6
06	1 46.5	1 46.8	1 41.6	0.6 0.1	6.6 0.8	12.6 1.6
07	1 46.8	1 47.0	1 41.9	0.7 0.1	6.7 0.8	12.7 1.6
08	1 47.0	1 47.3	1 42.1	0.8 0.1	6.8 0.9	12.8 1.6
09	1 47.3	1 47.5	1 42.4	0.9 0.1	6.9 0.9	12.9 1.6
10	1 47.5	1 47.8	1 42.6	1.0 0.1	7.0 0.9	13.0 1.6
11	1 47.8	1 48.0	1 42.8	1.1 0.1	7.1 0.9	13.1 1.6
12	1 48.0	1 48.3	1 43.1	1.2 0.2	7.2 0.9	13.2 1.7
13	1 48.3	1 48.5	1 43.3	1.3 0.2	7.3 0.9	13.3 1.7
14	1 48.5	1 48.8	1 43.6	1.4 0.2	7.4 0.9	13.4 1.7
15	1 48.8	1 49.0	1 43.8	1.5 0.2	7.5 0.9	13.5 1.7
16	1 49.0	1 49.3	1 44.0	1.6 0.2	7.6 1.0	13.6 1.7
17	1 49.3	1 49.5	1 44.3	1.7 0.2	7.7 1.0	13.7 1.7
18	1 49.5	1 49.8	1 44.5	1.8 0.2	7.8 1.0	13.8 1.7
19	1 49.8	1 50.1	1 44.8	1.9 0.2	7.9 1.0	13.9 1.7
20	1 50.0	1 50.3	1 45.0	2.0 0.3	8.0 1.0	14.0 1.8
21	1 50.3	1 50.6	1 45.2	2.1 0.3	8.1 1.0	14.1 1.8
22	1 50.5	1 50.8	1 45.5	2.2 0.3	8.2 1.0	14.2 1.8
23	1 50.8	1 51.1	1 45.7	2.3 0.3	8.3 1.0	14.3 1.8
24	1 51.0	1 51.3	1 45.9	2.4 0.3	8.4 1.1	14.4 1.8
25	1 51.3	1 51.6	1 46.2	2.5 0.3	8.5 1.1	14.5 1.8
26	1 51.5	1 51.8	1 46.4	2.6 0.3	8.6 1.1	14.6 1.8
27	1 51.8	1 52.1	1 46.7	2.7 0.3	8.7 1.1	14.7 1.8
28	1 52.0	1 52.3	1 46.9	2.8 0.4	8.8 1.1	14.8 1.9
29	1 52.3	1 52.6	1 47.1	2.9 0.4	8.9 1.1	14.9 1.9
30	1 52.5	1 52.8	1 47.4	3.0 0.4	9.0 1.1	15.0 1.9
31	1 52.8	1 53.1	1 47.6	3.1 0.4	9.1 1.1	15.1 1.9
32	1 53.0	1 53.3	1 47.9	3.2 0.4	9.2 1.2	15.2 1.9
33	1 53.3	1 53.6	1 48.1	3.3 0.4	9.3 1.2	15.3 1.9
34	1 53.5	1 53.8	1 48.3	3.4 0.4	9.4 1.2	15.4 1.9
35	1 53.8	1 54.1	1 48.6	3.5 0.4	9.5 1.2	15.5 1.9
36	1 54.0	1 54.3	1 48.8	3.6 0.5	9.6 1.2	15.6 2.0
37	1 54.3	1 54.6	1 49.0	3.7 0.5	9.7 1.2	15.7 2.0
38	1 54.5	1 54.8	1 49.3	3.8 0.5	9.8 1.2	15.8 2.0
39	1 54.8	1 55.1	1 49.5	3.9 0.5	9.9 1.2	15.9 2.0
40	1 55.0	1 55.3	1 49.8	4.0 0.5	10.0 1.3	16.0 2.0
41	1 55.3	1 55.6	1 50.0	4.1 0.5	10.1 1.3	16.1 2.0
42	1 55.5	1 55.8	1 50.2	4.2 0.5	10.2 1.3	16.2 2.0
43	1 55.8	1 56.1	1 50.5	4.3 0.5	10.3 1.3	16.3 2.0
44	1 56.0	1 56.3	1 50.7	4.4 0.6	10.4 1.3	16.4 2.1
45	1 56.3	1 56.6	1 51.0	4.5 0.6	10.5 1.3	16.5 2.1
46	1 56.5	1 56.8	1 51.2	4.6 0.6	10.6 1.3	16.6 2.1
47	1 56.8	1 57.1	1 51.4	4.7 0.6	10.7 1.3	16.7 2.1
48	1 57.0	1 57.3	1 51.7	4.8 0.6	10.8 1.4	16.8 2.1
49	1 57.3	1 57.6	1 51.9	4.9 0.6	10.9 1.4	16.9 2.1
50	1 57.5	1 57.8	1 52.1	5.0 0.6	11.0 1.4	17.0 2.1
51	1 57.8	1 58.1	1 52.4	5.1 0.6	11.1 1.4	17.1 2.1
52	1 58.0	1 58.3	1 52.6	5.2 0.7	11.2 1.4	17.2 2.2
53	1 58.3	1 58.6	1 52.9	5.3 0.7	11.3 1.4	17.3 2.2
54	1 58.5	1 58.8	1 53.1	5.4 0.7	11.4 1.4	17.4 2.2
55	1 58.8	1 59.1	1 53.3	5.5 0.7	11.5 1.4	17.5 2.2
56	1 59.0	1 59.3	1 53.6	5.6 0.7	11.6 1.5	17.6 2.2
57	1 59.3	1 59.6	1 53.8	5.7 0.7	11.7 1.5	17.7 2.2
58	1 59.5	1 59.8	1 54.1	5.8 0.7	11.8 1.5	17.8 2.2
59	1 59.8	2 00.1	1 54.3	5.9 0.7	11.9 1.5	17.9 2.2
60	2 00.0	2 00.3	1 54.5	6.0 0.8	12.0 1.5	18.0 2.3

INCREMENTS AND CORRECTIONS

8m

m 8 / s	SUN PLANETS ° ′	ARIES ° ′	MOON ° ′	v or Corrn d	v or Corrn d	v or Corrn d
00	2 00.0	2 00.3	1 54.5	0.0 0.0	6.0 0.9	12.0 1.7
01	2 00.3	2 00.6	1 54.8	0.1 0.0	6.1 0.9	12.1 1.7
02	2 00.5	2 00.8	1 55.0	0.2 0.0	6.2 0.9	12.2 1.7
03	2 00.8	2 01.1	1 55.2	0.3 0.0	6.3 0.9	12.3 1.7
04	2 01.0	2 01.3	1 55.5	0.4 0.1	6.4 0.9	12.4 1.8
05	2 01.3	2 01.6	1 55.7	0.5 0.1	6.5 0.9	12.5 1.8
06	2 01.5	2 01.8	1 56.0	0.6 0.1	6.6 0.9	12.6 1.8
07	2 01.8	2 02.1	1 56.2	0.7 0.1	6.7 0.9	12.7 1.8
08	2 02.0	2 02.3	1 56.4	0.8 0.1	6.8 1.0	12.8 1.8
09	2 02.3	2 02.6	1 56.7	0.9 0.1	6.9 1.0	12.9 1.8
10	2 02.5	2 02.8	1 56.9	1.0 0.1	7.0 1.0	13.0 1.8
11	2 02.8	2 03.1	1 57.2	1.1 0.2	7.1 1.0	13.1 1.9
12	2 03.0	2 03.3	1 57.4	1.2 0.2	7.2 1.0	13.2 1.9
13	2 03.3	2 03.6	1 57.6	1.3 0.2	7.3 1.0	13.3 1.9
14	2 03.5	2 03.8	1 57.9	1.4 0.2	7.4 1.0	13.4 1.9
15	2 03.8	2 04.1	1 58.1	1.5 0.2	7.5 1.1	13.5 1.9
16	2 04.0	2 04.3	1 58.4	1.6 0.2	7.6 1.1	13.6 1.9
17	2 04.3	2 04.6	1 58.6	1.7 0.2	7.7 1.1	13.7 1.9
18	2 04.5	2 04.8	1 58.8	1.8 0.3	7.8 1.1	13.8 2.0
19	2 04.8	2 05.1	1 59.1	1.9 0.3	7.9 1.1	13.9 2.0
20	2 05.0	2 05.3	1 59.3	2.0 0.3	8.0 1.1	14.0 2.0
21	2 05.3	2 05.6	1 59.5	2.1 0.3	8.1 1.1	14.1 2.0
22	2 05.5	2 05.8	1 59.8	2.2 0.3	8.2 1.2	14.2 2.0
23	2 05.8	2 06.1	2 00.0	2.3 0.3	8.3 1.2	14.3 2.0
24	2 06.0	2 06.3	2 00.3	2.4 0.3	8.4 1.2	14.4 2.0
25	2 06.3	2 06.6	2 00.5	2.5 0.4	8.5 1.2	14.5 2.1
26	2 06.5	2 06.8	2 00.7	2.6 0.4	8.6 1.2	14.6 2.1
27	2 06.8	2 07.1	2 01.0	2.7 0.4	8.7 1.2	14.7 2.1
28	2 07.0	2 07.3	2 01.2	2.8 0.4	8.8 1.2	14.8 2.1
29	2 07.3	2 07.6	2 01.5	2.9 0.4	8.9 1.3	14.9 2.1
30	2 07.5	2 07.8	2 01.7	3.0 0.4	9.0 1.3	15.0 2.1
31	2 07.8	2 08.1	2 01.9	3.1 0.4	9.1 1.3	15.1 2.1
32	2 08.0	2 08.4	2 02.2	3.2 0.5	9.2 1.3	15.2 2.2
33	2 08.3	2 08.6	2 02.4	3.3 0.5	9.3 1.3	15.3 2.2
34	2 08.5	2 08.9	2 02.6	3.4 0.5	9.4 1.3	15.4 2.2
35	2 08.8	2 09.1	2 02.9	3.5 0.5	9.5 1.3	15.5 2.2
36	2 09.0	2 09.4	2 03.1	3.6 0.5	9.6 1.4	15.6 2.2
37	2 09.3	2 09.6	2 03.4	3.7 0.5	9.7 1.4	15.7 2.2
38	2 09.5	2 09.9	2 03.6	3.8 0.5	9.8 1.4	15.8 2.2
39	2 09.8	2 10.1	2 03.8	3.9 0.6	9.9 1.4	15.9 2.3
40	2 10.0	2 10.4	2 04.1	4.0 0.6	10.0 1.4	16.0 2.3
41	2 10.3	2 10.6	2 04.3	4.1 0.6	10.1 1.4	16.1 2.3
42	2 10.5	2 10.9	2 04.6	4.2 0.6	10.2 1.4	16.2 2.3
43	2 10.8	2 11.1	2 04.8	4.3 0.6	10.3 1.5	16.3 2.3
44	2 11.0	2 11.4	2 05.0	4.4 0.6	10.4 1.5	16.4 2.3
45	2 11.3	2 11.6	2 05.3	4.5 0.6	10.5 1.5	16.5 2.3
46	2 11.5	2 11.9	2 05.5	4.6 0.7	10.6 1.5	16.6 2.4
47	2 11.8	2 12.1	2 05.7	4.7 0.7	10.7 1.5	16.7 2.4
48	2 12.0	2 12.4	2 06.0	4.8 0.7	10.8 1.5	16.8 2.4
49	2 12.3	2 12.6	2 06.2	4.9 0.7	10.9 1.5	16.9 2.4
50	2 12.5	2 12.9	2 06.5	5.0 0.7	11.0 1.6	17.0 2.4
51	2 12.8	2 13.1	2 06.7	5.1 0.7	11.1 1.6	17.1 2.4
52	2 13.0	2 13.4	2 06.9	5.2 0.7	11.2 1.6	17.2 2.4
53	2 13.3	2 13.6	2 07.2	5.3 0.8	11.3 1.6	17.3 2.5
54	2 13.5	2 13.9	2 07.4	5.4 0.8	11.4 1.6	17.4 2.5
55	2 13.8	2 14.1	2 07.7	5.5 0.8	11.5 1.6	17.5 2.5
56	2 14.0	2 14.4	2 07.9	5.6 0.8	11.6 1.6	17.6 2.5
57	2 14.3	2 14.6	2 08.1	5.7 0.8	11.7 1.7	17.7 2.5
58	2 14.5	2 14.9	2 08.4	5.8 0.8	11.8 1.7	17.8 2.5
59	2 14.8	2 15.1	2 08.6	5.9 0.8	11.9 1.7	17.9 2.5
60	2 15.0	2 15.4	2 08.9	6.0 0.9	12.0 1.7	18.0 2.6

9m

m 9 / s	SUN PLANETS ° ′	ARIES ° ′	MOON ° ′	v or Corrn d	v or Corrn d	v or Corrn d
00	2 15.0	2 15.4	2 08.9	0.0 0.0	6.0 1.0	12.0 1.9
01	2 15.3	2 15.6	2 09.1	0.1 0.0	6.1 1.0	12.1 1.9
02	2 15.5	2 15.9	2 09.3	0.2 0.0	6.2 1.0	12.2 1.9
03	2 15.8	2 16.1	2 09.6	0.3 0.0	6.3 1.0	12.3 1.9
04	2 16.0	2 16.4	2 09.8	0.4 0.1	6.4 1.0	12.4 2.0
05	2 16.3	2 16.6	2 10.0	0.5 0.1	6.5 1.0	12.5 2.0
06	2 16.5	2 16.9	2 10.3	0.6 0.1	6.6 1.0	12.6 2.0
07	2 16.8	2 17.1	2 10.5	0.7 0.1	6.7 1.1	12.7 2.0
08	2 17.0	2 17.4	2 10.8	0.8 0.1	6.8 1.1	12.8 2.0
09	2 17.3	2 17.6	2 11.0	0.9 0.1	6.9 1.1	12.9 2.0
10	2 17.5	2 17.9	2 11.2	1.0 0.2	7.0 1.1	13.0 2.1
11	2 17.8	2 18.1	2 11.5	1.1 0.2	7.1 1.1	13.1 2.1
12	2 18.0	2 18.4	2 11.7	1.2 0.2	7.2 1.1	13.2 2.1
13	2 18.3	2 18.6	2 12.0	1.3 0.2	7.3 1.2	13.3 2.1
14	2 18.5	2 18.9	2 12.2	1.4 0.2	7.4 1.2	13.4 2.1
15	2 18.8	2 19.1	2 12.4	1.5 0.2	7.5 1.2	13.5 2.1
16	2 19.0	2 19.4	2 12.7	1.6 0.3	7.6 1.2	13.6 2.2
17	2 19.3	2 19.6	2 12.9	1.7 0.3	7.7 1.2	13.7 2.2
18	2 19.5	2 19.9	2 13.1	1.8 0.3	7.8 1.2	13.8 2.2
19	2 19.8	2 20.1	2 13.4	1.9 0.3	7.9 1.3	13.9 2.2
20	2 20.0	2 20.4	2 13.6	2.0 0.3	8.0 1.3	14.0 2.2
21	2 20.3	2 20.6	2 13.9	2.1 0.3	8.1 1.3	14.1 2.2
22	2 20.5	2 20.9	2 14.1	2.2 0.3	8.2 1.3	14.2 2.2
23	2 20.8	2 21.1	2 14.3	2.3 0.4	8.3 1.3	14.3 2.3
24	2 21.0	2 21.4	2 14.6	2.4 0.4	8.4 1.3	14.4 2.3
25	2 21.3	2 21.6	2 14.8	2.5 0.4	8.5 1.3	14.5 2.3
26	2 21.5	2 21.9	2 15.1	2.6 0.4	8.6 1.4	14.6 2.3
27	2 21.8	2 22.1	2 15.3	2.7 0.4	8.7 1.4	14.7 2.3
28	2 22.0	2 22.4	2 15.5	2.8 0.4	8.8 1.4	14.8 2.3
29	2 22.3	2 22.6	2 15.8	2.9 0.5	8.9 1.4	14.9 2.4
30	2 22.5	2 22.9	2 16.0	3.0 0.5	9.0 1.4	15.0 2.4
31	2 22.8	2 23.1	2 16.2	3.1 0.5	9.1 1.4	15.1 2.4
32	2 23.0	2 23.4	2 16.5	3.2 0.5	9.2 1.5	15.2 2.4
33	2 23.3	2 23.6	2 16.7	3.3 0.5	9.3 1.5	15.3 2.4
34	2 23.5	2 23.9	2 17.0	3.4 0.5	9.4 1.5	15.4 2.4
35	2 23.8	2 24.1	2 17.2	3.5 0.6	9.5 1.5	15.5 2.5
36	2 24.0	2 24.4	2 17.4	3.6 0.6	9.6 1.5	15.6 2.5
37	2 24.3	2 24.6	2 17.7	3.7 0.6	9.7 1.5	15.7 2.5
38	2 24.5	2 24.9	2 17.9	3.8 0.6	9.8 1.6	15.8 2.5
39	2 24.8	2 25.1	2 18.2	3.9 0.6	9.9 1.6	15.9 2.5
40	2 25.0	2 25.4	2 18.4	4.0 0.6	10.0 1.6	16.0 2.5
41	2 25.3	2 25.6	2 18.6	4.1 0.6	10.1 1.6	16.1 2.5
42	2 25.5	2 25.9	2 18.9	4.2 0.7	10.2 1.6	16.2 2.6
43	2 25.8	2 26.1	2 19.1	4.3 0.7	10.3 1.6	16.3 2.6
44	2 26.0	2 26.4	2 19.3	4.4 0.7	10.4 1.6	16.4 2.6
45	2 26.3	2 26.7	2 19.6	4.5 0.7	10.5 1.7	16.5 2.6
46	2 26.5	2 26.9	2 19.8	4.6 0.7	10.6 1.7	16.6 2.6
47	2 26.8	2 27.2	2 20.1	4.7 0.7	10.7 1.7	16.7 2.6
48	2 27.0	2 27.4	2 20.3	4.8 0.8	10.8 1.7	16.8 2.7
49	2 27.3	2 27.7	2 20.5	4.9 0.8	10.9 1.7	16.9 2.7
50	2 27.5	2 27.9	2 20.8	5.0 0.8	11.0 1.7	17.0 2.7
51	2 27.8	2 28.2	2 21.0	5.1 0.8	11.1 1.8	17.1 2.7
52	2 28.0	2 28.4	2 21.3	5.2 0.8	11.2 1.8	17.2 2.7
53	2 28.3	2 28.7	2 21.5	5.3 0.8	11.3 1.8	17.3 2.7
54	2 28.5	2 28.9	2 21.7	5.4 0.9	11.4 1.8	17.4 2.8
55	2 28.8	2 29.2	2 22.0	5.5 0.9	11.5 1.8	17.5 2.8
56	2 29.0	2 29.4	2 22.2	5.6 0.9	11.6 1.8	17.6 2.8
57	2 29.3	2 29.7	2 22.5	5.7 0.9	11.7 1.9	17.7 2.8
58	2 29.5	2 29.9	2 22.7	5.8 0.9	11.8 1.9	17.8 2.8
59	2 29.8	2 30.2	2 22.9	5.9 0.9	11.9 1.9	17.9 2.8
60	2 30.0	2 30.4	2 23.2	6.0 1.0	12.0 1.9	18.0 2.9

10m   INCREMENTS AND CORRECTIONS   11m

m 10	SUN PLANETS	ARIES	MOON	v or Corrn d	v or Corrn d	v or Corrn d
s	° '	° '	° '	' '	' '	' '
00	2 30.0	2 30.4	2 23.2	0.0 0.0	6.0 1.1	12.0 2.1
01	2 30.3	2 30.7	2 23.4	0.1 0.0	6.1 1.1	12.1 2.1
02	2 30.5	2 30.9	2 23.6	0.2 0.0	6.2 1.1	12.2 2.1
03	2 30.8	2 31.2	2 23.9	0.3 0.1	6.3 1.1	12.3 2.2
04	2 31.0	2 31.4	2 24.1	0.4 0.1	6.4 1.1	12.4 2.2
05	2 31.3	2 31.7	2 24.4	0.5 0.1	6.5 1.1	12.5 2.2
06	2 31.5	2 31.9	2 24.6	0.6 0.1	6.6 1.1	12.6 2.2
07	2 31.8	2 32.2	2 24.8	0.7 0.1	6.7 1.2	12.7 2.2
08	2 32.0	2 32.4	2 25.1	0.8 0.1	6.8 1.2	12.8 2.2
09	2 32.3	2 32.7	2 25.3	0.9 0.2	6.9 1.2	12.9 2.3
10	2 32.5	2 32.9	2 25.6	1.0 0.2	7.0 1.2	13.0 2.3
11	2 32.8	2 33.2	2 25.8	1.1 0.2	7.1 1.2	13.1 2.3
12	2 33.0	2 33.4	2 26.0	1.2 0.2	7.2 1.3	13.2 2.3
13	2 33.3	2 33.7	2 26.3	1.3 0.2	7.3 1.3	13.3 2.3
14	2 33.5	2 33.9	2 26.5	1.4 0.2	7.4 1.3	13.4 2.3
15	2 33.8	2 34.2	2 26.7	1.5 0.3	7.5 1.3	13.5 2.4
16	2 34.0	2 34.4	2 27.0	1.6 0.3	7.6 1.3	13.6 2.4
17	2 34.3	2 34.7	2 27.2	1.7 0.3	7.7 1.3	13.7 2.4
18	2 34.5	2 34.9	2 27.5	1.8 0.3	7.8 1.4	13.8 2.4
19	2 34.8	2 35.2	2 27.7	1.9 0.3	7.9 1.4	13.9 2.4
20	2 35.0	2 35.4	2 27.9	2.0 0.4	8.0 1.4	14.0 2.5
21	2 35.3	2 35.7	2 28.2	2.1 0.4	8.1 1.4	14.1 2.5
22	2 35.5	2 35.9	2 28.4	2.2 0.4	8.2 1.4	14.2 2.5
23	2 35.8	2 36.2	2 28.7	2.3 0.4	8.3 1.5	14.3 2.5
24	2 36.0	2 36.4	2 28.9	2.4 0.4	8.4 1.5	14.4 2.5
25	2 36.3	2 36.7	2 29.1	2.5 0.4	8.5 1.5	14.5 2.5
26	2 36.5	2 36.9	2 29.4	2.6 0.5	8.6 1.5	14.6 2.6
27	2 36.8	2 37.2	2 29.6	2.7 0.5	8.7 1.5	14.7 2.6
28	2 37.0	2 37.4	2 29.8	2.8 0.5	8.8 1.5	14.8 2.6
29	2 37.3	2 37.7	2 30.1	2.9 0.5	8.9 1.6	14.9 2.6
30	2 37.5	2 37.9	2 30.3	3.0 0.5	9.0 1.6	15.0 2.6
31	2 37.8	2 38.2	2 30.6	3.1 0.5	9.1 1.6	15.1 2.6
32	2 38.0	2 38.4	2 30.8	3.2 0.6	9.2 1.6	15.2 2.7
33	2 38.3	2 38.7	2 31.0	3.3 0.6	9.3 1.6	15.3 2.7
34	2 38.5	2 38.9	2 31.3	3.4 0.6	9.4 1.6	15.4 2.7
35	2 38.8	2 39.2	2 31.5	3.5 0.6	9.5 1.7	15.5 2.7
36	2 39.0	2 39.4	2 31.8	3.6 0.6	9.6 1.7	15.6 2.7
37	2 39.3	2 39.7	2 32.0	3.7 0.6	9.7 1.7	15.7 2.7
38	2 39.5	2 39.9	2 32.2	3.8 0.7	9.8 1.7	15.8 2.8
39	2 39.8	2 40.2	2 32.5	3.9 0.7	9.9 1.7	15.9 2.8
40	2 40.0	2 40.4	2 32.7	4.0 0.7	10.0 1.8	16.0 2.8
41	2 40.3	2 40.7	2 32.9	4.1 0.7	10.1 1.8	16.1 2.8
42	2 40.5	2 40.9	2 33.2	4.2 0.7	10.2 1.8	16.2 2.8
43	2 40.8	2 41.2	2 33.4	4.3 0.8	10.3 1.8	16.3 2.9
44	2 41.0	2 41.4	2 33.7	4.4 0.8	10.4 1.8	16.4 2.9
45	2 41.3	2 41.7	2 33.9	4.5 0.8	10.5 1.8	16.5 2.9
46	2 41.5	2 41.9	2 34.1	4.6 0.8	10.6 1.9	16.6 2.9
47	2 41.8	2 42.2	2 34.4	4.7 0.8	10.7 1.9	16.7 2.9
48	2 42.0	2 42.4	2 34.6	4.8 0.8	10.8 1.9	16.8 2.9
49	2 42.3	2 42.7	2 34.9	4.9 0.9	10.9 1.9	16.9 3.0
50	2 42.5	2 42.9	2 35.1	5.0 0.9	11.0 1.9	17.0 3.0
51	2 42.8	2 43.2	2 35.3	5.1 0.9	11.1 1.9	17.1 3.0
52	2 43.0	2 43.4	2 35.6	5.2 0.9	11.2 2.0	17.2 3.0
53	2 43.3	2 43.7	2 35.8	5.3 0.9	11.3 2.0	17.3 3.0
54	2 43.5	2 43.9	2 36.1	5.4 0.9	11.4 2.0	17.4 3.0
55	2 43.8	2 44.2	2 36.3	5.5 1.0	11.5 2.0	17.5 3.1
56	2 44.0	2 44.4	2 36.5	5.6 1.0	11.6 2.0	17.6 3.1
57	2 44.3	2 44.7	2 36.8	5.7 1.0	11.7 2.0	17.7 3.1
58	2 44.5	2 45.0	2 37.0	5.8 1.0	11.8 2.1	17.8 3.1
59	2 44.8	2 44.2	2 37.2	5.9 1.0	11.9 2.1	17.9 3.1
60	2 45.0	2 45.5	2 37.5	6.0 1.1	12.0 2.1	18.0 3.2

m 11	SUN PLANETS	ARIES	MOON	v or Corrn d	v or Corrn d	v or Corrn d
s	° '	° '	° '	' '	' '	' '
00	2 45.0	2 45.5	2 37.5	0.0 0.0	6.0 1.2	12.0 2.3
01	2 45.3	2 45.7	2 37.7	0.1 0.0	6.1 1.2	12.1 2.3
02	2 45.5	2 46.0	2 38.0	0.2 0.0	6.2 1.2	12.2 2.3
03	2 45.8	2 46.2	2 38.2	0.3 0.1	6.3 1.2	12.3 2.4
04	2 46.0	2 46.5	2 38.4	0.4 0.1	6.4 1.2	12.4 2.4
05	2 46.3	2 46.7	2 38.7	0.5 0.1	6.5 1.2	12.5 2.4
06	2 46.5	2 47.0	2 38.9	0.6 0.1	6.6 1.3	12.6 2.4
07	2 46.8	2 47.2	2 39.2	0.7 0.1	6.7 1.3	12.7 2.4
08	2 47.0	2 47.5	2 39.4	0.8 0.2	6.8 1.3	12.8 2.5
09	2 47.3	2 47.7	2 39.6	0.9 0.2	6.9 1.3	12.9 2.5
10	2 47.5	2 48.0	2 39.9	1.0 0.2	7.0 1.3	13.0 2.5
11	2 47.8	2 48.2	2 40.1	1.1 0.2	7.1 1.4	13.1 2.5
12	2 48.0	2 48.5	2 40.3	1.2 0.2	7.2 1.4	13.2 2.5
13	2 48.3	2 48.7	2 40.6	1.3 0.2	7.3 1.4	13.3 2.5
14	2 48.5	2 49.0	2 40.8	1.4 0.3	7.4 1.4	13.4 2.6
15	2 48.8	2 49.2	2 41.1	1.5 0.3	7.5 1.4	13.5 2.6
16	2 49.0	2 49.5	2 41.3	1.6 0.3	7.6 1.5	13.6 2.6
17	2 49.3	2 49.7	2 41.5	1.7 0.3	7.7 1.5	13.7 2.6
18	2 49.5	2 50.0	2 41.8	1.8 0.3	7.8 1.5	13.8 2.6
19	2 49.8	2 50.2	2 42.0	1.9 0.3	7.9 1.5	13.9 2.7
20	2 50.0	2 50.5	2 42.3	2.0 0.4	8.0 1.5	14.0 2.7
21	2 50.3	2 50.7	2 42.5	2.1 0.4	8.1 1.6	14.1 2.7
22	2 50.5	2 51.0	2 42.7	2.2 0.4	8.2 1.6	14.2 2.7
23	2 50.8	2 51.2	2 43.0	2.3 0.4	8.3 1.6	14.3 2.7
24	2 51.0	2 51.5	2 43.2	2.4 0.5	8.4 1.6	14.4 2.8
25	2 51.3	2 51.7	2 43.4	2.5 0.5	8.5 1.6	14.5 2.8
26	2 51.5	2 52.0	2 43.7	2.6 0.5	8.6 1.6	14.6 2.8
27	2 51.8	2 52.2	2 43.9	2.7 0.5	8.7 1.7	14.7 2.8
28	2 52.0	2 52.5	2 44.2	2.8 0.5	8.8 1.7	14.8 2.8
29	2 52.3	2 52.7	2 44.4	2.9 0.6	8.9 1.7	14.9 2.9
30	2 52.5	2 53.0	2 44.6	3.0 0.6	9.0 1.7	15.0 2.9
31	2 52.8	2 53.2	2 44.9	3.1 0.6	9.1 1.7	15.1 2.9
32	2 53.0	2 53.5	2 45.1	3.2 0.6	9.2 1.8	15.2 2.9
33	2 53.3	2 53.7	2 45.4	3.3 0.6	9.3 1.8	15.3 2.9
34	2 53.5	2 54.0	2 45.6	3.4 0.7	9.4 1.8	15.4 3.0
35	2 53.8	2 54.2	2 45.8	3.5 0.7	9.5 1.8	15.5 3.0
36	2 54.0	2 54.5	2 46.1	3.6 0.7	9.6 1.8	15.6 3.0
37	2 54.3	2 54.7	2 46.3	3.7 0.7	9.7 1.9	15.7 3.0
38	2 54.5	2 55.0	2 46.6	3.8 0.7	9.8 1.9	15.8 3.0
39	2 54.8	2 55.2	2 46.8	3.9 0.7	9.9 1.9	15.9 3.0
40	2 55.0	2 55.5	2 47.0	4.0 0.8	10.0 1.9	16.0 3.1
41	2 55.3	2 55.7	2 47.3	4.1 0.8	10.1 1.9	16.1 3.1
42	2 55.5	2 56.0	2 47.5	4.2 0.8	10.2 2.0	16.2 3.1
43	2 55.8	2 56.2	2 47.7	4.3 0.8	10.3 2.0	16.3 3.1
44	2 56.0	2 56.5	2 48.0	4.4 0.8	10.4 2.0	16.4 3.1
45	2 56.3	2 56.7	2 48.2	4.5 0.9	10.5 2.0	16.5 3.2
46	2 56.5	2 57.0	2 48.5	4.6 0.9	10.6 2.0	16.6 3.2
47	2 56.8	2 57.2	2 48.7	4.7 0.9	10.7 2.1	16.7 3.2
48	2 57.0	2 57.5	2 48.9	4.8 0.9	10.8 2.1	16.8 3.2
49	2 57.3	2 57.7	2 49.2	4.9 0.9	10.9 2.1	16.9 3.2
50	2 57.5	2 58.0	2 49.4	5.0 1.0	11.0 2.1	17.0 3.3
51	2 57.8	2 58.2	2 49.7	5.1 1.0	11.1 2.1	17.1 3.3
52	2 58.0	2 58.5	2 49.9	5.2 1.0	11.2 2.1	17.2 3.3
53	2 58.3	2 58.7	2 50.1	5.3 1.0	11.3 2.2	17.3 3.3
54	2 58.5	2 59.0	2 50.4	5.4 1.0	11.4 2.2	17.4 3.3
55	2 58.8	2 59.2	2 50.6	5.5 1.1	11.5 2.2	17.5 3.4
56	2 59.0	2 59.5	2 50.8	5.6 1.1	11.6 2.2	17.6 3.4
57	2 59.3	2 59.7	2 51.1	5.7 1.1	11.7 2.2	17.7 3.4
58	2 59.5	3 00.0	2 51.3	5.8 1.1	11.8 2.3	17.8 3.4
59	2 59.8	3 00.2	2 51.6	5.9 1.1	11.9 2.3	17.9 3.4
60	3 00.0	3 00.5	2 51.8	6.0 1.2	12.0 2.3	18.0 3.5

12m   INCREMENTS AND CORRECTIONS   13m

m 12 s	SUN PLANETS ° '	ARIES ° '	MOON ° '	v or Corrn d , '	v or Corrn d , '	v or Corrn d , '
00	3 00.0	3 00.5	2 51.8	0.0 0.0	6.0 1.3	12.0 2.5
01	3 00.3	3 00.7	2 52.0	0.1 0.0	6.1 1.3	12.1 2.5
02	3 00.5	3 01.0	2 52.3	0.2 0.0	6.2 1.3	12.2 2.5
03	3 00.8	3 01.2	2 52.5	0.3 0.1	6.3 1.3	12.3 2.6
04	3 01.0	3 01.5	2 52.8	0.4 0.1	6.4 1.3	12.4 2.6
05	3 01.3	3 01.7	2 53.0	0.5 0.1	6.5 1.4	12.5 2.6
06	3 01.5	3 02.0	2 53.2	0.6 0.1	6.6 1.4	12.6 2.6
07	3 01.8	3 02.2	2 53.5	0.7 0.1	6.7 1.4	12.7 2.6
08	3 02.0	3 02.5	2 53.7	0.8 0.2	6.8 1.4	12.8 2.7
09	3 02.3	3 02.7	2 53.9	0.9 0.2	6.9 1.4	12.9 2.7
10	3 02.5	3 03.0	2 54.2	1.0 0.2	7.0 1.5	13.0 2.7
11	3 02.8	3 03.3	2 54.4	1.1 0.2	7.1 1.5	13.1 2.7
12	3 03.0	3 03.5	2 54.7	1.2 0.3	7.2 1.5	13.2 2.8
13	3 03.3	3 03.8	2 54.9	1.3 0.3	7.3 1.5	13.3 2.8
14	3 03.5	3 04.0	2 55.1	1.4 0.3	7.4 1.5	13.4 2.8
15	3 03.8	3 04.3	2 55.4	1.5 0.3	7.5 1.6	13.5 2.8
16	3 04.0	3 04.5	2 55.6	1.6 0.3	7.6 1.6	13.6 2.8
17	3 04.3	3 04.8	2 55.9	1.7 0.4	7.7 1.6	13.7 2.9
18	3 04.5	3 05.0	2 56.1	1.8 0.4	7.8 1.6	13.8 2.9
19	3 04.8	3 05.3	2 56.3	1.9 0.4	7.9 1.6	13.9 2.9
20	3 05.0	3 05.5	2 56.6	2.0 0.4	8.0 1.7	14.0 2.9
21	3 05.3	3 05.8	2 56.8	2.1 0.4	8.1 1.7	14.1 2.9
22	3 05.5	3 06.0	2 57.0	2.2 0.5	8.2 1.7	14.2 3.0
23	3 05.8	3 06.3	2 57.3	2.3 0.5	8.3 1.7	14.3 3.0
24	3 06.0	3 06.5	2 57.5	2.4 0.5	8.4 1.8	14.4 3.0
25	3 06.3	3 06.8	2 57.8	2.5 0.5	8.5 1.8	14.5 3.0
26	3 06.5	3 07.0	2 58.0	2.6 0.5	8.6 1.8	14.6 3.0
27	3 06.8	3 07.3	2 58.2	2.7 0.6	8.7 1.8	14.7 3.1
28	3 07.0	3 07.5	2 58.5	2.8 0.6	8.8 1.8	14.8 3.1
29	3 07.3	3 07.8	2 58.7	2.9 0.6	8.9 1.9	14.9 3.1
30	3 07.5	3 08.0	2 59.0	3.0 0.6	9.0 1.9	15.0 3.1
31	3 07.8	3 08.3	2 59.2	3.1 0.6	9.1 1.9	15.1 3.1
32	3 08.0	3 08.5	2 59.4	3.2 0.7	9.2 1.9	15.2 3.2
33	3 08.3	3 08.8	2 59.7	3.3 0.7	9.3 1.9	15.3 3.2
34	3 08.5	3 09.0	2 59.9	3.4 0.7	9.4 2.0	15.4 3.2
35	3 08.8	3 09.3	3 00.2	3.5 0.7	9.5 2.0	15.5 3.2
36	3 09.0	3 09.5	3 00.4	3.6 0.8	9.6 2.0	15.6 3.3
37	3 09.3	3 09.8	3 00.6	3.7 0.8	9.7 2.0	15.7 3.3
38	3 09.5	3 10.0	3 00.9	3.8 0.8	9.8 2.0	15.8 3.3
39	3 09.8	3 10.3	3 01.1	3.9 0.8	9.9 2.1	15.9 3.3
40	3 10.0	3 10.5	3 01.3	4.0 0.8	10.0 2.1	16.0 3.3
41	3 10.3	3 10.8	3 01.6	4.1 0.9	10.1 2.1	16.1 3.4
42	3 10.5	3 11.0	3 01.8	4.2 0.9	10.2 2.1	16.2 3.4
43	3 10.8	3 11.3	3 02.1	4.3 0.9	10.3 2.1	16.3 3.4
44	3 11.0	3 11.5	3 02.3	4.4 0.9	10.4 2.2	16.4 3.4
45	3 11.3	3 11.8	3 02.5	4.5 0.9	10.5 2.2	16.5 3.4
46	3 11.5	3 12.0	3 02.8	4.6 1.0	10.6 2.2	16.6 3.5
47	3 11.8	3 12.3	3 03.0	4.7 1.0	10.7 2.2	16.7 3.5
48	3 12.0	3 12.5	3 03.3	4.8 1.0	10.8 2.3	16.8 3.5
49	3 12.3	3 12.8	3 03.5	4.9 1.0	10.9 2.3	16.9 3.5
50	3 12.5	3 13.0	3 03.7	5.0 1.0	11.0 2.3	17.0 3.5
51	3 12.8	3 13.3	3 04.0	5.1 1.1	11.1 2.3	17.1 3.6
52	3 13.0	3 13.5	3 04.2	5.2 1.1	11.2 2.3	17.2 3.6
53	3 13.3	3 13.8	3 04.4	5.3 1.1	11.3 2.4	17.3 3.6
54	3 13.5	3 14.0	3 04.7	5.4 1.1	11.4 2.4	17.4 3.6
55	3 13.8	3 14.3	3 04.9	5.5 1.1	11.5 2.4	17.5 3.6
56	3 14.0	3 14.5	3 05.2	5.6 1.2	11.6 2.4	17.6 3.7
57	3 14.3	3 14.8	3 05.4	5.7 1.2	11.7 2.4	17.7 3.7
58	3 14.5	3 15.0	3 05.6	5.8 1.2	11.8 2.5	17.8 3.7
59	3 14.8	3 15.3	3 05.9	5.9 1.2	11.9 2.5	17.9 3.7
60	3 15.0	3 15.5	3 06.1	6.0 1.3	12.0 2.5	18.0 3.8

m 13 s	SUN PLANETS ° '	ARIES ° '	MOON ° '	v or Corrn d , '	v or Corrn d , '	v or Corrn d , '
00	3 15.0	3 15.5	3 06.1	0.0 0.0	6.0 1.4	12.0 2.7
01	3 15.3	3 15.8	3 06.4	0.1 0.0	6.1 1.4	12.1 2.7
02	3 15.5	3 16.0	3 06.6	0.2 0.0	6.2 1.4	12.2 2.7
03	3 15.8	3 16.3	3 06.8	0.3 0.1	6.3 1.4	12.3 2.8
04	3 16.0	3 16.5	3 06.1	0.4 0.1	6.4 1.4	12.4 2.8
05	3 16.3	3 16.8	3 07.3	0.5 0.1	6.5 1.5	12.5 2.8
06	3 16.5	3 17.0	3 07.5	0.6 0.1	6.6 1.5	12.6 2.8
07	3 16.8	3 17.3	3 07.8	0.7 0.2	6.7 1.5	12.7 2.9
08	3 17.0	3 17.5	2 07.0	0.8 0.2	6.8 1.5	12.8 2.9
09	3 17.3	3 17.8	3 07.3	0.9 0.2	6.9 1.6	12.9 2.9
10	2 17.5	3 18.0	3 08.5	1.0 0.2	7.0 1.6	13.0 2.9
11	3 17.8	3 18.3	3 08.7	1.1 0.2	7.1 1.6	13.1 2.9
12	3 18.0	3 18.5	3 08.0	1.2 0.3	7.2 1.6	13.2 3.0
13	3 18.3	3 18.8	3 08.2	1.3 0.3	7.3 1.6	13.3 3.0
14	3 18.5	3 19.0	3 09.5	1.4 0.3	7.4 1.7	13.4 3.0
15	3 18.8	3 19.3	3 09.7	1.5 0.3	7.5 1.7	13.5 3.0
16	3 19.0	3 19.5	3 09.9	1.6 0.4	7.6 1.7	13.6 3.1
17	3 19.3	3 19.8	3 09.2	1.7 0.4	7.7 1.7	13.7 3.1
18	3 19.5	3 20.0	3 10.4	1.8 0.4	7.8 1.8	13.8 3.1
19	3 19.8	3 20.3	3 10.7	1.9 0.4	7.9 1.8	13.9 3.1
20	3 20.0	3 20.5	3 10.9	2.0 0.5	8.0 1.8	14.0 3.2
21	3 20.3	3 20.8	3 10.1	2.1 0.5	8.1 1.8	14.1 3.2
22	3 20.5	3 21.0	3 11.4	2.2 0.5	8.2 1.8	14.2 3.2
23	3 20.8	3 21.3	3 11.6	2.3 0.5	8.3 1.9	14.3 3.2
24	3 21.0	3 21.6	3 11.8	2.4 0.5	8.4 1.9	14.4 3.2
25	3 21.3	3 21.8	3 12.1	2.5 0.6	8.5 1.9	14.5 3.3
26	3 21.5	3 22.1	3 12.3	2.6 0.6	8.6 1.9	14.6 3.3
27	3 21.8	3 22.3	3 12.6	2.7 0.6	8.7 2.0	14.7 3.3
28	3 22.0	3 22.6	3 12.8	2.8 0.6	8.8 2.0	14.8 3.3
29	3 22.3	3 22.8	3 13.0	2.9 0.7	8.9 2.0	14.9 3.4
30	3 22.5	3 23.1	3 13.3	3.0 0.7	9.0 2.0	15.0 3.4
31	3 22.8	3 23.3	3 13.5	3.1 0.7	9.1 2.0	15.1 3.4
32	3 23.0	3 23.6	3 13.8	3.2 0.7	9.2 2.1	15.2 3.4
33	3 23.3	3 23.8	3 14.0	3.3 0.7	9.3 2.1	15.3 3.4
34	3 23.5	3 24.1	3 14.2	3.4 0.8	9.4 2.1	15.4 3.5
35	3 23.8	3 24.3	3 14.5	3.5 0.8	9.5 2.1	15.5 3.5
36	3 24.0	3 24.6	3 14.7	3.6 0.8	9.6 2.2	15.6 3.5
37	3 24.3	3 24.8	3 14.9	3.7 0.8	9.7 2.2	15.7 3.5
38	3 24.5	3 25.1	3 15.2	3.8 0.9	9.8 2.2	15.8 3.6
39	3 24.8	3 25.3	3 15.4	3.9 0.9	9.9 2.2	15.9 3.6
40	3 25.0	3 25.6	3 15.7	4.0 0.9	10.0 2.3	16.0 3.6
41	3 25.3	3 25.8	3 15.9	4.1 0.9	10.1 2.3	16.1 3.6
42	3 25.5	3 26.1	3 16.1	4.2 0.9	10.2 2.3	16.2 3.6
43	3 25.8	3 26.3	3 16.4	4.3 1.0	10.3 2.3	16.3 3.7
44	3 26.0	3 26.6	3 16.6	4.4 1.0	10.4 2.3	16.4 3.7
45	3 26.3	3 26.8	3 16.9	4.5 1.0	10.5 2.4	16.5 3.7
46	3 26.5	3 27.1	3 17.1	4.6 1.0	10.6 2.4	16.6 3.7
47	3 26.8	3 27.3	3 17.3	4.7 1.1	10.7 2.4	16.7 3.8
48	3 27.0	3 27.6	3 17.6	4.8 1.1	10.8 2.4	16.8 3.8
49	3 27.3	3 27.8	3 17.8	4.9 1.1	10.9 2.5	16.9 3.8
50	3 27.5	3 28.1	3 18.0	5.0 1.1	11.0 2.5	17.0 3.8
51	3 27.8	3 28.3	3 18.3	5.1 1.1	11.1 2.5	17.1 3.8
52	3 28.0	3 28.6	3 18.5	5.2 1.2	11.2 2.5	17.2 3.9
53	3 28.3	3 28.8	3 18.8	5.3 1.2	11.3 2.5	17.3 3.9
54	3 28.5	3 29.1	3 19.0	5.4 1.2	11.4 2.6	17.4 3.9
55	3 28.8	3 29.3	3 19.2	5.5 1.2	11.5 2.6	17.5 3.9
56	3 29.0	3 29.6	3 19.5	5.6 1.3	11.6 2.6	17.6 4.0
57	3 29.3	3 29.8	3 19.7	5.7 1.3	11.7 2.6	17.7 4.0
58	3 29.5	3 30.1	3 20.0	5.8 1.3	11.8 2.7	17.8 4.0
59	3 29.8	3 30.3	3 20.2	5.9 1.3	11.9 2.7	17.9 4.0
60	3 30.0	3 30.6	3 20.4	6.0 1.4	12.0 2.7	18.0 4.1

14m INCREMENTS AND CORRECTIONS 15m

m 14 s	SUN PLANETS ° '	ARIES ° '	MOON ° '	v or Corrn d ' '	v or Corrn d ' '	v or Corrn d ' '
00	3 30.0	3 30.6	3 20.4	0.0 0.0	6.0 1.5	12.0 2.9
01	3 30.3	3 30.8	3 20.7	0.1 0.0	6.1 1.5	12.1 2.9
02	3 30.5	3 31.1	3 20.9	0.2 0.0	6.2 1.5	12.2 2.9
03	3 30.8	3 31.3	3 21.1	0.3 0.1	6.3 1.5	12.3 3.0
04	3 31.0	3 31.6	3 21.4	0.4 0.1	6.4 1.5	12.4 3.0
05	3 31.3	3 31.8	3 21.6	0.5 0.1	6.5 1.6	12.5 3.0
06	3 31.5	3 32.1	3 21.9	0.6 0.1	6.6 1.6	12.6 3.0
07	3 31.8	3 32.3	3 22.1	0.7 0.2	6.7 1.6	12.7 3.1
08	3 32.0	3 32.6	3 22.3	0.8 0.2	6.8 1.6	12.8 3.1
09	3 32.3	3 32.8	3 22.6	0.9 0.2	6.9 1.7	12.9 3.1
10	3 32.5	3 33.1	3 22.8	1.0 0.2	7.0 1.7	13.0 3.1
11	3 32.8	3 33.3	3 23.1	1.1 0.3	7.1 1.7	13.1 3.2
12	3 33.0	3 33.6	3 23.3	1.2 0.3	7.2 1.7	13.2 3.2
13	3 33.3	3 33.8	3 23.5	1.3 0.3	7.3 1.8	13.3 3.2
14	3 33.5	3 34.1	3 23.8	1.4 0.3	7.4 1.8	13.4 3.2
15	3 33.8	3 34.3	3 24.0	1.5 0.4	7.5 1.8	13.5 3.3
16	3 34.0	3 34.6	3 24.3	1.6 0.4	7.6 1.8	13.6 3.3
17	3 34.3	3 34.8	3 24.5	1.7 0.4	7.7 1.9	13.7 3.3
18	3 34.5	3 35.1	3 24.7	1.8 0.4	7.8 1.9	13.8 3.3
19	3 34.8	3 35.3	3 25.0	1.9 0.5	7.9 1.9	13.9 3.4
20	3 35.0	3 35.6	3 25.2	2.0 0.5	8.0 1.9	14.0 3.4
21	3 35.3	3 35.8	3 25.4	2.1 0.5	8.1 2.0	14.1 3.4
22	3 35.5	3 36.1	3 25.7	2.2 0.5	8.2 2.0	14.2 3.4
23	3 35.8	3 36.3	3 25.9	2.3 0.6	8.3 2.0	14.3 3.5
24	3 36.0	3 36.6	3 26.2	2.4 0.6	8.4 2.0	14.4 3.5
25	3 36.3	3 36.8	3 26.4	2.5 0.6	8.5 2.1	14.5 3.5
26	3 36.5	3 37.1	3 26.6	2.6 0.6	8.6 2.1	14.6 3.5
27	3 36.8	3 37.3	3 26.9	2.7 0.7	8.7 2.1	14.7 3.6
28	3 37.0	3 37.6	3 27.1	2.8 0.7	8.8 2.1	14.8 3.6
29	3 37.3	3 37.8	3 27.4	2.9 0.7	8.9 2.2	14.9 3.6
30	3 37.5	3 38.1	3 27.6	3.0 0.7	9.0 2.2	15.0 3.6
31	3 37.8	3 38.3	3 27.8	3.1 0.7	9.1 2.2	15.1 3.6
32	3 38.0	3 38.6	3 28.1	3.2 0.8	9.2 2.2	15.2 3.7
33	3 38.3	3 38.8	3 28.3	3.3 0.8	9.3 2.2	15.3 3.7
34	3 38.5	3 39.1	3 28.5	3.4 0.8	9.4 2.3	15.4 3.7
35	3 38.8	3 39.3	3 28.8	3.5 0.8	9.5 2.3	15.5 3.7
36	3 39.0	3 39.6	3 29.0	3.6 0.9	9.6 2.3	15.6 3.8
37	3 39.3	3 39.9	3 29.3	3.7 0.9	9.7 2.3	15.7 3.8
38	3 39.5	3 40.1	3 29.5	3.8 0.9	9.8 2.4	15.8 3.8
39	3 39.8	3 40.4	3 29.7	3.9 0.9	9.9 2.4	15.9 3.8
40	3 40.0	3 40.6	3 30.0	4.0 1.0	10.0 2.4	16.0 3.9
41	3 40.3	3 40.9	3 30.2	4.1 1.0	10.1 2.4	16.1 3.9
42	3 40.5	3 41.1	3 30.5	4.2 1.0	10.2 2.5	16.2 3.9
43	3 40.8	3 41.4	3 30.7	4.3 1.0	10.3 2.5	16.3 3.9
44	3 41.0	3 41.6	3 30.9	4.4 1.1	10.4 2.5	16.4 4.0
45	3 41.3	3 41.9	3 31.2	4.5 1.1	10.5 2.5	16.5 4.0
46	3 41.5	3 42.1	3 31.4	4.6 1.1	10.6 2.6	16.6 4.0
47	3 41.8	3 42.4	3 31.6	4.7 1.1	10.7 2.6	16.7 4.0
48	3 42.0	3 42.6	3 31.9	4.8 1.2	10.8 2.6	16.8 4.1
49	3 42.3	3 42.9	3 32.1	4.9 1.2	10.9 2.6	16.9 4.1
50	3 42.5	3 43.1	3 32.4	5.0 1.2	11.0 2.7	17.0 4.1
51	3 42.8	3 43.4	3 32.6	5.1 1.2	11.1 2.7	17.1 4.1
52	3 43.0	3 43.6	3 32.8	5.2 1.3	11.2 2.7	17.2 4.2
53	3 43.3	3 43.9	3 33.1	5.3 1.3	11.3 2.7	17.3 4.2
54	3 43.5	3 44.1	3 33.3	5.4 1.3	11.4 2.8	17.4 4.2
55	3 43.8	3 44.4	3 33.6	5.5 1.3	11.5 2.8	17.5 4.2
56	3 44.0	3 44.6	3 33.8	5.6 1.4	11.6 2.8	17.6 4.3
57	3 44.3	3 44.9	3 34.0	5.7 1.4	11.7 2.8	17.7 4.3
58	3 44.5	3 45.1	3 34.3	5.8 1.4	11.8 2.9	17.8 4.3
59	3 44.8	3 45.4	3 34.5	5.9 1.4	11.9 2.9	17.9 4.3
60	3 45.0	3 45.6	3 34.8	6.0 1.5	12.0 2.9	18.0 4.4

m 15 s	SUN PLANETS ° '	ARIES ° '	MOON ° '	v or Corrn d ' '	v or Corrn d ' '	v or Corrn d ' '
00	3 45.0	3 45.6	3 34.8	0.0 0.0	6.0 1.6	12.0 3.1
01	3 45.3	3 45.9	3 35.0	0.1 0.0	6.1 1.6	12.1 3.1
02	3 45.5	3 46.1	3 35.2	0.2 0.1	6.2 1.6	12.2 3.2
03	3 45.8	3 46.4	3 35.5	0.3 0.1	6.3 1.6	12.3 3.2
04	3 46.0	3 46.6	3 35.7	0.4 0.1	6.4 1.7	12.4 3.2
05	3 46.3	3 46.9	3 35.9	0.5 0.1	6.5 1.7	12.5 3.2
06	3 46.5	3 47.1	3 36.2	0.6 0.2	6.6 1.7	12.6 3.3
07	3 46.8	3 47.4	3 36.4	0.7 0.2	6.7 1.7	12.7 3.3
08	3 47.0	2 47.6	2 36.7	0.8 0.2	6.8 1.8	12.8 3.3
09	3 47.3	3 47.9	3 36.9	0.9 0.2	6.9 1.8	12.9 3.3
10	3 47.5	3 48.1	3 37.1	1.0 0.3	7.0 1.8	13.0 3.4
11	3 47.8	3 48.4	3 37.4	1.1 0.3	7.1 1.8	13.1 3.4
12	3 48.0	3 48.6	3 37.6	1.2 0.3	7.2 1.9	13.2 3.4
13	3 48.3	3 48.9	3 37.9	1.3 0.3	7.3 1.9	13.3 3.4
14	3 48.5	3 49.1	3 38.1	1.4 0.4	7.4 1.9	13.4 3.5
15	3 48.8	3 49.4	3 38.3	1.5 0.4	7.5 1.9	13.5 3.5
16	3 49.0	3 49.6	3 38.6	1.6 0.4	7.6 2.0	13.6 3.5
17	3 49.3	3 49.9	3 38.8	1.7 0.4	7.7 2.0	13.7 3.5
18	3 49.5	3 50.1	3 39.0	1.8 0.5	7.8 2.0	13.8 3.6
19	3 49.8	3 50.4	3 39.3	1.9 0.5	7.9 2.0	13.9 3.6
20	3 50.0	3 50.6	3 39.5	2.0 0.5	8.0 2.1	14.0 3.6
21	3 50.3	3 50.9	3 39.8	2.1 0.5	8.1 2.1	14.1 3.6
22	3 50.5	3 51.1	3 40.0	2.2 0.6	8.2 2.1	14.2 3.7
23	3 50.8	3 51.4	3 40.2	2.3 0.6	8.3 2.1	14.3 3.7
24	3 51.0	3 51.6	3 40.5	2.4 0.6	8.4 2.2	14.4 3.7
25	3 51.3	3 51.9	3 40.7	2.5 0.6	8.5 2.2	14.5 3.7
26	3 51.5	3 52.1	3 41.0	2.6 0.7	8.6 2.2	14.6 3.8
27	3 51.8	3 52.4	3 41.2	2.7 0.7	8.7 2.2	14.7 3.8
28	3 52.0	3 52.6	3 41.4	2.8 0.7	8.8 2.3	14.8 3.8
29	3 52.3	3 52.9	3 41.7	2.9 0.7	8.9 2.3	14.9 3.8
30	3 52.5	3 53.1	3 41.9	3.0 0.8	9.0 2.3	15.0 3.9
31	3 52.8	3 53.4	3 42.1	3.1 0.8	9.1 2.4	15.1 3.9
32	3 53.0	3 53.6	3 42.4	3.2 0.8	9.2 2.4	15.2 3.9
33	3 53.3	3 53.9	3 42.6	3.3 0.9	9.3 2.4	15.3 4.0
34	3 53.5	3 54.1	3 42.9	3.4 0.9	9.4 2.4	15.4 4.0
35	3 53.8	3 54.4	3 43.1	3.5 0.9	9.5 2.5	15.5 4.0
36	3 54.0	3 54.6	3 43.3	3.6 0.9	9.6 2.5	15.6 4.0
37	3 54.3	3 54.9	3 43.6	3.7 1.0	9.7 2.5	15.7 4.1
38	3 54.5	3 55.1	3 43.8	3.8 1.0	9.8 2.5	15.8 4.1
39	3 54.8	3 55.4	3 44.1	3.9 1.0	9.9 2.6	15.9 4.1
40	3 55.0	3 55.6	3 44.3	4.0 1.0	10.0 2.6	16.0 4.1
41	3 55.3	3 55.9	3 44.5	4.1 1.1	10.1 2.6	16.1 4.2
42	3 55.5	3 56.1	3 44.8	4.2 1.1	10.2 2.6	16.2 4.2
43	3 55.8	3 56.4	3 45.0	4.3 1.1	10.3 2.7	16.3 4.2
44	3 56.0	3 56.6	3 45.2	4.4 1.1	10.4 2.7	16.4 4.2
45	3 56.3	3 56.9	3 45.5	4.5 1.2	10.5 2.7	16.5 4.3
46	3 56.5	3 57.1	3 45.7	4.6 1.2	10.6 2.7	16.6 4.3
47	3 56.8	3 57.4	3 46.0	4.7 1.2	10.7 2.8	16.7 4.3
48	3 57.0	3 57.6	3 46.2	4.8 1.2	10.8 2.8	16.8 4.3
49	3 57.3	3 57.9	3 46.4	4.9 1.3	10.9 2.8	16.9 4.4
50	3 57.5	3 58.2	3 46.7	5.0 1.3	11.0 2.8	17.0 4.4
51	3 57.8	3 58.4	3 46.9	5.1 1.3	11.1 2.9	17.1 4.4
52	3 58.0	3 58.7	3 47.2	5.2 1.3	11.2 2.9	17.2 4.4
53	3 58.3	3 58.9	3 47.4	5.3 1.4	11.3 2.9	17.3 4.5
54	3 58.5	3 59.2	3 47.6	5.4 1.4	11.4 2.9	17.4 4.5
55	3 58.8	3 59.4	3 47.9	5.5 1.4	11.5 3.0	17.5 4.5
56	3 59.0	3 59.7	3 48.1	5.6 1.4	11.6 3.0	17.6 4.5
57	3 59.3	3 59.9	3 48.4	5.7 1.5	11.7 3.0	17.7 4.6
58	3 59.5	4 00.2	3 48.6	5.8 1.5	11.8 3.0	17.8 4.6
59	3 59.8	4 00.4	3 48.8	5.9 1.5	11.9 3.1	17.9 4.6
60	4 00.0	4 00.7	3 49.1	6.0 1.6	12.0 3.1	18.0 4.7

16ᵐ INCREMENTS AND CORRECTIONS 17ᵐ

m 16	SUN PLANETS	ARIES	MOON	v or Corrⁿ d	v or Corrⁿ d	v or Corrⁿ d	m 17	SUN PLANETS	ARIES	MOON	v or Corrⁿ d	v or Corrⁿ d	v or Corrⁿ d
s	° ′	° ′	° ′	′ ′	′ ′	′ ′	s	° ′	° ′	° ′	′ ′	′ ′	′ ′
00	4 00.0	4 00.7	3 49.1	0.0 0.0	6.0 1.7	12.0 3.3	00	4 15.0	4 15.7	4 03.4	0.0 0.0	6.0 1.8	12.0 3.5
01	4 00.3	4 00.9	3 49.3	0.1 0.0	6.1 1.7	12.1 3.3	01	4 15.3	4 15.9	4 03.6	0.1 0.0	6.1 1.8	12.1 3.5
02	4 00.5	4 01.2	3 49.5	0.2 0.1	6.2 1.7	12.2 3.4	02	4 15.5	4 16.2	4 03.9	0.2 0.1	6.2 1.8	12.2 3.6
03	4 00.8	4 01.4	3 49.8	0.3 0.1	6.3 1.7	12.3 3.4	03	4 15.8	4 16.5	4 04.1	0.3 0.1	6.3 1.8	12.3 3.6
04	4 01.0	4 01.7	3 50.0	0.4 0.1	6.4 1.8	12.4 3.4	04	4 16.0	4 16.7	4 04.3	0.4 0.1	6.4 1.9	12.4 3.6
05	4 01.3	4 01.9	3 50.3	0.5 0.1	6.5 1.8	12.5 3.4	05	4 16.3	4 16.0	4 04.6	0.5 0.1	6.5 1.9	12.5 3.6
06	4 01.5	4 02.2	3 50.5	0.6 0.2	6.6 1.8	12.6 3.5	06	4 16.5	4 17.2	4 04.8	0.6 0.2	6.6 1.9	12.6 3.7
07	4 01.8	4 02.4	3 50.7	0.7 0.2	6.7 1.8	12.7 3.5	07	4 16.8	4 17.5	4 05.1	0.7 0.2	6.7 2.0	12.7 3.7
08	4 02.0	4 02.7	3 51.0	0.8 0.2	6.8 1.9	12.8 3.5	08	4 17.0	4 17.7	4 05.3	0.8 0.2	6.8 2.0	12.8 3.7
09	4 02.3	4 02.9	3 51.2	0.9 0.2	6.9 1.9	12.9 3.5	09	4 17.3	4 17.0	4 05.5	0.9 0.3	6.9 2.0	12.9 3.8
10	4 02.5	4 03.2	3 51.5	1.0 0.3	7.0 1.9	13.0 3.6	10	4 17.5	4 18.2	4 05.8	1.0 0.3	7.0 2.0	13.0 3.8
11	4 02.8	4 03.4	3 51.7	1.1 0.3	7.1 2.0	13.1 3.6	11	4 17.8	4 18.5	4 06.0	1.1 0.3	7.1 2.1	13.1 3.8
12	4 03.0	4 03.7	3 51.9	1.2 0.3	7.2 2.0	13.2 3.6	12	4 18.0	4 18.7	4 06.2	1.2 0.4	7.2 2.1	13.2 3.9
13	4 03.3	4 03.9	3 52.2	1.3 0.4	7.3 2.0	13.3 3.7	13	4 18.3	4 18.0	4 06.5	1.3 0.4	7.3 2.1	13.3 3.9
14	4 03.5	4 04.2	3 52.4	1.4 0.4	7.4 2.0	13.4 3.7	14	4 18.5	4 19.2	4 06.7	1.4 0.4	7.4 2.2	13.4 3.9
15	4 03.8	4 04.4	3 52.6	1.5 0.4	7.5 2.1	13.5 3.7	15	4 18.8	4 19.5	4 07.0	1.5 0.4	7.5 2.2	13.5 3.9
16	4 04.0	4 04.7	3 52.9	1.6 0.4	7.6 2.1	13.6 3.7	16	4 19.0	4 19.7	4 07.2	1.6 0.5	7.6 2.2	13.6 4.0
17	4 04.3	4 04.9	3 53.1	1.7 0.5	7.7 2.1	13.7 3.8	17	4 19.3	4 19.0	4 07.4	1.7 0.5	7.7 2.2	13.7 4.0
18	4 04.5	4 05.2	3 53.4	1.8 0.5	7.8 2.1	13.8 3.8	18	4 19.5	4 20.2	4 07.7	1.8 0.5	7.8 2.3	13.8 4.0
19	4 04.8	4 05.4	3 53.6	1.9 0.5	7.9 2.2	13.9 3.8	19	4 19.8	4 20.5	4 07.9	1.9 0.6	7.9 2.3	13.9 4.1
20	4 05.0	4 05.7	3 53.8	2.0 0.6	8.0 2.2	14.0 3.9	20	4 20.0	4 20.7	4 08.2	2.0 0.6	8.0 2.3	14.0 4.1
21	4 05.3	4 05.9	3 54.1	2.1 0.6	8.1 2.2	14.1 3.9	21	4 20.3	4 20.0	4 08.4	2.1 0.6	8.1 2.4	14.1 4.1
22	4 05.5	4 06.2	3 54.3	2.2 0.6	8.2 2.3	14.2 3.9	22	4 20.5	4 21.2	4 08.6	2.2 0.6	8.2 2.4	14.2 4.1
23	4 05.8	4 06.4	3 54.6	2.3 0.6	8.3 2.3	14.3 3.9	23	4 20.8	4 21.5	4 08.9	2.3 0.7	8.3 2.4	14.3 4.2
24	4 06.0	4 06.7	3 54.8	2.4 0.7	8.4 2.3	14.4 4.0	24	4 21.0	4 21.7	4 09.1	2.4 0.7	8.4 2.5	14.4 4.2
25	4 06.3	4 06.9	3 55.0	2.5 0.7	8.5 2.3	14.5 4.0	25	4 21.3	4 21.0	4 09.3	2.5 0.7	8.5 2.5	14.5 4.2
26	4 06.5	4 07.2	3 55.3	2.6 0.7	8.6 2.4	14.6 4.0	26	4 21.5	4 22.2	4 09.6	2.6 0.8	8.6 2.5	14.6 4.3
27	4 06.8	4 07.4	3 55.5	2.7 0.7	8.7 2.4	14.7 4.0	27	4 21.8	4 22.5	4 09.8	2.7 0.8	8.7 2.5	14.7 4.3
28	4 07.0	4 07.7	3 55.7	2.8 0.8	8.8 2.4	14.8 4.1	28	4 22.0	4 22.7	4 10.1	2.8 0.8	8.8 2.6	14.8 4.3
29	4 07.3	4 07.9	3 56.0	2.9 0.8	8.9 2.4	14.9 4.1	29	4 22.3	4 22.0	4 10.3	2.9 0.8	8.9 2.6	14.9 4.4
30	4 07.5	4 08.2	3 56.2	3.0 0.8	9.0 2.5	15.0 4.1	30	4 22.5	4 23.2	4 10.5	3.0 0.9	9.0 2.6	15.0 4.4
31	4 07.8	4 08.4	3 56.5	3.1 0.9	9.1 2.5	15.1 4.2	31	4 22.8	4 23.5	4 10.8	3.1 0.9	9.1 2.7	15.1 4.4
32	4 08.0	4 08.7	3 56.7	3.2 0.9	9.2 2.5	15.2 4.2	32	4 23.0	4 23.7	4 11.0	3.2 0.9	9.2 2.7	15.2 4.4
33	4 08.3	4 08.9	3 56.9	3.3 0.9	9.3 2.6	15.3 4.2	33	4 23.3	4 23.0	4 11.3	3.3 1.0	9.3 2.7	15.3 4.5
34	4 08.5	4 09.2	3 57.2	3.4 0.9	9.4 2.6	15.4 4.2	34	4 23.5	4 24.2	4 11.5	3.4 1.0	9.4 2.7	15.4 4.5
35	4 08.8	4 09.4	3 57.4	3.5 1.0	9.5 2.6	15.5 4.3	35	4 23.8	4 24.5	4 11.7	3.5 1.0	9.5 2.8	15.5 4.5
36	4 09.0	4 09.7	3 57.7	3.6 1.0	9.6 2.6	15.6 4.3	36	4 24.0	4 24.7	4 12.0	3.6 1.1	9.6 2.8	15.6 4.6
37	4 09.3	4 09.9	3 57.9	3.7 1.0	9.7 2.7	15.7 4.3	37	4 24.3	4 24.0	4 12.2	3.7 1.1	9.7 2.8	15.7 4.6
38	4 09.5	4 10.2	3 58.1	3.8 1.0	9.8 2.7	15.8 4.3	38	4 24.5	4 25.2	4 12.5	3.8 1.1	9.8 2.9	15.8 4.6
39	4 09.8	4 10.4	3 58.4	3.9 1.1	9.9 2.7	15.9 4.4	39	4 24.8	4 25.5	4 12.7	3.9 1.1	9.9 2.9	15.9 4.6
40	4 10.0	4 10.7	3 58.6	4.0 1.1	10.0 2.8	16.0 4.4	40	4 25.0	4 25.7	4 12.9	4.0 1.2	10.0 2.9	16.0 4.7
41	4 10.3	4 10.9	3 58.8	4.1 1.1	10.1 2.8	16.1 4.4	41	4 25.3	4 25.0	4 13.2	4.1 1.2	10.1 2.9	16.1 4.7
42	4 10.5	4 11.2	3 59.1	4.2 1.2	10.2 2.8	16.2 4.5	42	4 25.5	4 26.2	4 13.4	4.2 1.2	10.2 3.0	16.2 4.7
43	4 10.8	4 11.4	3 59.3	4.3 1.2	10.3 2.8	16.3 4.5	43	4 25.8	4 26.5	4 13.6	4.3 1.3	10.3 3.0	16.3 4.8
44	4 11.0	4 11.7	3 59.6	4.4 1.2	10.4 2.9	16.4 4.5	44	4 26.0	4 26.7	4 13.9	4.4 1.3	10.4 3.0	16.4 4.8
45	4 11.3	4 11.9	3 59.8	4.5 1.2	10.5 2.9	16.5 4.5	45	4 26.3	4 26.0	4 14.1	4.5 1.3	10.5 3.1	16.5 4.8
46	4 11.5	4 12.2	4 00.0	4.6 1.3	10.6 2.9	16.6 4.6	46	4 26.5	4 27.2	4 14.4	4.6 1.3	10.6 3.1	16.6 4.8
47	4 11.8	4 12.4	4 00.3	4.7 1.3	10.7 2.9	16.7 4.6	47	4 26.8	4 27.5	4 14.6	4.7 1.4	10.7 3.1	16.7 4.9
48	4 12.0	4 12.7	4 00.5	4.8 1.3	10.8 3.0	16.8 4.6	48	4 27.0	4 27.7	4 14.8	4.8 1.4	10.8 3.2	16.8 4.9
49	4 12.3	4 12.9	4 00.8	4.9 1.3	10.9 3.0	16.9 4.6	49	4 27.3	4 27.0	4 15.1	4.9 1.4	10.9 3.2	16.9 4.9
50	4 12.5	4 13.2	4 01.0	5.0 1.4	11.0 3.0	17.0 4.7	50	4 27.5	4 28.2	4 15.3	5.0 1.5	11.0 3.2	17.0 5.0
51	4 12.8	4 13.4	4 01.2	5.1 1.4	11.1 3.1	17.1 4.7	51	4 27.8	4 28.5	4 15.6	5.1 1.5	11.1 3.2	17.1 5.0
52	4 13.0	4 13.7	4 01.5	5.2 1.4	11.2 3.1	17.2 4.7	52	4 28.0	4 28.7	4 15.8	5.2 1.5	11.2 3.3	17.2 5.0
53	4 13.3	4 13.9	4 01.7	5.3 1.5	11.3 3.1	17.3 4.8	53	4 28.3	4 28.0	4 16.0	5.3 1.5	11.3 3.3	17.3 5.0
54	4 13.5	4 14.2	4 02.0	5.4 1.5	11.4 3.1	17.4 4.8	54	4 28.5	4 29.2	4 16.3	5.4 1.6	11.4 3.3	17.4 5.1
55	4 13.8	4 14.4	4 02.2	5.5 1.5	11.5 3.2	17.5 4.8	55	4 28.8	4 29.5	4 16.5	5.5 1.6	11.5 3.4	17.5 5.1
56	4 14.0	4 14.7	4 02.4	5.6 1.5	11.6 3.2	17.6 4.8	56	4 29.0	4 29.7	4 16.7	5.6 1.6	11.6 3.4	17.6 5.1
57	4 14.3	4 14.9	4 02.7	5.7 1.6	11.7 3.2	17.7 4.9	57	4 29.3	4 29.0	4 17.0	5.7 1.7	11.7 3.4	17.7 5.2
58	4 14.5	4 15.2	4 02.9	5.8 1.6	11.8 3.2	17.8 4.9	58	4 29.5	4 30.2	4 17.2	5.8 1.7	11.8 3.4	17.8 5.2
59	4 14.8	4 15.4	4 03.1	5.9 1.6	11.9 3.3	17.9 4.9	59	4 29.8	4 30.5	4 17.5	5.9 1.7	11.9 3.5	17.9 5.2
60	4 15.0	4 15.7	4 03.4	6.0 1.7	12.0 3.3	18.0 5.0	60	4 30.0	4 30.7	4 17.7	6.0 1.8	12.0 3.5	18.0 5.3

18ᵐ   INCREMENTS AND CORRECTIONS   19ᵐ

m 18	SUN PLANETS	ARIES	MOON	v or Corrⁿ d		v or Corrⁿ d		v or Corrⁿ d		m 19	SUN PLANETS	ARIES	MOON	v or Corrⁿ d		v or Corrⁿ d		v or Corrⁿ d	
s	° ′	° ′	° ′	′	′	′	′	′	′	s	° ′	° ′	° ′	′	′	′	′	′	′
00	4 30.0	4 30.7	4 17.7	0.0	0.0	6.0	1.9	12.0	3.7	00	4 45.0	4 45.8	4 32.0	0.0	0.0	6.0	2.0	12.0	3.9
01	4 30.3	4 31.0	4 17.9	0.1	0.0	6.1	1.9	12.1	3.7	01	4 45.3	4 46.0	4 32.3	0.1	0.0	6.1	2.0	12.1	3.9
02	4 30.5	4 31.2	4 18.2	0.2	0.1	6.2	1.9	12.2	3.8	02	4 45.5	4 46.3	4 32.5	0.2	0.1	6.2	2.0	12.2	4.0
03	4 30.8	4 31.5	4 18.4	0.3	0.1	6.3	1.9	12.3	3.8	03	4 45.8	4 46.5	4 32.7	0.3	0.1	6.3	2.0	12.3	4.0
04	4 31.0	4 31.7	4 18.7	0.4	0.1	6.4	2.0	12.4	3.8	04	4 46.0	4 46.8	4 33.0	0.4	0.1	6.4	2.1	12.4	4.0
05	4 31.3	4 32.0	4 18.9	0.5	0.2	6.5	2.0	12.5	3.9	05	4 46.3	4 47.0	4 33.2	0.5	0.2	6.5	2.1	12.5	4.1
06	4 31.5	4 32.2	4 19.1	0.6	0.2	6.6	2.0	12.6	3.9	06	4 46.5	4 47.3	4 33.4	0.6	0.2	6.6	2.1	12.6	4.1
07	4 31.8	4 32.5	4 19.4	0.7	0.2	6.7	2.1	12.7	3.9	07	4 46.8	4 47.5	4 33.7	0.7	0.2	6.7	2.2	12.7	4.1
08	4 32.0	4 32.7	4 19.6	0.8	0.2	6.8	2.1	12.8	3.9	08	4 47.0	4 47.8	4 33.9	0.8	0.3	6.8	2.2	12.8	4.2
09	4 32.3	4 33.0	4 19.8	0.9	0.3	6.9	2.1	12.9	4.0	09	4 47.3	4 48.0	4 34.2	0.9	0.3	6.9	2.2	12.9	4.2
10	4 32.5	4 33.2	4 20.1	1.0	0.3	7.0	2.2	13.0	4.0	10	4 47.5	4 48.3	4 34.4	1.0	0.3	7.0	2.3	13.0	4.2
11	4 32.8	4 33.5	4 20.3	1.1	0.3	7.1	2.2	13.1	4.0	11	4 47.8	4 48.5	4 34.6	1.1	0.4	7.1	2.3	13.1	4.3
12	4 33.0	4 33.7	4 20.6	1.2	0.4	7.2	2.2	13.2	4.1	12	4 48.0	4 48.8	4 34.9	1.2	0.4	7.2	2.3	13.2	4.3
13	4 33.3	4 34.0	4 20.8	1.3	0.4	7.3	2.3	13.3	4.1	13	4 48.3	4 49.0	4 35.1	1.3	0.4	7.3	2.4	13.3	4.3
14	4 33.5	4 34.2	4 21.0	1.4	0.4	7.4	2.3	13.4	4.1	14	4 48.5	4 49.3	4 35.4	1.4	0.5	7.4	2.4	13.4	4.4
15	4 33.8	4 34.5	4 21.3	1.5	0.5	7.5	2.3	13.5	4.2	15	4 48.8	4 49.5	4 35.6	1.5	0.5	7.5	2.4	13.5	4.4
16	4 34.0	4 34.8	4 21.5	1.6	0.5	7.6	2.3	13.6	4.2	16	4 49.0	4 49.8	4 35.8	1.6	0.5	7.6	2.5	13.6	4.4
17	4 34.3	4 35.0	4 21.8	1.7	0.5	7.7	2.4	13.7	4.2	17	4 49.3	4 50.0	4 36.1	1.7	0.6	7.7	2.5	13.7	4.5
18	4 34.5	4 35.3	4 22.0	1.8	0.6	7.8	2.4	13.8	4.3	18	4 49.5	4 50.3	4 36.3	1.8	0.6	7.8	2.5	13.8	4.5
19	4 34.8	4 35.5	4 22.2	1.9	0.6	7.9	2.4	13.9	4.3	19	4 49.8	4 50.5	4 36.6	1.9	0.6	7.9	2.6	13.9	4.5
20	4 35.0	4 35.8	4 22.5	2.0	0.6	8.0	2.5	14.0	4.3	20	4 50.0	4 50.8	4 36.8	2.0	0.7	8.0	2.6	14.0	4.6
21	4 35.3	4 36.0	4 22.7	2.1	0.6	8.1	2.5	14.1	4.3	21	4 50.3	4 51.0	4 37.0	2.1	0.7	8.1	2.6	14.1	4.6
22	4 35.5	4 36.3	4 22.9	2.2	0.7	8.2	2.5	14.2	4.4	22	4 50.5	4 51.3	4 37.3	2.2	0.7	8.2	2.7	14.2	4.6
23	4 35.8	4 36.5	4 23.2	2.3	0.7	8.3	2.6	14.3	4.4	23	4 50.8	4 51.5	4 37.5	2.3	0.7	8.3	2.7	14.3	4.6
24	4 36.0	4 36.8	4 23.4	2.4	0.7	8.4	2.6	14.4	4.4	24	4 51.0	4 51.8	4 37.7	2.4	0.8	8.4	2.7	14.4	4.7
25	4 36.3	4 37.0	4 23.7	2.5	0.8	8.5	2.6	14.5	4.5	25	4 51.3	4 52.0	4 38.0	2.5	0.8	8.5	2.8	14.5	4.7
26	4 36.5	4 37.3	4 23.9	2.6	0.8	8.6	2.7	14.6	4.5	26	4 51.5	4 52.3	4 38.2	2.6	0.8	8.6	2.8	14.6	4.7
27	4 36.8	4 37.5	4 24.1	2.7	0.8	8.7	2.7	14.7	4.5	27	4 51.8	4 52.5	4 38.5	2.7	0.9	8.7	2.8	14.7	4.8
28	4 37.0	4 37.8	4 24.4	2.8	0.9	8.8	2.7	14.8	4.6	28	4 52.0	4 52.8	4 38.7	2.8	0.9	8.8	2.9	14.8	4.8
29	4 37.3	4 38.0	4 24.6	2.9	0.9	8.9	2.7	14.9	4.6	29	4 52.3	4 53.1	4 38.9	2.9	0.9	8.9	2.9	14.9	4.8
30	4 37.5	4 38.3	4 24.9	3.0	0.9	9.0	2.8	15.0	4.6	30	4 52.5	4 53.3	4 39.2	3.0	1.0	9.0	2.9	15.0	4.9
31	4 37.8	4 38.5	4 25.1	3.1	1.0	9.1	2.8	15.1	4.7	31	4 52.8	4 53.6	4 39.4	3.1	1.0	9.1	3.0	15.1	4.9
32	4 38.0	4 38.8	4 25.3	3.2	1.0	9.2	2.8	15.2	4.7	32	4 53.0	4 53.8	4 39.7	3.2	1.0	9.2	3.0	15.2	4.9
33	4 38.3	4 39.0	4 25.6	3.3	1.0	9.3	2.9	15.3	4.7	33	4 53.3	4 54.1	4 39.9	3.3	1.1	9.3	3.0	15.3	5.0
34	4 38.5	4 39.3	4 25.8	3.4	1.0	9.4	2.9	15.4	4.7	34	4 53.5	4 54.3	4 40.1	3.4	1.1	9.4	3.1	15.4	5.0
35	4 38.8	4 39.5	4 26.1	3.5	1.1	9.5	2.9	15.5	4.8	35	4 53.8	4 54.6	4 40.4	3.5	1.1	9.5	3.1	15.5	5.0
36	4 39.0	4 39.8	4 26.3	3.6	1.1	9.6	3.0	15.6	4.8	36	4 54.0	4 54.8	4 40.6	3.6	1.2	9.6	3.1	15.6	5.1
37	4 39.3	4 40.0	4 26.5	3.7	1.1	9.7	3.0	15.7	4.8	37	4 54.3	4 55.1	4 40.8	3.7	1.2	9.7	3.2	15.7	5.1
38	4 39.5	4 40.3	4 26.8	3.8	1.2	9.8	3.0	15.8	4.9	38	4 54.5	4 55.3	4 41.1	3.8	1.2	9.8	3.2	15.8	5.1
39	4 39.8	4 40.5	4 27.0	3.9	1.2	9.9	3.1	15.9	4.9	39	4 54.8	4 55.6	4 41.3	3.9	1.3	9.9	3.2	15.9	5.2
40	4 40.0	4 40.8	4 27.2	4.0	1.2	10.0	3.1	16.0	4.9	40	4 55.0	4 55.8	4 41.6	4.0	1.3	10.0	3.3	16.0	5.2
41	4 40.3	4 41.0	4 27.5	4.1	1.3	10.1	3.1	16.1	5.0	41	4 55.3	4 56.1	4 41.8	4.1	1.3	10.1	3.3	16.1	5.2
42	4 40.5	4 41.3	4 27.7	4.2	1.3	10.2	3.1	16.2	5.0	42	4 55.5	4 56.3	4 42.0	4.2	1.4	10.2	3.3	16.2	5.3
43	4 40.8	4 41.5	4 28.0	4.3	1.3	10.3	3.2	16.3	5.0	43	4 55.8	4 56.6	4 42.3	4.3	1.4	10.3	3.3	16.3	5.3
44	4 41.0	4 41.8	4 28.2	4.4	1.4	10.4	3.2	16.4	5.1	44	4 56.0	4 56.8	4 42.5	4.4	1.4	10.4	3.4	16.4	5.3
45	4 41.3	4 42.0	4 28.4	4.5	1.4	10.5	3.2	16.5	5.1	45	4 56.3	4 57.1	4 42.8	4.5	1.5	10.5	3.4	16.5	5.4
46	4 41.5	4 42.3	4 28.7	4.6	1.4	10.6	3.3	16.6	5.1	46	4 56.5	4 57.3	4 42.0	4.6	1.5	10.6	3.4	16.6	5.4
47	4 41.8	4 42.5	4 28.9	4.7	1.4	10.7	3.3	16.7	5.1	47	4 56.8	4 57.6	4 43.2	4.7	1.5	10.7	3.5	16.7	5.4
48	4 42.0	4 42.8	4 29.2	4.8	1.5	10.8	3.3	16.8	5.2	48	4 57.0	4 57.8	4 43.5	4.8	1.6	10.8	3.5	16.8	5.5
49	4 42.3	4 43.0	4 29.4	4.9	1.5	10.9	3.4	16.9	5.2	49	4 57.3	4 58.1	4 43.7	4.9	1.6	10.9	3.5	16.9	5.5
50	4 42.5	4 43.3	4 29.6	5.0	1.5	11.0	3.4	17.0	5.2	50	4 57.5	4 58.3	4 43.9	5.0	1.6	11.0	3.6	17.0	5.5
51	4 42.8	4 43.5	4 29.9	5.1	1.6	11.1	3.4	17.1	5.3	51	4 57.8	4 58.6	4 44.2	5.1	1.7	11.1	3.6	17.1	5.6
52	4 43.0	4 43.8	4 30.1	5.2	1.6	11.2	3.5	17.2	5.3	52	4 58.0	4 58.8	4 44.4	5.2	1.7	11.2	3.6	17.2	5.6
53	4 43.3	4 44.0	4 30.3	5.3	1.6	11.3	3.5	17.3	5.3	53	4 58.3	4 59.1	4 44.7	5.3	1.7	11.3	3.7	17.3	5.6
54	4 43.5	4 44.3	4 30.6	5.4	1.7	11.4	3.5	17.4	5.4	54	4 58.5	4 59.3	4 44.9	5.4	1.8	11.4	3.7	17.4	5.7
55	4 43.8	4 44.5	4 30.8	5.5	1.7	11.5	3.5	17.5	5.4	55	4 58.8	4 59.6	4 45.1	5.5	1.8	11.5	3.7	17.5	5.7
56	4 44.0	4 44.8	4 31.1	5.6	1.7	11.6	3.6	17.6	5.4	56	4 59.0	4 59.8	4 45.4	5.6	1.8	11.6	3.8	17.6	5.7
57	4 44.3	4 45.0	4 31.3	5.7	1.8	11.7	3.6	17.7	5.5	57	4 59.3	5 00.1	4 45.6	5.7	1.9	11.7	3.8	17.7	5.8
58	4 44.5	4 45.3	4 31.5	5.8	1.8	11.8	3.6	17.8	5.5	58	4 59.5	5 00.3	4 45.9	5.8	1.9	11.8	3.8	17.8	5.8
59	4 44.8	4 45.5	4 31.8	5.9	1.8	11.9	3.7	17.9	5.5	59	4 59.8	5 00.6	4 46.1	5.9	1.9	11.9	3.9	17.9	5.8
60	4 45.0	4 45.8	4 32.0	6.0	1.9	12.0	3.7	18.0	5.6	60	4 00.0	5 00.8	4 46.3	6.0	2.0	12.0	3.9	18.0	5.9

20ᵐ INCREMENTS AND CORRECTIONS 21ᵐ

m 20	SUN PLANETS	ARIES	MOON	v or Corrⁿ d	v or Corrⁿ d	v or Corrⁿ d
s	° ′	° ′	° ′	′ ′	′ ′	′ ′
00	5 00.0	5 00.8	4 46.3	0.0 0.0	6.0 2.1	12.0 4.1
01	5 00.3	5 01.1	4 46.6	0.1 0.0	6.1 2.1	12.1 4.1
02	5 00.5	5 01.3	4 46.8	0.2 0.1	6.2 2.1	12.2 4.2
03	5 00.8	5 01.6	4 47.0	0.3 0.1	6.3 2.2	12.3 4.2
04	5 01.0	5 01.8	4 47.3	0.4 0.1	6.4 2.2	12.4 4.2
05	5 01.3	5 02.1	4 47.5	0.5 0.2	6.5 2.2	12.5 4.3
06	5 01.5	5 02.3	4 47.8	0.6 0.2	6.6 2.3	12.6 4.3
07	5 01.8	5 02.6	4 48.0	0.7 0.2	6.7 2.3	12.7 4.3
08	5 02.0	5 02.8	4 48.2	0.8 0.3	6.8 2.3	12.8 4.4
09	5 02.3	5 03.1	4 48.5	0.9 0.3	6.9 2.4	12.9 4.4
10	5 02.5	5 03.3	4 48.7	1.0 0.3	7.0 2.4	13.0 4.4
11	5 02.8	5 03.6	4 49.0	1.1 0.4	7.1 2.4	13.1 4.5
12	5 03.0	5 03.8	4 49.2	1.2 0.4	7.2 2.5	13.2 4.5
13	5 03.3	5 04.1	4 49.4	1.3 0.4	7.3 2.5	13.3 4.5
14	5 03.5	5 04.3	4 49.7	1.4 0.5	7.4 2.5	13.4 4.6
15	5 03.8	5 04.6	4 49.9	1.5 0.5	7.5 2.6	13.5 4.6
16	5 04.0	5 04.8	4 50.2	1.6 0.5	7.6 2.6	13.6 4.6
17	5 04.3	5 05.1	4 50.4	1.7 0.6	7.7 2.6	13.7 4.7
18	5 04.5	5 05.3	4 50.6	1.8 0.6	7.8 2.7	13.8 4.7
19	5 04.8	5 05.6	4 50.9	1.9 0.6	7.9 2.7	13.9 4.7
20	5 05.0	5 05.8	4 51.1	2.0 0.7	8.0 2.7	14.0 4.8
21	5 05.3	5 06.1	4 51.3	2.1 0.7	8.1 2.8	14.1 4.8
22	5 05.5	5 06.3	4 51.6	2.2 0.8	8.2 2.8	14.2 4.9
23	5 05.8	5 06.6	4 51.8	2.3 0.8	8.3 2.8	14.3 4.9
24	5 06.0	5 06.8	4 52.1	2.4 0.8	8.4 2.9	14.4 4.9
25	5 06.3	5 07.1	4 52.3	2.5 0.9	8.5 2.9	14.5 5.0
26	5 06.5	5 07.3	4 52.5	2.6 0.9	8.6 2.9	14.6 5.0
27	5 06.8	5 07.6	4 52.8	2.7 0.9	8.7 3.0	14.7 5.0
28	5 07.0	5 07.8	4 53.0	2.8 1.0	8.8 3.0	14.8 5.1
29	5 07.3	5 08.1	4 53.3	2.9 1.0	8.9 3.0	14.9 5.1
30	5 07.5	5 08.3	4 53.5	3.0 1.0	9.0 3.1	15.0 5.1
31	5 07.8	5 08.6	4 53.7	3.1 1.0	9.1 3.1	15.1 5.2
32	5 08.0	5 08.8	4 54.0	3.2 1.1	9.2 3.1	15.2 5.2
33	5 08.3	5 09.1	4 54.2	3.3 1.1	9.3 3.2	15.3 5.2
34	5 08.5	5 09.3	4 54.4	3.4 1.2	9.4 3.2	15.4 5.3
35	5 08.8	5 09.6	4 54.7	3.5 1.2	9.5 3.2	15.5 5.3
36	5 09.0	5 09.8	4 54.9	3.6 1.2	9.6 3.3	15.6 5.3
37	5 09.3	5 10.1	4 55.2	3.7 1.3	9.7 3.3	15.7 5.4
38	5 09.5	5 10.3	4 55.4	3.8 1.3	9.8 3.3	15.8 5.4
39	5 09.8	5 10.6	4 55.6	3.9 1.3	9.9 3.4	15.9 5.4
40	5 10.0	5 10.8	4 55.9	4.0 1.4	10.0 3.4	16.0 5.5
41	5 10.3	5 11.1	4 56.1	4.1 1.4	10.1 3.5	16.1 5.5
42	5 10.5	5 11.4	4 56.4	4.2 1.4	10.2 3.5	16.2 5.5
43	5 10.8	5 11.6	4 56.6	4.3 1.5	10.3 3.5	16.3 5.6
44	5 11.0	5 11.9	4 56.8	4.4 1.5	10.4 3.6	16.4 5.6
45	5 11.3	5 12.1	4 57.1	4.5 1.5	10.5 3.6	16.5 5.6
46	5 11.5	5 12.4	4 57.3	4.6 1.6	10.6 3.6	16.6 5.7
47	5 11.8	5 12.6	4 57.5	4.7 1.6	10.7 3.7	16.7 5.7
48	5 12.0	5 12.9	4 57.8	4.8 1.6	10.8 3.7	16.8 5.7
49	5 12.3	5 13.1	4 58.0	4.9 1.7	10.9 3.7	16.9 5.8
50	5 12.5	5 13.4	4 58.3	5.0 1.7	11.0 3.8	17.0 5.8
51	5 12.8	5 13.6	4 58.5	5.1 1.7	11.1 3.8	17.1 5.8
52	5 13.0	5 13.9	4 58.7	5.2 1.8	11.2 3.8	17.2 5.9
53	5 13.3	5 14.1	4 59.0	5.3 1.8	11.3 3.9	17.3 5.9
54	5 13.5	5 14.4	4 59.2	5.4 1.8	11.4 3.9	17.4 5.9
55	5 13.8	5 14.6	4 59.5	5.5 1.9	11.5 3.9	17.5 6.0
56	5 14.0	5 14.9	4 59.7	5.6 1.9	11.6 4.0	17.6 6.0
57	5 14.3	5 15.1	4 59.9	5.7 1.9	11.7 4.0	17.7 6.0
58	5 14.5	5 15.4	5 00.2	5.8 2.0	11.8 4.0	17.8 6.1
59	5 14.8	5 15.6	5 00.4	5.9 2.0	11.9 4.1	17.9 6.1
60	5 15.0	5 15.9	5 00.7	6.0 2.1	12.0 4.1	18.0 6.2

m 21	SUN PLANETS	ARIES	MOON	v or Corrⁿ d	v or Corrⁿ d	v or Corrⁿ d
s	° ′	° ′	° ′	′ ′	′ ′	′ ′
00	5 15.0	5 15.9	5 00.7	0.0 0.0	6.0 2.2	12.0 4.3
01	5 15.3	5 16.1	5 00.9	0.1 0.0	6.1 2.2	12.1 4.3
02	5 15.5	5 16.4	5 01.1	0.2 0.1	6.2 2.2	12.2 4.4
03	5 15.8	5 16.6	5 01.4	0.3 0.1	6.3 2.3	12.3 4.4
04	5 16.0	5 16.9	5 01.6	0.4 0.1	6.4 2.3	12.4 4.4
05	5 16.3	5 17.1	5 01.8	0.5 0.2	6.5 2.3	12.5 4.5
06	5 16.5	5 17.4	5 02.1	0.6 0.2	6.6 2.4	12.6 4.5
07	5 16.8	5 17.6	5 02.3	0.7 0.3	6.7 2.4	12.7 4.6
08	5 17.0	5 17.9	5 02.6	0.8 0.3	6.8 2.4	12.8 4.6
09	5 17.3	5 18.1	5 02.8	0.9 0.3	6.9 2.5	12.9 4.6
10	5 17.5	5 18.4	5 03.0	1.0 0.4	7.0 2.5	13.0 4.7
11	5 17.8	5 18.6	5 03.3	1.1 0.4	7.1 2.5	13.1 4.7
12	5 18.0	5 18.9	5 03.5	1.2 0.4	7.2 2.6	13.2 4.7
13	5 18.3	5 19.1	5 03.8	1.3 0.5	7.3 2.6	13.3 4.8
14	5 18.5	5 19.4	5 04.0	1.4 0.5	7.4 2.7	13.4 4.8
15	5 18.8	5 19.6	5 04.2	1.5 0.5	7.5 2.7	13.5 4.8
16	5 19.0	5 19.9	5 04.5	1.6 0.6	7.6 2.7	13.6 4.9
17	5 19.3	5 20.1	5 04.7	1.7 0.6	7.7 2.8	13.7 4.9
18	5 19.5	5 20.4	5 04.9	1.8 0.6	7.8 2.8	13.8 4.9
19	5 19.8	5 20.6	5 05.2	1.9 0.7	7.9 2.8	13.9 5.0
20	5 20.0	5 20.9	5 05.4	2.0 0.7	8.0 2.9	14.0 5.0
21	5 20.3	5 21.1	5 05.7	2.1 0.8	8.1 2.9	14.1 5.1
22	5 20.5	5 21.4	5 05.9	2.2 0.8	8.2 2.9	14.2 5.1
23	5 20.8	5 21.6	5 06.1	2.3 0.8	8.3 3.0	14.3 5.1
24	5 21.0	5 21.9	5 06.4	2.4 0.9	8.4 3.0	14.4 5.2
25	5 21.3	5 22.1	5 06.6	2.5 0.9	8.5 3.0	14.5 5.2
26	5 21.5	5 22.4	5 06.9	2.6 0.9	8.6 3.1	14.6 5.2
27	5 21.8	5 22.6	5 07.1	2.7 1.0	8.7 3.1	14.7 5.3
28	5 22.0	5 22.9	5 07.3	2.8 1.0	8.8 3.2	14.8 5.3
29	5 22.3	5 23.1	5 07.6	2.9 1.0	8.9 3.2	14.9 5.3
30	5 22.5	5 23.4	5 07.8	3.0 1.1	9.0 3.2	15.0 5.4
31	5 22.8	5 23.6	5 08.0	3.1 1.1	9.1 3.3	15.1 5.4
32	5 23.0	5 23.9	5 08.3	3.2 1.1	9.2 3.3	15.2 5.4
33	5 23.3	5 24.1	5 08.5	3.3 1.2	9.3 3.3	15.3 5.5
34	5 23.5	5 24.4	5 08.8	3.4 1.2	9.4 3.4	15.4 5.5
35	5 23.8	5 24.6	5 09.0	3.5 1.3	9.5 3.4	15.5 5.6
36	5 24.0	5 24.9	5 09.2	3.6 1.3	9.6 3.4	15.6 5.6
37	5 24.3	5 25.1	5 09.5	3.7 1.3	9.7 3.5	15.7 5.6
38	5 24.5	5 25.4	5 09.7	3.8 1.4	9.8 3.5	15.8 5.7
39	5 24.8	5 25.6	5 10.0	3.9 1.4	9.9 3.5	15.9 5.7
40	5 25.0	5 25.9	5 10.2	4.0 1.4	10.0 3.6	16.0 5.7
41	5 25.3	5 26.1	5 10.4	4.1 1.5	10.1 3.6	16.1 5.8
42	5 25.5	5 26.4	5 10.7	4.2 1.5	10.2 3.7	16.2 5.8
43	5 25.8	5 26.6	5 10.9	4.3 1.5	10.3 3.7	16.3 5.8
44	5 26.0	5 26.9	5 11.1	4.4 1.6	10.4 3.7	16.4 5.9
45	5 26.3	5 27.1	5 11.4	4.5 1.6	10.5 3.8	16.5 5.9
46	5 26.5	5 27.4	5 11.6	4.6 1.6	10.6 3.8	16.6 5.9
47	5 26.8	5 27.6	5 11.9	4.7 1.7	10.7 3.8	16.7 6.0
48	5 27.0	5 27.9	5 12.1	4.8 1.7	10.8 3.9	16.8 6.0
49	5 27.3	5 28.1	5 12.3	4.9 1.8	10.9 3.9	16.9 6.1
50	5 27.5	5 28.4	5 12.6	5.0 1.8	11.0 3.9	17.0 6.1
51	5 27.8	5 28.6	5 12.8	5.1 1.8	11.1 4.0	17.1 6.1
52	5 28.0	5 28.9	5 13.1	5.2 1.9	11.2 4.0	17.2 6.2
53	5 28.3	5 29.1	5 13.3	5.3 1.9	11.3 4.0	17.3 6.2
54	5 28.5	5 29.4	5 13.5	5.4 1.9	11.4 4.1	17.4 6.2
55	5 28.8	5 29.7	5 13.8	5.5 2.0	11.5 4.1	17.5 6.3
56	5 29.0	5 29.9	5 14.0	5.6 2.0	11.6 4.2	17.6 6.3
57	5 29.3	5 30.2	5 14.3	5.7 2.0	11.7 4.2	17.7 6.3
58	5 29.5	5 30.4	5 14.5	5.8 2.1	11.8 4.2	17.8 6.4
59	5 29.8	5 30.7	5 14.7	5.9 2.1	11.9 4.3	17.9 6.4
60	5 30.0	5 30.9	5 15.0	6.0 2.2	12.0 4.3	18.0 6.5

22m INCREMENTS AND CORRECTIONS 23m

22m

s	SUN PLANETS	ARIES	MOON	v or Corrn d		v or Corrn d		v or Corrn d	
00	5 30.0	5 30.9	5 15.0	0.0	0.0	6.0	2.3	12.0	4.5
01	5 30.3	5 31.2	5 15.2	0.1	0.0	6.1	2.3	12.1	4.5
02	5 30.5	5 31.4	5 15.4	0.2	0.1	6.2	2.3	12.2	4.6
03	5 30.8	5 31.7	5 15.7	0.3	0.1	6.3	2.4	12.3	4.6
04	5 31.0	5 31.9	5 15.9	0.4	0.2	6.4	2.4	12.4	4.7
05	5 31.3	5 32.2	5 16.2	0.5	0.2	6.5	2.4	12.5	4.7
06	5 31.5	5 32.4	5 16.4	0.6	0.2	6.6	2.5	12.6	4.7
07	5 31.8	5 32.7	5 16.6	0.7	0.3	6.7	2.5	12.7	4.8
08	5 32.0	5 32.9	5 16.9	0.8	0.3	6.8	2.6	12.8	4.8
09	5 32.3	5 33.2	5 17.1	0.9	0.3	6.9	2.6	12.9	4.8
10	5 32.5	5 33.4	5 17.4	1.0	0.4	7.0	2.6	13.0	4.9
11	5 32.8	5 33.7	5 17.6	1.1	0.4	7.1	2.7	13.1	4.9
12	5 33.0	5 33.9	5 17.8	1.2	0.5	7.2	2.7	13.2	5.0
13	5 33.3	5 34.2	5 18.1	1.3	0.5	7.3	2.7	13.3	5.0
14	5 33.5	5 34.4	5 18.3	1.4	0.5	7.4	2.8	13.4	5.0
15	5 33.8	5 34.7	5 18.5	1.5	0.6	7.5	2.8	13.5	5.1
16	5 34.0	5 34.9	5 18.8	1.6	0.6	7.6	2.9	13.6	5.1
17	5 34.3	5 35.2	5 19.0	1.7	0.6	7.7	2.9	13.7	5.1
18	5 34.5	5 35.4	5 19.3	1.8	0.7	7.8	2.9	13.8	5.2
19	5 34.8	5 35.7	5 19.5	1.9	0.7	7.9	3.0	13.9	5.2
20	5 35.0	5 35.9	5 19.7	2.0	0.8	8.0	3.0	14.0	5.3
21	5 35.3	5 36.2	5 20.0	2.1	0.8	8.1	3.0	14.1	5.3
22	5 35.5	5 36.4	5 20.2	2.2	0.8	8.2	3.1	14.2	5.3
23	5 35.8	5 36.7	5 20.5	2.3	0.9	8.3	3.1	14.3	5.4
24	5 36.0	5 36.9	5 20.7	2.4	0.9	8.4	3.2	14.4	5.4
25	5 36.3	5 37.2	5 20.9	2.5	0.9	8.5	3.2	14.5	5.4
26	5 36.5	5 37.4	5 21.2	2.6	1.0	8.6	3.2	14.6	5.5
27	5 36.8	5 37.7	5 21.4	2.7	1.0	8.7	3.3	14.7	5.5
28	5 37.0	5 37.9	5 21.6	2.8	1.0	8.8	3.3	14.8	5.6
29	5 37.3	5 38.2	5 21.9	2.9	1.1	8.9	3.3	14.9	5.6
30	5 37.5	5 38.4	5 22.1	3.0	1.1	9.0	3.4	15.0	5.6
31	5 37.8	5 38.7	5 22.4	3.1	1.2	9.1	3.4	15.1	5.7
32	5 38.0	5 38.9	5 22.6	3.2	1.2	9.2	3.5	15.2	5.7
33	5 38.3	5 39.2	5 22.8	3.3	1.2	9.3	3.5	15.3	5.7
34	5 38.5	5 39.4	5 23.1	3.4	1.3	9.4	3.5	15.4	5.8
35	5 38.8	5 39.7	5 23.3	3.5	1.3	9.5	3.6	15.5	5.8
36	5 39.0	5 39.9	5 23.6	3.6	1.4	9.6	3.6	15.6	5.9
37	5 39.3	5 40.2	5 23.8	3.7	1.4	9.7	3.6	15.7	5.9
38	5 39.5	5 40.4	5 24.0	3.8	1.4	9.8	3.7	15.8	5.9
39	5 39.8	5 40.7	5 24.3	3.9	1.5	9.9	3.7	15.9	6.0
40	5 40.0	5 40.9	5 24.5	4.0	1.5	10.0	3.8	16.0	6.0
41	5 40.3	5 41.2	5 24.7	4.1	1.5	10.1	3.8	16.1	6.0
42	5 40.5	5 41.4	5 25.0	4.2	1.6	10.2	3.8	16.2	6.1
43	5 40.8	5 41.7	5 25.2	4.3	1.6	10.3	3.9	16.3	6.1
44	5 41.0	5 41.9	5 25.5	4.4	1.7	10.4	3.9	16.4	6.1
45	5 41.3	5 42.2	5 25.7	4.5	1.7	10.5	3.9	16.5	6.2
46	5 41.5	5 42.4	5 25.9	4.6	1.7	10.6	4.0	16.6	6.2
47	5 41.8	5 42.7	5 26.2	4.7	1.8	10.7	4.0	16.7	6.3
48	5 42.0	5 42.9	5 26.4	4.8	1.8	10.8	4.1	16.8	6.3
49	5 42.3	5 43.2	5 26.7	4.9	1.8	10.9	4.1	16.9	6.3
50	5 42.5	5 43.4	5 26.9	5.0	1.9	11.0	4.1	17.0	6.4
51	5 42.8	5 43.7	5 27.1	5.1	1.9	11.1	4.2	17.1	6.4
52	5 43.0	5 43.9	5 27.4	5.2	2.0	11.2	4.2	17.2	6.5
53	5 43.3	5 44.2	5 27.6	5.3	2.0	11.3	4.2	17.3	6.5
54	5 43.5	5 44.4	5 27.9	5.4	2.0	11.4	4.3	17.4	6.5
55	5 43.8	5 44.7	5 28.1	5.5	2.1	11.5	4.3	17.5	6.6
56	5 44.0	5 44.9	5 28.3	5.6	2.1	11.6	4.4	17.6	6.6
57	5 44.3	5 45.2	5 28.6	5.7	2.1	11.7	4.4	17.7	6.6
58	5 44.5	5 45.4	5 28.8	5.8	2.2	11.8	4.4	17.8	6.7
59	5 44.8	5 45.7	5 29.0	5.9	2.2	11.9	4.5	17.9	6.7
60	5 45.0	5 45.9	5 29.3	6.0	2.3	12.0	4.5	18.0	6.8

23m

s	SUN PLANETS	ARIES	MOON	v or Corrn d		v or Corrn d		v or Corrn d	
00	5 45.0	5 45.9	5 29.3	0.0	0.0	6.0	2.4	12.0	4.7
01	5 45.3	5 46.2	5 29.5	0.1	0.0	6.1	2.4	12.1	4.7
02	5 45.5	5 46.4	5 29.8	0.2	0.1	6.2	2.4	12.2	4.8
03	5 45.8	5 46.7	5 30.0	0.3	0.1	6.3	2.5	12.3	4.8
04	5 46.0	5 46.9	5 30.2	0.4	0.2	6.4	2.5	12.4	4.9
05	5 46.3	5 47.2	5 30.5	0.5	0.2	6.5	2.5	12.5	4.9
06	5 46.5	5 47.4	5 30.7	0.6	0.2	6.6	2.6	12.6	4.9
07	5 46.8	5 47.7	5 31.0	0.7	0.3	6.7	2.6	12.7	5.0
08	5 47.0	5 47.9	5 31.2	0.8	0.3	6.8	2.7	12.8	5.0
09	5 47.3	5 48.2	5 31.4	0.9	0.4	6.9	2.7	12.9	5.1
10	5 47.5	5 48.5	5 31.7	1.0	0.4	7.0	2.7	13.0	5.1
11	5 47.8	5 48.7	5 31.9	1.1	0.4	7.1	2.8	13.1	5.1
12	5 48.0	5 49.0	5 32.1	1.2	0.5	7.2	2.8	13.2	5.2
13	5 48.3	5 49.2	5 32.4	1.3	0.5	7.3	2.9	13.3	5.2
14	5 48.5	5 49.5	5 32.6	1.4	0.5	7.4	2.9	13.4	5.2
15	5 48.8	5 49.7	5 32.9	1.5	0.6	7.5	2.9	13.5	5.3
16	5 49.0	5 50.0	5 33.1	1.6	0.6	7.6	3.0	13.6	5.3
17	5 49.3	5 50.2	5 33.3	1.7	0.7	7.7	3.0	13.7	5.4
18	5 49.5	5 50.5	5 33.6	1.8	0.7	7.8	3.1	13.8	5.4
19	5 49.8	5 50.7	5 33.8	1.9	0.7	7.9	3.1	13.9	5.4
20	5 50.0	5 51.0	5 34.1	2.0	0.8	8.0	3.1	14.0	5.5
21	5 50.3	5 51.2	5 34.3	2.1	0.8	8.1	3.2	14.1	5.5
22	5 50.5	5 51.5	5 34.5	2.2	0.9	8.2	3.2	14.2	5.6
23	5 50.8	5 51.7	5 34.8	2.3	0.9	8.3	3.3	14.3	5.6
24	5 51.0	5 52.0	5 35.0	2.4	0.9	8.4	3.3	14.4	5.6
25	5 51.3	5 52.2	5 35.2	2.5	1.0	8.5	3.3	14.5	5.7
26	5 51.5	5 52.5	5 35.5	2.6	1.0	8.6	3.4	14.6	5.7
27	5 51.8	5 52.7	5 35.7	2.7	1.1	8.7	3.4	14.7	5.8
28	5 52.0	5 53.0	5 36.0	2.8	1.1	8.8	3.4	14.8	5.8
29	5 52.3	5 53.2	5 36.2	2.9	1.1	8.9	3.5	14.9	5.8
30	5 52.5	5 53.5	5 36.4	3.0	1.2	9.0	3.5	15.0	5.9
31	5 52.8	5 53.7	5 36.7	3.1	1.2	9.1	3.6	15.1	5.9
32	5 53.0	5 54.0	5 36.9	3.2	1.3	9.2	3.6	15.2	6.0
33	5 53.3	5 54.2	5 37.2	3.3	1.3	9.3	3.6	15.3	6.0
34	5 53.5	5 54.5	5 37.4	3.4	1.3	9.4	3.7	15.4	6.0
35	5 53.8	5 54.7	5 37.6	3.5	1.4	9.5	3.7	15.5	6.1
36	5 54.0	5 55.0	5 37.9	3.6	1.4	9.6	3.8	15.6	6.1
37	5 54.3	5 55.2	5 38.1	3.7	1.4	9.7	3.8	15.7	6.1
38	5 54.5	5 55.5	5 38.4	3.8	1.5	9.8	3.8	15.8	6.2
39	5 54.8	5 55.7	5 38.6	3.9	1.5	9.9	3.9	15.9	6.2
40	5 55.0	5 56.0	5 38.8	4.0	1.6	10.0	3.9	16.0	6.3
41	5 55.3	5 56.2	5 39.1	4.1	1.6	10.1	4.0	16.1	6.3
42	5 55.5	5 56.5	5 39.3	4.2	1.6	10.2	4.0	16.2	6.3
43	5 55.8	5 56.7	5 39.5	4.3	1.7	10.3	4.0	16.3	6.4
44	5 56.0	5 57.0	5 39.8	4.4	1.7	10.4	4.1	16.4	6.4
45	5 56.3	5 57.2	5 40.0	4.5	1.8	10.5	4.1	16.5	6.5
46	5 56.5	5 57.5	5 40.3	4.6	1.8	10.6	4.2	16.6	6.5
47	5 56.8	5 57.7	5 40.5	4.7	1.8	10.7	4.2	16.7	6.5
48	5 57.0	5 58.0	5 40.7	4.8	1.9	10.8	4.2	16.8	6.6
49	5 57.3	5 58.2	5 41.0	4.9	1.9	10.9	4.3	16.9	6.6
50	5 57.5	5 58.5	5 41.2	5.0	2.0	11.0	4.3	17.0	6.7
51	5 57.8	5 58.7	5 41.5	5.1	2.0	11.1	4.3	17.1	6.7
52	5 58.0	5 59.0	5 41.7	5.2	2.0	11.2	4.4	17.2	6.7
53	5 58.3	5 59.2	5 41.9	5.3	2.1	11.3	4.4	17.3	6.8
54	5 58.5	5 59.5	5 42.2	5.4	2.1	11.4	4.5	17.4	6.8
55	5 58.8	5 59.7	5 42.4	5.5	2.2	11.5	4.5	17.5	6.9
56	5 59.0	6 00.0	5 42.6	5.6	2.2	11.6	4.5	17.6	6.9
57	5 59.3	6 00.2	5 42.9	5.7	2.2	11.7	4.6	17.7	6.9
58	5 59.5	6 00.5	5 43.1	5.8	2.3	11.8	4.6	17.8	7.0
59	5 59.8	6 00.7	5 43.4	5.9	2.3	11.9	4.7	17.9	7.0
60	6 00.0	6 01.0	5 43.6	6.0	2.4	12.0	4.7	18.0	7.1

24m   INCREMENTS AND CORRECTIONS   25m

m 24	SUN PLANETS	ARIES	MOON	v or Corrn d	v or Corrn d	v or Corrn d
s	° ′	° ′	° ′	′ ′	′ ′	′ ′
00	6 00.0	6 01.0	5 43.6	0.0 0.0	6.0 2.5	12.0 4.9
01	6 00.3	6 01.2	5 43.8	0.1 0.0	6.1 2.5	12.1 4.9
02	6 00.5	6 01.5	5 44.1	0.2 0.1	6.2 2.5	12.2 5.0
03	6 00.8	6 01.7	5 44.3	0.3 0.1	6.3 2.6	12.3 5.0
04	6 01.0	6 02.0	5 44.6	0.4 0.2	6.4 2.6	12.4 5.1
05	6 01.3	6 02.2	5 44.8	0.5 0.2	6.5 2.7	12.5 5.1
06	6 01.5	6 02.5	5 45.0	0.6 0.2	6.6 2.7	12.6 5.1
07	6 01.8	6 02.7	5 45.3	0.7 0.3	6.7 2.7	12.7 5.2
08	6 02.0	6 03.0	5 45.5	0.8 0.3	6.8 2.8	12.8 5.2
09	6 02.3	6 03.2	5 45.7	0.9 0.4	6.9 2.8	12.9 5.3
10	6 02.5	6 03.5	5 46.0	1.0 0.4	7.0 2.9	13.0 5.3
11	6 02.8	6 03.7	5 46.2	1.1 0.4	7.1 2.9	13.1 5.3
12	6 03.0	6 04.0	5 46.5	1.2 0.5	7.2 2.9	13.2 5.4
13	6 03.3	6 04.2	5 46.7	1.3 0.5	7.3 3.0	13.3 5.4
14	6 03.5	6 04.5	5 46.9	1.4 0.6	7.4 3.0	13.4 5.5
15	6 03.8	6 04.7	5 47.2	1.5 0.6	7.5 3.1	13.5 5.5
16	6 04.0	6 05.0	5 47.4	1.6 0.7	7.6 3.1	13.6 5.6
17	6 04.3	6 05.2	5 47.7	1.7 0.7	7.7 3.1	13.7 5.6
18	6 04.5	6 05.5	5 47.9	1.8 0.7	7.8 3.2	13.8 5.6
19	6 04.8	6 05.7	5 48.1	1.9 0.8	7.9 3.2	13.9 5.7
20	6 05.0	6 06.0	5 48.4	2.0 0.8	8.0 3.3	14.0 5.7
21	6 05.3	6 06.3	5 48.6	2.1 0.9	8.1 3.3	14.1 5.8
22	6 05.5	6 06.5	5 48.8	2.2 0.9	8.2 3.3	14.2 5.8
23	6 05.8	6 06.8	5 48.1	2.3 0.9	8.3 3.4	14.3 5.8
24	6 06.0	6 07.0	5 48.3	2.4 1.0	8.4 3.4	14.4 5.9
25	6 06.3	6 07.3	5 49.6	2.5 1.0	8.5 3.5	14.5 5.9
26	6 06.5	6 07.5	5 49.8	2.6 1.1	8.6 3.5	14.6 6.0
27	6 06.8	6 07.8	5 50.0	2.7 1.1	8.7 3.6	14.7 6.0
28	6 07.0	6 08.0	5 50.3	2.8 1.1	8.8 3.6	14.8 6.0
29	6 07.3	6 08.3	5 50.5	2.9 1.2	8.9 3.6	14.9 6.1
30	6 07.5	6 08.5	5 50.8	3.0 1.2	9.0 3.7	15.0 6.1
31	6 07.8	6 08.8	5 51.0	3.1 1.3	9.1 3.7	15.1 6.2
32	6 08.0	6 09.0	5 51.2	3.2 1.3	9.2 3.8	15.2 6.2
33	6 08.3	6 09.3	5 51.5	3.3 1.3	9.3 3.8	15.3 6.2
34	6 08.5	6 09.5	5 51.7	3.4 1.4	9.4 3.8	15.4 6.3
35	6 08.8	6 09.8	5 52.0	3.5 1.4	9.5 3.9	15.5 6.3
36	6 09.0	6 10.0	5 52.2	3.6 1.5	9.6 3.9	15.6 6.4
37	6 09.3	6 10.3	5 52.4	3.7 1.5	9.7 4.0	15.7 6.4
38	6 09.5	6 10.5	5 52.7	3.8 1.6	9.8 4.0	15.8 6.5
39	6 09.8	6 10.8	5 52.9	3.9 1.6	9.9 4.0	15.9 6.5
40	6 10.0	6 11.0	5 53.1	4.0 1.6	10.0 4.1	16.0 6.5
41	6 10.3	6 11.3	5 53.4	4.1 1.7	10.1 4.1	16.1 6.6
42	6 10.5	6 11.5	5 53.6	4.2 1.7	10.2 4.2	16.2 6.6
43	6 10.8	6 11.8	5 53.9	4.3 1.8	10.3 4.2	16.3 6.7
44	6 11.0	6 12.0	5 54.1	4.4 1.8	10.4 4.2	16.4 6.7
45	6 11.3	6 12.3	5 54.3	4.5 1.8	10.5 4.3	16.5 6.7
46	6 11.5	6 12.5	5 54.6	4.6 1.9	10.6 4.3	16.6 6.8
47	6 11.8	6 12.8	5 54.8	4.7 1.9	10.7 4.4	16.7 6.8
48	6 12.0	6 13.0	5 55.1	4.8 2.0	10.8 4.4	16.8 6.9
49	6 12.3	6 13.3	5 55.3	4.9 2.0	10.9 4.5	16.9 6.9
50	6 12.5	6 13.5	5 55.5	5.0 2.0	11.0 4.5	17.0 6.9
51	6 12.8	6 13.8	5 55.8	5.1 2.1	11.1 4.5	17.1 7.0
52	6 13.0	6 14.0	5 56.0	5.2 2.1	11.2 4.6	17.2 7.0
53	6 13.3	6 14.3	5 56.2	5.3 2.2	11.3 4.6	17.3 7.1
54	6 13.5	6 14.5	5 56.5	5.4 2.2	11.4 4.7	17.4 7.1
55	6 13.8	6 14.8	5 56.7	5.5 2.2	11.5 4.7	17.5 7.1
56	6 14.0	6 15.0	5 57.0	5.6 2.3	11.6 4.7	17.6 7.2
57	6 14.3	6 15.3	5 57.2	5.7 2.3	11.7 4.8	17.7 7.2
58	6 14.5	6 15.5	5 57.4	5.8 2.4	11.8 4.8	17.8 7.3
59	6 14.8	6 15.8	5 57.7	5.9 2.4	11.9 4.9	17.9 7.3
60	6 15.0	6 16.0	5 57.9	6.0 2.5	12.0 4.9	18.0 7.4

m 25	SUN PLANETS	ARIES	MOON	v or Corrn d	v or Corrn d	v or Corrn d
s	° ′	° ′	° ′	′ ′	′ ′	′ ′
00	6 15.0	6 16.0	5 57.9	0.0 0.0	6.0 2.6	12.0 5.1
01	6 15.3	6 16.3	5 58.2	0.1 0.0	6.1 2.6	12.1 5.1
02	6 15.5	6 16.5	5 58.4	0.2 0.1	6.2 2.6	12.2 5.2
03	6 15.8	6 16.8	5 58.6	0.3 0.1	6.3 2.7	12.3 5.2
04	6 16.0	6 17.0	5 58.9	0.4 0.2	6.4 2.7	12.4 5.3
05	6 16.3	6 17.3	5 59.1	0.5 0.2	6.5 2.8	12.5 5.3
06	6 16.5	6 17.5	5 59.3	0.6 0.3	6.6 2.8	12.6 5.4
07	6 16.8	6 17.8	5 59.6	0.7 0.3	6.7 2.8	12.7 5.4
08	6 17.0	6 18.0	5 59.8	0.8 0.3	6.8 2.9	12.8 5.4
09	6 17.3	6 18.3	6 00.1	0.9 0.4	6.9 2.9	12.9 5.5
10	6 17.5	6 18.5	6 00.3	1.0 0.4	7.0 3.0	13.0 5.5
11	6 17.8	6 18.8	6 00.5	1.1 0.5	7.1 3.0	13.1 5.6
12	6 18.0	6 19.0	6 00.8	1.2 0.5	7.2 3.1	13.2 5.6
13	6 18.3	6 19.3	6 01.0	1.3 0.6	7.3 3.1	13.3 5.7
14	6 18.5	6 19.5	6 01.3	1.4 0.6	7.4 3.1	13.4 5.7
15	6 18.8	6 19.8	6 01.5	1.5 0.6	7.5 3.2	13.5 5.7
16	6 19.0	6 20.0	6 01.7	1.6 0.7	7.6 3.2	13.6 5.8
17	6 19.3	6 20.3	6 02.0	1.7 0.7	7.7 3.3	13.7 5.8
18	6 19.5	6 20.5	6 02.2	1.8 0.8	7.8 3.3	13.8 5.9
19	6 19.8	6 20.8	6 02.5	1.9 0.8	7.9 3.4	13.9 5.9
20	6 20.0	6 21.0	6 02.7	2.0 0.9	8.0 3.4	14.0 6.0
21	6 20.3	6 21.3	6 02.9	2.1 0.9	8.1 3.4	14.1 6.0
22	6 20.5	6 21.5	6 03.2	2.2 0.9	8.2 3.5	14.2 6.0
23	6 20.8	6 21.8	6 03.4	2.3 1.0	8.3 3.5	14.3 6.1
24	6 21.0	6 22.0	6 03.6	2.4 1.0	8.4 3.6	14.4 6.1
25	6 21.3	6 22.3	6 03.9	2.5 1.1	8.5 3.6	14.5 6.2
26	6 21.5	6 22.5	6 04.1	2.6 1.1	8.6 3.7	14.6 6.2
27	6 21.8	6 22.8	6 04.4	2.7 1.1	8.7 3.7	14.7 6.2
28	6 22.0	6 23.0	6 04.6	2.8 1.2	8.8 3.7	14.8 6.3
29	6 22.3	6 23.3	6 04.8	2.9 1.2	8.9 3.8	14.9 6.3
30	6 22.5	6 23.5	6 05.1	3.0 1.3	9.0 3.8	15.0 6.4
31	6 22.8	6 23.8	6 05.3	3.1 1.3	9.1 3.9	15.1 6.4
32	6 23.0	6 24.0	6 05.6	3.2 1.4	9.2 3.9	15.2 6.5
33	6 23.3	6 24.3	6 05.8	3.3 1.4	9.3 4.0	15.3 6.5
34	6 23.5	6 24.5	6 06.0	3.4 1.4	9.4 4.0	15.4 6.5
35	6 23.8	6 24.8	6 06.3	3.5 1.5	9.5 4.0	15.5 6.6
36	6 24.0	6 25.1	6 06.5	3.6 1.5	9.6 4.1	15.6 6.6
37	6 24.3	6 25.3	6 06.7	3.7 1.6	9.7 4.1	15.7 6.7
38	6 24.5	6 25.6	6 07.0	3.8 1.6	9.8 4.2	15.8 6.7
39	6 24.8	6 25.8	6 07.2	3.9 1.7	9.9 4.2	15.9 6.8
40	6 25.0	6 26.1	6 07.5	4.0 1.7	10.0 4.3	16.0 6.8
41	6 25.3	6 26.3	6 07.7	4.1 1.7	10.1 4.3	16.1 6.8
42	6 25.5	6 26.6	6 07.9	4.2 1.8	10.2 4.3	16.2 6.9
43	6 25.8	6 26.8	6 08.2	4.3 1.8	10.3 4.4	16.3 6.9
44	6 26.0	6 27.1	6 08.4	4.4 1.9	10.4 4.4	16.4 7.0
45	6 26.3	6 27.3	6 08.7	4.5 1.9	10.5 4.5	16.5 7.0
46	6 26.5	6 27.6	6 08.9	4.6 2.0	10.6 4.5	16.6 7.1
47	6 26.8	6 27.8	6 09.1	4.7 2.0	10.7 4.5	16.7 7.1
48	6 27.0	6 28.1	6 09.4	4.8 2.0	10.8 4.6	16.8 7.1
49	6 27.3	6 28.3	6 09.6	4.9 2.1	10.9 4.6	16.9 7.2
50	6 27.5	6 28.6	6 09.8	5.0 2.1	11.0 4.7	17.0 7.2
51	6 27.8	6 28.8	6 10.1	5.1 2.2	11.1 4.7	17.1 7.3
52	6 28.0	6 29.1	6 10.3	5.2 2.2	11.2 4.8	17.2 7.3
53	6 28.3	6 29.3	6 10.6	5.3 2.3	11.3 4.8	17.3 7.4
54	6 28.5	6 29.6	6 10.8	5.4 2.3	11.4 4.8	17.4 7.4
55	6 28.8	6 29.8	6 11.0	5.5 2.3	11.5 4.9	17.5 7.4
56	6 29.0	6 30.1	6 11.3	5.6 2.4	11.6 4.9	17.6 7.5
57	6 29.3	6 30.3	6 11.5	5.7 2.4	11.7 5.0	17.7 7.5
58	6 29.5	6 30.6	6 11.8	5.8 2.5	11.8 5.0	17.8 7.6
59	6 29.8	6 30.8	6 12.0	5.9 2.5	11.9 5.1	17.9 7.6
60	6 30.0	6 31.1	6 12.2	6.0 2.6	12.0 5.1	18.0 7.7

26ᵐ   INCREMENTS AND CORRECTIONS   27ᵐ

m 26	SUN PLANETS	ARIES	MOON	v or Corrⁿ d	v or Corrⁿ d	v or Corrⁿ d	m 27	SUN PLANETS	ARIES	MOON	v or Corrⁿ d	v or Corrⁿ d	v or Corrⁿ d
s	° ′	° ′	° ′	′ ′	′ ′	′ ′	s	° ′	° ′	° ′	′ ′	′ ′	′ ′
00	6 30.0	6 31.1	6 12.2	0.0 0.0	6.0 2.7	12.0 5.3	00	6 45.0	6 46.1	6 26.6	0.0 0.0	6.0 2.8	12.0 5.5
01	6 30.3	6 31.3	6 12.5	0.1 0.0	6.1 2.7	12.1 5.3	01	6 45.3	6 46.4	6 26.8	0.1 0.0	6.1 2.8	12.1 5.5
02	6 30.5	6 31.6	6 12.7	0.2 0.1	6.2 2.7	12.2 5.4	02	6 45.5	6 46.6	6 27.0	0.2 0.1	6.2 2.8	12.2 5.6
03	6 30.8	6 31.8	6 12.9	0.3 0.1	6.3 2.8	12.3 5.4	03	6 45.8	6 46.9	6 27.3	0.3 0.1	6.3 2.9	12.3 5.6
04	6 31.0	6 32.1	6 13.2	0.4 0.2	6.4 2.8	12.4 5.5	04	6 46.0	6 47.1	6 27.5	0.4 0.2	6.4 2.9	12.4 5.7
05	6 31.3	6 32.3	6 13.4	0.5 0.2	6.5 2.9	12.5 5.5	05	6 46.3	6 47.4	6 27.7	0.5 0.2	6.5 3.0	12.5 5.7
06	6 31.5	6 32.6	6 13.7	0.6 0.3	6.6 2.9	12.6 5.6	06	6 46.5	6 47.6	6 28.0	0.6 0.3	6.6 3.0	12.6 5.8
07	6 31.8	6 32.8	6 13.9	0.7 0.3	6.7 3.0	12.7 5.6	07	6 46.8	6 47.9	6 28.2	0.7 0.3	6.7 3.1	12.7 5.8
08	6 32.0	6 33.1	6 14.1	0.8 0.4	6.8 3.0	12.8 5.7	08	6 47.0	6 48.1	6 28.5	0.8 0.4	6.8 3.1	12.8 5.9
09	6 32.3	6 33.3	6 14.4	0.9 0.4	6.9 3.0	12.9 5.7	09	6 47.3	6 48.4	6 28.7	0.9 0.4	6.9 3.2	12.9 5.9
10	6 32.5	6 33.6	6 14.6	1.0 0.4	7.0 3.1	13.0 5.7	10	6 47.5	6 48.6	6 28.9	1.0 0.5	7.0 3.2	13.0 6.0
11	6 32.8	6 33.8	6 14.9	1.1 0.5	7.1 3.1	13.1 5.8	11	6 47.8	6 48.9	6 29.2	1.1 0.5	7.1 3.3	13.1 6.0
12	6 33.0	6 34.1	6 15.1	1.2 0.5	7.2 3.2	13.2 5.8	12	6 48.0	6 49.1	6 29.4	1.2 0.6	7.2 3.3	13.2 6.1
13	6 33.3	6 34.3	6 15.3	1.3 0.6	7.3 3.2	13.3 5.9	13	6 48.3	6 49.4	6 29.7	1.3 0.6	7.3 3.3	13.3 6.1
14	6 33.5	6 34.6	6 15.6	1.4 0.6	7.4 3.3	13.4 5.9	14	6 48.5	6 49.6	6 29.9	1.4 0.6	7.4 3.4	13.4 6.1
15	6 33.8	6 34.8	6 15.8	1.5 0.7	7.5 3.3	13.5 6.0	15	6 48.8	6 49.9	6 30.1	1.5 0.7	7.5 3.4	13.5 6.2
16	6 34.0	6 35.1	6 16.1	1.6 0.7	7.6 3.4	13.6 6.0	16	6 49.0	6 50.1	6 30.4	1.6 0.7	7.6 3.5	13.6 6.2
17	6 34.3	6 35.3	6 16.3	1.7 0.8	7.7 3.4	13.7 6.1	17	6 49.3	6 50.4	6 30.6	1.7 0.8	7.7 3.5	13.7 6.3
18	6 34.5	6 35.6	6 16.6	1.8 0.8	7.8 3.4	13.8 6.1	18	6 49.5	6 50.6	6 30.8	1.8 0.8	7.8 3.6	13.8 6.3
19	6 34.8	6 35.8	6 16.8	1.9 0.8	7.9 3.5	13.9 6.1	19	6 49.8	6 50.9	6 31.1	1.9 0.9	7.9 3.6	13.9 6.4
20	6 35.0	6 36.1	6 17.0	2.0 0.9	8.0 3.5	14.0 6.2	20	6 50.0	6 51.1	6 31.3	2.0 0.9	8.0 3.7	14.0 6.4
21	6 35.3	6 36.3	6 17.2	2.1 0.9	8.1 3.6	14.1 6.2	21	6 50.3	6 51.4	6 31.6	2.1 1.0	8.1 3.7	14.1 6.5
22	6 35.5	6 36.6	6 17.5	2.2 1.0	8.2 3.6	14.2 6.3	22	6 50.5	6 51.6	6 31.8	2.2 1.0	8.2 3.8	14.2 6.5
23	6 35.8	6 36.8	6 17.7	2.3 1.0	8.3 3.7	14.3 6.3	23	6 50.8	6 51.9	6 32.0	2.3 1.1	8.3 3.8	14.3 6.6
24	6 36.0	6 37.1	6 17.0	2.4 1.1	8.4 3.7	14.4 6.4	24	6 51.0	6 52.1	6 32.3	2.4 1.1	8.4 3.9	14.4 6.6
25	6 36.3	6 37.3	6 18.2	2.5 1.1	8.5 3.8	14.5 6.4	25	6 51.3	6 52.4	6 32.5	2.5 1.1	8.5 3.9	14.5 6.6
26	6 36.5	6 37.6	6 18.4	2.6 1.1	8.6 3.8	14.6 6.4	26	6 51.5	6 52.6	6 32.8	2.6 1.2	8.6 3.9	14.6 6.7
27	6 36.8	6 37.8	6 18.7	2.7 1.2	8.7 3.8	14.7 6.5	27	6 51.8	6 52.9	6 33.0	2.7 1.2	8.7 4.0	14.7 6.7
28	6 37.0	6 38.1	6 18.9	2.8 1.2	8.8 3.9	14.8 6.5	28	6 52.0	6 53.1	6 33.2	2.8 1.3	8.8 4.0	14.8 6.8
29	6 37.3	6 38.3	6 19.2	2.9 1.3	8.9 3.9	14.9 6.6	29	6 52.3	6 53.4	6 33.5	2.9 1.3	8.9 4.1	14.9 6.8
30	6 37.5	6 38.6	6 19.4	3.0 1.3	9.0 4.0	15.0 6.6	30	6 52.5	6 53.6	6 33.7	3.0 1.4	9.0 4.1	15.0 6.9
31	6 37.8	6 38.8	6 19.6	3.1 1.4	9.1 4.0	15.1 6.7	31	6 52.8	6 53.9	6 33.9	3.1 1.4	9.1 4.2	15.1 6.9
32	6 38.0	6 39.1	6 19.9	3.2 1.4	9.2 4.1	15.2 6.7	32	6 53.0	6 54.1	6 34.2	3.2 1.5	9.2 4.2	15.2 7.0
33	6 38.3	6 39.3	6 20.1	3.3 1.5	9.3 4.1	15.3 6.8	33	6 53.3	6 54.4	6 34.4	3.3 1.5	9.3 4.3	15.3 7.0
34	6 38.5	6 39.6	6 20.3	3.4 1.5	9.4 4.2	15.4 6.8	34	6 53.5	6 54.6	6 34.7	3.4 1.6	9.4 4.3	15.4 7.0
35	6 38.8	6 39.8	6 20.6	3.5 1.5	9.5 4.2	15.5 6.8	35	6 53.8	6 54.9	6 34.9	3.5 1.6	9.5 4.4	15.5 7.1
36	6 39.0	6 40.1	6 20.8	3.6 1.6	9.6 4.2	15.6 6.9	36	6 54.0	6 55.1	6 35.1	3.6 1.7	9.6 4.4	15.6 7.2
37	6 39.3	6 40.3	6 21.1	3.7 1.6	9.7 4.3	15.7 6.9	37	6 54.3	6 55.4	6 35.4	3.7 1.7	9.7 4.4	15.7 7.2
38	6 39.5	6 40.6	6 21.3	3.8 1.7	9.8 4.3	15.8 7.0	38	6 54.5	6 55.6	6 35.6	3.8 1.7	9.8 4.5	15.8 7.2
39	6 39.8	6 40.8	6 21.5	3.9 1.7	9.9 4.4	15.9 7.0	39	6 54.8	6 55.9	6 35.9	3.9 1.8	9.9 4.5	15.9 7.3
40	6 40.0	6 41.1	6 21.8	4.0 1.8	10.0 4.4	16.0 7.1	40	6 55.0	6 56.1	6 36.1	4.0 1.8	10.0 4.6	16.0 7.3
41	6 40.3	6 41.3	6 22.0	4.1 1.8	10.1 4.5	16.1 7.1	41	6 55.3	6 56.4	6 36.3	4.1 1.9	10.1 4.6	16.1 7.4
42	6 40.5	6 41.6	6 22.3	4.2 1.9	10.2 4.5	16.2 7.2	42	6 55.5	6 56.6	6 36.6	4.2 1.9	10.2 4.7	16.2 7.4
43	6 40.8	6 41.8	6 22.5	4.3 1.9	10.3 4.5	16.3 7.2	43	6 55.8	6 56.9	6 36.8	4.3 2.0	10.3 4.7	16.3 7.5
44	6 41.0	6 42.1	6 22.7	4.4 1.9	10.4 4.6	16.4 7.2	44	6 56.0	6 57.1	6 37.0	4.4 2.0	10.4 4.8	16.4 7.5
45	6 41.3	6 42.3	6 23.0	4.5 2.0	10.5 4.6	16.5 7.3	45	6 56.3	6 57.4	6 37.3	4.5 2.1	10.5 4.8	16.5 7.6
46	6 41.5	6 42.6	6 23.2	4.6 2.0	10.6 4.7	16.6 7.3	46	6 56.5	6 57.6	6 37.5	4.6 2.1	10.6 4.9	16.6 7.6
47	6 41.8	6 42.8	6 23.4	4.7 2.1	10.7 4.7	16.7 7.4	47	6 56.8	6 57.9	6 37.8	4.7 2.2	10.7 4.9	16.7 7.7
48	6 42.0	6 43.1	6 23.7	4.8 2.1	10.8 4.8	16.8 7.4	48	6 57.0	6 58.7	6 38.0	4.8 2.2	10.8 5.0	16.8 7.7
49	6 42.3	6 43.4	6 23.9	4.9 2.2	10.9 4.8	16.9 7.5	49	6 57.3	6 58.4	6 38.2	4.9 2.2	10.9 5.0	16.9 7.7
50	6 42.5	6 43.6	6 24.2	5.0 2.2	11.0 4.9	17.0 7.5	50	6 57.5	6 58.6	6 38.5	5.0 2.3	11.0 5.0	17.0 7.8
51	6 42.8	6 43.9	6 24.4	5.1 2.3	11.1 4.9	17.1 7.6	51	6 57.8	6 58.9	6 38.7	5.1 2.3	11.1 5.1	17.1 7.8
52	6 43.0	6 44.1	6 24.6	5.2 2.3	11.2 4.9	17.2 7.6	52	6 58.0	6 59.1	6 39.0	5.2 2.4	11.2 5.1	17.2 7.9
53	6 43.3	6 44.4	6 24.9	5.3 2.3	11.3 5.0	17.3 7.6	53	6 58.3	6 59.4	6 39.2	5.3 2.4	11.3 5.2	17.3 7.9
54	6 43.5	6 44.6	6 25.1	5.4 2.4	11.4 5.0	17.4 7.7	54	6 58.5	6 59.6	6 39.4	5.4 2.5	11.4 5.2	17.4 8.0
55	6 43.8	6 44.9	6 25.4	5.5 2.4	11.5 5.1	17.5 7.7	55	6 58.8	6 59.9	6 39.7	5.5 2.5	11.5 5.3	17.5 8.0
56	6 44.0	6 45.1	6 25.6	5.6 2.5	11.6 5.1	17.6 7.8	56	6 59.0	7 00.1	6 39.9	5.6 2.6	11.6 5.3	17.6 8.1
57	6 44.3	6 45.4	6 25.8	5.7 2.5	11.7 5.2	17.7 7.8	57	6 59.3	7 00.4	6 40.2	5.7 2.6	11.7 5.4	17.7 8.1
58	6 44.5	6 45.6	6 26.1	5.8 2.6	11.8 5.2	17.8 7.9	58	6 59.5	7 00.6	6 40.4	5.8 2.7	11.8 5.4	17.8 8.2
59	6 44.8	6 45.9	6 26.3	5.9 2.6	11.9 5.3	17.9 7.9	59	6 59.8	7 00.9	6 40.6	5.9 2.7	11.9 5.5	17.9 8.2
60	6 45.0	6 46.1	6 26.6	6.0 2.7	12.0 5.3	18.0 8.0	60	7 00.0	7 01.1	6 40.9	6.0 2.8	12.0 5.5	18.0 8.3

INCREMENTS AND CORRECTIONS

28^m ... **29^m**

m 28	SUN PLANETS	ARIES	MOON	v or Corrⁿ d	v or Corrⁿ d	v or Corrⁿ d
s	° ′	° ′	° ′	′ ′	′ ′	′ ′
00	7 00.0	7 01.1	6 40.9	0.0 0.0	6.0 2.9	12.0 5.7
01	7 00.3	7 01.4	6 41.1	0.1 0.0	6.1 2.9	12.1 5.7
02	7 00.5	7 01.7	6 41.3	0.2 0.1	6.2 2.9	12.2 5.8
03	7 00.8	7 01.9	6 41.6	0.3 0.1	6.3 3.0	12.3 5.8
04	7 01.0	7 02.2	6 41.8	0.4 0.2	6.4 3.0	12.4 5.9
05	7 01.3	7 02.4	6 42.1	0.5 0.2	6.5 3.1	12.5 5.9
06	7 01.5	7 02.7	6 42.3	0.6 0.3	6.6 3.1	12.6 6.0
07	7 01.8	7 02.9	6 42.5	0.7 0.3	6.7 3.2	12.7 6.0
08	7 02.0	7 03.2	6 42.8	0.8 0.4	6.8 3.2	12.8 6.1
09	7 02.3	7 03.4	6 43.0	0.9 0.4	6.9 3.3	12.9 6.1
10	7 02.5	7 03.7	6 43.3	1.0 0.5	7.0 3.3	13.0 6.2
11	7 02.8	7 03.9	6 43.5	1.1 0.5	7.1 3.4	13.1 6.2
12	7 03.0	7 04.2	6 43.7	1.2 0.6	7.2 3.4	13.2 6.3
13	7 03.3	7 04.4	6 44.0	1.3 0.6	7.3 3.5	13.3 6.3
14	7 03.5	7 04.7	6 44.2	1.4 0.7	7.4 3.5	13.4 6.4
15	7 03.8	7 04.9	6 44.4	1.5 0.7	7.5 3.6	13.5 6.4
16	7 04.0	7 05.2	6 44.7	1.6 0.8	7.6 3.6	13.6 6.5
17	7 04.3	7 05.4	6 44.9	1.7 0.8	7.7 3.7	13.7 6.5
18	7 04.5	7 05.7	6 45.2	1.8 0.9	7.8 3.7	13.8 6.6
19	7 04.8	7 05.9	6 45.4	1.9 0.9	7.9 3.8	13.9 6.6
20	7 05.0	7 06.2	6 45.6	2.0 1.0	8.0 3.8	14.0 6.7
21	7 05.3	7 06.4	6 45.9	2.1 1.0	8.1 3.8	14.1 6.7
22	7 05.5	7 06.7	6 46.1	2.2 1.0	8.2 3.9	14.2 6.7
23	7 05.8	7 06.9	6 46.4	2.3 1.1	8.3 3.9	14.3 6.8
24	7 06.0	7 07.2	6 46.6	2.4 1.1	8.4 4.0	14.4 6.8
25	7 06.3	7 07.4	6 46.8	2.5 1.2	8.5 4.0	14.5 6.9
26	7 06.5	7 07.7	6 47.1	2.6 1.2	8.6 4.1	14.6 6.9
27	7 06.8	7 07.9	6 47.3	2.7 1.3	8.7 4.1	14.7 7.0
28	7 07.0	7 08.2	6 47.5	2.8 1.3	8.8 4.2	14.8 7.0
29	7 07.3	7 08.4	6 47.8	2.9 1.4	8.9 4.2	14.9 7.1
30	7 07.5	7 08.7	6 48.0	3.0 1.4	9.0 4.3	15.0 7.1
31	7 07.8	7 08.9	6 48.3	3.1 1.5	9.1 4.3	15.1 7.2
32	7 08.0	7 09.2	6 48.5	3.2 1.5	9.2 4.4	15.2 7.2
33	7 08.3	7 09.4	6 48.7	3.3 1.6	9.3 4.4	15.3 7.3
34	7 08.5	7 09.7	6 49.0	3.4 1.6	9.4 4.5	15.4 7.3
35	7 08.8	7 09.9	6 49.2	3.5 1.7	9.5 4.5	15.5 7.4
36	7 09.0	7 10.2	6 49.5	3.6 1.7	9.6 4.6	15.6 7.4
37	7 09.3	7 10.4	6 49.7	3.7 1.8	9.7 4.6	15.7 7.5
38	7 09.5	7 10.7	6 49.9	3.8 1.8	9.8 4.7	15.8 7.5
39	7 09.8	7 10.9	6 50.2	3.9 1.9	9.9 4.7	15.9 7.6
40	7 10.0	7 11.2	6 50.4	4.0 1.9	10.0 4.8	16.0 7.6
41	7 10.3	7 11.4	6 50.6	4.1 1.9	10.1 4.8	16.1 7.6
42	7 10.5	7 11.7	6 50.9	4.2 2.0	10.2 4.8	16.2 7.7
43	7 10.8	7 11.9	6 51.1	4.3 2.0	10.3 4.9	16.3 7.7
44	7 11.0	7 12.2	6 51.4	4.4 2.1	10.4 4.9	16.4 7.8
45	7 11.3	7 12.4	6 51.6	4.5 2.1	10.5 5.0	16.5 7.8
46	7 11.5	7 12.7	6 51.8	4.6 2.2	10.6 5.0	16.6 7.9
47	7 11.8	7 12.9	6 52.1	4.7 2.2	10.7 5.1	16.7 7.9
48	7 12.0	7 13.2	6 52.3	4.8 2.3	10.8 5.1	16.8 8.0
49	7 12.3	7 13.4	6 52.6	4.9 2.3	10.9 5.2	16.9 8.0
50	7 12.5	7 13.7	6 52.8	5.0 2.4	11.0 5.2	17.0 8.1
51	7 12.8	7 13.9	6 53.0	5.1 2.4	11.1 5.3	17.1 8.1
52	7 13.0	7 14.2	6 53.3	5.2 2.5	11.2 5.3	17.2 8.2
53	7 13.3	7 14.4	6 53.5	5.3 2.5	11.3 5.4	17.3 8.2
54	7 13.5	7 14.7	6 53.8	5.4 2.6	11.4 5.4	17.4 8.3
55	7 13.8	7 14.9	6 54.0	5.5 2.6	11.5 5.5	17.5 8.3
56	7 14.0	7 15.2	6 54.2	5.6 2.7	11.6 5.5	17.6 8.4
57	7 14.3	7 15.4	6 54.5	5.7 2.7	11.7 5.6	17.7 8.4
58	7 14.5	7 15.7	6 54.7	5.8 2.8	11.8 5.6	17.8 8.5
59	7 14.8	7 15.9	6 54.9	5.9 2.8	11.9 5.7	17.9 8.5
60	7 15.0	7 16.2	6 55.2	6.0 2.9	12.0 5.7	18.0 8.6

m 29	SUN PLANETS	ARIES	MOON	v or Corrⁿ d	v or Corrⁿ d	v or Corrⁿ d
s	° ′	° ′	° ′	′ ′	′ ′	′ ′
00	7 15.0	7 16.2	6 55.2	0.0 0.0	6.0 3.0	12.0 5.9
01	7 15.3	7 16.4	6 55.4	0.1 0.0	6.1 3.0	12.1 5.9
02	7 15.5	7 16.7	6 55.7	0.2 0.1	6.2 3.0	12.2 6.0
03	7 15.8	7 16.9	6 55.9	0.3 0.1	6.3 3.1	12.3 6.0
04	7 16.0	7 17.2	6 56.1	0.4 0.2	6.4 3.1	12.4 6.1
05	7 16.3	7 17.4	6 56.4	0.5 0.2	6.5 3.2	12.5 6.1
06	7 16.5	7 17.7	6 56.6	0.6 0.3	6.6 3.2	12.6 6.2
07	7 16.8	7 17.9	6 56.9	0.7 0.3	6.7 3.3	12.7 6.2
08	7 17.0	7 18.2	6 57.1	0.8 0.4	6.8 3.3	12.8 6.3
09	7 17.3	7 18.4	6 57.3	0.9 0.4	6.9 3.4	12.9 6.3
10	7 17.5	7 18.7	6 57.6	1.0 0.5	7.0 3.4	13.0 6.4
11	7 17.8	7 18.9	6 57.8	1.1 0.5	7.1 3.5	13.1 6.4
12	7 18.0	7 19.2	6 58.0	1.2 0.6	7.2 3.5	13.2 6.5
13	7 18.3	7 19.4	6 58.3	1.3 0.6	7.3 3.6	13.3 6.5
14	7 18.5	7 19.7	6 58.5	1.4 0.7	7.4 3.6	13.4 6.6
15	7 18.8	7 20.0	6 58.8	1.5 0.7	7.5 3.7	13.5 6.6
16	7 19.0	7 20.2	6 59.0	1.6 0.8	7.6 3.7	13.6 6.7
17	7 19.3	7 20.5	6 59.2	1.7 0.8	7.7 3.8	13.7 6.7
18	7 19.5	7 20.7	6 59.5	1.8 0.9	7.8 3.8	13.8 6.8
19	7 19.8	7 21.0	6 59.7	1.9 0.9	7.9 3.9	13.9 6.8
20	7 20.0	7 21.2	7 00.0	2.0 1.0	8.0 3.9	14.0 6.9
21	7 20.3	7 21.5	7 00.2	2.1 1.0	8.1 4.0	14.1 6.9
22	7 20.5	7 21.7	7 00.4	2.2 1.1	8.2 4.0	14.2 7.0
23	7 20.8	7 22.0	7 00.7	2.3 1.1	8.3 4.1	14.3 7.0
24	7 21.0	7 22.2	7 00.9	2.4 1.2	8.4 4.1	14.4 7.1
25	7 21.3	7 22.5	7 01.1	2.5 1.2	8.5 4.2	14.5 7.1
26	7 21.5	7 22.7	7 01.4	2.6 1.3	8.6 4.2	14.6 7.2
27	7 21.8	7 23.0	7 01.6	2.7 1.3	8.7 4.3	14.7 7.2
28	7 22.0	7 23.2	7 01.9	2.8 1.4	8.8 4.3	14.8 7.3
29	7 22.3	7 23.5	7 02.1	2.9 1.4	8.9 4.4	14.9 7.3
30	7 22.5	7 23.7	7 02.3	3.0 1.5	9.0 4.4	15.0 7.4
31	7 22.8	7 24.0	7 02.6	3.1 1.5	9.1 4.5	15.1 7.4
32	7 23.0	7 24.2	7 02.8	3.2 1.6	9.2 4.5	15.2 7.5
33	7 23.3	7 24.5	7 03.1	3.3 1.6	9.3 4.6	15.3 7.5
34	7 23.5	7 24.7	7 03.3	3.4 1.7	9.4 4.6	15.4 7.6
35	7 23.8	7 25.0	7 03.5	3.5 1.7	9.5 4.7	15.5 7.6
36	7 24.0	7 25.2	7 03.8	3.6 1.8	9.6 4.7	15.6 7.7
37	7 24.3	7 25.5	7 04.0	3.7 1.8	9.7 4.8	15.7 7.7
38	7 24.5	7 25.7	7 04.3	3.8 1.9	9.8 4.8	15.8 7.8
39	7 24.8	7 26.0	7 04.5	3.9 1.9	9.9 4.9	15.9 7.8
40	7 25.0	7 26.2	7 04.7	4.0 2.0	10.0 4.9	16.0 7.9
41	7 25.3	7 26.5	7 05.0	4.1 2.0	10.1 5.0	16.1 7.9
42	7 25.5	7 26.7	7 05.2	4.2 2.1	10.2 5.0	16.2 8.0
43	7 25.8	7 27.0	7 05.4	4.3 2.1	10.3 5.1	16.3 8.0
44	7 26.0	7 27.2	7 05.7	4.4 2.2	10.4 5.1	16.4 8.1
45	7 26.3	7 27.5	7 05.9	4.5 2.2	10.5 5.2	16.5 8.1
46	7 26.5	7 27.7	7 06.2	4.6 2.3	10.6 5.2	16.6 8.2
47	7 26.8	7 28.0	7 06.4	4.7 2.3	10.7 5.3	16.7 8.2
48	7 27.0	7 28.2	7 06.6	4.8 2.4	10.8 5.3	16.8 8.2
49	7 27.3	7 28.5	7 06.9	4.9 2.4	10.9 5.4	16.9 8.2
50	7 27.5	7 28.7	7 07.1	5.0 2.5	11.0 5.4	17.0 8.4
51	7 27.8	7 29.0	7 07.4	5.1 2.5	11.1 5.5	17.1 8.4
52	7 28.0	7 29.2	7 07.6	5.2 2.6	11.2 5.5	17.2 8.5
53	7 28.3	7 29.5	7 07.8	5.3 2.6	11.3 5.6	17.3 8.5
54	7 28.5	7 29.7	7 08.1	5.4 2.7	11.4 5.6	17.4 8.6
55	7 28.8	7 30.0	7 08.3	5.5 2.7	11.5 5.7	17.5 8.6
56	7 29.0	7 30.2	7 08.5	5.6 2.8	11.6 5.7	17.6 8.7
57	7 29.3	7 30.5	7 08.8	5.7 2.8	11.7 5.8	17.7 8.7
58	7 29.5	7 30.7	7 09.0	5.8 2.9	11.8 5.8	17.8 8.8
59	7 29.8	7 31.0	7 09.3	5.9 2.9	11.9 5.9	17.9 8.8
60	7 30.0	7 31.2	7 09.5	6.0 3.0	12.0 5.9	18.0 8.9

30ᵐ INCREMENTS AND CORRECTIONS 31ᵐ

m 30 s	SUN PLANETS	ARIES	MOON	v or Corrⁿ d	v or Corrⁿ d	v or Corrⁿ d
00	7 30.0	7 31.2	7 09.5	0.0 0.0	6.0 3.1	12.0 6.1
01	7 30.3	7 31.5	7 09.7	0.1 0.0	6.1 3.1	12.1 6.2
02	7 30.5	7 31.7	7 10.0	0.2 0.1	6.2 3.2	12.2 6.2
03	7 30.8	7 31.0	7 10.2	0.3 0.2	6.3 3.2	12.3 6.3
04	7 31.0	7 32.2	7 10.5	0.4 0.2	6.4 3.3	12.4 6.3
05	7 31.3	7 32.5	7 10.7	0.5 0.3	6.5 3.3	12.5 6.4
06	7 31.5	7 32.7	7 10.9	0.6 0.3	6.6 3.4	12.6 6.4
07	7 31.8	7 32.0	7 11.2	0.7 0.4	6.7 3.4	12.7 6.5
08	7 32.0	7 33.2	7 11.4	0.8 0.4	6.8 3.5	12.8 6.5
09	7 32.3	7 33.5	7 11.6	0.9 0.5	6.9 3.5	12.9 6.6
10	7 32.5	7 33.7	7 11.9	1.0 0.5	7.0 3.6	13.0 6.6
11	7 32.8	7 33.0	7 12.1	1.1 0.6	7.1 3.6	13.1 6.7
12	7 33.0	7 34.2	7 12.4	1.2 0.6	7.2 3.7	13.2 6.7
13	7 33.3	7 34.5	7 12.6	1.3 0.7	7.3 3.7	13.3 6.8
14	7 33.5	7 34.7	7 12.8	1.4 0.7	7.4 3.8	13.4 6.8
15	7 33.8	7 35.0	7 13.1	1.5 0.8	7.5 3.8	13.5 6.9
16	7 34.0	7 35.2	7 13.3	1.6 0.8	7.6 3.9	13.6 6.9
17	7 34.3	7 35.5	7 13.6	1.7 0.9	7.7 3.9	13.7 7.0
18	7 34.5	7 35.7	7 13.8	1.8 0.9	7.8 4.0	13.8 7.0
19	7 34.8	7 36.0	7 14.0	1.9 1.0	7.9 4.0	13.9 7.1
20	7 35.0	7 36.2	7 14.3	2.0 1.0	8.0 4.1	14.0 7.1
21	7 35.3	7 36.5	7 14.5	2.1 1.1	8.1 4.1	14.1 7.2
22	7 35.5	7 36.7	7 14.7	2.2 1.1	8.2 4.2	14.2 7.2
23	7 35.8	7 37.0	7 15.0	2.3 1.2	8.3 4.2	14.3 7.3
24	7 36.0	7 37.2	7 15.2	2.4 1.2	8.4 4.3	14.4 7.3
25	7 36.3	7 37.5	7 15.5	2.5 1.3	8.5 4.3	14.5 7.4
26	7 36.5	7 37.7	7 15.7	2.6 1.3	8.6 4.4	14.6 7.4
27	7 36.8	7 38.0	7 15.9	2.7 1.4	8.7 4.4	14.7 7.5
28	7 37.0	7 38.3	7 16.2	2.8 1.4	8.8 4.5	14.8 7.5
29	7 37.3	7 38.5	7 16.4	2.9 1.5	8.9 4.5	14.9 7.6
30	7 37.5	7 38.8	7 16.7	3.0 1.5	9.0 4.6	15.0 7.6
31	7 37.8	7 39.0	7 16.9	3.1 1.6	9.1 4.6	15.1 7.7
32	7 38.0	7 39.3	7 17.1	3.2 1.6	9.2 4.7	15.2 7.7
33	7 38.3	7 39.5	7 17.4	3.3 1.7	9.3 4.7	15.3 7.8
34	7 38.5	7 39.8	7 17.6	3.4 1.7	9.4 4.8	15.4 7.8
35	7 38.8	7 40.0	7 17.9	3.5 1.8	9.5 4.8	15.5 7.9
36	7 39.0	7 40.3	7 18.1	3.6 1.8	9.6 4.9	15.6 7.9
37	7 39.3	7 40.5	7 18.3	3.7 1.9	9.7 4.9	15.7 8.0
38	7 39.5	7 40.8	7 18.6	3.8 1.9	9.8 5.0	15.8 8.0
39	7 39.8	7 41.0	7 18.8	3.9 2.0	9.9 5.0	15.9 8.1
40	7 40.0	7 41.3	7 19.0	4.0 2.0	10.0 5.1	16.0 8.1
41	7 40.3	7 41.5	7 19.3	4.1 2.1	10.1 5.1	16.1 8.2
42	7 40.5	7 41.8	7 19.5	4.2 2.1	10.2 5.2	16.2 8.2
43	7 40.8	7 42.0	7 19.8	4.3 2.2	10.3 5.2	16.3 8.3
44	7 41.0	7 42.3	7 20.0	4.4 2.2	10.4 5.3	16.4 8.3
45	7 41.3	7 42.5	7 20.2	4.5 2.3	10.5 5.3	16.5 8.4
46	7 41.5	7 42.8	7 20.5	4.6 2.3	10.6 5.4	16.6 8.4
47	7 41.8	7 43.0	7 20.7	4.7 2.4	10.7 5.4	16.7 8.5
48	7 42.0	7 43.3	7 21.0	4.8 2.4	10.8 5.5	16.8 8.5
49	7 42.3	7 43.5	7 21.2	4.9 2.5	10.9 5.5	16.9 8.6
50	7 42.5	7 43.8	7 21.4	5.0 2.5	11.0 5.6	17.0 8.6
51	7 42.8	7 44.0	7 21.7	5.1 2.6	11.1 5.6	17.1 8.7
52	7 43.0	7 44.3	7 21.9	5.2 2.6	11.2 5.7	17.2 8.7
53	7 43.3	7 44.5	7 22.1	5.3 2.7	11.3 5.7	17.3 8.8
54	7 43.5	7 44.8	7 22.4	5.4 2.7	11.4 5.8	17.4 8.8
55	7 43.8	7 45.0	7 22.4	5.5 2.8	11.5 5.8	17.5 8.9
56	7 44.0	7 45.3	7 22.6	5.6 2.8	11.6 5.9	17.6 8.9
57	7 44.3	7 45.5	7 22.8	5.7 2.9	11.7 5.9	17.7 9.0
58	7 44.5	7 45.8	7 23.1	5.8 2.9	11.8 6.0	17.8 9.0
59	7 44.8	7 46.0	7 23.3	5.9 3.0	11.9 6.0	17.9 9.1
60	7 45.0	7 46.3	7 23.8	6.0 3.1	12.0 6.1	18.0 9.2

m 31 s	SUN PLANETS	ARIES	MOON	v or Corrⁿ d	v or Corrⁿ d	v or Corrⁿ d
00	7 45.0	7 46.3	7 23.8	0.0 0.0	6.0 3.2	12.0 6.3
01	7 45.3	7 46.5	7 24.1	0.1 0.1	6.1 3.2	12.1 6.4
02	7 45.5	7 46.8	7 24.3	0.2 0.1	6.2 3.3	12.2 6.4
03	7 45.8	7 47.0	7 24.5	0.3 0.2	6.3 3.3	12.3 6.5
04	7 46.0	7 47.3	7 24.8	0.4 0.2	6.4 3.4	12.4 6.5
05	7 46.3	7 47.5	7 25.0	0.5 0.3	6.5 3.4	12.5 6.6
06	7 46.5	7 47.8	7 25.2	0.6 0.3	6.6 3.5	12.6 6.6
07	7 46.8	7 48.0	7 25.5	0.7 0.4	6.7 3.5	12.7 6.7
08	7 47.0	7 48.3	7 25.7	0.8 0.4	6.8 3.6	12.8 6.7
09	7 47.3	7 48.5	7 26.0	0.9 0.5	6.9 3.6	12.9 6.8
10	7 47.5	7 48.8	7 26.2	1.0 0.5	7.0 3.7	13.0 6.8
11	7 47.8	7 49.0	7 26.4	1.1 0.6	7.1 3.7	13.1 6.9
12	7 48.0	7 49.3	7 26.7	1.2 0.6	7.2 3.8	13.2 6.9
13	7 48.3	7 49.5	7 26.9	1.3 0.7	7.3 3.8	13.3 7.0
14	7 48.5	7 49.8	7 27.2	1.4 0.7	7.4 3.9	13.4 7.0
15	7 48.8	7 50.0	7 27.4	1.5 0.8	7.5 3.9	13.5 7.1
16	7 49.0	7 50.3	7 27.6	1.6 0.8	7.6 4.0	13.6 7.1
17	7 49.3	7 50.5	7 27.9	1.7 0.9	7.7 4.0	13.7 7.2
18	7 49.5	7 50.8	7 28.1	1.8 0.9	7.8 4.1	13.8 7.2
19	7 49.8	7 51.0	7 28.4	1.9 1.0	7.9 4.1	13.9 7.3
20	7 50.0	7 51.3	7 28.6	2.0 1.1	8.0 4.2	14.0 7.4
21	7 50.3	7 51.5	7 28.8	2.1 1.1	8.1 4.3	14.1 7.4
22	7 50.5	7 51.8	7 29.1	2.2 1.2	8.2 4.3	14.2 7.5
23	7 50.8	7 52.0	7 29.3	2.3 1.2	8.3 4.4	14.3 7.5
24	7 51.0	7 52.3	7 29.5	2.4 1.3	8.4 4.4	14.4 7.6
25	7 51.3	7 52.5	7 29.8	2.5 1.3	8.5 4.5	14.5 7.6
26	7 51.5	7 52.8	7 30.0	2.6 1.4	8.6 4.5	14.6 7.7
27	7 51.8	7 53.0	7 30.3	2.7 1.4	8.7 4.6	14.7 7.7
28	7 52.0	7 53.3	7 30.5	2.8 1.5	8.8 4.6	14.8 7.8
29	7 52.3	7 53.5	7 30.7	2.9 1.5	8.9 4.7	14.9 7.8
30	7 52.5	7 53.8	7 31.0	3.0 1.6	9.0 4.7	15.0 7.9
31	7 52.8	7 54.0	7 31.2	3.1 1.6	9.1 4.8	15.1 7.9
32	7 53.0	7 54.3	7 31.5	3.2 1.7	9.2 4.8	15.2 8.0
33	7 53.3	7 54.5	7 31.7	3.3 1.7	9.3 4.9	15.3 8.0
34	7 53.5	7 54.8	7 31.9	3.4 1.8	9.4 4.9	15.4 8.1
35	7 53.8	7 55.0	7 32.2	3.5 1.8	9.5 5.0	15.5 8.1
36	7 54.0	7 55.3	7 32.4	3.6 1.9	9.6 5.0	15.6 8.2
37	7 54.3	7 55.5	7 32.6	3.7 1.9	9.7 5.1	15.7 8.2
38	7 54.5	7 55.8	7 32.9	3.8 2.0	9.8 5.1	15.8 8.3
39	7 54.8	7 56.0	7 33.1	3.9 2.0	9.9 5.2	15.9 8.3
40	7 55.0	7 56.3	7 33.4	4.0 2.1	10.0 5.3	16.0 8.4
41	7 55.3	7 56.6	7 33.6	4.1 2.2	10.1 5.3	16.1 8.5
42	7 55.5	7 56.8	7 33.8	4.2 2.2	10.2 5.4	16.2 8.5
43	7 55.8	7 57.1	7 34.1	4.3 2.3	10.3 5.4	16.3 8.6
44	7 56.0	7 57.3	7 34.3	4.4 2.3	10.4 5.5	16.4 8.6
45	7 56.3	7 57.6	7 34.6	4.5 2.4	10.5 5.5	16.5 8.7
46	7 56.5	7 57.8	7 34.7	4.6 2.4	10.6 5.6	16.6 8.7
47	7 56.8	7 58.1	7 35.0	4.7 2.5	10.7 5.6	16.7 8.8
48	7 57.0	7 58.3	7 35.3	4.8 25	10.8 5.7	16.8 8.8
49	7 57.3	7 58.6	7 35.5	4.9 2.6	10.9 5.7	16.9 8.9
50	7 57.5	7 58.8	7 35.7	5.0 2.6	11.0 5.8	17.0 8.9
51	7 57.8	7 59.1	7 36.0	5.1 2.7	11.1 5.8	17.1 9.0
52	7 58.0	7 59.3	7 36.2	5.2 2.7	11.2 5.9	17.2 9.0
53	7 58.3	7 59.6	7 36.5	5.3 2.8	11.3 5.9	17.3 9.1
54	7 58.5	7 59.8	7 36.7	5.4 2.8	11.4 6.0	17.4 9.1
55	7 58.8	8 00.1	7 36.9	5.5 2.9	11.5 6.0	17.5 9.2
56	7 59.0	8 00.3	7 37.2	5.6 2.9	11.6 6.1	17.6 9.2
57	7 59.3	8 00.6	7 37.4	5.7 3.0	11.7 6.1	17.7 9.3
58	7 59.5	8 00.8	7 37.7	5.8 3.0	11.8 6.2	17.8 9.3
59	7 59.8	8 01.1	7 37.9	5.9 3.1	11.9 6.2	17.9 9.4
60	8 00.0	8 01.3	7 38.1	6.0 3.2	12.0 6.3	18.0 9.5

32^m INCREMENTS AND CORRECTIONS   33^m

m 32 s	SUN PLANETS	ARIES	MOON	v or Corrⁿ d	v or Corrⁿ d	v or Corrⁿ d
	° ′	° ′	° ′	′ ′	′ ′	′ ′
00	8 00.0	8 01.3	7 38.1	0.0 0.0	6.0 3.3	12.0 6.5
01	8 00.3	8 01.6	7 38.4	0.1 0.1	6.1 3.3	12.1 6.6
02	8 00.5	8 01.8	7 38.6	0.2 0.1	6.2 3.4	12.2 6.6
03	8 00.8	8 02.1	7 38.8	0.3 0.2	6.3 3.4	12.3 6.7
04	8 01.0	8 02.3	7 39.1	0.4 0.2	6.4 3.5	12.4 6.7
05	8 01.3	8 02.6	7 39.3	0.5 0.3	6.5 3.5	12.5 6.8
06	8 01.5	8 02.8	7 39.6	0.6 0.3	6.6 3.6	12.6 6.8
07	8 01.8	8 03.1	7 39.8	0.7 0.4	6.7 3.6	12.7 6.9
08	8 02.0	8 03.3	7 40.0	0.8 0.4	6.8 3.7	12.8 6.9
09	8 02.3	8 03.6	7 40.3	0.9 0.5	6.9 3.7	12.9 7.0
10	8 02.5	8 03.8	7 40.5	1.0 0.5	7.0 3.8	13.0 7.0
11	8 02.8	8 04.1	7 40.8	1.1 0.6	7.1 3.8	13.1 7.1
12	8 03.0	8 04.3	7 41.0	1.2 0.7	7.2 3.9	13.2 7.2
13	8 03.3	8 04.6	7 41.2	1.3 0.7	7.3 4.0	13.3 7.2
14	8 03.5	8 04.8	7 41.5	1.4 0.8	7.4 4.0	13.4 7.3
15	8 03.8	8 05.1	7 41.7	1.5 0.8	7.5 4.1	13.5 7.3
16	8 04.0	8 05.3	7 42.0	1.6 0.9	7.6 4.1	13.6 7.4
17	8 04.3	8 05.6	7 42.2	1.7 0.9	7.7 4.2	13.7 7.4
18	8 04.5	8 05.8	7 42.4	1.8 1.0	7.8 4.2	13.8 7.5
19	8 04.8	8 06.1	7 42.7	1.9 1.0	7.9 4.3	13.9 7.5
20	8 05.0	8 06.3	7 42.9	2.0 1.1	8.0 4.3	14.0 7.6
21	8 05.3	8 06.6	7 43.1	2.1 1.1	8.1 4.4	14.1 7.6
22	8 05.5	8 06.8	7 43.4	2.2 1.2	8.2 4.4	14.2 7.7
23	8 05.8	8 07.1	7 43.6	2.3 1.2	8.3 4.5	14.3 7.7
24	8 06.0	8 07.3	7 43.9	2.4 1.3	8.4 4.6	14.4 7.8
25	8 06.3	8 07.6	7 44.1	2.5 1.4	8.5 4.6	14.5 7.9
26	8 06.5	8 07.8	7 44.3	2.6 1.4	8.6 4.7	14.6 7.9
27	8 06.8	8 08.1	7 44.6	2.7 1.5	8.7 4.7	14.7 8.0
28	8 07.0	8 08.3	7 44.8	2.8 1.5	8.8 4.8	14.8 8.0
29	8 07.3	8 08.6	7 45.1	2.9 1.6	8.9 4.8	14.9 8.1
30	8 07.5	8 08.8	7 45.3	3.0 1.6	9.0 4.9	15.0 8.1
31	8 07.8	8 09.1	7 45.5	3.1 1.7	9.1 4.9	15.1 8.2
32	8 08.0	8 09.3	7 45.8	3.2 1.7	9.2 5.0	15.2 8.2
33	8 08.3	8 09.6	7 46.0	3.3 1.8	9.3 5.0	15.3 8.3
34	8 08.5	8 09.8	7 46.2	3.4 1.8	9.4 5.1	15.4 8.3
35	8 08.8	8 10.1	7 46.5	3.5 1.8	9.5 5.1	15.5 8.4
36	8 09.0	8 10.3	7 46.7	3.6 2.0	9.6 5.2	15.6 8.5
37	8 09.3	8 10.6	7 47.0	3.7 2.0	9.7 5.3	15.7 8.5
38	8 09.5	8 10.8	7 47.2	3.8 2.1	9.8 5.3	15.8 8.6
39	8 09.8	8 11.1	7 47.4	3.9 2.1	9.9 5.4	15.9 8.6
40	8 10.0	8 11.3	7 47.7	4.0 2.2	10.0 5.4	16.0 8.7
41	8 10.3	8 11.6	7 48.9	4.1 2.2	10.1 5.5	16.1 8.7
42	8 10.5	8 11.8	7 48.2	4.2 2.3	10.2 5.5	16.2 8.8
43	8 10.8	8 12.1	7 48.4	4.3 2.3	10.3 5.6	16.3 8.8
44	8 11.0	8 12.3	7 48.6	4.4 2.4	10.4 5.6	16.4 8.9
45	8 11.3	8 12.6	7 49.9	4.5 2.4	10.5 5.7	16.5 8.9
46	8 11.5	8 12.8	7 49.1	4.6 2.5	10.6 5.7	16.6 9.0
47	8 11.8	8 13.1	7 49.3	4.7 2.5	10.7 5.8	16.7 9.0
48	8 12.0	8 13.3	7 49.6	4.8 2.6	10.8 5.9	16.8 9.1
49	8 12.3	8 13.6	7 49.8	4.9 2.7	10.9 5.9	16.9 9.2
50	8 12.5	8 13.8	7 50.1	5.0 2.7	11.0 6.0	17.0 9.2
51	8 12.8	8 14.1	7 50.3	5.1 2.8	11.1 6.0	17.1 9.3
52	8 13.0	8 14.3	7 50.5	5.2 2.8	11.2 6.1	17.2 9.3
53	8 13.3	8 14.6	7 50.8	5.3 2.9	11.3 6.1	17.3 9.4
54	8 13.5	8 14.9	7 51.0	5.4 2.9	11.4 6.2	17.4 9.4
55	8 13.8	8 15.1	7 51.3	5.5 3.0	11.5 6.2	17.5 9.5
56	8 14.0	8 15.4	7 51.5	5.6 3.0	11.6 6.3	17.6 9.5
57	8 14.3	8 15.6	7 51.7	5.7 3.1	11.7 6.3	17.7 9.6
58	8 14.5	8 15.9	7 52.0	5.8 3.1	11.8 6.4	17.8 9.6
59	8 14.8	8 16.1	7 52.2	5.9 3.2	11.9 6.4	17.9 9.7
60	8 15.0	8 16.4	7 52.5	6.0 3.3	12.0 6.5	18.0 9.8

m 33 s	SUN PLANETS	ARIES	MOON	v or Corrⁿ d	v or Corrⁿ d	v or Corrⁿ d
	° ′	° ′	° ′	′ ′	′ ′	′ ′
00	8 15.0	8 16.4	7 52.5	0.0 0.0	6.0 3.4	12.0 6.7
01	8 15.3	8 16.6	7 52.7	0.1 0.1	6.1 3.4	12.1 6.8
02	8 15.5	8 16.9	7 52.9	0.2 0.1	6.2 3.5	12.2 6.8
03	8 15.8	8 17.1	7 53.2	0.3 0.2	6.3 3.5	12.3 6.9
04	8 16.0	8 17.4	7 53.4	0.4 0.2	6.4 3.6	12.4 6.9
05	8 16.3	8 17.6	7 53.6	0.5 0.3	6.5 3.6	12.5 7.0
06	8 16.5	8 17.9	7 53.9	0.6 0.3	6.6 3.7	12.6 7.0
07	8 16.8	8 18.1	7 54.1	0.7 0.4	6.7 3.7	12.7 7.1
08	8 17.0	8 18.4	7 54.4	0.8 0.4	6.8 3.8	12.8 7.1
09	8 17.3	8 18.6	7 54.6	0.9 0.5	6.9 3.9	12.9 7.2
10	8 17.5	8 18.9	7 54.8	1.0 0.6	7.0 3.9	13.0 7.3
11	8 17.8	8 19.1	7 55.1	1.1 0.6	7.1 4.0	13.1 7.3
12	8 18.0	8 19.4	7 55.3	1.2 0.7	7.2 4.0	13.2 7.4
13	8 18.3	8 19.6	7 55.6	1.3 0.7	7.3 4.1	13.3 7.4
14	8 18.5	8 19.9	7 55.8	1.4 0.8	7.4 4.1	13.4 7.5
15	8 18.8	8 20.1	7 56.0	1.5 0.8	7.5 4.2	13.5 7.5
16	8 19.0	8 20.4	7 56.3	1.6 0.9	7.6 4.2	13.6 7.6
17	8 19.3	8 20.6	7 56.5	1.7 0.9	7.7 4.3	13.7 7.6
18	8 19.5	8 20.9	7 56.7	1.8 1.0	7.8 4.4	13.8 7.7
19	8 19.8	8 21.1	7 57.0	1.9 1.1	7.9 4.4	13.9 7.7
20	8 20.0	8 21.4	7 57.2	2.0 1.1	8.0 4.5	14.0 7.8
21	8 20.3	8 21.6	7 57.5	2.1 1.2	8.1 4.5	14.1 7.9
22	8 20.5	8 21.9	7 57.7	2.2 1.2	8.2 4.6	14.2 7.9
23	8 20.8	8 22.1	7 57.9	2.3 1.3	8.3 4.6	14.3 8.0
24	8 21.0	8 22.4	7 58.2	2.4 1.3	8.4 4.7	14.4 8.0
25	8 21.3	8 22.6	7 58.4	2.5 1.4	8.5 4.7	14.5 8.1
26	8 21.5	8 22.9	7 58.7	2.6 1.5	8.6 4.8	14.6 8.2
27	8 21.8	8 23.1	7 58.9	2.7 1.5	8.7 4.9	14.7 8.2
28	8 22.0	8 23.4	7 59.1	2.8 1.6	8.8 4.9	14.8 8.3
29	8 22.3	8 23.6	7 59.4	2.9 1.6	8.9 5.0	14.9 8.3
30	8 22.5	8 23.9	7 59.6	3.0 1.7	9.0 5.0	15.0 8.4
31	8 22.8	8 24.1	7 59.8	3.1 1.7	9.1 5.1	15.1 8.4
32	8 23.0	8 24.4	8 00.1	3.2 1.8	9.2 5.1	15.2 8.5
33	8 23.3	8 24.6	8 00.3	3.3 1.8	9.3 5.2	15.3 8.5
34	8 23.5	8 24.9	8 00.6	3.4 1.9	9.4 5.2	15.4 8.6
35	8 23.8	8 25.1	8 00.8	3.5 2.0	9.5 5.3	15.5 8.7
36	8 24.0	8 25.4	8 01.0	3.6 2.0	9.6 5.4	15.6 8.7
37	8 24.3	8 25.6	8 01.3	3.7 2.1	9.7 5.4	15.7 8.8
38	8 24.5	8 25.9	8 01.5	3.8 2.1	9.8 5.5	15.8 8.8
39	8 24.8	8 26.1	8 01.8	3.9 2.2	9.9 5.5	15.9 8.9
40	8 25.0	8 26.4	8 02.0	4.0 2.2	10.0 5.6	16.0 8.9
41	8 25.3	8 26.6	8 02.2	4.1 2.3	10.1 5.6	16.1 9.0
42	8 25.5	8 26.9	8 02.5	4.2 2.3	10.2 5.7	16.2 9.0
43	8 25.8	8 27.1	8 02.7	4.3 2.4	10.3 5.8	16.3 9.1
44	8 26.0	8 27.4	8 02.9	4.4 2.5	10.4 5.8	16.4 9.2
45	8 26.3	8 27.6	8 03.2	4.5 2.5	10.5 5.9	16.5 9.2
46	8 26.5	8 27.9	8 03.4	4.6 2.6	10.6 5.9	16.6 9.3
47	8 26.8	8 28.1	8 03.7	4.7 2.6	10.7 6.0	16.7 9.3
48	8 27.0	8 28.4	8 03.9	4.8 2.7	10.8 6.0	16.8 9.4
49	8 27.3	8 28.6	8 04.1	4.9 2.7	10.9 6.1	16.9 9.4
50	8 27.5	8 28.9	8 04.4	5.0 2.8	11.0 6.1	17.0 9.5
51	8 27.8	8 29.1	8 04.6	5.1 2.8	11.1 6.2	17.1 9.5
52	8 28.0	8 29.4	8 04.9	5.2 2.9	11.2 6.3	17.2 9.6
53	8 28.3	8 29.6	8 05.1	5.3 3.0	11.3 6.3	17.3 9.7
54	8 28.5	8 29.9	8 05.3	5.4 3.0	11.4 6.4	17.4 9.7
55	8 28.8	8 30.1	8 05.6	5.5 3.1	11.5 6.4	17.5 9.8
56	8 29.0	8 30.4	8 05.8	5.6 3.1	11.6 6.5	17.6 9.8
57	8 29.3	8 30.6	8 06.1	5.7 3.2	11.7 6.5	17.7 9.9
58	8 29.5	8 30.9	8 06.3	5.8 3.2	11.8 6.6	17.8 9.9
59	8 29.8	8 31.1	8 06.5	5.9 3.3	11.9 6.6	17.9 10.0
60	8 30.0	8 31.4	8 06.8	6.0 3.4	12.0 6.7	18.0 10.1

34m INCREMENTS AND CORRECTIONS 35m

m 34	SUN PLANETS	ARIES	MOON	v or Corr^n d		v or Corr^n d		v or Corr^n d	
s	° ′	° ′	° ′	′	′	′	′	′	′
00	8 30.0	8 31.4	8 06.8	0.0	0.0	6.0	3.5	12.0	6.9
01	8 30.3	8 31.6	8 07.0	0.1	0.1	6.1	3.5	12.1	7.0
02	8 30.5	8 31.9	8 07.2	0.2	0.1	6.2	3.6	12.2	7.0
03	8 30.8	8 32.1	8 07.5	0.3	0.2	6.3	3.6	12.3	7.1
04	8 31.0	8 32.4	8 07.7	0.4	0.2	6.4	3.7	12.4	7.1
05	8 31.3	8 32.6	8 08.0	0.5	0.3	6.5	3.7	12.5	7.2
06	8 31.5	8 32.9	8 08.2	0.6	0.3	6.6	3.8	12.6	7.2
07	8 31.8	8 33.2	8 08.4	0.7	0.4	6.7	3.9	12.7	7.3
08	8 32.0	8 33.4	8 08.7	0.8	0.5	6.8	3.9	12.8	7.4
09	8 32.3	8 33.7	8 08.9	0.9	0.5	6.9	4.0	12.9	7.4
10	8 32.5	8 33.9	8 09.2	1.0	0.6	7.0	4.0	13.0	7.5
11	8 32.8	8 34.2	8 09.4	1.1	0.6	7.1	4.1	13.1	7.5
12	8 33.0	8 34.4	8 09.6	1.2	0.7	7.2	4.1	13.2	7.6
13	8 33.3	8 34.7	8 09.9	1.3	0.7	7.3	4.2	13.3	7.6
14	8 33.5	8 34.9	8 10.1	1.4	0.8	7.4	4.3	13.4	7.7
15	8 33.8	8 35.2	8 10.3	1.5	0.8	7.5	4.3	13.5	7.8
16	8 34.0	8 35.4	8 10.6	1.6	0.9	7.6	4.4	13.6	7.8
17	8 34.3	8 35.7	8 10.8	1.7	1.0	7.7	4.4	13.7	7.9
18	8 34.5	8 35.9	8 11.1	1.8	1.0	7.8	4.5	13.8	7.9
19	8 34.8	8 36.2	8 11.3	1.9	1.1	7.9	4.5	13.9	8.0
20	8 35.0	8 36.4	8 11.5	2.0	1.2	8.0	4.6	14.0	8.1
21	8 35.3	8 36.7	8 11.8	2.1	1.2	8.1	4.7	14.1	8.1
22	8 35.5	8 36.9	8 12.0	2.2	1.3	8.2	4.7	14.2	8.2
23	8 35.8	8 37.2	8 12.3	2.3	1.3	8.3	4.8	14.3	8.2
24	8 36.0	8 37.4	8 12.5	2.4	1.4	8.4	4.8	14.4	8.3
25	8 36.3	8 37.7	8 12.7	2.5	1.4	8.5	4.9	14.5	8.3
26	8 36.5	8 37.9	8 13.0	2.6	1.5	8.6	4.9	14.6	8.4
27	8 36.8	8 38.2	8 13.2	2.7	1.6	8.7	5.0	14.7	8.5
28	8 37.0	8 38.4	8 13.4	2.8	1.6	8.8	5.1	14.8	8.5
29	8 37.3	8 38.7	8 13.7	2.9	1.7	8.9	5.1	14.9	8.6
30	8 37.5	8 38.9	8 13.9	3.0	1.7	9.0	5.2	15.0	8.6
31	8 37.8	8 39.2	8 14.2	3.1	1.8	9.1	5.2	15.1	8.7
32	8 38.0	8 39.4	8 14.4	3.2	1.8	9.2	5.3	15.2	8.7
33	8 38.3	8 39.7	8 14.6	3.3	1.9	9.3	5.3	15.3	8.8
34	8 38.5	8 39.9	8 14.9	3.4	2.0	9.4	5.4	15.4	8.9
35	8 38.8	8 40.2	8 15.1	3.5	2.0	9.5	5.5	15.5	8.9
36	8 39.0	8 40.4	8 15.4	3.6	2.1	9.6	5.5	15.6	9.0
37	8 39.3	8 40.7	8 15.6	3.7	2.1	9.7	5.6	15.7	9.0
38	8 39.5	8 40.9	8 15.8	3.8	2.2	9.8	5.6	15.8	9.1
39	8 39.8	8 41.2	8 16.1	3.9	2.2	9.9	5.7	15.9	9.1
40	8 40.0	8 41.4	8 16.3	4.0	2.3	10.0	5.8	16.0	9.2
41	8 40.3	8 41.7	8 16.5	4.1	2.4	10.1	5.8	16.1	9.3
42	8 40.5	8 41.9	8 16.8	4.2	2.4	10.2	5.9	16.2	9.3
43	8 40.8	8 42.2	8 17.0	4.3	2.5	10.3	5.9	16.3	9.4
44	8 41.0	8 42.4	8 17.3	4.4	2.5	10.4	6.0	16.4	9.4
45	8 41.3	8 42.7	8 17.5	4.5	2.6	10.5	6.0	16.5	9.5
46	8 41.5	8 42.9	8 17.7	4.6	2.6	10.6	6.1	16.6	9.5
47	8 41.8	8 43.2	8 18.0	4.7	2.7	10.7	6.2	16.7	9.6
48	8 42.0	8 43.4	8 18.2	4.8	2.8	10.8	6.2	16.8	9.7
49	8 42.3	8 43.7	8 18.5	4.9	2.8	10.9	6.3	16.9	9.7
50	8 42.5	8 43.9	8 18.7	5.0	2.9	11.0	6.3	17.0	9.8
51	8 42.8	8 44.2	8 18.9	5.1	2.9	11.1	6.4	17.1	9.8
52	8 43.0	8 44.4	8 19.2	5.2	3.0	11.2	6.4	17.2	9.9
53	8 43.3	8 44.7	8 19.4	5.3	3.0	11.3	6.5	17.3	9.9
54	8 43.5	8 44.9	8 19.7	5.4	3.1	11.4	6.6	17.4	10.0
55	8 43.8	8 45.2	8 19.9	5.5	3.2	11.5	6.6	17.5	10.1
56	8 44.0	8 45.4	8 20.1	5.6	3.2	11.6	6.7	17.6	10.1
57	8 44.3	8 45.7	8 20.4	5.7	3.3	11.7	6.7	17.7	10.2
58	8 44.5	8 45.9	8 20.6	5.8	3.3	11.8	6.8	17.8	10.2
59	8 44.8	8 46.2	8 20.8	5.9	3.4	11.9	6.8	17.9	10.3
60	8 45.0	8 46.4	8 21.1	6.0	3.5	12.0	6.9	18.0	10.4

m 35	SUN PLANETS	ARIES	MOON	v or Corr^n d		v or Corr^n d		v or Corr^n d	
s	° ′	° ′	° ′	′	′	′	′	′	′
00	8 45.0	8 46.4	8 21.1	0.0	0.0	6.0	3.6	12.0	7.1
01	8 45.3	8 46.7	8 21.3	0.1	0.1	6.1	3.6	12.1	7.2
02	8 45.5	8 46.9	8 21.6	0.2	0.1	6.2	3.7	12.2	7.2
03	8 45.8	8 47.2	8 21.8	0.3	0.2	6.3	3.7	12.3	7.3
04	8 46.0	8 47.4	8 22.0	0.4	0.2	6.4	3.8	12.4	7.3
05	8 46.3	8 47.7	8 22.3	0.5	0.3	6.5	3.8	12.5	7.4
06	8 46.5	8 47.9	8 22.5	0.6	0.4	6.6	3.9	12.6	7.5
07	8 46.8	8 48.2	8 22.8	0.7	0.4	6.7	4.0	12.7	7.5
08	8 47.0	8 48.4	8 23.0	0.8	0.5	6.8	4.0	12.8	7.6
09	8 47.3	8 48.7	8 23.2	0.9	0.5	6.9	4.1	12.9	7.6
10	8 47.5	8 48.9	8 23.5	1.0	0.6	7.0	4.1	13.0	7.7
11	8 47.8	8 49.2	8 23.7	1.1	0.7	7.1	4.2	13.1	7.8
12	8 48.0	8 49.4	8 23.9	1.2	0.7	7.2	4.3	13.2	7.8
13	8 48.3	8 49.7	8 24.2	1.3	0.8	7.3	4.3	13.3	7.9
14	8 48.5	8 49.9	8 24.4	1.4	0.8	7.4	4.4	13.4	7.9
15	8 48.8	8 50.2	8 24.7	1.5	0.9	7.5	4.4	13.5	8.0
16	8 49.0	8 50.4	8 24.9	1.6	0.9	7.6	4.5	13.6	8.0
17	8 49.3	8 50.7	8 25.1	1.7	1.0	7.7	4.6	13.7	8.1
18	8 49.5	8 50.9	8 25.4	1.8	1.1	7.8	4.6	13.8	8.2
19	8 49.8	8 51.2	8 25.6	1.9	1.1	7.9	4.7	13.9	8.2
20	8 50.0	8 51.5	8 25.9	2.0	1.2	8.0	4.7	14.0	8.3
21	8 50.3	8 51.7	8 26.1	2.1	1.2	8.1	4.8	14.1	8.3
22	8 50.5	8 52.0	8 26.3	2.2	1.3	8.2	4.9	14.2	8.4
23	8 50.8	8 52.2	8 26.6	2.3	1.4	8.3	4.9	14.3	8.5
24	8 51.0	8 52.5	8 26.8	2.4	1.4	8.4	5.0	14.4	8.5
25	8 51.3	8 52.7	8 27.0	2.5	1.5	8.5	5.0	14.5	8.6
26	8 51.5	8 53.0	8 27.3	2.6	1.5	8.6	5.1	14.6	8.6
27	8 51.8	8 53.2	8 27.5	2.7	1.6	8.7	5.1	14.7	8.7
28	8 52.0	8 53.5	8 27.8	2.8	1.7	8.8	5.2	14.8	8.8
29	8 52.3	8 53.7	8 28.0	2.9	1.7	8.9	5.3	14.9	8.8
30	8 52.5	8 54.0	8 28.2	3.0	1.8	9.0	5.3	15.0	8.9
31	8 52.8	8 54.2	8 28.5	3.1	1.8	9.1	5.4	15.1	8.9
32	8 53.0	8 54.5	8 28.7	3.2	1.9	9.2	5.4	15.2	9.0
33	8 53.3	8 54.7	8 29.0	3.3	2.0	9.3	5.5	15.3	9.1
34	8 53.5	8 55.0	8 29.2	3.4	2.0	9.4	5.6	15.4	9.1
35	8 53.8	8 55.2	8 29.4	3.5	2.1	9.5	5.6	15.5	9.2
36	8 54.0	8 55.5	8 29.7	3.6	2.1	9.6	5.7	15.6	9.2
37	8 54.3	8 55.7	8 29.9	3.7	2.2	9.7	5.7	15.7	9.3
38	8 54.5	8 56.0	8 30.2	3.8	2.2	9.8	5.8	15.8	9.3
39	8 54.8	8 56.2	8 30.4	3.9	2.3	9.9	5.9	15.9	9.4
40	8 55.0	8 56.5	8 30.6	4.0	2.4	10.0	5.9	16.0	9.5
41	8 55.3	8 56.7	8 30.9	4.1	2.4	10.1	6.0	16.1	9.5
42	8 55.5	8 57.0	8 31.1	4.2	2.5	10.2	6.0	16.2	9.6
43	8 55.8	8 57.2	8 31.3	4.3	2.5	10.3	6.1	16.3	9.6
44	8 56.0	8 57.5	8 31.6	4.4	2.6	10.4	6.2	16.4	9.7
45	8 56.3	8 57.7	8 31.8	4.5	2.7	10.5	6.2	16.5	9.8
46	8 56.5	8 58.0	8 32.1	4.6	2.7	10.6	6.3	16.6	9.8
47	8 56.8	8 58.2	8 32.3	4.7	2.8	10.7	6.3	16.7	9.9
48	8 57.0	8 58.5	8 32.5	4.8	2.8	10.8	6.4	16.8	9.9
49	8 57.3	8 58.7	8 32.8	4.9	2.9	10.9	6.4	16.9	10.0
50	8 57.5	8 59.0	8 33.0	5.0	3.0	11.0	6.5	17.0	10.1
51	8 57.8	8 59.2	8 33.3	5.1	3.0	11.1	6.6	17.1	10.1
52	8 58.0	8 59.5	8 33.5	5.2	3.1	11.2	6.6	17.2	10.2
53	8 58.3	8 59.7	8 33.7	5.3	3.1	11.3	6.7	17.3	10.2
54	8 58.5	9 00.0	8 34.0	5.4	3.2	11.4	6.7	17.4	10.3
55	8 58.8	9 00.2	8 34.2	5.5	3.3	11.5	6.8	17.5	10.4
56	8 59.0	9 00.5	8 34.4	5.6	3.3	11.6	6.9	17.6	10.4
57	8 59.3	9 00.7	8 34.7	5.7	3.4	11.7	6.9	17.7	10.5
58	8 59.5	9 01.0	8 34.9	5.8	3.4	11.8	7.0	17.8	10.5
59	8 59.8	9 01.2	8 35.2	5.9	3.5	11.9	7.0	17.9	10.6
60	9 00.0	9 01.5	8 35.4	6.0	3.6	12.0	7.1	18.0	10.7

36ᵐ   INCREMENTS AND CORRECTIONS   37ᵐ

m 36 s	SUN PLANETS	ARIES	MOON	v or Corrⁿ d	v or Corrⁿ d	v or Corrⁿ d
	° ′	° ′	° ′	′ ′	′ ′	′ ′
00	9 00.0	9 01.5	8 35.4	0.0 0.0	6.0 3.7	12.0 7.3
01	9 00.3	9 01.7	8 35.6	0.1 0.1	6.1 3.7	12.1 7.4
02	9 00.5	9 02.0	8 35.9	0.2 0.1	6.2 3.8	12.2 7.4
03	9 00.8	9 02.2	8 36.1	0.3 0.2	6.3 3.8	12.3 7.5
04	9 01.0	9 02.5	8 36.4	0.4 0.2	6.4 3.9	12.4 7.5
05	9 01.3	9 02.7	8 36.6	0.5 0.3	6.5 4.0	12.5 7.6
06	9 01.5	9 03.0	8 36.8	0.6 0.4	6.6 4.0	12.6 7.7
07	9 01.8	9 03.2	8 37.1	0.7 0.4	6.7 4.1	12.7 7.7
08	9 02.0	9 03.5	8 37.3	0.8 0.5	6.8 4.1	12.8 7.8
09	9 02.3	9 03.7	8 37.5	0.9 0.5	6.9 4.2	12.9 7.8
10	9 02.5	9 04.0	8 37.8	1.0 0.6	7.0 4.3	13.0 7.9
11	9 02.8	9 04.2	8 38.0	1.1 0.7	7.1 4.3	13.1 8.0
12	9 03.0	9 04.5	8 38.3	1.2 0.7	7.2 4.4	13.2 8.0
13	9 03.3	9 04.7	8 38.5	1.3 0.8	7.3 4.4	13.3 8.1
14	9 03.5	9 05.0	8 38.7	1.4 0.9	7.4 4.5	13.4 8.2
15	9 03.8	9 05.2	8 39.0	1.5 0.9	7.5 4.6	13.5 8.2
16	9 04.0	9 05.5	8 39.2	1.6 1.0	7.6 4.6	13.6 8.3
17	9 04.3	9 05.7	8 39.5	1.7 1.0	7.7 4.7	13.7 8.3
18	9 04.5	9 06.0	8 39.7	1.8 1.1	7.8 4.7	13.8 8.4
19	9 04.8	9 06.2	8 39.9	1.9 1.2	7.9 4.8	13.9 8.5
20	9 05.0	9 06.5	8 40.2	2.0 1.3	8.0 4.9	14.0 8.5
21	9 05.3	9 06.7	8 40.4	2.1 1.3	8.1 4.9	14.1 8.6
22	9 05.5	9 07.0	8 40.6	2.2 1.3	8.2 5.0	14.2 8.6
23	9 05.8	9 07.2	8 40.9	2.3 1.4	8.3 5.0	14.3 8.7
24	9 06.0	9 07.5	8 41.1	2.4 1.5	8.4 5.1	14.4 8.8
25	9 06.3	9 07.7	8 41.4	2.5 1.5	8.5 5.2	14.5 8.8
26	9 06.5	9 08.0	8 41.6	2.6 1.6	8.6 5.2	14.6 8.9
27	9 06.8	9 08.2	8 41.8	2.7 1.6	8.7 5.3	14.7 8.9
28	9 07.0	9 08.5	8 42.1	2.8 1.7	8.8 5.4	14.8 9.0
29	9 07.3	9 08.7	8 42.3	2.9 1.8	8.9 5.4	14.9 9.1
30	9 07.5	9 09.0	8 42.6	3.0 1.8	9.0 5.5	15.0 9.1
31	9 07.8	9 09.2	8 42.8	3.1 1.9	9.1 5.5	15.1 9.2
32	9 08.0	9 09.5	8 43.0	3.2 1.9	9.2 5.6	15.2 9.2
33	9 08.3	9 09.8	8 43.3	3.3 2.0	9.3 5.7	15.3 9.3
34	9 08.5	9 10.0	8 43.5	3.4 2.1	9.4 5.7	15.4 9.4
35	9 08.8	9 10.3	8 43.8	3.5 2.1	9.5 5.8	15.5 9.4
36	9 09.0	9 10.5	8 44.0	3.6 2.2	9.6 5.8	15.6 9.5
37	9 09.3	9 10.8	8 44.2	3.7 2.3	9.7 5.9	15.7 9.6
38	9 09.5	9 11.0	8 44.5	3.8 2.3	9.8 6.0	15.8 9.6
39	9 09.8	9 11.3	8 44.7	3.9 2.4	9.9 6.0	15.9 9.7
40	9 10.0	9 11.5	8 44.9	4.0 2.4	10.0 6.1	16.0 9.7
41	9 10.3	9 11.8	8 45.2	4.1 2.5	10.1 6.1	16.1 9.8
42	9 10.5	9 12.0	8 45.4	4.2 2.6	10.2 6.2	16.2 9.9
43	9 10.8	9 12.3	8 45.7	4.3 2.6	10.3 6.3	16.3 9.9
44	9 11.0	9 12.5	8 45.9	4.4 2.7	10.4 6.3	16.4 10.0
45	9 11.3	9 12.8	8 46.1	4.5 2.7	10.5 6.4	16.5 10.0
46	9 11.5	9 13.0	8 46.4	4.6 2.8	10.6 6.4	16.6 10.1
47	9 11.8	9 13.3	8 46.6	4.7 2.9	10.7 6.5	16.7 10.2
48	9 12.0	9 13.5	8 46.9	4.8 2.9	10.8 6.6	16.8 10.2
49	9 12.3	9 13.8	8 47.1	4.9 3.0	10.9 6.6	16.9 10.3
50	9 12.5	9 14.0	8 47.3	5.0 3.0	11.0 6.7	17.0 10.3
51	9 12.8	9 14.3	8 47.6	5.1 3.1	11.1 6.8	17.1 10.4
52	9 13.0	9 14.5	8 47.8	5.2 3.2	11.2 6.8	17.2 10.5
53	9 13.3	9 14.8	8 48.0	5.3 3.2	11.3 6.9	17.3 10.5
54	9 13.5	9 15.0	8 48.3	5.4 3.3	11.4 6.9	17.4 10.6
55	9 13.8	9 15.3	8 48.5	5.5 3.3	11.5 7.0	17.5 10.6
56	9 14.0	9 15.5	8 48.8	5.6 3.4	11.6 7.1	17.6 10.7
57	9 14.3	9 15.8	8 49.0	5.7 3.5	11.7 7.1	17.7 10.8
58	9 14.5	9 16.0	8 49.2	5.8 3.5	11.8 7.2	17.8 10.8
59	9 14.8	9 16.3	8 49.5	5.9 3.6	11.9 7.2	17.9 10.9
60	9 15.0	9 16.5	8 49.7	6.0 3.7	12.0 7.3	18.0 11.0

m 37 s	SUN PLANETS	ARIES	MOON	v or Corrⁿ d	v or Corrⁿ d	v or Corrⁿ d
	° ′	° ′	° ′	′ ′	′ ′	′ ′
00	9 15.0	9 16.5	8 49.7	0.0 0.0	6.0 3.8	12.0 7.5
01	9 15.3	9 16.8	8 50.0	0.1 0.1	6.1 3.8	12.1 7.6
02	9 15.5	9 17.0	8 50.2	0.2 0.1	6.2 3.9	12.2 7.6
03	9 15.8	9 17.3	8 50.4	0.3 0.2	6.3 3.9	12.3 7.7
04	9 16.0	9 17.5	8 50.7	0.4 0.3	6.4 4.0	12.4 7.8
05	9 16.3	9 17.8	8 50.9	0.5 0.3	6.5 4.1	12.5 7.8
06	9 16.5	9 18.0	8 51.1	0.6 0.4	6.6 4.1	12.6 7.9
07	9 16.8	9 18.3	8 51.4	0.7 0.4	6.7 4.2	12.7 7.9
08	9 17.0	9 18.5	8 51.6	0.8 0.5	6.8 4.3	12.8 8.0
09	9 17.3	9 18.8	8 51.9	0.9 0.6	6.9 4.3	12.9 8.1
10	9 17.5	9 19.0	8 52.1	1.0 0.6	7.0 4.4	13.0 8.1
11	9 17.8	9 19.3	8 52.3	1.1 0.7	7.1 4.4	13.1 8.2
12	9 18.0	9 19.5	8 52.6	1.2 0.8	7.2 4.5	13.2 8.3
13	9 18.3	9 19.8	8 52.8	1.3 0.8	7.3 4.6	13.3 8.3
14	9 18.5	9 20.0	8 53.1	1.4 0.9	7.4 4.6	13.4 8.4
15	9 18.8	9 20.3	8 53.3	1.5 0.9	7.5 4.7	13.5 8.4
16	9 19.0	9 20.5	8 53.5	1.6 1.0	7.6 4.8	13.6 8.5
17	9 19.3	9 20.8	8 53.8	1.7 1.1	7.7 4.8	13.7 8.6
18	9 19.5	9 21.0	8 54.0	1.8 1.1	7.8 4.9	13.8 8.6
19	9 19.8	9 21.3	8 54.3	1.9 1.2	7.9 4.9	13.9 8.7
20	9 20.0	9 21.5	8 54.5	2.0 1.3	8.0 5.0	14.0 8.8
21	9 20.3	9 21.8	8 54.7	2.1 1.3	8.1 5.1	14.1 8.8
22	9 20.5	9 22.0	8 55.0	2.2 1.4	8.2 5.1	14.2 8.9
23	9 20.8	9 22.3	8 55.2	2.3 1.4	8.3 5.2	14.3 8.9
24	9 21.0	9 22.5	8 55.4	2.4 1.5	8.4 5.3	14.4 9.0
25	9 21.3	9 22.8	8 55.7	2.5 1.6	8.5 5.3	14.5 9.1
26	9 21.5	9 23.0	8 55.9	2.6 1.6	8.6 5.4	14.6 9.1
27	9 21.8	9 23.3	8 56.2	2.7 1.7	8.7 5.4	14.7 9.2
28	9 22.0	9 23.5	8 56.4	2.8 1.8	8.8 5.5	14.8 9.3
29	9 22.3	9 23.8	8 56.6	2.9 1.8	8.9 5.6	14.9 9.3
30	9 22.5	9 24.0	8 56.9	3.0 1.9	9.0 5.6	15.0 9.4
31	9 22.8	9 24.3	8 57.1	3.1 1.9	9.1 5.7	15.1 9.4
32	9 23.0	9 24.5	8 57.4	3.2 2.0	9.2 5.8	15.2 9.5
33	9 23.3	9 24.8	8 57.6	3.3 2.1	9.3 5.8	15.3 9.6
34	9 23.5	9 25.0	8 57.8	3.4 2.1	9.4 5.9	15.4 9.6
35	9 23.8	9 25.3	8 58.1	3.5 2.2	9.5 5.9	15.5 9.7
36	9 24.0	9 25.5	8 58.3	3.6 2.3	9.6 6.0	15.6 9.8
37	9 24.3	9 25.8	8 58.5	3.7 2.3	9.7 6.1	15.7 9.8
38	9 24.5	9 26.0	8 58.8	3.8 2.4	9.8 6.1	15.8 9.9
39	9 24.8	9 26.3	8 59.0	3.9 2.4	9.9 6.2	15.9 9.9
40	9 25.0	9 26.5	8 59.3	4.0 2.5	10.0 6.3	16.0 10.0
41	9 25.3	9 26.8	8 59.5	4.1 2.6	10.1 6.3	16.1 10.1
42	9 25.5	9 27.0	8 59.7	4.2 2.6	10.2 6.4	16.2 10.1
43	9 25.8	9 27.3	9 00.0	4.3 2.7	10.3 6.4	16.3 10.2
44	9 26.0	9 27.5	9 00.2	4.4 2.8	10.4 6.5	16.4 10.3
45	9 26.3	9 27.8	9 00.5	4.5 2.8	10.5 6.6	16.5 10.3
46	9 26.5	9 28.1	9 00.7	4.6 2.9	10.6 6.6	16.6 10.4
47	9 26.8	9 28.3	9 00.9	4.7 2.9	10.7 6.7	16.7 10.4
48	9 27.0	9 28.6	9 01.2	4.8 3.0	10.8 6.8	16.8 10.5
49	9 27.3	9 28.8	9 01.4	4.9 3.1	10.9 6.8	16.9 10.6
50	9 27.5	9 29.1	9 01.6	5.0 3.1	11.0 6.9	17.0 10.6
51	9 27.8	9 29.3	9 01.9	5.1 3.2	11.1 6.9	17.1 10.7
52	9 28.0	9 29.6	9 02.1	5.2 3.3	11.2 7.0	17.2 10.8
53	9 28.3	9 29.8	9 02.4	5.3 3.3	11.3 7.1	17.3 10.8
54	9 28.5	9 30.1	9 02.6	5.4 3.4	11.4 7.1	17.4 10.9
55	9 28.8	9 30.3	9 02.8	5.5 3.4	11.5 7.2	17.5 10.9
56	9 29.0	9 30.6	9 03.1	5.6 3.5	11.6 7.3	17.6 11.0
57	9 29.3	9 30.8	9 03.3	5.7 3.6	11.7 7.3	17.7 11.1
58	9 29.5	9 31.1	9 03.6	5.8 3.6	11.8 7.4	17.8 11.1
59	9 29.8	9 31.3	9 03.8	5.9 3.7	11.9 7.4	17.9 11.2
60	9 30.0	9 31.6	9 04.0	6.0 3.8	12.0 7.5	18.0 11.3

38m — INCREMENTS AND CORRECTIONS — 39m

38 s	SUN PLANETS ° ′	ARIES ° ′	MOON ° ′	v or Corrⁿ d	v or Corrⁿ d	v or Corrⁿ d
00	9 30.0	9 31.6	9 04.0	0.0 0.0	6.0 3.9	12.0 7.7
01	9 30.3	9 31.8	9 04.3	0.1 0.1	6.1 3.9	12.1 7.8
02	9 30.5	9 32.1	9 04.5	0.2 0.1	6.2 4.0	12.2 7.8
03	9 30.8	9 32.3	9 04.7	0.3 0.2	6.3 4.0	12.3 7.9
04	9 31.0	9 32.6	9 05.0	0.4 0.3	6.4 4.1	12.4 8.0
05	9 31.3	9 32.8	9 05.2	0.5 0.3	6.5 4.2	12.5 8.0
06	9 31.5	9 33.1	9 05.5	0.6 0.4	6.6 4.2	12.6 8.1
07	9 31.8	9 33.3	9 05.7	0.7 0.4	6.7 4.3	12.7 8.1
08	9 32.0	9 33.6	9 05.9	0.8 0.5	6.8 4.4	12.8 8.2
09	9 32.3	9 33.8	9 06.2	0.9 0.6	6.9 4.4	12.9 8.3
10	9 32.5	9 34.1	9 06.4	1.0 0.6	7.0 4.5	13.0 8.3
11	9 32.8	9 34.3	9 06.7	1.1 0.7	7.1 4.6	13.1 8.4
12	9 33.0	9 34.6	9 06.9	1.2 0.8	7.2 4.6	13.2 8.5
13	9 33.3	9 34.8	9 07.1	1.3 0.8	7.3 4.7	13.3 8.5
14	9 33.5	9 35.1	9 07.4	1.4 0.9	7.4 4.7	13.4 8.6
15	9 33.8	9 35.3	9 07.6	1.5 1.0	7.5 4.8	13.5 8.7
16	9 34.0	9 35.6	9 07.9	1.6 1.0	7.6 4.9	13.6 8.7
17	9 34.3	9 35.8	9 08.1	1.7 1.1	7.7 4.9	13.7 8.8
18	9 34.5	9 36.1	9 08.3	1.8 1.2	7.8 5.0	13.8 8.9
19	9 34.8	9 36.3	9 08.6	1.9 1.2	7.9 5.0	13.9 8.9
20	9 35.0	9 36.6	9 08.8	2.0 1.3	8.0 5.1	14.0 9.0
21	9 35.3	9 36.8	9 09.0	2.1 1.3	8.1 5.2	14.1 9.0
22	9 35.5	9 37.1	9 09.3	2.2 1.4	8.2 5.3	14.2 9.1
23	9 35.8	9 37.3	9 09.5	2.3 1.5	8.3 5.3	14.3 9.2
24	9 36.0	9 37.6	9 09.8	2.4 1.5	8.4 5.4	14.4 9.2
25	9 36.3	9 37.8	9 10.0	2.5 1.6	8.5 5.5	14.5 9.3
26	9 36.5	9 38.1	9 10.2	2.6 1.7	8.6 5.5	14.6 9.4
27	9 36.8	9 38.3	9 10.5	2.7 1.7	8.7 5.6	14.7 9.4
28	9 37.0	9 38.6	9 10.7	2.8 1.8	8.8 5.6	14.8 9.5
29	9 37.3	9 38.8	9 11.0	2.9 1.9	8.9 5.7	14.9 9.6
30	9 37.5	9 39.1	9 11.2	3.0 1.9	9.0 5.8	15.0 9.6
31	9 37.8	9 39.3	9 11.4	3.1 2.0	9.1 5.8	15.1 9.7
32	9 38.0	9 39.6	9 11.7	3.2 2.1	9.2 5.9	15.2 9.8
33	9 38.3	9 39.8	9 11.9	3.3 2.1	9.3 6.0	15.3 9.8
34	9 38.5	9 40.1	9 12.1	3.4 2.2	9.4 6.0	15.4 9.9
35	9 38.8	9 40.3	9 12.4	3.5 2.2	9.5 6.1	15.5 9.9
36	9 39.0	9 40.6	9 12.6	3.6 2.3	9.6 6.2	15.6 10.0
37	9 39.3	9 40.8	9 12.9	3.7 2.4	9.7 6.2	15.7 10.1
38	9 39.5	9 41.1	9 13.1	3.8 2.4	9.8 6.3	15.8 10.1
39	9 39.8	9 41.3	9 13.3	3.9 2.5	9.9 6.4	15.9 10.2
40	9 40.0	9 41.6	9 13.6	4.0 2.6	10.0 6.4	16.0 10.3
41	9 40.3	9 41.8	9 13.8	4.1 2.6	10.1 6.5	16.1 10.3
42	9 40.5	9 42.1	9 14.1	4.2 2.7	10.2 6.5	16.2 10.4
43	9 40.8	9 42.3	9 14.3	4.3 2.8	10.3 6.6	16.3 10.5
44	9 41.0	9 42.6	9 14.5	4.4 2.8	10.4 6.7	16.4 10.5
45	9 41.3	9 42.8	9 14.8	4.5 2.9	10.5 6.7	16.5 10.6
46	9 41.5	9 43.1	9 15.0	4.6 3.0	10.6 6.8	16.6 10.7
47	9 41.8	9 43.3	9 15.2	4.7 3.0	10.7 6.9	16.7 10.7
48	9 42.0	9 43.6	9 15.5	4.8 3.1	10.8 6.9	16.8 10.8
49	9 42.3	9 43.8	9 15.7	4.9 3.1	10.9 7.0	16.9 10.8
50	9 42.5	9 44.1	9 16.0	5.0 3.2	11.0 7.1	17.0 10.9
51	9 42.8	9 44.3	9 16.2	5.1 3.3	11.1 7.1	17.1 11.0
52	9 43.0	9 44.6	9 16.4	5.2 3.3	11.2 7.2	17.2 11.0
53	9 43.3	9 44.8	9 16.7	5.3 3.4	11.3 7.3	17.3 11.1
54	9 43.5	9 45.1	9 16.9	5.4 3.5	11.4 7.3	17.4 11.2
55	9 43.8	9 45.3	9 17.2	5.5 3.5	11.5 7.4	17.5 11.2
56	9 44.0	9 45.6	9 17.4	5.6 3.6	11.6 7.4	17.6 11.3
57	9 44.3	9 45.8	9 17.6	5.7 3.7	11.7 7.5	17.7 11.4
58	9 44.5	9 46.1	9 17.9	5.8 3.7	11.8 7.6	17.8 11.4
59	9 44.8	9 45.4	9 18.1	5.9 3.8	11.9 7.6	17.9 11.5
60	9 45.0	9 45.6	9 18.4	6.0 3.9	12.0 7.7	18.0 11.6

39 s	SUN PLANETS ° ′	ARIES ° ′	MOON ° ′	v or Corrⁿ d	v or Corrⁿ d	v or Corrⁿ d
00	9 45.0	9 46.6	9 18.4	0.0 0.0	6.0 4.0	12.0 7.9
01	9 45.3	9 46.9	9 18.6	0.1 0.1	6.1 4.0	12.1 8.0
02	9 45.5	9 47.1	9 18.8	0.2 0.1	6.2 4.1	12.2 8.0
03	9 45.8	9 47.4	9 19.1	0.3 0.2	6.3 4.1	12.3 8.1
04	9 46.0	9 47.6	9 19.3	0.4 0.3	6.4 4.2	12.4 8.2
05	9 46.3	9 47.9	9 19.5	0.5 0.3	6.5 4.3	12.5 8.2
06	9 46.5	9 48.1	9 19.8	0.6 0.4	6.6 4.3	12.6 8.3
07	9 46.8	9 48.4	9 20.0	0.7 0.5	6.7 4.4	12.7 8.4
08	9 47.0	9 48.6	9 20.3	0.8 0.5	6.8 4.5	12.8 8.4
09	9 47.3	9 48.9	9 20.5	0.9 0.6	6.9 4.5	12.9 8.5
10	9 47.5	9 49.1	9 20.7	1.0 0.7	7.0 4.6	13.0 8.6
11	9 47.8	9 49.4	9 21.0	1.1 0.7	7.1 4.7	13.1 8.6
12	9 48.0	9 49.6	9 21.2	1.2 0.8	7.2 4.7	13.2 8.7
13	9 48.3	9 49.9	9 21.5	1.3 0.9	7.3 4.8	13.3 8.8
14	9 48.5	9 50.1	9 21.7	1.4 0.9	7.4 4.9	13.4 8.8
15	9 48.8	9 50.4	9 21.9	1.5 1.0	7.5 4.9	13.5 8.9
16	9 49.0	9 50.6	9 22.2	1.6 1.1	7.6 5.0	13.6 9.0
17	9 49.3	9 50.9	9 22.4	1.7 1.1	7.7 5.1	13.7 9.0
18	9 49.5	9 51.1	9 22.6	1.8 1.2	7.8 5.1	13.8 9.1
19	9 49.8	9 51.4	9 22.9	1.9 1.3	7.9 5.2	13.9 9.2
20	9 50.0	9 51.6	9 23.1	2.0 1.3	8.0 5.3	14.0 9.2
21	9 50.3	9 51.9	9 23.4	2.1 1.4	8.1 5.3	14.1 9.3
22	9 50.5	9 52.1	9 23.6	2.2 1.4	8.2 5.4	14.2 9.3
23	9 50.8	9 52.4	9 23.8	2.3 1.5	8.3 5.5	14.3 9.4
24	9 51.0	9 52.6	9 24.1	2.4 1.6	8.4 5.5	14.4 9.5
25	9 51.3	9 52.9	9 24.3	2.5 1.6	8.5 5.6	14.5 9.5
26	9 51.5	9 53.1	9 24.6	2.6 1.7	8.6 5.7	14.6 9.6
27	9 51.8	9 53.4	9 24.8	2.7 1.8	8.7 5.7	14.7 9.6
28	9 52.0	9 53.6	9 25.0	2.8 1.8	8.8 5.8	14.8 9.7
29	9 52.3	9 53.9	9 25.3	2.9 1.9	8.9 5.9	14.9 9.8
30	9 52.5	9 54.1	9 25.5	3.0 2.0	9.0 5.9	15.0 9.9
31	9 52.8	9 54.4	9 25.7	3.1 2.0	9.1 6.0	15.1 9.9
32	9 53.0	9 54.6	9 26.0	3.2 2.1	9.2 6.1	15.2 10.0
33	9 53.3	9 54.9	9 26.2	3.3 2.2	9.3 6.1	15.3 10.1
34	9 53.5	9 55.1	9 26.5	3.4 2.2	9.4 6.2	15.4 10.1
35	9 53.8	9 55.4	9 26.7	3.5 2.3	9.5 6.3	15.5 10.2
36	9 54.0	9 55.6	9 26.9	3.6 2.4	9.6 6.3	15.6 10.2
37	9 54.3	9 55.9	9 27.2	3.7 2.4	9.7 6.4	15.7 10.3
38	9 54.5	9 56.1	9 27.4	3.8 2.5	9.8 6.5	15.8 10.4
39	9 54.8	9 56.4	9 27.7	3.9 2.6	9.9 6.5	15.9 10.5
40	9 55.0	9 56.6	9 27.9	4.0 2.6	10.0 6.6	16.0 10.5
41	9 55.3	9 56.9	9 28.1	4.1 2.7	10.1 6.6	16.1 10.6
42	9 55.5	9 57.1	9 28.4	4.2 2.8	10.2 6.7	16.2 10.7
43	9 55.8	9 57.4	9 28.6	4.3 2.8	10.3 6.8	16.3 10.7
44	9 56.0	9 57.6	9 28.8	4.4 2.9	10.4 6.8	16.4 10.8
45	9 56.3	9 57.9	9 29.1	4.5 3.0	10.5 6.9	16.5 10.9
46	9 56.5	9 58.1	9 29.3	4.6 3.0	10.6 7.0	16.6 10.9
47	9 56.8	9 58.4	9 29.6	4.7 3.1	10.7 7.0	16.7 11.0
48	9 57.0	9 58.6	9 29.8	4.8 3.2	10.8 7.1	16.8 11.1
49	9 57.3	9 58.9	9 30.0	4.9 3.2	10.9 7.2	16.9 11.1
50	9 57.5	9 59.1	9 30.3	5.0 3.3	11.0 7.2	17.0 11.2
51	9 57.8	9 59.4	9 30.5	5.1 3.4	11.1 7.3	17.1 11.3
52	9 58.0	9 59.6	9 30.8	5.2 3.4	11.2 7.4	17.2 11.3
53	9 58.3	9 59.9	9 31.0	5.3 3.5	11.3 7.4	17.3 11.4
54	9 58.5	10 00.1	9 31.2	5.4 3.6	11.4 7.5	17.4 11.5
55	9 58.8	10 00.4	9 31.5	5.5 3.6	11.5 7.6	17.5 11.5
56	9 59.0	10 00.6	9 31.7	5.6 3.7	11.6 7.6	17.6 11.6
57	9 59.3	10 00.9	9 32.0	5.7 3.8	11.7 7.7	17.7 11.7
58	9 59.5	10 01.1	9 32.2	5.8 3.8	11.8 7.8	17.8 11.7
59	9 59.8	10 01.4	9 32.4	5.9 3.9	11.9 7.8	17.9 11.8
60	10 00.0	10 01.6	9 32.7	6.0 4.0	12.0 7.9	18.0 11.9

INCREMENTS AND CORRECTIONS

40m   **41m**

m 40	SUN PLANETS	ARIES	MOON	v or Corrⁿ d	v or Corrⁿ d	v or Corrⁿ d	m 41	SUN PLANETS	ARIES	MOON	v or Corrⁿ d	v or Corrⁿ d	v or Corrⁿ d
s	° ′	° ′	° ′	′ ′	′ ′	′ ′	s	° ′	° ′	° ′	′ ′	′ ′	′ ′
00	10 00.0	10 01.6	9 32.7	0.0 0.0	6.0 4.1	12.0 8.1	00	10 15.0	10 16.7	9 47.0	0.0 0.0	6.0 4.2	12.0 8.3
01	10 00.3	10 01.9	9 32.9	0.1 0.1	6.1 4.1	12.1 8.2	01	10 15.3	10 16.9	9 47.2	0.1 0.1	6.1 4.2	12.1 8.4
02	10 00.5	10 02.1	9 33.1	0.2 0.1	6.2 4.2	12.2 8.2	02	10 15.5	10 17.2	9 47.5	0.2 0.1	6.2 4.3	12.2 8.4
03	10 00.8	10 02.4	9 33.4	0.3 0.2	6.3 4.3	12.3 8.3	03	10 15.8	10 17.4	9 47.7	0.3 0.2	6.3 4.4	12.3 8.5
04	10 01.0	10 02.6	9 33.6	0.4 0.3	6.4 4.3	12.4 8.4	04	10 16.0	10 17.7	9 47.9	0.4 0.3	6.4 4.4	12.4 8.6
05	10 01.3	10 02.9	9 33.9	0.5 0.3	6.5 4.4	12.5 8.4	05	10 16.3	10 17.9	9 48.2	0.5 0.3	6.5 4.5	12.5 8.6
06	10 01.5	10 03.1	9 34.1	0.6 0.4	6.6 4.5	12.6 8.5	06	10 16.5	10 18.2	9 48.4	0.6 0.4	6.6 4.6	12.6 8.7
07	10 01.8	10 03.4	9 34.3	0.7 0.5	6.7 4.5	12.7 8.6	07	10 16.8	10 18.4	9 48.7	0.7 0.5	6.7 4.6	12.7 8.8
08	10 02.0	10 03.6	9 34.6	0.8 0.5	6.8 4.6	12.8 8.6	08	10 17.0	10 18.7	9 48.9	0.8 0.6	6.8 4.7	12.8 8.9
09	10 02.3	10 03.9	9 34.8	0.9 0.6	6.9 4.7	12.9 8.7	09	10 17.3	10 18.9	9 49.1	0.9 0.6	6.9 4.8	12.9 8.9
10	10 02.5	10 04.1	9 35.1	1.0 0.7	7.0 4.7	13.0 8.8	10	10 17.5	10 19.2	9 49.4	1.0 0.7	7.0 4.8	13.0 9.0
11	10 02.8	10 04.4	9 35.3	1.1 0.7	7.1 4.8	13.1 8.8	11	10 17.8	10 19.4	9 49.6	1.1 0.8	7.1 4.9	13.1 9.1
12	10 03.0	10 04.7	9 35.5	1.2 0.8	7.2 4.9	13.2 8.9	12	10 18.0	10 19.7	9 49.8	1.2 0.8	7.2 5.0	13.2 9.1
13	10 03.3	10 04.9	9 35.8	1.3 0.9	7.3 4.9	13.3 9.0	13	10 18.3	10 19.9	9 50.1	1.3 0.9	7.3 5.0	13.3 9.2
14	10 03.5	10 05.2	9 36.0	1.4 0.9	7.4 5.0	13.4 9.0	14	10 18.5	10 20.2	9 50.3	1.4 1.0	7.4 5.1	13.4 9.3
15	10 03.8	10 05.4	9 36.2	1.5 1.0	7.5 5.1	13.5 9.1	15	10 18.8	10 20.4	9 50.6	1.5 1.0	7.5 5.2	13.5 9.3
16	10 04.0	10 05.7	9 36.5	1.6 1.1	7.6 5.1	13.6 9.2	16	10 19.0	10 20.7	9 50.8	1.6 1.1	7.6 5.3	13.6 9.4
17	10 04.3	10 05.9	9 36.7	1.7 1.1	7.7 5.2	13.7 9.2	17	10 19.3	10 20.9	9 51.0	1.7 1.2	7.7 5.3	13.7 9.5
18	10 04.5	10 06.2	9 37.0	1.8 1.2	7.8 5.3	13.8 9.3	18	10 19.5	10 21.2	9 51.3	1.8 1.2	7.8 5.4	13.8 9.5
19	10 04.8	10 06.4	9 37.2	1.9 1.3	7.9 5.3	13.9 9.4	19	10 19.8	10 21.4	9 51.5	1.9 1.3	7.9 5.5	13.9 9.6
20	10 05.0	10 06.7	9 37.4	2.0 1.4	8.0 5.4	14.0 9.5	20	10 20.0	10 21.7	9 51.8	2.0 1.4	8.0 5.5	14.0 9.7
21	10 05.3	10 06.9	9 37.7	2.1 1.4	8.1 5.5	14.1 9.5	21	10 20.3	10 21.9	9 52.0	2.1 1.5	8.1 5.6	14.1 9.8
22	10 05.5	10 07.2	9 37.9	2.2 1.5	8.2 5.5	14.2 9.6	22	10 20.5	10 22.2	9 52.2	2.2 1.5	8.2 5.7	14.2 9.8
23	10 05.8	10 07.4	9 38.2	2.3 1.6	8.3 5.6	14.3 9.7	23	10 20.8	10 22.4	9 52.5	2.3 1.6	8.3 5.7	14.3 9.9
24	10 06.0	10 07.7	9 38.4	2.4 1.6	8.4 5.7	14.4 9.7	24	10 21.0	10 22.7	9 52.7	2.4 1.7	8.4 5.8	14.4 10.0
25	10 06.3	10 07.9	9 38.6	2.5 1.7	8.5 5.7	14.5 9.8	25	10 21.3	10 23.0	9 52.9	2.5 1.7	8.5 5.9	14.5 10.0
26	10 06.5	10 08.2	9 38.9	2.6 1.8	8.6 5.8	14.6 9.9	26	10 21.5	10 23.2	9 53.2	2.6 1.8	8.6 5.9	14.6 10.1
27	10 06.8	10 08.4	9 39.1	2.7 1.8	8.7 5.9	14.7 9.9	27	10 21.8	10 23.5	9 53.4	2.7 1.9	8.7 6.0	14.7 10.2
28	10 07.0	10 08.7	9 39.3	2.8 1.9	8.8 5.9	14.8 10.0	28	10 22.0	10 23.7	9 53.7	2.8 1.9	8.8 6.1	14.8 10.2
29	10 07.3	10 08.9	9 39.6	2.9 2.0	8.9 6.0	14.9 10.1	29	10 22.3	10 24.0	9 53.9	2.9 2.0	8.9 6.2	14.9 10.3
30	10 07.5	10 09.2	9 39.8	3.0 2.0	9.0 6.1	15.0 10.1	30	10 22.5	10 24.2	9 54.1	3.0 2.1	9.0 6.2	15.0 10.4
31	10 07.8	10 09.4	9 40.1	3.1 2.1	9.1 6.1	15.1 10.2	31	10 22.8	10 24.5	9 54.4	3.1 2.1	9.1 6.3	15.1 10.4
32	10 08.0	10 09.7	9 40.3	3.2 2.2	9.2 6.2	15.2 10.3	32	10 23.0	10 24.7	9 54.6	3.2 2.2	9.2 6.4	15.2 10.5
33	10 08.3	10 09.9	9 40.5	3.3 2.2	9.3 6.3	15.3 10.3	33	10 23.3	10 25.0	9 54.9	3.3 2.3	9.3 6.4	15.3 10.6
34	10 08.5	10 10.2	9 40.8	3.4 2.3	9.4 6.3	15.4 10.4	34	10 23.5	10 25.2	9 55.1	3.4 2.4	9.4 6.5	15.4 10.7
35	10 08.8	10 10.4	9 41.0	3.5 2.4	9.5 6.4	15.5 10.5	35	10 23.8	10 25.5	9 55.3	3.5 2.4	9.5 6.6	15.5 10.7
36	10 09.0	10 10.7	9 41.3	3.6 2.4	9.6 6.5	15.6 10.5	36	10 24.0	10 25.7	9 55.6	3.6 2.5	9.6 6.6	15.6 10.8
37	10 09.3	10 10.9	9 41.5	3.7 2.5	9.7 6.5	15.7 10.6	37	10 24.3	10 26.0	9 55.8	3.7 2.6	9.7 6.7	15.7 10.9
38	10 09.5	10 11.2	9 41.7	3.8 2.6	9.8 6.6	15.8 10.7	38	10 24.5	10 26.2	9 56.1	3.8 2.6	9.8 6.8	15.8 10.9
39	10 09.8	10 11.4	9 42.0	3.9 2.6	9.9 6.7	15.9 10.7	39	10 24.8	10 26.5	9 56.3	3.9 2.7	9.9 6.8	15.9 11.0
40	10 10.0	10 11.7	9 42.2	4.0 2.7	10.0 6.8	16.0 10.8	40	10 25.0	10 26.7	9 56.5	4.0 2.8	10.0 6.9	16.0 11.1
41	10 10.3	10 11.9	9 42.4	4.1 2.8	10.1 6.8	16.1 10.9	41	10 25.3	10 27.0	9 56.8	4.1 2.8	10.1 7.0	16.1 11.1
42	10 10.5	10 12.2	9 42.7	4.2 2.8	10.2 6.9	16.2 10.9	42	10 25.5	10 27.2	9 57.0	4.2 2.9	10.2 7.1	16.2 11.2
43	10 10.8	10 12.4	9 42.9	4.3 2.9	10.3 7.0	16.3 11.0	43	10 25.8	10 27.5	9 57.2	4.3 3.0	10.3 7.1	16.3 11.3
44	10 11.0	10 12.7	9 43.2	4.4 3.0	10.4 7.0	16.4 11.1	44	10 26.0	10 27.7	9 57.5	4.4 3.0	10.4 7.2	16.4 11.3
45	10 11.3	10 12.9	9 43.4	4.5 3.0	10.5 7.1	16.5 11.1	45	10 26.3	10 28.0	9 57.7	4.5 3.1	10.5 7.3	16.5 11.4
46	10 11.5	10 13.2	9 43.6	4.6 3.1	10.6 7.2	16.6 11.2	46	10 26.5	10 28.2	9 58.0	4.6 3.2	10.6 7.3	16.6 11.5
47	10 11.8	10 13.4	9 43.9	4.7 3.2	10.7 7.2	16.7 11.3	47	10 26.8	10 28.5	9 58.2	4.7 3.3	10.7 7.4	16.7 11.6
48	10 12.0	10 13.7	9 44.1	4.8 3.2	10.8 7.3	16.8 11.3	48	10 27.0	10 28.7	9 58.4	4.8 3.3	10.8 7.5	16.8 11.6
49	10 12.3	10 13.9	9 44.4	4.9 3.3	10.9 7.4	16.9 11.4	49	10 27.3	10 29.0	9 58.7	4.9 3.4	10.9 7.5	16.9 11.7
50	10 12.5	10 14.2	9 44.6	5.0 3.4	11.0 7.4	17.0 11.5	50	10 27.5	10 29.2	9 58.9	5.0 3.5	11.0 7.6	17.0 11.8
51	10 12.8	10 14.4	9 44.8	5.1 3.4	11.1 7.5	17.1 11.5	51	10 27.8	10 29.5	9 59.2	5.1 3.5	11.1 7.7	17.1 11.8
52	10 13.0	10 14.7	9 45.1	5.2 3.5	11.2 7.6	17.2 11.6	52	10 28.0	10 29.7	9 59.4	5.2 3.6	11.2 7.7	17.2 11.9
53	10 13.3	10 14.9	9 45.3	5.3 3.6	11.3 7.6	17.3 11.7	53	10 28.3	10 30.0	9 59.6	5.3 3.7	11.3 7.8	17.3 12.0
54	10 13.5	10 15.2	9 45.6	5.4 3.6	11.4 7.7	17.4 11.7	54	10 28.5	10 30.2	9 59.9	5.4 3.7	11.4 7.9	17.4 12.0
55	10 13.8	10 15.4	9 45.8	5.5 3.7	11.5 7.8	17.5 11.8	55	10 28.8	10 30.5	10 00.1	5.5 3.8	11.5 8.0	17.5 12.1
56	10 14.0	10 15.7	9 46.0	5.6 3.8	11.6 7.8	17.6 11.9	56	10 29.0	10 30.7	10 00.3	5.6 3.9	11.6 8.0	17.6 12.2
57	10 14.3	10 15.9	9 46.3	5.7 3.8	11.7 7.9	17.7 11.9	57	10 29.3	10 31.0	10 00.6	5.7 3.9	11.7 8.1	17.7 12.2
58	10 14.5	10 16.2	9 46.5	5.8 3.9	11.8 8.0	17.8 12.0	58	10 29.5	10 31.2	10 00.8	5.8 4.0	11.8 8.2	17.8 12.3
59	10 14.8	10 16.4	9 46.7	5.9 4.0	11.9 8.0	17.9 12.1	59	10 29.8	10 31.5	10 01.1	5.9 4.1	11.9 8.2	17.9 12.4
60	10 15.0	10 16.7	9 47.0	6.0 4.1	12.0 8.1	18.0 12.2	60	10 30.0	10 31.7	10 01.3	6.0 4.2	12.0 8.3	18.0 12.5

42m   INCREMENTS AND CORRECTIONS   43m

m 42	SUN PLANETS	ARIES	MOON	v or Corrⁿ d		v or Corrⁿ d		v or Corrⁿ d	
s	° ′	° ′	° ′	′	′	′	′	′	′
00	10 30.0	10 31.7	10 01.3	0.0	0.0	6.0	4.3	12.0	8.5
01	10 30.3	10 32.0	10 01.5	0.1	0.1	6.1	4.3	12.1	8.6
02	10 30.5	10 32.2	10 01.8	0.2	0.1	6.2	4.4	12.2	8.6
03	10 30.8	10 32.5	10 02.0	0.3	0.2	6.3	4.5	12.3	8.7
04	10 31.0	10 32.7	10 02.3	0.4	0.3	6.4	4.5	12.4	8.8
05	10 31.3	10 33.0	10 02.5	0.5	0.4	6.5	4.6	12.5	8.9
06	10 31.5	10 33.2	10 02.7	0.6	0.4	6.6	4.7	12.6	8.9
07	10 31.8	10 33.5	10 03.0	0.7	0.5	6.7	4.7	12.7	9.0
08	10 32.0	10 33.7	10 03.2	0.8	0.6	6.8	4.8	12.8	9.1
09	10 32.3	10 34.0	10 03.4	0.9	0.6	6.9	4.9	12.9	9.1
10	10 32.5	10 34.2	10 03.7	1.0	0.7	7.0	5.0	13.0	9.2
11	10 32.8	10 34.5	10 03.9	1.1	0.8	7.1	5.0	13.1	9.3
12	10 33.0	10 34.7	10 04.2	1.2	0.9	7.2	5.1	13.2	9.4
13	10 33.3	10 35.0	10 04.4	1.3	0.9	7.3	5.2	13.3	9.4
14	10 33.5	10 35.2	10 04.6	1.4	1.0	7.4	5.2	13.4	9.5
15	10 33.8	10 35.5	10 04.9	1.5	1.1	7.5	5.3	13.5	9.6
16	10 34.0	10 35.7	10 05.1	1.6	1.1	7.6	5.4	13.6	9.6
17	10 34.3	10 36.0	10 05.4	1.7	1.2	7.7	5.5	13.7	9.7
18	10 34.5	10 36.2	10 05.6	1.8	1.3	7.8	5.5	13.8	9.8
19	10 34.8	10 36.5	10 05.8	1.9	1.3	7.9	5.6	13.9	9.8
20	10 35.0	10 36.7	10 06.1	2.0	1.4	8.0	5.7	14.0	9.9
21	10 35.3	10 37.0	10 06.3	2.1	1.5	8.1	5.7	14.1	10.0
22	10 35.5	10 37.2	10 06.5	2.2	1.6	8.2	5.8	14.2	10.1
23	10 35.8	10 37.5	10 06.8	2.3	1.6	8.3	5.9	14.3	10.1
24	10 36.0	10 37.7	10 07.0	2.4	1.7	8.4	6.0	14.4	10.2
25	10 36.3	10 38.0	10 07.3	2.5	1.8	8.5	6.0	14.5	10.3
26	10 36.5	10 38.2	10 07.5	2.6	1.8	8.6	6.1	14.6	10.3
27	10 36.8	10 38.5	10 07.7	2.7	1.9	8.7	6.2	14.7	10.4
28	10 37.0	10 38.7	10 08.0	2.8	2.0	8.8	6.2	14.8	10.5
29	10 37.3	10 39.0	10 08.2	2.9	2.1	8.9	6.3	14.9	10.6
30	10 37.5	10 39.2	10 08.5	3.0	2.1	9.0	6.4	15.0	10.6
31	10 37.8	10 39.5	10 08.7	3.1	2.2	9.1	6.4	15.1	10.7
32	10 38.0	10 39.7	10 08.9	3.2	2.3	9.2	6.5	15.2	10.8
33	10 38.3	10 40.0	10 09.2	3.3	2.3	9.3	6.6	15.3	10.8
34	10 38.5	10 40.2	10 09.4	3.4	2.4	9.4	6.7	15.4	10.9
35	10 38.8	10 40.5	10 09.7	3.5	2.5	9.5	6.7	15.5	11.0
36	10 39.0	10 40.7	10 09.9	3.6	2.6	9.6	6.8	15.6	11.1
37	10 39.3	10 41.0	10 10.1	3.7	2.6	9.7	6.9	15.7	11.1
38	10 39.5	10 41.3	10 10.4	3.8	2.7	9.8	6.9	15.8	11.2
39	10 39.8	10 41.5	10 10.6	3.9	2.8	9.9	7.0	15.9	11.3
40	10 40.0	10 41.8	10 10.8	4.0	2.8	10.0	7.1	16.0	11.3
41	10 40.3	10 42.0	10 11.1	4.1	2.9	10.1	7.2	16.1	11.4
42	10 40.5	10 42.3	10 11.3	4.2	3.0	10.2	7.2	16.2	11.5
43	10 40.8	10 42.5	10 11.6	4.3	3.0	10.3	7.3	16.3	11.5
44	10 41.0	10 42.8	10 11.8	4.4	3.1	10.4	7.4	16.4	11.6
45	10 41.3	10 43.0	10 12.0	4.5	3.2	10.5	7.4	16.5	11.7
46	10 41.5	10 43.3	10 12.3	4.6	3.3	10.6	7.5	16.6	11.8
47	10 41.8	10 43.5	10 12.5	4.7	3.3	10.7	7.6	16.7	11.8
48	10 42.0	10 43.8	10 12.8	4.8	3.4	10.8	7.7	16.8	11.9
49	10 42.3	10 44.0	10 13.0	4.9	3.5	10.9	7.7	16.9	12.0
50	10 42.5	10 44.3	10 13.2	5.0	3.5	11.0	7.8	17.0	12.0
51	10 42.8	10 44.5	10 13.5	5.1	3.6	11.1	7.9	17.1	12.1
52	10 43.0	10 44.8	10 13.7	5.2	3.7	11.2	7.9	17.2	12.2
53	10 43.3	10 45.0	10 13.9	5.3	3.8	11.3	8.0	17.3	12.3
54	10 43.5	10 45.3	10 14.2	5.4	3.8	11.4	8.1	17.4	12.3
55	10 43.8	10 45.5	10 14.4	5.5	3.9	11.5	8.1	17.5	12.4
56	10 44.0	10 45.8	10 14.7	5.6	4.0	11.6	8.2	17.6	12.5
57	10 44.3	10 46.0	10 14.9	5.7	4.0	11.7	8.3	17.7	12.5
58	10 44.5	10 46.3	10 15.1	5.8	4.1	11.8	8.4	17.8	12.6
59	10 44.8	10 46.5	10 15.4	5.9	4.2	11.9	8.4	17.9	12.7
60	10 45.0	10 46.8	10 15.6	6.0	4.3	12.0	8.5	18.0	12.8

m 43	SUN PLANETS	ARIES	MOON	v or Corrⁿ d		v or Corrⁿ d		v or Corrⁿ d	
s	° ′	° ′	° ′	′	′	′	′	′	′
00	10 45.0	10 46.8	10 15.6	0.0	0.0	6.0	4.4	12.0	8.7
01	10 45.3	10 47.0	10 15.9	0.1	0.1	6.1	4.4	12.1	8.8
02	10 45.5	10 47.3	10 16.1	0.2	0.1	6.2	4.5	12.2	8.8
03	10 45.8	10 47.5	10 16.3	0.3	0.2	6.3	4.6	12.3	8.9
04	10 46.0	10 47.8	10 16.6	0.4	0.3	6.4	4.6	12.4	9.0
05	10 46.3	10 48.0	10 16.8	0.5	0.4	6.5	4.7	12.5	9.1
06	10 46.5	10 48.3	10 17.0	0.6	0.4	6.6	4.8	12.6	9.1
07	10 46.8	10 48.5	10 17.3	0.7	0.5	6.7	4.9	12.7	9.2
08	10 47.0	10 48.8	10 17.5	0.8	0.6	6.8	4.9	12.8	9.3
09	10 47.3	10 48.0	10 17.8	0.9	0.7	6.9	5.0	12.9	9.4
10	10 47.5	10 49.3	10 18.0	1.0	0.7	7.0	5.1	13.0	9.4
11	10 47.8	10 49.5	10 18.2	1.1	0.8	7.1	5.1	13.1	9.5
12	10 48.0	10 49.8	10 18.5	1.2	0.9	7.2	5.2	13.2	9.6
13	10 48.3	10 50.0	10 18.7	1.3	0.9	7.3	5.3	13.3	9.6
14	10 48.5	10 50.3	10 19.0	1.4	1.0	7.4	5.4	13.4	9.7
15	10 48.8	10 50.5	10 19.2	1.5	1.1	7.5	5.4	13.5	9.8
16	10 49.0	10 50.8	10 19.4	1.6	1.2	7.6	5.5	13.6	9.9
17	10 49.3	10 51.0	10 19.7	1.7	1.2	7.7	5.6	13.7	9.9
18	10 49.5	10 51.3	10 19.9	1.8	1.3	7.8	5.7	13.8	10.0
19	10 49.8	10 51.5	10 20.2	1.9	1.4	7.9	5.7	13.9	10.1
20	10 50.0	10 51.8	10 20.4	2.0	1.5	8.0	5.8	14.0	10.2
21	10 50.3	10 52.0	10 20.6	2.1	1.5	8.1	5.9	14.1	10.2
22	10 50.5	10 52.3	10 20.9	2.2	1.6	8.2	5.9	14.2	10.3
23	10 50.8	10 52.5	10 21.1	2.3	1.7	8.3	6.0	14.3	10.4
24	10 51.0	10 52.8	10 21.3	2.4	1.7	8.4	6.1	14.4	10.4
25	10 51.3	10 53.0	10 21.6	2.5	1.8	8.5	6.2	14.5	10.5
26	10 51.5	10 53.3	10 21.8	2.6	1.9	8.6	6.2	14.6	10.6
27	10 51.8	10 53.5	10 22.1	2.7	2.0	8.7	6.3	14.7	10.7
28	10 52.0	10 53.8	10 22.3	2.8	2.0	8.8	6.4	14.8	10.7
29	10 52.3	10 54.0	10 22.5	2.9	2.1	8.9	6.5	14.9	10.8
30	10 52.5	10 54.3	10 22.8	3.0	2.2	9.0	6.5	15.0	10.9
31	10 52.8	10 54.5	10 23.0	3.1	2.2	9.1	6.6	15.1	10.9
32	10 53.0	10 54.8	10 23.3	3.2	2.3	9.2	6.7	15.2	11.0
33	10 53.3	10 55.0	10 23.5	3.3	2.4	9.3	6.7	15.3	11.1
34	10 53.5	10 55.3	10 23.7	3.4	2.5	9.4	6.8	15.4	11.2
35	10 53.8	10 55.5	10 24.0	3.5	2.5	9.5	6.9	15.5	11.2
36	10 54.0	10 55.8	10 24.2	3.6	2.6	9.6	7.0	15.6	11.3
37	10 54.3	10 56.0	10 24.4	3.7	2.7	9.7	7.0	15.7	11.4
38	10 54.5	10 56.3	10 24.7	3.8	2.8	9.8	7.1	15.8	11.5
39	10 54.8	10 56.5	10 24.9	3.9	2.8	9.9	7.2	15.9	11.5
40	10 55.0	10 56.8	10 25.2	4.0	2.9	10.0	7.3	16.0	11.6
41	10 55.3	10 57.0	10 25.4	4.1	3.0	10.1	7.3	16.1	11.7
42	10 55.5	10 57.3	10 25.6	4.2	3.0	10.2	7.4	16.2	11.7
43	10 55.8	10 57.5	10 25.9	4.3	3.1	10.3	7.5	16.3	11.8
44	10 56.0	10 57.8	10 26.1	4.4	3.2	10.4	7.5	16.4	11.9
45	10 56.3	10 58.0	10 26.4	4.5	3.3	10.5	7.6	16.5	12.0
46	10 56.5	10 58.3	10 26.6	4.6	3.3	10.6	7.7	16.6	12.0
47	10 56.8	10 58.5	10 26.8	4.7	3.4	10.7	7.8	16.7	12.1
48	10 57.0	10 58.8	10 27.1	4.8	3.5	10.8	7.8	16.8	12.2
49	10 57.3	10 59.0	10 27.3	4.9	3.6	10.9	7.9	16.9	12.3
50	10 57.5	10 59.3	10 27.5	5.0	3.6	11.0	8.0	17.0	12.3
51	10 57.8	10 59.6	10 27.8	5.1	3.7	11.1	8.0	17.1	12.4
52	10 58.0	10 59.8	10 28.0	5.2	3.8	11.2	8.1	17.2	12.5
53	10 58.3	11 00.1	10 28.3	5.3	3.8	11.3	8.2	17.3	12.5
54	10 58.5	11 00.3	10 28.5	5.4	3.9	11.4	8.3	17.4	12.6
55	10 58.8	11 00.6	10 28.7	5.5	4.0	11.5	8.3	17.5	12.7
56	10 59.0	11 00.8	10 29.0	5.6	4.1	11.6	8.4	17.6	12.8
57	10 59.3	11 01.1	10 29.2	5.7	4.1	11.7	8.5	17.7	12.8
58	10 59.5	11 01.3	10 29.5	5.8	4.2	11.8	8.6	17.8	12.9
59	10 59.8	11 01.6	10 29.7	5.9	4.3	11.9	8.6	17.9	13.0
60	11 00.0	11 01.8	10 29.9	6.0	4.4	12.0	8.7	18.0	13.1

44m INCREMENTS AND CORRECTIONS 45m

44 s	SUN PLANETS	ARIES	MOON	v or Corrⁿ d	v or Corrⁿ d	v or Corrⁿ d
00	11 00.0	11 01.8	10 29.9	0.0 0.0	6.0 4.5	12.0 8.9
01	11 00.3	11 02.1	10 30.2	0.1 0.1	6.1 4.5	12.1 9.0
02	11 00.5	11 02.3	10 30.4	0.2 0.1	6.2 4.6	12.2 9.0
03	11 00.8	11 02.6	10 30.6	0.3 0.2	6.3 4.7	12.3 9.1
04	11 01.0	11 02.8	10 30.9	0.4 0.3	6.4 4.7	12.4 9.2
05	11 01.3	11 03.1	10 31.1	0.5 0.4	6.5 4.8	12.5 9.2
06	11 01.5	11 03.3	10 31.4	0.6 0.4	6.6 4.9	12.6 9.3
07	11 01.8	11 03.6	10 31.6	0.7 0.5	6.7 5.0	12.7 9.4
08	11 02.0	11 03.8	10 31.8	0.8 0.6	6.8 5.0	12.8 9.5
09	11 02.3	11 04.1	10 32.1	0.9 0.7	6.9 5.1	12.9 9.6
10	11 02.5	11 04.3	10 32.3	1.0 0.7	7.0 5.2	13.0 9.6
11	11 02.8	11 04.6	10 32.6	1.1 0.8	7.1 5.3	13.1 9.7
12	11 03.0	11 04.8	10 32.8	1.2 0.9	7.2 5.4	13.2 9.8
13	11 03.3	11 05.1	10 33.0	1.3 1.0	7.3 5.5	13.3 9.9
14	11 03.5	11 05.3	10 33.3	1.4 1.0	7.4 5.5	13.4 9.9
15	11 03.8	11 05.6	10 33.5	1.5 1.1	7.5 5.6	13.5 10.0
16	11 04.0	11 05.8	10 33.8	1.6 1.2	7.6 5.6	13.6 10.1
17	11 04.3	11 06.1	10 34.0	1.7 1.3	7.7 5.7	13.7 10.2
18	11 04.5	11 06.3	10 34.2	1.8 1.3	7.8 5.8	13.8 10.2
19	11 04.8	11 06.6	10 34.5	1.9 1.4	7.9 5.9	13.9 10.3
20	11 05.0	11 06.8	10 34.7	2.0 1.5	8.0 5.9	14.0 10.4
21	11 05.3	11 07.1	10 34.9	2.1 1.6	8.1 6.0	14.1 10.5
22	11 05.5	11 07.3	10 35.2	2.2 1.6	8.2 6.1	14.2 10.5
23	11 05.8	11 07.6	10 35.4	2.3 1.7	8.3 6.2	14.3 10.6
24	11 06.0	11 07.8	10 35.7	2.4 1.8	8.4 6.2	14.4 10.7
25	11 06.3	11 08.1	10 35.9	2.5 1.9	8.5 6.3	14.5 10.8
26	11 06.5	11 08.3	10 36.1	2.6 1.9	8.6 6.4	14.6 10.8
27	11 06.8	11 08.6	10 36.4	2.7 2.0	8.7 6.5	14.7 10.9
28	11 07.0	11 08.8	10 36.6	2.8 2.1	8.8 6.5	14.8 11.0
29	11 07.3	11 09.1	10 36.9	2.9 2.2	8.9 6.6	14.9 11.1
30	11 07.5	11 09.3	10 37.1	3.0 2.2	9.0 6.7	15.0 11.1
31	11 07.8	11 09.6	10 37.3	3.1 2.3	9.1 6.7	15.1 11.2
32	11 08.0	11 09.8	10 37.6	3.2 2.4	9.2 6.8	15.2 11.3
33	11 08.3	11 10.1	10 37.8	3.3 2.4	9.3 6.9	15.3 11.3
34	11 08.5	11 10.3	10 38.0	3.4 2.5	9.4 7.0	15.4 11.4
35	11 08.8	11 10.6	10 38.3	3.5 2.6	9.5 7.0	15.5 11.5
36	11 09.0	11 10.8	10 38.5	3.6 2.7	9.6 7.1	15.6 11.6
37	11 09.3	11 11.1	10 38.8	3.7 2.7	9.7 7.2	15.7 11.6
38	11 09.5	11 11.3	10 39.0	3.8 2.8	9.8 7.3	15.8 11.7
39	11 09.8	11 11.6	10 39.2	3.9 2.9	9.9 7.3	15.9 11.8
40	11 10.0	11 11.8	10 39.5	4.0 3.0	10.0 7.4	16.0 11.9
41	11 10.3	11 12.1	10 39.7	4.1 3.0	10.1 7.5	16.1 11.9
42	11 10.5	10 12.3	10 40.0	4.2 3.1	10.2 7.6	16.2 12.0
43	11 10.8	11 12.6	10 40.2	4.3 3.2	10.3 7.6	16.3 12.1
44	11 11.0	11 12.8	10 40.4	4.4 3.3	10.4 7.7	16.4 12.2
45	11 11.3	11 13.1	10 40.7	4.5 3.3	10.5 7.8	16.5 12.2
46	11 11.5	11 13.3	10 40.9	4.6 3.4	10.6 7.9	16.6 12.3
47	11 11.8	11 13.6	10 41.1	4.7 3.5	10.7 7.9	16.7 12.4
48	11 12.0	11 13.8	10 41.4	4.8 3.6	10.8 8.0	16.8 12.5
49	10 12.3	11 14.1	10 41.6	4.9 3.6	10.9 8.1	16.9 12.5
50	11 12.5	11 14.3	10 41.9	5.0 3.7	11.0 8.2	17.0 12.6
51	11 12.8	11 14.6	10 42.1	5.1 3.8	11.1 8.2	17.1 12.7
52	11 13.0	11 14.8	10 42.3	5.2 3.9	11.2 8.3	17.2 12.8
53	11 13.3	11 15.1	10 42.6	5.3 3.9	11.3 8.4	17.3 12.8
54	11 13.5	11 15.3	10 42.8	5.4 4.0	11.4 8.5	17.4 12.9
55	11 13.8	11 15.6	10 43.1	5.5 4.1	11.5 8.5	17.5 13.0
56	11 14.0	11 15.8	10 43.3	5.6 4.2	11.6 8.6	17.6 13.1
57	11 14.3	11 16.1	10 43.5	5.7 4.2	11.7 8.7	17.7 13.1
58	11 14.5	11 16.3	10 43.8	5.8 4.3	11.8 8.8	17.8 13.2
59	11 14.8	11 16.6	10 44.0	5.9 4.4	11.9 8.8	17.9 13.3
60	11 15.0	11 16.8	10 44.3	6.0 4.5	12.0 8.9	18.0 13.4

45 s	SUN PLANETS	ARIES	MOON	v or Corrⁿ d	v or Corrⁿ d	v or Corrⁿ d
00	11 15.0	11 16.8	10 44.3	0.0 0.0	6.0 4.6	12.0 9.1
01	11 15.3	11 17.1	10 44.5	0.1 0.1	6.1 4.6	12.1 9.2
02	11 15.5	11 17.3	10 44.7	0.2 0.2	6.2 4.7	12.2 9.3
03	11 15.8	11 17.6	10 45.0	0.3 0.2	6.3 4.8	12.3 9.3
04	11 16.0	11 17.9	10 45.2	0.4 0.3	6.4 4.9	12.4 9.4
05	11 16.3	11 18.1	10 45.4	0.5 0.4	6.5 4.9	12.5 9.5
06	11 16.5	11 18.4	10 45.7	0.6 0.5	6.6 5.0	12.6 9.6
07	11 16.8	11 18.6	10 45.9	0.7 0.5	6.7 5.1	12.7 9.6
08	11 17.0	11 18.9	10 46.2	0.8 0.6	6.8 5.2	12.8 9.7
09	11 17.3	11 19.1	10 46.4	0.9 0.7	6.9 5.2	12.9 9.8
10	11 17.5	11 19.4	10 46.6	1.0 0.8	7.0 5.3	13.0 9.9
11	11 17.8	11 19.6	10 46.9	1.1 0.8	7.1 5.4	13.1 9.9
12	11 18.0	11 19.9	10 47.1	1.2 0.9	7.2 5.5	13.2 10.0
13	11 18.3	11 20.1	10 47.4	1.3 1.0	7.3 5.5	13.3 10.1
14	11 18.5	11 20.4	10 47.6	1.4 1.1	7.4 5.6	13.4 10.2
15	11 18.8	11 20.6	10 47.8	1.5 1.1	7.5 5.7	13.5 10.2
16	11 19.0	11 20.9	10 48.1	1.6 1.2	7.6 5.8	13.6 10.3
17	11 19.3	11 21.1	10 48.3	1.7 1.3	7.7 5.8	13.7 10.4
18	11 19.5	11 21.4	10 48.5	1.8 1.4	7.8 5.9	13.8 10.5
19	11 19.8	11 21.6	10 48.8	1.9 1.4	7.9 6.0	13.9 10.5
20	11 20.0	11 21.9	10 49.0	2.0 1.5	8.0 6.1	14.0 10.6
21	11 20.3	11 22.1	10 49.3	2.1 1.6	8.1 6.1	14.1 10.7
22	11 20.5	11 22.4	10 49.5	2.2 1.7	8.2 6.2	14.2 10.8
23	11 20.8	11 22.6	10 49.7	2.3 1.7	8.3 6.3	14.3 10.8
24	11 21.0	11 22.9	10 50.0	2.4 1.8	8.4 6.4	14.4 10.9
25	11 21.3	11 23.1	10 50.2	2.5 1.9	8.5 6.4	14.5 11.0
26	11 21.5	11 23.4	10 50.5	2.6 2.0	8.6 6.5	14.6 11.1
27	11 21.8	11 23.6	10 50.7	2.7 2.0	8.7 6.6	14.7 11.1
28	11 22.0	11 23.9	10 50.9	2.8 2.1	8.8 6.7	14.8 11.2
29	11 22.3	11 24.1	10 51.2	2.9 2.2	8.9 6.7	14.9 11.3
30	11 22.5	11 24.4	10 51.4	3.0 2.3	9.0 6.8	15.0 11.4
31	11 22.8	11 24.6	10 51.6	3.1 2.4	9.1 6.9	15.1 11.5
32	11 23.0	11 24.9	10 51.9	3.2 2.4	9.2 7.0	15.2 11.5
33	11 23.3	11 25.1	10 52.1	3.3 2.5	9.3 7.1	15.3 11.6
34	11 23.5	11 25.4	10 52.4	3.4 2.6	9.4 7.1	15.4 11.7
35	11 23.8	11 25.6	10 52.6	3.5 2.7	9.5 7.2	15.5 11.8
36	11 24.0	11 25.9	10 52.8	3.6 2.7	9.6 7.3	15.6 11.8
37	11 24.3	11 26.1	10 53.1	3.7 2.8	9.7 7.4	15.7 11.9
38	11 24.5	11 26.4	10 53.3	3.8 2.9	9.8 7.4	15.8 12.0
39	11 24.8	11 26.6	10 53.6	3.9 3.0	9.9 7.5	15.9 12.1
40	11 25.0	11 26.9	10 53.8	4.0 3.0	10.0 7.6	16.0 12.1
41	11 25.3	11 27.1	10 54.0	4.1 3.1	10.1 7.7	16.1 12.2
42	11 25.5	10 27.4	10 54.3	4.2 3.2	10.2 7.7	16.2 12.3
43	11 25.8	11 27.6	10 54.5	4.3 3.3	10.3 7.8	16.3 12.4
44	11 26.0	11 27.9	10 54.7	4.4 3.3	10.4 7.9	16.4 12.4
45	11 26.3	11 28.1	10 55.0	4.5 3.4	10.5 8.0	16.5 12.5
46	11 26.5	11 28.4	10 55.2	4.6 3.5	10.6 8.0	16.6 12.6
47	11 26.8	11 28.6	10 55.5	4.7 3.6	10.7 8.1	16.7 12.7
48	11 27.0	11 28.9	10 55.7	4.8 3.6	10.8 8.2	16.8 12.7
49	10 27.3	11 29.1	10 55.9	4.9 3.7	10.9 8.3	16.9 12.8
50	11 27.5	11 29.4	10 56.2	5.0 3.8	11.0 8.3	17.0 12.9
51	11 27.8	11 29.6	10 56.4	5.1 3.9	11.1 8.4	17.1 13.0
52	11 28.0	11 29.9	10 56.7	5.2 3.9	11.2 8.5	17.2 13.0
53	11 28.3	11 30.1	10 56.9	5.3 4.0	11.3 8.6	17.3 13.1
54	11 28.5	11 30.4	10 57.1	5.4 4.1	11.4 8.6	17.4 13.2
55	11 28.8	11 30.6	10 57.4	5.5 4.2	11.5 8.7	17.5 13.3
56	11 29.0	11 30.9	10 57.6	5.6 4.2	11.6 8.8	17.6 13.3
57	11 29.3	11 31.1	10 57.9	5.7 4.3	11.7 8.9	17.7 13.4
58	11 29.5	11 31.4	10 58.1	5.8 4.4	11.8 8.9	17.8 13.5
59	11 29.8	11 31.6	10 58.3	5.9 4.5	11.9 9.0	17.9 13.6
60	11 30.0	11 31.9	10 58.6	6.0 4.6	12.0 9.1	18.0 13.7

46ᵐ INCREMENTS AND CORRECTIONS 47ᵐ

m 46 s	SUN PLANETS ° '	ARIES ° '	MOON ° '	v or Corrn d ' '	v or Corrn d ' '	v or Corrn d ' '
00	11 30.0	11 31.9	10 58.6	0.0 0.0	6.0 4.7	12.0 9.3
01	11 30.3	11 32.1	10 58.8	0.1 0.1	6.1 4.7	12.1 9.4
02	11 30.5	11 32.4	10 59.0	0.2 0.2	6.2 4.8	12.2 9.5
03	11 30.8	11 32.6	10 59.3	0.3 0.2	6.3 4.9	12.3 9.5
04	11 31.0	11 32.9	10 59.5	0.4 0.3	6.4 5.0	12.4 9.6
05	11 31.3	11 33.1	10 59.8	0.5 0.4	6.5 5.0	12.5 9.7
06	11 31.5	11 33.4	11 00.0	0.6 0.5	6.6 5.1	12.6 9.8
07	11 31.8	11 33.6	11 00.2	0.7 0.5	6.7 5.2	12.7 9.8
08	11 32.0	11 33.9	11 00.5	0.8 0.6	6.8 5.3	12.8 9.9
09	11 32.3	11 34.1	11 00.7	0.9 0.7	6.9 5.3	12.9 10.0
10	11 32.5	11 34.4	11 01.0	1.0 0.8	7.0 5.4	13.0 10.1
11	11 32.8	11 34.6	11 01.2	1.1 0.9	7.1 5.5	13.1 10.2
12	11 33.0	11 34.9	11 01.4	1.2 0.9	7.2 5.6	13.2 10.2
13	11 33.3	11 35.1	11 01.7	1.3 1.0	7.3 5.7	13.3 10.3
14	11 33.5	11 35.4	11 01.9	1.4 1.1	7.4 5.7	13.4 10.4
15	11 33.8	11 35.6	11 02.1	1.5 1.2	7.5 5.8	13.5 10.5
16	11 34.0	11 35.9	11 02.4	1.6 1.2	7.6 5.9	13.6 10.5
17	11 34.3	11 36.2	11 02.6	1.7 1.3	7.7 6.0	13.7 10.6
18	11 34.5	11 36.4	11 02.9	1.8 1.4	7.8 6.0	13.8 10.7
19	11 34.8	11 36.7	11 03.1	1.9 1.5	7.9 6.1	13.9 10.8
20	11 35.0	11 36.9	11 03.3	2.0 1.6	8.0 6.2	14.0 10.9
21	11 35.3	11 37.2	11 03.6	2.1 1.6	8.1 6.3	14.1 10.9
22	11 35.5	11 37.4	11 03.8	2.2 1.7	8.2 6.4	14.2 11.0
23	11 35.8	11 37.7	11 04.1	2.3 1.8	8.3 6.4	14.3 11.1
24	11 36.0	11 37.9	11 04.3	2.4 1.9	8.4 6.5	14.4 11.2
25	11 36.3	11 38.2	11 04.5	2.5 1.9	8.5 6.6	14.5 11.2
26	11 36.5	11 38.4	11 04.8	2.6 2.0	8.6 6.7	14.6 11.3
27	11 36.8	11 38.7	11 05.0	2.7 2.1	8.7 6.7	14.7 11.4
28	11 37.0	11 38.9	11 05.2	2.8 2.2	8.8 6.8	14.8 11.5
29	11 37.3	11 39.2	11 05.5	2.9 2.2	8.9 6.9	14.9 11.5
30	11 37.5	11 39.4	11 05.7	3.0 2.3	9.0 7.0	15.0 11.6
31	11 37.8	11 39.7	11 06.0	3.1 2.4	9.1 7.1	15.1 11.7
32	11 38.0	11 39.9	11 06.2	3.2 2.5	9.2 7.1	15.2 11.8
33	11 38.3	11 40.2	11 06.4	3.3 2.6	9.3 7.2	15.3 11.9
34	11 38.5	11 40.4	11 06.7	3.4 2.6	9.4 7.3	15.4 11.9
35	11 38.8	11 40.7	11 06.9	3.5 2.7	9.5 7.4	15.5 12.0
36	11 39.0	11 40.9	11 07.2	3.6 2.8	9.6 7.4	15.6 12.1
37	11 39.3	11 41.2	11 07.4	3.7 2.9	9.7 7.5	15.7 12.2
38	11 39.5	11 41.4	11 07.6	3.8 2.9	9.8 7.6	15.8 12.2
39	11 39.8	11 41.7	11 07.9	3.9 3.0	9.9 7.7	15.9 12.3
40	11 40.0	11 41.9	11 08.1	4.0 3.1	10.0 7.8	16.0 12.4
41	11 40.3	11 42.2	11 08.3	4.1 3.2	10.1 7.8	16.1 12.5
42	11 40.5	10 42.4	11 08.6	4.2 3.3	10.2 7.9	16.2 12.6
43	11 40.8	11 42.7	11 08.8	4.3 3.3	10.3 8.0	16.3 12.6
44	11 41.0	11 42.9	11 09.1	4.4 3.4	10.4 8.1	16.4 12.7
45	11 41.3	11 43.2	11 09.3	4.5 3.5	10.5 8.1	16.5 12.8
46	11 41.5	11 43.4	11 09.5	4.6 3.6	10.6 8.2	16.6 12.9
47	11 41.8	11 43.7	11 09.8	4.7 3.6	10.7 8.3	16.7 12.9
48	11 42.0	11 43.9	11 10.0	4.8 3.7	10.8 8.4	16.8 13.0
49	11 42.3	11 44.2	11 10.3	4.9 3.8	10.9 8.4	16.9 13.1
50	11 42.5	11 44.4	11 10.5	5.0 3.9	11.0 8.5	17.0 13.2
51	11 42.8	11 44.7	11 10.7	5.1 4.0	11.1 8.6	17.1 13.3
52	11 43.0	11 44.9	11 11.0	5.2 4.0	11.2 8.7	17.2 13.3
53	11 43.3	11 45.2	11 11.2	5.3 4.1	11.3 8.8	17.3 13.4
54	11 43.5	11 45.4	11 11.5	5.4 4.2	11.4 8.8	17.4 13.5
55	11 43.8	11 45.7	11 11.7	5.5 4.3	11.5 8.9	17.5 13.6
56	11 44.0	11 45.9	11 11.9	5.6 4.3	11.6 9.0	17.6 13.6
57	11 44.3	11 46.2	11 12.2	5.7 4.4	11.7 9.1	17.7 13.7
58	11 44.5	11 46.4	11 12.4	5.8 4.5	11.8 9.1	17.8 13.8
59	11 44.8	11 46.7	11 12.6	5.9 4.6	11.9 9.2	17.9 13.9
60	11 45.0	11 46.9	11 12.9	6.0 4.7	12.0 9.3	18.0 14.0

m 47 s	SUN PLANETS ° '	ARIES ° '	MOON ° '	v or Corrn d ' '	v or Corrn d ' '	v or Corrn d ' '
00	11 45.0	11 46.9	11 12.9	0.0 0.0	6.0 4.8	12.0 9.5
01	11 45.3	11 47.2	11 13.1	0.1 0.1	6.1 4.8	12.1 9.6
02	11 45.5	11 47.4	11 13.4	0.2 0.2	6.2 4.9	12.2 9.7
03	11 45.8	11 47.7	11 13.6	0.3 0.2	6.3 5.0	12.3 9.7
04	11 46.0	11 47.9	11 13.8	0.4 0.3	6.4 5.1	12.4 9.8
05	11 46.3	11 48.2	11 14.1	0.5 0.4	6.5 5.1	12.5 9.9
06	11 46.5	11 48.4	11 14.3	0.6 0.5	6.6 5.2	12.6 10.0
07	11 46.8	11 48.7	11 14.6	0.7 0.6	6.7 5.3	12.7 10.1
08	11 47.0	11 48.9	11 14.8	0.8 0.6	6.8 5.3	12.8 10.1
09	11 47.3	11 49.2	11 15.0	0.9 0.7	6.9 5.5	12.9 10.2
10	11 47.5	11 49.4	11 15.3	1.0 0.8	7.0 5.5	13.0 10.3
11	11 47.8	11 49.7	11 15.5	1.1 0.9	7.1 5.6	13.1 10.4
12	11 48.0	11 49.9	11 15.7	1.2 1.0	7.2 5.7	13.2 10.5
13	11 48.3	11 50.2	11 16.0	1.3 1.0	7.3 5.8	13.3 10.5
14	11 48.5	11 50.4	11 16.2	1.4 1.1	7.4 5.9	13.4 10.6
15	11 48.8	11 50.7	11 16.5	1.5 1.2	7.5 5.9	13.5 10.7
16	11 49.0	11 50.9	11 16.7	1.6 1.3	7.6 6.0	13.6 10.8
17	11 49.3	11 51.2	11 16.9	1.7 1.3	7.7 6.1	13.7 10.8
18	11 49.5	11 51.4	11 17.2	1.8 1.4	7.8 6.2	13.8 10.9
19	11 49.8	11 51.7	11 17.4	1.9 1.5	7.9 6.3	13.9 11.0
20	11 50.0	11 51.9	11 17.7	2.0 1.6	8.0 6.3	14.0 11.1
21	11 50.3	11 52.2	11 17.9	2.1 1.7	8.1 6.4	14.1 11.2
22	11 50.5	11 52.4	11 18.1	2.2 1.7	8.2 6.5	14.2 11.2
23	11 50.8	11 52.7	11 18.4	2.3 1.8	8.3 6.6	14.3 11.3
24	11 51.0	11 52.9	11 18.6	2.4 1.9	8.4 6.7	14.4 11.4
25	11 51.3	11 53.2	11 18.8	2.5 2.0	8.5 6.7	14.5 11.5
26	11 51.5	11 53.4	11 19.1	2.6 2.1	8.6 6.8	14.6 11.6
27	11 51.8	11 53.7	11 19.3	2.7 2.1	8.7 6.9	14.7 11.6
28	11 52.0	11 53.9	11 19.6	2.8 2.2	8.8 7.0	14.8 11.7
29	11 52.3	11 54.2	11 19.8	2.9 2.3	8.9 7.0	14.9 11.8
30	11 52.5	11 54.5	11 20.0	3.0 2.4	9.0 7.1	15.0 11.9
31	11 52.8	11 54.7	11 20.3	3.1 2.5	9.1 7.2	15.1 12.0
32	11 53.0	11 55.0	11 20.5	3.2 2.5	9.2 7.3	15.2 12.0
33	11 53.3	11 55.2	11 20.8	3.3 2.6	9.3 7.4	15.3 12.1
34	11 53.5	11 55.5	11 21.0	3.4 2.7	9.4 7.4	15.4 12.2
35	11 53.8	11 55.7	11 21.2	3.5 2.8	9.5 7.5	15.5 12.3
36	11 54.0	11 56.0	11 21.5	3.6 2.9	9.6 7.6	15.6 12.4
37	11 54.3	11 56.2	11 21.7	3.7 2.9	9.7 7.7	15.7 12.4
38	11 54.5	11 56.5	11 22.0	3.8 3.0	9.8 7.8	15.8 12.5
39	11 54.8	11 56.7	11 22.2	3.9 3.1	9.9 7.8	15.9 12.6
40	11 55.0	11 57.0	11 22.4	4.0 3.2	10.0 7.9	16.0 12.7
41	11 55.3	11 57.2	11 22.7	4.1 3.2	10.1 8.0	16.1 12.7
42	11 55.5	11 57.5	11 22.9	4.2 3.3	10.2 8.1	16.2 12.8
43	11 55.8	11 57.7	11 23.1	4.3 3.4	10.3 8.2	16.3 12.9
44	11 56.0	11 58.0	11 23.4	4.4 3.5	10.4 8.2	16.4 13.0
45	11 56.3	11 58.2	11 23.6	4.5 3.6	10.5 8.3	16.5 13.1
46	11 56.5	11 58.5	11 23.9	4.6 3.6	10.6 8.4	16.6 13.1
47	11 56.8	11 58.7	11 24.1	4.7 3.7	10.7 8.5	16.7 13.2
48	11 57.0	11 59.0	11 24.3	4.8 3.8	10.8 8.6	16.8 13.3
49	11 57.3	11 59.2	11 24.6	4.9 3.9	10.9 8.6	16.9 13.4
50	11 57.5	11 59.5	11 24.8	5.0 4.0	11.0 8.7	17.0 13.5
51	11 57.8	11 59.7	11 25.1	5.1 4.0	11.1 8.8	17.1 13.5
52	11 58.0	12 00.0	11 25.3	5.2 4.1	11.2 8.9	17.2 13.6
53	11 58.3	12 00.2	11 25.5	5.3 4.2	11.3 8.9	17.3 13.7
54	11 58.5	12 00.5	11 25.8	5.4 4.3	11.4 9.0	17.4 13.8
55	11 58.8	12 00.7	11 26.0	5.5 4.4	11.5 9.1	17.5 13.9
56	11 59.0	12 01.0	11 26.2	5.6 4.4	11.6 9.2	17.6 13.9
57	11 59.3	12 01.2	11 26.5	5.7 4.5	11.7 9.3	17.7 14.0
58	11 59.5	12 01.5	11 26.7	5.8 4.6	11.8 9.3	17.8 14.1
59	11 59.8	12 01.7	11 27.0	5.9 4.7	11.9 9.4	17.9 14.2
60	12 00.0	12 02.0	11 27.2	6.0 4.8	12.0 9.5	18.0 14.3

INCREMENTS AND CORRECTIONS

48ᵐ — **48m** **49ᵐ** — **49m**

m 48 s	SUN PLANETS ° ′	ARIES ° ′	MOON ° ′	v or Corrⁿ d ′ ′	v or Corrⁿ d ′ ′	v or Corrⁿ d ′ ′
00	12 00.0	12 02.0	11 27.2	0.0 0.0	6.0 4.9	12.0 9.7
01	12 00.3	12 02.2	11 27.4	0.1 0.1	6.1 4.9	12.1 9.8
02	12 00.5	12 02.5	11 27.7	0.2 0.2	6.2 5.0	12.2 9.9
03	12 00.8	12 02.7	11 27.9	0.3 0.2	6.3 5.1	12.3 9.9
04	12 01.0	12 03.0	11 28.2	0.4 0.3	6.4 5.2	12.4 10.0
05	12 01.3	12 03.2	11 28.4	0.5 0.4	6.5 5.3	12.5 10.1
06	12 01.5	12 03.5	11 28.6	0.6 0.5	6.6 5.3	12.6 10.2
07	12 01.8	12 03.7	11 28.9	0.7 0.6	6.7 5.4	12.7 10.3
08	12 02.0	12 04.0	11 29.1	0.8 0.6	6.8 5.5	12.8 10.3
09	12 02.3	12 04.2	11 29.3	0.9 0.7	6.9 5.6	12.9 10.4
10	12 02.5	12 04.5	11 29.6	1.0 0.8	7.0 5.7	13.0 10.5
11	12 02.8	12 04.7	11 29.8	1.1 0.9	7.1 5.7	13.1 10.6
12	12 03.0	12 05.0	11 30.1	1.2 1.0	7.2 5.8	13.2 10.7
13	12 03.3	12 05.2	11 30.3	1.3 1.1	7.3 5.9	13.3 10.8
14	12 03.5	12 05.5	11 30.5	1.4 1.1	7.4 6.0	13.4 10.8
15	12 03.8	12 05.7	11 30.8	1.5 1.2	7.5 6.1	13.5 10.9
16	12 04.0	12 06.0	11 31.0	1.6 1.3	7.6 6.1	13.6 11.0
17	12 04.3	12 06.2	11 31.3	1.7 1.4	7.7 6.2	13.7 11.1
18	12 04.5	12 06.5	11 31.5	1.8 1.5	7.8 6.3	13.8 11.2
19	12 04.8	12 06.7	11 31.7	1.9 1.5	7.9 6.4	13.9 11.2
20	12 05.0	12 07.0	11 32.0	2.0 1.6	8.0 6.5	14.0 11.3
21	12 05.3	12 07.2	11 32.2	2.1 1.7	8.1 6.5	14.1 11.4
22	12 05.5	12 07.5	11 32.4	2.2 1.8	8.2 6.6	14.2 11.5
23	12 05.8	12 07.7	11 32.7	2.3 1.9	8.3 6.7	14.3 11.6
24	12 06.0	12 08.0	11 32.9	2.4 1.9	8.4 6.8	14.4 11.6
25	12 06.3	12 08.2	11 33.2	2.5 2.0	8.5 6.9	14.5 11.7
26	12 06.5	12 08.5	11 33.4	2.6 2.1	8.6 7.0	14.6 11.8
27	12 06.8	12 08.7	11 33.6	2.7 2.2	8.7 7.0	14.7 11.9
28	12 07.0	12 09.0	11 33.9	2.8 2.3	8.8 7.1	14.8 12.0
29	12 07.3	12 09.2	11 34.1	2.9 2.3	8.9 7.2	14.9 12.0
30	12 07.5	12 09.5	11 34.4	3.0 2.4	9.0 7.3	15.0 12.1
31	12 07.8	12 09.7	11 34.6	3.1 2.5	9.1 7.4	15.1 12.2
32	12 08.0	12 10.0	11 34.8	3.2 2.6	9.2 7.4	15.2 12.3
33	12 08.3	12 10.2	11 35.1	3.3 2.7	9.3 7.5	15.3 12.4
34	12 08.5	12 10.5	11 35.3	3.4 2.7	9.4 7.6	15.4 12.4
35	12 08.8	12 10.7	11 35.6	3.5 2.8	9.5 7.7	15.5 12.5
36	12 09.0	12 11.0	11 35.8	3.6 2.9	9.6 7.8	15.6 12.6
37	12 09.3	12 11.2	11 36.0	3.7 3.0	9.7 7.8	15.7 12.7
38	12 09.5	12 11.5	11 36.3	3.8 3.1	9.8 7.9	15.8 12.8
39	12 09.8	12 11.7	11 36.5	3.9 3.2	9.9 8.0	15.9 12.9
40	12 10.0	12 12.0	11 36.7	4.0 3.2	10.0 8.1	16.0 12.9
41	12 10.3	12 12.2	11 37.0	4.1 3.3	10.1 8.2	16.1 13.0
42	12 10.5	12 12.5	11 37.2	4.2 3.4	10.2 8.2	16.2 13.1
43	12 10.8	12 12.8	11 37.5	4.3 3.5	10.3 8.3	16.3 13.2
44	12 11.0	12 13.0	11 37.7	4.4 3.6	10.4 8.4	16.4 13.3
45	12 11.3	12 13.3	11 37.9	4.5 3.6	10.5 8.5	16.5 13.3
46	12 11.5	12 13.5	11 38.2	4.6 3.7	10.6 8.6	16.6 13.4
47	12 11.8	12 13.8	11 38.4	4.7 3.8	10.7 8.6	16.7 13.5
48	12 12.0	12 14.0	11 38.7	4.8 3.9	10.8 8.7	16.8 13.6
49	12 12.3	12 14.3	11 38.9	4.9 4.0	10.9 8.8	16.9 13.7
50	12 12.5	12 14.5	11 39.1	5.0 4.0	11.0 8.9	17.0 13.7
51	12 12.8	12 14.8	11 39.4	5.1 4.1	11.1 9.0	17.1 13.8
52	12 13.0	12 15.0	11 39.6	5.2 4.2	11.2 9.1	17.2 13.9
53	12 13.3	12 15.2	11 39.8	5.3 4.3	11.3 9.1	17.3 14.0
54	12 13.5	12 15.5	11 40.1	5.4 4.4	11.4 9.2	17.4 14.1
55	12 13.8	12 15.8	11 40.3	5.5 4.4	11.5 9.3	17.5 14.1
56	12 14.0	12 16.0	11 40.6	5.6 4.5	11.6 9.4	17.6 14.2
57	12 14.3	12 16.3	11 40.8	5.7 4.6	11.7 9.5	17.7 14.3
58	12 14.5	12 16.5	11 41.0	5.8 4.7	11.8 9.5	17.8 14.4
59	12 14.8	12 16.8	11 41.3	5.9 4.8	11.9 9.6	17.9 14.5
60	12 15.0	12 17.0	11 41.5	6.0 4.9	12.0 9.7	18.0 14.6

m 49 s	SUN PLANETS ° ′	ARIES ° ′	MOON ° ′	v or Corrⁿ d ′ ′	v or Corrⁿ d ′ ′	v or Corrⁿ d ′ ′
00	12 15.0	12 17.0	11 41.5	0.0 0.0	6.0 5.0	12.0 9.9
01	12 15.3	12 17.3	11 41.8	0.1 0.1	6.1 5.0	12.1 10.0
02	12 15.5	12 17.5	11 42.0	0.2 0.2	6.2 5.1	12.2 10.1
03	12 15.8	12 17.8	11 42.2	0.3 0.2	6.3 5.2	12.3 10.1
04	12 16.0	12 18.0	11 42.5	0.4 0.3	6.4 5.3	12.4 10.2
05	12 16.3	12 18.3	11 42.7	0.5 0.4	6.5 5.4	12.5 10.3
06	12 15.5	12 18.5	11 42.9	0.6 0.5	6.6 5.4	12.6 10.4
07	12 16.8	12 18.8	11 43.2	0.7 0.6	6.7 5.5	12.7 10.5
08	12 17.0	12 19.0	11 43.4	0.8 0.7	6.8 5.6	12.8 10.6
09	12 17.3	12 19.3	11 43.7	0.9 0.7	6.9 5.7	12.9 10.6
10	12 17.5	12 19.5	11 43.9	1.0 0.8	7.0 5.8	13.0 10.7
11	12 17.8	12 19.8	11 44.1	1.1 0.9	7.1 5.9	13.1 10.8
12	12 18.0	12 20.0	11 44.4	1.2 1.0	7.2 5.9	13.2 10.9
13	12 18.3	12 20.3	11 44.6	1.3 1.1	7.3 6.0	13.3 11.0
14	12 18.5	12 20.5	11 44.9	1.4 1.2	7.4 6.1	13.4 11.1
15	12 18.8	12 20.8	11 45.1	1.5 1.2	7.5 6.2	13.5 11.1
16	12 19.0	12 21.0	11 45.3	1.6 1.3	7.6 6.3	13.6 11.2
17	12 19.3	12 21.3	11 45.6	1.7 1.4	7.7 6.4	13.7 11.3
18	12 19.5	12 21.5	11 45.8	1.8 1.5	7.8 6.4	13.8 11.4
19	12 19.8	12 21.8	11 46.4	1.9 1.6	7.9 6.5	13.9 11.5
20	12 20.0	12 22.0	11 46.3	2.0 1.7	8.0 6.6	14.0 11.6
21	12 20.3	12 22.3	11 46.5	2.1 1.7	8.1 6.7	14.1 11.6
22	12 20.5	12 22.5	11 46.8	2.2 1.8	8.2 6.8	14.2 11.7
23	12 20.8	12 22.8	11 47.0	2.3 1.9	8.3 6.8	14.3 11.8
24	12 21.0	12 23.0	11 47.2	2.4 2.0	8.4 6.9	14.4 11.9
25	12 21.3	12 23.3	11 47.5	2.5 2.1	8.5 7.0	14.5 12.0
26	12 21.5	12 23.5	11 47.7	2.6 2.1	8.6 7.1	14.6 12.0
27	12 21.8	12 23.8	11 48.0	2.7 2.2	8.7 7.2	14.7 12.1
28	12 22.0	12 24.0	11 48.2	2.8 2.3	8.8 7.3	14.8 12.2
29	12 22.3	12 24.3	11 48.4	2.9 2.4	8.9 7.3	14.9 12.3
30	12 22.5	12 24.5	11 48.7	3.0 2.5	9.0 7.4	15.0 12.4
31	12 22.8	12 24.8	11 48.9	3.1 2.6	9.1 7.5	15.1 12.5
32	12 23.0	12 25.0	11 49.2	3.2 2.6	9.2 7.6	15.2 12.5
33	12 23.3	12 25.3	11 49.4	3.3 2.7	9.3 7.7	15.3 12.6
34	12 23.5	12 25.5	11 49.6	3.4 2.8	9.4 7.8	15.4 12.7
35	12 23.8	12 25.8	11 49.9	3.5 2.9	9.5 7.8	15.5 12.8
36	12 24.0	12 26.0	11 50.1	3.6 3.0	9.6 7.9	15.6 12.9
37	12 24.3	12 26.3	11 50.3	3.7 3.1	9.7 8.0	15.7 13.0
38	12 24.5	12 26.5	11 50.6	3.8 3.1	9.8 8.1	15.8 13.0
39	12 24.8	12 26.8	11 50.8	3.9 3.2	9.9 8.2	15.9 13.1
40	12 25.0	12 27.0	11 51.1	4.0 3.3	10.0 8.3	16.0 13.2
41	12 25.3	12 27.3	11 51.3	4.1 3.4	10.1 8.3	16.1 13.3
42	12 25.5	12 27.5	11 51.5	4.2 3.5	10.2 8.4	16.2 13.4
43	12 25.8	12 27.8	11 51.8	4.3 3.5	10.3 8.5	16.3 13.4
44	12 25.0	12 28.0	11 52.0	4.4 3.6	10.4 8.6	16.4 13.5
45	12 26.3	12 28.3	11 52.3	4.5 3.7	10.5 8.7	16.5 13.6
46	12 26.5	12 28.5	11 52.5	4.6 3.8	10.6 8.7	16.6 13.7
47	12 26.8	12 28.8	11 52.7	4.7 3.9	10.7 8.8	16.7 13.8
48	12 27.0	12 29.0	11 53.0	4.8 4.0	10.8 8.9	16.8 13.9
49	12 27.3	12 29.3	11 53.2	4.9 4.0	10.9 9.0	16.9 13.9
50	12 27.5	12 29.5	11 53.4	5.0 4.1	11.0 9.1	17.0 14.0
51	12 27.8	12 29.8	11 53.7	5.1 4.2	11.1 9.2	17.1 14.1
52	12 28.0	12 30.0	11 53.9	5.2 4.3	11.2 9.2	17.2 14.2
53	12 28.3	12 30.3	11 54.2	5.3 4.4	11.3 9.3	17.3 14.3
54	12 28.5	12 30.5	11 54.4	5.4 4.5	11.4 9.4	17.4 14.4
55	12 28.8	12 30.8	11 54.6	5.5 4.5	11.5 9.5	17.5 14.4
56	12 29.0	12 31.1	11 54.9	5.6 4.6	11.6 9.6	17.6 14.5
57	12 29.3	12 31.3	11 55.1	5.7 4.7	11.7 9.7	17.7 14.6
58	12 29.5	12 31.6	11 55.4	5.8 4.8	11.8 9.7	17.8 14.7
59	12 29.8	12 31.8	11 55.6	5.9 4.9	11.9 9.8	17.9 14.8
60	12 30.0	12 32.1	11 55.8	6.0 5.0	12.0 9.9	18.0 14.9

50ᵐ INCREMENTS AND CORRECTIONS 51ᵐ

m 50	SUN PLANETS	ARIES	MOON	v or Corrⁿ d		v or Corrⁿ d		v or Corrⁿ d	
s	° ′	° ′	° ′	′	′	′	′	′	′
00	12 30.0	12 32.1	11 55.8	0.0	0.0	6.0	5.1	12.0	10.1
01	12 30.3	12 32.3	11 56.1	0.1	0.1	6.1	5.1	12.1	10.2
02	12 30.5	12 32.6	11 56.3	0.2	0.2	6.2	5.2	12.2	10.3
03	12 30.8	12 32.8	11 56.5	0.3	0.3	6.3	5.3	12.3	10.4
04	12 31.0	12 33.1	11 56.8	0.4	0.3	6.4	5.4	12.4	10.4
05	12 31.3	12 33.3	11 57.0	0.5	0.4	6.5	5.5	12.5	10.5
06	12 31.5	12 33.6	11 57.3	0.6	0.5	6.6	5.6	12.6	10.6
07	12 31.8	12 33.8	11 57.5	0.7	0.6	6.7	5.6	12.7	10.7
08	12 32.0	12 34.1	11 57.7	0.8	0.7	6.8	5.7	12.8	10.8
09	12 32.3	12 34.3	11 58.0	0.9	0.8	6.9	5.8	12.9	10.9
10	12 32.5	12 34.6	11 58.2	1.0	0.8	7.0	5.9	13.0	10.9
11	12 32.8	12 34.8	11 58.5	1.1	0.9	7.1	6.0	13.1	11.0
12	12 33.0	12 35.1	11 58.7	1.2	1.0	7.2	6.1	13.2	11.1
13	12 33.3	12 35.3	11 58.9	1.3	1.1	7.3	6.1	13.3	11.2
14	12 33.5	12 35.6	11 58.2	1.4	1.2	7.4	6.2	13.4	11.3
15	12 33.8	12 35.8	11 59.4	1.5	1.3	7.5	6.3	13.5	11.4
16	12 34.0	12 36.1	11 59.7	1.6	1.3	7.6	6.4	13.6	11.4
17	12 34.3	12 36.3	11 59.9	1.7	1.4	7.7	6.5	13.7	11.5
18	12 34.5	12 36.6	12 00.1	1.8	1.5	7.8	6.6	13.8	11.6
19	12 34.8	12 36.8	12 00.4	1.9	1.6	7.9	6.6	13.9	11.7
20	12 35.0	12 37.1	12 00.6	2.0	1.7	8.0	6.7	14.0	11.8
21	12 35.3	12 37.3	12 00.8	2.1	1.8	8.1	6.8	14.1	11.9
22	12 35.5	12 37.6	12 01.1	2.2	1.9	8.2	6.9	14.2	12.0
23	12 35.8	12 37.8	12 01.3	2.3	1.9	8.3	7.0	14.3	12.0
24	12 36.0	12 38.1	12 01.6	2.4	2.0	8.4	7.1	14.4	12.1
25	12 36.3	12 38.3	12 01.8	2.5	2.1	8.5	7.2	14.5	12.2
26	12 36.5	12 38.6	12 02.0	2.6	2.2	8.6	7.2	14.6	12.3
27	12 36.8	12 38.8	12 02.3	2.7	2.3	8.7	7.3	14.7	12.4
28	12 37.0	12 39.1	12 02.5	2.8	2.4	8.8	7.4	14.8	12.5
29	12 37.3	12 39.3	12 02.8	2.9	2.4	8.9	7.5	14.9	12.5
30	12 37.5	12 39.6	12 03.0	3.0	2.5	9.0	7.6	15.0	12.6
31	12 37.8	12 39.8	12 03.2	3.1	2.6	9.1	7.7	15.1	12.7
32	12 38.0	12 40.1	12 03.5	3.2	2.7	9.2	7.7	15.2	12.8
33	12 38.3	12 40.3	12 03.7	3.3	2.8	9.3	7.8	15.3	12.9
34	12 38.5	12 40.6	12 03.9	3.4	2.9	9.4	7.9	15.4	13.0
35	12 38.8	12 40.8	12 04.2	3.5	2.9	9.5	8.0	15.5	13.0
36	12 39.0	12 41.1	12 04.4	3.6	3.0	9.6	8.1	15.6	13.1
37	12 39.3	12 41.3	12 04.7	3.7	3.1	9.7	8.2	15.7	13.2
38	12 39.5	12 41.6	12 04.9	3.8	3.2	9.8	8.2	15.8	13.3
39	12 39.8	12 41.8	12 05.1	3.9	3.3	9.9	8.3	15.9	13.4
40	12 40.0	12 42.1	12 05.4	4.0	3.4	10.0	8.4	16.0	13.5
41	12 40.3	12 42.3	12 05.6	4.1	3.5	10.1	8.5	16.1	13.6
42	12 40.5	12 42.6	12 05.9	4.2	3.5	10.2	8.6	16.2	13.6
43	12 40.8	12 42.8	12 06.1	4.3	3.6	10.3	8.7	16.3	13.7
44	12 41.0	12 43.1	12 06.3	4.4	3.7	10.4	8.8	16.4	13.8
45	12 41.3	12 43.3	12 06.6	4.5	3.8	10.5	8.8	16.5	13.9
46	12 41.5	12 43.6	12 06.8	4.6	3.9	10.6	8.9	16.6	14.0
47	12 41.8	12 43.8	12 07.0	4.7	4.0	10.7	9.0	16.7	14.1
48	12 42.0	12 44.1	12 07.3	4.8	4.0	10.8	9.1	16.8	14.1
49	12 42.3	12 44.3	12 07.5	4.9	4.1	10.9	9.2	16.9	14.2
50	12 42.5	12 44.6	12 07.8	5.0	4.2	11.0	9.3	17.0	14.3
51	12 42.8	12 44.8	12 08.0	5.1	4.3	11.1	9.3	17.1	14.4
52	12 43.0	12 45.1	12 08.2	5.2	4.4	11.2	9.4	17.2	14.5
53	12 43.3	12 45.3	12 08.5	5.3	4.5	11.3	9.5	17.3	14.6
54	12 43.5	12 45.6	12 08.7	5.4	4.5	11.4	9.6	17.4	14.6
55	12 43.8	12 45.8	12 09.0	5.5	4.6	11.5	9.7	17.5	14.7
56	12 44.0	12 46.1	12 09.2	5.6	4.7	11.6	9.8	17.6	14.8
57	12 44.3	12 46.3	12 09.4	5.7	4.8	11.7	9.8	17.7	14.9
58	12 44.5	12 46.6	12 09.7	5.8	4.9	11.8	9.9	17.8	15.0
59	12 44.8	12 46.8	12 09.9	5.9	5.0	11.9	10.0	17.9	15.1
60	12 45.0	12 47.1	12 10.2	6.0	5.1	12.0	10.1	18.0	15.2

m 51	SUN PLANETS	ARIES	MOON	v or Corrⁿ d		v or Corrⁿ d		v or Corrⁿ d	
s	° ′	° ′	° ′	′	′	′	′	′	′
00	12 45.0	12 47.0	12 10.2	0.0	0.0	6.0	5.2	12.0	10.3
01	12 45.3	12 47.3	12 10.4	0.1	0.1	6.1	5.2	12.1	10.4
02	12 45.5	12 47.6	12 10.6	0.2	0.2	6.2	5.3	12.2	10.5
03	12 45.8	12 47.8	12 10.9	0.3	0.3	6.3	5.4	12.3	10.6
04	12 46.0	12 48.1	12 11.1	0.4	0.3	6.4	5.5	12.4	10.6
05	12 46.3	12 48.3	12 11.3	0.5	0.4	6.5	5.6	12.5	10.7
06	12 45.5	12 48.6	12 11.6	0.6	0.5	6.6	5.7	12.6	10.8
07	12 46.8	12 48.8	12 11.8	0.7	0.6	6.7	5.8	12.7	10.9
08	12 47.0	12 49.1	12 12.1	0.8	0.7	6.8	5.8	12.8	11.0
09	12 47.3	12 49.4	12 12.3	0.9	0.8	6.9	5.9	12.9	11.1
10	12 47.5	12 49.6	12 12.5	1.0	0.9	7.0	6.0	13.0	11.2
11	12 47.8	12 49.9	12 12.8	1.1	0.9	7.1	6.1	13.1	11.2
12	12 48.0	12 50.1	12 13.0	1.2	1.0	7.2	6.2	13.2	11.3
13	12 48.3	12 50.4	12 13.3	1.3	1.1	7.3	6.3	13.3	11.4
14	12 48.5	12 50.6	12 13.5	1.4	1.2	7.4	6.4	13.4	11.5
15	12 48.8	12 50.9	12 13.7	1.5	1.3	7.5	6.4	13.5	11.6
16	12 49.0	12 51.1	12 14.0	1.6	1.4	7.6	6.5	13.6	11.7
17	12 49.3	12 51.4	12 14.2	1.7	1.5	7.7	6.6	13.7	11.8
18	12 49.5	12 51.6	12 14.4	1.8	1.5	7.8	6.7	13.8	11.8
19	12 49.8	12 51.9	12 14.7	1.9	1.6	7.9	6.8	13.9	11.9
20	12 50.0	12 52.1	12 14.9	2.0	1.7	8.0	6.9	14.0	12.0
21	12 50.3	12 52.4	12 15.2	2.1	1.8	8.1	7.0	14.1	12.1
22	12 50.5	12 52.6	12 15.4	2.2	1.9	8.2	7.0	14.2	12.2
23	12 50.8	12 52.9	12 15.6	2.3	2.0	8.3	7.1	14.3	12.3
24	12 51.0	12 53.1	12 15.9	2.4	2.1	8.4	7.2	14.4	12.4
25	12 51.3	12 53.4	12 16.1	2.5	2.1	8.5	7.3	14.5	12.4
26	12 51.5	12 53.6	12 16.4	2.6	2.2	8.6	7.4	14.6	12.5
27	12 51.8	12 53.9	12 16.6	2.7	2.3	8.7	7.5	14.7	12.6
28	12 52.0	12 54.1	12 16.8	2.8	2.4	8.8	7.6	14.8	12.7
29	12 52.3	12 54.4	12 17.1	2.9	2.5	8.9	7.6	14.9	12.8
30	12 52.5	12 54.6	12 17.3	3.0	2.6	9.0	7.7	15.0	12.9
31	12 52.8	12 54.9	12 17.5	3.1	2.7	9.1	7.8	15.1	13.0
32	12 53.0	12 55.1	12 17.8	3.2	2.7	9.2	7.9	15.2	13.0
33	12 53.3	12 55.4	12 18.0	3.3	2.8	9.3	8.0	15.3	13.1
34	12 53.5	12 55.6	12 18.3	3.4	2.9	9.4	8.1	15.4	13.2
35	12 53.8	12 55.9	12 18.5	3.5	3.0	9.5	8.2	15.5	13.3
36	12 54.0	12 56.1	12 18.7	3.6	3.1	9.6	8.2	15.6	13.4
37	12 54.3	12 56.4	12 19.0	3.7	3.2	9.7	8.3	15.7	13.5
38	12 54.5	12 56.6	12 19.2	3.8	3.3	9.8	8.4	15.8	13.6
39	12 54.8	12 56.9	12 19.5	3.9	3.3	9.9	8.5	15.9	13.6
40	12 55.0	12 57.1	12 19.7	4.0	3.4	10.0	8.6	16.0	13.7
41	12 55.3	12 57.4	12 19.9	4.1	3.5	10.1	8.7	16.1	13.8
42	12 55.5	12 57.6	12 20.2	4.2	3.6	10.2	8.8	16.2	13.9
43	12 55.8	12 57.9	12 20.4	4.3	3.7	10.3	8.8	16.3	14.0
44	12 56.0	12 58.1	12 20.6	4.4	3.8	10.4	8.9	16.4	14.1
45	12 56.3	12 58.4	12 20.9	4.5	3.9	10.5	9.0	16.5	14.2
46	12 56.5	12 58.6	12 21.1	4.6	3.9	10.6	9.1	16.6	14.2
47	12 56.8	12 58.9	12 21.4	4.7	4.0	10.7	9.2	16.7	14.3
48	12 57.0	12 59.1	12 21.6	4.8	4.1	10.8	9.3	16.8	14.4
49	12 57.3	12 59.4	12 21.8	4.9	4.2	10.9	9.4	16.9	14.5
50	12 57.5	12 59.6	12 22.1	5.0	4.3	11.0	9.4	17.0	14.6
51	12 57.8	12 59.9	12 22.3	5.1	4.4	11.1	9.5	17.1	14.7
52	12 58.0	13 00.1	12 22.6	5.2	4.5	11.2	9.6	17.2	14.8
53	12 58.3	13 00.4	12 22.8	5.3	4.5	11.3	9.7	17.3	14.8
54	12 58.5	13 00.6	12 23.0	5.4	4.6	11.4	9.8	17.4	14.9
55	12 58.8	13 00.9	12 23.3	5.5	4.7	11.5	9.9	17.5	15.0
56	12 59.0	13 01.1	12 23.5	5.6	4.8	11.6	10.0	17.6	15.1
57	12 59.3	13 01.4	12 23.8	5.7	4.9	11.7	10.0	17.7	15.2
58	12 59.5	13 01.6	12 24.0	5.8	5.0	11.8	10.1	17.8	15.3
59	12 59.8	13 01.9	12 24.2	5.9	5.1	11.9	10.2	17.9	15.4
60	13 00.0	13 02.1	12 24.5	6.0	5.2	12.0	10.3	18.0	15.5

52ᵐ   INCREMENTS AND CORRECTIONS   53ᵐ

m 52 s	SUN PLANETS ° ′	ARIES ° ′	MOON ° ′	v or Corrⁿ d ′ ′	v or Corrⁿ d ′ ′	v or Corrⁿ d ′ ′
00	13 00.0	13 02.1	12 24.5	0.0 0.0	6.0 5.3	12.0 10.5
01	13 00.3	13 02.4	12 24.7	0.1 0.1	6.1 5.3	12.1 10.6
02	13 00.5	13 02.6	12 24.9	0.2 0.2	6.2 5.4	12.2 10.7
03	13 00.8	13 02.9	12 25.2	0.3 0.3	6.3 5.5	12.3 10.8
04	13 01.0	13 03.1	12 25.4	0.4 0.3	6.4 5.6	12.4 10.9
05	13 01.3	13 03.4	12 25.7	0.5 0.4	6.5 5.7	12.5 10.9
06	13 01.5	13 03.6	12 25.9	0.6 0.5	6.6 5.8	12.6 11.0
07	13 01.8	13 03.9	12 26.1	0.7 0.6	6.7 5.9	12.7 11.1
08	13 02.0	13 04.1	12 26.4	0.8 0.7	6.8 6.0	12.8 11.2
09	13 02.3	13 04.4	12 26.6	0.9 0.8	6.9 6.0	12.9 11.3
10	13 02.5	13 04.6	12 26.9	1.0 0.9	7.0 6.1	13.0 11.4
11	13 02.8	13 04.9	12 27.1	1.1 1.0	7.1 6.2	13.1 11.5
12	13 03.0	13 05.1	12 27.3	1.2 1.1	7.2 6.3	13.2 11.6
13	13 03.3	13 05.4	12 27.6	1.3 1.1	7.3 6.4	13.3 11.6
14	13 03.5	13 05.6	12 27.8	1.4 1.2	7.4 6.5	13.4 11.7
15	13 03.8	13 05.9	12 28.0	1.5 1.3	7.5 6.6	13.5 11.8
16	13 04.0	13 06.1	12 28.3	1.6 1.4	7.6 6.7	13.6 11.9
17	13 04.3	13 06.4	12 28.5	1.7 1.5	7.7 6.7	13.7 12.0
18	13 04.5	13 06.6	12 28.8	1.8 1.6	7.8 6.8	13.8 12.1
19	13 04.8	13 06.9	12 29.0	1.9 1.7	7.9 6.9	13.9 12.2
20	13 05.0	13 07.1	12 29.2	2.0 1.8	8.0 7.0	14.0 12.3
21	13 05.3	13 07.4	12 29.5	2.1 1.8	8.1 7.1	14.1 12.3
22	13 05.5	13 07.6	12 29.7	2.2 1.9	8.2 7.2	14.2 12.4
23	13 05.8	13 07.9	12 30.0	2.3 2.0	8.3 7.3	14.3 12.5
24	13 06.0	13 08.2	12 30.2	2.4 2.1	8.4 7.4	14.4 12.6
25	13 06.3	13 08.4	12 30.4	2.5 2.2	8.5 7.4	14.5 12.7
26	13 06.5	13 08.7	12 30.7	2.6 2.3	8.6 7.5	14.6 12.8
27	13 06.8	13 08.9	12 30.9	2.7 2.4	8.7 7.6	14.7 12.9
28	13 07.0	13 09.2	12 31.1	2.8 2.5	8.8 7.7	14.8 13.0
29	13 07.3	13 09.4	12 31.4	2.9 2.5	8.9 7.8	14.9 13.0
30	13 07.5	13 09.7	12 31.6	3.0 2.6	9.0 7.9	15.0 13.1
31	13 07.8	13 09.9	12 31.9	3.1 2.7	9.1 8.0	15.1 13.2
32	13 08.0	13 10.2	12 32.1	3.2 2.8	9.2 8.0	15.2 13.3
33	13 08.3	13 10.4	12 32.3	3.3 2.9	9.3 8.1	15.3 13.4
34	13 08.5	13 10.7	12 32.6	3.4 3.0	9.4 8.2	15.4 13.5
35	13 08.8	13 10.9	12 32.8	3.5 3.1	9.5 8.3	15.5 13.6
36	13 09.0	13 11.2	12 33.1	3.6 3.2	9.6 8.4	15.6 13.7
37	13 09.3	13 11.4	12 33.3	3.7 3.2	9.7 8.5	15.7 13.7
38	13 09.5	13 11.7	12 33.5	3.8 3.3	9.8 8.6	15.8 13.8
39	13 09.8	13 11.9	12 33.8	3.9 3.4	9.9 8.7	15.9 13.9
40	13 10.0	13 12.2	12 34.0	4.0 3.5	10.0 8.8	16.0 14.0
41	13 10.3	13 12.4	12 34.2	4.1 3.6	10.1 8.8	16.1 14.1
42	13 10.5	13 12.7	12 34.5	4.2 3.7	10.2 8.9	16.2 14.2
43	13 10.8	13 12.9	12 34.7	4.3 3.8	10.3 9.0	16.3 14.3
44	13 11.0	13 13.2	12 35.0	4.4 3.9	10.4 9.1	16.4 14.3
45	13 11.3	13 13.4	12 35.2	4.5 3.9	10.5 9.2	16.5 14.4
46	13 11.5	13 13.7	12 35.2	4.6 4.0	10.6 9.3	16.6 14.5
47	13 11.8	13 13.9	12 35.7	4.7 4.1	10.7 9.4	16.7 14.6
48	13 12.0	13 14.2	12 35.9	4.8 4.2	10.8 9.5	16.8 14.7
49	13 12.3	13 14.4	12 36.2	4.9 4.3	10.9 9.5	16.9 14.8
50	13 12.5	13 14.7	12 36.4	5.0 4.4	11.0 9.6	17.0 14.9
51	13 12.8	13 14.9	12 36.6	5.1 4.5	11.1 9.7	17.1 15.0
52	13 13.0	13 15.2	12 36.9	5.2 4.6	11.2 9.8	17.2 15.1
53	13 13.3	13 15.4	12 37.1	5.3 4.6	11.3 9.9	17.3 15.1
54	13 13.5	13 15.7	12 37.4	5.4 4.7	11.4 10.0	17.4 15.2
55	13 13.8	13 15.9	12 37.6	5.5 4.8	11.5 10.1	17.5 15.3
56	13 14.0	13 16.2	12 37.8	5.6 4.9	11.6 10.2	17.6 15.4
57	13 14.3	13 16.4	12 38.1	5.7 5.0	11.7 10.2	17.7 15.5
58	13 14.5	13 16.7	12 38.3	5.8 5.1	11.8 10.3	17.8 15.6
59	13 14.8	13 16.9	12 38.5	5.9 5.2	11.9 10.4	17.9 15.7
60	13 15.0	13 17.2	12 38.8	6.0 5.3	12.0 10.5	18.0 15.8

m 53 s	SUN PLANETS ° ′	ARIES ° ′	MOON ° ′	v or Corrⁿ d ′ ′	v or Corrⁿ d ′ ′	v or Corrⁿ d ′ ′
00	13 15.0	13 17.2	12 38.8	0.0 0.0	6.0 5.4	12.0 10.7
01	13 15.3	13 17.4	12 39.0	0.1 0.1	6.1 5.4	12.1 10.8
02	13 15.5	13 17.7	12 39.3	0.2 0.2	6.2 5.5	12.2 10.9
03	13 15.8	13 17.9	12 39.5	0.3 0.3	6.3 5.6	12.3 11.0
04	13 16.0	13 18.2	12 39.7	0.4 0.4	6.4 5.7	12.4 11.1
05	13 16.3	13 18.4	12 40.0	0.5 0.4	6.5 5.8	12.5 11.1
06	13 16.5	13 18.7	12 40.2	0.6 0.5	6.6 5.9	12.6 11.2
07	13 16.8	13 18.9	12 40.5	0.7 0.6	6.7 6.0	12.7 11.3
08	13 17.0	13 19.2	12 40.7	0.8 0.7	6.8 6.1	12.8 11.4
09	13 17.3	13 19.4	12 40.9	0.9 0.8	6.9 6.2	12.9 11.5
10	13 17.5	13 19.7	12 41.2	1.0 0.9	7.0 6.2	13.0 11.6
11	13 17.8	13 19.9	12 41.4	1.1 1.0	7.1 6.3	13.1 11.7
12	13 18.0	13 20.2	12 41.6	1.2 1.1	7.2 6.4	13.2 11.8
13	13 18.3	13 20.4	12 41.9	1.3 1.2	7.3 6.5	13.3 11.9
14	13 18.5	13 20.7	12 42.1	1.4 1.2	7.4 6.6	13.4 11.9
15	13 18.8	13 20.9	12 42.4	1.5 1.3	7.5 6.7	13.5 12.0
16	13 19.0	13 21.2	12 42.6	1.6 1.4	7.6 6.8	13.6 12.1
17	13 19.3	13 21.4	12 42.8	1.7 1.5	7.7 6.9	13.7 12.2
18	13 19.5	13 21.7	12 43.1	1.8 1.6	7.8 7.0	13.8 12.3
19	13 19.8	13 21.9	12 43.3	1.9 1.7	7.9 7.0	13.9 12.4
20	13 20.0	13 22.2	12 43.6	2.0 1.8	8.0 7.1	14.0 12.5
21	13 20.3	13 22.4	12 43.8	2.1 1.9	8.1 7.2	14.1 12.6
22	13 20.5	13 22.7	12 44.0	2.2 2.0	8.2 7.3	14.2 12.7
23	13 20.8	13 22.9	12 44.3	2.3 2.1	8.3 7.4	14.3 12.8
24	13 21.0	13 23.2	12 44.5	2.4 2.1	8.4 7.5	14.4 12.8
25	13 21.3	13 23.4	12 44.7	2.5 2.2	8.5 7.6	14.5 12.9
26	13 21.5	13 23.7	12 45.0	2.6 2.3	8.6 7.7	14.6 12.0
27	13 21.8	13 23.9	12 45.2	2.7 2.4	8.7 7.8	14.7 13.1
28	13 22.0	13 24.2	12 45.5	2.8 2.5	8.8 7.8	14.8 13.2
29	13 22.3	13 24.4	12 45.7	2.9 2.6	8.9 7.9	14.9 13.3
30	13 22.5	13 24.7	12 45.9	3.0 2.7	9.0 8.0	15.0 13.4
31	13 22.8	13 24.9	12 46.2	3.1 2.8	9.1 8.1	15.1 13.5
32	13 23.0	13 25.2	12 46.4	3.2 2.9	9.2 8.2	15.2 13.6
33	13 23.3	13 25.4	12 46.7	3.3 2.9	9.3 8.3	15.3 13.6
34	13 23.5	13 25.7	12 46.9	3.4 3.0	9.4 8.4	15.4 13.7
35	13 23.8	13 26.0	12 47.1	3.5 3.1	9.5 8.5	15.5 13.8
36	13 24.0	13 26.2	12 47.4	3.6 3.2	9.6 8.6	15.6 13.9
37	13 24.3	13 26.5	12 47.6	3.7 3.3	9.7 8.6	15.7 14.0
38	13 24.5	13 26.7	12 47.9	3.8 3.4	9.8 8.7	15.8 14.1
39	13 24.8	13 27.0	12 48.1	3.9 3.5	9.9 8.8	15.9 14.2
40	13 25.0	13 27.2	12 48.3	4.0 3.6	10.0 8.9	16.0 14.3
41	13 25.3	13 27.5	12 48.6	4.1 3.7	10.1 9.0	16.1 14.4
42	13 25.5	13 27.7	12 48.8	4.2 3.7	10.2 9.1	16.2 14.4
43	13 25.8	13 27.9	12 49.0	4.3 3.8	10.3 9.2	16.3 14.5
44	13 26.0	13 28.2	12 49.3	4.4 3.9	10.4 9.3	16.4 14.6
45	13 26.3	13 28.5	12 49.5	4.5 4.0	10.5 9.4	16.5 14.7
46	13 26.5	13 28.7	12 49.8	4.6 4.1	10.6 9.5	16.6 14.8
47	13 26.8	13 29.0	12 50.0	4.7 4.2	10.7 9.5	16.7 14.9
48	13 27.0	13 29.2	12 50.2	4.8 4.3	10.8 9.6	16.8 15.0
49	13 27.3	13 29.5	12 50.5	4.9 4.4	10.9 9.7	16.9 15.1
50	13 27.5	13 29.7	12 50.7	5.0 4.5	11.0 9.8	17.0 15.2
51	13 27.8	13 30.0	12 51.0	5.1 4.5	11.1 9.9	17.1 15.2
52	13 28.0	13 30.2	12 51.2	5.2 4.6	11.2 10.0	17.2 15.3
53	13 28.3	13 30.5	12 51.4	5.3 4.7	11.3 10.1	17.3 15.4
54	13 28.5	13 30.7	12 51.7	5.4 4.8	11.4 10.2	17.4 15.5
55	13 28.8	13 31.0	12 51.9	5.5 4.9	11.5 10.3	17.5 15.6
56	13 29.0	13 31.2	12 52.1	5.6 5.0	11.6 10.3	17.6 15.7
57	13 29.3	13 31.5	12 52.4	5.7 5.1	11.7 10.4	17.7 15.8
58	13 29.5	13 31.7	12 52.6	5.8 5.2	11.8 10.5	17.8 15.9
59	13 29.8	13 32.0	12 52.9	5.9 5.3	11.9 10.6	17.9 16.0
60	13 30.0	13 32.2	12 53.1	6.0 5.4	12.0 10.7	18.0 16.1

54m   INCREMENTS AND CORRECTIONS   55m

m 54 s	SUN PLANETS	ARIES	MOON	v or Corrn d		v or Corrn d		v or Corrn d	
00	13 30.0	13 32.2	12 53.1	0.0	0.0	6.0	5.5	12.0	10.9
01	13 30.3	13 32.5	12 53.3	0.1	0.1	6.1	5.5	12.1	11.0
02	13 30.5	13 32.7	12 53.6	0.2	0.2	6.2	5.6	12.2	11.1
03	13 30.8	13 32.0	12 53.8	0.3	0.3	6.3	5.7	12.3	11.2
04	13 31.0	13 33.2	12 54.1	0.4	0.4	6.4	5.8	12.4	11.3
05	13 31.3	13 33.5	12 54.3	0.5	0.5	6.5	5.9	12.5	11.4
06	13 31.5	13 33.7	12 54.5	0.6	0.5	6.6	6.0	12.6	11.4
07	13 31.8	13 34.0	12 54.8	0.7	0.6	6.7	6.1	12.7	11.5
08	13 32.0	13 34.2	12 55.0	0.8	0.7	6.8	6.2	12.8	11.6
09	13 32.3	13 34.5	12 55.2	0.9	0.8	6.9	6.3	12.9	11.7
10	13 32.5	13 34.7	12 55.5	1.0	0.9	7.0	6.4	13.0	11.8
11	13 32.8	13 35.0	12 55.7	1.1	1.0	7.1	6.4	13.1	11.9
12	13 33.0	13 35.2	12 56.0	1.2	1.1	7.2	6.5	13.2	12.0
13	13 33.3	13 35.5	12 56.2	1.3	1.2	7.3	6.6	13.3	12.1
14	13 33.5	13 35.7	12 56.4	1.4	1.3	7.4	6.7	13.4	12.2
15	13 33.8	13 36.0	12 56.7	1.5	1.4	7.5	6.8	13.5	12.3
16	13 34.0	13 36.2	12 56.9	1.6	1.5	7.6	6.9	13.6	12.4
17	13 34.3	13 36.5	12 57.2	1.7	1.5	7.7	7.0	13.7	12.4
18	13 34.5	13 36.7	12 57.4	1.8	1.6	7.8	7.1	13.8	12.5
19	13 34.8	13 37.0	12 57.6	1.9	1.7	7.9	7.2	13.9	12.6
20	13 35.0	13 37.2	12 57.9	2.0	1.8	8.0	7.3	14.0	12.7
21	13 35.3	13 37.5	12 58.1	2.1	1.9	8.1	7.4	14.1	12.8
22	13 35.5	13 37.7	12 58.3	2.2	2.0	8.2	7.4	14.2	12.9
23	13 35.8	13 38.0	12 58.6	2.3	2.1	8.3	7.5	14.3	13.0
24	13 36.0	13 38.2	12 58.8	2.4	2.2	8.4	7.6	14.4	13.1
25	13 36.3	13 38.5	12 59.1	2.5	2.3	8.5	7.7	14.5	13.2
26	13 36.5	13 38.7	12 59.3	2.6	2.4	8.6	7.8	14.6	13.3
27	13 36.8	13 39.0	12 59.5	2.7	2.5	8.7	7.9	14.7	13.4
28	13 37.0	13 39.2	12 59.8	2.8	2.5	8.8	8.0	14.8	13.4
29	13 37.3	13 39.5	13 00.0	2.9	2.6	8.9	8.1	14.9	13.5
30	13 37.5	13 39.7	13 00.3	3.0	2.7	9.0	8.2	15.0	13.6
31	13 37.8	13 40.0	13 00.5	3.1	2.8	9.1	8.3	15.1	13.7
32	13 38.0	13 40.2	13 00.7	3.2	2.9	9.2	8.4	15.2	13.8
33	13 38.3	13 40.5	13 01.0	3.3	3.0	9.3	8.4	15.3	13.9
34	13 38.5	13 40.7	13 01.2	3.4	3.1	9.4	8.5	15.4	14.0
35	13 38.8	13 41.0	13 01.5	3.5	3.2	9.5	8.6	15.5	14.1
36	13 39.0	13 41.2	13 01.7	3.6	3.3	9.6	8.7	15.6	14.2
37	13 39.3	13 41.5	13 01.9	3.7	3.4	9.7	8.8	15.7	14.3
38	13 39.5	13 41.7	13 02.2	3.8	3.5	9.8	8.9	15.8	14.4
39	13 39.8	13 42.0	13 02.4	3.9	3.5	9.9	9.0	15.9	14.4
40	13 40.0	13 42.2	13 02.6	4.0	3.6	10.0	9.1	16.0	14.5
41	13 40.3	13 42.5	13 02.9	4.1	3.7	10.1	9.2	16.1	14.6
42	13 40.5	13 42.7	13 03.1	4.2	3.8	10.2	9.3	16.2	14.7
43	13 40.8	13 43.0	13 03.4	4.3	3.9	10.3	9.4	16.3	14.8
44	13 41.0	13 43.2	13 03.6	4.4	4.0	10.4	9.4	16.4	14.9
45	13 41.3	13 43.5	13 03.8	4.5	4.1	10.5	9.5	16.5	15.0
46	13 41.5	13 43.7	13 04.1	4.6	4.2	10.6	9.6	16.6	15.1
47	13 41.8	13 44.0	13 04.3	4.7	4.3	10.7	9.7	16.7	15.2
48	13 42.0	13 44.3	13 04.6	4.8	4.4	10.8	9.8	16.8	15.3
49	13 42.3	13 44.5	13 04.8	4.9	4.5	10.9	9.9	16.9	15.4
50	13 42.5	13 44.8	13 05.0	5.0	4.5	11.0	10.0	17.0	15.4
51	13 42.8	13 45.0	13 05.3	5.1	4.6	11.1	10.1	17.1	15.5
52	13 43.0	13 45.3	13 05.5	5.2	4.7	11.2	10.2	17.2	15.6
53	13 43.3	13 45.5	13 05.7	5.3	4.8	11.3	10.3	17.3	15.7
54	13 43.5	13 45.8	13 06.0	5.4	4.9	11.4	10.4	17.4	15.8
55	13 43.8	13 46.0	13 06.2	5.5	5.0	11.5	10.4	17.5	15.9
56	13 44.0	13 46.3	13 06.5	5.6	5.1	11.6	10.5	17.6	16.0
57	13 44.3	13 46.5	13 06.7	5.7	5.2	11.7	10.6	17.7	16.1
58	13 44.5	13 46.8	13 06.9	5.8	5.3	11.8	10.7	17.8	16.2
59	13 44.8	13 47.0	13 07.2	5.9	5.4	11.9	10.8	17.9	16.3
60	13 45.0	13 47.3	13 07.4	6.0	5.5	12.0	10.9	18.0	16.4

m 55 s	SUN PLANETS	ARIES	MOON	v or Corrn d		v or Corrn d		v or Corrn d	
00	13 45.0	13 47.3	13 07.4	0.0	0.0	6.0	5.6	12.0	11.1
01	13 45.3	13 47.5	13 07.7	0.1	0.1	6.1	5.6	12.1	11.2
02	13 45.5	13 47.8	13 07.9	0.2	0.2	6.2	5.7	12.2	11.3
03	13 45.8	13 48.0	13 08.1	0.3	0.3	6.3	5.8	12.3	11.4
04	13 46.0	13 48.3	13 08.4	0.4	0.4	6.4	5.9	12.4	11.5
05	13 46.3	13 48.5	13 08.6	0.5	0.5	6.5	6.0	12.5	11.6
06	13 46.5	13 48.8	13 08.8	0.6	0.6	6.6	6.1	12.6	11.7
07	13 46.8	13 49.0	13 09.1	0.7	0.6	6.7	6.2	12.7	11.7
08	13 47.0	13 49.3	13 09.3	0.8	0.7	6.8	6.3	12.8	11.8
09	13 47.3	13 49.5	13 09.6	0.9	0.8	6.9	6.4	12.9	11.9
10	13 47.5	13 49.8	13 09.8	1.0	0.9	7.0	6.5	13.0	12.0
11	13 47.8	13 50.0	13 10.0	1.1	1.0	7.1	6.6	13.1	12.1
12	13 48.0	13 50.3	13 10.3	1.2	1.1	7.2	6.7	13.2	12.2
13	13 48.3	13 50.5	13 10.5	1.3	1.2	7.3	6.8	13.3	12.3
14	13 48.5	13 50.8	13 10.8	1.4	1.3	7.4	6.8	13.4	12.4
15	13 48.8	13 51.0	13 11.0	1.5	1.4	7.5	6.9	13.5	12.5
16	13 49.0	13 51.3	13 11.2	1.6	1.5	7.6	7.0	13.6	12.6
17	13 49.3	13 51.5	13 11.5	1.7	1.6	7.7	7.1	13.7	12.7
18	13 49.5	13 51.8	13 11.7	1.8	1.7	7.8	7.2	13.8	12.8
19	13 49.8	13 52.0	13 12.0	1.9	1.8	7.9	7.3	13.9	12.9
20	13 50.0	13 52.3	13 12.2	2.0	1.9	8.0	7.4	14.0	13.0
21	13 50.3	13 52.5	13 12.4	2.1	1.9	8.1	7.5	14.1	13.0
22	13 50.5	13 52.8	13 12.7	2.2	2.0	8.2	7.6	14.2	13.1
23	13 50.8	13 53.0	13 12.9	2.3	2.1	8.3	7.7	14.3	13.2
24	13 51.0	13 53.3	13 13.1	2.4	2.2	8.4	7.8	14.4	13.3
25	13 51.3	13 23.5	13 13.4	2.5	2.3	8.5	7.9	14.5	13.4
26	13 51.5	13 53.8	13 13.6	2.6	2.4	8.6	8.0	14.6	13.5
27	13 51.8	13 54.0	13 13.9	2.7	2.5	8.7	8.0	14.7	13.6
28	13 52.0	13 54.3	13 14.1	2.8	2.6	8.8	8.1	14.8	13.7
29	13 52.3	13 54.5	13 14.3	2.9	2.7	8.9	8.2	14.9	13.8
30	13 52.5	13 54.8	13 14.6	3.0	2.8	9.0	8.3	15.0	13.9
31	13 52.8	13 55.0	13 14.8	3.1	2.9	9.1	8.4	15.1	14.0
32	13 53.0	13 55.3	13 15.1	3.2	3.0	9.2	8.5	15.2	14.1
33	13 53.3	13 55.5	13 15.3	3.3	3.1	9.3	8.6	15.3	14.2
34	13 53.5	13 55.8	13 15.5	3.4	3.1	9.4	8.7	15.4	14.2
35	13 53.8	13 56.0	13 15.8	3.5	3.2	9.5	8.8	15.5	14.3
36	13 54.0	13 56.3	13 16.0	3.6	3.3	9.6	8.9	15.6	14.4
37	13 54.3	13 56.5	13 16.2	3.7	3.4	9.7	9.0	15.7	14.5
38	13 54.5	13 56.8	13 16.5	3.8	3.5	9.8	9.1	15.8	14.6
39	13 54.8	13 57.0	13 16.7	3.9	3.6	9.9	9.2	15.9	14.7
40	13 55.0	13 57.3	13 17.0	4.0	3.7	10.0	9.3	16.0	14.8
41	13 55.3	13 57.5	13 17.2	4.1	3.8	10.1	9.3	16.1	14.9
42	13 55.5	13 57.8	13 17.4	4.2	3.9	10.2	9.4	16.2	15.0
43	13 55.8	13 58.0	13 17.7	4.3	4.0	10.3	9.5	16.3	15.1
44	13 56.0	13 58.3	13 17.9	4.4	4.1	10.4	9.6	16.4	15.2
45	13 56.3	13 58.5	13 18.2	4.5	4.2	10.5	9.7	16.5	15.3
46	13 56.5	13 58.8	13 18.4	4.6	4.3	10.6	9.8	16.6	15.4
47	13 56.8	13 59.0	13 18.6	4.7	4.3	10.7	9.9	16.7	15.4
48	13 57.0	13 59.3	13 18.9	4.8	4.4	10.8	10.0	16.8	15.5
49	13 57.3	13 59.5	13 19.1	4.9	4.5	10.9	10.1	16.9	15.6
50	13 57.5	13 59.8	13 19.3	5.0	4.6	11.0	10.2	17.0	15.7
51	13 57.8	14 00.0	13 19.6	5.1	4.7	11.1	10.3	17.1	15.8
52	13 58.0	14 00.3	13 19.8	5.2	4.8	11.2	10.4	17.2	15.9
53	13 58.3	14 00.5	13 20.1	5.3	4.9	11.3	10.5	17.3	16.0
54	13 58.5	14 00.8	13 20.3	5.4	5.0	11.4	10.5	17.4	16.1
55	13 58.8	14 01.0	13 20.5	5.5	5.1	11.5	10.6	17.5	16.2
56	13 59.0	14 01.3	13 20.8	5.6	5.2	11.6	10.7	17.6	16.3
57	13 59.3	14 01.5	13 21.0	5.7	5.3	11.7	10.8	17.7	16.4
58	13 59.5	14 01.8	13 21.3	5.8	5.4	11.8	10.9	17.8	16.5
59	13 59.8	14 02.0	13 21.5	5.9	5.5	11.9	11.0	17.9	16.6
60	14 00.0	14 02.3	13 21.7	6.0	5.6	12.0	11.1	18.0	16.7

56ᵐ INCREMENTS AND CORRECTIONS 57ᵐ

56ᵐ

m 56 / s	SUN PLANETS ° ′	ARIES ° ′	MOON ° ′	v or Corrn d	v or Corrn d	v or Corrn d
00	14 00.0	14 02.3	13 21.7	0.0 0.0	6.0 5.7	12.0 11.3
01	14 00.3	14 02.6	13 22.0	0.1 0.1	6.1 5.7	12.1 11.4
02	14 00.5	14 02.8	13 22.2	0.2 0.2	6.2 5.8	12.2 11.5
03	14 00.8	14 03.1	13 22.4	0.3 0.3	6.3 5.9	12.3 11.6
04	14 01.0	14 03.3	13 22.7	0.4 0.4	6.4 6.0	12.4 11.7
05	14 01.3	14 03.6	13 22.9	0.5 0.5	6.5 6.1	12.5 11.8
06	14 01.5	14 03.8	13 23.2	0.6 0.6	6.6 6.2	12.6 11.9
07	14 01.8	14 04.1	13 23.4	0.7 0.7	6.7 6.3	12.7 12.0
08	14 02.0	14 04.3	13 23.6	0.8 0.8	6.8 6.4	12.8 12.1
09	14 02.3	14 04.6	13 23.9	0.9 0.8	6.9 6.5	12.9 12.1
10	14 02.5	14 04.8	13 24.1	1.0 0.9	7.0 6.6	13.0 12.2
11	14 02.8	14 05.1	13 24.4	1.1 1.0	7.1 6.7	13.1 12.3
12	14 03.0	14 05.3	13 26.6	1.2 1.1	7.2 6.8	13.2 12.4
13	14 03.3	14 05.6	13 24.8	1.3 1.2	7.3 6.9	13.3 12.5
14	14 03.5	14 05.8	13 25.1	1.4 1.3	7.4 7.0	13.4 12.6
15	14 03.8	14 06.1	13 25.3	1.5 1.4	7.5 7.1	13.5 12.7
16	14 04.0	14 06.3	13 25.6	1.6 1.5	7.6 7.2	13.6 12.8
17	14 04.3	14 06.6	13 25.8	1.7 1.6	7.7 7.3	13.7 12.9
18	14 04.5	14 06.8	13 26.0	1.8 1.7	7.8 7.3	13.8 13.0
19	14 04.8	14 07.1	13 26.3	1.9 1.8	7.9 7.4	13.9 13.1
20	14 05.0	14 07.3	13 26.5	2.0 1.9	8.0 7.5	14.0 13.2
21	14 05.3	14 07.6	13 26.7	2.1 2.0	8.1 7.6	14.1 13.3
22	14 05.5	14 07.8	13 27.0	2.2 2.1	8.2 7.7	14.2 13.4
23	14 05.8	14 08.1	13 27.2	2.3 2.2	8.3 7.8	14.3 13.5
24	14 06.0	14 08.3	13 27.5	2.4 2.3	8.4 7.9	14.4 13.6
25	14 06.3	14 08.6	13 27.7	2.5 2.4	8.5 8.0	14.5 13.7
26	14 06.5	14 08.8	13 27.9	2.6 2.4	8.6 8.1	14.6 13.7
27	14 06.8	14 09.1	13 28.2	2.7 2.5	8.7 8.2	14.7 13.8
28	14 07.0	14 09.3	13 28.4	2.8 2.6	8.8 8.3	14.8 13.9
29	14 07.3	14 09.6	13 28.7	2.9 2.7	8.9 8.4	14.9 14.0
30	14 07.5	14 09.8	13 28.9	3.0 2.8	9.0 8.5	15.0 14.1
31	14 07.8	14 10.1	13 29.1	3.1 2.9	9.1 8.6	15.1 14.2
32	14 08.0	14 10.3	13 29.4	3.2 3.0	9.2 8.7	15.2 14.3
33	14 08.3	14 10.6	13 29.6	3.3 3.1	9.3 8.8	15.3 14.4
34	14 08.5	14 10.8	13 29.8	3.4 3.2	9.4 8.9	15.4 14.5
35	14 08.8	14 11.1	13 30.1	3.5 3.3	9.5 8.9	15.5 14.6
36	14 09.0	14 11.3	13 30.3	3.6 3.4	9.6 9.0	15.6 14.7
37	14 09.3	14 11.6	13 30.6	3.7 3.5	9.7 9.1	15.7 14.8
38	14 09.5	14 11.8	13 30.8	3.8 3.6	9.8 9.2	15.8 14.9
39	14 09.8	14 12.1	13 31.0	3.9 3.7	9.9 9.3	15.9 15.0
40	14 10.0	14 12.3	13 31.3	4.0 3.8	10.0 9.4	16.0 15.1
41	14 10.3	14 12.6	13 31.5	4.1 3.9	10.1 9.5	16.1 15.2
42	14 10.5	14 12.8	13 31.8	4.2 4.0	10.2 9.6	16.2 15.3
43	14 10.8	14 13.1	13 32.0	4.3 4.0	10.3 9.7	16.3 15.3
44	14 11.0	14 13.3	13 32.2	4.4 4.1	10.4 9.8	16.4 15.4
45	14 11.3	14 13.6	13 32.5	4.5 4.2	10.5 9.9	16.5 15.5
46	14 11.5	14 13.8	13 32.7	4.6 4.3	10.6 10.0	16.6 15.6
47	14 11.8	14 14.1	13 32.9	4.7 4.4	10.7 10.1	16.7 15.7
48	14 12.0	14 14.3	13 33.2	4.8 4.5	10.8 10.2	16.8 15.8
49	14 12.3	14 14.6	13 33.4	4.9 4.6	10.9 10.3	16.9 15.9
50	14 12.5	14 14.8	13 33.7	5.0 4.7	11.0 10.4	17.0 16.0
51	14 12.8	14 15.1	13 33.9	5.1 4.8	11.1 10.5	17.1 16.1
52	14 13.0	14 15.3	13 33.9	5.2 4.9	11.2 10.5	17.2 16.2
53	14 13.3	14 15.6	13 34.1	5.3 5.0	11.3 10.6	17.3 16.3
54	14 13.5	14 15.8	13 34.6	5.4 5.1	11.4 10.7	17.4 16.4
55	14 13.8	14 16.1	13 34.9	5.5 5.2	11.5 10.8	17.5 16.5
56	14 14.0	14 16.3	13 35.1	5.6 5.3	11.6 10.9	17.6 16.6
57	14 14.3	14 16.6	13 35.3	5.7 5.4	11.7 11.0	17.7 16.7
58	14 14.5	14 16.8	13 35.6	5.8 5.5	11.8 11.1	17.8 16.8
59	14 14.8	14 17.1	13 35.8	5.9 5.6	11.9 10.2	17.9 16.9
60	14 45.0	14 17.3	13 36.1	6.0 5.7	12.0 11.3	18.0 17.0

57ᵐ

m 57 / s	SUN PLANETS ° ′	ARIES ° ′	MOON ° ′	v or Corrn d	v or Corrn d	v or Corrn d
00	14 15.0	14 17.3	13 36.1	0.0 0.0	6.0 5.8	12.0 11.5
01	14 15.3	14 17.6	13 36.3	0.1 0.1	6.1 5.8	12.1 11.6
02	14 15.5	14 17.8	13 36.5	0.2 0.2	6.2 5.9	12.2 11.7
03	14 15.8	14 18.1	13 36.8	0.3 0.3	6.3 6.0	12.3 11.8
04	14 16.0	14 18.3	13 37.0	0.4 0.4	6.4 6.1	12.4 11.9
05	14 16.3	14 18.6	13 37.2	0.5 0.5	6.5 6.2	12.5 12.0
06	14 16.5	14 18.8	13 37.5	0.6 0.6	6.6 6.3	12.6 12.1
07	14 16.8	14 19.1	13 37.7	0.7 0.7	6.7 6.4	12.7 12.2
08	14 17.0	14 19.3	13 38.0	0.8 0.8	6.8 6.5	12.8 12.3
09	14 17.3	14 19.6	13 38.2	0.9 0.9	6.9 6.6	12.9 12.4
10	14 17.5	14 19.8	13 38.4	1.0 1.0	7.0 6.7	13.0 12.5
11	14 17.8	14 20.1	13 38.7	1.1 1.1	7.1 6.8	13.1 12.6
12	14 18.0	14 20.3	13 38.9	1.2 1.2	7.2 6.9	13.2 12.7
13	14 18.3	14 20.6	13 39.2	1.3 1.2	7.3 7.0	13.3 12.7
14	14 18.5	14 20.9	13 39.4	1.4 1.3	7.4 7.1	13.4 12.8
15	14 18.8	14 21.1	13 39.6	1.5 1.4	7.5 7.2	13.5 12.9
16	14 19.0	14 21.4	13 39.9	1.6 1.5	7.6 7.3	13.6 13.0
17	14 19.3	14 21.6	13 40.1	1.7 1.6	7.7 7.4	13.7 13.1
18	14 19.5	14 21.9	13 40.3	1.8 1.7	7.8 7.5	13.8 13.2
19	14 19.8	14 22.1	13 40.6	1.9 1.8	7.9 7.6	13.9 13.3
20	14 20.0	14 22.4	13 40.8	2.0 1.9	8.0 7.7	14.0 13.4
21	14 20.3	14 22.6	13 41.1	2.1 2.0	8.1 7.8	14.1 13.5
22	14 20.5	14 22.9	13 41.3	2.2 2.1	8.2 7.9	14.2 13.6
23	14 20.8	14 23.1	13 41.5	2.3 2.2	8.3 8.0	14.3 13.7
24	14 21.0	14 23.4	13 41.8	2.4 2.3	8.4 8.1	14.4 13.8
25	14 21.3	14 23.6	13 42.0	2.5 2.4	8.5 8.1	14.5 13.9
26	14 21.5	14 23.9	13 42.3	2.6 2.5	8.6 8.2	14.6 14.0
27	14 21.8	14 24.1	13 42.5	2.7 2.6	8.7 8.3	14.7 14.1
28	14 22.0	14 24.4	13 42.7	2.8 2.7	8.8 8.4	14.8 14.2
29	14 22.3	14 24.6	13 43.0	2.9 2.8	8.9 8.5	14.9 14.3
30	14 22.5	14 24.9	13 43.2	3.0 2.9	9.0 8.6	15.0 14.4
31	14 22.8	14 25.1	13 43.4	3.1 3.0	9.1 8.7	15.1 14.5
32	14 23.0	14 25.4	13 43.7	3.2 3.1	9.2 8.8	15.2 14.6
33	14 23.3	14 25.6	13 43.9	3.3 3.2	9.3 8.9	15.3 14.7
34	14 23.5	14 25.9	13 44.2	3.4 3.3	9.4 9.0	15.4 14.8
35	14 23.8	14 26.1	13 44.4	3.5 3.4	9.5 9.1	15.5 14.9
36	14 24.0	14 26.4	13 44.6	3.6 3.5	9.6 9.2	15.6 15.0
37	14 24.3	14 26.6	13 44.9	3.7 3.5	9.7 9.3	15.7 15.0
38	14 24.5	14 26.9	13 45.1	3.8 3.6	9.8 9.4	15.8 15.1
39	14 24.8	14 27.1	13 45.4	3.9 3.7	9.9 9.5	15.9 15.2
40	14 25.0	14 27.4	13 45.6	4.0 3.8	10.0 9.6	16.0 15.3
41	14 25.3	14 27.6	13 45.8	4.1 3.9	10.1 9.7	16.1 15.4
42	14 25.5	14 27.9	13 46.1	4.2 4.0	10.2 9.8	16.2 15.5
43	14 25.8	14 28.1	13 46.3	4.3 4.1	10.3 9.9	16.3 15.6
44	14 26.0	14 28.4	13 46.5	4.4 4.2	10.4 10.0	16.4 15.7
45	14 26.3	14 28.6	13 46.8	4.5 4.3	10.5 10.1	16.5 15.8
46	14 26.5	14 28.9	13 47.0	4.6 4.4	10.6 10.2	16.6 15.9
47	14 26.8	14 29.1	13 47.3	4.7 4.5	10.7 10.3	16.7 16.0
48	14 27.0	14 29.4	13 47.5	4.8 4.6	10.8 10.4	16.8 16.1
49	14 27.3	14 29.6	13 47.7	4.9 4.7	10.9 10.4	16.9 16.2
50	14 27.5	14 29.9	13 48.0	5.0 4.8	11.0 10.5	17.0 16.3
51	14 27.8	14 30.1	13 48.2	5.1 4.9	11.1 10.6	17.1 16.4
52	14 28.0	14 30.4	13 48.5	5.2 5.0	11.2 10.7	17.2 16.5
53	14 28.3	14 30.6	13 48.7	5.3 5.1	11.3 10.8	17.3 16.6
54	14 28.5	14 30.9	13 48.9	5.4 5.2	11.4 10.9	17.4 16.7
55	14 28.8	14 31.1	13 49.2	5.5 5.3	11.5 11.0	17.5 16.8
56	14 29.0	14 31.4	13 49.4	5.6 5.4	11.6 11.1	17.6 16.9
57	14 29.3	14 31.6	13 49.7	5.7 5.5	11.7 11.2	17.7 17.0
58	14 29.5	14 31.9	13 49.9	5.8 5.6	11.8 11.3	17.8 17.1
59	14 29.8	14 32.1	13 50.1	5.9 5.7	11.9 11.4	17.9 17.2
60	14 30.0	14 32.4	13 50.4	6.0 5.8	12.0 11.5	18.0 17.3

58m INCREMENTS AND CORRECTIONS 59m

m 58	SUN PLANETS	ARIES	MOON	v or Corrⁿ d		v or Corrⁿ d		v or Corrⁿ d	
s	° ′	° ′	° ′	′	′	′	′	′	′
00	14 30.0	14 32.4	13 50.4	0.0	0.0	6.0	5.9	12.0	11.7
01	14 30.3	14 32.6	13 50.6	0.1	0.1	6.1	5.9	12.1	11.8
02	14 30.5	14 32.9	13 50.8	0.2	0.2	6.2	6.0	12.2	11.9
03	14 30.8	14 33.1	13 51.1	0.3	0.3	6.3	6.1	12.3	12.0
04	14 31.0	14 33.4	13 51.3	0.4	0.4	6.4	6.2	12.4	12.1
05	14 31.3	14 33.6	13 51.6	0.5	0.5	6.5	6.3	12.5	12.2
06	14 31.5	14 33.9	13 51.8	0.6	0.6	6.6	6.4	12.6	12.3
07	14 31.8	14 34.1	13 52.0	0.7	0.7	6.7	6.5	12.7	12.4
08	14 32.0	14 34.4	13 52.3	0.8	0.8	6.8	6.6	12.8	12.5
09	14 32.3	14 34.6	13 52.5	0.9	0.8	6.9	6.7	12.9	12.6
10	14 32.5	14 34.9	13 52.8	1.0	1.0	7.0	6.8	13.0	12.7
11	14 32.8	14 35.1	13 53.0	1.1	1.1	7.1	6.9	13.1	12.8
12	14 33.0	14 35.4	13 53.2	1.2	1.2	7.2	7.0	13.2	12.9
13	14 33.3	14 35.6	13 53.5	1.3	1.3	7.3	7.1	13.3	13.0
14	14 33.5	14 35.9	13 53.7	1.4	1.4	7.4	7.2	13.4	13.1
15	14 33.8	14 36.1	13 53.9	1.5	1.5	7.5	7.3	13.5	13.2
16	14 34.0	14 36.4	13 54.2	1.6	1.6	7.6	7.4	13.6	13.3
17	14 34.3	14 36.6	13 54.4	1.7	1.7	7.7	7.5	13.7	13.4
18	14 34.5	14 36.9	13 54.7	1.8	1.8	7.8	7.6	13.8	13.5
19	14 34.8	14 37.1	13 54.9	1.9	1.9	7.9	7.7	13.9	13.6
20	14 35.0	14 37.3	13 55.1	2.0	2.0	8.0	7.8	14.0	13.7
21	14 35.3	14 37.6	13 55.4	2.1	2.0	8.1	7.9	14.1	13.7
22	14 35.5	14 37.9	13 55.6	2.2	2.1	8.2	8.0	14.2	13.8
23	14 35.8	14 38.1	13 55.9	2.3	2.2	8.3	8.1	14.3	13.9
24	14 66.0	14 38.4	13 56.1	2.4	2.3	8.4	8.2	14.4	14.0
25	14 36.3	14 38.6	13 56.3	2.5	2.4	8.5	8.3	14.5	14.1
26	14 36.5	14 38.9	13 56.6	2.6	2.5	8.6	8.4	14.6	14.2
27	14 36.8	14 39.2	13 56.8	2.7	2.6	8.7	8.5	14.7	14.3
28	14 37.0	14 39.4	13 57.0	2.8	2.7	8.8	8.6	14.8	14.4
29	14 37.3	14 39.7	13 57.3	2.9	2.8	8.9	8.7	14.9	14.5
30	14 37.5	14 39.9	13 57.5	3.0	2.9	9.0	8.7	15.0	14.6
31	14 37.8	14 40.2	13 57.8	3.1	3.0	9.1	8.9	15.1	14.7
32	14 38.0	14 40.4	13 58.0	3.2	3.1	9.2	9.0	15.2	14.8
33	14 38.3	14 40.7	13 58.2	3.3	3.2	9.3	9.1	15.3	14.9
34	14 38.5	14 40.9	13 58.5	3.4	3.3	9.4	9.2	15.4	15.0
35	14 38.8	14 41.2	13 58.7	3.5	3.4	9.5	9.3	15.5	15.1
36	14 39.0	14 41.4	13 59.0	3.6	3.5	9.6	9.4	15.6	15.2
37	14 39.3	14 41.7	13 59.2	3.7	3.6	9.7	9.5	15.7	15.3
38	14 39.5	14 41.9	13 59.4	3.8	3.7	9.8	9.6	15.8	15.4
39	14 39.8	14 42.2	13 59.7	3.9	3.8	9.9	9.7	15.9	15.5
40	14 40.0	14 42.4	13 59.9	4.0	3.9	10.0	9.8	16.0	15.6
41	14 40.3	14 42.7	14 00.1	4.1	4.0	10.1	9.8	16.1	15.7
42	14 40.5	14 42.9	14 00.4	4.2	4.1	10.2	9.9	16.2	15.8
43	14 40.8	14 43.2	14 00.6	4.3	4.2	10.3	10.0	16.3	15.9
44	14 41.0	14 43.4	14 00.9	4.4	4.3	10.4	10.1	16.4	16.0
45	14 41.3	14 43.7	14 01.1	4.5	4.4	10.5	10.2	16.5	16.1
46	14 41.5	14 43.9	14 01.3	4.6	4.5	10.6	10.3	16.6	16.2
47	14 41.8	14 44.2	14 01.6	4.7	4.6	10.7	10.4	16.7	16.3
48	14 42.0	14 44.4	14 01.8	4.8	4.7	10.8	10.5	16.8	16.4
49	14 42.3	14 44.7	14 02.1	4.9	4.8	10.9	10.6	16.9	16.5
50	14 42.5	14 44.9	14 02.3	5.0	4.9	11.0	10.7	17.0	16.6
51	14 42.8	14 45.2	14 02.5	5.1	5.0	11.1	10.8	17.1	16.7
52	14 43.0	14 45.4	14 02.8	5.2	5.1	11.2	10.9	17.2	16.8
53	14 43.3	14 45.7	14 03.0	5.3	5.2	11.3	11.0	17.3	16.9
54	14 43.5	14 45.9	14 03.3	5.4	5.3	11.4	11.1	17.4	17.0
55	14 43.8	14 46.2	14 03.5	5.5	5.4	11.5	11.2	17.5	17.1
56	14 44.0	14 46.4	14 03.7	5.6	5.5	11.6	11.3	17.6	17.2
57	14 44.3	14 46.7	14 04.0	5.7	5.6	11.7	11.4	17.7	17.3
58	14 44.5	14 46.9	14 04.2	5.8	5.7	11.8	11.5	17.8	17.4
59	14 44.8	14 47.2	14 04.4	5.9	5.8	11.9	10.6	17.9	17.5
60	14 45.0	14 47.4	14 04.7	6.0	5.9	12.0	11.7	18.0	17.6

m 59	SUN PLANETS	ARIES	MOON	v or Corrⁿ d		v or Corrⁿ d		v or Corrⁿ d	
s	° ′	° ′	° ′	′	′	′	′	′	′
00	14 45.0	14 47.4	14 04.7	0.0	0.0	6.0	6.0	12.0	11.9
01	14 45.3	14 47.7	14 04.9	0.1	0.1	6.1	6.0	12.1	12.0
02	14 45.5	14 47.9	14 05.2	0.2	0.2	6.2	6.1	12.2	12.1
03	14 45.8	14 48.2	14 05.4	0.3	0.3	6.3	6.2	12.3	12.2
04	14 46.0	14 48.4	14 05.6	0.4	0.4	6.4	6.3	12.4	12.3
05	14 46.3	14 48.7	14 05.9	0.5	0.5	6.5	6.4	12.5	12.4
06	14 46.5	14 48.9	14 06.1	0.6	0.6	6.6	6.5	12.6	12.5
07	14 46.8	14 49.2	14 06.4	0.7	0.7	6.7	6.6	12.7	12.6
08	14 47.0	14 49.4	14 06.6	0.8	0.8	6.8	6.7	12.8	12.7
09	14 47.3	14 49.7	14 06.8	0.9	0.9	6.9	6.8	12.9	12.8
10	14 47.5	14 49.9	14 07.1	1.0	1.0	7.0	6.9	13.0	12.9
11	14 47.8	14 50.2	14 07.3	1.1	1.1	7.1	7.0	13.1	13.0
12	14 48.0	14 50.4	14 07.5	1.2	1.2	7.2	7.1	13.2	13.1
13	14 48.3	14 50.7	14 07.8	1.3	1.3	7.3	7.2	13.3	13.2
14	14 48.5	14 50.9	14 08.0	1.4	1.4	7.4	7.3	13.4	13.3
15	14 48.8	14 51.2	14 08.3	1.5	1.5	7.5	7.4	13.5	13.4
16	14 49.0	14 51.4	14 08.5	1.6	1.6	7.6	7.5	13.6	13.5
17	14 49.3	14 51.7	14 08.7	1.7	1.7	7.7	7.6	13.7	13.6
18	14 49.5	14 51.9	14 09.0	1.8	1.8	7.8	7.7	13.8	13.7
19	14 49.8	14 52.2	14 09.2	1.9	1.9	7.9	7.8	13.9	13.8
20	14 50.0	14 52.4	14 09.5	2.0	2.0	8.0	7.9	14.0	13.9
21	14 50.3	14 52.7	14 09.7	2.1	2.1	8.1	8.0	14.1	14.0
22	14 50.5	14 52.9	14 09.9	2.2	2.2	8.2	8.1	14.2	14.1
23	14 50.8	14 53.2	14 10.2	2.3	2.3	8.3	8.2	14.3	14.2
24	14 51.0	14 53.4	14 10.4	2.4	2.4	8.4	8.3	14.4	14.3
25	14 51.3	14 53.7	14 10.6	2.5	2.5	8.5	8.4	14.5	14.4
26	14 51.5	14 53.9	14 10.9	2.6	2.6	8.6	8.5	14.6	14.5
27	14 51.8	14 54.2	14 11.1	2.7	2.7	8.7	8.6	14.7	14.6
28	14 52.0	14 54.4	14 11.4	2.8	2.8	8.8	8.7	14.8	14.7
29	14 52.3	14 54.7	14 11.6	2.9	2.9	8.9	8.8	14.9	14.8
30	14 52.5	14 54.9	14 11.8	3.0	3.0	9.0	8.9	15.0	14.9
31	14 52.8	14 55.2	14 12.1	3.1	3.1	9.1	9.0	15.1	15.0
32	14 53.0	14 55.4	14 12.3	3.2	3.2	9.2	9.1	15.2	15.1
33	14 53.3	14 55.7	14 12.6	3.3	3.3	9.3	9.2	15.3	15.2
34	14 53.5	14 55.9	14 12.8	3.4	3.4	9.4	9.3	15.4	15.3
35	14 53.8	14 56.2	14 13.0	3.5	3.5	9.5	9.4	15.5	15.4
36	14 54.0	14 56.4	14 13.3	3.6	3.6	9.6	9.5	15.6	15.5
37	14 54.3	14 56.7	14 13.5	3.7	3.7	9.7	9.6	15.7	15.6
38	14 54.5	14 56.9	14 13.8	3.8	3.8	9.8	9.7	15.8	15.7
39	14 54.8	14 57.2	14 14.0	3.9	3.9	9.9	9.8	15.9	15.8
40	14 55.0	14 57.5	14 14.2	4.0	4.0	10.0	9.9	16.0	15.9
41	14 55.3	14 57.7	14 14.5	4.1	4.1	10.1	10.0	16.1	16.0
42	14 55.5	14 58.0	14 14.7	4.2	4.2	10.2	10.1	16.2	16.1
43	14 55.8	14 58.2	14 14.9	4.3	4.3	10.3	10.2	16.3	16.2
44	14 56.0	14 58.5	14 15.2	4.4	4.4	10.4	10.3	16.4	16.3
45	14 56.3	14 58.7	14 15.4	4.5	4.5	10.5	10.4	16.5	16.4
46	14 56.5	14 59.0	14 15.7	4.6	4.6	10.6	10.5	16.6	16.5
47	14 56.8	14 59.2	14 15.9	4.7	4.7	10.7	10.6	16.7	16.6
48	14 57.0	14 59.5	14 16.1	4.8	4.8	10.8	10.7	16.8	16.7
49	14 57.3	14 59.7	14 16.4	4.9	4.9	10.9	10.8	16.9	16.8
50	14 57.5	15 00.0	14 16.6	5.0	5.0	11.0	10.9	17.0	16.9
51	14 57.8	15 00.2	14 16.9	5.1	5.1	11.1	11.0	17.1	17.0
52	14 58.0	15 00.5	14 17.1	5.2	5.2	11.2	11.1	17.2	17.1
53	14 58.3	15 00.7	14 17.3	5.3	5.3	11.3	11.2	17.3	17.2
54	14 58.5	15 01.0	14 17.6	5.4	5.4	11.4	11.3	17.4	17.3
55	14 58.8	15 01.2	14 17.8	5.5	5.5	11.5	11.4	17.5	17.4
56	14 59.0	15 01.5	14 18.0	5.6	5.6	11.6	11.5	17.6	17.5
57	14 59.3	15 01.7	14 18.3	5.7	5.7	11.7	11.6	17.7	17.6
58	14 59.5	15 02.0	14 18.5	5.8	5.8	11.8	11.7	17.8	17.7
59	14 59.8	15 02.2	14 18.8	5.9	5.9	11.9	11.8	17.9	17.8
60	15 00.0	15 02.5	14 19.0	6.0	6.0	12.0	11.9	18.0	17.9

TABLES FOR INTERPOLATING SUNRISE, MOONRISE, ETC.

TABLE I - FOR LATITUDE

Tabular Interval 10°	5°	2°	5m	10m	15m	20m	25m	30m	35m	40m	45m	50m	55m	60m	1h05m	1h10m	1h15m	1h20m
° '	° '	° '	m	m	m	m	m	m	m	m	m	m	m	m	h m	h m	h m	h m
0 30	0 15	0 06	0	0	1	1	1	1	1	2	2	2	2	2	0 02	0 02	0 02	0 02
1 00	0 30	0 12	0	1	1	2	2	3	3	3	4	4	4	5	05	05	05	05
1 30	0 45	0 18	1	1	2	3	3	4	4	5	5	6	7	7	07	07	07	07
2 00	1 00	0 24	1	2	3	4	5	5	6	7	7	8	9	10	10	10	10	10
2 30	1 15	0 30	1	2	4	5	6	7	8	9	9	10	11	12	12	13	13	13
3 00	1 30	0 36	1	3	4	6	7	8	9	10	11	12	13	14	0 15	0 15	0 16	0 16
3 30	1 45	0 42	2	3	5	7	8	10	11	12	13	14	16	17	18	18	19	19
4 00	2 00	0 48	2	4	6	8	9	11	13	14	15	16	18	19	20	21	22	22
4 30	2 15	0 54	2	4	7	9	11	13	15	16	18	19	21	22	23	24	25	26
5 00	2 30	1 00	2	5	7	10	12	14	16	18	20	22	23	25	26	27	28	29
5 30	2 45	1 06	3	5	8	11	13	16	18	20	22	24	26	28	0 29	0 30	0 31	0 32
6 00	3 00	1 12	3	6	9	12	14	17	20	22	24	26	29	31	32	33	34	36
6 30	3 15	1 18	3	6	10	13	16	19	22	24	26	29	31	34	36	37	38	40
7 00	3 30	1 24	3	7	10	14	17	20	23	26	29	31	34	37	39	41	42	44
7 30	3 45	1 30	4	7	11	15	18	22	25	28	31	34	37	40	43	44	46	48
8 00	4 00	1 36	4	8	12	16	20	23	27	30	34	37	41	44	0 47	0 48	0 51	0 53
8 30	4 15	1 42	4	8	13	17	21	25	29	33	36	40	44	48	0 51	0 53	0 56	0 58
9 00	4 30	1 48	4	9	13	18	22	27	31	35	39	43	47	52	0 55	0 58	1 01	1 04
9 30	4 45	1 54	5	9	14	29	24	28	33	38	42	47	51	56	1 00	1 04	1 08	1 12
10 00	5 00	2 00	5	10	15	20	25	30	35	40	45	50	55	60	1 05	1 10	1 15	1 20

Table I is for interpolating the LMT of sunrise, twilight, moonrise. etc., for latitude. It is to be entered, in the appropriate column on the left, with the difference between true latitude and the nearest tabular latitude which is less than the true latitude; and with the argument at the top which is the nearest value of the difference between the times for the tabular latitude and the next higher one; the correction so obtained is applied to the time for the tabular latitude; the sign of the correction can be seen by inspection. It is to be noted that the interpolation is not linear, so that when using this table it is essential to take out the tabular phenomenon for the latitude less than the true latitude.

TABLE II - FOR LONGITUDE

Difference between the times for given date and preceding date (for east longitude) or for given date and following date (for west longitude)

Long East or West	10m	20m	30m	40m	50m	60m	10m	1h+20m	30m	40m	1h+50m	60m	2h10m	2h20m	2h30m	2h40m	2h50m	3h00m
°	m	m	m	m	m	m	m	m	m	m	m	m	h m	h m	h m	h m	h m	h m
0	0	0	0	0	0	0	0	0	0	0	0	0	0 00	0 00	0 00	0 00	0 00	0 00
10	0	1	1	1	1	2	2	2	2	3	3	3	04	04	04	04	05	05
20	1	1	2	2	3	3	4	4	5	6	6	7	07	08	08	09	09	10
30	1	2	2	3	4	5	6	7	7	8	9	10	11	12	12	13	14	15
40	1	2	3	4	6	7	8	9	10	11	12	13	14	16	17	18	19	20
50	1	3	3	6	7	8	10	11	12	14	15	17	0 18	0 19	0 21	0 22	0 24	0 23
60	2	3	5	7	8	10	12	13	15	17	18	20	22	23	25	27	28	30
70	2	4	6	8	10	12	14	16	17	19	21	23	25	27	29	31	33	35
80	2	4	7	9	11	13	16	18	20	22	24	27	29	31	33	36	38	40
90	2	5	7	10	12	15	17	20	22	25	27	30	32	35	37	40	42	45
100	3	6	8	11	14	17	19	22	25	28	31	33	0 36	0 39	0 42	0 44	0 47	0 50
110	3	6	9	12	15	18	21	24	27	31	34	37	40	43	46	49	0 52	0 55
120	3	7	10	13	17	20	23	27	30	33	37	40	43	47	50	53	0 57	1 00
130	4	7	11	14	18	22	25	29	32	36	40	43	47	51	54	0 58	1 01	1 05
140	4	8	12	16	19	23	27	31	35	39	43	47	51	54	0 58	1 02	1 06	1 10
150	4	8	13	17	21	25	29	33	38	42	46	50	0 54	0 58	1 03	1 07	1 11	1 15
160	4	9	13	18	22	27	31	36	40	44	49	53	0 58	1 02	1 07	1 11	1 16	1 20
170	5	9	14	19	24	28	33	38	42	47	52	57	1 01	1 06	1 11	1 16	1 20	1 25
180	5	10	15	20	25	30	35	40	45	50	55	60	1 05	1 10	1 15	1 20	1 25	1 30

Table II is for interpolating the LMT of moonrise, moonset and the Moon's meridian passage for longitude, it is entered with longitude and the difference between the times for the given date and for the preceding date (in east longitudes) or following date (in west longitudes). The correction is normally *added* for west longitudes and *subtracted* for east longitudes, but if, as occasionally happens, the times become earlier each day instead of later, the sign of correction must be reversed.

ALTITUDE CORRECTION TABLES 0°–35° — MOON

App. Alt.	0°–4° Corrⁿ	5°–9° Corrⁿ	10°–14° Corrⁿ	15°–19° Corrⁿ	20°–24° Corrⁿ	25°–29° Corrⁿ	30°–34° Corrⁿ	App. Alt.
	0° ′	5° ′	10° ′	15° ′	20° ′	25° ′	30° ′	
00	34.5	58.2	62.1	62.8	62.2	60.8	58.9	00
10	36.5	58.5	62.2	62.8	62.2	60.8	58.8	10
20	38.3	58.7	62.2	62.8	62.1	60.7	58.8	20
30	40.0	58.9	62.3	62.8	62.1	60.7	58.7	30
40	41.5	59.1	62.3	62.8	62.0	60.6	58.6	40
50	42.9	59.3	62.4	62.7	62.0	60.6	58.5	50
	1°	6°	11°	16°	21°	26°	31°	
00	44.2	59.5	62.4	62.7	62.0	60.5	58.5	00
10	45.4	59.7	62.4	62.7	61.9	60.4	58.4	10
20	46.5	59.9	62.5	62.7	61.9	60.4	58.3	20
30	47.5	60.0	62.5	62.7	61.9	60.3	58.2	30
40	48.4	60.2	62.5	62.7	61.8	60.3	58.2	40
50	49.3	60.3	62.6	62.7	61.8	60.2	58.1	50
	2°	7°	12°	17°	22°	27°	32°	
00	50.1	60.5	62.6	62.7	61.7	60.1	58.0	00
10	50.8	60.6	62.6	62.6	61.7	60.1	57.9	10
20	51.5	60.7	62.6	62.6	61.6	60.0	57.8	20
30	52.2	60.9	62.7	62.6	61.6	59.9	57.8	30
40	52.8	61.0	62.7	62.6	61.6	59.9	57.7	40
50	53.4	61.1	62.7	62.6	61.5	59.8	57.6	50
	3°	8°	13°	18°	23°	28°	33°	
00	53.9	61.2	62.7	62.5	61.5	59.7	57.5	00
10	54.4	61.3	62.7	62.5	61.4	59.7	57.4	10
20	54.9	61.4	62.7	62.5	61.4	59.6	57.4	20
30	55.3	61.5	62.8	62.5	61.3	59.5	57.3	30
40	55.7	61.6	62.8	62.4	61.3	59.5	57.2	40
50	56.1	61.6	62.8	62.4	61.2	59.4	57.1	50
	4°	9°	14°	19°	24°	29°	34°	
00	56.4	61.7	62.8	62.4	61.2	59.3	57.0	00
10	56.8	61.8	62.8	62.4	61.1	59.3	56.9	10
20	57.1	61.9	62.8	62.3	61.1	59.2	56.9	20
30	57.4	61.9	62.8	62.3	61.0	59.1	56.8	30
40	57.7	62.0	62.8	62.3	61.0	59.1	56.7	40
50	58.0	62.1	62.8	62.2	60.9	59.0	56.6	50

HP	L	U	L	U	L	U	L	U	L	U	L	U	L	U	HP
54.0	0.3	0.9	0.3	0.9	0.4	1.0	0.5	1.1	0.6	1.2	0.7	1.3	0.9	1.5	54.0
54.3	0.7	1.1	0.7	1.2	0.8	1.2	0.8	1.3	0.9	1.4	1.1	1.5	1.2	1.7	54.3
54.6	1.1	1.4	1.1	1.4	1.1	1.4	1.2	1.5	1.3	1.6	1.4	1.7	1.5	1.8	54.6
54.9	1.4	1.6	1.5	1.6	1.5	1.6	1.6	1.7	1.6	1.8	1.8	1.9	1.9	2.0	54.9
55.2	1.8	1.8	1.8	1.8	1.9	1.8	1.9	1.9	2.0	2.0	2.1	2.1	2.2	2.2	55.2
55.5	2.2	2.0	2.2	2.0	2.3	2.1	2.3	2.1	2.4	2.2	2.4	2.3	2.5	2.4	55.5
55.8	2.6	2.2	2.6	2.2	2.6	2.3	2.7	2.3	2.7	2.4	2.8	2.4	2.9	2.5	55.8
56.1	3.0	2.4	3.0	2.5	3.0	2.5	3.0	2.5	3.1	2.6	3.1	2.6	3.2	2.7	56.1
56.4	3.3	2.7	3.4	2.7	3.4	2.7	3.4	2.7	3.4	2.8	3.5	2.8	3.5	2.9	56.4
56.7	3.7	2.9	3.7	2.9	3.8	2.9	3.8	2.9	3.8	3.0	3.8	3.0	3.9	3.0	56.7
57.0	4.1	3.1	4.1	3.1	4.1	3.1	4.1	3.1	4.2	3.2	4.2	3.2	4.2	3.2	57.0
57.3	4.5	3.3	4.5	3.3	4.5	3.3	4.5	3.3	4.5	3.3	4.5	3.4	4.6	3.4	57.3
57.6	4.9	3.5	4.9	3.5	4.9	3.5	4.9	3.5	4.9	3.5	4.9	3.5	4.9	3.6	57.6
57.9	5.3	3.8	5.7	3.8	5.2	3.8	5.2	3.7	5.2	3.7	5.2	3.7	5.2	3.7	57.9
58.2	5.6	4.0	5.6	4.0	5.6	4.0	5.6	4.0	5.6	3.9	5.6	3.9	5.6	3.9	58.2
58.5	6.0	4.2	6.0	4.2	6.0	4.2	6.0	4.2	6.0	4.1	5.9	4.1	5.9	4.1	58.5
58.8	6.4	4.4	6.4	4.4	6.4	4.4	6.3	4.4	6.3	4.3	6.3	4.3	6.2	4.2	58.8
59.1	6.8	4.6	6.8	4.6	6.7	4.6	6.7	4.6	6.7	4.5	6.6	4.5	6.6	4.4	59.1
59.4	7.2	4.8	7.1	4.8	7.1	4.8	7.1	4.8	7.0	4.7	7.0	4.7	6.9	4.6	59.4
59.7	7.5	5.1	7.5	5.0	7.5	5.0	7.5	5.0	7.4	4.9	7.7	4.8	7.2	4.8	59.7
60.0	7.9	5.3	7.9	5.3	7.9	5.2	7.8	5.2	7.8	5.0	7.7	5.0	7.6	4.9	60.0
60.3	8.3	5.5	8.3	5.5	8.2	5.4	8.2	5.4	8.2	5.2	8.1	5.3	7.9	5.1	60.3
60.6	8.7	5.7	8.7	5.7	8.6	5.7	8.6	5.6	8.5	5.5	8.4	5.4	8.2	5.3	60.6
60.9	9.1	5.9	9.0	5.9	9.0	5.9	8.9	5.8	8.8	5.7	8.7	5.6	8.6	5.4	60.9
61.2	9.5	6.2	9.4	6.1	9.4	6.1	9.3	6.0	9.2	5.9	9.1	5.8	8.9	5.6	61.2
61.5	9.8	6.4	9.8	6.3	9.7	6.3	9.7	6.2	9.5	6.1	9.4	5.9	9.2	5.8	61.5

DIP

Ht. of Eye (m)	Corrⁿ	Ht. of Eye (ft.)	Ht. of Eye (m)	Corrⁿ	Ht. of Eye (ft.)
2.4		8.0	9.5		31.5
2.6	−2.8	8.6	9.9	−5.5	32.7
2.8	−2.9	9.2	10.3	−5.6	33.9
3.0	−3.0	9.8	10.6	−5.7	35.1
3.2	−3.1	10.5	11.0	−5.8	36.3
3.4	−3.2	11.2	11.4	−5.9	37.6
3.6	−3.3	11.9	11.8	−6.0	38.9
3.8	−3.4	12.6	12.2	−6.1	40.1
4.0	−3.5	13.3	12.6	−6.2	41.5
4.3	−3.6	14.1	13.0	−6.3	42.8
4.5	−3.7	14.9	13.4	−6.4	44.2
4.7	−3.8	15.7	13.8	−6.5	45.5
5.0	−3.9	16.5	14.2	−6.6	46.9
5.2	−4.0	17.4	14.7	−6.7	48.4
5.5	−4.1	18.3	15.1	−6.8	49.8
5.8	−4.2	19.1	15.5	−6.9	51.3
6.1	−4.3	20.1	16.0	−7.0	52.8
6.3	−4.4	21.0	16.5	−7.1	54.3
6.6	−4.5	22.0	16.9	−7.2	55.8
6.9	−4.6	22.9	17.4	−7.3	57.4
7.2	−4.7	23.9	17.9	−7.4	58.9
7.5	−4.8	24.9	18.4	−7.5	60.5
7.9	−4.9	26.0	18.8	−7.6	62.1
8.2	−5.0	27.1	19.7	−7.7	63.8
8.5	−5.1	28.1	19.8	−7.8	65.4
8.8	−5.2	29.2	20.4	−7.9	67.1
9.2	−5.3	30.4	20.9	−8.0	68.8
9.5	−5.4	31.5	21.4	−8.1	70.5

MOON CORRECTION
TABLE

The correction is in two parts; the first correction is taken from the upper part of the table with argument apparent altitude, and the second from the lower part, with argument HP, in the same column as that from which the first correction was taken. Separate corrections are given in the lower part for lower (L) and up-per(U) limbs. All corrections are to be **added** to apparent altitude, *but 30′ is to be subtracted from the altitude of the upper limb.*

For corrections for pressure and temperature see page A4.

For bubble sextant observations ignore dip, take the mean of upper and lower limb corrections and subtract 15′ from the altitude.

App. Alt. = Apparent altitude = Sextant altitude corrected for index error and dip.

ALTITUDE CORRECTION TABLES 35°–90°— MOON

App. Alt.	35°–39° Corrⁿ	40°–44° Corrⁿ	45°–49° Corrⁿ	50°–54° Corrⁿ	55°–59° Corrⁿ	60°–64° Corrⁿ	65°–69° Corrⁿ	70°–74° Corrⁿ	75°–79° Corrⁿ	80°–84° Corrⁿ	85°–89° Corrⁿ	App. Alt.
′	° ′	° ′	° ′	° ′	° ′	° ′	° ′	° ′	° ′	° ′	° ′	′
	35	**40**	**45**	**50**	**55**	**60**	**65**	**70**	**75**	**80**	**85**	
00	56.5	53.7	50.5	46.9	43.1	38.9	34.6	30.0	25.3	20.5	15.6	00
10	56.4	53.6	50.4	46.8	42.9	38.8	34.4	29.9	25.2	20.4	15.5	10
20	56.3	53.5	50.2	46.7	42.8	38.7	34.3	29.7	25.0	20.2	15.3	20
30	56.2	53.4	50.1	46.5	42.7	38.5	34.1	29.6	24.9	20.0	15.1	30
40	56.2	53.3	50.0	46.4	42.5	38.4	34.0	29.4	24.7	19.9	15.0	40
50	56.1	53.2	49.9	46.3	42.4	38.2	33.8	29.3	24.5	19.7	14.8	50
	36	**41**	**46**	**51**	**56**	**61**	**66**	**71**	**76**	**81**	**86**	
00	56.0	53.1	49.8	46.2	42.3	38.1	33.7	29.1	24.4	19.6	14.6	00
10	55.9	53.0	49.7	46.0	42.1	37.9	33.5	29.0	24.2	19.4	14.5	10
20	55.8	52.9	49.5	45.9	42.0	37.8	33.4	28.8	24.1	19.2	14.3	20
30	55.7	52.8	49.4	45.8	41.9	37.7	33.2	28.7	23.9	19.1	14.2	30
40	55.6	52.6	49.3	45.7	41.7	37.5	33.1	28.5	23.8	18.9	14.0	40
50	55.5	52.5	49.2	45.5	41.6	37.4	32.9	28.3	23.6	18.7	13.8	50
	37	**42**	**47**	**52**	**57**	**62**	**67**	**72**	**77**	**82**	**87**	
00	55.4	52.4	49.1	45.4	41.4	37.2	32.8	28.2	23.4	18.6	13.7	00
10	55.3	52.3	49.0	45.3	41.3	37.1	32.6	28.0	23.3	18.4	13.5	10
20	55.2	52.2	48.8	45.2	41.2	36.9	32.5	27.9	23.1	18.2	13.3	20
30	55.1	52.1	48.7	45.0	41.0	36.8	32.3	27.7	22.9	18.1	13.2	30
40	55.0	52.0	48.6	44.9	40.9	36.6	32.2	27.6	22.8	17.9	13.0	40
50	55.0	51.9	48.5	44.8	40.8	36.5	32.0	27.4	22.6	17.8	12.8	50
	38	**43**	**48**	**53**	**58**	**63**	**68**	**73**	**78**	**83**	**88**	
00	54.9	51.8	48.4	44.6	40.6	36.4	31.9	27.2	22.5	17.6	12.7	00
10	54.8	51.7	48.3	44.5	40.5	36.2	31.7	27.1	22.3	17.4	12.5	10
20	54.7	51.6	48.1	44.4	40.3	36.1	31.6	26.9	22.1	17.3	12.3	20
30	54.6	51.5	48.0	44.2	40.2	35.9	31.4	26.8	22.0	17.1	12.2	30
40	54.5	51.4	47.9	44.1	40.1	35.8	31.3	26.6	21.8	16.9	12.0	40
50	54.4	51.2	47.8	44.0	39.9	35.6	31.1	26.5	21.7	16.8	11.8	50
	39	**44**	**49**	**54**	**59**	**64**	**69**	**74**	**79**	**84**	**89**	
00	54.3	51.1	47.7	43.9	39.8	35.5	31.0	26.3	21.5	16.6	11.7	00
10	54.2	51.0	47.5	43.7	39.6	35.3	30.8	26.1	21.3	16.4	11.5	10
20	54.1	50.9	47.4	43.6	39.5	35.2	30.7	26.0	21.2	16.3	11.4	20
30	54.0	50.8	47.3	43.5	39.4	35.0	30.5	25.8	21.0	16.1	11.2	30
40	53.9	50.7	47.2	43.3	39.2	34.9	30.4	25.7	20.9	16.0	11.0	40
50	53.8	50.6	47.0	43.2	39.1	34.7	30.2	25.5	20.7	15.8	10.9	50

HP	L	U	L	U	L	U	L	U	L	U	L	U	L	U	L	U	L	U	L	U	L	U	HP
′	′	′	′	′	′	′	′	′	′	′	′	′	′	′	′	′	′	′	′	′	′	′	′
54.0	1.1	1.7	1.3	1.9	1.5	2.1	1.7	2.4	2.0	2.6	2.3	2.9	2.6	3.2	2.9	3.5	3.2	3.8	3.5	4.1	3.8	4.5	54.0
54.3	1.4	1.8	1.6	2.0	1.8	2.2	2.0	2.5	2.2	2.7	2.5	3.0	2.8	3.2	3.1	3.5	3.3	3.8	3.6	4.1	3.9	4.4	54.3
54.6	1.7	2.0	1.9	2.2	2.1	2.4	2.3	2.6	2.5	2.8	2.7	3.0	3.0	3.3	3.2	3.5	3.5	3.8	3.8	4.0	4.0	4.3	54.6
54.9	2.0	2.2	2.2	2.3	2.3	2.5	2.5	2.7	2.7	2.9	2.9	3.1	3.2	3.3	3.4	3.5	3.6	3.8	3.9	4.0	4.1	4.3	54.9
55.2	2.3	2.3	2.5	2.4	2.6	2.6	2.8	2.8	3.0	2.9	3.2	3.1	3.4	3.3	3.6	3.5	3.8	3.7	4.0	4.0	4.2	4.2	55.2
55.5	2.7	2.5	2.8	2.6	2.9	2.7	3.1	2.9	3.2	3.0	3.4	3.2	3.6	3.4	3.7	3.5	3.9	3.7	4.1	3.9	4.3	4.1	55.5
55.8	3.0	2.6	3.1	2.7	3.2	2.8	3.3	3.0	3.5	3.1	3.6	3.3	3.8	3.4	3.9	3.6	4.1	3.7	4.2	3.9	4.4	4.0	55.8
56.1	3.3	2.8	3.4	2.9	3.5	3.0	3.6	3.1	3.7	3.2	3.8	3.3	4.0	3.4	4.1	3.6	4.2	3.7	4.4	3.8	4.5	4.0	56.1
56.4	3.6	2.9	3.7	3.0	3.8	3.1	3.9	3.2	3.9	3.3	4.0	3.4	4.1	3.5	4.3	3.6	4.4	3.7	4.5	3.8	4.6	3.9	56.4
56.7	3.9	3.1	4.0	3.1	4.1	3.2	4.1	3.3	4.2	3.3	4.3	3.4	4.3	3.5	4.4	3.6	4.5	3.7	4.6	3.8	4.7	3.8	56.7
57.0	4.3	3.2	4.3	3.3	4.3	3.3	4.4	3.4	4.4	3.4	4.5	3.5	4.5	3.5	4.6	3.6	4.7	3.6	4.7	3.7	4.8	3.8	57.0
57.3	4.6	3.4	4.6	3.4	4.6	3.4	4.7	3.5	4.7	3.5	4.7	3.6	4.7	3.6	4.8	3.6	4.8	3.7	4.9	3.7	4.9	3.7	57.3
57.6	4.9	3.6	4.9	3.6	4.9	3.6	4.9	3.6	4.9	3.6	4.9	3.6	4.9	3.6	4.9	3.6	5.0	3.6	5.0	3.6	5.0	3.6	57.6
57.9	5.2	3.7	5.2	3.7	5.2	3.7	5.2	3.7	5.2	3.7	5.1	3.6	5.1	3.6	5.1	3.6	5.1	3.6	5.1	3.6	5.1	3.6	57.9
58.2	5.5	3.9	5.5	3.8	5.5	3.8	5.4	3.8	5.4	3.7	5.4	3.7	5.3	3.7	5.3	3.6	5.2	3.6	5.2	3.5	5.2	3.5	58.2
58.5	5.9	4.0	5.8	4.0	5.8	3.9	5.7	3.9	5.6	3.8	5.6	3.8	5.5	3.7	5.5	3.6	5.4	3.6	5.3	3.5	5.3	3.4	58.5
58.8	6.2	4.2	6.1	4.1	6.0	4.1	6.0	4.0	5.9	3.9	5.8	3.8	5.7	3.7	5.6	3.6	5.5	3.5	5.4	3.5	5.3	3.4	58.8
59.1	6.5	4.3	6.4	4.3	6.3	4.2	6.2	4.1	6.1	4.0	6.0	3.9	5.9	3.8	5.8	3.6	5.7	3.5	5.6	3.4	5.4	3.3	59.1
59.4	6.8	4.5	6.7	4.4	6.6	4.3	6.5	4.2	6.4	4.1	6.2	3.9	6.1	3.8	6.0	3.7	5.8	3.5	5.7	3.4	5.5	3.2	59.4
59.7	7.1	4.7	7.0	4.5	6.9	4.4	6.8	4.3	6.6	4.1	6.5	4.0	6.3	3.8	6.1	3.7	6.0	3.5	5.8	3.3	5.6	3.2	59.7
60.0	7.5	4.8	7.3	4.7	7.2	4.5	7.0	4.4	6.9	4.2	6.7	4.0	6.5	3.9	6.3	3.7	6.1	3.5	5.9	3.3	5.7	3.1	60.0
60.3	7.8	5.0	7.6	4.8	7.5	4.7	7.3	4.5	7.1	4.3	6.9	4.1	6.7	3.9	6.5	3.7	6.3	3.5	6.0	3.2	5.8	3.0	60.3
60.6	8.1	5.1	7.9	5.0	7.7	4.8	7.6	4.6	7.3	4.4	7.1	4.2	6.9	3.9	6.7	3.7	6.4	3.4	6.2	3.2	5.9	2.9	60.6
60.9	8.4	5.3	8.2	5.1	8.0	4.9	7.8	4.7	7.6	4.5	7.3	4.2	7.1	4.0	6.8	3.7	6.6	3.4	6.3	3.2	6.0	2.9	60.9
61.2	8.7	5.4	8.5	5.2	8.3	5.0	8.1	4.8	7.8	4.5	7.6	4.3	7.3	4.0	7.0	3.7	6.7	3.4	6.4	3.1	6.1	2.8	61.2
61.5	9.1	5.6	8.8	5.4	8.6	5.1	8.3	4.9	8.1	4.6	7.8	4.3	7.5	4.0	7.2	3.7	6.9	3.4	6.5	3.1	6.2	2.7	61.5

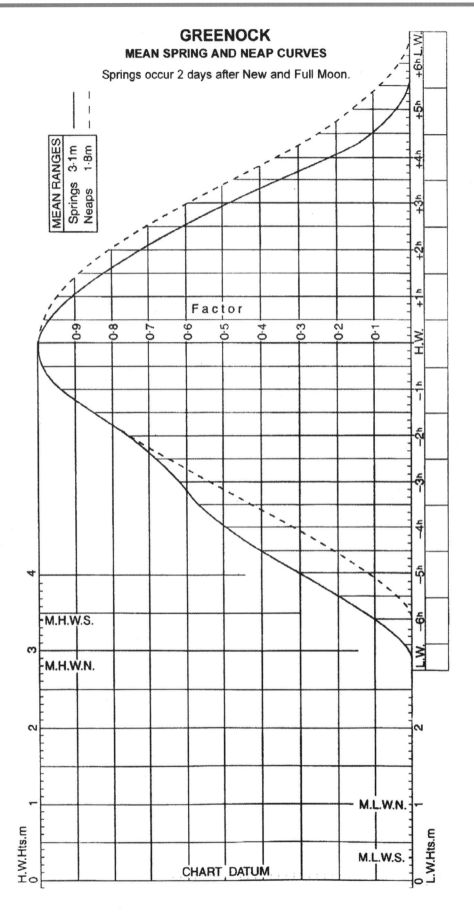

GREENOCK
MEAN SPRING AND NEAP CURVES
Springs occur 2 days after New and Full Moon.

MEAN RANGES
Springs 3·1m
Neaps 1·8m

Factor

H.W.

M.H.W.S.

M.H.W.N.

M.L.W.N.

M.L.W.S.

CHART DATUM

H.W.Hts.m

L.W.Hts.m

L.W.

SCOTLAND - GREENOCK

Lat 55°57'N   LONG 4°46'W

TIME ZONE UT (GMT) TIMES AND HEIGHTS OF HIGH AND LOW WATERS YEAR 2006

JANUARY

Date	Time	m	Time	m	Time	m	Time	m
1 SU	0052	3.3	0615	0.6	1317	3.6	1849	0.3
2 M	0144	3.3	0703	0.6	1400	3.7	1937	0.2
3 TU	0234	3.3	0753	0.6	1444	3.7	2027	0.2
4 W	0323	3.3	0843	0.7	1529	3.7	2118	0.3
5 TH	0412	3.3	0934	0.8	1616	3.7	2213	0.4
6 F	0501	3.2	1028	0.9	1707	3.6	2312	0.5
7 SA	0551	3.1	1127	1.0	1802	3.4		
8 SU	0017	0.6	0643	3.0	1233	1.1	1904	3.2
9 M	0123	0.7	0742	3.0	1345	1.1	2026	3.1
10 TU	0226	0.8	0901	3.0	1456	1.0	2149	3.1
11 W	0324	0.8	1011	3.1	1556	0.9	2253	3.1
12 TH	0418	0.8	1104	3.2	1646	0.7	2346	3.1
13 F	0505	0.8	1149	3.4	1730	0.6		
14 SA ○	0034	3.1	0548	0.8	1230	3.5	1808	0.6
15 SU	0117	3.1	0627	0.8	1308	3.5	1843	0.6
16 M	0155	3.1	0704	0.8	1344	3.6	1917	0.6
17 TU	0230	3.1	0738	0.8	1418	3.6	1950	0.6
18 W	0302	3.0	0813	0.8	1451	3.5	2025	0.6
19 TH	0335	3.0	0849	0.8	1525	3.5	2101	0.6
20 F	0409	3.0	0926	0.8	1601	3.4	2139	0.6
21 SA	0445	3.0	1007	0.9	1639	3.3	2223	0.7
22 SU	0524	2.9	1054	1.0	1721	3.2	2314	0.8
23 M	0608	2.8	1150	1.1	1809	3.0		
24 TU	0012	0.9	0701	2.7	1253	1.2	1907	2.9
25 W	0115	1.0	0812	2.7	1404	1.1	2021	2.9
26 TH	0222	1.0	0940	2.8	1517	1.0	2146	2.9
27 F	0328	0.9	1045	3.0	1617	0.7	2255	3.0
28 SA	0426	0.8	1135	3.3	1707	0.4	2353	3.2
29 SU ●	0517	0.6	1220	3.5	1752	0.2		
30 M	0047	3.2	0604	0.5	1306	3.6	1837	0.0
31 TU	0138	3.3	0650	0.4	1350	3.8	1922	0.0

FEBRUARY

Date	Time	m	Time	m	Time	m	Time	m
1 W	0226	3.3	0736	0.4	1434	3.8	2007	0.0
2 TH	0309	3.4	0822	0.4	1516	3.9	2054	0.1
3 F	0349	3.4	0908	0.5	1558	3.8	2142	0.2
4 SA	0427	3.3	0956	0.6	1641	3.6	2236	0.4
5 SU	0507	3.2	1048	0.8	1725	3.4	2338	0.7
6 M	0550	3.1	1152	1.0	1815	3.1		
7 TU	0051	0.9	0640	2.9	1317	1.1	1919	2.8
8 W	0206	1.0	0746	2.8	1441	1.1	2143	2.7
9 TH	0311	1.0	0948	2.9	1546	0.9	2252	2.9
10 F	0407	0.9	1050	3.1	1636	0.7	2342	3.0
11 SA	0454	0.7	1137	3.2	1717	0.6		
12 SU	0026	3.0	0534	0.7	1218	3.4	1753	0.5
13 M ○	0106	3.0	0610	0.6	1255	3.4	1825	0.4
14 TU	0141	3.0	0642	0.6	1328	3.4	1854	0.4
15 W	0212	3.0	0711	0.6	1358	3.4	1923	0.4
16 TH	0238	3.0	0741	0.5	1427	3.4	1952	0.4
17 F	0304	3.0	0814	0.5	1459	3.4	2024	0.4
18 SA	0332	3.1	0848	0.5	1532	3.4	2100	0.4
19 SU	0402	3.0	0926	0.6	1607	3.3	2140	0.5
20 M	0435	2.9	1009	0.7	1645	3.2	2227	0.7
21 TU	0511	2.8	1102	0.9	1728	3.0	2325	0.9
22 W	0558	2.7	1207	1.0	1824	2.8		
23 TH	0032	1.0	0709	2.6	1324	1.1	1942	2.7
24 F	0148	1.1	0904	2.6	1456	0.9	2130	2.7
25 SA	0311	1.0	1024	2.9	1602	0.6	2249	2.9
26 SU	0414	0.7	1117	3.2	1651	0.2	2346	3.1
27 M	0503	0.5	1204	3.4	1735	0.0		
28 TU ●	0036	3.2	0547	0.4	1249	3.6	1816	-0.1

MARCH

Date	Time	m	Time	m	Time	m	Time	m
1 W	0123	3.3	0630	0.2	1316	3.8	1859	-0.2
2 TH	0205	3.4	0712	0.2	1416	3.9	1941	-0.1
3 F	0242	3.4	0755	0.2	1457	3.9	2025	0.0
4 SA	0317	3.4	0837	0.3	1537	3.8	2110	0.2
5 SU	0352	3.4	0921	0.4	1614	3.6	2158	0.5
6 M	0429	3.3	1009	0.6	1655	3.3	2255	0.8
7 TU	0510	3.1	1109	0.9	1741	3.0		
8 W	0019	1.1	0558	2.9	1252	1.1	1839	2.6
9 TH	0145	1.2	0659	2.8	1422	1.0	2141	2.6
10 F	0252	1.1	0923	2.7	1525	0.9	2241	2.7
11 SA	0348	1.0	1031	3.0	1614	0.7	2326	2.9
12 SU	0434	0.8	1117	3.1	1653	0.5		
13 M	0005	3.0	0511	0.6	1157	3.2	1727	0.4
14 TU ○	0042	3.0	0544	0.5	1232	3.3	1757	0.4
15 W	0114	3.0	0613	0.5	1303	3.3	1824	0.4
16 TH	0143	3.0	0640	0.4	1330	3.3	1850	0.3
17 F	0206	3.0	0708	0.4	1359	3.3	1918	0.3
18 SA	0229	3.1	0740	0.3	1431	3.3	1951	0.3
19 SU	0256	3.1	0814	0.3	1505	3.3	2027	0.3
20 M	0325	3.1	0853	0.4	1540	3.2	2108	0.4
21 TU	0356	3.0	0937	0.6	1617	3.1	2156	0.6
22 W	0429	2.9	1032	0.7	1700	2.9	2254	0.9
23 TH	0513	2.7	1141	0.9	1758	2.7		
24 F	0004	1.0	0626	2.6	1303	0.9	1926	2.6
25 SA	0126	1.1	0837	2.6	1437	0.7	2124	2.7
26 SU	0254	1.0	1001	2.9	1541	0.4	2237	2.9
27 M	0356	0.7	1054	3.2	1628	0.1	2329	3.1
28 TU	0444	0.4	1142	3.4	1711	-0.1		
29 W ●	0015	3.2	0525	0.3	1228	3.6	1752	-0.2
30 TH	0058	3.3	0606	0.1	1312	3.7	1833	-0.2
31 F	0136	3.4	0647	0.1	1354	3.8	1914	-0.1

APRIL

Date	Time	m	Time	m	Time	m	Time	m
1 SA	0211	3.4	0727	0.1	1434	3.7	1956	0.1
2 SU	0246	3.5	0809	0.2	1513	3.6	2040	0.4
3 M	0321	3.5	0852	0.3	1551	3.4	2127	0.6
4 TU	0358	3.4	0938	0.6	1631	3.1	2220	0.9
5 W	0438	3.2	1037	0.8	1720	2.8	2342	1.2
6 TH	0527	3.0	1222	1.0	1824	2.5		
7 F	0551	3.1	1127	1.0	1802	3.4		
8 SA	0220	1.2	0814	2.7	1450	0.8	2212	2.7
9 SU	0316	1.0	0956	2.9	1539	0.7	2254	2.8
10 M	0403	0.8	1044	3.0	1619	0.5	2332	2.9
11 TU	0441	0.6	1123	3.1	1653	0.4		
12 W	0007	3.0	0513	0.5	1158	3.1	1723	0.4
13 TH ○	0040	3.0	0542	0.4	1228	3.1	1750	0.3
14 F	0108	3.0	0609	0.4	1257	3.2	1818	0.3
15 SA	0132	3.0	0639	0.3	1329	3.2	1848	0.3
16 SU	0157	3.1	0712	0.3	1405	3.2	1924	0.3
17 M	0226	3.2	0749	0.3	1441	3.2	2004	0.3
18 TU	0257	3.2	0831	0.3	1519	3.1	2049	0.5
19 W	0330	3.1	0919	0.5	1600	3.0	2140	0.7
20 TH	0406	3.0	1019	0.6	1649	2.8	2240	0.9
21 F	0455	2.8	1130	0.7	1757	2.6	2350	1.0
22 SA	0617	2.7	1253	0.7	1932	2.6		
23 SU	0110	1.0	0813	2.7	1412	0.5	2107	2.7
24 M	0229	0.9	0932	3.0	1512	0.2	2213	2.9
25 TU	0331	0.7	1028	3.2	1601	0.0	2303	3.1
26 W	0420	0.4	1116	3.4	1645	-0.1	2347	3.2
27 TH ●	0503	0.2	1203	3.5	1727	-0.1		
28 F	0028	3.3	0544	0.1	1248	3.6	1808	0.0
29 SA	0107	3.4	0624	0.1	1332	3.5	1850	0.1
30 SU	0143	3.4	0705	0.1	1414	3.5	1934	0.3

○ Full Moon   ● New Moon

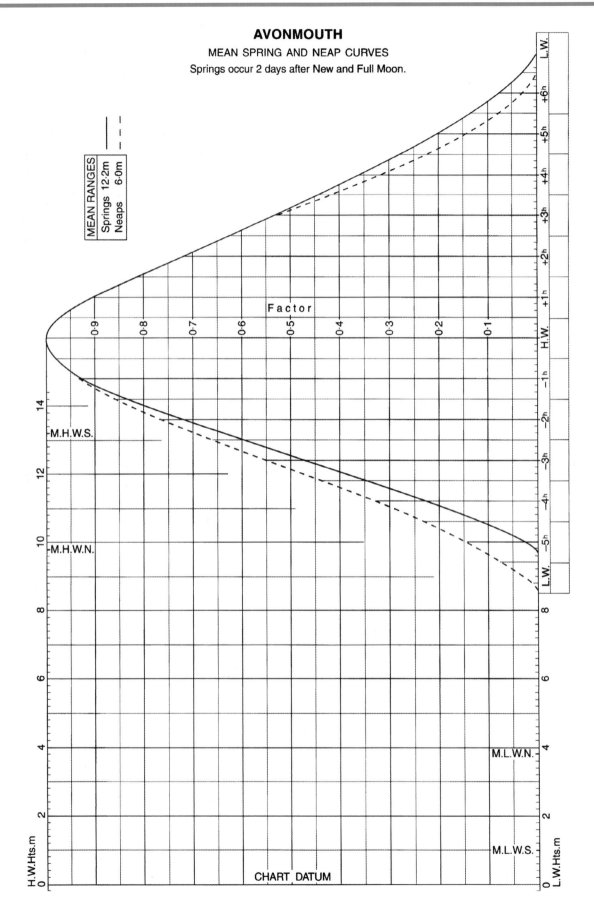

AVONMOUTH
MEAN SPRING AND NEAP CURVES
Springs occur 2 days after New and Full Moon.

ENGLAND – PORT OF BRISTOL (AVONMOUTH)

Lat 51°30'N   LONG 2°44'W

TIME ZONE UT (GMT)   TIMES AND HEIGHTS OF HIGH AND LOW WATERS   YEAR 2006

JANUARY

Day	Time	m	Day	Time	m
1 SU	0212 / 0749 / 1439 / 2017	1.7 / 13.2 / 1.4 / 13.0	16 M	0244 / 0822 / 1510 / 2046	1.9 / 12.3 / 2.2 / 12.0
2 M	0301 / 0837 / 1529 / 2105	1.5 / 13.3 / 1.3 / 13.1	17 TU	0321 / 0857 / 1542 / 2118	2.1 / 12.2 / 2.4 / 11.8
3 TU	0347 / 0924 / 1614 / 2151	1.5 / 13.3 / 1.3 / 13.0	18 W	0349 / 0928 / 1607 / 2147	2.3 / 12.0 / 2.5 / 11.7
4 W	0429 / 1010 / 1657 / 2235	1.6 / 13.1 / 1.4 / 12.7	19 TH	0411 / 0957 / 1628 / 2215	2.4 / 11.8 / 2.6 / 11.4
5 TH	0509 / 1056 / 1737 / 2320	1.8 / 12.8 / 1.6 / 12.2	20 F	0435 / 1025 / 1652 / 2243	2.4 / 11.5 / 2.6 / 11.2
6 F	0548 / 1144 / 1817	2.1 / 12.2 / 2.1	21 SA	0504 / 1056 / 1724 / 2317	2.5 / 11.3 / 2.7 / 10.9
7 SA	0008 / 0630 / 1239 / 1902	11.6 / 2.6 / 11.6 / 2.6	22 SU	0540 / 1135 / 1802	2.8 / 10.9 / 3.0
8 SU	0103 / 0720 / 1343 / 1956	11.0 / 3.1 / 11.0 / 3.1	23 M	0000 / 0623 / 1225 / 1849	10.5 / 3.3 / 10.4 / 3.5
9 M	0211 / 0826 / 1453 / 2107	10.5 / 3.6 / 10.7 / 3.5	24 TU	0056 / 0721 / 1331 / 1956	10.1 / 3.7 / 10.1 / 3.9
10 TU	0323 / 0951 / 1600 / 2225	10.4 / 3.7 / 10.7 / 3.4	25 W	0211 / 0847 / 1454 / 2133	9.8 / 4.0 / 10.0 / 3.9
11 W	0428 / 1103 / 1701 / 2330	107 / 3.3 / 11.0 / 3.0	26 TH	0343 / 1019 / 1620 / 2300	10.2 / 3.6 / 10.5 / 3.3
12 TH	0525 / 1202 / 1756	11.2 / 2.8 / 11.4	27 F	0458 / 1134 / 1729	11.0 / 2.8 / 11.4
13 F	0024 / 0615 / 1254 / 1844	2.5 / 11.7 / 2.4 / 11.8	28 SA	0008 / 0557 / 1238 / 1826	2.6 / 12.0 / 2.1 / 12.3
14 SA ○	0115 / 0701 / 1344 / 1929	2.1 / 12.1 / 2.2 / 12.0	29 SU ●	0109 / 0650 / 1339 / 1919	1.9 / 12.9 / 1.5 / 13.0
15 SU	0202 / 0743 / 1429 / 2010	2.0 / 12.3 / 2.1 / 12.1	30 M	0207 / 0740 / 1435 / 2008	1.4 / 13.5 / 1.0 / 13.5
			31 TU	0259 / 0828 / 1525 / 2054	1.0 / 13.9 / 0.6 / 13.7

FEBRUARY

Day	Time	m	Day	Time	m
1 W	0344 / 0913 / 1608 / 2137	0.8 / 14.1 / 0.5 / 13.8	16 TH	0340 / 0907 / 1556 / 2124	1.9 / 12.3 / 2.2 / 12.1
2 TH	0423 / 0955 / 1645 / 2217	0.8 / 14.0 / 0.6 / 13.5	17 F	0359 / 0933 / 1610 / 2148	2.1 / 12.2 / 2.3 / 11.9
3 F	0456 / 1035 / 1716 / 2254	1.0 / 13.5 / 1.1 / 12.9	18 SA	0414 / 0958 / 1625 / 2213	2.1 / 12.0 / 2.2 / 11.8
4 SA	0525 / 1115 / 1745 / 2332	1.5 / 12.8 / 1.7 / 12.1	19 SU	0436 / 1026 / 1650 / 2243	2.1 / 11.8 / 2.3 / 11.5
5 SU	0553 / 1156 / 1816	2.2 / 11.8 / 2.4	20 M	0506 / 1100 / 1722 / 2321	2.3 / 11.4 / 2.6 / 11.0
6 M	0013 / 0627 / 1247 / 1856	11.1 / 2.9 / 10.7 / 3.3	21 TU	0542 / 1145 / 1802	2.8 / 10.7 / 3.1
7 TU	0107 / 0716 / 1402 / 1955	10.2 / 3.8 / 9.9 / 4.0	22 W	0011 / 0631 / 1246 / 1859	10.3 / 3.5 / 10.0 / 3.9
8 W	0237 / 0836 / 1531 / 2138	9.6 / 4.4 / 9.7 / 4.3	23 TH	0123 / 0749 / 1412 / 2039	9.7 / 4.1 / 9.6 / 4.3
9 TH	0401 / 1039 / 1643 / 2306	9.8 / 4.1 / 10.1 / 3.7	24 F	0308 / 0952 / 1601 / 2243	9.7 / 3.9 / 10.1 / 3.7
10 F	0508 / 1145 / 1742	10.5 / 3.3 / 10.8	25 SA	0442 / 1123 / 1719 / 2359	10.7 / 2.9 / 11.2 / 2.7
11 SA	0006 / 0602 / 1239 / 1831	2.9 / 11.3 / 2.6 / 11.5	26 SU	0546 / 1230 / 1816	11.9 / 1.9 / 12.4
12 SU	0058 / 0648 / 1328 / 1915	2.2 / 12.0 / 2.0 / 12.0	27 M	0100 / 0638 / 1330 / 1906	1.7 / 13.1 / 1.1 / 13.3
13 M ○	0146 / 0728 / 1414 / 1953	1.8 / 12.4 / 1.8 / 12.3	28 TU ●	0156 / 0726 / 1423 / 1952	1.0 / 13.9 / 0.5 / 13.9
14 TU	0230 / 0805 / 1456 / 2027	1.6 / 12.6 / 1.8 / 12.3			
15 W	0309 / 0838 / 1531 / 2057	1.7 / 12.5 / 1.9 / 12.2			

MARCH

Day	Time	m	Day	Time	m
1 W	0246 / 0811 / 1510 / 2035	0.5 / 14.4 / 0.1 / 14.2	16 TH	0245 / 0810 / 1506 / 2028	1.5 / 12.6 / 1.7 / 12.4
2 TH	0329 / 0853 / 1550 / 2115	0.2 / 14.5 / 0.0 / 14.2	17 F	0317 / 0839 / 1532 / 2055	1.7 / 12.4 / 2.0 / 12.3
3 F	0405 / 0933 / 1622 / 2151	0.3 / 14.3 / 0.4 / 13.8	18 SA	0338 / 0905 / 1545 / 2119	1.9 / 12.3 / 2.2 / 12.2
4 SA	0433 / 1009 / 1647 / 2224	0.8 / 13.7 / 1.0 / 13.1	19 SU	0351 / 0930 / 1557 / 2145	2.0 / 12.2 / 2.1 / 12.0
5 SU	0455 / 1043 / 1708 / 2256	1.4 / 12.8 / 1.7 / 12.2	20 M	0410 / 0959 / 1621 / 2216	1.9 / 12.0 / 2.1 / 11.7
6 M	0516 / 1118 / 1734 / 2330	2.1 / 11.6 / 2.5 / 11.1	21 TU	0439 / 1035 / 1651 / 2254	2.1 / 11.5 / 2.4 / 11.2
7 TU	0546 / 1158 / 1809	2.9 / 10.3 / 3.4	22 W	0514 / 1119 / 1730 / 2344	2.6 / 10.8 / 3.0 / 10.4
8 W	0014 / 0628 / 1307 / 1904	9.9 / 3.9 / 9.2 / 4.4	23 TH	0601 / 1220 / 1826	3.3 / 9.9 / 3.9
9 TH	0150 / 0744 / 1507 / 2050	9.0 / 4.7 / 8.9 / 4.8	24 F	0056 / 0718 / 1352 / 2008	9.6 / 4.1 / 9.4 / 4.4
10 F	0339 / 1024 / 1623 / 2247	9.3 / 4.4 / 9.6 / 4.0	25 SA	0252 / 0940 / 1551 / 2233	9.7 / 3.9 / 10.0 / 3.6
11 SA	0447 / 1127 / 1722 / 2345	10.2 / 3.4 / 10.6 / 2.9	26 SU	0426 / 1110 / 1704 / 2343	10.8 / 2.7 / 11.3 / 2.4
12 SU	0541 / 1217 / 1809	11.2 / 2.4 / 11.5	27 M	0528 / 1213 / 1758	12.1 / 1.6 / 12.6
13 M	0034 / 0624 / 1304 / 1849	2.1 / 12.0 / 1.8 / 12.1	28 TU	0040 / 0618 / 1308 / 1845	1.4 / 13.2 / 0.8 / 13.5
14 TU ○	0122 / 0703 / 1349 / 1925	1.6 / 12.5 / 1.5 / 12.4	29 W ●	0133 / 0704 / 1359 / 1928	0.7 / 14.0 / 0.2 / 14.1
15 W	0206 / 0738 / 1430 / 1958	1.4 / 12.6 / 1.5 / 12.5	30 TH	0221 / 0748 / 1444 / 2009	0.3 / 14.4 / 0.0 / 14.3
			31 F	0303 / 0829 / 1522 / 2048	0.2 / 14.4 / 0.2 / 14.1

APRIL

Day	Time	m	Day	Time	m
1 SA	0339 / 0907 / 1553 / 2123	0.4 / 14.0 / 0.6 / 13.6	16 SU	0311 / 0838 / 1519 / 2052	1.8 / 12.3 / 2.1 / 12.3
2 SU	0406 / 0942 / 1616 / 2155	1.0 / 13.3 / 1.3 / 12.9	17 M	0330 / 0908 / 1537 / 2123	1.9 / 12.2 / 2.0 / 12.1
3 M	0425 / 1015 / 1635 / 2225	1.6 / 12.3 / 1.9 / 11.9	18 TU	0353 / 0942 / 1602 / 2158	1.9 / 12.0 / 2.1 / 11.8
4 TU	0445 / 1047 / 1700 / 2256	2.3 / 11.2 / 2.7 / 10.8	19 W	0423 / 1021 / 1635 / 2240	2.1 / 11.5 / 2.4 / 11.2
5 W	0514 / 1124 / 1734 / 2337	3.0 / 10.0 / 3.5 / 9.7	20 TH	0502 / 1109 / 1717 / 2333	2.6 / 10.7 / 3.0 / 10.5
6 TH	0557 / 1226 / 1828	4.0 / 8.9 / 2.4.5	21 F	0554 / 1212 / 1817	3.3 / 10.0 / 3.8
7 F	0114 / 0714 / 1438 / 2012	8.9 / 4.7 / 8.7 / 4.9	22 SA	0049 / 0720 / 1346 / 2015	9.9 / 3.8 / 9.7 / 4.1
8 SA	0309 / 0948 / 1551 / 2215	9.2 / 4.5 / 9.4 / 4.1	23 SU	0240 / 0922 / 1528 / 2207	10.1 / 3.4 / 10.4 / 3.3
9 SU	0414 / 1055 / 1648 / 2313	10.0 / 3.4 / 10.4 / 3.0	24 M	0401 / 1041 / 1637 / 2313	11.1 / 2.4 / 11.5 / 2.2
10 M	0506 / 1144 / 1734	11.0 / 2.5 / 11.3	25 TU	0501 / 1142 / 1731	12.2 / 1.5 / 12.5
11 TU	0002 / 0549 / 1230 / 1814	2.2 / 11.8 / 1.9 / 12.0	26 W	0010 / 0552 / 1237 / 1817	1.4 / 13.1 / 0.9 / 13.3
12 W	0048 / 0628 / 1314 / 1850	1.7 / 12.2 / 1.6 / 12.3	27 TH ●	0102 / 0638 / 1327 / 1900	0.8 / 13.7 / 0.5 / 13.7
13 TH ○	0132 / 0704 / 1356 / 1924	1.5 / 12.4 / 1.6 / 12.5	28 F	0149 / 0721 / 1412 / 1941	0.6 / 13.9 / 0.4 / 13.8
14 F	0212 / 0737 / 1432 / 1955	1.5 / 12.5 / 1.7 / 12.5	29 SA	0233 / 0803 / 1451 / 2020	0.6 / 13.7 / 0.7 / 13.6
15 SA	0246 / 0809 / 1501 / 2024	1.7 / 12.4 / 1.9 / 12.4	30 SU	0310 / 0842 / 1524 / 2056	0.9 / 13.3 / 1.1 / 13.1

SCOTLAND, WEST COAST

No.	PLACE	Lat. N	Long. W	High Water 0000 and 1200	High Water 0600 and 1800	Low Water 0000 and 1200	Low Water 0600 and 1800	MHWS	MHWN	MLWN	MLWS	ML Z₀ m	
				Zone UT(GMT)									
404	**GREENOCK** .... (see page 138)			**0000** and **1200**	**0600** and **1800**	**0000** and **1200**	**0600** and **1800**	3.4	2.8	1.0	0.3		
	Loch Fyne												
394	East Loch Tarbert	55 52	5 24	−0005	−0005	0000	−0005	+0.2	+0.1	0.0	0.0	2.03	
395	Inveraray	56 14	5 04	+0011	+0011	+0034	+0034	−0.1	+0.1	−0.5	−0.2	⊙	
	Kyles of Bute												
396	Rubha a'Bhodaich	55 55	5 09	−0020	−0010	−0007	−0007	−0.2	−0.1	+0.2	+0.2	1.78	
396a	Tighnabruich	55 55	5 13	+0007	−0010	−0002	−0015	0.0	+0.2	+0.4	+0.5	2.09	
	Firth of Clyde (cont.)												
398	Miliport	55 45	4 56	−0005	−0025	−0025	−0005	0.0	−0.1	0.0	+0.1	1.99	
399	Rothesay Bay	55 51	5 03	−0020	−0015	−0010	−0002	+0.2	+0.2	+0.2	+0.2	1.90	
399a	Wemyss bay	55 53	4 53	−0005	−0005	−0005	−0005	0.0	0.0	+0.1	+0.1	⊙	
	Loch Long												
399b	Coulport	56 03	4 53	−0011	−0011	−0008	−0008	0.0	0.0	0.0	0.0	2.01	
399c	Lochgoilhead	56 10	4 54	+0015	0000	−0005	−0005	−0.2	−0.3	−0.3	−0.3	1.71	
401	Arrochar	56 12	4 45	−0005	−0005	−0005	−0005	0.0	0.0	−0.1	−0.1	⊙	
	Gare Loch												
402	Rosneath	56 01	4 47	−0005	−0005	−0005	−0005	0.0	−0.1	0.0	0.0	2.02	
402a	Faslane	56 04	4 49	−0010	−0010	−0010	−0010	0.0	0.0	−0.1	−0.2	1.87	
402b	Garelochhead	56 05	4 50	0000	0000	0000	0000	0.0	0.0	0.0	−0.1	⊙	
	River Clyde												
403	Helensburgh	56 00	4 44	0000	0000	0000	0000	0.0	0.0	0.0	0.0	⊙	
404	GREENOCK	55 57	4 46	STANDARD PORT				See Table V				1.97	
405	Port Glasgow	55 56	4 41	+0010	+0005	+0010	+0020	+0.2	+0.1	0.0	0.0	⊙	
406	Bowling	55 56	4 29	+0020	+0010	+0030	+0055	+0.6	+0.5	+0.3	+0.1	⊙	
406a	Clydebank (Rothesay Dock)	55 54	4 24	+0025	+0015	+0035	+0100	+1.0	+0.8	+0.5	+0.4	2.70	c
407	Glasgow	55 51	4 16	+0025	+0015	+0035	+0105	+1.3	+1.1	+0.7	+0.4	2.90	c
	Firth of Clyde (cont.)												
408	Brodick Bay	55 35	5 08	−0013	−0013	−0008	−0008	−0.2	−0.1	0.0	+0.1	1.90	
409	Lamlash	55 32	5 07	−0016	−0036	−0024	−0004	−0.2	−0.2	⊙	⊙	⊙	
410	Ardrossan	55 38	4 49	−0020	−0010	−0010	−0010	−0.2	−0.2	+0.1	+0.1	1.86	
411	Irvine	55 36	4 41	−0020	−0020	−0030	−0010	−0.3	−0.3	−0.1	0.0	⊙	
412	Troon	55 33	4 41	−0025	−0025	−0020	−0020	−0.2	−0.2	0.0	0.0	1.91	
413	Ayr	55 28	4 39	−0025	−0025	−0030	−0015	−0.4	−0.3	+0.1	+0.1	⊙	
414	Girvan	55 15	4 52	−0025	−0040	−0035	−0010	−0.3	−0.3	−0.1	0.0	1.82	
	Loch Ryan												
414a	Stranraer	54 55	5 03	−0030	−0025	−0010	−0010	−0.2	−0.1	0.0	+0.1	1.90	
452	**LIVERPOOL** .... (see page 146)			**0000** and **1200**	**0600** and **1800**	**0200** and **1400**	**0800** and **2000**	9.3	7.4	2.9	0.9		
415	Portpatrick	54 50	5 07	+0018	+0026	0000	−0035	−5.5	−4.4	−2.0	−0.6	2.06	
	Luce Bay												
419	Drummore	54 41	4 53	+0030	+0040	+0015	+0020	−3.4	−2.5	−0.9	−0.3	3.32	
420	Offshore Platform	54 50	4 53	+0030	−0030	−0015	+0005	−2.8	−2.1	−1.0	−0.3	3.57	
420a	Port William	54 46	4 35	+0030	+0030	−0025	0000	−2.9	−2.2	−0.8	⊙	⊙	
	Wigtown Bay												
421	Isle of Whithorn	54 42	4 22	+0020	+0025	+0025	+0005	−2.4	−2.0	−0.8	−0.2	3.74	
422	Garlieston	54 47	4 22	+0025	+0035	+0030	+0005	−2.3	−1.7	−0.5	⊙	⊙	
	Solway Firth												
422a	Kirkcudbright Bay	54 48	4 04	+0015	+0015	+0010	0000	−1.8	−1.5	−0.5	−0.1	⊙	
424	Hestan Islet	54 50	3 48	+0025	+0025	+0020	+0025	−1.0	−1.1	−0.5	0.0	4.21	
425	Southerness Point	54 52	3 36	+0030	−0030	−0030	+0010	−0.7	−0.7	⊙	⊙	⊙	
426	Annan Waterfoot	54 58	3 16	+0050	+0105	+0220	−0310	−2.2	−2.6	−2.7	‡	⊙	★
430	Torduff Point	54 58	3 09	+0105	+0140	+0520	+0410	−4.1	−4.9	‡	‡	⊙	★
431	Redkirk	54 59	3 06	+0110	+0215	+0715	+0445	−5.5	−6.2	‡	‡	⊙	★
	England												
432	Silloth	54 52	3 24	+0030	+0040	+0045	+0055	−0.1	−0.3	−0.6	−0.1	⊙	
433	Maryport	54 43	3 30	+0017	+0032	+0020	+0005	−0.7	−0.8	−0.4	0.0	⊙	
434	Workington	54 39	3 34	+0020	+0020	+0020	+0010	−1.2	−1.1	−0.3	0.0	4.54	
435	Whitehaven	54 33	3 36	+0005	+0015	+0010	+0005	−1.3	−1.1	−0.5	+0.1	4.53	
436	Tarn Point	54 17	3 25	+0005	+0005	+0010	0000	−1.0	−1.0	−0.4	0.0	⊙	
437	Duddon Bar	54 09	3 20	+0003	+0003	+0008	+0002	−0.8	−0.8	−0.3	0.0	⊙	

⊙ No data.
★ See notes on page 328.
§ Dries out except for river water.

‡ The tide does not normally fall below Chart Datum.
c For intermediate heights, use harmonic constants (see Part III).

ENGLAND, WEST COAST; ISLE OF MAN; WALES

No.	PLACE	Lat. N	Long. W	TIME DIFFERENCES High Water Zone UT(GMT)		Low Water		HEIGHT DIFFERENCES (IN METRES) MHWS	MHWN	MLWN	MLWS	ML Z₀ m	
439	**BARROW (RAMSDEN DOCK)**	(see page 142)		**0000** and **1200**	**0600** and **1800**	**0100** and **1300**	**0700** and **1900**	**9.3**	**7.1**	**3.0**	**1.1**	5.05	
	Morecambe Bay												
439a	Roa Island...........................	54 04	3 10	−0006	−0004	−0004	−0001	0.0	0.0	0.0	0.0	4.97	
439b	Haws Point...........................	54 03	3 10	−0007	−0004	−0002	−0005	+0.1	0.0	0.0	0.0	4.89	
439c	Halfway Shoal.......................	54 02	3 12	−0014	−0012	−0012	−0010	−0.3	−0.2	−0.1	0.0	4.91	
452	**LIVERPOOL**	(see page 146)		**0000** and **1200**	**0600** and **1800**	**0200** and **1400**	**0700** and **1900**	**9.3**	**7.4**	**2.9**	**0.9**		
440	Ulverston...........................	54 11	3 04	+0020	+0040	⊙	⊙	00	−0.1	⊙	⊙	⊙	
440a	Arnside.............................	54 12	2 51	+0100	+0135	⊙	⊙	+0.5	+0.2	⊙	⊙	⊙	
440b	Morecambe...........................	54 04	2 52	+0005	+0010	+0030	+0015	+0.2	0.0	0.0	+0.2	⊙	
441	Heysham.............................	54 02	2 55	+0005	+0005	+0015	0000	+0.1	0.0	0.0	+0.2	5.10	
	River Lune												
442	Glasson Dock	54 00	2 51	+0020	+0030	+0220	+0220	−2.7	−3.0	⊙	⊙	⊙	★
442a	Lancaster...........................	54 03	2 49	+0110	+0030	§	§	−5.0	−4.9	§	§	⊙	
	River Wyre												
443	Wyre Lighthouse.....................	53 57	3 02	−0010	−0010	+0005	0000	−0.1	−0.1	⊙	⊙	⊙	
444	Fleetwood...........................	53 56	3 00	−0008	−0008	−0003	−0003	−0.1	−0.1	+0.1	+0.3	5.03	
445	Blackpool	53 49	3 04	−0015	−0005	−0005	−0015	−0.4	−0.4	−0.1	+0.1	⊙	
	River Ribble												
446	Preston	53 46	2 45	+0010	+0010	+0335	+0310	−4.0	−4.1	−2.8	−0.8	⊙	★
	Liverpool Bay												
447	Southport	53 39	3 01	−0020	−0010	⊙	⊙	−0.3	−0.3	⊙	⊙	⊙	
448	Formby..............................	53 32	3 07	−0015	−0010	−0020	−0020	−0.3	−0.1	0.0	+0.1	5.15	
	River Mersey												
451	Gladstone Dock	53 27	3 01	−0003	−0003	−0003	−0003	−0.1	−0.1	0.0	−0.1	5.15	
452	LIVERPOOL (ALFRED DOCK)	53 22	3 01	STANDARD PORT				See Table V				5.14	
453	Eastham.............................	53 19	2 57	+0010	+0010	+0009	+0009	+0.3	+0.1	−0.1	−0.3	5.17	
455	Hale Head...........................	53 19	2 48	+0030	+0025	⊙	⊙	−2.4	−2.5	⊙	⊙	⊙	
456	Widnes	53 21	2 44	+0040	+0045	+0400	+0345	−4.2	−4.4	−2.5	−0.3	⊙	
456a	Fiddler's Ferry	53 22	2 39	+0100	+0115	+0540	+0450	−5.9	−6.3	−2.4	−0.4	⊙	
	River Dee												
461	Hilbre Island.......................	53 23	3 13	−0015	−0012	−0010	−0015	−0.3	−0.2	+0.2	+0.4	5.15	
462	Mostyn Docks........................	53 19	3 16	−0020	−0015	−0020	−0020	−0.8	−0.7	⊙	⊙	⊙	
463	Connah's Quay	53 13	3 03	0000	+0015	+0355	+0340	−4.6	−4.4	§	§	⊙	★
464	Chester.............................	53 12	4 54	+0105	+0105	+0500	+0500	−5.3	−5.4	§	§	⊙	★
	Isle of Man												
466	Peel................................	54 14	4 42	+0005	+0005	−0015	−0025	−4.1	−3.1	−1.4	−0.5	2.92	
467	Ramsey..............................	54 19	4 22	+0005	+0015	−0005	−0015	−1.9	−1.5	−0.6	0.0	4.16	
468	Douglas.............................	54 09	4 28	+0005	+0015	−0015	−0025	−2.4	−2.0	−0.5	−0.1	3.79	
468a	Port St. Mary.......................	54 04	4 44	+0005	+0015	−0010	−0030	−3.4	−2.6	−1.3	−0.4	3.25	
469	Calf Sound	54 04	4 48	+0005	+0005	−0015	−0025	−3.2	−2.6	−0.9	−0.3	⊙	
469a	Port Erin...........................	54 05	4 46	−0005	+0015	−0010	−0050	−4.1	−3.2	−1.3	−0.5	2.73	
	Wales												
470	Colwyn Bay..........................	53 18	3 43	−0020	−0020	⊙	⊙	−1.5	−1.3	⊙	⊙	⊙	
471	Llandudno...........................	53 20	3 50	−0020	−0020	−0035	−0040	−1.7	−1.4	−0.7	−0.3	4.10	
478	**HOLYHEAD**	(see page 150)		**0000** and **1200**	**0600** and **1800**	**0500** and **1700**	**1100** and **2300**	**5.6**	**4.4**	**2.0**	**0.7**		
471a	Conwy...............................	53 17	3 50	+0025	+0035	+0120	+0105	+2.3	+1.8	+0.6	+0.4	4.43	
	Menai Strait												
472	Beaumaris...........................	53 16	4 05	+0025	+0010	+0055	+0035	+2.0	+1.6	+0.5	+0.1	4.22	
473	Menai Bridge........................	53 13	4 09	+0030	+0010	+0100	+0035	+1.7	+1.4	+0.3	0.0	4.05	
474	Port Dinorwic.......................	53 11	4 13	−0015	−0025	+0030	0000	0.0	0.0	0.0	+0.1	3.38	
475	Caernarfon..........................	53 09	4 16	−0030	−0030	+0015	−0005	−0.4	−0.4	−0.1	−0.1	3.04	
475a	Fort Belan..........................	53 07	4 20	−0040	−0015	−0025	−0005	−1.0	−0.9	−0.2	−0.1	2.83	

SEASONAL CHANGES IN MEAN LEVEL

	No.		Jan. 1	Feb. 1	Mar. 1	Apr. 1	May 1	June 1	July 1	Aug. 1	Sep. 1	Oct. 1	Nov. 1	Dec. 1	Jan. 1
394	−	398	+0.1	0.0	−0.1	−0.1	−0.1	−0.1	0.0	0.0	0.0	0.0	+0.1	+0.1	+0.1
399	−	407	+0.2	+0.1	0.0	−0.1	−0.1	−0.1	−0.1	−0.1	0.0	0.0	+0.1	+0.2	+0.2
408	−	414a	+0.1	0.0	−0.1	−0.1	−0.1	−0.1	0.0	0.0	0.0	0.0	+0.1	+0.1	+0.1
415	−	444	0.0	0.0	0.0	−0.1	−0.1	0.0	0.0	0.0	0.0	0.0	+0.1	+0.1	0.0
445	−	464	0.0	0.0	−0.1	−0.1	0.0	0.0	0.0	0.0	0.0	0.0	+0.1	+0.1	0.0
466	−	478	+0.1	0.0	0.0	−0.1	−0.1	−0.1	0.0	0.0	0.0	0.0	+0.1	+0.1	+0.1

WALES; ENGLAND, WEST COAST

No.	PLACE	Lat. N		Long. W		TIME DIFFERENCES High Water Zone UT(GMT)		Low Water		MHWS	MHWN	MLWN	MLWS	ML Z₀ m	
523	**PORT OF BRISTOL (AVONMOUTH)** .... (see page 142)					**0600** and **1800**	**1100** and **2300**	**0300** and **1500**	**0800** and **2000**	**13.2**	**9.8**	**3.8**	**1.0**		
513	Barry	51	23	3	16	−0030	−0015	−0125	−0030	−1.8	−1.3	+0.2	0.0	6.09	
513a	Flat Holm	51	23	3	07	−0015	−0015	−0045	−0045	−1.3	−1.1	−0.2	+0.2	6.2	x
513b	Steep Holm	51	20	3	06	−0020	−0020	−0050	−0050	−1.6	−1.2	−0.2	−0.2	6.1	x
514	Cardiff	51	27	3	09	−0015	−0015	−0100	−0030	−1.0	−0.6	+0.1	0.0	6.45	
515	Newport	51	33	2	59	−0020	−0010	0000	−0020	−1.1	−1.0	−0.6	−0.7	6.03	★
	River Wye	51	39	2	40	+0020	+0020	☉	☉	☉	☉	☉	☉	☉	★
516	Chepstow														
523	**PORT OF BRISTOL (AVONMOUTH)** .... (see page 162)					**0000** and **1200**	**0600** and **1800**	**0000** and **1200**	**0700** and **1900**	**13.2**	**9.8**	**3.8**	**1.0**		
	River Severn														
517	Sudbrook	51	35	2	43	+0010	+0010	+0025	+0015	+0.2	+0.1	−0.1	+0.1	6.86	
	England														
518	Beachley (Aust)	51	36	2	38	+0010	+0015	+0040	+0025	−0.2	−0.2	−0.5	−0.3	6.42	
519	Inward Rocks	51	39	2	37	+0020	+0020	+0105	+0045	−1.0	−1.1	−1.4	−0.6	5.74	★c
520	Narlwood Rocks	51	39	2	36	+0025	+0025	+0120	+0100	−1.9	−2.0	−2.3	−0.8	☉	★
521	White House	51	40	2	33	+0025	+0025	+0145	+0120	−3.0	−3.1	−3.6	−1.0	3.94	★c
522	Berkeley	51	42	2	30	+0030	+0045	+0245	+0220	−3.8	−3.9	−3.4	−0.5	3.44	★c
522a	Sharpness Dock	51	43	2	29	+0035	+0050	+0305	+0245	−3.9	−4.2	−3.3	−0.4	☉	★
522b	Wellhouse Rock	51	44	2	29	+0040	+0055	+0320	+0305	−4.1	−4.4	−3.1	−0.2	3.25	★c
522c	Epney	51	42	2	24	+0130	☉	☉	☉	−9.4	☉	☉	☉	☉	★
522d	Minsterworth	51	50	2	23	+0140	☉	☉	☉	−10.1	☉	☉	☉	☉	★
522e	Llanthony	51	51	2	21	+0215	☉	☉	☉	−10.7	☉	☉	☉	☉	★
523	**PORT OF BRISTOL (AVONMOUTH)** ... **(Royal Portbury Dock)** (see page 162)					**0200** and **1400**	**0800** and **2000**	**0300** and **1500**	**0800** and **2000**	**13.2**	**9.8**	**3.8**	**1.0**	6.96	★
	River Avon														
523a	Shirehampton	51	29	2	41	0000	0000	+0035	+0010	−0.7	−0.7	−0.8	0.0	☉	
523b	Sea Mills	51	29	2	39	+0005	+0005	+0105	+0030	−1.4	−1.5	−1.7	0.1	☉	
524	Cumberland Basin Entrance	51	27	2	37	+0010	+0010	§	§	−2.9	−3.0	§	§	☉	
524a	Portishead	51	30	2	45	−0002	0000	☉	☉	−0.1	−0.1	☉	☉	☉	
525	Clevedon	51	27	2	52	−0010	−0020	−0025	−0015	−0.4	−0.2	+0.2	0.0	6.8	x
525a	St. Thomas Head	51	24	2	56	0000	0000	−0030	−0030	−0.4	−0.2	+0.1	+0.1	6.7	x
526	English and Welsh Grounds	51	28	2	59	−0008	−0008	−0030	−0030	−0.5	−0.8	−0.3	0.0	6.5	ax
527	Weston-super-Mare	51	21	2	59	−0020	−0030	−0130	−0030	−1.2	−1.0	−0.8	−0.2	6.1	x
	River Parrett														
528	Burnham-on-Sea	51	14	3	00	−0020	−0025	−0030	0000	−2.3	−1.9	−1.4	−1.1°	☉	
529	Bridgwater	51	08	3	00	−0015	−0030	+0305	+0455	−8.6	−8.1	§	§	☉	★
530	Hinkley Point	51	13	3	08	−0020	−0025	−0100	−0040	−1.7	−1.4	−0.2	−0.2	6.0	x
531	Watchet	51	11	3	20	−0035	−0050	−0145	−0040	−1.9	−1.5	+0.1	+0.1	5.87	
532	Minehead	51	13	3	28	−0037	−0052	−0155	−0045	−2.6	−1.9	−0.2	0.0	5.71	
533	Porlock Bay	51	13	3	38	−0045	−0055	−0205	−0050	−3.0	−2.2	−0.1	0.1	5.62	
534	Lynmouth	51	14	3	49	−0055	−0115	☉	☉	−3.6	−2.7	☉	☉	☉	
496	**MILFORD HAVEN** (see page 154)					**0100** and **1300**	**0700** and **1900**	**0100** and **1300**	**0700** and **1900**	**7.0**	**5.2**	**2.5**	**0.7**		
535	Ilfracombe	51	13	4	07	−0016	−0016	−0041	−0031	+2.3	+ 1.8	+0.6	+0.3	5.04	
	Rivers Taw and Torridge														
536	Appledore	51	03	4	12	−0020	−0025	+0015	−0045	+0.5	0.0	−0.9	−0.5	3.68	★c
537	Yelland Narsh	51	04	4	10	−0010	−0015	+0100	−0015	+0.1	−0.4	−1.2	−0.6	3.02	★c
538	Fremington	51	05	4	07	−0010	−0015	+0030	−0030	−1.1	−1.8	−2.2	−0.5	☉	★
539	Barnstaple	51	05	4	04	0000	−0015	−0155	−0245	−2.9	−3.8	−2.2	−0.4	☉	★
540	Bideford	51	01	4	12	−0020	−0025	0000	0000	−1.1	−1.6	−2.5	−0.7	☉	★
541	Clovelly	51	00	4	24	−0030	−0030	−0020	−0040	+1.3	+1.1	+0.2	+0.2	☉	
542	Lundy	51	10	4	40	−0025	−0025	−0020	−0035	+0.9	+0.7	+0.3	+0.1	4.35	
543	Bude	50	50	4	33	−0040	−0040	−0035	−0045	+0.7	+0.6	☉	☉	☉	
544	Boscastle	50	41	4	42	−0045	−0010	−0110	−0100	+0.3	+0.4	+0.2	+0.2	4.02	
544a	Port Isaac	50	35	4	50	−0100	−0100	−0100	−0100	+0.5	+0.6	0.0	+0.2	4.13	

SEASONAL CHANGES IN MEAN LEVEL

No.			Jan. 1	Feb. 1	Mar. 1	Apr. 1	May 1	June 1	July 1	Aug. 1	Sep. 1	Oct. 1	Nov. 1	Dec. 1	Jan. 1
476	−	482	+0.1	0.0	0.0	−0.1	−0.1	−0.1	0.0	0.0	0.0	0.0	+0.1	+0.1	+0.1
482a	−	512	0.0	0.0	0.0	0.0	0.0	0.0	−0.1	0.0	0.0	0.0	+0.1	+0.1	0.0
513	−	534	0.0	0.0	0.0	−0.1	−0.1	−0.1	0.0	0.0	+0.1	+0.1	+0.1	0.0	0.0
535	−	544a	+0.1	0.0	0.0	−0.1	−0.1	−0.1	0.0	0.0	0.0	0.0	+0.1	+0.1	+0.1

FOR FINDING THE HEIGHT OF THE TIDE AT
TIMES BETWEEN HIGH AND LOW WATER

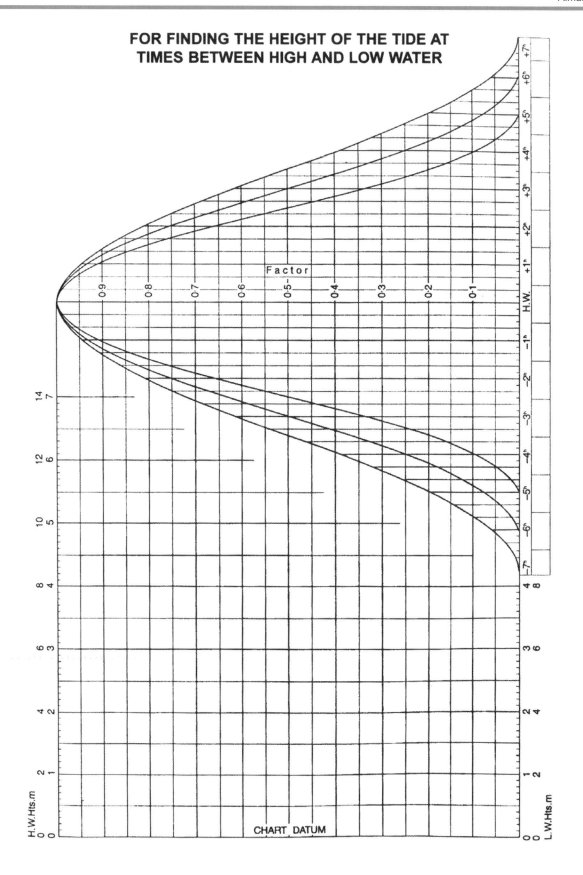

CANADA - VANCOUVER

Lat 49°17'N   LONG 123°07'W

TIME ZONE +0800 TIMES AND HEIGHTS OF HIGH AND LOW WATERS **YEAR 2006**

JANUARY

Day	Time	m	Time	m	Time	m	Time	m
1 SU	0008	0.0	0746	4.9	1255	3.7	1705	4.4
2 M	0053	0.1	0823	5.0	1351	3.5	1807	4.2
3 TU	0136	0.3	0859	5.0	1451	3.2	1914	4.0
4 W	0220	0.7	0935	5.0	1554	2.8	2028	3.7
5 TH	0303	1.2	1010	5.0	1656	2.4	2154	3.4
6 F	0348	1.8	1044	4.9	1753	1.9	2341	3.3
7 SA	0440	2.5	1118	4.8	1847	1.5		
8 SU	0138	3.6	0549	3.1	1152	4.6	1937	1.1
9 M	0312	4.0	0719	3.5	1229	4.4	2026	0.9
10 TU	0420	4.3	0850	3.7	1309	4.3	2114	0.7
11 W	0509	4.6	1003	3.8	1354	4.2	2201	0.6
12 TH	0550	4.7	1058	3.7	1444	4.1	2245	0.6
13 F	0625	4.7	1142	3.7	1532	4.1	2325	0.6
14 SA ○	0658	4.8	1222	3.6	1619	4.0		
15 SU	0002	0.6	0729	4.7	1301	3.5	1703	4.0
16 M	0035	0.7	0758	4.7	1341	3.3	1747	3.9
17 TU	0105	0.9	0823	4.7	1423	3.2	1835	3.7
18 W	0133	1.2	0847	4.7	1506	2.9	1928	3.5
19 TH	0201	1.5	0909	4.7	1550	2.7	2027	3.4
20 F	0230	1.9	0932	4.6	1634	2.4	2138	3.3
21 SA	0303	2.4	0955	4.5	1719	2.1	2314	3.2
22 SU	0343	2.8	1021	4.4	1805	1.8		
23 M	0126	3.4	0436	3.2	1049	4.4	1852	1.5
24 TU	0258	3.8	0557	3.6	1123	4.3	1942	1.1
25 W	0358	4.1	0743	3.8	1207	4.3	2034	0.8
26 TH	0445	4.4	0911	3.9	1302	4.3	2124	0.6
27 F	0526	4.6	1012	3.9	1405	4.3	2218	0.3
28 SA	0603	4.7	1102	3.7	1511	4.1	2307	0.2
29 SU ●	0638	4.8	1150	3.5	1618	4.4	2353	0.1
30 M	0711	4.9	1239	3.3	1724	4.4		
31 TU	0036	0.3	0742	4.9	1330	2.9	1827	4.2

FEBRUARY

Day	Time	m	Time	m	Time	m	Time	m
1 W	0117	0.6	0813	5.0	1423	2.5	1931	4.0
2 TH	0157	1.1	0843	5.0	1516	2.1	2041	3.8
3 F	0238	1.8	0914	4.9	1610	1.7	2205	3.6
4 SA	0322	2.4	0944	4.8	1703	1.4	2350	3.7
5 SU	0416	3.0	1016	4.5	1758	1.2		
6 M	0134	3.9	0537	3.5	1050	4.3	1854	1.1
7 TU	0259	4.2	0731	3.7	1131	4.1	1952	1.0
8 W	0401	4.4	0910	3.7	1227	3.9	2050	1.0
9 TH	0447	4.5	1011	3.6	1337	3.9	2142	0.9
10 F	0524	4.6	1051	3.5	1446	3.9	2228	0.9
11 SA	0555	4.6	1126	3.4	1544	3.9	2307	0.9
12 SU ○	0623	4.6	1159	3.2	1633	3.9	2341	1.0
13 M	0647	4.6	1232	3.0	1718	3.9		
14 TU	0011	1.1	0709	4.6	1306	2.8	1802	3.9
15 W	0039	1.3	0729	4.6	1340	2.6	1847	3.8
16 TH	0107	1.6	0748	4.5	1414	2.3	1936	3.7
17 F	0135	1.9	0808	4.5	1450	2.1	2030	3.6
18 SA	0206	2.3	0828	4.4	1528	1.8	2134	3.6
19 SU	0242	2.7	0849	4.4	1609	1.6	2258	3.6
20 M	0324	3.1	0912	4.3	1656	1.4		
21 TU	0046	3.8	0422	3.5	0938	4.2	1751	1.3
22 W	0217	4.0	0553	3.8	1019	4.1	1853	1.1
23 TH	0321	4.2	0755	3.8	1125	4.0	1958	0.9
24 F	0409	4.4	0913	3.7	1246	4.0	2101	0.7
25 SA	0448	4.6	1004	3.5	1411	4.1	2158	0.5
26 SU	0522	4.6	1049	3.3	1528	4.2	2247	0.5
27 M ●	0553	4.7	1134	2.9	1637	4.3	2332	0.6
28 TU	0622	4.8	1219	2.5	1740	4.3		

MARCH

Day	Time	m	Time	m	Time	m	Time	m
1 W	0013	0.9	0650	4.9	1304	2.0	1841	4.2
2 TH	0054	1.4	0718	4.9	1350	1.6	1943	4.1
3 F	0134	1.9	0747	4.8	1437	1.3	2052	4.0
4 SA	0217	2.5	0815	4.7	1524	1.1	2212	4.0
5 SU	0307	3.0	0844	4.4	1613	1.0	2341	4.1
6 M	0413	3.4	0914	4.2	1707	1.1		
7 TU	0104	4.2	0559	3.6	0949	3.9	1807	1.2
8 W	0218	4.3	0804	3.6	1041	3.7	1913	1.3
9 TH	0317	4.4	0918	3.4	1209	3.5	2018	1.3
10 F	0402	4.4	0959	3.2	1351	3.5	2115	1.3
11 SA	0437	4.4	1030	3.1	1506	3.6	2201	1.3
12 SU	0506	4.4	1100	2.8	1600	3.7	2240	1.4
13 M	0530	4.4	1130	2.6	1646	3.8	2313	1.4
14 TU ○	0551	4.4	1159	2.4	1729	3.9	2344	1.7
15 W	0610	4.4	1229	2.1	1812	3.9		
16 TH	0013	1.9	0628	4.4	1259	1.8	1856	4.0
17 F	0043	2.2	0646	4.3	1330	1.6	1943	4.0
18 SA	0115	2.5	0705	4.3	1403	1.4	2035	4.0
19 SU	0150	2.8	0725	4.2	1438	1.2	2136	4.0
20 M	0231	3.2	0744	4.2	1518	1.1	2250	4.1
21 TU	0323	3.4	0804	4.0	1606	1.1		
22 W	0012	4.1	0437	3.6	0834	3.9	1703	1.1
23 TH	0128	4.2	0638	3.7	0933	3.8	1811	1.1
24 F	0230	4.3	0813	3.5	1114	3.7	1924	1.1
25 SA	0317	4.4	0905	3.3	1257	3.7	2032	1.0
26 SU	0356	4.5	0948	2.9	1431	3.8	2130	1.0
27 M	0428	4.6	1030	2.5	1548	4.0	2221	1.1
28 TU	0458	4.6	1112	2.0	1653	4.2	2306	1.4
29 W ●	0526	4.7	1154	1.5	1753	4.3	2349	1.8
30 TH	0554	4.7	1235	1.1	1853	4.3		
31 F	0032	2.2	0622	4.7	1317	0.8	1954	4.3

APRIL

Day	Time	m	Time	m	Time	m	Time	m
1 SA	0117	2.7	0650	4.5	1359	0.6	2059	4.4
2 SU	0206	3.1	0718	4.3	1443	0.7	2207	4.4
3 M	0306	3.4	0747	4.1	1529	0.8	2316	4.4
4 TU	0432	3.5	0817	3.8	1620	1.1		
5 W	0023	4.3	0632	3.5	0854	3.6	1718	1.3
6 TH	0125	4.3	0812	3.3	1008	3.3	1823	1.5
7 F	0219	4.3	0859	3.0	1213	3.2	1931	1.7
8 SA	0301	4.3	0930	2.8	1404	3.3	2031	1.8
9 SU	0335	4.3	0958	2.5	1514	3.4	2121	1.9
10 M	0402	4.2	1026	2.2	1607	3.6	2203	2.0
11 TU	0425	4.2	1054	2.0	1653	3.8	2240	2.2
12 W	0445	4.2	1123	1.7	1737	4.0	2315	2.4
13 TH ○	0504	4.2	1151	1.4	1820	4.1	2349	2.6
14 F	0524	4.2	1221	1.1	1904	4.2		
15 SA	2.8	3.0	4.2	0.3	0.9	3.2	4.3	0.3
16 SU	0100	3.1	0604	4.2	1327	0.8	2042	4.3
17 M	0142	3.3	0624	4.1	1404	0.7	2139	4.4
18 TU	0232	3.5	0646	4.0	1446	0.7	2239	4.4
19 W	0339	3.6	0715	3.9	1535	0.8	2342	4.4
20 TH	0517	3.6	0802	3.7	1633	1.0		
21 F	0042	4.4	0657	3.4	0938	3.5	1739	1.1
22 SA	0134	4.5	0758	3.1	1135	3.4	1849	1.3
23 SU	0218	4.5	0843	2.7	1323	3.5	1957	1.5
24 M	0255	4.5	0925	2.2	1453	3.7	2058	1.7
25 TU	0327	4.6	1005	1.6	1605	3.9	2152	2.0
26 W	0358	4.6	1046	1.1	1708	4.1	2242	2.4
27 TH ●	0428	4.6	1126	0.7	1807	4.4	2330	2.7
28 F	0457	4.5	1206	0.4	1904	4.5		
29 SA	0018	3.0	0527	4.4	1247	0.3	2000	4.6
30 SU	0109	3.2	0558	4.3	1328	0.4	2055	4.6

UNITED STATES - SAN FRANCISCO (GOLDEN GATE)

Lat 37°48'N   LONG 122°28'W

TIME ZONE +0800   TIMES AND HEIGHTS OF HIGH AND LOW WATERS   YEAR 2006

JANUARY

Day	DoW	Time	m	Time	m	Time	m	Time	m
1	SU	0114	1.5	0528	0.9	1136	2.1	1833	-0.5
2	M	0155	1.6	0624	0.9	1228	2.0	1918	-0.4
3	TU	0237	1.6	0725	0.8	1324	1.9	2004	-0.2
4	W	0319	1.7	0834	0.8	1425	1.7	2051	-0.1
5	TH	0402	1.7	0949	0.6	1536	1.5	2140	0.2
6	F	0446	1.8	1106	0.5	1701	1.3	2232	0.4
7	SA	0532	1.9	1220	0.3	1839	1.2	2329	0.6
8	SU	0619	1.9	1326	0.1	2014	1.2		
9	M	0030	0.8	0706	2.0	1424	-0.1	2130	1.3
10	TU	0133	0.9	0754	2.0	1513	-0.2	2229	1.4
11	W	0231	1.0	0840	2.0	1557	-0.2	2318	1.4
12	TH	0324	1.0	0925	2.0	1637	-0.2	2359	1.5
13	F	0412	1.0	1006	1.9	1713	-0.2		
14	SA ○	0036	1.5	0455	1.0	1046	1.9	1747	-0.2
15	SU	0109	1.5	0535	0.9	1123	1.9	1819	-0.2
16	M	0139	1.5	0615	0.9	1200	1.8	1850	-0.1
17	TU	0207	1.5	0657	0.9	1238	1.8	1921	0.0
18	W	0234	1.5	0742	0.9	1319	1.6	1952	0.2
19	TH	0302	1.6	0833	0.8	1404	1.4	2023	0.3
20	F	0331	1.6	0930	0.7	1500	1.2	2056	0.5
21	SA	0403	1.6	1033	0.6	1614	1.1	2134	0.6
22	SU	0440	1.7	1138	0.5	1759	1.0	2221	0.8
23	M	0523	1.7	1240	0.3	1958	1.1	2325	0.9
24	TU	0612	1.8	1337	0.1	2119	1.2		
25	W	0039	1.0	0706	1.9	1428	-0.1	2210	1.3
26	TH	0146	1.1	0801	2.0	1517	-0.2	2250	1.4
27	F	0245	1.0	0855	2.1	1602	-0.4	2327	1.5
28	SA	0338	0.9	0948	2.1	1646	-0.5		
29	SU ●	0003	1.6	0429	0.9	1040	2.2	1729	-0.5
30	M	0038	1.6	0521	0.7	1131	2.1	1811	-0.4
31	TU	0114	1.7	0615	0.6	1224	2.0	1852	-0.2

FEBRUARY

Day	DoW	Time	m	Time	m	Time	m	Time	m
1	W	0107	1.8	0748	0.5	1414	1.8	1934	-0.1
2	TH	0228	1.8	0814	0.4	1421	1.6	2016	0.2
3	F	0308	1.9	0921	0.3	1533	1.4	2102	0.4
4	SA	0351	1.9	1034	0.2	1703	1.2	2155	0.7
5	SU	0439	1.9	1149	0.2	1849	1.4	2300	0.9
6	M	0533	1.9	1302	0.1	2022	1.2		
7	TU	0016	1.0	0632	1.8	1406	0.0	2129	1.3
8	W	0129	1.0	0732	1.8	1459	-0.1	2217	1.4
9	TH	0232	1.0	0827	1.8	1543	-0.1	2257	1.5
10	F	0322	0.9	0915	1.8	1621	-0.1	2331	1.5
11	SA	0405	0.9	0958	1.9	1653	-0.1		
12	SU ○	0000	1.5	0444	0.8	1037	1.8	1723	-0.1
13	M	0026	1.5	0520	0.8	1113	1.8	1750	0.0
14	TU	0048	1.6	0555	0.7	1149	1.7	1816	0.1
15	W	0110	1.6	0631	0.6	1227	1.6	1842	0.2
16	TH	0132	1.6	0709	0.6	1307	1.5	1909	0.3
17	F	0157	1.6	0751	0.5	1352	1.2	1936	0.5
18	SA	0224	1.6	0839	0.4	1448	1.2	2005	0.6
19	SU	0256	1.7	0935	0.4	1604	1.1	2038	0.8
20	M	0336	1.7	1040	0.3	1758	1.0	2126	0.9
21	TU	0427	1.7	1152	0.2	2000	1.1	2249	1.1
22	W	0529	1.7	1300	0.0	2103	1.2		
23	TH	0025	1.1	0637	1.8	1400	-0.1	2143	1.3
24	F	0139	1.0	0743	1.9	1452	-0.2	2218	1.4
25	SA	0238	0.9	0844	2.0	1539	-0.3	2250	1.5
26	SU	0331	0.8	0940	2.0	1622	-0.3	2322	1.6
27	M ●	0422	0.6	1034	2.0	1703	-0.3	2354	1.7
28	TU	0512	0.4	1128	2.0	1742	-0.2		

MARCH

Day	DoW	Time	m	Time	m	Time	m	Time	m
1	W	0027	1.8	0603	0.3	1222	1.9	1821	0.0
2	TH	0101	1.9	0656	0.2	1320	1.7	1901	0.0
3	F	0137	1.9	0751	0.1	1423	1.5	1943	0.5
4	SA	0216	1.9	0851	0.1	1537	1.3	2030	0.7
5	SU	0259	1.9	0957	0.1	1708	1.2	2128	0.9
6	M	0350	1.8	1111	0.1	1849	1.2	2246	1.0
7	TU	0451	1.7	1228	0.1	2009	1.3		
8	W	0014	1.0	0601	1.6	1336	0.0	2105	1.4
9	TH	0129	1.0	0711	1.6	1431	0.0	2146	1.4
10	F	0226	0.9	0811	1.6	1515	0.0	2220	1.5
11	SA	0312	0.8	0902	1.7	1550	-0.2	2248	1.5
12	SU	0352	0.7	0946	1.7	1620	0.1	2312	1.6
13	M	0427	0.6	1026	1.7	1647	0.1	2333	1.6
14	TU ○	0501	0.5	1105	1.6	1713	0.2	2353	1.6
15	W	0533	0.4	1143	1.6	1738	0.3		
16	TH	0013	1.6	0606	0.3	1223	1.5	1803	0.4
17	F	0035	1.7	0641	0.2	1307	1.4	1829	0.5
18	SA	0100	1.7	0720	0.2	1356	1.3	1857	0.7
19	SU	0128	1.7	0804	0.1	1457	1.2	1928	0.8
20	M	0203	1.7	0857	0.1	1617	1.1	2006	0.9
21	TU	0247	1.7	1000	0.1	1804	1.1	2108	1.0
22	W	0346	1.6	1113	0.0	1932	1.2	2251	1.1
23	TH	0459	1.6	1225	0.0	2023	1.3		
24	F	0026	1.0	0617	1.7	1327	-0.1	2100	1.4
25	SA	0135	0.9	0730	1.7	1420	-0.2	2133	1.5
26	SU	0232	0.7	0835	1.8	1507	-0.2	2205	1.6
27	M	0324	0.5	0935	1.8	1549	-0.1	2236	1.7
28	TU	0413	0.2	1033	1.8	1629	0.0	2306	1.8
29	W ●	0501	0.0	1129	1.7	1709	0.1	2340	1.9
30	TH	0549	-0.1	1226	1.6	1749	0.3		
31	F	0014	2.0	0637	-0.2	1325	1.5	1830	0.5

APRIL

Day	DoW	Time	m	Time	m	Time	m	Time	m
1	SA	0050	1.9	0728	-0.2	1429	1.4	1915	0.7
2	SU	0129	1.9	0822	-0.2	1541	1.3	2007	0.9
3	M	0214	1.8	0922	-0.1	1704	1.2	2114	1.0
4	TU	0306	1.6	1030	0.0	1828	1.3	2241	1.0
5	W	0411	1.5	1143	0.1	1935	1.3		
6	TH	0007	1.0	0526	1.5	1249	0.1	2023	1.4
7	F	0116	0.9	0641	1.4	1344	0.1	2100	1.4
8	SA	0209	0.7	0746	1.4	1427	0.1	2129	1.5
9	SU	0253	0.6	0842	1.5	1503	0.2	2154	1.5
10	M	0332	0.5	0931	1.5	1535	0.2	2216	1.6
11	TU	0407	0.3	1016	1.4	1603	0.3	2236	1.6
12	W ●	0439	0.2	1100	1.4	1631	0.4	2257	1.7
13	TH ○	0511	0.1	1143	1.4	1658	0.5	2320	1.7
14	F	0543	0.0	1228	1.3	1726	0.6	2345	1.7
15	SA	0618	-0.1	1317	1.3	1756	0.7		
16	SU	0014	1.7	0657	-0.2	1411	1.2	1829	0.9
17	M	0047	1.7	0742	-0.2	1514	1.2	1908	0.9
18	TU	0128	1.7	0835	-0.2	1627	1.2	2002	1.0
19	W	0219	1.6	0935	-0.2	1744	1.2	2123	1.1
20	TH	0324	1.6	1043	-0.1	1845	1.3	2302	
21	F	0440	1.6	1149	-0.1	1932	1.4		
22	SA	0025	0.9	0601	1.5	1248	-0.1	2009	1.5
23	SU	0130	0.6	0719	1.5	1341	0.0	2044	1.6
24	M	0225	0.4	0830	1.5	1428	0.0	2117	1.7
25	TU	0316	0.1	0936	1.6	1512	0.2	2150	1.9
26	W	0403	-0.1	1037	1.5	1554	0.3	2223	1.9
27	TH ●	0449	-0.3	1136	1.5	1636	0.5	2257	2.0
28	F	0534	-0.4	1234	1.5	1719	0.6	2333	2.0
29	SA	0620	-0.4	1333	1.4	1804	0.7		
30	SU	0011	1.9	0707	-0.4	1434	1.4	1854	0.9

UNITED STATES - SAN FRANCISCO BAY ENTRANCE (GOLDEN GATE)

Lat 37°49'N   LONG 122°30'W

TIME ZONE +0800 — POSITIVE (+) DIRECTION 065 NEGATIVE (-) DIRECTION 245 — YEAR 2006

JANUARY

Day	Slack Time	Max Time	Rate
1 SU	0249	0453	-2.2
	0745	1043	2.8
	1325	1700	-5.7
	2056		
2 M		0002	4.3
	0334	0543	-2.3
	0842	1137	2.8
	1420	1750	-5.4
	2144		
3 TU		0049	4.2
	0418	0634	-2.6
	0945	1234	2.7
	1519	1842	-4.9
	2231		
4 W		0136	3.9
	0501	0727	-2.9
	1054	1337	2.6
	1626	1936	-4.2
	2320		
5 TH		0225	3.6
	0545	0822	-3.2
	1205	1446	2.5
	1740	2033	-3.4
6 F	0011	0315	3.3
	0628	0920	-3.5
	1361	1601	2.5
	1859	2134	-2.7
7 SA	0104	0408	3.0
	0713	1018	-3.8
	1423	1719	2.7
	2019	2240	-2.1
8 SU	0201	0503	2.7
	0800	1117	-4.1
	1525	1831	3.0
	2134	2350	-1.7
9 M	0300	0559	2.5
	0849	1215	-4.4
	1622	1933	3.3
	2242		
10 TU		0101	-1.6
	0357	0653	2.4
	0938	1309	-4.5
	1714	2027	3.5
	2340		
11 W		0203	-1.5
	0451	0744	2.4
	1026	1358	-4.7
	1802	2116	3.6
12 TH	0030	0251	-1.6
	0540	0831	2.4
	1112	1442	-4.7
	1846	2159	3.7
13 F	0114	0329	-1.6
	0624	0914	2.4
	1158	1523	-4.7
	1928	2238	3.6
14 SA O	0154	0404	-1.7
	0705	0954	2.4
	1238	1602	-4.7
	2007	2314	3.5
15 SU	0232	0438	-1.8
	0745	1033	2.3
	1318	1640	-4.6
	2044	2347	3.4
16 M	0307	0515	-1.9
	0826	1113	2.2
	1358	1719	-4.3
	2119		
17 TU		0018	3.2
	0342	0553	-2.1
	0909	1155	2.1
	1440	1759	-4.0
	2152		
18 W		0051	3.0
	0415	0634	-2.3
	0958	1241	2.0
	1525	1840	-3.5
	2224		
19 TH		0125	2.8
	0447	0717	-2.4
	1052	1331	1.8
	1618	1925	-3.0
	2257		
20 F		0202	2.5
	0520	0803	-2.7
	1151	1427	1.7
	1720	2013	-2.5
	2332		
21 SA		0244	2.3
	0555	0852	-2.9
	1254	1529	1.7
	1834	2107	-2.0
22 SU	0014	0330	2.1
	0634	0944	-3.1
	1356	1638	1.8
	1953	2206	-1.6
23 M	0105	0422	1.9
	0717	1039	-3.5
	1456	1748	2.2
	2108	2308	-1.4
24 TU	0207	0517	1.9
	0806	1135	-3.9
	1551	1853	2.6
	2215		
25 W		0011	-1.4
	0310	0613	2.0
	0858	1231	-4.4
	1642	1949	3.2
	2314		
26 TH		0111	-1.6
	0408	0707	2.3
	0951	1324	-4.9
	1731	2038	3.7
27 F	0004	0206	-1.8
	0501	0759	2.4
	1043	1416	-5.4
	1818	2124	4.1
28 SA	0051	0256	-2.1
	0552	0850	2.9
	1135	1506	-5.7
	1903	2208	4.4
29 SU •	0133	0344	-2.5
	0642	0940	3.2
	1228	1554	-5.9
	1948	2250	4.5
30 M	0214	0431	-2.9
	0734	1031	3.4
	1321	1642	-5.7
	2032	2332	4.4
31 TU	0253	0518	-3.2
	0829	1124	3.4
	1417	1730	-5.2
	2115		

FEBRUARY

Day	Slack Time	Max Time	Rate
1 W		0014	4.2
	0332	0606	-3.5
	0928	1220	3.3
	1517	1820	-4.5
	2159		
2 TH		0058	3.8
	0411	0655	-3.7
	1031	1320	3.1
	1622	1912	-3.7
	2245		
3 F		0144	3.3
	0453	0747	-3.9
	1138	1427	2.8
	1735	2007	-2.8
	2335		
4 SA		0234	2.8
	0538	0843	-3.9
	1248	1543	2.7
	1853	2109	-2.0
5 SU	0032	0330	2.4
	0628	0943	-3.9
	1359	1706	2.7
	2014	2221	-1.5
6 M	0139	0434	2.1
	0724	1050	-3.9
	1506	1821	2.9
	2130	2352	-1.2
7 TU	0248	0542	2.0
	0823	1158	-4.0
	1606	1923	3.2
	2234		
8 W		0120	-1.3
	0351	0645	2.1
	0921	1301	-4.1
	1700	2016	3.4
	2326		
9 TH		0214	-1.5
	0445	0739	2.2
	1014	1352	-4.3
	1747	2101	3.5
10 F	0009	0250	-1.7
	0531	0825	2.4
	1103	1433	-4.4
	1829	2139	3.6
11 SA	0046	0317	-1.9
	0612	0904	2.6
	1147	1509	-4.5
	1906	2213	3.6
12 SU O	0120	0342	-2.1
	0650	0940	2.7
	1228	1543	-4.5
	1940	2241	3.5
13 M	0151	0411	-2.3
	0727	1016	2.7
	1307	1617	-4.4
	2011	2307	3.3
14 TU	0220	0443	-2.6
	0803	1053	2.7
	1346	1652	-4.1
	2040	2334	3.2
15 W	0248	0518	-2.8
	0841	1131	2.6
	1426	1719	-3.7
	2107		
16 TH		0002	2.9
	0314	0555	-3.0
	0922	1213	2.4
	1510	1808	-3.2
	2133		
17 F		0034	2.7
	0341	0635	-3.1
	1008	1258	2.2
	1600	1851	-2.7
	2200		
18 SA		0109	2.3
	0409	0718	-3.2
	1100	1350	2.1
	1700	1938	-2.2
	2233		
19 SU		0151	2.0
	0443	0807	-3.3
	1201	1451	1.9
	1813	2033	-1.7
	2315		
20 M		0240	1.7
	0526	0901	-3.3
	1311	1602	2.0
	1935	2134	-1.3
21 TU	0015	0339	1.6
	0621	1002	-3.5
	1420	1721	2.2
	2053	2242	-1.2
22 W	0138	0445	1.6
	0726	1105	-3.8
	1523	1832	2.2
	2158	2351	-1.3
23 TH	0256	0551	1.9
	0833	1207	-4.3
	1618	1929	3.3
	2252		
24 F		0054	-1.6
	0359	0652	2.3
	0935	1305	-4.9
	1709	2017	3.8
	2337		
25 SA		0149	-2.1
	0453	0747	2.8
	1034	1358	-5.3
	1755	2059	4.2
26 SU •	0017	0237	-2.7
	0543	0839	3.4
	1130	1448	-5.6
	1838	2139	4.5
27 M •	0055	0322	-3.3
	0633	0929	3.8
	1224	1536	-5.6
	1920	2218	4.5
28 TU	0131	0406	-3.8
	0723	1020	4.0
	1319	1622	-5.2
	2001	2257	4.3

MARCH

Day	Slack Time	Max Time	Rate
1 W	0206	0450	-4.3
	0814	1111	4.0
	1415	1709	-4.7
	2042	2336	4.0
2 TH	0242	0534	-4.5
	0908	1204	3.8
	1514	1757	-3.9
	2124		
3 F		0018	3.5
	0319	0621	-4.5
	1006	1301	3.5
	1617	1847	-3.0
	2208		
4 SA		0103	2.9
	0400	0711	-4.3
	1105	1405	3.1
	1727	1942	-2.2
	2300		
5 SU		0154	2.3
	0447	0805	-4.0
	1218	1521	2.8
	1843	2045	-1.5
6 M	0005	0254	1.8
	0544	0907	-3.7
	1331	1648	2.7
	2003	2205	-1.1
7 TU	0125	0409	1.6
	0651	1020	-3.5
	1442	1805	2.8
	2116		
8 W		0016	-1.1
	0242	0530	1.6
	0801	1141	-3.5
	1545	1905	3.0
	2214		
9 TH		0121	-1.4
	0345	0639	1.9
	0905	1251	-3.7
	1638	1954	3.2
	2259		
10 F		0203	-1.7
	0436	0731	2.2
	1001	1339	-3.9
	1722	2035	3.4
	2336		
11 SA		0232	-2.1
	0519	0814	2.5
	1050	1416	-4.1
	1801	2109	3.5
12 SU	0008	0252	-2.4
	0557	0851	2.8
	1135	1447	-4.1
	1835	2137	3.5
13 M	0037	0314	-2.7
	0633	0925	2.9
	1216	1519	-4.1
	1906	2201	3.4
14 TU O	0104	0340	-3.1
	0708	0959	3.1
	1257	1551	-3.9
	1934	2225	3.2
15 W	0129	0410	-3.4
	0742	1034	3.1
	1337	1625	-3.6
	1959	2250	3.0
16 TH	0153	0443	-3.7
	0816	1110	3.0
	1418	1701	-3.3
	2023	2318	2.8
17 F	0215	0519	-3.8
	0853	1149	2.9
	1502	1740	-2.8
	2047	2350	2.5
18 SA	0239	0558	-3.8
	0933	1232	2.7
	1551	1823	-2.3
	2114		
19 SU		0025	2.1
	0307	0641	-3.8
	1021	1322	2.5
	1650	1911	-1.8
	2148		
20 M		0107	1.8
	0342	0730	-3.7
	1121	1423	2.3
	1802	2006	-1.4
	2234		
21 TU		0200	1.5
	0429	0827	-3.6
	1233	1535	2.2
	1922	2111	-1.1
	2346		
22 W		0307	1.3
	0535	0931	-3.6
	1347	1656	2.5
	2035	2223	-1.1
23 TH	0131	0422	1.4
	0655	1038	-3.8
	1454	1808	2.9
	2134	2335	-1.4
24 F	0253	0535	1.8
	0815	1144	-4.2
	1551	1903	3.4
	2221		
25 SA		0038	-2.0
	0354	0640	2.4
	0925	1245	-4.6
	1641	1948	3.9
	2302		
26 SU		0129	-2.8
	0446	0738	3.1
	1027	1339	-4.9
	1726	2028	4.2
	2338		
27 M •		0215	-3.5
	0535	0830	3.7
	1126	1429	-5.0
	1809	2106	4.3
28 TU	0012	0258	-4.3
	0623	0920	4.2
	1222	1517	-4.8
	1849	2144	4.2
29 W •	0046	0339	-4.8
	0710	1009	4.4
	1317	1603	-4.4
	1929	2222	4.0
30 F	0120	0422	-5.2
	0759	1058	4.4
	1413	1649	-3.8
	2009	2300	3.6
31 TU	0155	0505	-5.2
	0849	1149	4.2
	1510	1735	-3.1
	2050	2341	3.1

CANADA; UNITED STATES

No.	PLACE	Lat. N	Long W	TIME DIFFERENCES HHW	LLW	HEIGHT DIFFERENCES (IN METRES) MHHW	MLHW	MHLW	MLLW	ML Z_o m
				Zone +0800						
9133	**VANCOUVER**....................................	(seepage165)				**4.4**	**3.9**	**2.9**	**1.1**	
	Sutil Channel									
9105	Whaletown Bay........................	50 06	125 03	−0004	−0004	+0.3	+0.6	+0.5	+0.5	3.51
	Deer Passage									
9107	Redonda Bay	50 15	124 57	+0013	+0010	+0.1	+0.2	+0.2	+0.2	3.25
	Bute Inlet									
9111	Waddington Bay	50 56	124 51	+0010	+0008	0.0	+0.1	+0.1	0.0	3.07
9113	Lund..	49 59	124 46	−0005	−0002	+0.2	+0.4	+0.3	+0.4	3.36
	Sechelt Inlet									
9122	Egmont	49 45	123 56	−0003	−0004	−0.1	+0.1	+0.2	+0.3	3.20
9123	Porpoise Bay	49 29	123 45	P	P	−2.1	−1.6	−1.1	−0.4	1.75
9125	Pender Harbour........................	49 38	124 02	0000	+0004	−0.1	+0 2	+0.2	+0.3	3.17
9129	Squamish.................................	49 42	123 09	−0010	-0010	−0.2	+0.1	+0.1	+0.3	3.14
	Burrard Inlet									
9131	Point Atkinson.............................C	49 20	123 15	−0013	−0013	−0.2	+0.1	+0.1	+0.2	3.08
9133	VANCOUVER.............................	49 17	123 07	STANDARD PORT			See Table V			3.06
9134	Lake Buntzen	49 23	122 52	+0100	+0100	−0.3	0.0	0.0	+0.1	3.00
	Fraser River									★x
9136	Send Heads	49 06	123 18	−0020	0020	−0.3	−0.2	+0.1	+0.1	2.96 ★
9138	New Westminter	49 12	122 55	+0044	+0225	−2.4	☉	☉	☉	1.3 ★
9139	Port Coquitlam	49 14	122 46	+0215	+0345	−3.2	☉	☉	☉	☉ ★
9140	Port Haney	49 13	122 36	+0158	+0414	−3.6	☉	☉	☉	☉
9141	Sumas	49 08	122 05	+0409	+0713	−4.1	☉	☉	☉	☉
9142	Tsawwassen	49 00	123 08	−0012	−0019	−0.4	−0.1	+0.1	+0.2	2.96
9142a	White Rock	49 01	122 48	−0016	−0027	−0.6	−0.3	0.0	+0.1	2.80
	United States									
9143	Blaine	49 00	122 46	−0016	−0025	−1.7	−1.5	−1.2	−1.1	1.72
9143a	Cherry Point ....U	48 52	122 45	−0018	−0029	−1.8	−1.5	−1.2	−1.1	1.67
9144	Ferndale	48 50	122 43	−0022	−0029	−1.9	−1.5	−1.2	−1.1	1.65
9145	Point Migley	48 45	122 43	−020	−0040	−2.1	−1.6	−1.3	−1.1	1.58
9147	Bellingham..............................	48 45	122 30	−0031	−0045	−2.0	−1.7	−1.2	−1.1	1.55
9149	Anacortes	48 31	122 37	−0043	−0102	−2.1	−1.7	−1.2	−1.1	1.52
9065	**VICTORIA**	(see page 162)				**2.6**	**2.3**	**2.0**	**0.8**	
9151	Aleck Bay	48 26	122 51	−0038	+0035	−0.6	−0.3	−0.5	−0.8	1.40
9133	**VANCOUVER**............................	(see page 165)				**4.4**	**3.9**	**2.9**	**1.1**	
9152	Strawberry Bay	48 34	122 43	−0055	−0109	−2.1	−1.7	−1.3	−1.1	1.49
9153	Peavine Pass	48 36	122 48	−0040	−0110	−2.1	−1.6	−1.4	−1.1	1.49
9155	Echo Bay	48 45	122 54	−0013	−0023	−2.0	−1.6	−1.2	−1.1	1.58
9156	Alden Point	48 47	122 58	−0010	0000	−2.0	−1.9	−1.3	−1.1	1.58
9158	Turn Point	48 41	123 14	−0050	−0040	−2.3	−1.9	−1.4	−1.1	1.43
	San Juan Island									
9159	Friday Harbour	48 33	123 00	−0030	−0053	−2.2	−1.9	−1.3	−1.1	1.43
9065	**VICTORIA**	(see page 162)				**2.6**	**2.3**	**2.0**	**0.8**	
9160	Kanaka Bay	48 29	123 05	+0045	+0040	−0.6	−0.4	−0.6	−0.8	1.38 d
9133	**VANCOUVER**..........................	(see page 165)				**4.4**	**3.9**	**2.9**	**1.1**	
	Whidbey Island									
9163	Yokeko Point	48 25	122 37	−0043	−0040	−1.3	−1.1	−1.2	−1.1	1.86
9169	Point Partridge	48 14	122 46	−0125	−0140	−2.3	−1.8	−1.4	−1.1	1.43

SEASONAL CHANGES IN MEAN LEVEL

No.		Jan. 1	Feb. 1	Mar. 1	Apr. 1	May 1	June 1	July 1	Aug. 1	Sep. 1	Oct. 1	Nov. 1	Dec. 1	Jan. 1
9023	− 9060	0.0	+0.1	+0.1	+0.1	0.0	0.0	0.0	−0.1	−0.1	−0.1	0.0	0.0	0.0
9061	− 9067	0.0	+0.1	+0.1	+0.1	0.0	0.0	0.0	0.0	−0.1	−0.1	−0.1	0.0	0.0
9068	− 9159	+0.1	+0.1	0.0	0.0	0.0	0.0	0.0	0.0	−0.1	−0.1	0.0	0.0	+0.1
9160	− 9169	0.0	+0.1	+0.1	0.0	0.0	0.0	0.0	0.0	−0.1	−0.1	−0.1	0.0	0.0

UNITED STATES

No.	PLACE	Lat. N	Long W	TIME DIFFERENCES HHW / LLW Zone +0800		HEIGHT DIFFERENCES (IN METRES) MHHW	MLHW	MHLW	MLLW	ML Z$_o$ m
9050	**TOFINO**............	(see page 159)				**3.4**	**3.0**	**1.4**	**0.7**	
	Siuslaw River									
9245	Entrance.................	44 01	124 08	−0033	−0027	−1.2	−1.1	−0.6	−0.7	1.23
9246	Florence..................	43 58	124 06	+0014	+0021	−1.5	−1.4	−0.7	−0.7	1.07
	Umpqua River									
9249	Entrance.................	43 41	124 12	−0033	−0028	−1.3	−1.3	−0.6	−0.7	1.13
9250	Gardiner.................	43 44	124 07	+0027	−0033	−1.4	−1.4	−0.7	−0.7	1.07
	Coos Bay									
9252	Entrance (Charleston)............U	43 21	124 19	−0038	−0031	−1.2	−0.1	−0.6	−0.7	1.25
9253	Port of Coos Bay	43 23	124 13	−0050	+0055	−1.2	−1.2	−0.7	−0.7	1.19
9254	Bandon.................	43 07	124 25	−0041	−0033	−1.3	−1.3	−0.7	−0.7	1.15
9256	Port Orford	42 44	124 30	−0058	−0047	−1.2	−1.2	−0.6	−0.7	1.21
9305	**SAN FRANSISCO**	(See page 168)				**1.7**	**1.4**	**0.7**	**0.0**	
9259	Wedderdurm............	42 26	124 25	+0017	+0018	+0.2	+0.2	0.0	0.0	1.10
9262	Chetco Cove	42 03	124 17	+0010	+0004	+0.3	+0.3	+0.1	0.0	1.13
9264	Crescent City ....U	41 45	124 11	+0008	+0002	+0.3	+0.3	+0.1	0.0	1.14
9268	Trinidad Harbour........	41 03	124 09	+0006	−0001	+0.3	+0.2	+0.1	0.0	1.11
	Humboldt Bay									
9270	North Spit ....U	40 46	124 13	+0024	+0020	+0.4	+0.3	+0.1	0.0	1.13
9271	Eureka..................	40 48	124 10	+0050	+0033	+0.5	+0.4	+0.1	0.0	1.20
9281	Shelter Cove............	40 02	124 04	−0023	−0022	+0.1	0.0	0.0	0.0	1.01
9284	Fort Bragg Landing.......	39 27	123 49	−0014	−0025	0.0	0.0	0.0	0.0	0.94
9287	Point Area...............	38 57	123 44	−0026	−0026	0.0	0.0	0.0	0.0	0.94
9288	Arena Cove............U	38 55	123 43	−0029	−0027	0.0	0.0	0.0	0.0	0.97
9290	Fort Ross Cove	38 31	123 15	−0050	−0030	0.0	−0.1	0.0	0.0	0.91
9293	Point Reyes	38 00	122 58	−0051	−0031	0.0	0.0	0.0	0.0	0.96
9295	Southeast Farallon Island........	37 42	123 00	−0040	−0020	−0.1	−0.1	0.0	0.0	0.91
	SAN FRANCISCO BAY									
9295a	Sausalito.................	37 51	122 29	+0010	+0014	−0.1	−0.1	0.0	0.0	0.91
9295b	Richmond................	37 56	122 24	+0027	+0025	+0.1	+0.1	0.0	0.0	0.99
9295c	Richmond Inner Harbour	37 55	122 22	+0024	+0036	0.0	0.0	0.0	0.0	0.99
9296	Point San Quentin..........	37 57	122 28	+0039	+0050	0.0	0.0	0.0	0.0	0.95
	Carquinez Strait									
9297	Mare Island	38 04	122 15	+0132	+0158	0.0	0.0	−0.1	0.0	0.95
9298	Benicia	38 03	122 08	+0219	+0213	−0.1	−0.1	−0.1	0.0	0.89
9298a	Port Chicago............U	38 03	122 02	+0242	+0238	−0.2	−0.2	−0.2	0.0	0.78
	Sacroamento River									
9299	Collinsville..............	38 04	121 51	+0353	+0358	−0.5	−0.5	−0.3	−0.0	0.62
9300	Three Mile Slough	38 06	121 42	+0431	+0436	−0.5	−0.4	−0.3	0.0	0.63
	San Joaquin Riverr									
9303	Three Mile Slough	38 05	121 41	+0510	+0530	−0.7	−0.7	−0.3	0.0	0.55
9304	Stockton	37 58	121 17	+0650	+0710	−0.7	−0.5	−0.4	0.0	0.62
9305	SAN FRANCISCO (Golden Gate)	37 48	122 28	STANDARD PORT		See Table V				0.97
9306	Oakland (Grove Street)	37 48	122 17	+0033	+0042	+0.1	−0.8	0.0	0.0	1.01
9306a	North Point, Pier 41	37 49	122 25	+0013	+0011	+0.1	−1.1	0.0	0.0	1.01
9306b	Rincon Pont, Pier 22$^{1/2}$...........	37 47	122 23	+0023	+0025	+0.2	−1.1	0.0	0.0	1.04
9306c	Hunters Point	37 44	122 21	+0025	+0039	+0.3		0.0	0.00	1.10
9306d	Oyster Point Marina	37 40	122 23	+0041	+0100	+0.4	+0.4	0.0	0.0	1.15
9307	Coyote Point Marina	37 36	122 19	+0042	+0108	+0.5	+0.4	+0.1	0.0	1.20
9307a	San Mateo Bridge............	37 35	122 15	+0044	+0111	+0.6	+0.5	+0.1	0.0	1.25
9307b	Redwood Creek, Marker 8..........	37 32	122 12	+0053	+0128	+0.7	+0.6	+0.1	0.0	1.31
9307c	Redwood City	37 30	122 13	+0048	+0115	+0.7	+0.7	+0.1	0.0	1.34
9308	Dumbarton Bridge	37 30	122 07	+0050	+0115	+0.8	+0.8	+0.1	0.0	1.39
9309	Alamede	37 46	122 18	+0029	+0039	+0.2	+0.2	0.0	0.0	1.08
	PACIFIC COAST									
9312	Halfmoon Bay.............	37 30	122 29	−0106	−0050	−1.2	−0.1	0.0	0.0	0.91
9315	Ano Nuevo Island	37 06	122 20	−0124	−0104	−0.2	−0.2	0.0	0.0	0.82

SEASONAL CHANGES IN MEAN LEVEL

No	Jan. 1	Feb. 1	Mar. 1	Apr. 1	May 1	June 1	July 1	Aug. 1	Sep. 1	Oct. 1	Nov.1	Dec. 1	Jan. 1
9050	0.0	+0.1	+0.1	+0.1	+0.0	0.0	0.0	−0.1	−0.1	−0.1	0.0	0.0	0.0
9065	0.0	+0.1	+0.1	+0.1	+0.0	0.0	0.0	0.0	−0.1	−0.1	−0.1	0.0	0.0
9133	+0.1	+0.1	0.0	0.0	0.0	0.0	0.0	0.0	−0.1	−0.1	0.0	0.0	+0.1
9172 − 9197	+0.1	+0.1	0.0	0.0	0.0	0.0	0.0	0.0	−0.1	0.0	0.0	0.0	+0.1
9172 − 9197	0.0	+0.1	+0.1	0.0	0.0	0.0	0.0	0.0	−0.1	−0.1	−0.1	0.0	0.0
9208 − 9220	+0.1	+0.1	+0.1	0.0	0.0	0.0	−0.1	−0.1	−0.1	−0.1	0.0	0.0	+0.1
9222	+0.2	+0.2	+0.1	0.0	−0.1	−0.1	−0.2	−0.2	−0.1	0.0	+0.1	+0.1	+0.2
9223 − 9256	+0.1	+0.1	0.0	0.0	0.0	0.0	−0.1	−0.1	−0.1	0.0	0.0	0.0	+0.1
9259 − 9293	+0.1	−0.1	0.0	−0.1	−0.1	−0.1	0.0	0.0	0.0	0.0	+0.1	+0.1	+0.1
9295 − 9315						Negligible							

Glossary of Abbreviations

A:	After draught	**eg**	for example
AIS	Automatic Identification System	**EGC**	Enhanced Group Calling
ALC	Articulated Loading Column	**EGNOS**	European Geostationary Navigation Overlay Service
ALRS	Admiralty List of Radio Signal		
AMVER	Automated Mutual Assistance Vessel Rescue System	**ELSBM**	Exposed Location Single Buoy Mooring
ARCS	Admiralty Raster Chart Service	**ELT**	Emergency Locating Transmitter
ARPA	Automatic Radar Plotting Aids	**ENC**	Electronic Navigation Chart
ASF	Additional Secondary Factor (Correction)	**ENE**	East North East
		EP	Estimated Position
ATT	Admiralty Tide Tables	**EPIRB**	Emergency Position Indicating Radio Beacon
AUSREP	Australian Ship Reporting System		
BA	British Admiralty	**ERBL**	Electronic Range and Bearing Line
BCPA	Bearing of Closest Point of Approach	**ESE**	East South East
C	Compass (Course or Bearing)	**ETA**	Estimated Time of Arrival
°C	Degree Centigrade or Celsius	**ETD**	Estimated Time of Departure
C/A	Coarse Acquisition	**ETO**	Electro Technical Officer
CALM	Catenary Anchor Leg Mooring	**F**	Forward Draught
C$_b$	Cumulonimbus cloud	**°F**	Degree Fahrenheit
CD	Compact Disc	**FFA**	Fire Fighting Appliances
CES	Coast Earth Station	**G**	Gyro (Course or Bearing)
CIR	Cross Index Range	**GC**	Great Circle
COLREGS	Collision Regulations (International Regulations for Preventing Collisions at Sea, 1972)	**GDOP**	Geometric Dilution of Precision
		GHA	Greenwich Hour Angle
		GHz	Gigahertz
conn	Conning (Control of the ship)	**GLONASS**	Global Navigation Satellite System
cos	Cosine (trigonometric function)	**GMDSS**	Global Maritime Distress and Safety System
cot	Cotangent (trigonometric function)		
C/P	Charter Party	**GMT**	Greenwich Mean Time
CPA	Closest Point of Approach	**GNSS**	Global Navigation Satellite System
CPP	Controllable Pitch Propeller	**GPS**	Global Positioning System
CRS	Coast Radio Station	**GRI**	Group Repetition Interval
CSC	Cargo Ship Safety Certificate	**GT**	Gross Tonnage
CSP	Commence Search Point	**h**	Hour
CZD	Calculated Zenith Distance	**hav**	Haversine
d	Day	**HDOP**	Horizontal Dilution of Precision
D/F	Direction Finder	**HF**	High Frequency
DGPS	Differential Global Positioning System	**hp or HP**	Horse Power
DMA	Defence Mapping Agency	**HW**	High Water
DMP	Difference of Meridional Parts	**IALA**	International Association of Marine Aids to Navigation Lighthouse Authorities
DP	Dynamic Positioning		
DR	Dead Reckoning		
DSC	Digital Selective Calling	**IAMSAR**	International Aeronautical and Maritime Search and Rescue
DTG	Distance To Go		
DWT	Dead Weight Tonnage	**IBS**	Integrated Bridge System
E	East	**ICS**	International Chamber of Shipping
EBL	Electronic Bearing Line	**ID**	Identity
ECDIS	Electronic Chart Display and Information System	**IEC**	International Electro-technical Commission

IHO	International Hydrographic Office	MRCC	Maritime Rescue Co-ordination Centre
IMO	International Maritime Organisation	MSAS	Multifunctional Satellite-based Augmentation System
IRPCS	International Regulations for Preventing Collisions at Sea	MSI	Maritime Safety Information
ISM	International Safety Management (The international management code for the safe operation of ships and for pollution prevention)	MSL	Mean Sea Level
		MSN	Merchant Shipping Notice
		MSR	Mean Spring Range
		MTL	Mean Tidal Level
ISPS	International Ship and Port Facility Security Code	MTSAT	Multi-functional Transport Satellite
		N	North
ITCZ	Inter Tropical Convergence Zone	NBDP	Narrow Band Direct Printing
ITP	Intercept Terminal Point	NE	North East
kHz	Kilohertz	NLT	Not Less Than
km	Kilometre	nm	Nautical Mile
kn	Knot	NMT	Not More Than
kts	Knots	NNE	North North East
KW	Kilowatt	NNW	North North West
LANBY	Large Automated Navigation Buoy	No	Number
LAYCAN	Laytime Cancellation	NP	Nautical Publication
LEOSAR	Low Earth Orbit Search and Rescue Satellite	NT	Net Tonnage
		NUC	Not Under Command
LIT	Longitude In Time	NW	North West
LHA	Local Hour Angle	OOW	Officer Of the Watch
LL	Lower Limb	OSC	Ob Scene Co-ordinator
LMT	Local Mean Time	PC	Passenger Ship Safety Certificate
LOA	Length Over All	PDOP	Position Dilution of Precision North Pole
LOP	Line Of Position		
LORAN	Long Range Navigation	P_n	North Pole
LR	Long Range	PI	Parallel Indexing
LSA	Life Saving Appliances	P_s	South Pole
LW	Low Water	PPS	Precise Positioning Service
M	Metre	RAM	Restricted in Ability to Manoeuvre
m	Minute	RCC	Rescue Co-ordination Centre
MARPOL	Marine Pollution Prevention Regulations	RFA	Royal Fleet Auxiliary
		RIO	Radar Information Overlay
Max	Maximum	RL	Rhumb Line
METROUTE	Meteorological Routeing Service	RN	Royal Navy
MCA	Marine Coastguard Agency (UK)	RNC	Raster Navigation Chart
MF	Medium Frequency	ROR	Rule Of the Road
MGN	Marine Guidance Note	R/T	Radio Telephone or Telephony
MHHW	Mean Higher High Water	RTF	Radio Transmitter Frequency
MHLW	Mean Higher Low Water	s	Second
MHW	Mean High Water	S	South
MHWI	Mean High Water Interval	SA	Selective Availability
MHWN	Mean High Water Neap	SALM	Single Anchor Leg Mooring
MHWS	Mean High Water Spring	SALS	Single Anchor Leg Storage
MHz	Megahertz	SAR	Search and Rescue
MIN	Marine Information Notice	SARSAT	Search and Rescue Satellite
MKD	Minimum Keyboard and Display	SART	Search and Rescue Radar Transponder
MLHW	Mean Lower High Water		
MLLW	Mean Lower Low Water	SBAS	Satellite Based Augmentation System
MLW	Mean Low Water	SBE	Stand-by Engine
MLWS	Mean Low Water Spring	SE	South East
MMSI	Maritime Mobile Station Identifier	SEC	Safety Equipment Certificate (for cargo ships)
MP	Meridional Part		

SES	Ship Earth Station		**UK**	United Kingdom
SD	Semi Diameter		**UKC**	Under Keel Clearance
SHA	Sidereal Hour Angle		**UKHO**	United Kingdom Hydrographic Office
sin	Sine (trigonometric function)		**UL**	Upper Limb
SITREP	Situation Report		**UMS**	Unattended machinery Space
SMC	Search and Rescue Mission Co-ordinator		**µs**	Microsecond
			US	United States
SMS	Safety Management System		**USA**	United States of America
SOLAS	Safety of Life at Sea Convention		**UT**	Universal Time
SPS	Standard Positioning Service		**UTC**	Universal Time Co-ordinated
SRR	Search and Rescue Region		**VDOP**	Vertical Dilution of Precision
SRU	Search and Rescue Region		**VDR**	Voyage Data Recorder
SSE	South South East		**VHF**	Very High Frequency
SSW	South South West		**vol**	Volume
STCW	Standards of Training Certification and Watchkeeping		**VRM**	Variable Range Marker
			VTIS	Vessel Traffic Information Service
SW	South West		**VTS**	Vessel Traffic Service
tan	Tangent (trigonometric function)		**W**	West
T	True (course or bearing)		**WAAS**	Wide Area Augmentation System
TCPA	Time of Closest Point of Approach		**WGS**	World Geodetic System
TDMA	Time Distribution Management Arrangement		**WNW**	West North West
			WO	Wheel Over
TRS	Tropical Revolving Storm		**WSW**	West South West
T&P	Temporary and Preliminary Notices		**WWNWS**	World Wide Navigation Warning Service
TSS	Traffic Separation Scheme			
TTC	Tracking and Telemetry Control		**XTE**	Cross Track Error
TZD	True Zenith Distance			
UAIS	Universal Automatic Identification System			

References

Admiralty Ocean Passages of the World NP 136 5th Ed (2004) UKHO

Admiralty List of Radio Signals NP 281(1) (2005/06) UKHO

Admiralty List of Radio Signals NP 282 (2005/06) UKHO

Admiralty Tide Tables Vol 1 NP 201-06 (2006) UKHO

Admiralty Tide Tables Vol 4 NP 204-06 (2006) UKHO

Gnomonic chart – Indian and Southern Ocean (1914) UKHO

Mariners Routeing Guide (5502) Malacca and Singapore Straits (1997) UKHO

Nautical Almanac (2006) HMNAO and UKHO

Ship's Routeing 8th Ed (2003) IMO

Bibliography

Bowditch (1995) The American Practical Navigator. DMA

ICS (1998) Bridge Procedures Guide 3rd Ed. Marisee Publications

ICS (1998) Guide to Helicopter/Ship Operations 2nd Ed. Witherby

IMO (2003) Ship's Routeing 8th Ed.

Metoffice (1978) Meteorology for Mariners 3rd Ed. HMSO

MOD (1987) Admiralty Manual of Navigation Vol 1. HMSO

Royal Navy (2004) Astro Navigation – Admiralty Manual of Navigation Vol 2. Nautical Institute

Sonnenberg G (1988) Radar and Electronic Navigation 6th Ed. Butterworth

Swift A (2004) Bridge Team Management 2nd Ed. Nautical Institute

UKHO (2005/06) Admiralty List of Radio Signals NP 283(1)

UKHO (2004) Admiralty Ocean Passages of the World NP 136 5th Ed.

UKHO (2004) The Mariners Handbook NP 100 8th Ed.

Wall A, Bole A, O'Dineley W (2005) Radar and ARPA Manual. Elsevier

Index

Templates

RADAR PLOTTING SHEET

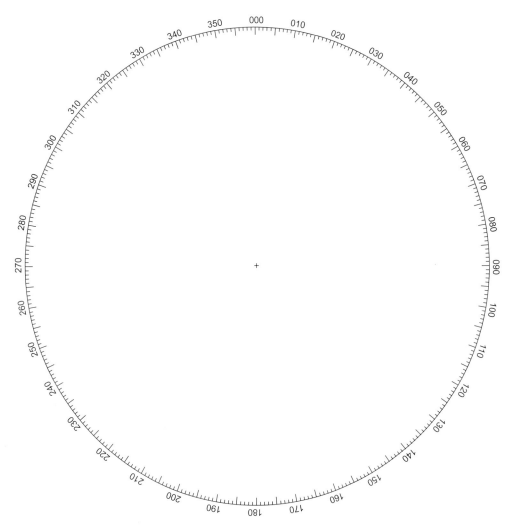

Range Scale: Nautical Miles

| | 1 | 2 | 3 | 4 | 5 | 6 | 7 | 8 | 9 | 10 | 11 | 12 |

Target	1	2	3	4
Bearing				
Range				
CPA				
TCPA				
BCPA				
Course				
Speed				
Aspect				
Action/New CPA				
New TCPA				
New BCPA				

AZIMUTH

Date		A = tan lat ÷ tan LHA	
GMT		B = tan dec ÷ sin LHA	
GHA		C = A ± B	
Increment		tan Az = 1 ÷ (C × $coslat$)	
SHA		Az	
Sub-total			
360° if required			
Longitude		True Bearing	
LHA Sun			
Declination		Gyro Bearing	
dCorr^n		Gyro Error	
Declination			

AMPLITUDE

Date		sin Declination	
Lat		cos Latitude	
LMT sunrise/set		sin Amplitude	
Increment		Amplitude	
LMT for Latitude			
LIT		True Bearing	
GMT			
Declination		Gyro Bearing	
dCorr^n		Gyro Error	
Declination			

POLARIS

DR Latitude		Date and Z T		
DR Longitude		Zone		
Course/Speed		Greenwich date		
GMT		**Altitude**		
GHA Aries		Sext Alt		
Increment		IE		
Sub-total		Obs Alt		
Longitude		Dip		
- 360° ?		App Alt		
LHA Aries		T Corr^n		
		True Alt		
		a_o		
		a_1		
		a_2		
Azimuth				
Position line		Latitude		

MARQ ST HILAIRE

DR Latitude				
DR Longitude				
Body				
C T				
C E				
GMT				
Almanac data				
Tabulated GHA				
Increment				
vCorr^n	SHA			
GHA				

Longitude				
- 360° if required				
LHA				
Declination				
dCorr^n				
Declination				
cos ZX				
CZD				
Altitude				
Sext Alt				
IE				
Obs Alt				
Dip				
App Alt				
T Corr^n				
True Alt				
TZD				
Intercept				
Azimuth				
A				
B				
C				
tan Az				
True Az				
P/L				

MERIDIAN PASSAGE/ANGLE ON SEXTANT

POSITION AT MERIDIAN PASSAGE

DR Latitude		Date and Z T		
DR Longitude		Zone		
Course/Speed		Greenwich date		
For ITP				
d.lat				
dep				
mean lat				
d.long				
ITP				
1st Approx		**1st run up posn**		
LMT merpass		d.lat		
LIT		dep		
GMT		mean lat (from ITP)		
Initial GMT		d.long		

Run		1st run up Lat	
Speed		1st run up Long	
Distance Run			
2nd Approx		**2nd run up posn**	
LMT merpass		d.lat	
LIT		dep	
GMT merpass		mean lat (from ITP)	
Initial GMT		d.long	
Run		2nd run up Lat	
Speed		2nd run up Long	
Distance Run			
		Altitude	
Declination		Sext Alt	
dCorr^n		IE	
Declination		Obs Alt	
		Dip	

Setting sextant		App Alt	
Lat N		T Corr^n	
TA = D – L + 90°		True Alt	
		L = D – TA + 90°	
Sext Alt		From Plot	
IE		dep	
Obs Alt		mean lat	
Dip		d.long	
App Alt			
T Corr^n		For T bearing of	
True Alt		Position Line =	
(working back)		**Observed Posn**	
		Latitude	
		Longitude	

GREAT CIRCLE CALCULATIONS

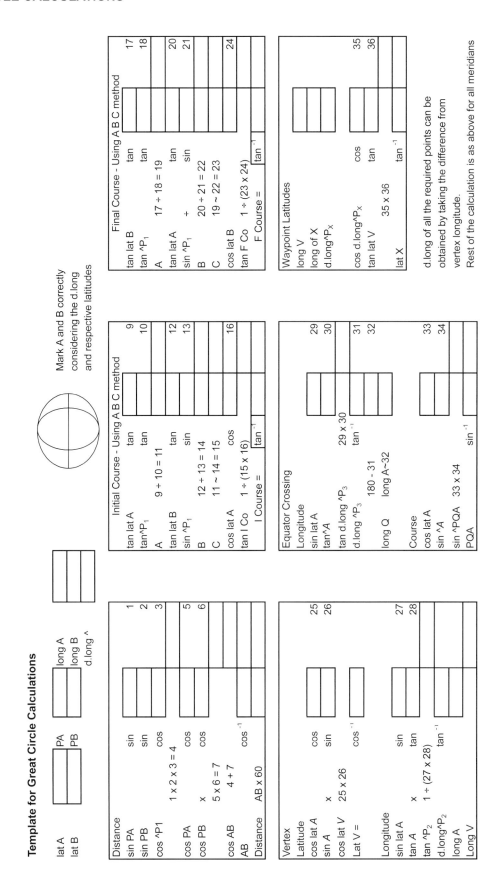

RENDEZVOUS – DOUBLE APPROXIMATION

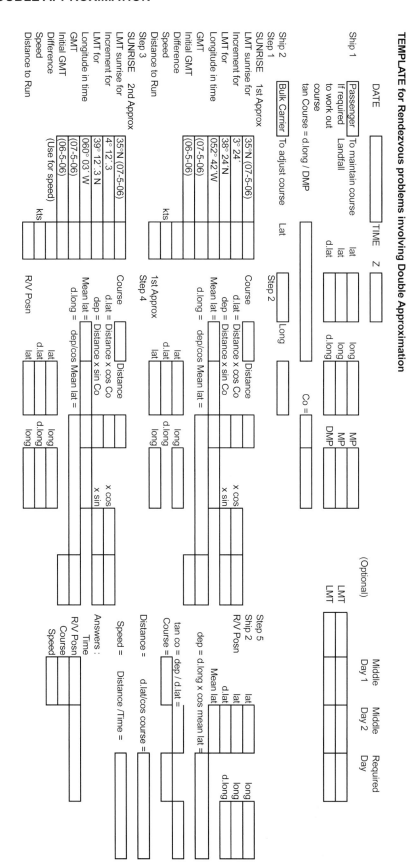

TEMPLATE for Rendezvous problems involving Double Approximation

DATE [ ]   TIME [ ] Z

Ship 1   Passenger   To maintain course
         If required   Landfall
         to work out
         course
         tan Course = d.long / DMP

Ship 2   Bulk Carrier   To adjust course

Step 1   Lat [ ]   lat [ ]   long [ ]
SUNRISE   1st Approx   lat [ ]   long [ ]
LMT sunrise for   35° N (07-5-06)   d.lat [ ]   d.long [ ]
Increment for   3° 24'
LMT for   38° 24' N   Step 2   Long [ ]
Longitude in time   052° 42' W
GMT   (07-5-06)
Initial GMT   (06-5-06)   Co = [ ]   MP [ ]
                                    MP [ ]
Difference   DMP [ ]
GMT
Distance to Run
Speed [ ] kts

Step 2
SUNRISE   2nd Approx
LMT sunrise for   35° N (07-5-06)
Increment for   4° 12'.3
LMT for   39° 12'.3 N
Longitude in time   060° 03' W
GMT   (07-5-06)
Initial GMT   (06-5-06)
Difference   (Use for speed)
GMT
Speed [ ] kts
Distance to Run

Course [ ] Distance
d.lat = Distance x cos Co [ ] x cos
dep = Distance x sin Co [ ] x sin
Mean lat [ ]
d.long = dep/cos Mean lat = [ ]

Step 2   lat [ ]   long [ ]
1st Approx   d.lat [ ]   d.long [ ]
             lat [ ]   long [ ]

Step 4
Course [ ] Distance
d.lat = Distance x cos Co [ ] x cos
dep = Distance x sin Co [ ] x sin
Mean lat [ ]
d.long = dep/cos Mean lat = [ ]

(Optional)   LMT
             LMT

Middle Day 1   Middle Day 2   Required Day

Step 5
Ship 2   lat [ ]   long [ ]
R/V Posn   d.lat [ ]   long [ ]
           lat [ ]   d.long [ ]
tan co = dep / d.lat = [ ]
dep = d.long x cos mean lat = [ ]
Mean lat [ ]
Course = [ ]

Distance = [ ]   d.lat/cos course = [ ]

Speed = [ ]   Distance /Time = [ ]

Answers :
   Time
   R/V Posn
   Course
   Speed [ ]

INDEX TO SELECTED STARS, 2015

Name	No	Mag	SHA	Dec
Acamar	7	3·2	315	S 40
Achernar	5	0·5	335	S 57
Acrux	30	1·3	173	S 63
Adhara	19	1·5	255	S 29
Aldebaran	10	0·9	291	N 17
Alioth	32	1·8	166	N 56
Alkaid	34	1·9	153	N 49
Al Na'ir	55	1·7	28	S 47
Alnilam	15	1·7	276	S 1
Alphard	25	2·0	218	S 9
Alphecca	41	2·2	126	N 27
Alpheratz	1	2·1	358	N 29
Altair	51	0·8	62	N 9
Ankaa	2	2·4	353	S 42
Antares	42	1·0	112	S 26
Arcturus	37	0·0	146	N 19
Atria	43	1·9	107	S 69
Avior	22	1·9	234	S 60
Bellatrix	13	1·6	279	N 6
Betelgeuse	16	Var.*	271	N 7
Canopus	17	−0·7	264	S 53
Capella	12	0·1	281	N 46
Deneb	53	1·3	50	N 45
Denebola	28	2·1	183	N 14
Diphda	4	2·0	349	S 18
Dubhe	27	1·8	194	N 62
Elnath	14	1·7	278	N 29
Eltanin	47	2·2	91	N 51
Enif	54	2·4	34	N 10
Fomalhaut	56	1·2	15	S 30
Gacrux	31	1·6	172	S 57
Gienah	29	2·6	176	S 18
Hadar	35	0·6	149	S 60
Hamal	6	2·0	328	N 24
Kaus Australis	48	1·9	84	S 34
Kochab	40	2·1	137	N 74
Markab	57	2·5	14	N 15
Menkar	8	2·5	314	N 4
Menkent	36	2·1	148	S 36
Miaplacidus	24	1·7	222	S 70
Mirfak	9	1·8	309	N 50
Nunki	50	2·0	76	S 26
Peacock	52	1·9	53	S 57
Pollux	21	1·1	243	N 28
Procyon	20	0·4	245	N 5
Rasalhague	46	2·1	96	N 13
Regulus	26	1·4	208	N 12
Rigel	11	0·1	281	S 8
Rigil Kentaurus	38	−0·3	140	S 61
Sabik	44	2·4	102	S 16
Schedar	3	2·2	350	N 57
Shaula	45	1·6	96	S 37
Sirius	18	−1·5	259	S 17
Spica	33	1·0	158	S 11
Suhail	23	2·2	223	S 43
Vega	49	0·0	81	N 39
Zubenelgenubi	39	2·8	137	S 16

No	Name	Mag	SHA	Dec
1	Alpheratz	2·1	358	N 29
2	Ankaa	2·4	353	S 42
3	Schedar	2·2	350	N 57
4	Diphda	2·0	349	S 18
5	Achernar	0·5	335	S 57
6	Hamal	2·0	328	N 24
7	Acamar	3·2	315	S 40
8	Menkar	2·5	314	N 4
9	Mirfak	1·8	309	N 50
10	Aldebaran	0·9	291	N 17
11	Rigel	0·1	281	S 8
12	Capella	0·1	281	N 46
13	Bellatrix	1·6	279	N 6
14	Elnath	1·7	278	N 29
15	Alnilam	1·7	276	S 1
16	Betelgeuse	Var.*	271	N 7
17	Canopus	−0·7	264	S 53
18	Sirius	−1·5	259	S 17
19	Adhara	1·5	255	S 29
20	Procyon	0·4	245	N 5
21	Pollux	1·1	243	N 28
22	Avior	1·9	234	S 60
23	Suhail	2·2	223	S 43
24	Miaplacidus	1·7	222	S 70
25	Alphard	2·0	218	S 9
26	Regulus	1·4	208	N 12
27	Dubhe	1·8	194	N 62
28	Denebola	2·1	183	N 14
29	Gienah	2·6	176	S 18
30	Acrux	1·3	173	S 63
31	Gacrux	1·6	172	S 57
32	Alioth	1·8	166	N 56
33	Spica	1·0	158	S 11
34	Alkaid	1·9	153	N 49
35	Hadar	0·6	149	S 60
36	Menkent	2·1	148	S 36
37	Arcturus	0·0	146	N 19
38	Rigil Kentaurus	−0·3	140	S 61
39	Zubenelgenubi	2·8	137	S 16
40	Kochab	2·1	137	N 74
41	Alphecca	2·2	126	N 27
42	Antares	1·0	112	S 26
43	Atria	1·9	107	S 69
44	Sabik	2·4	102	S 16
45	Shaula	1·6	96	S 37
46	Rasalhague	2·1	96	N 13
47	Eltanin	2·2	91	N 51
48	Kaus Australis	1·9	84	S 34
49	Vega	0·0	81	N 39
50	Nunki	2·0	76	S 26
51	Altair	0·8	62	N 9
52	Peacock	1·9	53	S 57
53	Deneb	1·3	50	N 45
54	Enif	2·4	34	N 10
55	Al Na'ir	1·7	28	S 47
56	Fomalhaut	1·2	15	S 30
57	Markab	2·5	14	N 15

*0·1 — 1·2

ALTITUDE CORRECTION TABLES 10°-90°—SUN,STARS,PLANETS

OCT.—MAR. SUN APR.—SEPT.

App. Alt.	Lower Limb	Upper Limb	App. Alt.	Lower Limb	Upper Limb
° ′	′	′	° ′	′	′
9 33	+10.8	−21.5	9 39	+10.6	−21.2
9 45	+10.9	−21.4	9 50	+10.7	−21.1
9 56	+11.0	−21.3	10 02	+10.8	−21.0
10 08	+11.1	−21.2	10 14	+10.9	−20.9
10 20	+11.2	−21.1	10 27	+11.0	−20.8
10 33	+11.3	−21.0	10 40	+11.1	−20.7
10 46	+11.4	−20.9	10 53	+11.2	−20.6
11 00	+11.5	−20.8	11 07	+11.3	−20.5
11 15	+11.6	−20.7	11 22	+11.4	−20.4
11 30	+11.7	−20.6	11 37	+11.5	−20.3
11 45	+11.8	−20.5	11 53	+11.6	−20.2
12 01	+11.9	−20.4	12 10	+11.7	−20.1
12 18	+12.0	−20.3	12 27	+11.8	−20.0
12 36	+12.1	−20.2	12 45	+11.9	−19.9
12 54	+12.2	−20.1	13 04	+12.0	−19.8
13 14	+12.3	−20.0	13 24	+12.1	−19.7
13 34	+12.4	−19.9	13 44	+12.2	−19.6
13 55	+12.5	−19.8	14 06	+12.3	−19.5
14 17	+12.6	−19.7	14 29	+12.4	−19.4
14 41	+12.7	−19.6	14 53	+12.5	−19.3
15 05	+12.8	−19.5	15 18	+12.6	−19.2
15 31	+12.9	−19.4	15 45	+12.7	−19.1
15 59	+13.0	−19.3	16 13	+12.8	−19.0
16 27	+13.1	−19.2	16 43	+12.9	−18.9
16 58	+13.2	−19.1	17 14	+13.0	−18.8
17 30	+13.3	−19.0	17 47	+13.1	−18.7
18 05	+13.4	−18.9	18 23	+13.2	−18.6
18 41	+13.5	−18.8	19 00	+13.3	−18.5
19 20	+13.6	−18.7	19 41	+13.4	−18.4
20 02	+13.7	−18.6	20 24	+13.5	−18.3
20 46	+13.8	−18.5	21 10	+13.6	−18.2
21 34	+13.9	−18.4	21 59	+13.7	−18.1
22 25	+14.0	−18.3	22 52	+13.8	−18.0
23 20	+14.1	−18.2	23 49	+13.9	−17.9
24 20	+14.2	−18.1	24 51	+14.0	−17.8
25 24	+14.3	−18.0	25 58	+14.1	−17.7
26 34	+14.4	−17.9	27 11	+14.2	−17.6
27 50	+14.5	−17.8	28 31	+14.3	−17.5
29 13	+14.6	−17.7	29 58	+14.4	−17.4
30 44	+14.7	−17.6	31 33	+14.5	−17.3
32 24	+14.8	−17.5	33 18	+14.6	−17.2
34 15	+14.9	−17.4	35 15	+14.7	−17.1
36 17	+15.0	−17.3	37 24	+14.8	−17.0
38 34	+15.1	−17.2	39 48	+14.9	−16.9
41 06	+15.2	−17.1	42 28	+15.0	−16.8
43 56	+15.3	−17.0	45 29	+15.1	−16.7
47 07	+15.4	−16.9	48 52	+15.2	−16.6
50 43	+15.5	−16.8	52 41	+15.3	−16.5
54 46	+15.6	−16.7	56 59	+15.4	−16.4
59 21	+15.7	−16.6	61 50	+15.5	−16.3
64 28	+15.8	−16.5	67 15	+15.6	−16.2
70 10	+15.9	−16.4	73 14	+15.7	−16.1
76 24	+16.0	−16.3	79 42	+15.8	−16.0
83 05	+16.1	−16.2	86 31	+15.9	−15.9
90 00			90 00		

STARS AND PLANETS

App Alt.	Corrn
° ′	′
9 55	−5.3
10 07	−5.2
10 20	−5.1
10 32	−5.0
10 46	−4.9
10 59	−4.8
11 14	−4.7
11 29	−4.6
11 44	−4.5
12 00	−4.4
12 17	−4.3
12 35	−4.2
12 53	−4.1
13 12	−4.0
13 32	−3.9
13 53	−3.8
14 16	−3.7
14 39	−3.6
15 03	−3.5
15 29	−3.4
15 56	−3.3
16 25	−3.2
16 55	−3.1
17 27	−3.0
18 01	−2.9
18 37	−2.8
19 16	−2.7
19 56	−2.6
20 40	−2.5
21 27	−2.4
22 17	−2.3
23 11	−2.2
24 09	−2.1
25 12	−2.0
26 20	−1.9
27 34	−1.8
28 54	−1.7
30 22	−1.6
31 58	−1.5
33 43	−1.4
35 38	−1.3
37 45	−1.2
40 06	−1.1
42 42	−1.0
45 34	−0.9
48 45	−0.8
52 16	−0.7
56 09	−0.6
60 26	−0.5
65 06	−0.4
70 09	−0.3
75 32	−0.2
81 12	−0.1
87 03	0.0
90 00	

App. Alt. Additional Corrn

2015

VENUS

Jan. 1–May 3
Dec. 4–Dec. 31

°	′
60	+0.1

May 4–June 22
Oct. 13–Dec. 3

°	′
41	+0.2
76	+0.1

June 23–July 14
Sept. 19–Oct. 12

°	′
34	+0.3
60	+0.2
80	+0.1

July 15–July 30
Sept. 2–Sept. 18

°	′
29	+0.4
51	+0.3
68	+0.2
83	+0.1

July 31–Sept. 1

°	′
26	+0.5
46	+0.4
60	+0.3
73	+0.2
84	+0.1

MARS

Jan. 1–Dec. 31

°	′
60	+0.1

DIP

Ht. of Eye	Corrn	Ht. of Eye	Ht. of Eye	Corrn
m	′	ft.	m	′
2.4	−2.8	8.0	1.0	− 1.8
2.6	−2.9	8.6	1.5	− 2.2
2.8	−3.0	9.2	2.0	− 2.5
3.0	−3.1	9.8	2.5	− 2.8
3.2	−3.2	10.5	3.0	− 3.0
3.4	−3.3	11.2	See table ←	
3.6	−3.4	11.9	m	′
3.8	−3.5	12.6	20	− 7.9
4.0	−3.6	13.3	22	− 8.3
4.3	−3.7	14.1	24	− 8.6
4.5	−3.8	14.9	26	− 9.0
4.7	−3.9	15.7	28	− 9.3
5.0	−4.0	16.5		
5.2	−4.1	17.4	30	− 9.6
5.5	−4.2	18.3	32	− 10.0
5.8	−4.3	19.1	34	− 10.3
6.1	−4.4	20.1	36	− 10.6
6.3	−4.5	21.0	38	− 10.8
6.6	−4.6	22.0		
6.9	−4.7	22.9	40	− 11.1
7.2	−4.8	23.9	42	− 11.4
7.5	−4.9	24.9	44	− 11.7
7.9	−5.0	26.0	46	− 11.9
8.2	−5.1	27.1	48	− 12.2
8.5	−5.2	28.1		
8.8	−5.3	29.2	ft.	′
9.2	−5.4	30.4	2	− 1.4
9.5	−5.5	31.5	4	− 1.9
9.9	−5.6	32.7	6	− 2.4
10.3	−5.7	33.9	8	− 2.7
10.6	−5.8	35.1	10	− 3.1
11.0	−5.9	36.3		
11.4	−6.0	37.6	See table ←	
11.8	−6.1	38.9	ft.	′
12.2	−6.2	40.1	70	− 8.1
12.6	−6.3	41.5	75	− 8.4
13.0	−6.4	42.8	80	− 8.7
13.4	−6.5	44.2	85	− 8.9
13.8	−6.6	45.5	90	− 9.2
14.2	−6.7	46.9	95	− 9.5
14.7	−6.8	48.4		
15.1	−6.9	49.8	100	− 9.7
15.5	−7.0	51.3	105	− 9.9
16.0	−7.1	52.8	110	− 10.2
16.5	−7.2	54.3	115	− 10.4
16.9	−7.3	55.8	120	− 10.6
17.4	−7.4	57.4	125	− 10.8
17.9	−7.5	58.9		
18.4	−7.6	60.5	130	− 11.1
18.8	−7.7	62.1	135	− 11.3
19.3	−7.8	63.8	140	− 11.5
19.8	−7.9	65.4	145	− 11.7
20.4	−8.0	67.1	150	− 11.9
20.9	−8.1	68.8	155	− 12.1
21.4		70.5		

App. Alt. = Apparent altitude = Sextant altitude corrected for index error and dip.